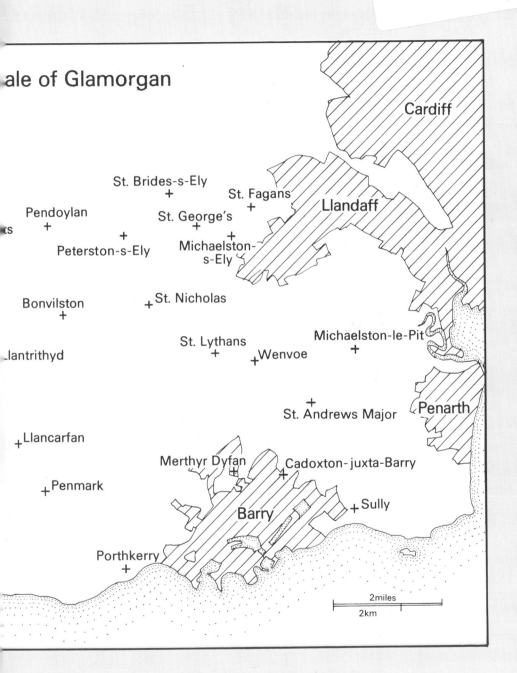

ale of Glamorgan

Cardiff

St. Brides-s-Ely
+

St. Fagans
+

Llandaff

Pendoylan
+

St. George's
+

Peterston-s-Ely
+

Michaelston-
s-Ely
+

Bonvilston
+

St. Nicholas
+

lantrithyd

St. Lythans
+

Wenvoe
+

Michaelston-le-Pit
+

St. Andrews Major
+

Penarth

Llancarfan
+

Merthyr Dyfan
+

Cadoxton-juxta-Barry
+

Penmark
+

Barry

Sully
+

Porthkerry
+

2miles

2km

Medieval Churches

of the

Vale of Glamorgan

'Lord, I have loved the habitation of Thy house:
And the place where thine honour dwelleth'

(St. George's church—inscription above south porch)

Llantrithyd church—Basset-Mansel tomb ▶

Medieval Churches
of the
Vale of Glamorgan

by

Geoffrey R. Orrin, B.A.

With an Historical Introduction by

Dr. F. G. Cowley

1988
D. BROWN AND SONS LIMITED
COWBRIDGE

British Library Cataloguing in Publication Data
Orrin, Geoffrey R.
Medieval Churches of the Vale of Glamorgan
1. South Glamorgan. Vale of Glamorgan (District). Churches, history.
Architectural features
I. Title
726'.5'0942989

ISBN 0-905928-80-6

Printed in Wales by
D. Brown & Sons Ltd., Bridgend, Mid Glamorgan

Dedication

To the memory of
The Right Reverend John Richard Worthington Poole-Hughes, M.A. (OXON),
Bishop of Llandaff (1975–1985) and Assistant Bishop of Hereford.

Contents

List of Colour Plates

List of Monochrome Plates

xi

The publishers wish to acknowledge
the generous financial assistance of
the late Right Reverend John Poole-Hughes,
The Thomas Ellis Memorial Fund of the University of Wales
and
Barclays Bank plc

Foreword

by the BISHOP OF LLANDAFF

I am most pleased to be associated with Geoffrey Orrin's book on the Churches in the Vale of Glamorgan and I commend it to its readers with enthusiasm, confident in the belief that they will derive much pleasure from its pages. The story it tells is a noble one as it traces the long history enshrined within the walls of these holy places. 'The lot is fallen unto me in a fair ground: yea, I have a goodly heritage', says the Psalmist. Geoffrey Orrin has helped us appreciate some of the visible aspects of that goodly heritage.

+ Roy Landav:

Acknowledgements

The author and publishers would like to thank the following for permission to reproduce photographs and church plans in this book:—

Reverend John W. Binny, rector of Eglwys Brewis with St. Athan, Flemingston and Gileston, for permission to reproduce the first page of Flemingston parish register of marriages, dated 1578; the Librarian, South Glamorgan County Library for Mansel Franklen photographs of the nave of Ewenny Priory church prior to restoration, the south transept of Ewenny Priory church with the figure of Colonel John Picton Turbervill, Llanmihangel church 1889, and 14th-century sedilia in St. Fagan's church. Also for a photograph of a drawing of St. Bride's-super-Ely church by David Jones of Wallington (commenced in 1881 and finished in 1888.) in his notebook in Cardiff Central Library (M.S.1.187.), and a photograph of the interior of Llanfrynach church prior to restoration in 1922 taken from a pamphlet in Cardiff Central Library entitled *Llanfrynach church, Glamorganshire: an ancient parish church* . . . by the Reverend Frederick R. Williams; E. A. J. Carr, Director CADW—Welsh Historic Monuments for church plan of Ewenny Priory church; Glamorgan Archive Service, Cardiff for photograph of Llanblethian church nave prior to restoration; Glamorgan-Gwent Archaeological Trust for church plan of Cowbridge church; J. Alan Hey for coloured photograph of Cowbridge church stained glass; Reverend David Jenkins, rector of Llantwit Major for photograph of the interior of Llantwit Major church prior to restoration in 1899 and 1905; Brian C. Luxton for photograph of St. Cadoc's church, Cadoxton-juxta-Barry interior prior to restoration in 1885 from his book entitled:- *St. Cadoc's: a history of the old village church of Cadoxton-juxta-Barry*, 1980.; the Director, National Museum of Wales, Cardiff for photograph of sepia drawing by W. W. Young c.1830 of Llantrithyd Place and church; the Librarian, National Library of Wales, Aberystwyth for photograph of first page of Flemingston parish register of marriages; Dr. E. Clive Rouse for two photographs of wall paintings in Llantwit Major church, measured copies drawn by him from the scaffolding; Miss Hilary Thomas for coloured photograph of the Berkerolles tomb at St. Athan's; Howard J. Thomas, Royal Commission on Ancient and Historical Monuments in Wales, Aberystwyth for church plan of St. Andrew's Major church.

Preface

The idea of writing a book on the medieval churches of the Vale of Glamorgan was first suggested to me in 1981 by my colleague Clive Towse, a faithful worshipper at the Cathedral Church of Llandaff. He saw in the Vale of Glamorgan an area similar to Gower whose churches I described in 1979 in my book entitled *The Gower Churches*. With this end in view I approached the Bishop of Llandaff, the Rt. Reverend J. R. W. Poole-Hughes who endorsed the undertaking by writing a letter asking that the co-operation and support of the clergy be given to me. I am deeply grateful for the constant support and encouragement of both Bishop Poole-Hughes and his successor Bishop Roy Davies and for the considerable financial assistance of the Diocese of Llandaff. I would also like to take this opportunity to thank the clergy of the Vale churches, including those who have retired, for the trouble so many have taken to make this book a comprehensive study. The Rt. Reverend Roy Davies, Bishop of Llandaff has done me the honour of contributing the foreword for which I thank him warmly.

To date there has been no exhaustive survey of the ecclesiastical architecture of the Vale of Glamorgan although the major churches have all been described to some extent over the past century and some lesser churches have featured in articles in the Vale series of books edited by Stewart Williams. It was Dr. John Guy's intention to write a book on the Vale of Glamorgan churches in the 1960s when he was a theological student at St. David's College, Lampeter but he was diverted into other interests such as pluralism and non-resident clergy in the old diocese of Llandaff and produced his excellent two-volume Ph.D. thesis on those topics in 1983.

I am grateful to him for the use of his notes on the Vale churches which provided the basis of his series of articles on the churches published in the *South Wales Echo* in 1963. It was my original intention to write a book on the Vale churches similar to my *Gower Churches* but the Vale churches turned out to be more sophisticated architectural structures with special associations with local families of note. Consequently over the last three years the book has grown almost beyond the author's control but I hope it will provide a definitive study of the Vale churches. I decided to describe in this study only those churches in the Vale which are of medieval foundation. This was to avoid dealing with many of the (to my mind) less important Victorian churches built at the end of the 19th century and the beginning of the 20th in the more populated areas of the south-east region of the Vale; an undertaking which would have unbalanced the scale of the study, and needlessly extended its scope.

Unfortunately many of the Vale churches have to be kept locked to avoid vandalism which is a sad reflection on our society today. However, it is fairly easy to obtain a key to the churches by enquiring at the local post office or village shop. Sometimes there is a note in the church porch giving the address of the key holder.

I can claim at least one merit for this book and that is that I have personally visited every church mentioned several times in the course of the past six years and that the features described are a true record of the churches as they were at the time of writing.

I have pleasure in acknowledging the generous collaboration of my colleague, Dr. F. G. Cowley, who not only contributed the historical introduction but also provided invaluable advice on the historical background of each church. I am also deeply indebted to my colleague Dr. David Painting for reading the original manuscript and suggesting many improvements to the text. I cannot adequately express my thanks to Mark Child of Swindon, a well-known writer on church architecture, for answering innumerable queries relating to architectural features which I encountered in the Vale churches. Throughout my work I have been especially indebted to my colleague Clive Towse for his enthusiastic research on my behalf, his sustaining interest, and his fund of knowledge of genealogy and heraldry.

My thanks go also to my other colleagues in the University College of Swansea Library: Paul Reynolds for translating the Latin inscriptions and for allowing me to draw upon his rich store of biblical knowledge; Barbara Jones for translating the Welsh inscriptions and mottoes and David Bevan, College archivist, for his sound advice on a wide range of subjects. The colour and monochrome photographs which illustrate the book were taken by Bill Pring, L.R.P.S., senior photographic technician and I am grateful to him for his patience and photographic expertise. I am grateful also to Guy Lewis, senior cartographer in the Department of Geography for drawing the excellent plans of Llancarfan, Llantwit Major and St. Fagans churches and the map of the Vale churches and to Anthony L. Jones of Pencoed for his artistic illustration of the heraldic glossary. I am also indebted to Hazel Pember and Carole Williams of the Inter-Library Loans Department who supplied many of the books listed in my bibliography. My thanks go also to Susan Simpson and Wendy Gibbon for typing the first draft of the manuscript, and to Meta Soo and Elaine Hutchinson for typing amendments to the text. The design and production of this book owe much to the enthusiastic support of Bob Whitaker of D. Brown & Sons Ltd. of Bridgend.

I have received so much help from so many people in the preparation of this book that it would seem invidious not to mention everyone who has been of assistance but I must single out the following for my special thanks:— Reverend Dr. John Baldwin of Llandaff—campanologist; E. G. W. Bill, Librarian, Lambeth Palace Library, London; B. S. Q. F. Buchanan, archivist, J. W. Walker & Sons Ltd. of Brandon, Suffolk; Peter Burnard of Surbiton—

record agent and genealogist; John Cory of St. Brides-super-Ely—church-warden; Dr. Chrystal Davies of Fairwater Vicarage, Cardiff—co-editor of the *Welsh Churchman*; Iolo Davies of Dean Close School, Cheltenham—campanologist and author; J. Iorwerth Davies, Librarian, Mid Glamorgan County Council; R. O. Dennys, Arundel Herald of Arms Extraordinary, College of Arms, London; Reverend B. B. Edmonds of Sudbury—organ historian; Ieuan Edwards, Librarian, South Glamorgan County Council; Dr. J. C. Eisel of Ullingswick, Hereford—campanologist; Mrs. E. A. L. Estève-Coll, Librarian, Victoria and Albert Museum, London; Keith Evans, Assistant Librarian, National Library of Wales, Aberystwyth; Alfred Fisher, Chairman, The British Society of Master Glass Painters, London; Mrs. R. C. Griffen of Warminster, Wiltshire; Birkin Haward of Ipswich—art historian; Betty Horley, Secretary to the Bishop of Llandaff; Peter Howell of Banbury, Oxfordshire—author; A. Lloyd Hughes, Archivist, Department of Documentation, Welsh Folk Museum, St. Fagans, Cardiff; Brian Ll. James, Sub-Librarian, University College of Cardiff; Anthony L. Jones of Pencoed, Mid Glamorgan—heraldic artist; Dr. Brian Kemp of Reading University—church monuments historian; D. G. Lambert, Diocesan Registrar of Llandaff; J. M. Lewis, Senior Assistant Keeper, Department of Archaeology and Numismatics, National Museum of Wales, Cardiff; Richard Lewis, Assistant Librarian, National Library of Wales, Aberystwyth; M. E. Ling, Reference Librarian, Cardiff Central Library; Brian Luxton of Barry—local historian; Canon S. H. Mogford of Cardiff—former rector of Llanblethian church with Cowbridge; Mrs. Patricia Moore, Glamorgan archivist, Cardiff; R. C. Norris of Mountain Ash—organ builder; Dr. P. D. Oldham of Penmark—campanologist; Colin Pascoe—organist Llantwit Major church; Frank Roper of Penarth—sculptor and stained glass artist; Dr. E. Clive Rowse of Gerrards Cross, Buckinghamshire—mural painting restorer and historian; Dr Elfyn Scourfield, Keeper, Welsh Folk Museum, St. Fagans; Janet Seeley, Assistant Librarian, Council for the Care of Churches, London; Dr. Michael Siddons of Croesyceiliog, Cwmbran, Gwent—heraldic specialist and writer; Alfred Spanier, researcher, British Library Newspaper Library, Colindale, London; John Taylor & Co. Ltd. of Loughborough—bellfounders; Brian Thomas, Librarian, West Glamorgan County Council; Hilary M. Thomas of Llandough—local historian; Howard J. Thomas, Royal Commission on Ancient and Historical Monuments in Wales, Aberystwyth; Hubert P. Thomas, Principal, Celtic Studios, Swansea; D. F. Thurlow, tonal director, Nicholson & Co., Worcester—organ builders; Mr. & Mrs. J. Picton Turbervill of Ewenny Priory; Walter Vile of St. Fagans—local historian; J. D. Warner-Davies, Principal archivist, City of Birmingham Public Library; John Watts-Williams, Assistant Keeper, Church Records, National Library of Wales, Aberystwyth; Whitechapel Bell Foundry, London; Glennys Wild, Keeper, Department of Applied Art, City of Birmingham Museum and Art Gallery; Alfred L. Wilkinson of Harwich—retired stained glass artist; Robert J. Williams rector of Reynoldston; J. Wippell & Co. of Exeter—church furnishers. If by mischance some one has been omitted from this list of acknowledgements will they please accept my sincere thanks for any contributions they have made to this study.

Any errors or omissions that remain are entirely the author's own responsibility. Finally to my wife Julie I owe a debt of gratitude for the forbearance with which she accepted the Vale Churches as a long term presence in our home and for accompanying me on many journeys to the Vale.

Geoffrey R. Orrin
Reynoldston, June, 1987

Historical
and
Architectural
Introductions

Llangan church—9th-century wheel cross in churchyard to the west of the church

Historical Introduction

The origins of the Christian Church in Glamorgan lie shrouded in an obscurity which neither the archaeologist nor the historian has yet been able to penetrate. The bare chronological framework of fact regarding the introduction and progress of the faith in Roman Britain is clear enough. It had obtained a footing in Britain by about 200 A.D., give or take a decade, and it had been brought hither in an unspectacular way either by traders or by soldiers transferred to Britain from other parts of the Roman Empire. There is no reliable evidence for a deliberately mounted mission such as that led by St. Augustine at the end of the 6th century. The Christian faith was one of a number of eastern religions which found their way into Britain in Roman times and the early Christians had to gain their converts in competition with these as well as with the older indigenous pagan cults. A period of persecution, probably in the mid 3rd century, produced a small batch of martyrs for the faith—Alban at the town and fort of Verulamium and Julius and Aaron at or near the legionary fortress of Caerleon. The intermittent persecution of Christians by the Roman authorities ended in 313 A.D. with an edict of toleration and later in the century—in 395 A.D.—Christianity was recognised as the state religion of the Roman Empire.

Well before these dates, however, the Christian communities in Britain were sufficiently numerous to have acquired an organization similar to that already existing in Roman Gaul. The British bishops, like their counterparts in Gaul, had their seats in towns and cities and ruled over territorial dioceses. With the assistance of priests and deacons they ministered to the Christian communities within these dioceses. We know that bishops were despatched to the Council of Arles in 314 A.D. from York, Lincoln and London and non-episcopal representatives from a fourth, unnamed centre, perhaps Cirencester. British bishops were also present at the Councils of Sardica in 342 and Arminium in 359. Later in the century the Romano-British Church produced two of its most famous sons. The heretic Pelagius was born somewhere in Britain about the year 380 A.D. and Patrick, the future apostle of the Irish, was also born somewhere in western Britain about this time.

During the present century archaeologists have uncovered numerous finds which illustrate this Christian presence in lowland Britain. Mosaic floors and mural paintings bearing Christian themes and motifs have been discovered on the sites of Roman villas; a number of lead baptismal tanks have also been

Bonvilston church—figure of pre-Norman date on west wall of nave

found and more recently a complete set of Eucharistic vessels was recovered from a ploughed field at Water Newton (Cambridgeshire). Remains of what may have been Christian churches have also been uncovered at Silchester, St. Albans and within the Saxon shore fort of Richborough. Unfortunately nothing has yet been found within what is now Wales to match these spectacular discoveries from lowland Britain. A pewter bowl bearing a debased Chi Rho monogram has been found at Caerwent and its finder, Mr. George Boon, has suggested that this small Roman town, the capital of the Silures, contained a Christian house church. These solitary finds in one place represent the sum total of the material evidence for a 4th century Christian presence in the area which was yet to become Wales.

By the beginning of the 5th century, Roman power throughout western Europe was crumbling under barbarian attack. Britain was being attacked by the Picts from the north and by the Scotti or Irish from the west. British leaders were now told by the Roman authorities to fend for themselves. At first Anglo-Saxon war-bands were invited into Britain as mercenaries to assist in its defence but the trickle of mercenaries became a flood and by about 500 A.D. most of lowland Britain was occupied by pagan Anglo-Saxons. Some Christian communities may have survived but the organization of the Christian church in this lowland region was smashed, not to be re-established until the century after St. Augustine landed in Kent in 597 A.D.

But Christian communities and some form of church organization did survive in the west in the Roman province of Britannia Prima, the area which today comprises Wales and the English counties of Cornwall, Devon and Somerset—and we may be sure that Christian communities of some size already existed in the rich lowlands of Glamorgan which we now know were intensively settled and farmed in Roman times.

Here in western Britain about 540 A.D. Gildas was writing his famous jeremiad of contemporary ills, the *Ruin of Britain*. Gildas's main object was to denounce the sins of his contemporaries but in passing he provides some interesting facts about the church of his own day. Everything he tells us presupposes a long tradition of established Christianity throughout western Britain. The Church was organised on the western model with its hierarchy of bishop, priest and deacon. It was a Church, too, which through the passage of time had become complacent, lax and even corrupt. The clergy ministered to the people in purpose-built churches where the celebration of the Eucharist was the central act of worship. In Gildas's day paganism was no longer looked upon as a powerful rival though pagan idols still survived—'devilish monstrosities . . . some of which we can see today, stark as ever, inside or outside deserted city walls; outlines still ugly, faces still grim'.

Gildas, tantalizingly for the historian, names no ecclesiastical centres and gives hardly a hint of the way the Church was territorially organized in his time. He speaks almost exclusively of a secular Church ruled over by bishops who presumably operated from the older, decaying civil settlements or from the newer tribal centres which were replacing them. On two occasions, how-

Llantwit Major church—head of churchyard cross showing the figure of St. Illtyd

ever, he speaks of a minority in the Church who were true to their calling and worthy of his praise. He may have been referring to the new monastic movement which was already transforming the life of the western Church. Christian monasticism had its origins in Egypt. In the last decades of the 3rd century men who were disillusioned by the luxury and laxity of life in the great city of Alexandria fled to the desert and there founded hermitages and monasteries where they aimed to live a life more in keeping with the precepts of Christ. Stories of the spiritual exploits of these 'desert fathers', men like St. Anthony and St. Pachomius, were taken back to the west by Christian pilgrims and tourists and in time monasteries of similar type were established in southern and central Gaul. It was either directly from Egypt or more probably from these Gallic monasteries that the monastic ideal was transmitted to western Britain and to our own Glamorgan. This new monastic movement reinforced and re-invigorated the Church which survived the collapse of Roman power in western Britain.

Glamorgan, like other coastal areas of Wales, was geographically well-placed to receive these new influences. With most of lowland Britain occupied by pagan Anglo-Saxons, the western seaways acquired a new importance and were frequently used not merely by traders in luxury goods but by Christian churchmen and missionaries. The early Christian inscribed stones dating from the 5th and 6th centuries which have been found in the coastal areas of South Wales are material testimony to these influences. The style of writing employed and the formulae used have enabled archaeologists to trace back their cultural origins to the Lyon and Vienne areas of Gaul.

The older influences of the Roman past and the new influences of Gallic monasticism are personified in Illtyd, the first Christian of the Vale of whose life we have details. There is no contemporary or near-contemporary *Life* of this saint whose life spanned the end of the 5th and beginning of the 6th century, but within a century and a half of his death the Breton author of the *Life of St. Samson* records valuable details of his achievements. He was abbot of the great monastery of Llantwit Major which was also a school of the highest reputation. Illtyd, writes our Breton author, was 'of all the Britons best skilled in Holy Scripture . . . as well as in every kind of learning, such as geometry, rhetoric, grammar, arithmetic and the knowledge of all arts; in divination, too, he was well proven and he had foreknowledge of the future'. Llantwit Major was perhaps the earliest of the major monasteries of Glamorgan. Others were Llancarfan founded by St. Cadog, Llandough founded by the obscure Docco and Llandaff which was a small monastery before it became the seat of a bishopric. These monasteries were not merely enclosed communities designed to nourish the piety and learning of an ecclesiastical élite. They were centres of pastoral care and their inmates carried the Christian faith to the surrounding countryside, administering the sacraments and founding churches dependent on the parent monasteries.

In Ireland the great monasteries came to rule over great confederations of dependent monasteries and churches and eventually superseded the diocesan

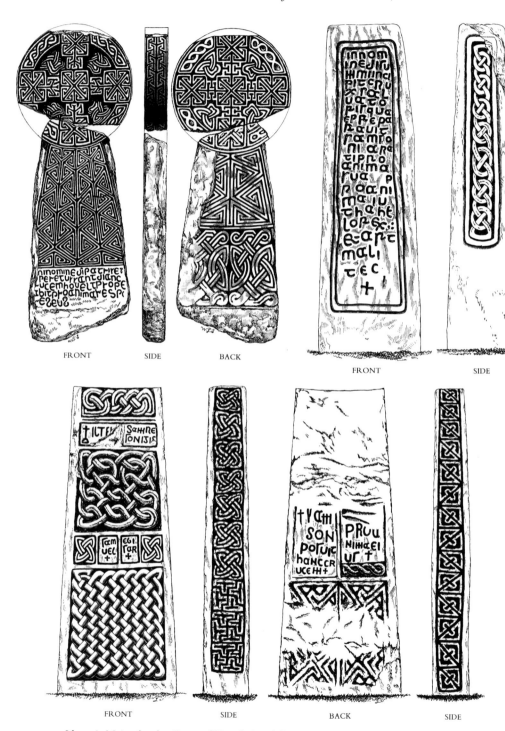

FRONT   SIDE   BACK   FRONT   SIDE

FRONT   SIDE   BACK   SIDE

Llantwit Major church—Cross of Houelt (*top left*); Cross of Samson, Samuel and Ebisar
(*below*); inscribed pillar of Samson, King Juthahel and Artmal (*top right*)

organization established in Patrician times. Many bishops became mere functionaries within the monastic community, retained to carry out those offices which only a bishop could perform—the conferring of holy orders and the administration of the sacrament of confirmation. This did not happen in Wales, least of all in South-east Wales. In the *Life of St. Samson* we learn of Bishop Dubricius (Dyfrig), a shadowy figure with a base in Erging, who exercised episcopal supervision over the monastery of Llantwit Major and by inference over a wide area of South-east Wales. Further west Teilo was bishop as well as abbot of Llandeilo Fawr and seems to have exercised authority over a small territorial diocese as well as supervising a more extensive confederation of dependent monasteries.

The bishops and the monasteries they supervised were the primary agents in establishing centres of worship and providing for the pastoral care of people in the Vale of Glamorgan in this early Christian period. But numerous churches must also have been founded by kings and rich landlords for a peasantry on whose services and tribute they depended. A late 7th-century charter (later incorporated into the *Book of Llandaff*) records how King Ithel gave *ecclesia Elidon* to Bishop Euddogwy and a 9th-century charter from the same source gives details of a grant by Aguod ap Ieuaf of the vill of Penn Onn and its church Lann Tilull to Bishop Cerennyr. *Ecclesia Elidon* has been identified as St. Lythan's and Lann Tilull as St.-y-Nyll, which became in medieval times a dependent chapel in the parish of St. Bride's-super-Ely. Information for this early period is sparse indeed but what there is suggests that many Vale churches were already established before 900.

What were these early structures like? Again, we can only hazard an intelligent guess for their foundations have been masked by later buildings or perhaps covered by later churchyard burials. Archbishop Dunstan, when he was dedicating the Sussex church of Mayfield in the 10th century, found it out of line and re-oriented it by pushing it with his shoulder. Doubtless many of the humbler Vale churches were of this kind—small and flimsily constructed of wood. The Vale has always had access to good building stone, however, and there is no reason to suggest that all the churches were of this kind. The major church within the monastic enclosure at Llantwit Major, and others like it, may well have been constructed of stone. But all of the pre-Conquest churches of Glamorgan must have been small and primitive judging by the modest size of the medieval structures which succeeded them.

By the beginning of the 10th century the monastic centres of Llantwit Major, Llancarfan and Llandough reached the apogee of their power and influence. They enjoyed the patronage and largess of local kings and princes and provided marked burial places for them within the monastic enclosure, as the surviving inscribed stones of Llantwit Major testify. They were landlords of extensive estates and repositories of fine manuscripts and rich metalwork. However, their riches and their location near the coast rendered them easy victims to the raiding Viking and Anglo-Saxon war-bands which ravaged South Wales at the end of the 10th and beginning of the 11th century. They never regained their

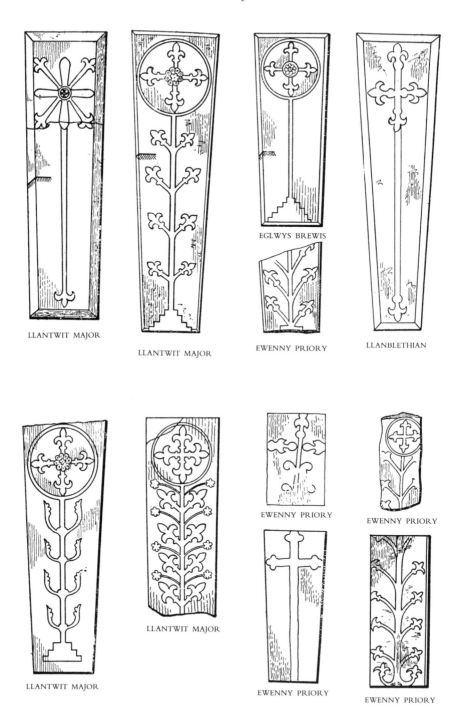

LLANTWIT MAJOR

LLANTWIT MAJOR

EGLWYS BREWIS

EWENNY PRIORY

LLANBLETHIAN

LLANTWIT MAJOR

LLANTWIT MAJOR

EWENNY PRIORY

EWENNY PRIORY

EWENNY PRIORY

EWENNY PRIORY

Incised sepulchral slabs from Llantwit Major and other Vale churches

former influence and power. Even before the raids they had long since lost their monastic character. They had become collegiate bodies of clerics known in Wales as *clasau*, but similar in function and organization to the minsters of Anglo-Saxon England. The raids mark one stage in their transformation from *clas* churches into large but ordinary village churches.

What was a period of decline for the older monastic centres was one of marked expansion for episcopal government in the area. The valuable researches of Dr. Wendy Davies on the *Book of Llandaff* have now clearly demonstrated that the establishment of a single bishopric in South-east Wales based on Llandaff dates essentially from the time of Bishop Joseph (*c.* 1027-1045) and that Llandaff had already embarked on a process which can only be described as one of ecclesiastical aggrandisement: the 'doctoring', manipulation and editing of charters and other texts to enable Llandaff to take over and absorb the rights, traditions and properties belonging to older monastic and episcopal centres in South Wales. This attempt to provide a respectable pedigree for Llandaff as an ancient see reached its fulfilment in the text of that remarkable amalgam of fact and fiction, the *Book of Llandaff* which belongs to the episcopate of Urban (1107-1133).

With the Anglo-Norman conquest of Glamorgan in the last decade of the 11th century and the election of Urban as bishop of Llandaff in 1107 the Church in the area entered one of the most formative periods in its history. Urban made a profession of canonical obedience to Anselm, archbishop of Canterbury and his diocese was the first of the Welsh sees to be effectively incorporated into the province of Canterbury. The political conquest and the establishment of ecclesiastical control from Canterbury helped to break down the isolation of the Welsh Church and to broaden the channels through which new reforming influences could flow. At this period the papacy had assumed a vigorous leadership of the Church which was to revitalize its life and tighten its organization. The popes were determined to wrest the Church at all levels from the domination of laymen, to stamp out simony (the purchase and sale of church offices) and to enforce the existing canon law forbidding clerical marriage. The impact of these reforming ideals were to be felt as keenly in Glamorgan as elsewhere and was to result in the complete refashioning of the machinery of pastoral care and the establishment of the parochial system as its main component.

The period saw the completion of the process by which parish boundaries were precisely demarcated. It now seems clear that the parochial boundaries of most of the major churches were already in existence before Urban became bishop of Llandaff in 1107. But the Anglo-Norman colonisation of lowland Glamorgan created new units and new patterns of settlement which made necessary a deliberate drawing of new boundaries and an adjustment of the old. An example of this can be illustrated from the history of Llancarfan parish. About 1140 Archbishop Theobald complained that 'chapels had been lately built in the parish of Llancarfan' without authorisation. These chapels were probably the forerunners of the parish churches of Penmark, Barry, Porthkerry

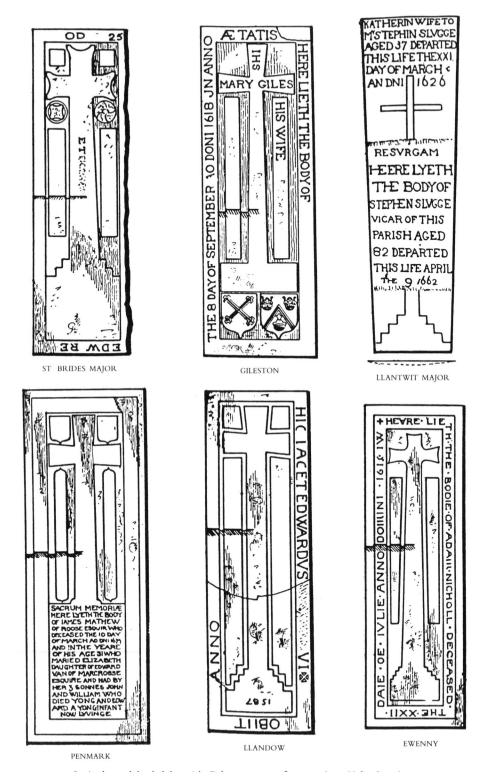

Incised sepulchral slabs with Calvary crosses from various Vale churches

and Cwmcidy and eventually acquired their own parochial boundaries. Merthyr Dyfan too seems to have been a post-conquest church whose parochial territory was further divided in the late 12th century to form new parishes for the daughter churches of Cadoxton and Uchelolau (Highlight). This process of parochial demarcation (which had probably been completed by the mid-13th century) was made all the more necessary because the Church was placing particular emphasis on everyone's obligation to pay tithe for the support of the clergy. The incumbent of a church needed to know the exact area from which he could draw tithe.

But the parochial system was not merely a matter of boundaries. During this period a succession of canon lawyer-popes, in an attempt to make the parish church an effective instrument of pastoral care, gradually created and defined the offices of patron, rector and vicar. The position and rights of the village lord who in the 11th century 'granted' a village church to a parson were transformed by the new canon law. The popes insisted that laymen should have a right of patronage or advowson only, that is, the right of 'presenting' a cleric to the bishop for 'institution' to a living. If the bishop considered the presentee a worthy person to be incumbent he would then institute and induct him as rector of the living. In cases where a rector could not reside or where the rectorial tithes had been granted to a monastery, the rector or the monastery was to present to the bishop a suitable person as vicar or stipendiary priest to perform the services. We know from surviving episcopal acts that these regulations were being applied to Glamorgan churches by the bishops of Llandaff in the 12th and 13th centuries.

Before the end of the 12th century the rural deans make their first appearance in the records of Llandaff diocese. They acted as valuable links between the bishop and the archdeacon on the one hand and the parish clergy on the other and in Glamorgan supervised groups of parishes which formed the territorial deaneries of Groneath and Llandaff. Sometime before 1291 Groneath had been subdivided to form a third deanery, that of Kenfig, but this had ceased to exist by the time the *Valor Ecclesiasticus* was drawn up in 1535.

The Anglo-Norman conquest also assisted the introduction into Glamorgan of new monastic institutions. The key abbeys involved in the establishment of Benedictine monasticism were Tewkesbury and Gloucester. Robert Fitz-Hamon made lavish grants from his newly-conquered territory to these two abbeys, granting the ancient monastic centres of Llandough and Llantwit Major to Tewkesbury and that of Llancarfan to Gloucester. In time Tewkesbury established a dependent priory at St. Mary's, Cardiff and Gloucester a similar priory at St. Michael's, Ewenny. The new, reformed Cistercian order, too, acquired foundations within the lordship at Neath (at first a Savigniac house but transferred to the Cistercian order in 1147) and Margam (1147). These two abbeys were to become the richest Cistercian houses in Wales.

The new monasteries impinged on the parochial life of the Vale at a number of levels. They held extensive lands in the Vale and must have recruited many of their monks and lay brothers from this area. A development which had

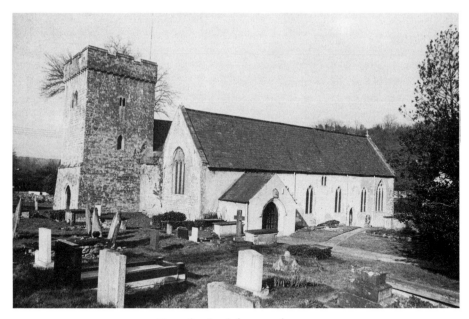

Llancarfan church from south-west

Ewenny Priory church from north side in 1897

important consequences for the future was the granting of the rectorial tithes of Vale churches to monasteries within and outside Glamorgan. Of the 45 Vale churches treated in this volume some 14 were eventually thus appropriated and had their great tithes siphoned off to monasteries. Some of these churches were the richest in the Vale and when, at the Dissolution, the property of the monasteries were sold to laymen or corporate institutions outside the county this substantial source of income was lost to the Church for ever.

The building of the monastic churches at Ewenny from 1141 and at Margam in the 1180s was on a scale hitherto unseen in Glamorgan. They may have prompted patrons and parish clergy to undertake the rebuilding of village churches in Glamorgan. We know from the architecture of many Vale churches that the period 1150 and 1300 was one of great building activity, one which saw the building of new churches and the rebuilding of older, more primitive structures on more ambitious lines. Many additions and modifications to structures were of course made after 1300—towers and porches were added and new style windows inserted. One or two churches—Bonvilston for example—were practically rebuilt in the 19th century. But generally it can be said that between 1150 and 1350 the Vale churches assumed the form we are familiar with today.

Although the structural form of the Vale churches had become fixed by the mid-14th century, a 20th-century visitor, were it possible for him to be transported back in time, would have observed marked differences in the 'look' of churches both from without and from within. In medieval times the Vale churches concealed their outside stonework under a coat of limewash. Church roofs if they were not stone-tiled were sometimes thatched—the use of blue slate dates from the late 18th century onwards. Within the churches the walls were plastered and used for mural paintings of biblical scenes and incidents in the lives of the saints. Niches were adorned with painted images of saints. It is a truism of modern media studies that what is seen is more readily assimilated and remembered than what is heard. In an age when most laymen were illiterate, parish priests would use these 'visual aids' to reinforce their sermons and homilies. Some fine examples of medieval mural painting have survived at Colwinston and Llantwit Major.

Wooden altars were customary in England and presumably in Wales from early times but the Council of Winchester (1070) urged the desirability of stone altars in churches. Bishop Wulfstan of Worcester (1062-95) was substituting stone altars for wooden ones during his episcopate and since Bishop Urban of Llandaff had been a priest of Worcester, their introduction into his own diocese could not have been long delayed. The stone altar, stressing the sacrificial aspect of the Mass, now assumed a position near or against the east wall of the chancel, a position it has retained in both Roman Catholic and Anglican churches until the liturgical reforms of recent times. The growing importance of the chancel as a holy place echoed the legislation of the reforming papacy which laid emphasis on the separateness of the clergy as a body apart from the laity. The chancel became their preserve—not only a place where Mass was celebrated and where the clergy sat for the recitation of the divine office but a part of the fabric for the repair of which the rector took financial responsibility. The rood-screen—a wooden structure surmounted by the image of Christ crucified—completed this separation. These physical features of the late medieval parish churches are important because they embodied theological concepts which were to come under attack from the Protestant reformers. Transubstantiation, the sacrificial aspect of the Mass, the role of the priest as an intermediary between God and man, and of the saints as intercessors were concepts which were to dominate the theological debates of the 16th century.

In England and Wales the Reformation changes were initially prompted by Henry VIII's determination to have his marriage to Catherine of Aragon annulled. The legislation which passed through the Reformation Parliament between 1532 and 1534 effectively put an end to the pope's jurisdiction in England and Wales and substituted in its place the royal supremacy. In 1536 the abbey of Margam and in 1539 the abbey of Neath and the priory of Ewenny were dissolved. But as long as Henry VIII lived no major changes were made in sacramental doctrine and the Mass continued to be said in Latin with the old ceremonial. On the accession of Edward VI, however, power fell into the hands of those who were eager for radical Protestant change. The heresy laws were suspended, communion allowed to be administered in both kinds, images in churches removed and priests permitted to marry. The first Prayer Book, wholly in English and largely the work of Archbishop Thomas Cranmer was issued in 1549. It was a distillation of the medieval Latin liturgies translated into an English at once sonorous and majestic. It was followed in 1552 by a radically revised second Prayer Book in which references to the sacrificial aspects of the Mass were eliminated. Chantries in parish churches, institutions specially endowed for the recitation of Masses for departed souls, had been dissolved in 1547 and this had already resulted in major losses of vestments and plate from parish churches. In 1553 a more thorough raid was made of church goods when commissioners were ordered to confiscate from churches all ornaments and vestments beyond the minimum laid down in the 1552 Prayer Book. The inventories for Glamorgan have survived and some of them have been printed (*Cardiff Records*, i, 379-86). They show the enormous losses of plate, ornaments and vestments which the Vale churches sustained at this time. During her short reign (1553-58) Mary attempted to put back the clock and restore Roman Catholicism and the papal supremacy. But the burnings of Protestants and the alliance with Spain alienated public opinion and strengthened anti-papal feeling.

On the accession of Elizabeth the pendulum of change which had swung so violently in previous reigns came to rest. Elizabeth was unable to restore, as perhaps she would have wished, the religious situation as it existed in the reign of her father. Her church settlement which was intended to satisfy the desires of the majority of her subjects, was based on a re-issue of the second Prayer Book of 1552 with some significant changes of a conservative kind. The ornaments of the church and the dress of the clergy were to be those in use in 1548 when the traditional priestly vestments were still worn. The so-called 'Black Rubric' of 1552 which declared that no adoration of the Real Presence was intended by kneeling at the Communion was dropped.

It is difficult to determine the reactions of the parish priests and people of the Vale to the momentous changes of the 16th century. Few of them had the ability or means to convey their thoughts to posterity. Most of them seem to have accepted the changes and conformed—but with reservations. It must be remembered that many parishioners of the Vale at this period, and indeed well into the modern period, were Welsh speaking and for them the new English liturgy had little meaning. For the Glamorgan poet Thomas ap Ieuan ap Rhys (*c*. 1510-*c*. 1560) the new Protestant teaching was an alien faith imposed on the Welsh. He lamented the liturgical and sacramental changes: the great stone altars cast down and replaced by communion tables like widows' boards and the removal of those accessories—incense, the rood and holy-water stoups—which had given colour, drama and consolation to so many medieval worshippers. Not until the new liturgy was made available in Welsh in the second half of the 16th century did the threat of active opposition to the Elizabethan settlement recede. Even then a brave minority refused to conform. One of the most prominent recusants in the Vale was Sir Thomas Stradling (1499-1571). He acquired a certain notoriety in the early years of Elizabeth's reign from a miracle which was alleged to have occurred in his park. On the night of 20th March, 1559, the Tuesday before Good Friday, an old ash tree in his park was struck down by lightning. Sir Thomas, viewing the damage the following morning, found in the split stump of the tree the clear impression of a cross fourteen inches long. He made a drawing of the cross and had four pictures of it painted. He kept one of the pictures for himself but gave two to well-wishers and a fourth he sent to his daughter at Louvain. By 1561 news of the alleged miracle had reached Elizabeth's minister, Cecil. He feared it would become a rallying point for those who favoured the old faith and a threat to the security of the throne. Thomas Stradling was thrown into the Tower and a commission appointed to enquire into the 'miracle'. John Santlowe, the vicar of St. Donat's and one of the witnesses questioned, hastened to emphasize that 'he had never said any kind of service since he was vicar, but only according to the Queen's proceedings since the old service was abolished.' Sir Thomas was released in 1563 but never subscribed to the Act of Uniformity. The government allowed him, in his infirmity, to remain unmolested. The recusant rolls of Elizabeth's reign show a number of priests administering the sacraments according to the Roman rite and pockets of recusants loyal to the old faith in the Vale parishes of Colwinston, Penllin, Llancarfan, Kenfig/Pyle and Newcastle. But these recusants lacked the protective umbrella which only powerful landowners of the stature of the Marquis of Worcester could provide. The old faith in the Vale gradually withered and died as the 17th century advanced.

The tensions inherent in the Elizabethan church settlement—the tug between those who wished to retain traditional Catholic ceremonial and doctrine, those who wished for a more Protestant Prayer Book and those who wanted to scrap

ANNO DOMINI. 1559.   XIII. KALEND. APRILIS.

Hanc crucis effigiem,pie lector,fraxinus ipso ,   *Fraxinus hæreticos duros , hominesq,rebelles:*
Quem legis hìc, anno , mense,dieq,dedit.   *Mites corde viros tecta medulla notat.*
Arbor apud Vuallos Stradlingi creuit in aruis: *Fraxinei Christi obscurant insignia trunci ,*
Hic torquatus eques(si modò quæris) erat.   *Obscurata tegunt signa , virosq,premunt.*
Tempestas oritur ,fortis confringitur arbor: *Sed Libani Cedros tandem,hæreticosq, rebelles*
Exhibet hanc mollis deinde medulla crucem.   *Confringet summi ferrea virga Dei.*
Formam charta docet , nux auellana colorem: *Tunc cultusq,Dei,pietasq,,fidesq, vigebunt:*
Mensura,expressit quam tibi pictor,erat.   *Exeret & celsum crux tua,Christe,caput.*

IOANNES   FENNVS.

The 'miracle' of St. Donat's: the Latin verses by John Fenn tell the 'gentle reader'
of the finding of the image of the Cross in an ash tree split during a great
storm in April, 1559, and go on to turn the incident into symbolic representation of
the triumph of Christ (From Nicholas Harpsfield, *Dialogi Sex,* Paris, 1566)

episcopal government altogether—were yet to be worked out. The religious history of the greater part of the 17th century is largely taken up with the story of how one party and now another gained the upper hand and attempted to impose its own views. Charles I's support of the High Church party associated with Archbishop Laud and suspicions that there might be a return to Roman Catholicism were among the issues which bedevilled relations between Charles and his Parliaments and led to the outbreak of the Civil War.

In 1643 the Long Parliament abolished episcopacy and made efforts to see that altars, crosses, statues, candlesticks and other ornaments were removed from churches. Two years later Archbishop Laud was executed, the Prayer Book abolished and the Directory, a Parliamentary service book, put in its place. In 1650 an Act for the Propagation of the Gospel in Wales was passed. This was a deliberate attempt to puritanize Wales. Commissioners were appointed to examine incumbents and to eject from their livings those found guilty of delinquency, malignancy and non-residence.

Initially the application of this legislation in Glamorgan may have been felt less severely because so many of the major landed families in the area—the Stradlings of St. Donat's, the Bassetts of Beaupré, the Aubreys of Llantrithyd, the Carnes of Ewenny and the Mansels of Margam—were loyal supporters of Charles I. But when the fortunes of war began to go against the royalists, new leaders emerged. Men like Bussy Mansel (the grandson of Sir Thomas Mansel) and Colonel Philip Jones were not only officers in the Parliamentary army but men of great local power who were sympathetic to the Puritan cause. The battle of St. Fagans in 1648 was decisive and laid the church in Glamorgan wide open to Puritan persecution. We know that some 35 incumbents in Glamorgan were ejected from their livings before 1650 and some 20 after the Act of Propagation. The sufferings of these clergy and their families were harsh. The services of the church in many parishes were now suspended for long periods. John Walker in his *Sufferings of the Clergy* tells us that Llancarfan church was 'shut up, and the parish had services very seldom'. Radical 'enthusiasts' descended on other churches, men like Alsop, who took possession of Penarth and Lavernock, 'telling the people that he was sent by the Lord unto them, to pitch his tent among them. As he did undisturbed until the Restoration.' Wherever large bodies of Puritan soldiers gathered there were incidents. Puritan troopers burst into Llandaff cathedral at service time, seized the chalice from the celebrant's hands and marched off some of the communicants to gaol. Walter, the weaver, mounted the pulpit and preached for three hours against the ceremonies of the church. Few churches in the Vales were sufficiently rich in statuary and decoration to attract the more violent of the Puritan iconoclasts but we may be sure that any ornaments or furniture remaining which were in any way reminiscent of the Catholic past were now removed. The interiors of the Vale churches took on an uncared-for, barn-like appearance which they retained well into the 19th century. The modern churchman will naturally sympathize with the plight of the persecuted Church at this time, but it should be remembered that the Puritans had not smashed a smoothly-running, faultless

Church. Some of the evicted incumbants were drunkards, as even John Walker admitted, and many more were pluralists who never set foot in the parishes from which they drew their income. Walker's own words were echoed by those of the Reverend Thomas Fuller writing at the beginning of the conflict: 'there be drunkards on both sides and swearers on both sides, pious on both sides and profane on both sides.'

With the restoration of Charles II in 1660 there were some hopes at first of devising a church settlement sufficiently comprehensive to include the Presbyterians and the more moderate Independents. These hopes were dashed by the failure of the Savoy Conference and the return of the Cavalier Parliament in 1661. The Act of Uniformity (1662) insisted that all church ministers should accept the newly-revised Prayer Book and those who refused were ejected from their livings. Some 23 ministers were ejected from Glamorgan livings during the period 1660-1662. There now followed a period of persecution of dissenters which lasted intermittently throughout the reigns of Charles II and James II. It was brought to an end by the Toleration Act of 1689. This Act was in many ways a crucial one for the Established Church. It relieved Nonconformists of the money fine for which they had previously been liable for not attending service in the parish church. Those dissenters who had previously lacked the courage or financial resources to brave the censures of the law now left the Established Church and attended their own places of worship. But the Act also unintentionally provided a licence for the apathetic. Many now absented themselves from all forms of organised worship.

Historians have long been aware of the imperfections and short-comings of the Established Church during the 18th and early 19th century. Free thinkers like Gibbon and caricaturists like Rowlandson and Cruikshank projected a vivid image of the 'fat slumbers of the Church', of well-fed, complacent, pluralist incumbents and lean, thread-bare curates. It was an image eagerly taken up by historians of the church in the following century and they reinforced the general picture of a Church characterised by torpor, slackness and neglect of organised churchmanship coupled with an obsessive suspicion of anything that smacked of zeal, 'enthusiasm', or popery. More recently historians have been examining the life of the Church within the context of the age rather than from hindsight. They have challenged the more sweeping generalizations and have convincingly demonstrated that a strong current of reform was running through the Church even before the Methodist Revival had made its influence felt. The sterling work of the S.P.C.K. in distributing bibles and religious literature in rural parishes, the establishment of a diocesan library at Cowbridge to encourage the further education of the clergy and the achievements of the circulating schools of Griffith Jones in promoting literacy and catachetical instruction were all part of this ground-swell of reform. Many Glamorgan clergy were particularly appreciative of the circulating schools. 'Our churches', wrote the curate of Gelligaer in 1741, 'are now near as full again of auditors as they used to be . . . our solemn assemblies are thronged and what is more to be taken notice of, there is a visible change for the better in the lives and behaviour of the people, which induces me to hope that God pours down His blessing in great abundance upon this new way ... of reviving religion among us'. Thanks to the researches of the past generation of historians a much more sympathetic interpretation of the life of the Church during the period is now beginning to emerge.

The Church was operating under considerable constraints. These were partly a legacy of its constitution, partly a reaction against the sectarian bitterness and violence of the previous century. The bishops of Llandaff, like bishops of other dioceses, were still essentially medieval officers ruling over a medieval institution. Apart from their meagre personal income (amounting to about £400 at the beginning of the century), they had no central financial fund at their disposal and no central administrative body or diocesan committee to implement reform. They exercised what executive authority they had through their archdeacons, rural deans and incumbents. Bishops were chosen as much for their political value as for their qualities as pastoral leaders. They had long since ceased to act as powerful ministers of state but the government still expected their support in the House of Lords. This meant residence in London for the winter and spring of each year, leaving them the summer months to administer their dioceses. The records of the triennial visitations that have survived for Llandaff diocese however show that these duties were punctiliously performed and go far to dispel the image of an uncaring, absentee diocesan.

The clergy who held the livings and manned the parishes of the Vale fell into two groups: the graduates who had received their education at Oxford and Cambridge and those—later to be known as 'literates'—who were educated at the grammar schools of Cowbridge, Usk and Abergavenny or in local parsonage houses. Neither group received much more than a smattering of theological or pastoral training to fit them for their work but there were many handbooks of advice and instruction for clerics beginning their careers and these had a wide circulation. The possession of a degree certainly enhanced the prospects of clerical promotion but in the last resort patronage was all important. The patronage of most of the Vale livings was held by gentry families and a cleric who was a member of such a family or related to a family which had served a gentry house in some professional capacity such as a steward, had a better chance of acquiring the more desirable livings than an 'outsider'. In the 18th and early 19th centuries the Church in the Vale was very much a family affair.

Livings in Llandaff diocese were notoriously poor. At the beginning of the 18th century only 39 livings in the diocese had an income of over £50. As was explained earlier the greater tithes of many churches were in the hands of laymen or of corporate bodies outside the county. Some livings were too slender individually to support a parson and his family and it became customary for the more highly-favoured clergy to acquire more than one living to secure a decent livelihood. Given the low value of church livings a certain amount of pluralism was inevitable and the problem was not a new one in the 18th century. But no amount of apologetics can excuse the more notorious cases. Miles Bassett (d. 1813) was vicar of Aberafan, vicar of Swansea and perpetual

Llancarfan church—carving on pillar
of south arcade

St. Bride's Major church—carved head of
label stop on the north wall of nave

Llantwit Major church—figure of winged cherub-head on monument

curate of Bonvilston, Oystermouth and St. Ismaels, Ferryside. Dr. J. T. Casberd (d. 1843) was canon of Llandaff, canon of Wells and vicar of Penmark as well as being vicar of Llantwit and Llysworney. Pluralism on this scale took many of the clergy into the ranks of the middling gentry. Men like Bassett and Casberd could not personally serve all the livings they held in plurality and they were forced to delegate the task to curates who performed the church services for lowly stipends varying from £20 to £50 a year. It has been claimed with some justice that the Church in Llandaff diocese between 1660 and 1816 was kept alive by its curates.

Most of the Vale churches had at least one service on Sunday; either Morning or Evening Prayer. Holy Communion was celebrated less frequently. The Book of Common Prayer of 1549 and the 21st canon of 1604 had recommended a minimum of three celebrations a year, on the great festivals of Christmas, Easter and Whitsun and this became the norm for many rural parishes. In the Vale, however, many churches had four or five celebrations a year in the second half of the 18th century and a few (Bonvilston, Llantrithyd and St. Nicholas) could boast a monthly celebration. But not all who attended, communicated. Many considered that taking Communion was 'for the quality' or for those who were particularly pious.

Outside the main centres like Cowbridge and Llantwit, the Vale churches were dank and cheerless places. Matthew Bramble, a character in Smollett's *Humphry Clinker* might well have included them in his general observations on the ancient parish churches of England with their 'gross, stagnated air, surcharged with damps from vaults, tombs and charnel houses'. They were, he observed, 'so many magazines of rheums created for the benefit of the medical profession . . . in the winter months especially . . . more bodies are lost than souls saved'. As the 18th century advanced the fabric of many Vale churches were showing the effects of age and weather. The build-up of earth from repeated burials around the southern side of chancels and naves was one cause of the damp which seeped through the walls. But wind and weather had also taken their toll over the centuries leaving rotting roofs and crumbling masonry. Bishop Shute Barrington's *Diocese Book* compiled from the returns of his primary visitation—in itself a testimony to his pastoral concern—gives a fair picture of the fabric defects of the Vale churches at this time. A few examples will suffice. At St. Bride's Major it was noted that 'the church wants better seats, west end of tower wants pointing and other repairs, some of the walls being mouldered away'. At Wick the 'south side of the roof damaged by the wind; porch wants repairing and the tower pointing, chancel not level and paved as church is'. At Llangan 'north west end of roof sinks, a purling being broke there and also on the opposite side . . . chancel lathes in the south side decayed . . .'. At St. Mary Hill, 'church chancel and porch neither level nor paved, pine end of chancel leans out of perpendicular and the wall opens within and without. Side walls in bad condition. Part of the roof on the north side damaged, seats want repairing.' The fabric of the Vale churches was not completely neglected in the 18th and early 19th centuries. Repair work and a certain amount of restoration

Colwinston church—figure of Madonna and Child in niche in chancel wall

Llantwit Major church—Jacobean figure in north wall of Western church

and refurbishing of furniture was undertaken but the church rate levied by churchwardens was often insufficient for major works and the patrons of livings were not uniformly generous in contributing to the costs involved.

The religious climate of the Hanoverian Church was one of moderation. It was a natural reaction of a society that had experienced the worst effects of bigotry and fanaticism in the previous century. 'Moderation', wrote David Hume, 'is of advantage to every establishment . . . extremes of all kinds are to be avoided'. In such a society it was inevitable that Methodism would have a mixed reception. Methodism originated as a revivalist movement within the established Church. It grew naturally out of the reformist activities of the S.P.C.K. at the beginning of the century. The churchmen who led the Methodist movement placed great emphasis on the need for personal conversion and took the Christian message outside the parish church to vast audiences that the Church had failed to reach. The movement's appeal was to the heart rather than the head.

It soon divided into two broad theological groups. The leaders of the indigenous Welsh movement, Howell Harris and Daniel Rowlands, ordered their religious thought on the theology of John Calvin. The latter stressed the absolute corruption of man's nature, the election by God of those who are to be saved and justification by faith alone. These Calvinistic Methodists of Wales had their counterparts in the movement led by George Whitfield in England. The followers of John Wesley by contrast emphasised man's free will. They argued that the doctrine of the election of some involved the reprobation of others. It made God into a tyrant and took away from man any responsibility for his own salvation. Both brands of Methodism—the Calvinistic and the Arminian or Wesleyan—acquired substantial pockets of adherents in the Vale and they survived and flourished largely through the sympathetic support of landed gentry families who held the patronage of a number of Vale churches: the Joneses of Fonmon, the Thomases of Wenvoe and the Edwins of Llanmihangel. It is no surprise to find Methodist supporters and sympathisers as incumbents in the parishes of which they were patrons; John Richards at Porthkerry, Philip Thomas at Michaelston-le-Pit, John Hodges at Wenvoe and David Jones at Llangan.

But most incumbents of the Vale, backed by their patrons, strenuously opposed the setting up of Methodist societies in their parishes. The strength of their opposition is aptly summed up by the Reverend W. Miles, vicar of Llanblethian in his reply to the visitation queries of 1763; 'There is a methodist meeting house at Aberthyn in this parish—tinkers, thatchers, weavers and other vermin.'

The Methodist leaders had from the first protested their loyalty to the Established Church and insisted that members of their societies should attend Sunday service at their parish church. But towards the end of the century pressures within the movement grew for the Methodists to ordain their own ministers. The Wesleyans resisted this pressure until after the death of their leader in 1791 and the Calvinistic Methodists until 1811. The Church has often

Cadoxton-juxta-Barry church interior prior to restoration in 1885

been blamed for failing to contain the movement and harness its energies but it is hard to see how it could have done so. The Methodists had set up their own independent organisation in competition to the parish church and had done so without obtaining official authorisation either at parochial or diocesan level. Their meeting houses were already well established in many Vale villages before the final break. Even more crucial in making the breach inevitable was the ambivalent ideas which the leaders themselves held on what constituted a validly ordained ministry. Wesley had himself, as early as 1784, acted as a bishop in 'consecrating' two superintendents for the Methodist congregations in America. In the circumstances it is difficult to see how the pressure from laymen within the movement for non-episcopal 'ordinations' of this kind could be resisted. The secession was nevertheless a grave blow. Many devout Christians were lost to the Church and they now attended their own denominational chapels. Some Methodists, particularly in the Vale, continued to resort to their parish churches for the Communion service but as the 19th century advanced these Wesleyans and Calvinistic Methodists became increasingly identified with the Nonconformists of the older dissent in their criticism of the Established Church and later in the pressure for Disestablishment of the Church.

The Religious Census of 1851 showed how deeply entrenched Nonconformity was in the Vale. There were about 50 regular meeting houses of the four main denominations: the Independents, the Baptists, the Wesleyans and the Calvinistic Methodists. Of these the latter were numerically the largest. There was also one chapel of the Unitarians or General Baptists at Wick and two or three small and short-lived congregations of Mormons. On Census Sunday, 30th March, 1851 it would seem that about half the population attended chapel or meeting while only a fifth attended the parish church. But the problems posed by the situation in the Vale were far less pressing than those in other parts of the diocese. Thanks to the relatively high level of agricultural wages the population of the Vale remained fairly stable throughout the 19th century. It was an area, too, plentifully supplied with churches. There was no pressing need for a movement of church extension. The situation was far graver in the large, upland parishes of the diocese where the iron and coal industries had brought together large and growing concentrations of population. Nonconformity with its more flexible organisation and its ability to respond more quickly to the needs of a growing population had in these areas stolen an even more dramatic march on the Church. There was a desperate need for more places of worship and for more clergy to serve them. It was to these problems that a new bishop, Alfred Ollivant (1849-82), was to direct most of his energies in the first half of his episcopate.

Before Ollivant's appointment, the Established Church at national level and with government initiative had already taken the first steps to set its house in order. The Tithe Commutation Act (1836), the Established Church Act (1836), the Pluralities Act (1836), the Ecclesiastical Duties and Revenues Act (1840), the New Parishes Act (1843) and the setting up of the Ecclesiastical Commissioners in 1835 to manage the estates of the church and make a more equitable

Llangan church—head of churchyard cross

distribution of its income, were well designed to remove long-standing abuses and to provide the church with more efficient machinery to discharge its pastoral functions. The effects of these administrative reforms were not felt immediately and Ollivant had to plan his own strategy and provide finances for carrying it out without much help from the Ecclesiastical Commissioners. Using the directing agency of the Llandaff Church Diocesan Extension Society (set up in 1850) and with assistance from the well-to-do and from such organisations as the Pastoral Aid Society, the Incorporated Church Building Society and the Additional Curates Society, Ollivant was able during his episcopate to build, rebuild or restore 170 churches in the diocese and to provide the Church in the coalfield with something like the level of clerical manpower it needed to perform its mission.

But the Church could not have been reformed and transformed solely through the agency of legislation and church extension. It needed a fresh infusion of spiritual vigour and this was provided by two movements within the Church: the Evangelical Movement and the Oxford Movement.

The church extension movement had brought to the fore a number of evangelical clergymen whose activities were to make a lasting impression on the life of the Church in the third quarter of the 19th century. As a group the evangelicals had their origin in the 18th century. They laid special stress on personal conversion and salvation by faith in the atoning death of Christ, on the supreme importance of the scriptures and preaching at the expense of tradition, the sacraments and liturgical worship. At many points they had much in common with the Methodists but they remained loyal to the Church and worked within the framework of the parochial system. In the 1850s and 1860s evangelicals like John Griffith at Merthyr, John Hanmer Griffiths at Neath, Richard Llewelyn at Maesteg and W. Leigh Morgan at Cardiff brought a vigour to their preaching and a commitment to their pastoral role which projected a new image of the Anglican minister particularly in the industrial and urban parishes.

The followers of the Oxford Movement were spokesmen for a completely different brand of churchmanship. The movement was started in 1833 by a group of Oxford dons who were concerned for the security of the Church in a period of reform when all established institutions were coming under attack or criticism. They viewed the church not as a man-made institution but as a divine society founded by Christ and endowed with supernatural powers. The ministers of the Church, its bishops, priests and deacons, derived their authority not from the State but by direct descent, through the laying on of hands, from the Apostles themselves. They were dispensers of divinely instituted sacraments which were regarded as the chief means of grace and the guarantee of personal salvation and holiness. These ideals were propagated by a series of ninety tracts published between 1833 and 1841 which were distributed to churchmen throughout the country. The introduction of ceremonial and ritual into the services of the Church was not initially the concern of the Tractarians—Pusey himself had once innocently asked a colleague 'What is a cope?'—but the development grew naturally out of their high conception of the Church and of its sacraments and was assisted by the work of the Cambridge Camden Society.

This society was founded in 1839 by two Cambridge undergraduates, John Mason Neale and Benjamin Webb, with the object of studying ecclesiastical art. It became through its periodical, *The Ecclesiologist*, an influential pressure group promoting the restoration of old churches, the building of new ones and the furnishing of both according to the society's own strict canons of what was acceptable in ecclesiastical art and what should be rejected. The ecclesiologists were anxious to alter the arrangements of the typical parish church of the early 19th century, to rid it of its dominant three-decker pulpit, its galleries and pews and to restore the sanctuary to the place of honour it had enjoyed in medieval times with an altar raised on steps and with a proper reredos. Later they advocated the introduction of lecterns, choir stalls in the chancel, lighted candles and frontals on the altar, screens, side chapels, sedilia, piscinae and credence tables. They urged in fact a return to what they considered parish churches might have looked like in the 14th century. The publications of the ecclesiologists were widely circulated among squires and clergy in the second half of the 19th century and greatly influenced the way old churches were restored and new churches built.

Llandaff diocese in mid-century was an area where most of the clergy could be labelled 'low' or 'broad' church and Bishop Ollivant in 1857 could still comfort himself that the activities of the Tractarians, which were causing concern to other diocesans, had not yet disturbed the tranquillity of his own diocese. Among the first Tractarians to be appointed to livings within the diocese was Evan Lewis, instituted to the parish of Aberdare (a Bute living) in 1859. Lewis was at Jesus College, Oxford when the Oxford Movement was in full swing and his brother, David, had served as curate to John Henry Newman, one of the movement's founders, when the latter was vicar of St. Mary's, Oxford. But Lewis was not a ritualist and his ministry at Aberdare did not provoke the disturbances soon to be caused by Tractarians in a number of parishes in Monmouthshire. In the Glamorgan part of the diocese the key events in the spread of Tractarian ideals were the conversion to Roman Catholicism of the third Marquis of Bute in 1868 and the adoption of the ideals of the movement in the same decade by members of the Talbot family of Margam and Penrice.

The Marquis of Bute was the patron of a number of Glamorgan livings and this patronage was exercised after his conversion, by trustees, all of whom were sympathetic to the movement. As a result of presentations by these trustees, Aberdare, Dowlais, St. Mary's, Cardiff and Roath became major centres of the Anglo-Catholic movement within the Church. It has been suggested that the children of C. R. M. Talbot—Theodore, Emily and Olive—first came under the influence of the Oxford Movement through the influence of their governess, Miss Neale, a sister of J. M. Neale, the ecclesiologist and Tractarian hymn-writer, and their promotion of the Tractarian cause is apparent in the support they gave in the 1860s to the Anglo-Catholic parson of Llanmadoc and Cheriton, the Rev. J. D. Davies. But another key event was certainly the meeting in 1869 of Theodore Talbot with Father Arthur Stanton of St. Alban's, Holborn, then one of the most noted centres of the Anglo-Catholic movement in London. Theodore devoted much of his time to social work in that slum parish and on his return eagerly set about restoring the parish church of Margam (1872-3) in accordance with the principles of the ecclesiologists: 'Let us begin by demolishing the Squire's and Parson's pews', he remarked to workmen dismantling the interior of the old church, 'there must be no vested interest here'. After Theodore's tragic death through a riding accident in 1876, his work for the movement was taken up by his sisters and Margam became the centre of the Anglo-Catholic revival in West Glamorgan.

The Vale lay outside the main centres where the Evangelicals and Tractarians wielded their greatest influence and although there were incumbents with Tractarian sympathies—Reverend J. B. Gwyn at Merthyr Mawr, Reverend Daniel Evans at Llanmaes and Fr. Jenner at Wenvoe—none of the Vale churches became a stronghold of party interest as many of them had been before the secession of the Methodists. But in the second half of the century the Church in the Vale was responding to all the new influences that were abroad in the Church—to the reforming activities of the newly-activated rural deans as well as to the pervasive influences generated by the Evangelical and Tractarian movements. Bishop Ollivant had begun a practice of summoning his rural deans to annual meetings and they became useful instruments of his reforming zeal. The clergy of the Vale had always numbered a large proportion of Oxford and Cambridge graduates among its ranks. By birth and education they belonged to the gentry class and shared their society and interests perhaps at the expense of their poorer parishioners. They were now beginning to show a deeper spiritual and moral commitment to their pastoral office, a greater sensitivity to the needs of their parishioners and of society at large. They increased the number of services within the parish church and improved their quality. The dull drone which characterised services at the beginning of the century gave place to more orderly and lively services with congregational hymn-singing led by small trained choirs. The latter development had been stimulated by the formation of the Llandaff Diocesan Church Choral Society in 1861. This society did much to raise the standards of choral worship within the diocese. The clergy were also taking a more active role in general parish affairs. They founded and promoted day schools and Sunday schools and attempted, with a good deal of success, to channel the energies of their more boisterous parishioners away from the rumbustious and sometimes violent activities of the village *mabsant* into parish clubs and societies. The churches were becoming better manned. Between 1850 and 1910 the number of ordained clergy in the four Welsh dioceses rose from 700 to 1,543. Much of this increased manpower went to serve the newly-carved out parishes in urban and industrial areas but rural areas like the Vale also benefited. Increased clerical manpower and a succession of Pluralities Acts (1838, 1850, 1885) stopped the scandal of absentee clergymen drawing comparatively large incomes from numerous livings.

Bonvilston church—Early-English-style
capital on organ chamber arch (*left*)

Wenvoe church—elaborately carved
19th-century corbel of chancel arch (*right*)

St. Donat's church—winged cherub-head on monument in nave

The fabric of the churches was also immeasurably improved and here the influence of the ecclesiologists was paramount. Many of the principles enunciated so confidently by the ecclesiologists and Gothic revivalists can now be seen to have been misconceived and some of them were arrant nonsense. The remark of Pugin to a priest 'How do you expect to achieve the conversion of England dressed in a cope like that?' illustrates the dottier, more bizarre side of the movement. It has been claimed that the restoration of rural churches was prompted as much by the antiquarian interests of patrons and incumbents as by religious zeal. This may well have been so but the wave of restoration work undertaken in the second half of the century preserved the Vale churches from impending destruction by wind and weather and enabled a priceless heritage of architecture to be passed on to our own generation. More importantly, the Vale churches became fitter and seemlier places for worship. The influence of the ecclesiologists can be seen in the new furnishings introduced in the second half of the 19th and early 20th centuries—in the lecterns and choir stalls, in the open seating which replaced the box pews, in the increased importance accorded to the chancel and altar and also in the way masonry was restored to emphasise the medieval features of the church. For the best examples of the art of the ecclesiologists, however, one must go outside the group of churches treated in this volume to Merthyr Mawr and St. German's, Cardiff. The old church at Merthyr Mawr was taken down in the late 1840s and a new church rebuilt in accordance with the principles of the ecclesiologists by the diocesan architect, John Prichard from plans drawn up by Benjamin Ferrey, a pupil of the elder Pugin. It was consecrated in 1851. St. German's, Cardiff is a larger and more mature work, designed by Bodley and Garner and opened in 1884. It has what is perhaps the most aesthetically satisfying interior of any church in Wales.

In the second half of the century the professional training of the clergy was still exercising the concern of the diocesan. St. David's College, Lampeter opened its doors to new students in 1827 and trained many priests who were subsequently to work in Llandaff diocese but the diocese had to wait until 1892 for its own theological college. The college of St. Michael and All Angels had its first home at Aberdare but moved to Llandaff in 1911. Patronised by the High Church Talbot family at Margam and with a teaching staff Tractarian in its sympathies it produced a number of clergy in the Anglo-Catholic tradition. But even in the present century some ordinands still went outside the diocese for their theological training like the Mirfield-trained Canon Harold Rew, a noted Tractarian author, who spent the later years of his ministry as rector of St. Bride's-super-Ely.

At the beginning of this century a new cloud hung over the Church—the threat of Disestablishment. In 1912 the parishioners of St. Andrew Major, Dinas Powis, forwarded a strongly-worded protest to the Prime Minister 'against the proposal to dismember the church by cutting off from the province of Canterbury the four Welsh dioceses, and to despoil it by confiscating to secular uses endowments consecrated to the service of God.' The parish vestry urged 'upon all Christian people, irrespective of political party, to write in uncompromising

Llantrithyd church—cartouche with Aubrey arms over south doorway

resistance to any Bill embodying such proposals.' These fears were shared by most clergy and well-informed laymen in the period leading up to Disestablishment. They feared the Church would suffer financial bankruptcy, that it would become isolated from the main stream of Anglican life and thought, and more importantly, particularly after the Nonconformist revival of 1911-2, that its pastoral mission would be seriously impeded by continuing Nonconformist expansion. Yet in retrospect none of these fears were justified. The Act of Disestablishment was passed in 1914 and came into operation in 1920. At first there was, it is true, a sense of isolation felt particularly keenly by the higher clergy. Dr. David Walker has pictured A. G. Edwards, the first archbishop of the newly-constituted province as a 'curiously isolated figure', at the 1920 Lambeth Conference 'seeking consolation in unexpected quarters like an invalid whose operation is still an uncomfortably recent experience.' But this feeling of being an anomalous appendage of the Established Church of England had been overcome by the 1950s when the province was seen to be making distinctive contributions to the counsels of the Anglican Communion at large. There developed, too, a growing sense of identity with Welsh interests reinforced in 1966 by the introduction of a new Church in Wales service book in Welsh and English. The Nonconformist 'threat', for such it had seemed to churchmen in the 1920s, has also receded. There is now a growing awareness of fellowship and common purpose with other denominations in the face of influences which are secularising British society. The issue of a joint pastoral letter from the bishops of the Church in Wales and the Roman Catholic Church in Wales on Easter day, 1986, was one landmark in the progress of this growing sense of Christian fellowship. The tide of materialism and secularism has resulted in a marked decline in church membership among all denominations. A *Western Mail* survey which appeared in 1965 showed Church in Wales membership falling from 200,000 in 1953 to 180,000—a ten per cent drop. Further losses are known to have taken place since. A more recent survey organised by MARC Europe and the Bible Society, however, shows Church in Wales Sunday attendances holding up well as against other denominations.

Two major problems facing the present-day Church are the continuing decline in the number of full-time clergy serving the Church and the need to remodel the ecclesiastical geography of the province (at diocesan and parochial level) to meet the needs of changed economic and social circumstances. In the early 1930s the Church in Wales had nearly 1,600 full-time clergy. This figure had dropped to under 1,300 in 1957 and by 1984 had dropped even more dramatically to 689. The Church in Wales has now less clergy than it had in 1850 before the great period of Victorian expansion in clerical manpower had begun. The Church in the Vale has felt these losses as keenly as other areas and grouped parishes now look like being a permanent feature of Church life.

But society in the Vale has also radically changed. It is still an area with a rich agricultural industry but farm mechanisation has substantially reduced the numbers of those who work on the land. Many of the old landed estates have been broken up. The old powerful alliance of resident squire and parson which gave social cohesion to village and parish in Victorian times has disappeared for ever. Some of the Vale villages are dying, others have been transformed into large dormitory villages providing homes for people who work in the major towns and cities in the vicinity. The train, the bus and the car have created a more mobile society. The parishes whose boundaries were defined in the 12th century no longer reflect the settlement patterns of the present day and new territorial groupings are needed if the Church is to pursue a more effective pastoral ministry in the future.

While there is little room for complacency, one achievement of the Church during the past few decades deserves special mention. In 1948 the Reverend Ewart Lewis, a future vicar of Cowbridge, wrote a stimulating essay on *The Church in Wales, the Catholic Church and the Future*. In it he urged church people not to rest 'till what here and there happens once a month becomes a principal feature of each Sunday's worship through the Church in Wales, a corporate act of prayer and praise commemorating the whole redemptive work of God and sealed and hallowed by the reception of the Body and Blood by all present.' This vision has been realised and the parish eucharist is now the central act of Sunday worship in most of the Vale churches and indeed in most parishes of the Church in Wales.

F. G. Cowley
July, 1986

Introduction to the Church Architecture and Furnishings in the Vale of Glamorgan Churches

The Vale of Glamorgan, or Bro Morgannwg as it is called in Welsh, is an area of great interest to the antiquarian and historian. In it are to be found prehistoric stone circles, tumuli and menhirs, remains of Roman masonry from fortress and villa, monastic granges and religious houses. Apart from these more tangible monuments there is a wealth of tradition, legend and folklore. But perhaps the most attractive and characteristic of all the archaeological features of the Vale are its ancient parish churches. The churches are only a mile or two apart from one another; they are nearly all of medieval origin and most incorporate some medieval fabric.

Ecclesiastically, the Vale of Glamorgan comprises the Rural Deaneries of Llantwit Major and Cowbridge, Penarth and Barry, with a few parishes from the Deaneries of Bridgend and Llandaff. One of the key factors in the development of ecclesiastical architecture in Glamorgan—and the Vale in particular— was that within the area there was a plentiful supply of a good quality building stone, lias limestone, of which the best known variety was the pale cream-coloured layer of Sutton stone quarried near Ogmore. This was the major building stone used in the Vale of Glamorgan and was used throughout the Middle Ages but was superseded in the 16th century by Rhaetic sandstone because it was cheaper and easier to quarry. This stone is found in the Bridgend and Cowbridge areas, the best known being the Quarella stone. Rhaetic sandstone was the most popular stone for dressed work in the 17th century by which time it had completely superseded Sutton stone.

In contrast to the great churches of the Vale such as Ewenny Priory church, Llantwit Major and Llancarfan, the village churches are comparatively small in size and do not display the sophisticated architectural details found in English parish churches. The reason for this was that lias limestone does not easily lend itself to the fine manipulation necessary for ecclesiastical sculpture. Ecclesiastical architecture in Wales owed its development to the influence of the monasteries where building work was being carried on throughout the early medieval period. Furthermore part of the tithes and ecclesiastical revenues of Welsh churches were paid to English overlords or were appropriated to Norman

Ewenny Priory church—
south transept
with figure of
Colonel J. P. Turbervill

St. Mary Hill church—
former Norman
chancel arch
now in window
of north nave

Abbeys, thus depriving the local churches of much-needed funds for the upkeep and adornment of their structures.

The late appearance of some architectural features in Wales as compared with England should not be regarded as exceptional or surprising, for some new fashions in architecture, well-established in England, took fifty years or more to make an appearance in the poorer rural areas of Wales.

No Celtic churches have come down to us, but many of the existing churches were no doubt built on sites consecrated by ancient ecclesiastical associations. It is likely that some pre-Norman structures survived for some time after the Conquest until the Normans established themselves sufficiently to build stone structures in their place.

The churches of the Vale of Glamorgan are of many different types and sizes and exhibit all styles of Romanesque and Gothic architecture. At Ewenny Priory church we have the finest example of early Norman architecture and it is perhaps the best specimen of a fortified ecclesiastical building in Wales. The presbytery is one of the rare instances in the country of Romanesque vaulting on a large scale. In the smaller churches at Marcross, Monknash and Wick round Norman chancel arches rest on simple chamfered abaci. The chancel arch at Marcross displays bold chevron ornament at its apex and single-leaf patterns on the chamfer of the jambs. The south doorway at Marcross has a round Norman arch springing from capitals decorated with conventional leaf ornament. The hood mould is decorated with billet ornament and terminates in human heads as label stops. At St. Bride's-super-Ely church the decoration of the outer doorway of the south porch (brought from Margam Abbey in 1849) is a splendid specimen of Norman workmanship. The inner arch is adorned with chevron decoration above scalloped capitals and the chamfered outer arch springs from square abaci above trumpet capitals. Traces of Norman work can be seen in many churches usually in the round-headed inner arches of the south doorways as at Monknash and St. Fagans churches. The low chancel arch at Llancarfan church is Transitional Norman, as is the pointed chancel arch with chevron moulding at Penmark church.

The Early English style of architecture in the Vale is exemplified in the Eastern church at Llantwit Major and in the tower and crossing at Cowbridge church. The nave of Llancarfan church is of 13th-century date and the arcade to the nave has four acutely-pointed Early English arches springing from square pillars. Many of the smaller churches in the Vale such as Eglwys Brewis, Llansannor, Michaelston-le-Pit, St. Lythan's and Welsh St. Donat's were built in the Early English style of architecture of the 13th century.

St. Athan's church with its Berkerolles Chapel and St. Fagans with its beautifully-carved sedilia and Decorated chancel windows are examples of 14th-century Decorated architecture. At Llantwit Major the stone reredos in the chancel is the finest piece of late 14th-century sculpture in the area. The finely-sculptured cusped tomb recesses in the chancel of St. George-super-Ely church are other examples of 14th-century Decorated work. The chancel arch at Pendoylan with its compound piers comprising three demi-shafts with

Marcross church—
Norman south doorway

St. Bride's-super-Ely church—south porch with Norman arch

castellated capitals displaying four-leaf decoration is early Perpendicular work of the late 14th century.

The buttressed towers at Llanblethian, Peterston-super-Ely, St. Hilary and St. Bride's Major are specimens of 15th-century Perpendicular architecture. The south aisle at Cowbridge church with its 15th-century arcade also belongs to this period of architecture.

The Tudor period of architecture is represented in the Vale only in additions to buildings such as the 16th-century porches at Ewenny Priory church and Llansannor church, the addition of the Button Chapel at St. Lythan's church and the insertion of a five-light Tudor window in the north wall of the nave of Cowbridge church. The chancel at Llantrithyd was rebuilt in the 17th century (1656) and that at Llandow was restored in 1712.

Many of the churches were restored in the 19th century but according to Dr. H. M. Thompson in his *Manuscript notes on the old churches of Glamorgan* (1935) 'many were restored so judiciously that the results belie the bad name which that period has for such work.' Many of the Vale churches owe their present appearance to the work of 19th-century restorers and builders. During the 19th century thousands of pounds were provided by members of wealthy land-owning families in the Vale to restore the churches which they attended personally and over which they extended a local patronage.

In 1860 John Bruce Pryce of Dyffryn contributed £1,000 towards the restoration of St. Nicholas' church. Baroness Harriet Windsor of St. Fagans Castle restored and enlarged St. Fagans church in 1860 at a cost of £2,200, while at St. Hilary Mrs. Charlotte Traherne restored the church in memory of her husband, the Reverend John Montgomery Traherne at a cost of £2,000 in 1862. The Turbervill family of Ewenny spent a small fortune throughout the 19th century rebuilding and restoring Ewenny Priory church.

The work of restoration of the Vale churches continued throughout the latter part of the 19th century culminating in a period of great activity during the last two decades when the following churches were restored:— St. Mary Hill (1884), Cadoxton-juxta-Barry (1885), St. Andrew's Major (1885), St. George-super-Ely (1886), Llantwit Major (1888), Llanmihangel (1889), Monknash (1890), Peterston-super-Ely (1891), Welsh St. Donat's (1891), Marcross (1893), Pendoylan (1893), Llysworney (1894), Sully (1895), Llánblethian (1896), Llantrithyd (1897) and Llantwit Major (1899).

The most famous church architect of the period was Sir George Gilbert Scott (1810–78) who restored St. Hilary's church in 1862, and another distinguished ecclesiologist was Scott's one-time assistant George Edmund Street (1824–91) who restored and enlarged St. Fagans church in 1860. Charles Buckeridge (1832–73), who restored Llandough church in 1869, was a pupil of Sir George Gilbert Scott and was primarily an ecclesiastical architect. W. D. Caröe (1857–1938), a London architect of Danish descent, who did his best work in Wales, restored the chancel of Llantwit Major church in 1905 on behalf of the Ecclesiastical Commissioners. Another London architect, William Weir, a pupil of Philip Webb (1831–1915) restored Eglwys Brewis church in 1900 for the

Society for the Protection of Ancient Buildings. The Merrett memorial window at Michaelston-le-Pit church is the work of Sir Ninian Comper (1864-1960), and the reredos and pulpit at Wenvoe are also attributed to him.

However, some of the architects involved in the church restoration were local figures. The dominant firm was Prichard and Seddon, the diocesan architects. John Prichard (1817-86) was a pupil of T. L. Walker who had been chief assistant to A. C. Pugin (the elder). Prichard superintended the restoration of many churches throughout the diocese. He was also the architect responsible for the extensive restoration of Llandaff Cathedral between 1844 and 1857. He formed a partnership with John P. Seddon in 1853. Prichard undertook the commissions in Glamorgan while Seddon did those in Monmouthshire. The architects F. R. Kempson and C. B. Fowler were in partnership in Glamorgan in the last decade of the 19th century. F. R. Kempson was responsible for the restoration of Michaelston-super-Ely church in 1908, and C. B. Fowler restored Llanblethian church in 1896. The other local architect of repute was George Eley Halliday, who restored Llantwit Major church in 1899, and 1905 in collaboration with J. W. Rodger.

The usual plan of the church in the Vale of Glamorgan was the rectangular nave and the smaller, narrower, rectangular chancel. The Reverend Professor E. Tyrrell-Green of St. David's College, Lampeter, writing in 1917 stated that the early Celtic churches influenced the arrangement of later structures in Wales in the separation of the nave from the chancel by a more or less solid screen—'the Celtic church plan of a narrow doorway-like chancel arch'. A primitive narrow chancel arch giving scanty access to a secluded dimly-lit chancel is a feature of many of the Vale churches. The dimensions of these chancel arches are hardly more than that of a large doorway and the way towards the chancel at Marcross and Eglwys Brewis churches is rendered even more difficult by small walls on each side of the archway. According to Sir Stephen Glynne this was also the arrangement at Monknash church before a 19th-century restoration removed these dwarf walls.

Because the walls of division between nave and chancel obstructed the view of the elevation of the Host, apertures called hagioscopes or squints were constructed at a later date through which the congregation could see what was taking place at the high altar. These squints occur at Llandow, St. Bride's Major and Wick churches on each side of the chancel arch. At a higher level of the rood-loft a sanctum squint occurs at Llanfrynach piercing the chancel wall. In some of the Vale churches the chancel is often out of alignment with the nave (the so-called 'weeping chancel'). This phenomenon has been interpreted as symbolizing Christ's drooping head on the Cross of Calvary. Most chancels incline to the north (as in iconography Christ's head leans towards His right shoulder), but some chancels lean towards the south. The chancels at Bonvilston and Llysworney are inclined to the north but the chancel at St. Mary Church leans to the south.

Medieval stone altar slabs are uncommon. The custom of celebrating the Eucharist on the tombs of martyrs first caused stone altars to be introduced in the church. The upper surface or 'mensa' was inscribed with five crosses (one in the centre and one in each corner), symbolizing the five wounds of Christ. After the Reformation the Puritans who could not accept the sacrificial aspect of the mass objected to stone altars and substituted a wooden 'holy table' on which to commemorate the Last Supper. Thus the stone altars were taken from their rightful place and thrown out into the churchyard or placed face downwards under the tower space or in the floor of the porch. In the Church of England the legality of stone altars was disputed in the 19th century but in recent times those that have survived have been restored to the positions they occupied three centuries earlier. Several of these pre-Reformation stone altars can be found in the Vale churches at Ewenny Priory, St. Donat's, St. George-super-Ely, Llantwit Major (the Western church), Merthyr Dyfan and Wick. At Colwinston one of these stone altar slabs still lies on the south side of the churchyard.

A reredos is a decorated wall or screen rising from ground level behind the altar below the east window. The term 'retable' is synonymous with 'reredos' but it has been applied to the step or gradine which is occasionally found at the back of the altar. The reredos took many forms. The simplest form of reredos was an embroidered curtain or dossal suspended at the back of the altar. Later in the 14th or 15th centuries the stone or alabaster reredos consisted of niches of sculptured figures representing saints. There is a most remarkable late 14th-century stone reredos at Llantwit Major church which is constructed in the form of a wall a few feet from the east wall, through which pass a north and a south door. The reredos has a facade of twenty-two recessed and canopied niches. The piece consists of five bays of unequal lengths and the central bay is a double tier of niches, five below and seven above.

Also at Llantwit Major church is a 13th-century Jesse niche. In the lower portion of the niche we have Jesse lying down asleep with a stem proceeding from his left side and branching off in two directions encircling crowned heads. It has been suggested that this was originally the reredos of the high altar.

The panels of the reredos were invariably decorated with religious scenes particularly the Crucifixion and Passion of Our Lord. At St. Hilary's church the centre panel of the polished marble reredos is a representation of the Last Supper after Leonardo da Vinci. It depicts the emotions and expressions of the twelve Apostles just after Jesus has told them that one of them will betray Him.

The beautifully-carved reredos of Austrian oak at Llanblethian church is a *tour de force* in imitation of the stone sculptures which were carved throughout the church in the 14th century. The reredos depicts a scene from the Supper at Emmaus on the altar panel flanked by two towers with pinnacles which have foliated crockets and finials.

At Llansannor church there is a carved oak reredos decorated in English gold leaf. The central panel contains a representation of Our Lord upon the cross with the attendant figures of the Blessed Virgin Mary and St. John on either side. Four panels on each side of the reredos contain shields bearing emblems of the Passion.

St. Hilary's church—marble reredos depicting the Last Supper after Leonardo da Vinci

Wenvoe church—reredos by Sir Ninian Comper

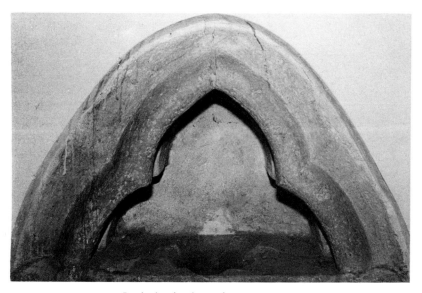

Cowbridge church—13th-century piscina

The beautifully-carved reredos at Wenvoe church by Sir Ninian Comper has ogee arches with foliated crockets and finials with pinnacles between, which end in bosses in the backdrop. The seven carved statuettes include the Virgin Mary and Child, St. George slaying the Dragon and St. Peter and St. Paul with bishops of the church.

Arched sepulchral recessed tombs are to be found in several Vale churches which were probably intended to receive the bones of their founders, but many of the effigies or slabs have disappeared from these recesses.

Piscinas are very numerous but they are usually only found in pre-Reformation structures. A piscina is simply a drain to take away the water used to wash the communion vessels and the celebrant's hands during the celebration of the mass. They are nearly always placed near the altar sometimes in a recess in the south wall of the sanctuary. The presence of a piscina is usually evidence that somewhere in the vicinity there was originally an altar, which proved to be the case in the Stradling Chapel at St. Donat's church and the south chapel at Llanblethian church.

In the south-east corner of the sanctuary of St. Mary Church is a free-standing piscina on a twisted and fluted pillar. At Llanmihangel and Llysworney churches pillar piscinas with Norman cushion capitals which were originally free-standing have been embedded in a recess in the south wall of the chancel. Later in the 13th century it was customary for piscinas to have two drains, one for the water used for washing the priest's hands, the other for the water used

*St. Mary Church—*19th-century aumbry
in north wall of chancel

for rinsing the chalice and paten. In St. Mary Hill church there is a crude double-drain piscina which dates from the 13th century. Many piscinas are simply cut into the window-sill of the south-east window of the chancel as at Welsh St. Donat's. At Llancarfan church the piscina with moulded circular bowl is carved out of the stone bench or rude sedile. In the north wall of the chancel of some of the Vale churches are recesses which are called aumbries or lockers. In the Middle Ages these recesses were often fitted with wooden doors and were used for the safe-keeping of eucharistic vessels. Aumbries were also used for the reservation of the Blessed Sacrament and pyx. At St. Mary Church in the north wall of the chancel is a 19th-century aumbry done in the First Pointed Victorian Gothic style with trefoil arch, dogtooth moulding and stiff-leaf foliage.

Sedilia are seats by the altar for the celebrant, deacon and sub-deacon while the choir sings the *Kyrie eleison, Gloria in excelsis* and the *Credo,* and they are normally situated to the west of the piscina in the south wall of the chancel. Some of the seats were stepped, giving the priest the most elevated seat and the sub-deacon the lowest seat but usually they were level. Sedilia are rare in the Vale churches and the only surviving medieval specimen is that belonging to the Decorated style of architecture of the 14th century at St. Fagans church. The fine sedilia and piscina is a particularly harmonious piece done in the 14th century as a panel and stepped downwards from the east. It is of four bays with cinquefoils and caps. The labels of the arches terminate in carved heads as label stops and in the spandrels are large leaf forms with a tailed monster in the westernmost one. The piscina has a credence shelf and quatrefoil drain hole.

The need for piscinas and sedilia ceased with the introduction of the reformed liturgy and they were only reintroduced in a few Anglo-Catholic churches in Victorian times. One excellent example of this in the Vale is at Llandough-by-Cowbridge church where the stone sedilia done in First Pointed Victorian Gothic style provide double seats for the priest and clerk beneath offset canopies

St. Fagans church—14th-century sedilia in south wall of chancel

whose arches are returned above quarter-round moulding on the outside wall. The seats are stepped downwards towards the west. The trefoil-headed pillar piscina with moulded capital and base includes a credence shelf.

The medieval rood screen, beautifully carved and enriched with coloured ornamentation, was the crowning feature of nearly every parish church nave. Over the rood screen was the beam on which was placed the rood (an image of Christ on the Cross of Calvary with the figures of the Blessed Virgin Mary and St. John representing the attendant church). It provided a place for the reading of the Gospel at mass and in some churches a choir. However, there is a paucity of remains of rood screens in the Vale. The only extant example of the great screen is to be found at Llancarfan, where the only surviving part is now placed at the west end of the Raglan Chapel. It exhibits a multifoiled ogee arch in the centre with openwork tracery lights below the head beam and applied blind tracery on the wainscot panels. Three other screens remain *in situ* at Llanmaes, Llantrithyd and Porthkerry but all considerably restored. That at Llantrithyd was recoloured in 1941 in pale blue, red and gilt, its original colour scheme. At Ewenny Priory church is the only wooden screen of 14th-century date surviving in the Vale. It is placed as a dividing screen between the presbytery and choir.

No rood-lofts have survived in the Vale of Glamorgan. The majority of them were taken down and burned along with their images by the Protestant and Puritan reformers in the 16th and 17th centuries. Others were simply lost through neglect or swept away during the 19th century by well-intentioned

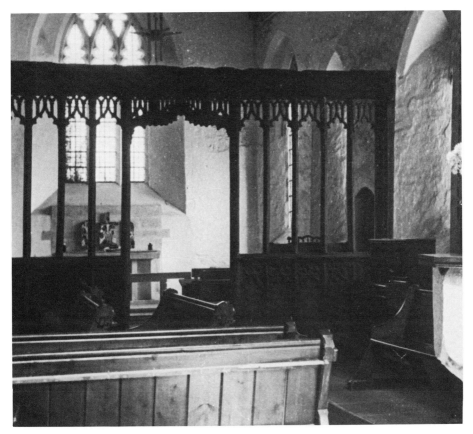

Llancarfan church—Raglan Chapel screen

incumbents who regarded their structures as obsolete. Today the only visual evidence of a former rood-loft in some churches is the presence of the rood-loft staircase which is usually set in the wall to the north of the chancel, by the stone corbels which once supported the bressummer or main beam of the loft, or by a window set high in the wall of the nave to light the loft. In the Vale churches many rood-loft staircases remain either as a straight staircase within the north wall as at St. Donat's church, or as a spiral staircase within a projection on the north wall of the nave as at Colwinston, Llanmaes and Llansannor. The rood staircase is placed approximately four or five metres from the east end of the northern wall of the nave and the staircase ascends in an easterly direction upwards until a doorway is reached at the north end of the loft. At Llanfrynach the staircase is steeper and the entrance door is consequently nearer to the east end of the nave. Pendoylan has a well-preserved spiral staircase within the chancel wall. The original rood-loft doors with their applied tracery remain at Llanblethian and Llangan while the wooden crenellated door-head is still visible at Marcross church. The rood-loft door at Gileston retains a portion of the iron

plate once attached to the drop handle and is coeval with the ironwork of the
15th-century south door.

Sometimes access to the rood-loft was by way of a staircase from the interior
of the chancel at its north-western corner which does not interfere with the
external aspect of the church. This arrangement can be seen at Marcross and
Monknash, and the outline of a 15th-century rood-loft doorway at Eglwys
Brewis church indicates a similar entrance from within the chancel. However,
at Welsh St. Donat's the staircase leads from the chancel within a projection on
the north wall of the chancel to the rood-loft. At Peterston-super-Ely church
the entrance to the former rood-loft and staircase is contained in the wall of the
chancel arch and shares with Cadoxton-juxta-Barry the unusual feature of
having its rood-loft entrance placed on the south side of the building. In
cruciform churches such as Michaelston-le-Pit and St. George-super-Ely where
the tower is placed at the crossing it appears to have been customary to combine
access to both tower and rood-loft.

The stone corbels which supported the rood-loft are frequently to be seen *in
situ* on the chancel wall and are an accurate indication of the height and width of
some of these rood-lofts. At Llancarfan it appears that the rood-loft extended
for a full bay west of the chancel arch, approximately three metres above the
present ground level, forming a loft over three metres wide. Here as at St.
Andrew's Major church, the rood-loft spanned both nave and aisle.

The rood-lofts were usually lit by a small window placed high in the
northern wall sometimes supplemented by a corresponding light on the south
side as at Gileston. After the destruction of these lofts many of the windows
were built up as is the case at Peterston-super-Ely church.

The churches of the Vale of Glamorgan are rich in incised sepulchral stone
slabs dating from the 12th century. From the 13th to the 15th century the
sepulchral stone slabs usually tapered in their length being widest at the top.
The crosses, some with a circle and some without, represent every conceivable
design in which a cross appears. The stem generally has a stepped base representing the cross at Calvary or a fleur-de-lys decoration at the base in imitation
of the professional cross carried in the hand. These sepulchral slabs developed
from the carved lids of stone coffins which were either raised above the level of
the ground in churchyards or were allowed to remain exposed in the floors of
churches to provide permanent memorials to those buried beneath. A number
of these stone slabs in the 12th century had coped tops but the majority were
flat. The carving was invariably in low relief and the motifs were mainly
decorative or symbolic. However, as early as the beginning of the 12th century
they took the form of an effigy of the deceased. At St. Bride's Major church a
stone coffin with incised coffin-lid was discovered in the churchyard in 1845 and
was brought into the church. The empty stone coffin was placed on the south
side of the chancel and the incised coffin-lid bearing a representation of Johan le
Botiler of Dunraven (*c.* 1285) was placed in the floor under the altar. The
engraving shows the knight in the cross-legged attitude with hauberk and
chausses, wearing a long surcoat. The device of crossed legs had nothing to do

St. Bride's Major church—incised sepulchral slab of Johan le Botiler (c.1285)

After Boutell

Ewenny Priory church—tomb of the founder Maurice de Londres

with the crusades but merely reflected contemporary artistic style. In the same church in the north-east corner of the sanctuary is an early 13th-century sepulchral slab which is incised with three different types of cross and probably marks the burial place of a former priest.

The cross was the dominant motif on sepulchral slabs. Numerous 13th-century sepulchral slabs with floriated crosses exist at Llanblethian church, placed against the inside walls of the tower, and in the Western church at Llantwit Major. A sepulchral slab in the south transept of Ewenny Priory church commemorates the founder, Maurice de Londres. It is a beautiful slab of fine design and excellent workmanship in a perfect state of preservation. The stem of a graceful floriated cross divides the Norman-French inscription and around the chamfered edge runs a raised Early English leaf-scroll. Some slabs are carved with symbols indicating the calling or profession of the deceased. At Marcross church, on the south side of the chancel floor, is an incised sepulchral slab in memory of an early 13th-century priest, for it bears an Early English floriated cross with the open Bible on one side and a chalice on the other.

Several sepulchral slabs bear on either side of the massive tapering stem one or more rectangular objects which are termed 'billets'. These billets are thought to represent a last survival of the disposition of the Virgin Mary and St. John on each side of the Cross of Calvary. However, T. C. Evans, also known under his

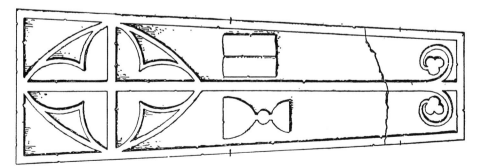

Marcross church—13th-century incised sepulchral slab

Llantwit Major church—semi-effigial slab

bardic title 'Cadrawd', expounded the theory that the billets represented smaller crosses appearing below the arms of the central cross, thus forming the 'Calvary' arrangement. Many of these billeted slabs have a large space left at the base for an inscription or epitaph, like the ones which exist in the south chancel of Penmark to James Mathew of Rhoose (d. 1631) and on the east wall of the south porch at Llandow to Thomas Powell (d. 1658).

The names of John Shirrey and Edward Turberville 1624 and 1643 respectively, which are inscribed on two fragments of a sepulchral slab at Llanmaes church, were added years after the cross was carved, as the lettering is engraved contrary to the standing of the cross. T. H. Thomas in his article entitled *Calvary Crosses, Glamorgan* in 1904 (*Transactions of the Cardiff Naturalists' Society*, Vol. 37, 1904 pp. 55-56) noted that the defacement of one of the fragments of the slab occurred in 1643, the year in which the Great Order for the destruction of 'crucifixions, crosses and all images of any one or more persons of the Trinity' was promulgated. However, Thomas believed that the destruction had commenced earlier and many slabs may have been removed and adapted later on by stone-cutters who carved 17th-century names upon 16th-century or even earlier stone slabs.

Set into the north wall of the nave of Porthkerry church is a fine 17th-century sepulchral slab with raised Calvary cross and billets which is remarkable for the excellence of its lettering. It is a memorial to Reynold Portrey (d. 1629) who was apparently some kind of physician. In the 17th and 18th centuries massive carved slabs of marble were often used with an achievement in low-relief and the inscription incised in Roman letters. In the sanctuary floor of Gileston church there are two such slabs. One (dedicated in 1618 to Matthew and Mary Giles) displays a Calvary cross with billets and the coat of arms of the Giles family and that of his wife's family, the Flemings; the other tombstone depicts the coat of arms of Willis impaling those of Giles and commemorates Mary Allen (d. 1734) 'relict of Richard Carne of Ewenny and late wife of William Willis, sole heiress of the Manor of Gileston.'

Semi-effigial monuments are rare in the Vale of Glamorgan churches. Memorials of this kind in which parts of the human figure are represented as the head or bust derive their origin apparently from the need to combine a monumental effigy with a monumental cross upon the sepulchral slab. One of the earliest semi-effigial slabs is preserved in the Western church at Llantwit Major. This is a 13th-century coped stone with a centre ridge decorated with a row of fifteen lozenge-shaped figures terminating above in a quatrefoil, within which is a bared head with prominent ears and closed eyes. The other semi-effigial sepulchral slab in the Vale is at Llanmihangel church. On the north wall of the nave is a representation of a tomb-chest carved in low-relief consisting of an effigy of the upper part of a small figure of a layman with ruff round the neck and the hands clasped in prayer. It is a memorial to Griffith Grant (d. 1591). In this slab, where the upper part of the coffin-lid is entirely cut away and its place occupied by a semi-effigy, a cross appears below the figure.

By the early 13th century more elaborate memorial monuments were beginning to appear in which the slab with now a high-relief effigy was placed on a tomb-chest standing in the church. The sides of these tomb-chests were adorned with arcading, heraldic shields and foliage and by the end of the century figures of 'weepers', that is, relatives or friends of the deceased, were added. At a later date the more important tomb-chests were provided with stone canopies. A number of memorial effigies survive from the medieval period in the Vale churches, some placed upon tomb-chests, others set under a canopied recess in the wall of the church. They can be divided into two groups, military and civilian effigies. The earliest of the effigies representing a cross-legged knight is found in the south transept of Ewenny Priory church. The effigy is mutilated and badly worn and is believed to represent Sir Payn de Turberville.

In St. Athan's church in the south chapel or Berkerolles Chapel, are two tomb-chests belonging to members of the Berkerolles family of East Orchard,

Llanmihangel church—effigy of Griffith Grant (d.1591)

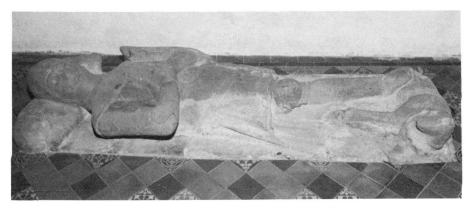

Llansannor church—effigy of Gronw ab Ifor

Sir William (d. 1329) and Sir Roger Berkerolles (d. 1351) with their wives. Both knights are dressed in a suit of chain mail which is supplemented by plate armour strapped to the front of the legs and arms. They both wear a bascinet, a close-fitting pointed helmet from which hangs a mail guard for the sides of the face and neck, called a 'camail'. The armour is typical of the early part of the 14th century. The tomb of Sir Roger Berkerolles is the finer of the two and stands under a canopied recess beneath a heavily-moulded ogee arch with crockets and finial. Both tombs are adorned with blind arcading and beneath each of the arches are 'weepers' representing various orders of society.

In the chancel of Llansannor church lies the cross-legged effigy of a knight, who is believed to be Gronw ab Ifor. The armour of the effigy includes a bascinet and camail which places it in the latter part of the 14th century. By about 1415 the knight's body was wholly encased in plate armour and this is illustrated by the effigy in St. Hilary's church of Thomas Basset of Beaupré (d. 1423) who lies recumbent upon a tomb in attitude of prayer wearing a

St. Hilary's church—tomb of Sir Thomas Basset (d.1423)

complete suit of armour. It demonstrates clearly the transition from mail to plate armour.

Later development in medieval armour is seen on the Butler tomb set under a canopy in the north wall of the chancel of St. Bride's Major church (*c.* 1540). The details of the armour worn by Sir John Butler which includes tassets (plates which overlap upwards from the hips to the waist) and the tuilles that hang from them are those introduced and developed in the late 15th century. Sir John Butler is shown bare-headed and later medieval military effigies, particularly those dating after 1450 were commonly shown bare-headed.

The second group of effigies includes civilians or persons not of knightly rank. Under a richly-moulded segmental arch in the north wall of St. Hilary's church is the effigy of a young civilian which is probably of early 13th-century date. The effigy is believed to represent a member of the De Cardiff family. Other male effigies of this group may be seen at Llantrithyd, Llantwit Major and Llanblethian churches. At Llantrithyd church under a recess in the north wall of the nave lies the effigy of a civilian clad in a loose garment with rounded low neck which reaches to the ankles. It dates from the 13th century and does not appear to be in its original position.

At Llantwit Major in the Western church is a sepulchral slab bearing the effigy of a medieval priest or layman dressed in a long loose tunic buttoned to the throat. The left hand holds a glove and the right hand is raised and lies upon the breast. The slab is coffin-shaped and belongs to the latter part of the 14th century.

An effigy in Llanblethian church in the south wall of the south chapel is of Sutton stone and of 13th-century character, very similar to the effigy in the nave of Llantrithyd church viz. a layman recumbent with hands clasped in prayer with a greyhound at the feet.

At Flemingston and Llantwit Major churches there are female effigies. In a fine recess in the south wall of the south chapel of Flemingston church is a stone effigy of the early 14th century depicting Lady Joan Le Fleming. This effigy does not appear to be in its original position. The second female effigy which lies in the Western church at Llantwit Major is that of a lady of the late 16th century. She is dressed in a kirtle intricately embroidered with long sleeves, a tasselled girdle, wide ruff, lace cap and high pleated hat with small feather. Above her right shoulder is the bust of a child complete with ruff and cap. This monument records the death of the wife and child of Richard Hopkins who were probably buried in Llantwit Major church circa 1580.

The 16th century brought major changes in posture since the effect of the Renaissance was to encourage the depiction of the dead as they had appeared in life. Thus by the middle of the 16th century the kneeling attitude had appeared. The kneeling effigy usually appeared at prayer before a *prie-dieu* and this attitude became popular on hanging wall-monuments where married couples faced each other over the prayer desk. Among the many fine monuments that remain in the Vale of Glamorgan churches there is nothing quite so elaborate as the Basset-Mansel tomb (1597) in Llantrithyd church. It fills the northern side of the chancel from floor to ceiling and project almost halfway across the chancel. The monument depicts John Basset and his wife, Elizabeth, kneeling in prayer before a *prie-dieu*. The lower part of the monument, which is of massive design, supports the recumbent effigies of Sir Anthony Mansel and his wife, Elizabeth (née Basset). Around this tomb as 'weepers' are the seven children of the Mansels. Sir Anthony Mansel is depicted in full armour of the period with a sword at his side. At St. Donat's church in the Stradling Chapel we have a fine mural monument which resembles the Basset-Mansel tomb in Llantrithyd church. The figures of Sir Edward Stradling (d. 1609) and his wife, Agnes (d. 1610) are shown kneeling on cushions on opposite sides of a centre altar.

In the south aisle of Cowbridge church is an early 17th-century mural monument erected by Sir Edward Carne to his parents. It depicts William Carne of Nash Manor and Great House, Cowbridge with his wife, Elizabeth, both kneeling, each against a prayer desk bearing an open book, while beneath in high relief are his three sons and three daughters as 'weepers'. It was quite common from the latter part of the 16th century for the whole family of the deceased to be depicted, the husband and wife as life-size effigies, either recumbent or kneeling, with the children kneeling in a row along the front of the monument as illustrated in the monument above and also at Llantrithyd church.

Demi-figures were less common but they remained in vogue during the 17th century and the early part of the 18th century and featured on hanging wall-monuments. On the north wall of the chancel of St. Bride's Major church is an elegant monument to the memory of John Wyndham, Esq., Serjeant-at-law (d. 1697) and his wife, Jane (d. 1698). The two demi-figures face each other beneath an open pediment on which stand the Wyndham arms between decorative swags. Beneath the cornice on each side of the demi-figures and inscription tablet free-standing Corinthian columns are encased in drapery.

The wall tablet with inscription panel and no effigy was to become the most popular of all forms of funerary monuments. These grew increasingly frequent as time passed and varied from period to period according to changing tastes in architecture and decoration. Its architectural form consisted of a rectangular or oval inscription panel flanked by columns or pilasters beneath an entablature and pediment. On the north wall of the chancel of Penmark church is a fine 17th-century hanging wall-monument with twisting side columns supporting a broken pediment. The monument with its oval inscription panel commemorates Thomas Lewis, Esq., (d.1869) of Penmark Place, eldest son of Sir Thomas Lewis. In Wenvoe church on the north wall of the nave are two fine monuments to members of the Thomas family of Wenvoe Castle dating from the 17th and 18th centuries. The one on the west side bears an oval tablet wife, Jane (d. 1688), daughter of Sir John Stradling of St. Donat's. The inscription tablet is on a rectangular panel flanked by black marble free-standing Corinthian columns supporting a moulded cornice. The triangular pediment has a broken arch to admit the standing figure of a female with her two children on a pedestal between two reclining figures, all in classical attire.

St. Donat's church—monument to Sir Edward Stradling (d.1609)
and his wife, Agnes

The other mural monument commemorates Sir Edmond Thomas (d. 1723) and his wife, Mary. The monument has two rectangular inscription tablets on a brown-coloured border enclosed above and to the sides by swags as drapery and surmounted by three cherubic angels' heads. The piece is framed by pilasters beneath a moulded cornice and segmental pediment with both this and the tympanum broken to admit a painted achievement displaying the arms of Thomas of Wenvoe.

Church monuments in the 19th century were influenced by two major stylistic movements in the arts. As far as funerary monuments were concerned the Greek movement was the dominant force in the first half of the 19th century, while the Gothic Revival predominated in the Victorian period. Black and white marble was used for the construction of monuments in the early part

St. Bride's Major church—monument
to John Wyndham (d. 1697) and his wife, Jane

of the 19th century. The design of these monuments was profoundly influenced
by Greek style. They were basically rectangular in shape surmounted in most
cases by a triangular pediment of shallow pitch and frequently enriched by
'acroteria' (quadrant-like bodies) projecting upwards at the ends of the pediment.

Examples of early 19th-century monuments in Greek Revivalist style in the
Vale of Glamorgan are to be found at St. Bride's Major and Wick churches. On
the south wall of the chancel at St. Bride's Major church is a monument to
Thomas Wyndham Esq. of Dunraven Castle (1763-1814) beautifully executed
in white marble and signed by Sebastian Gahagan of Bath. On it are carved in
high relief the effigies in Greek Revivalist style of Wyndham dying upon a
couch and his two infant sons (who predeceased him) calling him up to heaven.
On the north wall of Wick church is another monument in neo-classical style to

Wenvoe church—monument to William Thomas (d.1636) *(left)*
Wenvoe church—monument to Sir Edmond Thomas (d.1723) *(right)*

Frances Hewett (née Prichard) (d. 1828). The memorial depicts a figure in loose classical dress seemingly distraught leaning against the ubiquitous urn, a symbol of death derived from antiquity. The inscription has a frieze of Greek-key decoration.

The Gothic Revival originated in the mid-18th century, inspired by a romantic interest in the Middle Ages. As far as funerary monuments were concerned the transition from the neo-classical period was gradual but after 1850 Gothic remained the dominant style for the rest of the century.

A monument in the south-east corner of the nave of Penmark church to three members of the Jones family of Fonmon Castle who died in the latter part of the 19th century is typical of the Victorian Gothic Revival. It is divided into three panels surmounted by trefoil-headed Gothic arches with foliage in the spandrels below which hang three heraldic shields. A hanging wall-monument on the north wall of the nave, of St. George-super-Ely church, erected in 1838

St. Bride's Major church—monument to Thomas Wyndham (d.1814) and his two sons *(left)*

Wick church—memorial to Frances Hewett (d.1828) *(right)*

to Mary, (d. 1812) relict of John Llewellin, Esquire, of Coedriglan has a Gothic frame comprising a crocketed and finialed gable over cinquefoiled arches between flanking pinnacled shafts. On the north wall of the nave of St. Hilary's church is a late 19th-century marble monument with head and shoulders portrait carved in relief of the deceased Major William West James Basset of Beaupré (d.1871).

Memorials in the 20th century are now in general more modest than they have been since the 11th century. The late Victorians started the fashion of dedicating useful pieces of church furniture as memorials instead. Today memorial stained glass windows are by far the most favourite type of memorial.

Monumental brasses are rare in the Vale of Glamorgan and only one exists at Llandough-by-Cowbridge church, dedicated to Wenllian Walsche, the wife of Walter Moreton (d. 1427). The brass is let into a finely-carved slab of limestone in the floor of the sanctuary on the north side of the altar. Above the inscription in black-letter Latin the figure of a woman is depicted wearing a horned head-dress and veil and kirtle beneath a cinquefoiled ogee canopy with cusps and crockets.

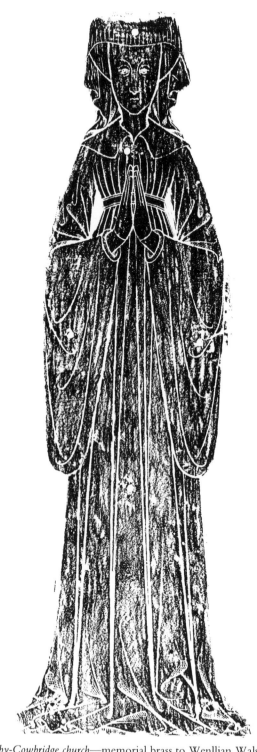

Llandough-by-Cowbridge church—memorial brass to Wenllian Walsche (d. 1427)

St. George-super-Ely church—Victorian Gothic monument on north wall of nave *(left)*
Pendoylan church—memorial monument to Rev. John Williams, rector of
Llanmihangel and Flemingston *(right)*

In the sanctuary and chancel of the Vale churches are tombstones to the important members of the Vale of Glamorgan families of rank. They were usually buried in this privileged position because they were frequently patrons or generous benefactors of the church. Many of the clergy buried there also belonged to notable families. In the 18th and 19th centuries it became fashionable to construct vaults under the church usually below the chancel wherein the local gentry or clergy were buried. Such family vaults exist in many of the Vale churches. At Pendoylan church the construction of the Hensol Castle vault in 1870 caused the collapse of the east wall of the chancel. In 1889 during the restoration of Llanmihangel church workmen disappeared into the vault of the Edwins when they placed a ladder in that part of the church for the purpose of removing two mural monuments from the east wall. In 1899 a vault was

Michaelston-super-Ely church—
16th-century heraldic plaque

Llanblethian church—
19th-century hatchment

constructed in the chancel of Peterston-super-Ely church for Edward Turberville Llewellin (d. 1890) and his wife, Elizabeth (d. 1879).

In many of the Vale churches there are heraldic memorials to the important
families of the area who once worshipped there. These take the form of family
heraldic achievements on monuments, heraldic stained glass or funerary hatchments. A funerary hatchment is the escutcheon of a deceased person painted on
canvas stretched across a lozenge-shaped wooden frame. It was hung on the
front of the deceased's house after the funeral for approximately six months and
was then placed in the church either where he worshipped or where he was
buried or where he was patron or where he owned estates. Hatchments date
from the late 17th century to the 19th century. Two funerary hatchments are
extant in the Vale of Glamorgan at Llantwit Major and Llanblethian churches.
The former commemorates the Reverend Robert Nicholl-Carne, M.A., of
Nash Manor and Dimlands House, Llantwit Major (d. 1849). The latter is
unidentified but commemorates a person descended from the marriage of a
male member of the Bourne family and a female Spurling or Stanford.

Several of the Vale churches have beautiful old oak roofs of late medieval
date. They can be divided into two main types, the arch-braced truss and the
wagon or barrel roof. A typical example of the arch-braced, open collar-truss
type roof of 15th-century date can be seen in the nave of Welsh St. Donat's
church, where the principal rafters are cut out of large oak scantlings which rest
on short wallplates supported by stone corbels. The intervals between the
purlins and the wallplate are filled with curved windbraces. Although the
windbrace originated as a practical device giving rigidity, its artistic possibilities
were soon realized with the result that it was carved in various ornamental
forms. Similar roofs exist in Llanfrynach and Llansannor churches. At Llantwit
Major the Western church has a splendid 15th-century arch-braced roof of Irish
bog oak with collar-beam trusses. The principal rafters, which are supported on
wooden corbels carved in the form of human heads, have trenched purlins with
a crenellated moulding on their upper edges. At the intersection of the lower
purlins with the principal rafters are alternate heraldic and floriated bosses.

The second main type of roof is the open wagon roof which is formed by a
series of closely-set arch braces seated on the wallplate rising to the ridge piece.
The effect from below is that of a canvas-covered farm wagon and hence the
name. The resulting square panels might be boarded or plastered while the
points of intersection between the rafters and purlins were usually decorated
with carved foliage bosses or heads of angels or saints.

An example of this type of roof is to be seen in Cowbridge church where the
nave has a wagon-truss roof with gilded bosses at the intersections of the purlins
and main braces. At Penmark the nave has a high wagon or barrel roof with an
arcade pattern on the wallplates. In some churches such as Llanmihangel the
western part of the roof of the nave has an open arch-braced roof but the part of
the roof nearer to the chancel is filled in or panelled. This arrangement is also
quite common in many chancels. At St. Hilary's church, which was completely
restored in 1862, the roofs of the nave and south aisle have a king-post

Welsh St. Donat's church (above left);
Llantwit Major church (Western church)— arch-braced roofs *(below left)*
Llanfrynach church—15th-century arch-braced roof *(above)*

North side. South side.

H. Longueville Jones. del.   J. H. Le Keux. Sc.

Llantwit Major church—heraldic and floriated roof bosses

Cowbridge church—wagon-truss roof with gilded bosses

St. Hilary's church—kingpost roof of nave

arrangement with cambered tie-beams and curved braces. At Bonvilston church the chancel has an arch-braced roof with diagonal braces and at Llangan the nave has a modern trussed-rafter roof which was a common form of roof construction in the 13th century.

The interiors of the early Norman churches were lit by simple round-headed openings pierced through thick walls with a deep internal splay. There are many original Norman and Early English windows in the Vale of Glamorgan churches but there has been much insertion of late windows, doorways, etc., mostly of the Perpendicular style. Dr. H. M. Thompson thought that there were probably two periods of especial activity in church restoration and renovation and the first of these occurred in the 15th and 16th centuries, the second in the 19th century. The first of these periods has given us insertions on the south and north sides of the nave of many square-headed windows. They are normally of two or three lights occasionally four and distinguished from the earlier windows by being foliated in cinquefoil instead of trefoil heads with the addition of cusping.

Peterston-super-Ely church illustrates these points better than any other church in the Vale. Also refenestration at Porthkerry church must have removed narrow deeply-splayed lights to make room for Perpendicular windows with a hood mould and label terminations. At St. Athan's church there are several original windows of the Decorated period of the 14th century with reticulated tracery especially in the south transept. Few original windows occur on the north side of the nave. Sometimes one may find a high-placed window intended to light the rood-loft as at Llanmihangel church. But windows on the north side are almost always 19th-century insertions. The frequent absence of windows on the north side of the church has been attributed to the superstitious custom of keeping out the Devil from that side of the church as was shown by the practice of blocking up north or 'devil's doors'. The north door to the nave was known as the 'devil's door' and it was often left open during the service of Baptism in the belief that any evil spirits in the child would escape through it.

The majority of windows in the east end of the chancel above the altar of the Vale churches were inserted during the 19th century and were invariably contemporary with the restoration of the church during that period. The original east windows were then placed in the side walls of the chancel as at Llanmihangel church in 1889. These windows were generally constructed in the Perpendicular style of the 15th century with rectilinear-style tracery in the head as at Penmark church. Windows inserted in the nave of St. Bride's Major in the middle of the 19th century are constructed in the Decorated and Geometrical styles of the 14th century.

Many other windows of the Decorated and early Perpendicular period at Cowbridge, St. Fagans and Llantwit Major churches were restored in the 19th century. Some of these windows at Cowbridge and Llantwit Major had been blocked up for many years with masonry as shown in several 19th-century prints and engravings.

Good quality building stone such as Bath and Portland was imported into the Vale of Glamorgan during the 19th century to dress doorways and for use in the construction of new windows. Many windows at Flemingston church are dressed with Portland stone and windows in the Perpendicular style at Llansannor are constructed out of Bath stone. Many of the stone corbels or label stops were carved with quaint heads and figures representing builders, masons, architects, patrons and other benefactors of the church.

Medieval stained glass in the Vale of Glamorgan is rare and only occurs at St. Bride's-super-Ely church. There the east window consists of roundels of 14th- and 15th-century stained glass set in an opaque glass background. The window was designed by George G. Pace of York in 1956 using medieval stained glass which he had collected over the years.

Pendoylan church—Insole memorial window by W. F. Dixon

However, there is a wealth of 19th-century stained glass in the Vale churches by many well-known stained glass artists. The revival of stained glass in the 19th century was a by-product of the Anglo-Catholic Movement and the Victorian Gothic Revival in architecture. The most prolific firm of stained glass makers was Clayton & Bell of London. John Richard Clayton (1827-1913) and Alfred Bell (1832-95) became partners in 1855 and their studio soon became one of the largest in the Victorian period.

Unfortunately many windows of the larger English firms generally remained unsigned. Thus Clayton & Bell windows nearly always have to be identified by recognition of style or by reference to diocesan faculties which gave permission for the insertion of these windows. Fine examples of Clayton & Bell's work can be seen in the east windows of St. Hilary, St. Nicholas and Llantwit Major churches. Clayton & Bell's most original pupil was William Francis Dixon (1848-1928) who designed the stained glass window in the nave of Pendoylan church in memory of Mary Ann Insole, wife of James Harvey Insole of Llandaff and Tŷ Fry.

Besides Clayton & Bell and Heaton, Butler & Bayne one other firm which stood out during the peak of the High Victorian period of the Gothic Revival was that of Lavers and Barraud. This firm was established in 1855 by Nathaniel W. Lavers (1828-1911) and he was joined in 1858 by Francis Philip Barraud (1824-1900). Nathaniel Westlake (1833-1921) joined Lavers & Barraud by early 1860. A fine example of their work appears in the north wall of the nave at Llandow church. Windows by James Powell & Sons of Whitefriars, London, who flourished from 1835 to 1973 and were one of the most important and progressive stained glass firms of the 19th century, can be seen in the south aisle of Cowbridge church and in the north wall of the nave at Llanblethian church.

John Hardman & Co. of Birmingham was another of the major firms of 19th-century stained glass makers. However, the firm's work only appears in the Vale of Glamorgan at St. Fagans church where all the stained glass windows but one are by John Hardman. His chief designer at that period was his nephew John Hardman Powell (1827-95). The reason for the profusion of Hardman glass was that George Edmund Street (1824-81), the architect who restored St. Fagans church in 1860, employed John Hardman to make the stained glass for his early churches.

The last thirty years of the 19th century were marked by the appearance in the stained glass field of many of the new firms which were formed by skilled designers and craftsmen who split off from the big firms such as Clayton & Bell in a period of prolific output and demand. The principal firms were Burlison and Grylls, A. L. Moore and Jones & Willis. Both John Burlison (1843-91) and Thomas John Grylls (1845-1913) trained in the studios of Clayton & Bell. In 1868 Burlison & Grylls founded a stained glass studio at 23, Newman Street, London. The only identifiable window by Burlison & Grylls appears in the south side of the nave at St. Bride's Major church. The beautiful east window of Llysworney church which commemorates John Devereux Vann Loder Nicholl-Carne (d. 1905), was designed by Arthur L. Moore in 1908. Another window by Moore can be seen in the south-east wall of the nave of St. Athan's church. A stained glass window in the north-east wall of the nave of Peterston-super-Ely church portraying in its three lights the figure of Christ blessing little children, Christ as the Light of the World and Christ as the Good Shepherd is the work of the firm of Jones & Willis of London and Birmingham.

Towards the end of the 19th century there was a growing dissatisfaction with the factory-like production methods which many large Victorian firms had adopted to meet the great demand for stained glass. By 1890 a new generation of Arts and Crafts Movement workers demanded that the designer of a window should be responsible for all stages of its execution from the initial sketch to the fixing of the finished work in the church. Nevertheless by the beginning of the 20th century British stained glass held a leading position in the world.

In the 20th century British stained glass remained more traditional in style than in other European countries. The end of the Great War of 1914-1918 brought about a further demand for stained glass windows as memorials for

St. Hilary's church—stained glass east window by Clayton and Bell

Llanblethian church—memorial stained glass window to Reverend William Franklen Evans *(left)*
Cowbridge church—heraldic glass from window of south (Llanquian) aisle *(right)*

those men of the parish who lost their lives fighting for King and Country. There are several memorial windows in the churches of the Vale of Glamorgan installed circa 1920 by London stained glass artists such as Percy Bacon (Bonvilston church) and Robert J. Newbery (Llanblethian and Llandow churches). South Wales is comparatively rich in 20th-century glass both by followers of the Arts and Crafts Movement from 1910 onwards and by the Celtic Studios of Swansea and those glaziers connected with the Swansea College of Art.

The large round-headed window in the west wall of Ewenny Priory church depicts the Nativity and was designed by William Glasby of London in 1929. The David Jones of Llangan memorial window in St. Canna's church is also attributed to him. A two-light stained glass window in the north aisle of Ewenny Priory church which depicts the figures of St. Elizabeth, mother of John the Baptist and St. Luke, 'the beloved Physician', was designed by Messrs. G. Maile & Sons Ltd. of Regents Park, London in 1935. The stained glass east window of Wick church, erected in 1940, is also the work of the same firm which was founded in 1785. The Merrett memorial west window in Michaelston-le-Pit church depicts the four Archangels of the Bible and was designed by Sir Ninian Comper in 1952. Notable windows by Alfred L.

Michaelston-le-Pit church—Merrett memorial window in west wall of nave

Wilkinson are to be seen in the east window of Sully church and the memorial window to Assistant Bishop Richard W. Jones in the nave of Peterston-super-Ely church.

Hubert Thomas of Celtic Studios, Swansea, is the designer of two memorial stained glass windows in the nave of Llanmaes church to the Reverend Henry Campbell Davies and his wife which were erected in the 1960s. Another window by the same stained glass artist appears in the south transept of St. George-super-Ely church to Llewellyn Edmund Traherne (d. 1914) and his wife, Dorothy Emma Olivia Traherne (d. 1957).

The Elizabeth Gullen memorial window erected in the nave of Colwinston church in 1963, which depicts light itself radiating from the centre of the window to its four corners, is the work of John Petts, a contemporary stained glass artist of Abergavenny, Monmouthshire.

Frank Roper of Penarth, who is better known for his work as a sculptor, designed the modern stained glass window in Llysworney church depicting

Peterston-super-Ely church—memorial window to Assistant Bishop R. W. Jones

Christ the King and Christ the Good Shepherd. The space above the doorway to the tower at Wenvoe church is filled with stained glass depicting the Jesse tree with the Virgin and Child framed within the tree. This stained glass design is also the work of Frank Roper. An example of the work of H. W. Harvey, a modern traditional stained glass artist of York, appears in the nave of Merthyr Dyfan church depicting the Holy Family. This window was erected in 1974.

A stained glass window in the nave of St. Bride's Major church portraying the figures of St. Francis and St. Helena was designed by James A. Crombie, a contemporary glazier from Bristol. The most recent stained glass window to be erected in the Vale of Glamorgan churches is at St. Curig's church, Porthkerry.

It was erected on St. David's Day, 1987 to the memory of John Jickells (1920–1985) by his widow, Mrs. Noreen Jickells. The stained glass depicts a pattern of butterflies, symbols of the Resurrection, as well as expressing the beauty and mystery of God's creation. The window was designed by John Petts, stained glass artist of Abergavenny, Monmouthshire.

The subject matter of early stained glass windows illustrated in a figurative form Old and New Testament stories and characters. Thus the stained glass gave man a visual meaning of God's word and the windows often complemented the wall paintings. Christ was usually the central figure of all the iconography. Naturally the most common scenes are those of the Passion, the Crucifixion, the Taking down from the Cross (Deposition) followed by the Resurrection, Mary Magdalene mistaking Christ for the Gardener (Noli me tangere) and the Ascension.

The east window at St. Hilary's church depicts scenes from the Passion, Crucifixion, Resurrection and Glorious Ascension of Our Lord. While at Cowbridge church the east window illustrates the birth, life and death of Christ with scenes from the Annunciation, the Visitation, the Epiphany, the Presentation in the Temple, the Flight into Egypt, Jesus with the Doctors in the Temple, the Carriage of the Cross and finally, in the centre light, the Crucifixion and Resurrection.

The figure of Christ as the Good Shepherd appears prominently in the stained glass windows of the Vale churches. Other memorial windows of the Victorian period invariably referred to the theme of resurrection, as seen in the Morson window in Cowbridge church which depicts the raising of Jairus' daughter, the raising of Lazarus and the raising of the widow's son.

The Virgin Mary has her own cycle in stained glass. We have scenes in glass depicting the Annunciation and the Visitation with Elizabeth in the west windows of St. Fagans church. Other windows in the Vale churches portray the Nativity and its associated scenes of the Adoration of the Magi and the Shepherds, the Flight into Egypt, the Presentation in the Temple and Finding Jesus with the Doctors in the Temple.

Angels naturally abound in the stained glass (particularly in the tracery lights) attending all the momentous occasions and holy personages and often carrying musical instruments. The Archangels of the Bible were also very popular subjects and Gabriel, Michael, Raphael and Uriel all appear in the Merrett memorial window by Sir Ninian Comper in Michaelston-le-Pit church.

The Four Evangelists are always accompanied by their emblems—the ox (St. Luke), the lion (St. Mark), the man (St. Matthew) and the eagle (St. John). Two beautiful stained glass windows by John Hardman in St. Fagans church also depict the four Evangelists. The east window at Llandough-by-Cowbridge church depicts Christ appearing in Glory holding the orb of the world.

Some windows in the Vale churches are filled with heraldic stained glass such as the Boteler memorial window in Penmark church, the Hubert de Burgh Thomas window in Colwinston church, the Nicholl-Carne memorial window in St. Donat's church and the window in the Llanquian aisle at Cowbridge that commemorates various benefactors of the former Cowbridge Grammar School—including Sir Edward Stradling, Sir Leoline Jenkins and Jesus College, Oxford.

The patron saints of the church also appear in stained glass. At St. Bride's-super-Ely church we have the figure of St. Brigid, at Llangan St. Canna, at St. Donat's St. Donat, at St. Nicholas St. Nicholas and at Sully we have St. John the Baptist. Christ's early relations appear in groups such as the Holy Family in a stained glass window in the nave of Merthyr Dyfan church.

In the Middle Ages all churches displayed wall paintings. The main object of medieval wall paintings, apart from embellishing the church, was to impart religious knowledge. There were no printed books until the end of the 15th century and such service books and bibles as there were had to be laboriously copied in manuscript by the monks and only privileged persons possessed them. The Bible story and the lives of the saints were taught to the parishioners by paintings on church walls—'the Biblia Pauperum' or 'Poor Man's Bible'. The Crucifixion and scenes from Christ's Passion and the life of the Virgin Mary were the most common narrative themes. Another subject frequently found was the Tree of Jesse or the ancestry of Christ. The Doom or Last Judgement was another theme without which no medieval church was complete and was usually situated in a prominent position over the chancel arch.

In the Vale of Glamorgan very few medieval wall paintings remain extant, but in Llantwit Major church fine examples of these wall paintings still exist in the chancel and nave. On the north wall of the chancel is the 13th-century figure of Mary Magdalene holding a jar of precious ointment in her right hand and next to it is a fragmentary figure of the Virgin Mary, also of 13th-century date. Of the wall paintings in the nave of the church the finest is that of St. Christopher, the patron saint of travellers. His larger than life figure occupies its usual position opposite the south entrance so that a parishioner had only to look through the door to see the image of St. Christopher and receive his protection, for superstition had it that whoever beheld his image was safe that day from sudden death.

In Llanmaes church the western part of the north wall of the nave is covered with medieval paintings which are said to represent St. George and the Dragon with the Princess standing at the gate of the castle and what are thought to be three priests in eucharistic vestments. On the west wall of the chancel arch in Colwinston church, surrounding the northern niche, are traces of medieval wall paintings which depict the consecration of St. Nicholas as Bishop of Myra and the picturesque story of the young mother whose baby was miraculously saved from death by boiling while his mother attended the bishop's consecration.

The Reformation brought about a violent reaction against all forms of decoration and images reminiscent of the Roman past. An order in council of 1547 was promulgated for the obliteration and destruction of popish and superstitious books and images, 'so that the memory of them shall not remain in their churches and houses.' Consequently many of the beautiful wall paintings were covered by limewash and their place taken by texts of scripture or the

Llantwit Major church—wall paintings of St. Christopher (*left*) and Mary Magdelene (*right*)

'sentences' as they were known. These included the Creed, the Lord's Prayer and the Ten Commandments. Furthermore the Royal Arms were ordered to be displayed in every church by Henry VIII after the Act of Supremacy.

At Eglwys Brewis church the walls are literally covered with such texts from scripture. On the south side of the chancel arch is the Lord's Prayer and on the north wall of the nave is the Apostles' Creed. To the east of the Creed are painted the Royal Arms of England of William III and Mary (1689-1702). At Llantwit Major church to the east of the figure of St. Christopher is a much-faded painting of the Royal Arms of King James I with the inscription 'God Save King James 1604'. A large painted panel containing the text of the Apostles' Creed exists at Llancarfan church on the south wall of the south aisle.

Many other medieval wall paintings were lost in Victorian times by the senseless practice of stripping the plaster from the walls to show 'the beautiful stonework'. Consequently hundreds of wall paintings were destroyed in the 19th century in this way, as at Llanblethian church for example in 1896, while

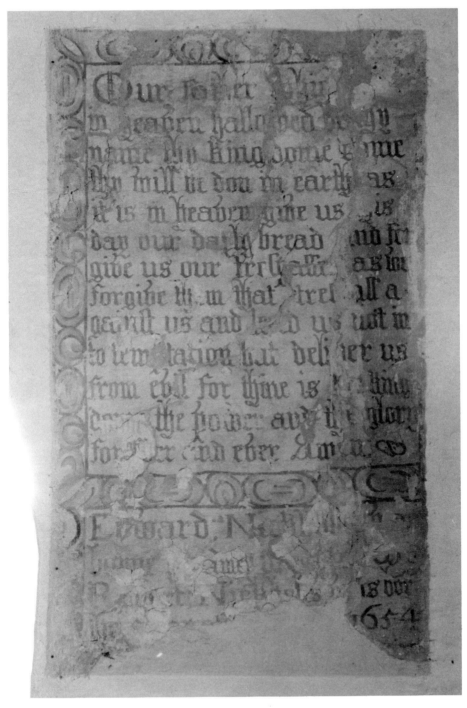

Eglwys Brewis church—The Lord's Prayer painted on the chancel wall

Colwinston church—wall paintings on chancel arch

fragments of other medieval wall paintings remain unrestored beneath the walls
of Cadoxton-juxta-Barry and Llansannor churches.

The word pulpit is derived from the Latin word 'pulpitum' meaning a
platform. In the Middle Ages it was made of wood or stone and was carved
with symbolic scenes. Generally speaking few medieval pulpits exist today as
sermons were usually delivered in medieval times before the altar at the west
end of the chancel or from the rood-loft. There is however a fine stone one at
Newton Nottage, a church not dealt with in this survey.

Pulpits were generally introduced in 1603 on the accession of James I when a
canon was issued ordering churchwardens to provide a pulpit in every church.
The earliest pulpit in the Vale of Glamorgan churches is probably that at
Penmark church. It is a Jacobean pulpit from which the Reverend John Wesley
preached in 1777. The pulpit at Llancarfan church has 16th-century-style
linenfold panels and the cornice is adorned with Tudor-style floral decoration.
It dates as do the vast majority of pulpits in the Vale churches from 19th-
century restorations. Three-decker pulpits which were common in the late 17th
and 18th centuries were removed in Victorian times. The high-backed box
pews necessitated the preacher standing on the top deck with the reader
occupying the middle deck and the clerk the lowest. In Michaelston-le-Pit
church there is a version of the three-decker pulpit which has been skilfully
adapted to meet local needs. The lowest part forms the choir stalls, the centre

Eglwys Brewis church—Royal Arms of William and Mary

the reading desk and the upper part of the pulpit proper. Heavy ornate stone pulpits in the Victorian Gothic style are to be found at Cowbridge, Llanblethian, St. Bride's Major and St. Nicholas. The pulpit at Llanblethian, erected in 1896, is of unique design and no expense was spared in its construction. It is composed of Penarth alabaster, red Forest of Dean stone, Quarella stone from Bridgend and red Irish marble. Pulpits are panelled with tracery recalling windows of the period. The panels in each of the facets of the

Penmark church—Jacobean pulpit

Llanblethian church—19th-century pulpit

pulpit at Llanblethian are richly carved with blind tracery on a marble background and each panel has trefoil-headed arches beneath an ogee arch. The spandrels are filled with rectilinear-style tracery which is in keeping with the 15th-century Perpendicular architecture of the church.

The panels of wooden pulpits were often carved with depictions of saints or other devotional figures. Wenvoe church has a finely-carved oak pulpit with the three figures in high relief showing Jesus in the centre panel with the Apostles St. Andrew and St. Peter on either side. The head of each panel is a double ogee arch with foliated pinnacles which extend into the plainly-moulded cornice. The design of the pulpit is attributed to Sir Ninian Comper.

The hour glass or sermon glass came into general use in the Established church in the 16th and 17th centuries for the purpose of regulating the length of the sermon. Hence it was usually attached to the pulpit or the adjacent wall within easy reach of the preacher. Many of these hour glasses were destroyed during the Victorian restorations when new pulpits were erected in the churches. However, the bracket for an hour glass remains attached to the pulpit at Marcross church.

St. Nicholas' church—19th century pulpit

Pulpits usually stand on the north side of the nave. The pulpit constructed in the 19th century for St. Nicholas' church was found to be too large to go into its former position on the north side of the nave and consequently had to be placed on the south side.

With regard to church organs in the Vale of Glamorgan, Iolo Morganwg states in one of his manuscripts that Jasper Tudor, Earl of Pembroke gave the organs to the churches at Cowbridge, Llantwit Major, St. Athan's and St. Fagans and that all the organs were taken down during the reigns of Henry VIII and Edward VI. Organ playing had been listed amongst the faults and abuses of religion by the Lower House of Convocation in 1536 and in 1563 that same body called for the removal of all organs from places of worship. During the period of the Commonwealth many organs were destroyed but after the Restoration in 1660 organs were again brought into use in church services.

Most of the churches of the Vale have an organ of some kind depending on the size of the building and the nature of the music sung in it. Several of the richer organs in the Vale churches came from private houses or redundant churches or chapels. The organ at Llantwit Major church built by C. H. Walker of Manchester Square, London, came from The Ham, the residence of Illtyd Nicholl before he moved to Llanmaes at the turn of the century. The organ by Albert E. Pease of Stoke Newington at St. Bride's Major church was brought from the parish church of St. John the Baptist, Ystradyfodwg which was closed

Llantwit Major church—19th-century organ built by C. H. Walker *(left)*
Flemingston church—early 19th-century organ built by Joseph Walker *(right)*

through subsidence and the organ at Penmark church came from Moriah
Chapel, Abercynon, in 1946.

Some of the smaller parish churches such as St. Mary Church and
Llandough-by-Cowbridge have organs that were built by the 'Positive' Organ
Co. Ltd. of London. This firm flourished in the early years of this century as
suppliers of small organs, mostly of one manual, to country and mission
churches. The instruments were built to standard designs and purchased from a
catalogue.

In the second half of the 19th century substantial changes took place in the
layout and furnishings of Anglican churches and these affected the position of
the organ and its design. The ecclesiologists and Tractarians who were mainly
responsible for these changes wanted to get rid of the box pews, western
galleries and three-decker pulpits which cluttered churches and to return to
what they considered were the ideals of the Middle Ages. The main focus was
to be on the altar. Immediately in front of the altar in the chancel area choir

stalls were introduced for a surpliced choir to lead the congregation in hymn singing. As a result of these changes the organ was now brought forward from the western gallery which it had usually occupied to a position nearer the altar and choir. New organs were designed to fit unobtrusively into their changed setting.

During the restoration of Cowbridge church in 1893 the old organ which stood in a gallery at the west end of the nave was disposed of and a new three-manual organ built by J. Nicholson of Worcester was installed at the east end of the south aisle near the choir. Also the one-manual 'Positive' organ erected in the west end of the nave of St. Athan's church in 1911 was removed at some time in this century and located in the crossing to be near the choir and chancel. When Bonvilston church was almost entirely rebuilt in 1863 a custom-made organ built by W. G. Vowles of Bristol was installed in a specially constructed organ chamber which was part of the design of the restored church.

The two-manual organ by Evans and Barr of Belfast at St. Andrew's Major church, which was installed in the north aisle in 1919, was moved into the Lee Chapel in 1922 so as to be near the choir and chancel. At St. Nicholas' church the two-manual organ built by J. S. Dane & Sons of Swansea in 1875 is located under the drop arch to the side chapel on the south side of the chancel. The earliest instrument in the Vale churches is most probably the one-manual organ at Flemingston church built by Joseph W. Walker (d. 1870), the founder of the firm of J. W. Walker in the early part of the 19th century.

After the Norman Conquest the stone font became a regular part of the furniture of every parish church. This accounts for the fact that so many of the ancient fonts which have come down to us display details of Norman style in their construction and decoration. The massive size of the Norman fonts provided ample evidence for the practice of total immersion of the infant at the administration of Holy Baptism, which was not uncommon at the period when the fonts were constructed. Despite the fact that many churches were drastically restored and others were rebuilt out of all recognition in the 19th century the Norman fonts were retained in a great many cases so that they remain the only material link with the original Norman church.

The majority of Norman fonts of the 12th and 13th centuries in the Vale of Glamorgan are tub-shaped with roll-moulding and are mostly worked out of Sutton stone which as we have seen was quarried near Ogmore. The early Norman font at Ewenny Priory church is an exception. It is goblet-shaped with roll-moulding and has been recut at some time in the past. Fine examples of Norman fonts exist at Llantwit Major and St. Donat's churches which are decorated with 'shingle' or 'fish-scale' ornamentation. The most remarkable Norman font is to be seen at St. Lythan's church; it is barrel-shaped and decorated with six rows of large chevron moulding in a continuous pattern. It has no base or stem and the font rests squarely upon a modern base. The 'Chrism' or consecrated oil blessed by the Bishop was mingled with the baptismal water. In order to preserve this water the bowls were lined with lead (as at Marcross church).

Wick—Norman

St. Hilary—Norman

St. Lythan's—Norman with
chevron decoration

Llantwit Major—Norman with
scale decoration

St. Donat's—Norman with
scale decoration

Welsh St. Donat's—
late Norman

Llancarfan—nonagonal
(nine-sided)

Flemingston—13th-century

Bonvilston—13th-century

MEDIEVAL FONTS

Llangan—13th-century

Pendoylan—14th-century

St. George-super-Ely—
early 15th-century

Peterston-super-Ely—
15th-century font and cover

St. Fagans—
15th-century

Llantrithyd—Tudor

Cowbridge—19th-century
octagonal

Sully—19th-century

LATE MEDIEVAL AND POST-REFORMATION FONTS

Scallops appear on the underside of the basin at Llancarfan, Monknash and Welsh St. Donat's churches. The font at Llancarfan is unusual for it has a nonagonal (nine-sided) bowl. The only example in the Vale of Glamorgan of Norman arcading with trefoil arches appears on the defunct font at Llantrithyd church which lies neglected on the south side of the churchyard. Some of the Norman fonts have been recut and carving introduced at a later date as at Ewenny Priory church and Peterston-super-Ely church. The 13th-century font at Flemingston church was designed to look like a Norman cushion capital. It has a modern cover with an acorn finial with open scroll trusses on a plain central shaft.

In the 13th century it was decreed that fonts should be fitted with a lid or cover secured by a lock to prevent the theft of holy water for superstitious purposes. Consequently some fonts show the scars or marks on the rim where rivets holding these locks were removed in later years.

The octagonal-shaped font originated at the end of the Norman period. Many of the fonts of the 14th and 15th centuries were made octagonal in shape because the figure eight was considered to be a mystical number and symbolic of regeneration. A 15th-century font at St. George-super-Ely church is octagonal and each panel displays a quatrefoil in a circle. The best example of a late Perpendicular font is to be seen at Llantrithyd church where the font has an octagonal goblet-shaped bowl with moulded rim. The bowl is decorated on each panel with a piece of scroll-edged strapwork and typical Tudor flower decoration. The pedestal shaft rests on an octagonal base.

At Sully church a 19th-century font, which is said to have been made for the Great Exhibition of 1851, is goblet-shaped and beautifully and elaborately carved with angels' bodies. Also at Sully church is an old wooden capstan font. Victorian fonts of octagonal shape can be seen at Cowbridge and Wenvoe churches.

Most fonts have flat oak covers but at Gileston church the oak cover is conical and has eight carved panels of Jacobean design. In St. Athan's church the font has a twelve-sided pyramidal oak cover with ribs down each angle surmounted by a finial. The most elaborate font cover is at Peterston-super-Ely church which consists of three stages of finely-carved woodwork.

As to the position of the fonts, in general they are mostly placed to the left of the south door of the nave on entering the church. But in some of the Vale churches they are to be found in the centre of the nave near the west end as at Marcross, Penmark and Welsh St. Donat's.

On the right-hand side of the doorway of many of the Vale churches is a stoup for holy water, usually set in a small niche, sometimes supported on a slender pillar shaft. Some are octagonal or hexagonal in shape. As they passed through the church door the parishioners dipped the fingers of their right hand into the holy water and crossed themselves, a token of the renewal of their baptism.

Accommodation was increased in several of the Vale churches in the 18th century by the addition of a west gallery (which was cheaper than an aisle in a poor parish). They sometimes housed a choir or an orchestra. Such galleries existed at Cowbridge, Llantrithyd, Michaelston-super-Ely and Sully churches, but all of these were swept away during restorations of the churches in the latter part of the 19th century. Access to the west gallery at Llantrithyd church was obtained by an outside staircase, and the doorway, now built-in, leading to this gallery can still be seen on the south side of the tower.

The western tower was generally a late medieval addition to the rectangular chancel and nave and many of the present Vale towers were built in the 14th and 15th centuries. The towers at Llanmaes and Wenvoe were removed from the north side of the chancel and rebuilt in their present position in 1632 and 1699 respectively. The ashlar-faced tower of St. Fagans church has a stone plaque with the arms of the Lewis family and the date 1730 which suggests a rebuilding of the tower at that time.

The usual design was the unbuttressed tower marked by a wide-spreading or battered base below a stringcourse a metre or so from the ground which is repeated at a higher level at Llanfrynach and Pendoylan. The battlemented stage of the tower is corbelled out in typical Welsh fashion and there are three merlons on each face with narrow embrasures. The belfry stage is either lit by square-headed Perpendicular windows or else pierced by slit-loopholes. The entrance to the tower is either through a western or southern door as at Sully, where the lower stage of the tower forms a porch with entrance on the south side. Windows and doorways have been introduced from time to time in the western walls of many of the towers.

The belfry is usually reached from within by a stone staircase to the first level and then by ladders to the upper stages. However, at Colwinston, Llanfrynach and St. Mary Church a projection on the south side of the tower contains a spiral staircase leading to the upper stages of the tower. At Merthyr Dyfan the projection housing the staircase is on the north side and at Llanmihangel church a projection was built on the north side of the tower in 1909 to facilitate access to the belfry.

The Somerset type of Perpendicular tower is represented in the Vale at Llanblethian church. Other buttressed 15th-century towers are present at Peterston-super-Ely, St. Bride's Major and St. Hilary. The massive tower at Cowbridge church was remodelled in the 19th century with the result that it is unique in its rather eccentric form.

The other predominant type of tower in the Vale is the saddleback. Generally the axis of the saddleback tower is east to west and occasionally a second north-south saddleback links each pair of opposing gables as at Llansannor and St. George-super-Ely. Charles B. Fowler, the architect, thought that the concept of the saddleback tower was imported from Normandy where he had seen so many of this type. One peculiarity about the church towers in Wales and in particular in the Vale of Glamorgan is that the upper stage of these towers is usually corbelled out to form a corbel table which not only helps to support the parapet but also forms a decorative feature.

Where there is no tower there is often a western bellcote; sometimes as at

St. Hilary's church—upper stage of 15th-century buttressed tower with corbel table

Peterston-super-Ely church—15th-century buttressed tower

St. Bride's-super-Ely church in 1881—saddleback tower
From a drawing by David Jones of Wallington

Llangan, Flemingston and Llandough-by-Cowbridge, two bells hang side by
side in the simple arch which holds them. At Gileston the western bellcote is
corbelled out in the style of corbel tables of tower battlements and has a
chimney-like appearance. Similarly, at Eglwys Brewis the western bellcote is of
unusual design with an embattled square turret with corbel table.

Few of the bells which these medieval towers were built to carry have
survived. However, pre-Reformation bells exist in the towers of Colwinston,
Llanfrynach, Llanmaes, Llysworney and Porthkerry churches, all with Latin
inscriptions invoking popular saints. The bell at Llysworney is said to have been
cast by John Gosselin (d.1453) of the Bristol Medieval Foundry between 1449
and 1453. The fourth bell by Henry Gefferies of Bristol bears the inscription
'Sancta Maria ora pro nobis, hg' and is believed to have been cast circa 1550.

Bells of the 17th century by Thomas Stone, an itinerant bellfounder (whose
name appears in full on a bell at St. Mary Church instead of his usual initials
T.S.) occur at Llanmaes, Llanmihangel, Monknash and St. Mary Church.
Thomas Stone cast bells between 1627 and 1655. He favoured the use of Latin
inscriptions and he probably carried with him notes of suitable stock inscriptions in Latin for use in Welsh churches in preference to the use of English.

The principal firm of Welsh bellfounders was the Evans family of Chepstow
and their bells hang in many Vale churches. Two bells cast by the first Evan
Evans (fl. 1686-1724) at Pendoylan church are thought to be the earliest cast by
that foundry. The ring of eight bells at Cowbridge church cast by Evan and
William Evans (*fl.* 1718-27), bellfounders of Chepstow in 1722 is probably the

Cowbridge church—Tenor bell, removed for repairs in 1935

only complete original Evans octave surviving in the Principality.

The firm of Rudhall of Gloucester cast several bells in the Vale of Glamorgan. A ring of six bells cast by Abraham Rudhall in 1718 hangs in the belfry at Bonvilston church. A large single bell cast by John Rudhall in 1800 occurs in Ewenny Priory church. At Llanmaes church there is a bell dated 1777 by William Bilbie of Chewstoke, Somerset, who cast bells between 1775 and 1790.

Two bells by John Pennington of Monmouth occur at Merthyr Dyfan church dated 1676 and one at Llancarfan dated 1664. A bell cast by Jefferies & Price of Bristol (1839-1854) hangs in the tower at St. George-super-Ely church.

The bellcotes at Llangan and Flemingston churches hold bells cast by John Warner & Sons of London (founded 1853). Llewellins and James of Bristol (1851-1930), John Taylor of Loughborough (est. 1840) and Mears and Stainbank of the Whitechapel Foundry London recast several bells in the Vale during the latter part of the 19th century. At St. Donat's church are six hemispherical bells or 'gongs' recast by the Whitechapel Foundry in 1913 from the single bell in the church and two other bells from the castle. Two bells in the belfry of

Peterston-super-Ely church contain Welsh inscriptions:—'Gogoniant i Dduw yn yr Uchelder' (Glory to God in the Highest) and 'Ti dduw a Folwn' (We praise thee, O God).

Three churches in the Vale retain their sanctus bells *in situ*; they are at Llantrithyd, St. Nicholas and Welsh St. Donat's. Two hang from a wooden frame in the east side of the chancel arch, while the one at St. Nicholas is suspended high above the south side of the sanctuary. These bells were rung at certain times during the celebration of the mass, principally at 'the sanctus' (hence the name) and at the elevation of the consecrated elements. C. B. Fowler writing in his *Rambling sketches from the old churches in the Diocese of Llandaff* (1896) mentions a sanctus bell at Porthkerry church with the inscription 'Santa Maria ora pro nobis' but no such bell exists today. However, a large bell in the tower of Porthkerry church bears the same inscription and was cast by Henry Gefferies of Bristol circa 1550. Fowler may have been thinking of this bell.

At Marcross church on the south side of the chancel there is a low-side window now shuttered where a hand bell was rung during the mass to inform those parishioners who could not be present at the service so that they might bow their knees at the high point of the mass.

The porch is a late medieval addition to the fabric of the church. The general position of the porch is on the south side of the church near the west end and they were built on the south side first as a protection for the south door from the prevailing south-west winds and usually on the side nearest to the population of the village. Cowbridge, St. Bride's Major and St. Donat's of the Vale churches have the unusual feature of having their porches built on the north side of the church. At Sully church the lower part of the west tower forms a porch

Llantrithyd church—sanctus bell above chancel arch *(left)*
Welsh St. Donat's church—sanctus bell above chancel arch *(right)*

with entrance on the south side. Porches were used for both secular and
religious purposes. Banns were read in the porch and the first part of the
baptismal service also took place there. Inside the porch are the customary stone
benches where generations of children once received instruction from the parish
priest in elementary education and religious knowledge.

The porches in the Vale are generally large and windowless and sometimes
out of proportion to the rest of the fabric and those which have survived are
crudely constructed. Nearly all the porches in the Vale churches are of late date
namely, 15th or early 16th century. The notable exception is the storeyed porch
at Llantwit Major which may be of late 13th- or perhaps early 14th-century
date. There the porch is unusually large and covers the entrance through an
early Norman doorway. Access to the upper chamber is through a pointed
doorway in the south wall of the church west of the Norman door. The steps to
the parvise ascend in the thickness of the south wall and it is thought that this
room was used as a dwelling place by the priest.

The roof of the porch was generally vaulted and
the bosses at the intersection of the ribs carried
interesting designs. At Llandough-by-Cowbridge
church the roof displays floriated bosses and a
central rib is carved with the head of Christ. At
Penmark the roof of the nave has an arcade pattern
on the wallplates which is repeated on the frieze in
the south porch.

The principal decorative features of the porch
usually consisted of an image of the patron saint of
the church and a cross in the apex of the gable.
Above the south porch at St. Mary Church is a
trefoiled niche containing the sculpted figures of the
Archangel Gabriel and the Virgin Mary
representing the Annunciation and thus the
dedication of the church. At Monknash the porch is
crudely built and is typical of many Glamorgan
porches; the gable is surmounted by a Latin cross
with the date 1628 inscribed on it. Several porches display empty niches above
the inner doorway which once contained statuettes of the patron saints as at
Penmark. The outer doorway of the south porch at St. Fagans church is 15th-
century, but the foliated cross immediately above is a 19th-century addition to
an older stump. The 15th-century inner doorway of the porch at Gileston
church is unique in the Vale of Glamorgan; it bears six heraldic shields
belonging to local families of note carved upon it and is in an excellent state of
preservation.

At Llanblethian church the south porch is built in the Perpendicular style and
the outer arch is pointed and surmounted by a dripstone. It is decorated with
crockets and pinnacles with grotesque gargoyles leering from either side of the
porch. Other porches with Perpendicular doorways are to be found at Pen-

Gileston church—15th-century inner doorway of south porch,
carved with heraldic shields

mark, Llancarfan, Colwinston and Llansannor. The porch at Llansannor has a
fine 16th-century doorway with four-centred outer arch surmounted by a
square label and pointed inner arch. Above the outer doorway is a replica of the
original sundial placed there by Thomas Truman in 1741. Above the porch at
St. George-super-Ely is a tablet with the inscription 'Lord I have loved the
habitation of thy house and the place where thine honour dwelleth.'

The outer doorway of the south porch at St. Bride's-super-Ely is a splendid example of Norman workmanship. It was brought there from Margam Abbey in 1849 during the restoration of the church. The inner arch is adorned by chevron decoration above little scalloped capitals and the chamfered outer arch is surmounted by a row of chevron ornaments which form lozenges.

Several porches were completely rebuilt during the 19th century as at Bonvilston where the porch is typically Victorian with high-pitched roof and an inner arch trefoil-headed with pierced cusps springing from the sides. An outer moulded arch springs from abaci above capitals with Early English-style, stiff-leaf foliage. There are trefoil-headed side windows, bench seats internally and a hood mould with label stops.

In many porches there are the remains of holy-water stoups where parishioners dipped their fingers and made the sign of the cross on their forehead and breast to remind themselves of their baptismal vows. These stoups were usually placed in a niche on the right-hand side of the doorway of the porch.

Sundials are fairly common in the Vale of Glamorgan. Their use goes back to the Middle Ages when mass or scratch dials were common. They told the times of church services but later they were developed to mark the hours of the day. They were usually situated near the main entrance above the porch doorway. They survive as an incised circle with a central hole (which once held the gnomon) and a number of radiating lines. An ancient mass dial can be seen on the south wall of the south transept at Ewenny Priory church. The four radiating lines probably represented the four main daily offices; prime or the first hour, terce or the third hour, sext which was noon and none the ninth hour. Later sundials can be seen at Llanblethian, Llansannor, Llancarfan and Penmark churches.

At one time every churchyard had a cross which was erected in the burial ground as a religious symbol at a time when individual monuments were uncommon. There are several churchyard crosses in the Vale of Glamorgan. Many of them retain their steps but the shaft and crosses have all but disappeared. They were destroyed by Cromwell's soldiers in the 17th century and the iconoclasts broke up most of the heads which bore sculptured images. These crosses were placed midway between the main entrance to the churchyard and the south porch east of the principal path. The cross was used as a 'station' (a stopping place where prayers might be said) in church processions on special church festivals such as Rogation and Palm Sunday. The cross also played an important role in the secular life of the community. From it, public announcements and proclamations were made. These crosses were originally used as outdoor preaching places. The mounted shaft type of cross which was most common, consisted of steps, base (plinth or socket), shaft, capital and head. The base usually consisted of from one to six steps made of individual stones forming a round, square or rectangular structure.

At Llangan, St. Mary Hill and St. Donat's we have rare examples of medieval churchyard crosses which still retain their original 15th-century carved heads. The one at Llangan is the most beautiful and finely-sculptured 15th-century

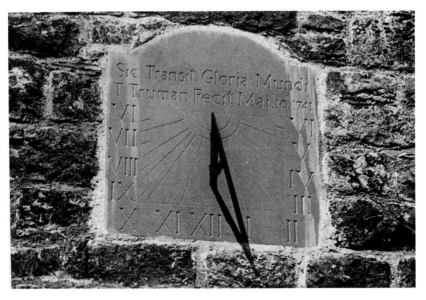

Llansannor church—sundial above south porch

St. Donat's church—
churchyard cross

St. Donat's church—head of churchyard cross *(left)*
Llangan church—rear of churchyard cross *(right)*

cross in Glamorgan. It has two tiers of carved figures. The two broad faces have double canopies with the Crucifixion on one side and a Pietà on the other. The two narrow faces have single canopies with figures of saints and ecclesiastics. The upper part of the head of the cross is square in plan having four equal faces with a saint under a single canopy. The churchyard cross at St. Mary Hill has a fine head and on the front is a representation of the Crucifixion, with the Embalming on the reverse and figures of saints on the other two sides, all surmounted by finely-carved canopies. In the churchyard at St. Donat's are two crosses. One on the north side is modern and records the restoration of the church in 1878. The other in its traditional position on the south side is of 15th-century date. The Crucifixion is carved on one side and on the other is the Blessed Virgin Mary seated and crowned. There are canopied figures on the other sides and along the top of the cross-head. Some churchyard crosses were restored at the beginning of this century as at Llantwit Major and Porthkerry. At Llanfrynach the churchyard cross is of a peculiar composition, the base being an inverted column with roll-moulding capped by a Norman cushion capital.

The lychgate is the gabled gateway to the church beneath which the coffin is set down to wait the arrival of the priest for the first part of the burial service.

Peterston-super-Ely church—lychgate

The word lychgate is derived from the Old English word 'lic' (cf. German 'Leiche') meaning corpse. Very few lychgates pre-date the 17th century. Several lychgates appear in the Vale at entrances to the church. Many of them, such as at Michaelston-le-Pit, Peterston-super-Ely, Porthkerry and Sully were erected as memorials to those men of the parish who lost their lives in the Great War 1914-1918. At St. Hilary's church the lychgate, constructed of stone and teak, was erected in 1900 on the east side of the churchyard as a memorial to George Montgomery Traherne of St. Hilary and Coedriglan (d. 1896) by his widow Mrs. Harriet Traherne. Affixed to the lychgate is a marble tablet recording the safe return of fifteen men from the parish who served in the Great War, 1914-18.

There is only one piece of pre-Reformation church plate left in the Vale of Glamorgan and the diocese of Llandaff and that is the silver paten at Llanmaes church, circa 1495. Llanmaes also possesses a silver chalice which was originally an Elizabethan drinking cup. Round the bowl is engraved a broad belt of loosely-interlaced foliated strap ornament forming four medallions in which are engraved four heads in profile. The cup is hall-marked 1569. Round the top is a band of beautifully-engraved foliated ornament.

The Vale possesses several silver chalices of the Elizabethan period. The bowls of these chalices are usually in the form of an inverted cone slightly bell-shaped

Llanmaes church—chalice and paten

and the foot is invariably round and about the same diameter as the lip of the bowl. The ornament usually consists of belts of intersecting foliated strap ornament. The earliest pieces of Elizabethan church plate in the Vale are a cup and cover at Sully church dated 1576, hall-marked 1566. However, the paten at Llanmaes church is of pre-Reformation date according to G.E. Halliday who assigned it the date 1495.

Many of these valuable eucharistic vessels are no longer in daily use and are either on permanent loan to the National Museum of Wales or locked away in bank vaults because they are too expensive to insure for everyday use.

In 1535 Henry VIII, by virtue of the Act of Supremacy, appointed Thomas Cromwell to be his Vicar-General. The keeping of parish registers was ordered by Cromwell in 1538 when he issued a mandate 'ordering every person, vicar or curate to enter in a book every wedding, christening and burial in his parish with the names of the parties'. The parish was to provide a 'sure coffer' with two locks, the parson having the custody of one key, the churchwardens that of

Cowbridge church—Elizabethan chalice and the Seys flagon

the other. The entries were to be made every Sunday after service in the presence of one of the wardens under a penalty of a fine of 3s 4d to be used to repair the church.

The language of the registers varies between Latin and English but after 1733 Latin was seldom used. In 1813 an Act of Parliament required baptisms, marriages and burials to be registered in three separate volumes which were printed according to a prescribed form. When civil registration was introduced in 1837 a new form of marriage register was introduced to conform with the civil registers. There are gaps in the records of some parishes because there was some delay in obtaining a new register and the entries for the intervening years, which were usually kept in loose papers, were lost.

Parish registers contain additional information other than bland unvarnished records of baptisms, marriages and burials. Unusual natural occurrences such as eclipses, comets and meteors are occasionally recorded in the registers as well as storms, frost and fires. In the coastal parishes in the Vale of Glamorgan there are several entries for burials after shipwrecks, as in the registers of Porthkerry and Monknash.

In the register of baptisms and burials for 1758-1812 at St. Donat's church one entry gives detailed information about three persons buried on the 6th September 1774 who were on their passage from Bristol to Ireland:— 'These unhappy persons with 24 more perished in the ship *Elizabeth* of Bristol among whom was Captain Weekes her master. The said ship was wrecked on the rocks near Marcross-Cwm.'

In the Llanmaes parish register of burials is the entry of the death of Ioan Yorath who was reputed to have died at the age of 180 years. Near the figure which sets the age at 'about 180' there is evidence under a powerful microscope of an erasure and it is thought there has been some alteration but if there is any truth in the statement that he was 'in the fights at Bosworthe' it would certainly make him considerably over a hundred years old. Also a contemporary note in the parish registers at Llanmaes records that a ruined belfry stood on the north side of the chancel before the tower was erected at the west end in 1632. At Michaelston-le-Pit church the parish registers date from 1738 and the first entry in the marriage section records the wedding of the rector, Thomas Hancorne. The earliest parish registers in the Vale of Glamorgan are to be found at St. Donat's church and Flemingston church dating back to the year 1570.

Several parish registers in the Vale which were recorded in a Glamorgan Record Office survey in 1951 have unfortunately gone missing at Llanmihangel, Gileston, and St. Mary Hill churches. Hearsay evidence recorded in a National Library of Wales questionnaire in 1940 stated that 'some old registers were seen burning at Bonvilston House after the death of a Mr. Bassett.' Most parish registers are now deposited either at the National Library of Wales at Aberystwyth or at the Glamorgan Record Office in Cardiff.

The religious changes of the 16th century marked the end of church building in Glamorgan. By this time the heavily-populated Vale especially was well provided with medieval churches and new work was only initiated when the state of the fabric prompted rebuilding or repair work. When the tower of Llanmaes was rebuilt and the chancel of Llantrithyd church renovated, the builders used a local version of the Perpendicular style. The Reformation changes entailed the removal of rood-screens, stone altar slabs, medieval stained glass, the lime-washing of medieval wall paintings and the blocking-up of rood-stairs.

The Victorian Gothic church revival halted the decay of the fabric of many churches in the Vale. Some churches were almost completely rebuilt, others repaired and most were restored at least once during the latter part of the 19th century. Dr. H. M. Thompson in his *Manuscript notes on the old churches of Glamorgan* (1935) described the churches in the Vale as 'medieval church buildings built in a modest form for a simple people.'

Nearly every church in the Vale of Glamorgan has some feature peculiar to itself. The church at St. Mary Hill exhibits the distempered bust of a former incumbent under the chancel arch and the original Norman chancel arch is now

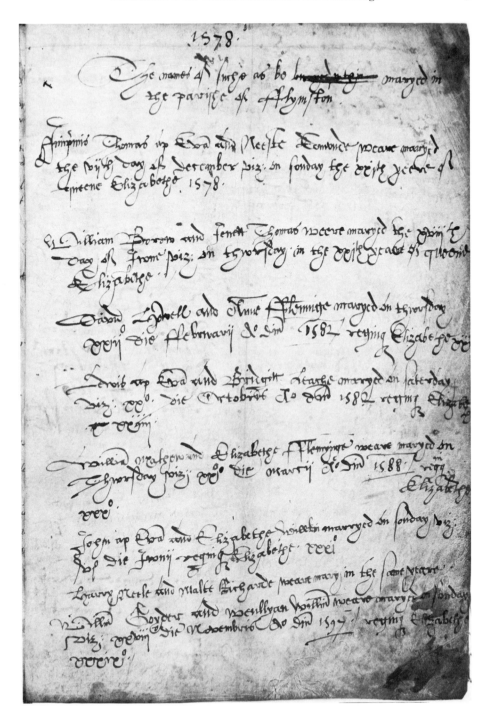

Flemingston church—First page of parish register of marriages dated 1578

built into the north wall of the nave. A gravestone at St. Nicholas' church has the opening bar of Chopin's 20th Prelude carved upon it, while the church at Michaelston-le-Pit has a quasi three-decker pulpit skilfully adapted to local needs. St. George's church has a weather-vane on the tower which is a representation of St. George and the Dragon. Several churches such as Gileston and Llansannor once stood in the private grounds of manor houses.

Despite the passage of time and changes wrought by the Victorian restorers the Vale churches have still retained their intrinsic character and individuality. Although these churches are 'unique repositories of the county's past' and often beautiful, both architecturally and as historic monuments, we ought never to forget their principal purpose, which is and always has been to serve their communities as living places of worship in the Vale of Glamorgan.

Descriptions of the Forty-five Churches

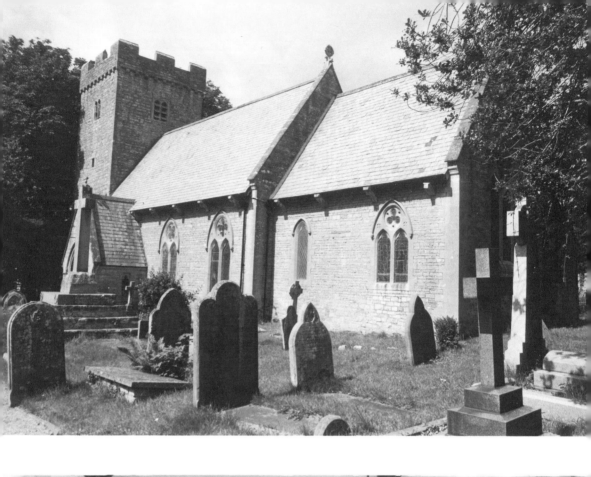

Bonvilston Church

The parish church of Bonvilston is dedicated to St. Mary the Virgin. The present church dates almost entirely from 1863 when the original 12th-century church was virtually rebuilt, only the tower and the chancel arch remaining of the earlier structure. Repairs carried out in 1824 at a cost of £120 (raised by local subscription) were inadequate to arrest the decay of the building which had long been sadly neglected. The church as it stands today is an example of First Pointed Victorian Gothic architecture and it appears that the reconstruction followed very closely the plan of the original building. Evidence for this can be found in the alignment of the nave and chancel, as the latter had a definite inclination to the north, the east window being out of line with the chancel arch. This phenomenon can be seen in many churches and is claimed to represent the inclination of Christ's head on the Cross of Calvary—the so-called 'weeping chancel'. The architects were Messrs. Prichard and Seddon and the cost of the rebuilding amounted to £1,600.

In 1180 the Abbey of Tewkesbury had the right to two parts of the tithes here. The earliest recorded incumbent was Richard, described as 'Decanus de Bonvelist' who was priest at Bonvilston from 1189 to 1201. In the early part of the 13th century different members of the Bonville family gave lands to Margam Abbey together with the advowson of the church, all of which gifts were confirmed by the Bishop of Llandaff in 1234. The church of Bonvilston was valued at £4 in 1254 (Taxation of Norwich) and £6-13s-4d in 1291 (*Taxatio Ecclesiastica*). In 1535 (*Valor Ecclesiasticus*) it was worth £8-1s-2d, the vicar apparently holding all the revenue except the pension of 16s-10d. In 1563 the Bishop of Llandaff's returns describe the living as a 'curacy' and it is so styled in 1603 when the curate had for service '£10 or the small tithes' and the impropriation worth £13-6s-8d was held by Thomas Bassett, Esq. in fee from the King. The parish of Bonvilston was for many years in the patronage of the Bassett family of Beaupré who on occasions placed members of their own family in the living. William Bassett was vicar here from 1614 to 1644, John Bassett from 1764 to 1779 and Miles Bassett from 1779 to 1811. In 1763, 1765, 1810 and 1817 the 'curacy' received grants from Queen Anne's Bounty amounting to £900, that in 1765 being to meet the private benefaction made in 1764 by the Reverend Miles Bassett, patron and impropriator consisting of the vicarial tithes, £12 per annum and a rent-charge of £3 per annum. In 1771 (Bishop Barrington's *Llandaff Diocesan Book*) the living was worth £25. In 1835 it was styled a perpetual curacy worth gross £83 and John James Bassett was patron and impropriator. With the Disestablishment of the Welsh Church in 1920 private patronage was abolished and the perpetual curacy became styled as a vicarage. The living of Bonvilston was linked with the rectory of St. Nicholas in 1953 and with St. George-super-Ely in 1970 to form a grouped benefice.

The church consists of chancel, nave, north transept and embattled western tower containing six bells. The chancel arch is of 15th-century date with continuous moulding springing from three moulded abbreviated capitals, and is clearly all the pre-restoration work that remains in this part of the church. The east window is of three trefoiled lights with a cinquefoil in the apex surmounted by a hood mould with carved heads as label stops. The stained glass in the window depicts at the top the Ascension of Our Lord surrounded by heads of angels; on either side in the trefoiled lights there are disciples. In the centre is the Crucifixion, on the north side are the women at the Cross and on the south side disciples. In the bottom panes appear the Shepherds, the Holy Family and the Magi. The window was erected by John Homfray in memory of his daughter, Ann Maria (d.1863), wife of Richard Bassett.

The chancel is lit on the south side by a trefoiled lancet with dripstone and a two-light Early English-style window with plate tracery in the head. The stained glass depicts the Risen Christ appearing to Mary Magdalene whom she mistook for the gardener on Easter morning. The window was erected in January, 1891 in memory of Richard Bassett of Bonvilston (d.1891) by his second wife, Honor and their sons, William and Hugh. A brass plaque on the south wall of the chancel commemorates Joseph Hugh Brain (d.1914) of Bonvilston House, churchwarden and member of the church choir from 1903 to 1914.

The close connection of the Bassett family with this church can be clearly traced by reference to the memorials in the sanctuary and chancel. On the north side of the chancel is a marble monument on which is emblazoned the Bassett arms 'Argent, a chevron between three hunting horns, stringed sable' to the memory of John Bassett of Bonvilston (d.1824) son of the Reverend John Bassett. Opposite on the south wall is another memorial tablet displaying the Bassett arms with family motto in Welsh 'Gwell angau na chywilydd' (Better death than dishonour) to the memory of Christopher Bassett, Captain, R.N. (d.1764) and his brother, the aforementioned Reverend John Bassett, Prebendary of Llandaff. The chancel has an arch-braced roof with diagonal braces with the arches supported by plain stone corbels with decorated wallplate.

The present choir stalls, altar rails, pulpit and lectern of carved oak, designed by Messrs. J. Wippell of Exeter, were erected in the church in 1908 as a memorial to Joseph Benjamin Brain (d.1907) and his wife, Ellen Allwood Brain (d.1908) by their sons and daughters. (See brass plaque on south wall of chancel). The pulpit and choir-stalls are a matching set and of unusual design, a mixture of classical motifs in the 18th-century style executed in Victorian times. The pulpit is very harmonious and very square with corner posts rather than stiles. The open sides have round arches in pairs on square abaci above round pillars with an obvious entasis. They have finely-done little circular mouldings and square bases. The mouldings of the cornice are continued around the corner posts and include the egg and tongue decoration which is repeated around the head of the arches. The same decoration runs beneath the bottom rail. Beneath the open arches a middle rail with dentil runs above a pair of sunken or coffered panels on each face. With the exception of the lower row of egg and tongue decoration, the bays of the choir-stalls may be described exactly as each side of the pulpit.

A custom-made organ, built by W. G. Vowles of Bristol towards the end of the 19th century, completely occupies the space in the north transept which may have been built solely for that purpose. The organ was restored in 1978 and the cost of the work was borne by several generous parishioners in memory of departed loved ones. The mouldings of the Early English-style pointed arch are deeply recessed above flat abaci surmounting caps of typical stiff-leaf decoration on the ends of decisive stalks, displaying small leaf forms. The organ conceals a rather ornate rose window with sexfoil in the centre surmounted by an external dripstone.

Another family for long connected with the parish, the Samuels (one of them, Evan, was churchwarden in 1847) can be traced genealogically from 1795 to 1863 on a memorial tablet on the south-east wall of the nave.

The windows of the nave comprise on the north side a two-light trefoil-headed window with quatrefoil above surmounted by dripstone with carved heads as label stops, and on the south side a pair of two-light trefoil-headed windows with plate tracery and a single trefoiled lancet with trefoil in the apex, all surmounted by hood moulds and carved heads as label terminations.

The stained glass in the centre window of the south nave depicts the figures of the Blessed Virgin Mary and Child with St. Nicholas, the patron saint of ship-wrecked sailors in the top panes and, in the bottom panes, scenes from Christ walking on the water and comforting the anxious disciples on the sea of Galilee during a storm with the words 'Peace, be still'. This window, designed by Percy Bacon of London, was erected in 1920 by Mrs. Harriet Diana Williams in memory of Charles Laurence Wyndham Williams, Midshipman, R.N. who lost his life on H.M.S. *Russell* in April 1916.

Affixed to the south-west wall of the nave above the doorway to the belfry staircase is a rectangular block of carved stone depicting a male figure standing beneath a rounded arch. The figure is clothed with a girdle and a pair of boots that reach almost to the knees. The arms are bent horizontally across the waist, with the fingers touching. On each side of the figure are vine scrolls and there is a simple volluted scroll at the base. It appears to be of 12th-century character, if not earlier, and may be part of a panel of a memorial. The sculpture bears a remarkable similarity to that on the stone pulpit at Newton Nottage church. This stone was found in the tower belfry and was fixed in the nave at the end of the last century. The nave, like the chancel, has an arch-braced roof with diagonal braces and the arches are supported on plain stone corbels with a decorated wallplate.

The circular font has a 13th-century bowl divided into six panels by characteristic leaf forms done in high relief. They spring in pairs from little flat columns with a vertical leaf between each main pair. The leading tips touch making a pointed oval of each panel. The bowl has a thick rim and modern foliage spurs connect the circular base to its square plinth. This font is reputed to be the smallest font in the diocese of Llandaff.

The south porch is a typical Victorian structure with an inner arch, trefoil-headed with pierced cusps springing from the sides and an outer moulded arch. It springs from a slight abacus continued as a string part of the way round the porch. The capitals beneath have stiff-leaf foliage and, below the necking, slender shafts with a vertical fillet and end in little round bases on square plinths. There are trefoil-headed side windows, bench seats internally and a hood mould with a very unusual design of label stop. The inner south doorway of the church has a pointed arch. On each side of the porch is a splendid pair of footscrapers.

The tower opens to the nave by a plain pointed arch which is filled with a beautifully-carved oak screen. The screen is of three bays, the central one a door, each of two trefoil-headed lights with panelling beneath. The cornice is plainly moulded with a row of brattishing. In the head are variously-shaped trefoils, some pointed. The tower is square and lofty with a corbel table below the battlement. The west door has a pointed arch and above it is a two-light cinquefoil-headed window beneath ogee arches under a square head and label. The belfry windows are of two lights with pointed heads under a square head and the mullions of these windows are worked out of headstones, the inscriptions being quite distinct. On the south face of the tower are two small apertures at a lower level. The tower contains a ring of six bells with tenor 12 cwt in F sharp and treble 5 cwt in D sharp cast by Abraham Rudhall of Gloucester in 1718. The ring of bells was given, as will be seen from the inscription on the tenor bell, by the family of Miles Button of Cottrell in 1718. The bells were quarter turned and rehung in 1918 by Mears & Stainbank of London. They were provided with modern fittings in the existing frame in 1936 by Gillett & Johnston, bellfounders of Croydon. The inscriptions on the bells are as follows:-

Treble—BARBARA CUM IUVENUM TURBA COMITISQ PUELLAE ME
   TRIBUERE DEI VOCIFERARE DECUS
   2   PROSPERITY TO THIS PARISH A 🔔 R. 1718.
   3   GOD SAVE THE CHURCH AND KING A 🔔 R. 1718.
   4   PROSPERITY TO ALL OUR BENEFACTORS A 🔔 R. 1718.
   5   IOHN SAMVELL IAMES MAYO CH:WARDENS A 🔔·R. 1718.
   6   GLORIA DETUR DEO GRATIA MILONI BUTTON A 🔔 R. 1718.

Arthur Wright, the noted campanologist, gave the following rendering of the legend of the treble bell:- 'Barbara with a group of young men and her daughter companion gave me to proclaim loudly God's Glory'. The Barbara of the inscription was thought to be the mother, the first wife of Miles Button, the 'comes puella', Barbara, junior, and son may have been among the 'iuvenum turba'. The inscription of the tenor bell is translated as 'Glory be given to God through the goodness of Miles Button'. The ringing chamber in the ground floor of the tower houses a series of boards recording the ringing of peals on the bells, the earliest being 1822.

The churchyard cross is constructed of Forest of Dean stone from a design prepared by William Clarke of Llandaff and was restored by public subscription as a memorial to the men of the parish who fell in the Great War, 1914-1918. The names of the five servicemen who gave their lives is inscribed on the top step of the cross facing south.

The church plate consists of an Elizabethan silver chalice with a paten cover hall-marked 1576. The same date is engraved on the handle of the cover. Round the bowl is the usual band of foliated intersecting strap ornament. There is also a paten standing on a foot hall-marked 1710. On the underside is scratched 'Donat Bonvilestone' 1711. The registers of baptisms and burials date from 1761, and marriages from 1758, though the marriage registers for 1813-1837 are apparently lost. A reply to a National Library of Wales questionnaire in 1940 stated that 'some old registers were seen burning at Bonvilston House after the death of a Mr. Bassett'.

Cadoxton-juxta-Barry Church

The parish church of Cadoxton-juxta-Barry is dedicated to St. Cadoc, a 6th-century saint who founded the celebrated monastery at Llancarfan. The church was built in the latter part of the 12th century, but the earliest recorded reference to the church is contained in the Taxation of Norwich (1254) when it was described as 'Ecclesia de Caddokeston' and valued at 7 marks. In the *Taxatio Ecclesiastica* 1291 it was worth £3-6s-8d and was described as a small church. Cadoxton remained a rectory but the tax assessment showed a marked decline in the value of the living. In 1535 (*Valor Ecclesiasticus*) it was classified among the Rectories and valued at £5-10s-4d. The parson was resident in 1563. From 1681 until 1777 the benefice of Cadoxton-juxta-Barry was held conjointly with that of Merthyr Dyfan. In 1771 (Bishop Barrington's *Llandaff Diocesan Book*) the living was worth £65; the incumbent was the Reverend William Jenkins and the patron was Edward Popham, Esq. According to the diocesan report in 1809 the yearly value of this benefice arising from rent of glebe and tithes was £69-10s-7d. In 1835 the living was worth gross £117 and R. F. Jenner and others were the patrons. At the beginning of this century the Wenvoe Castle Estate held two out of three presentations to the living, while the Old Court Estate had the advowson on every third presentation. On the 18th December, 1902 John Smith Longdon became rector through the patronage of Laura Frances Jenner of Wenvoe Castle. This was the last presentation to the living made by a lay patron, for the Disestablishment and Disendowment of the Welsh Church in 1920 brought an end to private patronage and the living became the gift of the Bishop of Llandaff and the Diocesan Board of Patronage. St. Cadoc's, the old village church of Cadoxton-juxta-Barry is now held with St. Mary's church, Barry, built in 1905.

The church consists of chancel, nave, south porch and western tower containing three bells. The chancel arch is a drop arch with regular voussoirs above the point of spring until the keystone at the crown which is curiously cramped and out of centre. The blocks below are of differing sizes and the soffit or jambs are canted. They continue uninterrupted from floor to crown. Above the chancel arch painted on the wall is a cross fleurée with the monogram IHC (derived from the first three letters of the Greek word IHCOYC (Jesus) in the centre.) The east window is of two lights with Y-tracery and was erected in 1828. When Sir Stephen Glynne visited the church in 1865 he described the east window as 'modern and poor' which was quite an apt description.

The altar table and reredos is a very attractive piece and is a mass of applied Decorated-style tracery. It is basically a series of panels, some plain, but most admitting some quite complicated tracery forms in which the ogee arch predominates. The reredos itself is of three panels, the outer ones of two-light cinquefoil-headed tracery beneath ogee arches, enclosed by pointed arches beneath a depressed arch. The central panel, naturally higher than the rest, symbolically shows three angels in unity beneath a multifoiled ogee arch with crockets and finial; there are circles with cinquefoils in the spandrels and the same motif is repeated in the lower part of the flanking panels. There are side panels to the reredos with a plain moulded cornice including single floral motifs above three panels. As a centrepiece to the altar table below, the Lamb of God with the Banner of Victory is enclosed within the multifoils of a circle. The altar table and the reredos were erected in loving memory of their three young children by John and Jane Llewellyn of The Court, Cadoxton in St. John's Welsh church on Christmas Day, 1926, and was removed and re-erected in St. Cadoc's church when St. John's church closed in 1951. The Laudian communion rails and the raised sanctuary floor probably date back to the beginning of the 17th century when Archbishop William Laud introduced such innovations in the chancel.

Above on the south side of the altar on the east wall of the chancel is a white marble memorial tablet to the Reverend Gabriel Powell (d. 1858), rector of the parish from 1830 to 1858, and his youngest daughter Anne, and on the other side is another tablet in memory of the Reverend Ebenezer Morris (d. 1902), rector of the parish for 31 years.

The chancel is lit on the south side by a Perpendicular two-light cinquefoil-headed window with square label, and beneath this window in a rectangular recess is a 13th-century piscina which resembles the capital of a column. It is decorated with Early English star moulded panels and was obviously once a free-standing pillar piscina. On the exterior of the south wall beneath the whitewash can be seen the crude outline of a diminutive priest's door with pointed arch, which is now blocked up; a small blocked up window lies to the west of it. The earliest monumental inscription in the church is on a small slab in a blocked window in the north wall of the chancel dated 1646 to the Reverend George Fowler, Gent. and Master of Arts, rector of the parish from 1639 to 1646. On the same wall is a memorial monument decorated with two classical columns in relief commemorating Watkin Thomas, Gent. (d. 1666), his wife, Ann (d. 1677) and their daughter, Jane (d. 1704). She was the wife of the Reverend Edmund Estance, rector of the parish from 1670 to 1705.

Several members of the Andrews family of Cadoxton Court lie buried beneath the chancel. It was this family as resident Lords who rebuilt and lengthened the nave and added the west tower in the 15th century.

The rood-loft doorway with pointed arch behind the pulpit leads, by way of a spiral staircase contained in a projection in the south wall of the of the nave, to a low and narrow square-headed opening above, which once gave access to the former rood-loft. St. Cadoc's church shares with Peterston-super-Ely church the unusual feature of having its rood-loft entrance placed on the south side of the building. A rough stone corbel also remains to the left of the chancel arch which once supported the rood-loft beam.

On the east wall of the nave, north of the chancel arch, is a monumental inscription surmounting a relief sculpture of an upturned boat, commemorating Herbert Matthews of *Wenvoe Arms*, Cadoxton, who lost his life at sea in the S.S. *'Highgate'* on the 19th February, 1890. Opposite on the south side of the chancel arch is a mural memorial tablet to Elizabeth John (d. 1774) and her husband, Edward (d. 1799), the village fiddler.

The south side of the nave is lit by two Perpendicular three-light cinquefoil-headed windows with external square labels. The south-east window depicts the figures of Faith, Hope and Charity and was erected in 1887 by Caroline Spickett in memory of her parents. Beneath this window is an 18th-century tombstone in a good state of preservation embedded in the wall of the nave, which commemorates Mary Harry (d. 1751) and her husband John (d. 1767). Adjacent to this stone is another small tombstone in fine condition made of 'Bull Clifft' marble, its top corners adorned with winged cherub-heads. It was erected in memory of three children of John and Elizabeth Spickett of Brinhill; Joan (d. 1757) aged 22 weeks, Edward (d. 1759), aged 21 weeks and Elizabeth (d. 1773), aged 17 years (who died from the small pox). The stone ends with the following rhyming epitaph:—

'This Sillent grave will us keep
Untill that Glourious day
Then shall we awake out of Sleep
And Leave this Bed of Clay.'

The windows on the north side of the nave comprise two small windows deeply splayed one above the other in the north-east corner, one square-headed, the other trefoil-headed to light the former rood-loft. In the centre of the north of the nave, set high in the wall, is a round-headed light deeply splayed, and towards the west end a three-light Perpendicular window with cinquefoil-heads and square label. Around the walls of the nave are placed the fourteen stations of the cross, which are a series of painted carvings in relief depicting incidents in the Passion of Our Lord. They were given in memory of May Powell who died 14th December, 1981.

At the west end of the nave, set in the wall north of the tower arch, is a tombstone recording the burial of John John (d. 1794) with the following rhyme:—

'Pain was my Pleasure, Physic was my Food
Groans was my Devotion, drugs did me no good
Christ was my Physician to know the way thats best
To ease me of my pain and set my Soul at rest'.

According to William Thomas' diary of 1794 he died of a 'Long Lingring Dropsy of 46 years of age'. The nave has a wagon-truss roof of Somerset design and craftsmanship. The Norman font is tub-shaped with bold roll-mouldings around the rim and centre and stands on a modern wooden platform. The font cover is a replica of an earlier one made in 1886 by David Spickett. On the right-hand side of the south doorway on entering is an octagonal-shaped holy-water stoup.

The large Perpendicular south porch, which has stone benches inside, has simple continuous pointed arches within and without. The east jamb of the outer doorway of the porch has the following graffiti cut into the masonry: IT. 1715/WH 1722; and in the west jamb: HT 1654. In the porch are two inscriptions set into the stone seat which extends along the west side; one close to the outer door, is to Mary Turbervill (d. 1727); the other commemorates John Langton (d. 1705) and his wife, Ann (d. 1760), aged 99 years. In 1934 a crude lancet window, hewn out of a block of stone, was found in the purlieus of the churchyard. Dr. H. M. Thompson, the Cardiff antiquarian, thought that it could possibly have once been a window in the tower. It is now cemented to the eastern stone bench in the porch.

The tower arch opens to the nave by a drop arch with very regular voussoirs without a keystone which are uninterrupted from floor to crown. This archway is very similar to the chancel arch but smaller. The tower is plain without buttresses or stringcourse with a saddleback roof. The belfry has four trefoil-headed lights on each face and below on the south face is a small round-headed aperture, and below that a trefoil-headed light (now partly blocked up) and a round-headed light at ground level. The west door of the tower has a drop arch and is of early 15th-century date. It is surmounted by a hood mould with rectangular stops. Above it is a Perpendicular single-light with trefoiled head, deeply splayed and labelled. At the north-east corner of the tower is a projecting stair-turret with round-headed window to light the staircase. The tower contains three bells which were rehung and recast in 1826 by Thomas Mears of London. In 1931, due to the poor financial state of the parish, the Parochial Church Council decided to have only the middle bell (in F sharp and weighing approximately 220 lbs.) recast by Mears & Stainbank of the Whitechapel foundry who had cast the original bell in 1826.

The church was restored in 1885 and the work of restoration was limited to the renovation of the nave and lower part of the tower. The walls of the nave were rebuilt and a new nave roof was raised. The floor of the nave was excavated to a depth of six inches and filled with fine concrete, and the old paving was carefully replaced in the aisle and entrance near the south door. Wooden flooring was laid six inches above the aisle to carry new pews of pitch pine which replaced the old-fashioned and dilapidated box pews. During the course of restoration, the old rood-loft staircase which had been walled up since the Reformation was exposed to view and inside were discovered human skulls, together with an octagonal holy-water stoup which was subsequently replaced in its traditional position to the right of the south doorway. Beneath the whitewash on the interior walls of the nave the remains of extensive frescoes or wall paintings were discovered, but with the collapse of the north and south walls these were unfortunately destroyed. The font was moved to its present position in the nave and a new font cover was provided. The floor of the tower was repaved, a new west door was fitted and a new belfry floor put in. The cost of the restoration amounted to £600 and the work was carried into effect under the supervision of John Price Jones, architect, of Cardiff, by the contractors, Jones Brothers of Cardiff.

The churchyard cross was restored in 1922 as a memorial to the men of Cadoxton who fell in the Great War, 1914-1918. The design of the cross, a copy of one in Bonvilston churchyard, was prepared by John Payne, sculptor, of Barry, and the work was carried out under the supervision of Alfred Owen, architect, of Barry. The three lower Calvary steps were restored and a fourth course of the same stone, lias limestone, was added. The Calvary was surmounted by a base and plain cross of blue Forest of Dean stone. The names of those men of the parish who fell in the Second World War, 1939-1945, were inscribed on the third course.

In the 18th century, the era of non-resident rectors, several incumbents were absentee rectors. Cornelius Norwood, rector of Cadoxton and Merthyr Dyfan (1757-1766), lived in Corsham, Wiltshire, where he was a schoolmaster. A noted pluralist, William Price—who was the longest-surviving rector for nearly 53 years—was non-resident throughout the period (1777-1830). He lived in England where he was incumbent of other parishes and the church was served by curates who rarely resided in the parish.

The church plate includes an Elizabethan chalice and cover with a belt of intersecting strap ornament round the bowl. Both cup and cover are hall-marked 1576. The register of baptisms dates from 1753, marriages from 1754 and burials from 1752.

Colwinston Church

The parish church of Colwinston is dedicated to St. Michael and was probably built in the 12th century. The church was granted to the Abbey of St. Peter's, Gloucester, in 1141 but eventually formed part of the endowments of that abbey's dependent priory at Ewenny. Initially Ewenny Priory only enjoyed the right of advowson and a deed of Bishop Nicholas (1148-83) records the monks as presenting two parsons to the church, William, the priest and Philip, son of Master Ralph. This suggests that the church was one of moieties, *i.e.* a church divided into two benefices. Churches of this kind could have originated in one of two ways; they were either former *clas* churches in which two or more clerics shared the endowments as successors of the original *claswyr*, or churches whose endowments had been divided among co-heirs. Bishop Nicholas declared that on the death of both parsons the church should revert to the monks of Ewenny. This seems to have happened by the end of the 12th century.

In 1254 (Taxation of Norwich) it was valued at 5 marks. In the valuation of 1291 it was coupled with the parochial churches of St. Michael's Ewenny and St. Bride's Major with the prior of Ewenny as the rector. The three churches were jointly valued at £40. In 1535 (*Valor Ecclesiasticus*) the Rectory brought 26s-8d to the Priory and the living was ranked as a vicarage worth £6-10s-4d. In 1603 the vicarage was worth £10: the impropriation worth £10 belonged to John Carne, Esquire, as a fee but was leased to one Mary Jones, widow. In 1754 and 1767 the vicarage of Colwinston received grants from Queen Anne's Bounty amounting to £400 to meet private benefactions which amounted to £400. In 1771 (Bishop Barrington's Primary Visitation of the Diocese) the living was worth £70; the incumbent was the Reverend John Nicholl and the patron was David Thomas, Gent. In 1835 it was a vicarage worth gross £122. Miss Anna Thomas was patron and impropriator. Colwinston was grouped with Llysworney with Llandow in 1970 to form one benefice.

The church consists of chancel, nave, south porch and western tower containing one bell. It is built in the Early English style of architecture. The chancel arch is Norman and semicircular of Sutton stone and springs from impost blocks chamfered on the lower side. The restored east window is of two cinquefoiled lights with square label. The stained glass window depicts the figures of St. Michael and St. George, the two warrior saints, and is a memorial to Lieutenant Gordon Fairfax Raymond Prichard (whose head and shoulders portrait appears at the base of the left-hand light) of the Lincolnshire regiment who was killed at Nitrals Nek, South Africa on the 11th July, 1900. The window was designed by Messrs. Clayton & Bell of London and was erected in the church by his family in 1901. Prior to a fire which badly damaged the chancel of the church in 1971 there was on each side of the altar on the east wall of the sanctuary a brass tablet upon which were written the ten commandments from the Book of Exodus, Chapter XX. The oak altar rails were presented to the church in 1934 by parishioners as a memorial to the Reverend Robert Curre Thomas (d.1930), vicar of the parish for 24 years.

The chancel is lit on the south side by two Early English lancets of Sutton stone with trefoiled heads, both deeply splayed. In the window-sill of the one nearest the altar is a square drain piscina. On either side of the altar are two stone corbels similar to those above the chancel arch, and in the north wall of the sanctuary is a square aumbry. In the south wall of the chancel is the customary priest's door with pointed arch. On the north wall of the sanctuary is a white marble monument with composite capitals supporting a broken pediment which displays the arms of Iestyn ap Gwrgant 'Gules three chevrons argent' for Thomas. The monument was erected to the memory of David Thomas of Pwllywrach (d. 1769) and several other members of his immediate family. A brass memorial plaque on the north wall of the chancel commemorates Herbert Charles Collins Prichard (d. 1893), eldest son of Charles John Collins and Mary Anna Prichard of Pwllywrach and his wife, Mary Anna Prichard (d. 1898), eldest daughter of David Thomas (and sister of Hubert de Burgh Thomas). The plaque also commemorates Charles John Collins Prichard of Pwllywrach (d. 1903), who restored the church in 1879. Emblazoned on the plaque are the arms of Prichard 'Argent a dragon's head erased at the neck vert holding in the mouth a sinister hand gules, issuant from it guttée-de-sang' impaling the arms of Thomas 'Gules three chevrons argent'. Several memorial tablets on the chancel walls commemorate other members of the Thomas and Prichard families of Pwllywrach, the manor house just outside the village.

In the north wall of the chancel under an Early English canopied niche with scroll-moulding lies the effigy of a man in the shape of a coffin carved from Sutton stone. The effigy is much worn and the face no longer visible. The hands are clasped in the attitude of prayer and the surcoat reaches to the ankles. The row of dogtooth ornament along the side places it in the early part of the 13th century. The north wall of the chancel is reinforced by a massive stone buttress. Painted on the wall above the chancel arch there was once beautiful scrollwork bearing the words 'Holy, Holy, Holy.' This was painted out when the church was redecorated in 1971 on the direction of the architect.

Above the chancel arch remain three stone corbels and another one on the south wall of the nave which formerly supported the rood-loft. The entrance to the rood-loft is retained in the north wall, the stone steps being built into the thickness of the wall. Above it is another round-headed door at the higher level of the loft but much further east. High in the north side of the chancel arch a square opening pierces the wall towards the chancel, probably a sanctum squint which gave a view of the altar from the former rood-loft. On each side of the chancel arch are two large trefoil-headed niches. Between the one on the south side and the chancel arch is another which is obviously not *in situ*. It has little crockets and a finial above the trefoiled arch with a pinnacle on either side. It is of 14th-century date and is probably a fragment of a reredos. Surrounding the northern niche are traces of medieval mural paintings, which according to Mrs. Eve Baker of London, a specialist in mural work, are said to depict the enthronement of Thomas à Becket displaying the arms of the See of Canterbury 'Azure an archiepiscopal cross in pale or, surmounted by a pall proper charged with four crosses pattée fitchée sable,' and the martyrdom of St. Vitus who was boiled in oil when he was twelve. He is always shown with his nurse standing on one side and his father on the other. John Parkinson of the Royal Commission on Ancient and Historical Monuments in Wales has recently put forward the theory that the wall paintings depict the consecration of St. Nicholas, Bishop of Myra and the young mother who left her baby in the bathtub (which in those days was heated by placing the filled bathtub over a low fire) to attend the service. She returned to the house which by then was full of smoke and steam and in terror imagined her child scalded to death but she found him sitting in the bath quite unharmed. She knelt down to thank God that St. Nicholas had saved her baby's life. I am inclined to favour the latter theory since the two scenes are linked by a common theme in the life of St. Nicholas. The wall paintings are reckoned to be 600 years old and are painted in tempera on a fine lime plaster background in lampblack and earth colours.

The oak pulpit has a deeply-moulded cornice. The front panel is decorated with a small quatrefoil above two round-lobed trefoil lights and the sides have two rectangular coffered panels below two small round-lobed trefoil lights. On the sides are representations of buttresses whose bases develop out of the plain moulded bottom rail which is supported on three sides only. The centre support displays a trefoil-headed light. Access to the pulpit is by way of three steps with plain supporting hand rails.

The windows of the nave comprise on the south side two windows of three lights with rounded heads and labelled. The window in the south-east wall of the nave is a memorial in stained glass to Hubert de Burgh Thomas (d. 1878) of Pwllywrach and his coat of arms 'Gules three chevrons argent with a crest of a paschal lamb' is emblazoned on a shield in the centre light with his family initials in the other lights. The window was designed and erected by his sister, Mary Collins Prichard in 1879 'in memoriam fratis dilectissimi' (in memory of a beloved brother) so the inscription reads. A memorial tablet to Hubert de Burgh Thomas and his brother, the Reverend Robert Curre Thomas, rector of the parish for 24 years (1905-1929), was erected by the Prichard family on the north wall of the chancel. Above the south doorway is a black and white marble tablet erected to the memory of John Prichard Thomas (d. 1857) aged 28 years, surgeon of Pontypridd, son of John and Martha Thomas of the Golden Mile Farm in the parish.

The stained glass window of three lights in the south-west wall of the nave is a memorial to Elizabeth Gullen (1946-1960) and was erected in September

1963. The subject of the window is light itself with the centre light depicting light radiating to the corners of the three windows with the words 'Let there be light'. The window was designed by John Petts of Abergavenny, Monmouthshire. The nave is lit on the north side by a two-light round-headed window with square label. The stained glass in the window depicts Christ as the Good Shepherd and Merciful Lord and is a memorial to two infants, David Thomas of Pwllywrach (d. 1845) aged 7 days, and James Gordon Simonds (d. 1901). The nave has an arch-braced roof with collar-beam ties.

The font of Sutton stone has an octagonal bowl chamfered below on an octagonal stem with a square base with chamfered edges. The south porch is large, its outer doorway is late Perpendicular with a square hood moulding, but the inner south door of the church is sharply pointed. On the east wall of the porch is a marble memorial tablet in 'honour of twenty-three men of the parish who served in the Great War, 1914-1918' since every one who fought in that conflict came home safely, which must be very rare. A brass plaque in the nave commemorates Major Hubert de Burgh Prichard the only soldier from the parish who fell in the Second World War.

The massive square tower has a battlement and corbel table beneath. The belfry is lit on each face by a round-headed louvred window. The west doorway has a four-centred arch and the blocks which form the sides are barely canted. Above it is a square-headed window with three round-headed lights of 16th-century type. A projection on its south wall contains a spiral staircase leading to the belfry. The tower houses a pre-Reformation bell which bears the Latin inscription: 'SANCTE MICHAEL ORA PRO NOBIS'—(Pray for us St. Michael.) There were originally three bells in the tower but two were broken and the metal sold in 1722 to pay for the reseating of the church. The tower was re-roofed, the belfry refloored and the bell framing renewed in 1930 at a cost of £150.

The church was restored in 1879 when new windows were inserted in the nave and a new pulpit, communion table, lectern and chancel furniture were introduced. During the work of restoration the old rood-loft staircase was uncovered in the north wall of the nave and new doors were fitted at the entrance and upper doorway. Also a new door was placed in the porch. The alterations gave increased accommodation and the renovation of the roofs, walls and windows added greatly to the comfort of the congregation. The work of restoration was satisfactorily carried out by Thomas Thomas of Colwinston under the superintendence of Henry J. Williams, architect of Bristol. The cost of the restoration amounted to £800 and the church was reopened for divine service after restoration on Monday, 22nd September, 1879, by the Rt. Reverend Dr. Alfred Ollivant, Bishop of Llandaff. The offertories of the day's services went towards reseating the church.

A memorial tablet in the church records the death of the Reverend Evan Jones in 1843 at the ripe age of 90 years 'curate of Colwinston 48 years and vicar of 11 years altogether 59 years, a faithful minister of the Gospel.' On the south side of the churchyard is a pre-Reformation mensa or altar slab. After the

Reformation they were forbidden in the Established church when only wooden tables were permitted. These slabs were torn from their rightful place and thrown out into the churchyard but recently many of these mensas have been restored to the church. All that remains of the churchyard cross is a rather stumpy cross on an old pillar resting on three steps. The chancel and the east wall of the nave are white-washed on the outside which was a common feature in the churches of the Vale of Glamorgan in former times.

The church plate includes a silver-plated flagon presented by D. Thomas in 1853. The register of baptisms and burials dates from the year 1766 and marriages from 1771.

Cowbridge Church

The parish church of Cowbridge is dedicated to the Holy Cross on which Our Saviour died and has often been referred to as the 'Cathedral of the Vale'. The church was formerly a chapel of ease to Llanblethian, which is borne out by John Leland's remark in his *Itinerary of England and Wales* that 'the saying is that Lanlithan is the hed paroch chirch of Cowbridge'. The chapel of the Holy Cross was built sometime in the 13th century. It had no separate endowment and in the Norwich Taxation of 1254 it was probably listed as one of the 'chapels' attached to Llanblethian. Very little is known about the church of the Holy Cross before the year 1473 when Lady Anne Neville of Warwick, consort of Richard, Duke of Gloucester (afterwards Richard III), built the south aisle of the church which was allocated to the Nerber family of Llanquian after the chapel of St. James at Llanquian was either destroyed or ceased to be used in the early part of the 15th century. The south aisle has long been referred to as the Llanquian aisle. In 1484 Richard III as Lord of Glamorgan granted a petition from the townspeople of the borough of Cowbridge for the provision of a chaplain in the church of the Holy Cross. This provision of a chaplain seems to have continued until 1550 when one Richard Eles was in receipt of a salary of £4 per annum.

At this time the church was also served by a chantry priest. The chantry chapel on the north side of the chancel was founded by a burgess, William Prior, who endowed it with land and burgages which in 1546 brought in a rent of £11-5s-11d, of which the chantry priest received a stipend of £6. The chantry was suppressed and its endowment was appropriated to the Crown in 1548. The priest was granted a pension of £5. In the *Valor Ecclesiasticus* (1535) the vicar of Llanblethian received £2-13s-4d from the chapel of Cowbridge. In 1563 it was described as a 'chapel which hath christening and burying services in it' annexed to Llanblethian. In 1603 it was styled a chapel and in 1835 a 'curacy' of Llanblethian when the patrons and impropriators were the Dean and Chapter of Gloucester. The impropriation afterwards passed to the Ecclesiastical Commissioners and the patronage to the Bishop of Llandaff. In 1966 the benefice of Llanblethian with Cowbridge was grouped with St. Mary Church and Llandough.

The church consists of chancel with north chapel, a choir under the central tower containing eight bells, a nave with south aisle extending the whole length of the arcade of the nave and choir, and a north porch. The east window is

Cowbridge Church

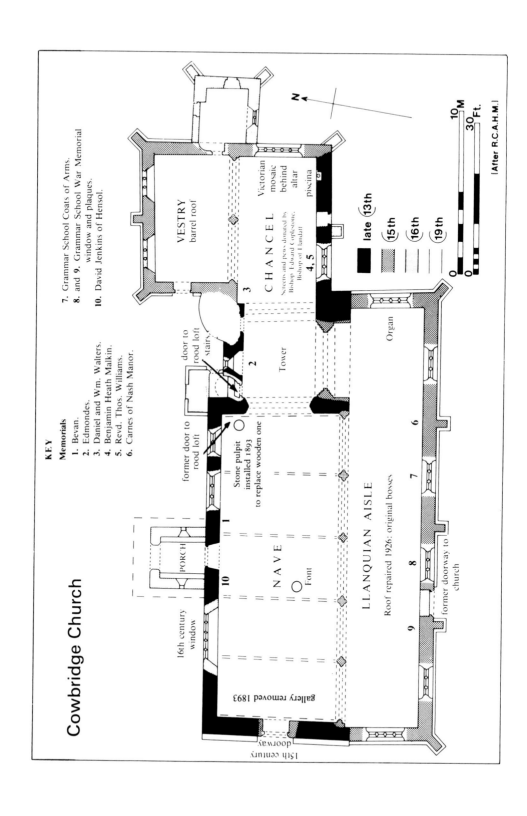

KEY

Memorials

1. Bevan.
2. Edmondes.
3. Daniel and Wm. Walters.
4. Benjamin Heath Malkin.
5. Revd. Thos. Williams.
6. Carnes of Nash Manor.

7. Grammar School Coats of Arms.
8. and 9. Grammar School War Memorial window and plaques.
10. David Jenkins of Hensol.

16th century window

PORCH

NAVE
Font

gallery removed 1893

15th century doorway

Stone pulpit installed 1893 to replace wooden one

former door to rood loft

door to rood loft stairs

VESTRY
barrel roof

Tower

CHANCEL
Screens and pews donated by Bishop Edward Copleston, Bishop of Llandaff

Victorian mosaic behind altar
piscina

Organ

LLANQUIAN AISLE

Roof repaired 1926: original bosses

former doorway to church

late 13th
15th
16th
19th

N

[After R.C.A.H.M.]

0   10 M
0   30 Ft.

basically of 14th-century rectilinear form. It has five cinquefoiled lights in a
2:1:2 arrangement. The two centre mullions continue straight into the head of
the window with two trefoiled tracery lights beneath a sexfoil. Each outer pair
of main lights is treated as a pointed window, the arches springing from the
centre mullions. Again there are small tracery lights beneath a sexfoil of which
two are trefoil-headed. The whole window is surmounted by a hood mould
which terminates in rectangular stops. The five main lights are filled with
Victorian stained glass which is said to have been presented to the church in the
19th century by a member of the Edmondes family of Old Hall. The ten stained
glass panels illustrate the birth, life, death and resurrection of Our Lord and
depict scenes from the Annunciation, the Visitation of Our Lady, the Epiphany,
the Presentation in the Temple, the Flight into Egypt, Jesus with the Doctors in
the Temple, the Road to Calvary, the Descent from the Cross, and finally in
the centre light, the Crucifixion and Glorious Resurrection.

Beneath the window is a reredos of three panels inlaid with mosaic below an
embattled cresting and a row of crosses. The left-hand panel includes two sacred
monograms: CHI RHO (the first two letters of the Greek word XPICTOC
'The Anointed One' (Christ) and beneath the crown IHS (derived from the first
letters of IHCOYC (Jesus). The cross with the 'P' is a standard style of medieval
consecration cross. The panel also has a Trinity star or Star of David. The centre
panel includes a cross pommée within a quatrefoil surrounded by the emblems
of the four Evangelists, Matthew, Mark, Luke and John. The right-hand panel
has a crown above a fleur-de-lys, a cross pattée formée and the nails of the
Passion.

In the south-east corner of the sanctuary is a piscina of Sutton stone under a
trefoil-arched recess with octofoil drain. This was uncovered by one of the
masons during the restoration of the church in 1893. On the north side of the
chancel the composite arches spring above shafts with concave mouldings
between, and single rolls following their horizontal outline to give the impression of a capital. The bases of the shaft are similarly treated. The space between
each arch is filled by wood and glass partitions with rectangular lights in the
head. Below, the panelling is treated as a screen—an embattled cresting on an
otherwise plain cornice. Beneath this is a series of panels, plain below, but the
top row has applied tracery: cinquefoils in the head with leaf forms on some of
the cusping and trefoils in the spandrels. A brass plaque records that the infilling
of these arches was a gift from the Cowbridge Grammar School Old Boys'
Association 'in memory of Richard Williams, M.C., M.A., headmaster 1919-
1938 and of his devoted and inspired service to his school. In memory also of
those boys of the school who gave their lives in the Second World War, 1939-
1945'. To the north of the chancel stands the choir vestry, formerly the chantry
chapel, and the clergy vestry beyond it to the east, which overlaps the chancel
and choir vestry. This may have been an almonry since a small blocked opening
exists which may originally have been the place where alms in the form of
bread loaves were distributed to the poor of the parish.

The east window of the former chantry chapel (now the vestry) is of three cinquefoiled lights with rectilinear tracery in the head. The window contains stained glass panels depicting coats of arms of various benefactors of Cowbridge Grammar School which were transferred from Seys room and Founders' room in 1978. They include the coats of arms of the Rt. Reverend Dr. Richard Lewis, Bishop of Llandaff (1883-1905), Emily Charlotte Talbot of Margam Abbey (1840-1918), George Thomas Clark (1809-1898) and Sir Thomas Mansel Franklen (1840-1928). The right-hand panel which displays the coat of arms of Cowbridge Grammar School commemorates David Percival Jones, M.A., mathematics master from 1894 to 1912.

Besides the high altar there were once two other altars in Cowbridge church, one in the chapel on the north side of the chancel, which was the altar served by the chantry priest, and the second at the east end of the south aisle, which was probably the altar of St. Nicholas referred to in a clause of a mortgage deed of 1516 which allowed the redemption of the mortgage by repayment in gold marks and groats 'in the Rood church of Cowbridge upon the altar of St. Nicholas between the rising of the sun and the going down of the same'. The present oak altar rails were installed in 1965 in accordance with the design of George Gaze Pace, architect of York. They were given in memory of the Reverend Ewart Lewis, M.A., vicar of Cowbridge from 1949 to 1963.

The chancel is of uncommon length and was furnished on the lines of a college chapel through the generosity of Bishop Edward Copleston when he lived at Llandough Castle. Interest in the choir and chancel is heightened by the fact that for upwards of three and a half centuries the scholars and masters of the Grammar School have sat and knelt there in worship. The chancel is lit on the south side by two Perpendicular windows of three cinquefoiled lights with rectilinear tracery in the head surmounted by a hood mould. These two windows contain stained glass which commemorate two past headmasters of Cowbridge Grammar School. The south-east window illustrates the theme of resurrection and depicts the raising of Jairus' daughter, the raising of Lazarus and the raising of the widow's son. Beneath are the coats of arms of Cowbridge Grammar School and Jesus College, Oxford (which owned the school from 1685-1918) and the Agnus Dei with the banner of victory. This window was erected through the generosity of past and present boys in memory of the Reverend J. C. F. Morson, M.A. (headmaster 1870-1875) shortly after his death. In 1899 this window was removed from the south wall of the aisle to the south chancel. The other window in the chancel to the west of Morson's window is a memorial to his predecessor the Reverend Thomas Williams (1864-1870), though it bears no reference to him. The window depicts Samuel replying to God's voice, the Sermon on the Mount and the figure of Timothy, a disciple of Paul.

The rood-loft staircase doorway, which has a depressed semicircular arch, still remains in the west end of the north wall of the tower. There is no sign of the upper doorway onto the rood-loft but it may be assumed that the loft was entered by a doorway opening westwards into the nave in the north spandrel of the west arch of the tower. The close links which have existed between the church and school for over three and a half centuries are reflected particularly in the memorials in the chancel and other parts of the church. From its foundation in 1608 till recent times, headmasters of Cowbridge Grammar School were nearly always curates of the parish as well, and the same may be true of many assistant masters. The chancel is full of memorial monuments to members of the Edmondes family and several headmasters lie buried beneath its floor. Between two memorial tablets to members of the Edmondes family in the north wall of the tower is a broad pointed lancet containing a window which depicts the Blessed Virgin Mary captioned by the first lines of the *Magnificat*. On the south wall of the chancel is a memorial tablet to the topographer Dr. Benjamin Heath Malkin (1769-1842), author of *The Scenery, Antiquities and Biography of South Wales* (1804).

The arches to the central tower above the choir are all pointed and treated differently both as regards construction and mouldings. They are equilateral and the mouldings are quite broad and shallow, all of which indicates a late 13th-century date. The arch to the east springs directly from the north and south walls. The mouldings of the compound southern arch—some of which are shallow and concave and therefore typical of the period—are continued unchanged down the jambs with no intervening capital. The inner arch on the west side springs from the round moulded abaci above an engaged pair of slender shafts on a central drum which also has a fillet along its length.

The central tower is a massive fortified structure with four stages of heavy buttresses on the north side and embattled. The embrasures are small and few, the merlons wide by comparison and solid. The tower has an external stair turret which is approached by a doorway with pointed arch. It is battlemented and its upper stage—like that of the tower proper—is corbelled out in typical Welsh fashion. The tower is square, and above all is a castellated octagon which at one time was probably surmounted by a spire. Tradition has it that the spire was struck by lightning and burnt in 1480. The tower has small single and double lights: some square-headed and others trefoiled.

The tower houses a ring of eight bells cast by Evan and William Evans of Chepstow in 1722. At that time the revenues of the borough were mortgaged over nine years to borrow £246 'for new casting the s'd bells and for adding Four New Bells more ... so as to have a ring peal or sett of eight bells'. Consequently it was only natural that the bells should have the Cowbridge Borough seal impressed on each bell as part of their inscriptions, together with the names of some borough officials as benefactors. The bells, which are now the only complete original Evans' octave surviving, were tuned and rehung in a steel frame by John Taylor & Co. bellfounders, Loughborough in 1935.

The bell inscriptions are as follows:—

Treble in E	EVAN EVANS, Wm EVANS BELLFOUNDERS 1722
No. 2. in D sharp	BENEFACTOR RICHARD GREGORY RECTOR
	BENEFACTR DANL. DURELL SCHOOLEMASTER 1722

Memorial to Judge David Jenkins of Hensol (d. 1664)

Photograph by John Russell

No. 3. in C sharp	BENE(FACTRESSE)S MRS. MAGT MATHEWS MRS. HESTER WILKINS E.E. W.E. 1722
No. 4. in B	Wm DAVIS IOHN STYDER ALDN. BENES. E.E. W.E. 1722
No. 5. in A	RICH. BATES THOS. BATES ALDERMAN E.E. W.E. 1722
No. 6 in C sharp	THOS. WILKINS, IE(VA)N WILLIAMS GENT ALDERN. BENEFACTS. E.E. W.E. 1722
No. 7 in F sharp	EDWD. CARNE ROG(ER) WILKINS ESQR BAYLIFFS BENEFACTS. E.E. W.E. 1722
Tenor in E.	EDW STRADLING ESQR DEP MAYOR E.E. W.E. 1722.

The Reverend Daniel Durel, M.A. (whose name is wrongly spelt on the 2nd bell) was headmaster of Cowbridge Grammar School from 1721 to 1763. The old sanctus bell bears no inscription. It was used as a fire bell and a curfew bell until 1896 and rests at the top of the turret stair leading to the belfry.

The nave has a wagon-truss roof with gilded bosses at the intersections of the purlins and principal rafters. The windows on the north of the nave comprise a two-light and a three-light window with cinquefoiled heads and rectilinear tracery in the heads surmounted by hood mouldings. The stained glass in the three-light window depicts the Sermon on the Mount, Mary Magdalene and the risen Lord on Easter morning, and Christ blessing little children. Beneath in the centre panel is the coat of arms of Cowbridge with the motto 'Awn Rhagom' (Let us go forward). This window was erected in memory of Eva Caroline Tilley (d. 1896), Mayoress of the Borough and wife of Alderman David Tilley, also their children, Herbert David Tilley (d. 1882) and George Eaton Tilley (d. 1888).

The pulpit, which was installed at the restoration of the church in 1893, is a heavy ornate piece between plain moulded top and bottom rails with large leaf forms on the underside of the drum. The stiles between the panels are three stage buttresses with set-offs and double gables surmounted by a finial with foliated crockets. Each panel is treated as a mullioned and transomed window of two cinquefoil-headed lights with a dagger-shaped quatrefoil between and regular quatrefoils below the transom. The head is formed by an ogee arch on slender pink marble shafts with 13th-century-style caps and bases. The arch develops into a finial which rises into the top rail.

On the north wall of the nave to the west of the porch is a marble monument to Judge David Jenkins of Hensol (d. 1664) who lies buried in the church. Underneath is his coat of arms 'Three cocks gules between a chevron gules' with the family motto 'Fe Dal Am Daro' (No one provokes me with impunity). He was incarcerated in the Tower of London for his opposition to Cromwell, but was released in 1656. To the west of this monument is a five-light Tudor window with rounded heads and external square label.

The west window of the nave is similar in design to the East window. It has

South (Llanquian) aisle

five cinquefoil-headed lights in a 2:1:2 arrangement with the two centre mullions continuing straight into the head. All the tracery lights are trefoils and those within the centre mullions are divided vertically by a castellated transom. The outer pair of main lights are treated as pointed windows and have little quatrefoils filling the spaces in the head. The whole is surmounted by a dripstone. The west doorway has a simple typical Tudor arch with concave mouldings which are looking the worse for its weight above. The font is plain octagonal with chamfered rim and a taper down to the moulded necking or string that separates the bowl from the stem. It is set upon a moulded base. The Victorian north porch, rebuilt in 1859, has a depressed outer arch and a pointed inner arch. Inside are the customary stone benches.

The arcade of the south aisle has five bays and the pillars of the arcade consist of four engaged shafts as a central core, separated by a fairly deep hollow and two fillets (which was quite a common arrangement during the early Perpendicular period). The necking follows the shape of the pier below and is plainly moulded. There is the illusion of a capital even though the shape of the shaft is carried above the neck with the hollow splayed out to meet what almost becomes an octagonal upper moulding. The windows of the south aisle comprise four windows of three cinquefoiled lights with rectilinear tracery in the apex surmounted by hood moulds. The two windows in the middle of the south aisle have stained glass; one window is a memorial to Old Boys of Cowbridge Grammar School who fell in the Great War, 1914-1918, and depicts the warrior saints, St. George, St. Michael and St. Martin. Below are the coat of arms of the school and those of Jesus College, Oxford. The window was designed by Messrs. James Powell of Whitefriars, London. The adjacent window contains stained glass panels displaying coats of arms of various benefactors of the school transferred from the old Cowbridge Grammar School in 1978 by the Old Boys' Association and South Glamorgan County Council Education Committee as a token of the close association between church and school for more than three centuries. The window displays in the centre light the coats of arms of Jesus College, Oxford, Sir Edward Stradling (1529-1609) and Sir Leoline Jenkins (1623-1685); in the left-hand light are the coats of arms of Evan Seys (1604-1681) and Major-General Trevor Bruce Tyler C.S.I. (1858-1893), one of the most distinguished of the School's Old Boys; in the right-hand light are the coats of arms of Frederic W. Edmondes, Archdeacon of Llandaff (1841-1918). Below is a memorial to the Reverend William Franklen Evans, headmaster of the school for twenty-nine years (1890-1918), which consists of three shields. Two above bear the arms of Jesus College, Oxford and Felsted School, and one below displays the coat of arms of Cowbridge Grammar School. The east window of the south aisle has four cinquefoiled lights with the central mullion diverging in the head to form a pointed arch over each pair of lights. The head is filled with Victorian Perpendicular-style tracery lights. The three-manual organ, built by Nicholson & Co. Ltd. of Worcester in 1893, stands at the east end of the south aisle. It was fitted with an electric blower in 1954 and was restored in 1966 in memory of Albert William Morgan, organist from 1947 to 1964 and churchwarden from 1959 to 1964. The south aisle has a cradle roof.

The most outstanding monument in the church is the 17th-century Carne memorial on the south wall of the south aisle. It depicts William Carne of Nash Manor and Great House, Cowbridge with his wife, Elizabeth (daughter of Edward Van of Marcross and Llantwit Major) both kneeling against a prayer-desk bearing an open book while beneath in high relief are his three sons and three daughters as 'weepers'. The monument of pink veined marble displays the heraldic achievement of the Carne family above a plain cornice flanked by obelisks. It has Corinthian capitals and pillars on high bases. The sculpture rests on a marble shelf supported by consoles which display decorative motifs and a shield on which are emblazoned the six quarterings of the Carne arms. Beneath is a rectangular inscription panel in Latin which is decorated with winged cherub-heads and below that an apron with a winged skull symbolizing not death but the passage to immortality through death. Heraldry abounds throughout the piece with the Carne and Mansel arms prominently displayed.

17th-century Carne memorial in the south (Llanquian) aisle

Photograph by John Russell

The nave before removal of the screen which now divides the choir and south aisle

In the centre of the monument between the two principal figures are emblazoned the six quarterings of the Carne arms, once colourfully painted but now sadly faded. The memorial was erected in 1626 by the eldest son, Sir Edward Carne who was Receiver-General for South Wales in the early 17th century.

The south aisle is divided from the choir by a square-framed screen of five bays with embattled cresting which was originally erected across the chancel in 1850. The opening, which is between the first and third bays, has a low pointed arch with leaves and fruit in the spandrels, and springs above plain moulded caps on small shafts. Each bay has two lights and slender muntins which extend into the head with foliage in the cusps between ogee arches. In the pierced tracery above are quatrefoils, mouchette shapes and each pair of lights is covered by a single tracery arch. Below the lights are plain panels. The south wall of the aisle is reinforced by four two-stage buttresses, and in the middle of the south wall is a built-in doorway which was probably the main entrance to the church in earlier times. About a metre from the ground a stringcourse runs along the whole length of the south wall of the south aisle. The west window of the aisle is of four cinquefoiled lights and above, trefoil-headed tracery lights. It does not have moulded jambs and is set well back in the wall.

The church has been restored a number of times. In 1722 the tower was repaired; in 1766 the roof of the north aisle was renewed with timber grown in the churchyard. In 1777 two windows in the south chancel and the east window were blocked up. In the early part of 1848 the tracery of some of the old windows in the chancel which had been blocked up for several years, as shown in a drawing by J. Garsed (c.1840) of the south view of the church, was restored and partly filled with stained glass. The architect was Edward Haycock of Shrewsbury and the restoration work was due to the Chancellor of Llandaff Cathedral. During the years 1850-1852 when the vicar of Cowbridge was the Reverend Thomas Edmondes the church was restored by John Prichard, the diocesan architect, at a cost of £1,800 of which the Cowbridge Corporation donated £50 'as a subscription towards the restoration of the fabric and rearrangement of the sittings in the parish church of Cowbridge'. A grant of £150 was obtained from the Incorporated Church Building Society for repewing the church 'on condition that 258 of the 645 seats should be set apart and declared to be free (i.e. unappropriated) for the use of the poor of the parish for ever'. The word free was not actually placed on the seats because many of the middle and lower classes, for whose use these 'free' seats were intended, objected to 'sitting in seats which bore any distinctive mark, on the plea of its marking their inferiority of station and their poverty more conspicuous in the House of God where all worshippers ought to be on an equality.' Also the school trustees subscribed £100 towards the restoration of Cowbridge church on condition that the members of the school should occupy their accustomed pews. During this drastic restoration, new windows were inserted in the south aisle and in the west end of the nave. In 1859 the north porch was rebuilt.

In 1893 the church underwent a further restoration when the work included the renovation of the tower and rehanging of the bells, the replastering of the interior, the removal of the gallery at the west end of the nave, the erection of a new organ in the south aisle and the erection of a new pulpit. The cost of this restoration amounted to £800 and the work was carried out by Messrs. Hatherley and Carr of Bristol, under the supervision of Messrs. Bruton and Williams, architects of Cardiff.

In 1913 a start was made to raise funds for the restoration of the tower and nave roof. A sum of £450 was raised which was expended on the renovation of the tower and repairs to the roof. The outbreak of war in 1914 prevented the work of restoration being carried any further. Although attempts were made after cessation of hostilities in 1918 to raise money for further restoration, it was not until 1924 that it was decided to proceed with the work. In 1926 the roof of the nave was completely renewed and the leaning arcade to the south aisle was taken down and rebuilt stone by stone on sound foundations. The work of restoration which was carried out according to plans prepared by Thomas Guy Clarke, architect of Llandaff, amounted to over £4,000. In 1935 the church bells which had been silent for several years due to the poor state of the bellframe, were retuned and rehung in a new steel bellframe by Taylors of Loughborough. On the 7th December, 1935 eight members of the Llandaff and Monmouth Diocesan Association of Change Ringers rang the first complete peal on the bells, consisting of 5,040 changes in three hours and ten minutes.

The church plate includes an Elizabethan silver chalice hall-marked 1576, also a silver flagon donated by Margaret Seys in 1680, a paten cover inscribed on the underside 'The gift of E.S. (Evan Seys) to the church of Cowbridge', hall-marked 1715, another silver paten inscribed 'the gift of Cissell Jenkins' and a

Cowbridge church—stained glass window in chancel ▶

further silver paten inscribed 'In honorem Dei D.D. hanc patinem T.E. hujus parochiae Vicus 1835 to 1883'. The registers date from 1718 but there are gaps in the early years.

Eglwys Brewis Church

The parish church of Eglwys Brewis is dedicated to St. Brice, a 5th-century bishop. The dedication of the church is thought to be St. Brice merely because of its similarity to the Welsh name Brewis. The origin of the church is obscure but it probably derives its name 'Eglwys Brewis' from William de Braose, Bishop of Llandaff (1266–1287) meaning 'the church of Braose'. The church has the unusual distinction of standing within the boundaries of the Royal Air Force station at St. Athan and draws its congregation from service personnel and their families attached to the station. The present structure dates from the 13th century and is probably the crudest and smallest church in the Vale of Glamorgan and in the diocese of Llandaff.

In 1254 (Taxation of Norwich) the church was worth £2 when it was called 'Eglis Priwes', £5 in 1291 (*Taxatio Ecclesiastica*) and £4-0s-2d in 1535 (*Valor Ecclesiasticus*). The first recorded incumbent of Eglwys Brewis was 'Ricardus de Egluspirwys' in 1443. The parson was resident in 1563 and during the 16th century the advowson of the church went with the manor. In 1645 the Reverend William Edwards was ejected from the living of Eglwys Brewis by the Parliamentarians. In 1771 (Bishop Barrington's Primary Visitation of the Diocese) the living was worth £40; the incumbent was the Reverend Thomas Bassett and the patrons were Evan Seys and Robert Jones of Fonmon Castle. The living was styled a Rectory in 1835 worth gross £93 when the Reverend Richard Bassett (1832–1852) was the incumbent and J. D. Llewelyn was the patron. In 1912 the small parish of Eglwys Brewis (previously served from St. Hilary) was joined with the parish of St. Athan and the rector of St. Athan, the Reverend George Morganwg Jenkins became rector of the benefice of Eglwys Brewis with St. Athan. In 1978 these two parishes were linked with Flemingston and Gileston to form a grouped benefice.

The church consists of chancel, nave, south porch and embattled western bellcote formerly containing one bell. The chancel arch is crudely pointed of 13th-century date and on each side of it are two stone blocks which appear to indicate the original width of the arch which was enlarged in the 15th century. The east window is Early English of two trefoiled lights. In the east wall of the chancel on either side of the altar are two strangely-shaped niches, that on the north side being coffin-shaped, that on the south side oblong. In the south-east corner of the sanctuary stands a pillar piscina. In the floor of the sanctuary and chancel are several tombstones belonging to the Davies family but probably the most interesting tombstone (apart from the one bearing a floriated cross) is that of Mary Bassett who died in 1643 at the age of 12 years, the daughter of Miles Bassett, Gent. The sanctuary is divided from the rest of the chancel by a low wooden altar rail designed by the architect Philip Webb (1831-1915) in 1900. The chancel is lit on the south side by a two-light window with rounded heads and square label and on the north side by two modern square-headed lattice windows, one single the other of two lights. In the south wall of the chancel is a priest's door with pointed arch. On the north side of the chancel is a stone step and the outline of a 15th-century doorway which once led to the rood-loft.

On the south side of the chancel arch is the Lord's Prayer painted in fresco and below it are several lines which are unfortunately defaced by damp and age. However, one can discern the names Edward Nichyll and Robert Nichyll and the date 1654. David Jones of Wallington, the noted antiquarian, visited the church in 1881 and he was of the opinion that these two names represented the churchwardens of the time. The Reverend David Nicholl was rector of Eglwys Brewis in 1660 and members of the Nicholl family appear to have resided in the parish for a number of years.

On the north side of the chancel arch are painted the first and third verses of the 119th psalm 'Blessed are they that are undefiled and walk in ye way of ye Lord which do no inequity and walk in his wayes'. There are no windows in the north wall of the nave. In the centre of the north wall is emblazoned in fresco the Royal Arms of England of William III and Mary (1689-1702). The arms are quarterly, first and fourth grand quarters France modern and England, second quarter Scotland, third quarter Ireland. Supporters are dexter:- 'A lion rampant guardant or, imperially crowned' and sinister:- 'A unicorn rampant argent, armed crined and gorged with a coronet composed of crosses pattée and fleurs-de-lys and chained or'. It has an inescutcheon (a small shield in the middle of the main one) which are the arms of Nassau 'Azure, billetée a lion rampant or' charged upon the Royal Stuart shield.

On the west of the Royal Arms is painted the Apostles' Creed while on the east side, much worn by age, are two panels which also contain extracts from the Bible. One of these panels is taken from the 6th chapter of St. Matthew ending with the 'Amen' found in verse 13. The other passage appears to be taken from the Gospel of St. John. On the south wall of the nave near the door is yet another text from Psalm 41, verses 1-2, 'Blessed is ye that [considereth] the poor and needy . . .'. The reason for the profusion of wall lettering of quotations from the Scriptures can be explained by reference to Canon no. 82 of the Ecclesiastical Canons of 1603 which ordered 'the ten commandments be set up in the east end of every church and chapel where the people may best see and read the same and other chosen sentences written upon the walls of the said churches and chapels in places convenient'.

The nave is lit on the south side by a pair of two-light round-headed windows both labelled. The south-east window has two roundels of stained glass depicting the Virgin Mary and Infant Jesus and St. George slaying the dragon. Near the south doorway is an octagonal holy-water stoup. The roofs of the nave and chancel are modern with the old gable supports retained and strengthened. The Norman font is of Sutton stone and is circular with cable pattern moulding round the rim standing on two stone steps set diagonally to each other. The one-manual organ, built by the 'Positive' Organ Co. Ltd., of London about 1914, stands in the north-west corner of the nave.

The south porch has a 16th-century outer doorway within which is a pointed south doorway leading into the church which is a step lower in level. There are stone benches each side and in the east wall is a small aperture. Near the door on the same side is a holy-water stoup. The western bellcote is of uncommon design with an embattled square turret with corbel table. The modern bell, which is devoid of any inscription, now stands near the font at the west end of the nave.

In 1900 during the incumbency of the Reverend H. C. Davies (1894-1906) Eglwys Brewis church was restored under the auspices of the Society for the Protection of Ancient Buildings in accordance with specifications of their architect, William Weir. Weir was a pupil of the architect, Philip Webb (1831-1915) and he spent most of his apprenticeship in the 1890s learning the repair method from him. Eglwys Brewis church was the first church for which William Weir was given sole charge of the work. Great care was taken to retain the original character of the church and the work was regarded more as a 'reparation' than a restoration. The work consisted mainly in strengthening the walls, especially the chancel arch which was of 13th-century date. It was in a very poor state due to the fact that it had been built of small stones embedded in clay. The Society for the Protection of Ancient Buildings had made specific recommendations to Weir about the treatment of the chancel arch. Weir rebuilt the damaged core by interspersing seams of concrete with coarse bands of flat stones which were inserted through one side of the wall leaving the other side intact throughout. This method was known as 'Webb's sandwich'.

Parts of the east side of the chancel arch were also repaired, including a bulge above the apex of the arch and the 15th-century doorway on the north side to the former rood-loft. The east wall of the chancel was also strengthened and the dropped relieving arch above the east window was raised. On removal of the whitewash and plaster, the coffin-shaped niche on the north side of the wall was uncovered and restored to its original state. The old oak principals of the roof were repaired but the old deal timbers of the roof, which were of slight construction, were replaced by sturdier ones of oak. The work on the church, which started in the spring of 1900, was completed by September of that year at a cost of £500.

As it now stands, apart from the work of reparation mentioned above and the remodelling of the nave in the 15th century, the structure of the church remains virtually unaltered since the church was built in the 13th century.

The church plate consists of an Elizabethan silver chalice similar to the cup at St. Hilary dated 1577 and a large pewter paten. The registers date from 1750.

Ewenny Priory Church

The Priory church of Ewenny is dedicated to St. Michael the Archangel and was probably rebuilt on the site of an earlier church by William de Londres, Lord of Ogmore early in the 12th century. The church was dedicated during the episcopate of Urban, bishop of Llandaff (1107-1134) and a letter of Gilbert Foliot, abbot of Gloucester, which records the dedication, seems to imply that the church belonged to Gloucester at this period. In the 'List of Donations' in the Gloucester cartulary it is recorded that Robert, Earl of Gloucester made the Priory of Ewenny free of toll throughout all his lands during the abbacy of Walter de Lacy (1130-1139). It is probable that a cell of a few monks was established at Ewenny before 1141 and in that year Maurice de Londres, son of William de Londres, raised the cell to conventual status. The record of the gift reads as follows:- 'In the year 1141 Maurice de Londonia, son of William de Londonia, gave to the church of St. Peter of Gloucester, the church of St. Michael of Ewenny, the church of St. Bridget (St. Bride's Major) with the chapel of Ugemore (Wick), de Lanfey (Lampha), the church of St. Michael of Colvestone (Colwinston) with the lands, meadows and all other things belonging unto them freely and willingly in free almoigne in order that it might become a convent of monks'. The gift was made on condition that when the churches granted had been appropriated to the Priory 'there shall be therein a convent of at least thirteen monks of the order of Gloucester'. Some years later this gift was confirmed by William de Londres, son of Maurice de Londres and grandson of the William who built the Priory. The Priory belonged to the Benedictine order of Monks.

In 1254 (Taxation of Norwich) it was valued at 20 marks. In 1291 (*Taxatio Ecclesiastica*) it is included in the same valuation as St. Bride's Major and Colwinston, namely £40, and belonged to the Prior of Ewenny. In 1535 (*Valor Ecclesiasticus*) the total income of Ewenny was £78-8s-8d; the Rectory was worth £9-2s-4d; there was no separate vicarage as the monks resided on the spot. At the Dissolution of the Monasteries in 1537 Ewenny Priory was leased to Sir Edward Carne who covenanted for a curate. Sir Edward was the last English Ambassador to the Holy See before Henry VIII broke off relations with the Papacy. In 1545 Sir Edward Carne purchased Ewenny Priory, then one of the dissolved houses of Glamorgan, from the Crown for £727-6s-4d and built an imposing mansion within the Abbey walls which remained in his family till the 18th century when it passed to the Turbervills.

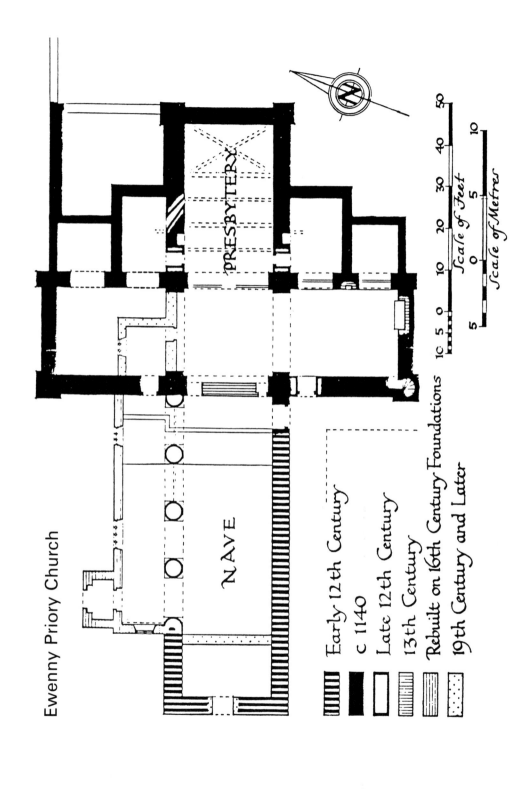

Ewenny Priory Church

NAVE

PRESBYTERY

Early 12th Century
c 1140
Late 12th Century
13th Century
Rebuilt on 16th Century Foundations
19th Century and Later

Scale of Feet
10 5 0 10 20 30 40 50

Scale of Metres
5 0 5 10

Ewenny was a curacy in 1563 and also in 1603 when the curate received £10 for service and the impropriation worth £4-10s-0d was held by John Carne, Esquire in fee from the King. The Carne family occupied Ewenny Priory for almost two hundred years and in 1741 the Priory passed to the Turbervill family. Richard Turbervill, the son of Frances Carne and Edward Turbervill, was the last descendant of Sir Edward Carne at Ewenny. In 1771 (Bishop Barrington's *Llandaff Diocesan Book*) the living was worth £40; the incumbent was the Reverend Edmund Williams and the patron was Richard Turbervill. On his death in that year he left his estate to Richard Turbervill Picton. In the latter part of the 18th century the then lady owner of the Priory, Mrs. Elizabeth Turbervill (who did not reside there) allowed the place to become greatly neglected. The eastern part of the church formerly used by the monks was used as a farm shed, and as such it appears in a watercolour painted circa 1797 by J.M.W. Turner in the Pyke Thompson collection of the National Museum of Wales. On the death of Richard Turbervill's widow in 1797 Richard Turbervill Picton took possession of the estate and changed his name to Turbervill. While the Priory was uninhabited for a period in the 18th century a considerable part of the original building fell down.

In 1835 Ewenny Priory church was styled a 'donative chapel' worth gross £47 per annum; R. T. Turbervill was the patron and impropriator. In 1867 Ewenny passed to Lt. Colonel Thomas Picton-Warlow who took the name of Turbervill as did his brother Colonel John Picton-Warlow when he in turn succeeded to the estate in 1891. Lt. Colonel Thomas Picton Turbervill who died in 1891 provided funds for the restoration of the church in 1895-1896.

In 1898 by Act of Parliament the living, which was a donative one, became a presentative. The Reverend Thomas Davies Bevan was presented, instituted and inducted by Lt. Colonel Thomas Picton Turbervill on the 18th November 1890 as the last vicar to hold his donative benefice. From 1925 to 1984 Ewenny Priory church was annexed to Merthyr Mawr church. From 1984 to date the living of Ewenny had been designated a suspended benefice and the priest-in-charge of Ewenny is the Rt. Reverend David Reece, Assistant Bishop of Llandaff.

The Priory Church of Ewenny is a remarkable example of pure Norman work throughout. The roof of the presbytery is a fine example of Romanesque vaulting on a large scale. It consists of three vaulted bays of which the first two are barrel-vaulted with squared vaulting ribs springing from pilasters with reeded capitals which are corbelled off at the lowest stringcourse. The latter is decorated with a simple chevron. A secondary moulded rib is thrown across the vault between each pair of arches. The easternmost bay has a groined vault with similar ribs which on the eastern side spring from half-columns standing on the string and set obliquely across the corners of the presbytery. The presbytery is lit by three round-headed windows with deeply-splayed embrasures in the east wall and single windows of similar design in the side walls of the eastern bay. The centre window in the east wall is filled with stained glass with a representation of the figure of St. Michael the Archangel, the patron saint of the

Stone-ribbed vaulted roof of presbytery

South transept

church. He is depicted as a winged warrior because he fights against the powers of darkness. This window and the other four windows with patterned stained glass were erected between 1869 and 1885 when the presbytery was restored by Lt. Colonel Thomas Picton Turbervill.

The altar table, which stands free of the eastern wall, has been reconstructed using the original slab which has been redressed with a wide chamfer on the underside. Three of the original five incised consecration crosses are still clearly visible. In the south wall of the presbytery is a double piscina with octofoil and sexfoil drains and moulded scalloped edge reset under a modern arch. At each side of the presbytery are small round-headed doorways which led to the side chapels now in ruins.

The presbytery is paved with glazed earthenware tiles, exact replicas of the original ones found when the foundations of the transept chapels were excavated; some of them form geometrical patterns while others bear the arms of the Abbey of Gloucester (the cross keys of St. Peter and the sword of Paul), of William Parker, the last abbot of Gloucester, and the Beauchamps, Berkerolles and Turbervilles, all of whom were considerable benefactors of this Priory. In the north wall of the presbytery is an aumbry under a round-headed arch and a hagioscope or squint which focuses on the high altar through the thickness of the wall from the ruined side chapel.

Since the Reformation the presbytery has been used as the family burial place of the proprietors of the Priory, the Carnes and the Turbervills. At the east end of the north wall of the presbytery is a brass plaque containing the names of all the owners of the estate who lie buried below the floor at the east end. The earliest name is that of John Carne, son of Sir John Carne, who died in 1643 and the latest that of Margaret Elizabeth Turbervill who died in March 1867. On the same wall above the stringcourse is a white marble monument surmounted by a draped urn which commemorates Colonel Gervas Powell Turbervill (d.1861) and his first wife, Elizabeth (d.1844), daughter of Stephen Dowell of Brawish Grove, Berkshire. At the west end of the north wall is another white marble tablet erected by his wife and children to the memory of Colonel John Picton Turbervill (1837-1924), who was owner of Ewenny Priory for over thirty years. He lies buried nearby in the family burial ground 'under the shadow of the walls he loved so well.' Opposite on the south wall are several memorial tablets to members of the Turbervill family; among them one to Edith Picton Turbervill (1872-1960), Member of Parliament for the Wrekin division of Shropshire (1929-31) and daughter of Colonel John Picton Turbervill. Above the stringcourse on the south wall is a grey stone tablet bearing a Calvary cross at the base of which is the figure of the Paschal Lamb holding aloft the banner of victory representing the Risen Christ. At the intersection of the arms of the cross is the sacred monogram IHS and below on the shaft is a quartered shield displaying 1st and 4th quarters 'Chequy or and gules a fess erminois' (Turbervill), 2nd and 3rd quarters 'Sable a chevron between three fleurs-de-lys argent' (Powell). The monument was erected to the memory of Elizabeth Margaret Turbervill (d.1867) by her cousin Colonel John Picton Turbervill.

Norman archway in south wall of nave

Oak screen dividing presbytery and south transept

The oak screen which divides the presbytery from the crossing is of three bays, the centre being the opening, square-framed and clearly of different periods. The upper part has heavy reticulated tracery fashioned in a series of quatrefoils above ten trefoil lights on each side with pierced spandrels. However, the wainscot has inserted linenfold panels of 19th-century date, seven on each side of two different kinds. The rebates on either side of the door standards indicate that there was a door here originally. The mullions are very worn and bear out what Colonel J. P. Turbervill observed in his book: *Ewenny Priory: monastery and fortress* (1901): 'The upright bars of the wooden screen still show the deep cuts worn in them by the friction of ropes with which the beasts were tied up.' This reference is to the condition of the Priory church at the very end of the 18th century as depicted in J. M. W. Turner's watercolour of the interior of the church which gave it more the appearance of a farm shed than a religious building. The screen was repaired in 1867 when a new door was made to take the place of the plank door shown in Turner's drawing. It is claimed that the presbytery screen must have been removed from the nave where it served as a fence screen to the altar of the parish church; the slots for the fixing of the screen still remain on the piers.

The massive central tower rises above the crossing beneath round, lantern arches perfectly plain, of two orders; the inner one springs from the two corbelled shafts with reeded capitals and moulded bases; the outer springs from a flat pilaster capped with a projecting string of chevron ornament. The top stage of the tower is corbelled out in typical Welsh fashion and the style of the merlons with very narrow embrasures by comparison is certainly more military than ecclesiastical. The battlements are arranged in steps and each coped merlon is pierced with a large cross eyelet. There are three embrasures in each face. At the corners are very small pinnacles which serve to offset the otherwise heavy appearance produced by the massive battlements. The row of projecting brackets would have held a fighting platform as at Cheriton church in Gower. The belfry stage with two single round-headed lights on each face is separated from the stage below by a flat stringcourse. The single bell in the tower has the inscription: 'I. RUDHALL GLOCESTER FECIT 1800'. The tower was restored in 1877 by Lt. Colonel Thomas Picton Turbervill but no alterations whatever were made in the original design.

The south transept has remained almost untouched since the day when it was built. It is lit at the south end by three plain round-headed lights arranged in the form of a triangle so that the centre one is placed above the other two. One peculiarity of these windows is that they are by no means in the centre of the south wall. This may be due to the fact that the stair turret takes up part of the south wall. A small doorway in the south-west corner of the transept leads up to the tower by a circular stone staircase and along a passage contrived in the west wall. This passage opens to the church by an arcade of seven small round arches upon short shafts with moulded bases and cushion capitals. The gallery so formed overlooking the south transept is divided by alternate round and square columns but the northernmost pillars are of round pattern thus breaking the

West entrance c. 1795

Ewenny Priory in 1775

(from Francis Grose *The Antiquities of Endland and Wales*)

symmetry of the arcade. The passage leads ultimately to the upper chamber of the tower and from here it is possible to reach the wall-walk behind the battlements of the south transept and the space above the vault over the presbytery.

In the south wall at ground level is a canopied niche of 13th-century date which once contained the broken effigy believed to be that of Sir Payn de Turberville which now lies upon a base in the middle of the transept. The south transept has two blocked Norman arches in the east wall which once opened into the chapels now in ruins. The arches are of two plain members springing from a central square pier and responds, each capped with an abacus decorated with chevron moulding. The northern arch has its hood mould decorated with billets; the southern one is quite plain. In the central pier is a trefoiled niche of Early English design with heavy roll-moulding. The arches and chapels belonged to the earlier Priory church and so appear low in comparison with the rest of the transept. The work up to and including the heavy stringcourse with chevron moulding belongs to the church which was built for the newly-established conventual community circa 1141. But the work above the chevron stringcourse represents a remodelling and heightening of the church which took place at the end of the 12th century.

In the south transept are several tombs and sepulchral slabs, many of which were removed there from the north aisle when it was restored in 1896. There are three sepulchral slabs to the De Londres family. The principal one is that of Maurice de Londres who died in the middle of the 12th century. The perfect inscription in Norman-French is in Lombardic characters and reads:-

'ICI:GIST:MORICE:DE:LVNDRES:LE FVN-
DUR:DEU:LI:RENDE:SUN:LABVR:A.M.'

(Here lies Morice de Londres, the Founder,
God reward him for his work. Amen.)

The shaft of a beautiful floriated cross divides two lines of the inscription while around the chamfered edge runs a border of Early English scroll-leaf. The slab is early 13th century in date and was presumably erected sometime after his death.

An incised sepulchral slab of much simpler workmanship with only a cross bearing the inscription:- 'HIC IACET W(ILLEMUS) DE LON(DONIA)' (Here lies William de Londres) has been attributed by Dr. C. A. Ralegh Radford to Maurice de Londres' grandson William, the third of that name who held the Lordship of Ogmore. It now lies broken into four pieces in the north-east corner of the transept.

The third De Londres' slab is incised with the full-length figure of Hawise de Londres (d.1274) but the head and shoulders are missing. She was the daughter and heiress of Thomas de Londres (d.1196) and great-great-granddaughter of William de Londres who built the Priory in the 12th century. The inscription in Norman-French is hardly decipherable but Dr. Ralegh Radford thought it may have read thus:-

'(PRIEZ):PUR:LA (NOB)LE:DAME:HAWISE:DE:LONDRES: (PENSEZ ET
CHANTER):PUR:LA:SON:ALME:DUET:PAT.NOST.'
(Pray for the noble Lady Hawise de Londres: remember and chant for her
soul two Paternosters.)

The slab is now broken into two pieces which are propped against the east
wall of the transept but prior to 1895 it was used as a seat in the porch for many
generations.

The free-standing tomb-chest which stands to the south of the sepulchral slab
of Maurice de Londres has on all four sides six coats of arms within a shield
which are various quarterings of the Carne family. They include the Carne
arms 'Gules, a pelican in her piety proper', the Giles arms 'Sable a crosslet
saltirewise argent', the Walden arms 'Azure a lion rampant', the Fleming arms
'A chevron between three coronets out of each issuing two feathers' and other
unidentified coats of arms, probably English acquired by marriage. Lying upon
this tomb-chest is the mutilated effigy of a knight in chain mail with a long
surcoat with pointed shield and sword. This effigy may well represent Sir Payn
de Turberville of Coity, who was benefactor of the Priory in the 13th century.

To the south of this stands a large tomb-chest of black and white polished
marble and the inscription records that the tomb was erected by Martha,
daughter of Sir Hugh Wyndham in memory of her husband Edward Carne of
Ewenny (d.1650). The west end of the tomb-chest displays six quarterings of
the arms of the Carne family impaling the arms of Wyndham 'Azure a chevron
between three lions' heads erased or'. The tomb also commemorates his great-
grandson John Carne (d.1700) the last male of the line, aged 15 years. On the
flat surface of the tomb is inscribed a rather pompous inscription by a Thomas
of Tregoes to the latter:-

'HERE LY'S EWENNY'S HOPE, EWENNY'S PRIDE
IN HIM BOTH FLOVRIS'D AND IN HIM BOTH DY'D
DEATH HAVEING SEIS'D HIM, LINGER'D LOATHE TO BE
THE RVINE OF THIS WORTHY FAMILY'.

In the floor of the south transept are three sepulchral slabs with Calvary
crosses and billets which mark the graves of former priors. One of these slabs
has been re-used since the Reformation and bears the following inscription:

'HEARE LIETH THE BODIE OF ADAM NICHOLL DECEASED
THE XXII DAIE OF IVLIE ANNO DOMINI 1615. IW'

On the east, south and west walls of the south transept are several interesting
monuments to members of the Carne and Turbervill families who were owners
of Ewenny Priory in the 18th and 19th centuries. On the east wall is a fine
marble monument surmounted by a classical urn and decorated below with a
winged cherub-head. It was erected to the memory of Richard Turbervill,
Esq., of Ewenny Priory (d. 1771), M.P. for Glamorgan in 1767 and his wife,
Elizabeth, (d. 1797), only daughter of Richard Herbert, Esq., of Cilybebill, near
Neath. The monument on the south wall commemorates Richard Carne of

Ewenny Priory church—south transept from presbytery ▶

Ewenny Priory (d. 1713) who married Mary, eldest daughter of Dr. James Allen of Gileston by Winifred Giles, daughter and heiress of Major William Giles of Gileston. This monument is carved in the form of an exquisite Baroque cartouche. The cartouche, which has an oval inscription tablet, incorporates drapes and foliage with cherub-heads and a skull at the base. At the top is a quartered shield displaying 1st and 4th quarters 'Gules a pelican in her piety proper' (Carne), 2nd and 3rd quarters 'Sable a cross crosslet saltirewise argent', (Giles). The marble monument on the west wall, which is flanked by fluted composite columns, is surmounted by a plain sarcophagus with gadrooned top and tapering sides. It was erected in memory of Richard Turbervill Turbervill of Ewenny Priory (d. 1817), eldest son of Thomas Picton of Poyston, Pembrokeshire. (He assumed the name and arms of Turbervill by Royal Licence in 1797.) The monument also commemorates his wife, Elizabeth (d. 1828), eldest daughter of the Reverend Gervas Powell of Llanharan House, Glamorgan and their eldest son, Richard Turbervill Turbervill (d. 1848).

All along the east and north walls of the transept are arranged a considerable number of sculptured stones most of which belong to the Norman period but amongst them are fragments of purely Celtic design. Embedded in the floor of the transept are several tombstones to the memory of various members of the Carne and Turbervill families. The outside wall of the south transept bears a mass dial with four radiating lines that probably represent the four main daily offices: prime or the first hour, terce or the third hour, sext which was noon and none the ninth hour.

The nave of the monastic church is today in use as the parish church of Ewenny. In order to understand properly the plan of the church it must be remembered that the nave has always formed the parish church while the rest of the building was used by the monks. A wall of separation across the western arch of the lantern has always existed from earliest times acting at once as the reredos of the parochial church and the rood screen of the priory. It is a solid, rough wall approximately three metres in height of 13th-century date. In Elizabethan times the entire space between screen and lantern arch was built up. Placed upon the wall is a carved oak beam with a cavetto moulding in front decorated with patera and finished above with a battlemented cornice. On either side of the reredos are two processional doorways which formerly led through the screen into the Priory church. The upper part of the western arch of the crossing is now filled with a panelled screen containing twelve rectangular lights which effectively seals off the nave from the Priory church.

The present nave is approximately five metres shorter and the roof about two metres lower than the original. The existing west wall was built circa 1803 and the beautiful Norman archway of the west door decorated with chevron moulding was removed to form the entrance to the upper garden where it still stands today. The nave is lit on the south side by three large round-headed windows with deeply-splayed embrasures set high in the south wall which date from the 12th century. One jamb of a fourth window has been blocked up in the south-west corner of the wall. Towards the east end of the south wall is a

Nave before restoration

Photographed by Sir T. Mansel Franklen in 1889

small two-light Tudor window which was opened out in order to provide additional light at that end of the nave. Almost below it in the south-east corner is the round-headed processional doorway leading from the cloisters which were once situated on the south side of the nave. The doorway is of two orders; the inner plain, the outer with chevron decoration beneath a hood mould adorned with narrow cable and nail-headed ornament. The shafts of the outer order are decorated with reeded capitals and have plain moulded bases. In the north wall of the nave above the massive piers of the arcade may be seen the three round-headed Norman clerestory windows which were blocked up when the Tudor north aisle was built and restored in 1870-1885.

The pulpit which stands on the north side of the nave is partly boarded and partly panelled with fine marquetry work. These appear to be raised or fielded and the crosses and the petals within are composed of various kinds of wood such as mahogany, maple, sycamore and rosewood. It has a plain moulded cornice with Gothic style stiff-leaf foliage in pairs of 13th-century style. Each side has been decorated in two halves, the upper section comprises a single square panel and the lower four smaller square panels. The stem is an engaged column with a semicircular base with two little spurs resting on a square plinth. The carved and inlaid reading desk is equally fine.

The large round-headed window in the west wall of the nave was inserted in the church in 1929 to beautify the church and provide additional light. The stained glass is illustrative of the Nativity and the Angel appearing before the shepherds. It was erected to the memory of Ethel Lucie Turbervill (d.1929) by her husband, Charles Grenville Turbervill from a design prepared by William Glasby of London, and Cook and Edwards, architects. The roof of the nave is a plain open timber construction.

On the south wall of the nave hangs a Roll of Honour carved in oak to the fifty-three men and one woman of the parish who served in the Great War, 1914-1918, and adjacent to it is a marble tablet to the two youngest sons and two grandsons of Colonel John Picton Turbervill of Ewenny Priory–Arthur Picton-Warlow (d.1917), Wilfrid Picton-Warlow (d.1914), Cortlandt Richard MacGregor (d.1915) and Kenneth Cortlandt MacGregor (d.1915), all of whom were killed on active service abroad.

Beneath the blocked-up window at the western end of the south wall a memorial tablet to the memory of David William, the village blacksmith (d.1742) is inscribed with the following epitaph:-

'My sledge and hammer lie decay'd
My bellows too have lost their wind
My fires extinct, my force allay'd
My vice is in the dust confin'd
My coal is spent, my iron's gone
My nails are drove, my work is done.'

The font, which stands at the west end of the nave, has a circular bowl and is decorated with a horizontal round and hollow mouldings at rim, centre and base. There is reason to believe that it has been recut and it now stands on a modern base.

The present north aisle was built in 1895-96 to replace a Tudor aisle which had collapsed in 1803. The Tudor aisle had replaced the original Norman aisle. The north aisle is separated from the nave by an arcade of four bays. The massive circular piers have moulded bases and reeded capitals; the arches two square members. The aisle is lit by three Laudian windows, two in the north wall of three and four round-headed lights and one of two round-headed lights at the west end. All the windows have square labels. The stained glass in the west window depicts the figures of St. Elizabeth, mother of John the Baptist, and St. Luke 'the beloved physician'. It was erected in 1935 by the daughters of the Reverend Thomas Davies Bevan, M.A., vicar of the parish for 35 years (d.1925). The window was designed by Messrs. G. Maile & Son Ltd., of London. At the east end of the aisle a round-headed doorway which formerly led to the north transept now leads to the modern vestry. Towards the east end of the aisle stands a pipe organ built by Messrs. Norman & Beard of Norwich and London, which was erected in the church in 1903 at a cost of £750. A memorial plaque on the north wall of the aisle to the memory of Lt. Colonel Thomas Picton Turbervill (1827-1891) records that the nave was repaired between 1895 and 1896 by his widow, his brother Colonel John Picton Turbervill and his brother-in-law Harry Connop. The Tudor south porch was rebuilt in 1895-1896 and still retains the Tudor outer arch with its square label. The inner doorway of the porch has a plain rounded arch.

The Turbervill family have for centuries past been benefactors of Ewenny Priory and its present condition owes a great deal to the care and continuing effort of preservation by the family during the 19th century. Successive restorations were carried out by Richard Turbervill Turbervill (1800-1817), by Lt. Colonel Thomas Picton Turbervill (1870-1891) and finally by Colonel John Picton Turbervill (1895-1896). Richard T. Turbervill set about restoring the church in 1800. He did not attempt to restore the whole of the church but was content to make the church fit to be used as a place of worship. He pulled down the ruined north transept, shortened the nave at the west end by about five metres and lowered the roof covering the clerestory windows above the arcade. Two of the round-headed Norman windows on the south side of the nave were converted into two large oblong windows to provide additional light. The level of the floor was raised, thereby covering the bases of the pillars. From the churchwardens' accounts we learn that the necessary alterations and repairs, which included the procuring of a new bell for the tower, lasted over a period of more than twenty years. During this time a heavy church rate was levied amounting in one year to two shillings in the pound to cover the cost of the repairs. This money was spent only on the parish church and no work was carried out on the monastic part of the Priory church.

The church remained in this condition for more than fifty years until about 1870 when Lt. Colonel Thomas Picton Turbervill continued the work of restoration on the advice of Professor Edward Freeman, the historian and famous Victorian ecclesiologist, who took a great interest in the building. At the time of Freeman's first visit to the church in 1867, three enormous buttresses of solid masonry almost entirely concealed both sides of the presbytery. The windows in the south transept were unglazed while those in the presbytery had been filled with masonry. Lt. Colonel Thomas Picton Turbervill had two of the great buttresses on both sides of the presbytery removed, leaving only the one at the east end. The interior of the presbytery was then repaired, the windows at the east end being opened out and glazed as well as those in the side walls. All traces of whitewash which had been liberally applied were removed, the old oak screen was repaired and the whole of the presbytery paved with glazed earthenware tiles, exact copies of some of the designs of those found in the side chapel on the south side. The large tombs which encumbered the presbytery were then removed to the south transept. The floor of the transept was repaired, concreted and the walls cleaned and cemented.

In 1875 the present pulpit was erected in the nave and the old-fashioned pews replaced by the present ones. A year or two later the tower was restored but no alterations whatever were made in the original design. The oak flooring of the belfry was renewed in 1886 and three years later the great arch separating the nave from the choir was opened out and the separating wall brought down to its original level.

After the death in 1891 of Lt. Colonel Thomas Picton Turbervill (who had willed a considerable sum of money to be spent on further restoration of the church) his widow, his brother, Colonel John Picton Turbervill and his brother-in-law, Harry Connop decided to restore the north aisle and the nave of the church. The work commenced in June 1895 under the guidance of John Thomas Micklethwaite, a well-known architect. It was decided that the new north aisle should be narrower than that built in the 16th century and in keeping with the original Norman aisle. During the preparation of the site of the new aisle it was necessary to remove several tombstones which were replaced afterwards as near as possible to their former position. A large quantity of bones which were disturbed were reverently re-interred on the north-east side of the churchyard. During the excavation of the north aisle old tombstones and Celtic crosses of pre-Norman date were discovered and placed in the south transept.

The Tudor porch was pulled down and rebuilt in a new position, every stone being marked and replaced carefully. The masonry blocking up the arcade was removed revealing little or no damage to the moulding of the arches. The floor of the nave was brought down to its original level, exposing the bases of the piers of the arcade. The two large Tudor windows in the south wall of the nave were removed and the Norman windows restored. The flat plaster ceiling was taken down and a plain oak roof erected at the height of the original one. The clerestory windows above the north arcade were restored. A new vestry was built on the site of the ruined north transept and a few of the most perfect tiles from the side chapels were placed on either side of the small round arch leading from the aisle into the vestry. The cost of the restoration amounted to £1,000 which was donated by the Turbervill family and a few county families. The workmen on the Turbervill estate carried out the whole of the building work.

Nothing now remains of the conventual buildings which lay in the usual position on the south side of the church, except for a few fragments incorporated in the Georgian mansion which now occupies the site. The monastic part of the Priory church is now under the guardianship of the Welsh Historic Monuments (CADW).

The church plate consists of a handsome silver flagon with lid and handle hall-marked 1750; also a silver chalice of late 17th-century date and a silver paten standing on a foot, circa 1750. Both hall-marks have unfortunately been obliterated. The register of burials dates from 1714, baptisms from 1754 and marriages from 1755.

Flemingston Church

The parish church of Flemingston is dedicated to St. Michael the Archangel and the original church was probably built by a member of the Le Fleming family in the early 13th century. The present structure of the church dates from the early 14th century in the Early English and Decorated styles. The church is first recorded in the Taxation of Norwich in 1254, when it was valued at 4 marks. In the *Taxatio Ecclesiastica* of Pope Nicholas IV in 1291 it was worth £2 and in 1535 (*Valor Ecclesiasticus*) it was valued at £5-6s-8d. The parson was resident in 1563. The patronage of the living seems always to have been vested in the Lord of the Manor. In 1665 it belonged to a member of the Thomas family of Flemingston Court and passed by marriage to the Edwins of Llanmihangel Place and to the Wyndhams. In 1771 (Bishop Barrington's Primary Visitation of the Diocese) the living was worth £50; the incumbent was the Reverend William Church and the patron was Lady Charlotte Edwin. In 1835 it was a Rectory worth gross £200 in the patronage of Lord Dunraven. Flemingston church was joined with Gileston in 1914 and both parishes were linked with St. Athan with Eglwys Brewis in 1978 to form a grouped benefice.

The church consists of chancel, nave with south transept, south porch and western bellcote containing two bells. The restored chancel arch is pointed with plain mouldings and springs directly from the chancel wall. The east window is of two cinquefoiled lights and the tracery in the head is a combination of cusped Geometrical and Flowing tracery. It radiates from the centre of a circle, two opposing ogee shapes giving the appearance of four arms and dividing the feature into as many lozenge-shaped lights. It is surmounted by a dripstone with square label stops. The stained glass depicts the Crucifixion and Ascension of Our Lord; beneath the Saviour's Cross stand Mary, his mother, and the 'beloved disciple', John, looking sorrowfully on at the scene. In the other light Our Lord is seen ascending into Heaven in the act of blessing His Apostles and, through them, His church on earth. The window was erected in 1907 by Miss Ann Jenkins of Penarth in memory of her parents, David James and Jane Elizabeth Jenkins who lived at Flemingston Court and was designed by Messrs. Clayton & Bell, Regent Street, London.

The chancel is lit on the south side by two broad trefoil lancets with ogee-foliated heads which are 19th-century insertions. The south-east window which is stained, depicts the Presentation of the Infant Jesus in the temple with Simeon the 'just and devote' man taking the Infant Saviour in his arms, uttering the canticle *Nunc dimittis*. It was erected in memory of Rees Morris, priest, rector of

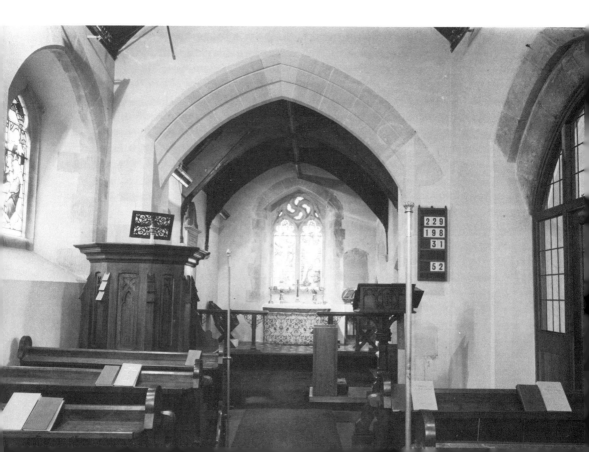

the parish from 1895 to 1926, Mary, his wife and their only son, Harold David by their daughters. Between the two chancel windows on the south side is a priest's door with pointed arch. In the south-east corner of the sanctuary is a cinquefoiled headed niche containing a damaged piscina. On the east wall, south of the altar, is an 18th-century memorial tablet to members of the Hallett family. The chancel has an arch-braced timber roof with foliated bosses with emblems carved on the bases of the principal rafters, which are identical with those at St. Mary Church. On the north wall of the chancel is a brass memorial plaque to the memory of Elizabeth, wife of the Reverend S. James, rector who 'for 23 years worshipped in this spot' and died 2nd February, 1890, aged 79 years.

In 1848 when Sir Stephen Glynne visited the church, there was a rood-loft door high on the south side of the chancel arch, but a restoration of the church ten years later in 1858 swept away all traces of this rood-loft. The wooden pulpit has a deep moulded cornice with heavy buttresses as stiles which are even deeper on the drum. It has narrow sunken panels of different widths and is decorated with a pointed quatrefoil above a trefoil of different sizes. There are two similar panels on the door of the pulpit and before the closed drum is a moulded rail. The arch from the nave to the south transept has an obtusely-pointed arch of two members which springs directly from the side walls. The transept itself is very large in proportion to the church. In the south wall of the transept is a fine sepulchral arch with mouldings and little shafts with their circular caps and bases and astragals between. It has prominent roll-mouldings with deep hollows and is of 13th-century character. Beneath the arch lies the stone effigy of a lady depicting Joan Le Fleming, a member of the Flemingston branch of the Norman family who held Flemingston a hundred years or more after the Norman incursion into Glamorgan. Her head rests upon a small square cushion with an oblong stone under it, and she is wearing a wimple which covers neck and chin, leaving the face exposed. The eyes are closed while the hands are clasped on the breast in the attitude of prayer. The dress is long, reaching to the feet which rest upon a lion whose head is missing. The inscription which is in Norman-French and Lombardic characters faces the wall and leads one to suppose that it is not in its original position. The wording reads as follows:— 'DAME: IHONE: FLEMENG: GIVT ICI: DEV DE: LALME: EIT: MERCI: KI: DU: P: LALME: PRIERTA: CARANTE: IVRS:' (Lady Joan Fleming lies here and may God have mercy on her soul. Whoso prays for the soul of the deceased will receive forty days' pardon.) The effigy is later than the arched recess—of 14th-century date. In the south wall of the transept to the left of the effigy is a trefoil-headed recess containing a piscina with sexfoil drain. The south window of the transept is of three cinquefoiled lights, cusped with intersecting tracery forming three quatrefoils. It is surmounted by a dripstone with large square label stops. The transept is lit on the west side by an original trefoil lancet and on the east side by a modern broad trefoil lancet which is coeval with the two south chancel windows. The transept has an open timber roof with curved windbraces.

On the north wall of the nave are two modern windows of two lights with ogee-foliated heads, containing stained glass designed by Messrs. Clayton & Bell of London. The stained glass in the easternmost window depicts the Adoration of the Shepherds and was erected in 1921 in memory of David James and Jane Elizabeth Jenkins by their children. The other stained glass window in the north wall of the nave adjoining the Iolo memorial, depicts Joseph and Mary finding Jesus in the temple confounding the Doctors. This window is dedicated to the memory of Edward Williams (d. 1886) of Middlesborough, son of Taliesin Williams and grandson of Iolo Morganwg, and also his wife, Elizabeth (d. 1889). This window was erected in 1920 by William Illtyd Williams, a great-grandson of Iolo Morganwg. In the north wall of the nave lies another stone effigy under a plain recess. The figure is crudely scratched on the surface of the slab and is female, since part of the name 'Elizabeth' can be deciphered. On the north wall of the nave is a memorial monument in memory of the Reverend William Davies (d. 1829), curate of Llanmihangel and Flemingston. He was killed when thrown from his horse in 1829 and lies buried beneath the memorial erected to his memory, as it was his wish that he should be buried as near as possible to the memorial of Iolo Morganwg.

In the north-west corner of the nave is a fine memorial monument to Iolo Morganwg and his son Taliesin ab Iolo. It is composed of twin tablets in the form of an open book in white marble, inscribed in Welsh and English, and was erected in 1855, by Caroline, Countess of Dunraven, and other titled admirers of the old Glamorgan bard and antiquary. The English version reads as follows:— 'In memory of Edward Williams (Iolo Morganwg) of this village, stone mason, bard and antiquary. Born at Penon in the adjoining parish of Llancarvan on the 10th day of March (old style) A.D. 1746, died on the 18th December, 1826'. A stonemason by trade he taught himself to become both poet and historian and eventually literary forger. Out of a particular desire to prove that Glamorgan had a richer tradition than any other county, he fabricated folk tales, genealogies, historic records and manuscripts. After his death his son, Taliesin, bound his papers into volumes which are now deposited at the National Library of Wales, Aberystwyth. His remains, together with those of his son Taliesin, lie buried in Flemingston churchyard. His grave was at one time marked by an inscribed tombstone describing his character and achievements, which was erected in 1855 'by those persons who appreciated his literary genius'. The tablet also commemorates his son, Taliesin, who, like his father, was a bard.

The nave is lit on the south side by a modern single broad lancet with ogee-foliated head. At the west end of the nave are two single trefoil lancets deeply splayed. The nave has an arch-braced roof with curved windbraces between the wallplate and purlins. The south porch is set very close to the west end of the nave. It has a segmental pointed outer arch with an inner arch dying into the side walls; the inner south doorway is plain pointed of Bath stone. The 13th-century font was designed to look like a cushion capital with the underside characteristically rounded into a short circular stem. There are two roll-mouldings at the base of the stem which rests on a square plinth. The modern cover has an acorn finial with open scroll trusses on a plain central shaft. The organ is an early valuable chamber organ thought to be built by the early 19th-century organ builder, Joseph Walker. Over the west end of the nave is a gable bellcote with open arches, containing two bells. The bells bear the date 1858 and were cast by John Warner & Sons, London.

The general fabric of the church was thoroughly restored in 1858 at the sole expense of Caroline, Countess of Dunraven. The work of restoration included the insertion of several modern windows in the nave and chancel with dressings of Portland stone. A new Decorated-style window was inserted at the east end and the chancel arch 'a rude misshapen one, bulging out and without mouldings' was removed and replaced by the present one. The whitewash on the exterior walls of the church was removed and an obtuse lancet high in the west end of the nave was closed. The west end of the nave wall was strengthened on either side by a solid buttress. The old bells were recast and rehung in the bellcote.

There once stood on the apex of the transept gable a blue lias limestone sundial which had a great reputation for accuracy. It bore the inscription 'WILL. HALL. CHURCHWARDEN A.D. 1728'. (The name Will. Hall, churchwarden appears to be an abbreviation of William Hallett, whose family lies buried in the chancel.) The sundial was erected by a former rector, the Reverend Edward Prichard, who died in 1742 at the advanced age of 109 years. Prichard was a remarkable man. He possessed a great knowledge of astronomy and, in addition, he conducted a school in the village where he taught Latin, Greek, Hebrew and Mathematics. He was a close friend of the celebrated Sir Isaac Newton, who on more than one occasion visited Flemingston to consult with him.

The church plate is of unusual design and is said to be unique in the diocese of Llandaff. The bowl of the silver chalice is small and oviform in shape, richly chased, standing on a baluster stem. The foot is engraved with a peacock's feather design. The cup is hall-marked 1607. The paten cover is neither hall-marked nor dated and is quite plain. Another paten cover is inscribed 'Flemingstone 1862'. The parish registers are among the earliest in the diocese, dating back (as do those of St. Donat's church) to the year 1570.

Gileston Manor House and church, 1887

Photograph by Sir T. Mansel Franklen

Gileston Church

The parish church of Gileston is dedicated to St. Giles, although it was originally dedicated to St. Mabon when the Welsh name of the parish was Llanfabon-y-fro. The parish of Gileston takes its name from the family of Giles who held the manor in 1350 with the advowson of the church by service of one knight's fee worth £4-12s-2d per annum. It is believed therefore that the present dedication has grown out of the name of the manor, not as usually the name of the manor out of the dedication. The manor and advowson of the church remained in the Giles family until the close of the 17th century. The church was worth £2 in 1291 (*Taxatio Ecclesiastica*) and £5-18s-0d in 1535 (*Valor Ecclesiasticus*). The living was vacant in 1563 but there was a curate there to do service. According to the *Notitia Episcopatum* of 1665 when the Giles family were still patrons of Gileston it was listed as worth £15. By 1728 this had become £25 and by 1771 £30. In 1807 the 'rectory' of Gileston received £200 from Queen Anne's Bounty and in 1809 another £200 to meet the benefactions of £100 each from the Reverend J. Edwardes, husband of the heiress of the manor, who was the patron and also the rector. In 1914 the living of Gileston was coupled with that of Flemingston. Thus the rector living at Flemingston had to cross 'alien' territory to reach his church at Gileston, since Gileston parish was an enclave within the parish of St. Athan. The parishes of Gileston and Flemingston were joined with those of St. Athan and Eglwys Brewis in 1978 to form a grouped benefice.

The church consists of chancel, nave, south porch and small embattled western tower containing one bell. The present church dates from the 15th century but an earlier church existed on this spot. The chancel arch is plain pointed of large blocks, regular-sized voussoirs. The east window is of two cinquefoiled lights, square-headed and labelled. The oak reredos is of five panels, all but the centre with a castellated cresting. The canopy in the centre is a trefoil set on little hammerbeams with long pointed quatrefoils in the spandrels and crockets on the arch above, which is surmounted by a plain cross. At the head of each flanking panel trefoils spring again from the likeness of hammer-beams, beneath pointed arches with panelling in the spandrels and various leaf decorations applied conservatively. The canopy and cresting are surmounted by crocketed finials.

The chancel is lit on the south side by two trefoil lancets both deeply splayed. In the sanctuary floor are several interesting sepulchral slabs and tombstones.

One dated 1618 to (Matthew) and Mary Giles displays a Latin cross with billets
at each side below the base with the coat of arms of the Giles family 'Sable a
cross crosslet in saltire argent' and that of his wife's family, the Flemings 'A
chevron between three coronets out of each issuing two feathers.' On the south
side of the sanctuary is a remarkable tombstone to Mary Allen (d. 1734),
daughter of James Allen, Gent., and his wife, Winifred, 'relict of Richard Carne
of Ewenny and late wife of William Willis, clerk, sole heiress of the manor of
Gileston.' The tombstone shows the coat of arms of Willis 'Azure a chevron
between three mullets' impaling those of Giles 'Sable a cross crosslet in saltire
argent.' On the north side of the sanctuary are two more incised sepulchral
slabs, displaying floriated crosses.

On the south wall of the chancel between the two windows is a marble
memorial tablet to Major William Giles (d. 1673), the son of Matthew Giles,
Gent., and the last of the male line of the Giles family. The tablet is surmounted
by the Giles crest and coat of arms of four quarterings, first and fourth, 'Sable a
cross potent', second and third, 'Sable a cross crosslet in saltire argent'.

A white, veined, marble monument on the north wall of the chancel commemorates Ann, the wife of the Reverend William Willis (d. 1760), Lord of the
Manor. She was an heiress of the Giles family whose only daughter, Margaret,
carried the estate into the Edwardes family. Adjacent to this on the same wall is
a white, marble monument in memory of the Reverend John Edwardes, M.A.,
(1765-1847) Lord of the Manor and rector of the parish for 44 years and his son,
the Reverend Frederic Francis Edwardes, (1801-1882) Lord of the Manor and
rector of the parish for 35 years. The monument was erected by Mrs. Charlotte
Johnes and Lady Elizabeth Hills-Johnes, granddaughters of the Reverend John
Edwardes and nieces of the Reverend F. F. Edwardes. The memorial tablet is
surmounted by the crest and coat of arms of the Edwardes family which are as
follows:— Crest—'A demi-lion or holding between the paws a bowen's knot.'
Arms quarterly first quarter—'Sable a lion rampant within an orle of
cinquefoils or'; second quarter—'Gules a chevron or, between three bowen's
knots'; third quarter—'Sable, three bucks' heads, caboshed, argent'; fourth
quarter—'Chequy or and sable a fesse argent'. The motto 'Aspera ad virtutem
est via' translates 'The road to virtue is rough'.

The chancel has an arch-braced roof with curved windbraces between the
purlins and wallplate. The plainly-moulded corbels of the nave and chancel
roofs from which the roof braces spring have carved bosses in the shape of
human faces on their undersides. The chancel screen is early Perpendicular and
the piece is full of ogee arches, particularly in the cinquefoiled fenestration
tracery of the two bays each of two lights. The doorway has a cinquefoiled
head, the centre being an ogee arch and there are flowers and leaves in the
spandrels.

A door with four-centred arch in the north wall of the nave leads to the
rood-loft staircase which is in an excellent state of preservation. The door still
retains a portion of the iron plate once attached to the drop handle and is of
similar character to the south door. A portion of the stairway is roofed by a late

13th-century sepulchral slab and the north wall of the nave was evidently widened to take the rood-loft staircase. Two lights which formerly lit the rood-loft remain *in situ*; a shortened trefoil lancet high in the north wall of the nave and a similar window high in the opposite south wall deeply splayed. There are no other windows on the north side of the nave.

The nave is lit on the south side by a two-light cinquefoiled window with square head and label, a shortened trefoil lancet in the south-east corner and a two-light window with ogee-foliated heads beneath a square head and label in the south-west corner. The nave has an arch-braced roof with a continuous internal curve with curved windbraces between the purlins. At the intersections of the tie-beam and purlins there are bosses of Tudor rose decoration. The aisle of the nave is paved with old tombstones whose inscriptions the feet of generations of worshippers have rendered almost illegible.

The oak pulpit in the south-east corner of the nave has applied Gothic tracery in the three panels. There is a castellated cresting and a running vine in the cornice. The top panel in each case has a cinquefoil beneath a pointed arch. The smaller ones below include cinquefoils—the cusps decorated with beads—beneath an ogee arch with quatrefoils in the spandrels. The Norman font of Sutton stone is plain and cylindrical without mouldings or ornament set on a round stem. The oak cover is conical and has eight carved panels of Jacobean-style design. The 14th-century west doorway is built-in. The south porch is early Perpendicular and is large in proportion to the church. The inner arch of the south doorway has an obtusely-pointed arch composed of different-sized voussoirs. Above the inner doorway is a niche with an ogee-crocketed canopy which once held a crucifix. Near the door is an octagonal holy-water stoup and also an ancient piscina. The outer doorway has an arch surmounted by a dripstone with carved heads as stops. A little gable at the apex of the porch supports a cross fleurée.

The most interesting feature of the church is the unusual south door which is unique in the diocese. It bears six carved shields upon it and has remained for some five hundred and thirty years in an almost perfect state of preservation. The wrought-iron hinges are as when first attached to the oak and so is the drophandle. The coats of arms and foliage carved between the ribs in the upper portion of the door is not cut in the solid but is planted on and rebated into the frame and ribs. The six escutcheons are the heraldic arms of local families. They are as follows:—

1. Walsh of Llandough 'Ermine a bend, gules a mullet for difference.'
2. Umfraville of Penmark (1104-1350) 'Or 6 cinquefoils gules—3, 2 and 1.'
3. Giles family 'A hand couped holding a sword'—the crest of the Giles family.
4. Giles of Gileston—'Sable, a cross crosslet in saltire argent'—the arms of the Giles family who held Gileston in 1262.
5. Fleming—'A chevron between 3 coronets, out of each issuing two feathers'.

6.   Cradock family—'A boar's head couped'—this was the seal of Sir Mathew
     Cradock.

The door is probably of a date between 1450 and 1480.

The western bell turret is corbelled out in the usual style of the corbel tables
of tower battlements so common in the Vale of Glamorgan and has a chimney-
like appearance. It contains a single bell which bears the inscription ANO. D.M.
1ò00 CB. P.B. The churchyard cross which is set upon four steps, was destroyed
by Cromwell's soldiers who considered these crosses to be a sign of idolatry.
However, in 1900 it was restored by taking a piece of ornamental stone from
the corner of the church, carving it and placing it on a broken shaft. The top of
the shaft has a cross with six finials.

The church was partially restored in 1885 when the Reverend Montague
Welby of Gileston Manor complained to the patron of the living, Lady Hills-
Johnes, that Gileston church was unfit for divine worship. Consequently the old
box pews were removed and replaced with new oak seats and the existing
wood flooring was removed. The church underwent a more extensive restoration in 1903 when the church was reseated throughout with oak seats and a
new pulpit and two new priest's stalls were erected. Also a new reredos of oak
was placed in the sanctuary. The old plaster ceiling of the nave was taken down
to reveal the old 15th-century oak roof. The chancel roof was also renewed
with oak and the bell turret was taken down and completely rebuilt. The
chancel arch was restored so that it no longer gave the impression of being 'very
rude' as described by Sir Stephen Glynne when he visited the church in July
1871. The cost of restoration amounted to approximately £1,000 and the
architect was G. E. Halliday.

The church plate includes a silver chalice with its paten cover, both of which
are inscribed 'The gift of Mrs. Mary Carne to the parish of Gilestone in the
county of Glamorgan, 1721'. The church once possessed a fair linen cloth
embroidered with the lady's hair 'The cloth for Gilestone church 1721'. Mrs.
Mary Carne was the daughter of Major William Giles and Winifred, daughter
of James Allen. She married Richard Carne of Ewenny.

The register of marriages dates from the year 1701, baptisms and burials from
1813.

Llanblethian Church

The parish church of Llanblethian is dedicated to St. John the Baptist although it was originally dedicated to St. Bleddian, the Welsh form of St. Lupus. The church was formerly known as Llanbleddian Fawr to distinguish it from Llanbleddian Fach (St. Lythan's). Llanblethian is the ancient parish church of the benefice of Llanblethian with Cowbridge and as a mother church it served a large area with chapelries at Cowbridge, Llanquian, Llansannor and Welsh St. Donat's. The earliest reference to the existence of a church at Llanblethian is an undated confirmatory charter of Nicholas ap Gwrgant, Bishop of Llandaff (1148-1183) in which we learn that Llanblethian, together with its chapels, had become a possession of St. Mary's Abbey, Tewkesbury. By the middle of the 13th century Llansannor had become a rectory, but Welsh St. Donat's remained attached to Llanblethian until the Disestablishment of the Welsh Church in 1920 when it was joined with Ystradowen.

The church of Llanblethian with its chapels was valued at 18 marks in 1254 (Taxation of Norwich) and the vicarage worth 40s was already established. In 1291 (*Taxatio Ecclesiastica*) the church was included in the same valuation as Llantwit Major and assigned to the Abbot of Tewkesbury. The vicarage was valued separately at £5. In 1535 (*Valor Ecclesiasticus*) the living was classified as a vicarage worth (including the chapel of Cowbridge) £10-12s-4d and the rectorial tithes still went to Tewkesbury. At the Dissolution of the Monasteries the patronage of Llanblethian church passed to the Dean and Chapter of Gloucester, who continued to appoint vicars until the Disestablishment of the Welsh Church. In 1603 it was styled a vicarage worth £43-6s-8d; the impropriation worth £48 was held by Anthony Mansell, Esquire, under the Chapter of Gloucester. In 1771 (Bishop Barrington's *Llandaff Diocesan Book*) Llanblethian was valued at £90. In 1835 it was a vicarage worth (with its chapels) gross £280, and the patrons and impropriators were the Dean and Chapter of Gloucester. In 1966 the parish of Llanblethian with Cowbridge was grouped with the parishes of Llandough-by-Cowbridge and St. Mary Church to form one benefice.

The church consists of chancel, nave, south chapel with crypt, south porch and western tower containing six bells. The chancel arch is Victorian, done in a pointed 14th-century style with the inner arch corbelled out at the point of spring on two little demi-caps. The east window is Perpendicular, of three cinquefoiled lights with rectilinear tracery in the head surmounted by a drip-

stone with carved heads as label stops. The stained glass in the window is a memorial to the Reverend Isaac Davies Lewis (d. 1885). The theme of the window is a text taken from St. John's Gospel (XXI, 16) which describes how Jesus gave Simon Peter the chance to cancel out his three-fold denial with the three-times repeated question, 'Do you love me?' The text of the verse is inscribed in the two outer lights and the centre light shows Jesus giving Simon Peter the post-Resurrection commission, 'Feed my sheep'.

The beautifully-carved reredos of Austrian oak is a *tour de force* in imitation of the stone sculptures which were carved throughout the church in the 14th century. The reredos depicts a scene from the Supper at Emmaus on the altar panel, flanked by two towers with pinnacles which have foliated crockets and finials. This piece, which was carved by William Clarke of Llandaff, stretches the width of the chancel and is panelled throughout with the likeness of standard and flowing window tracery. The reredos was erected in the church in 1911 in memory of Frederick William Dunn (1844-1911), People's Warden of Llanblethian church for twenty years. He was instrumental in securing the restoration of the church in 1896 and of the tower in 1907.

The chancel is lit on the south side by two broad trefoil-headed lights and the stained glass depicts the figures of Faith and Hope and was erected in 1896 in memory of Edward Charles John Nicholl (d. 1893). In the north wall of the chancel is a round-headed Norman lancet: deeply splayed, depicting the figure of Charity; it was erected in 1896 to the memory of William Thomas (d. 1892), churchwarden from 1864 to 1890, and his wife, Jane (d. 1888). The chancel has an arch-braced roof with curved windbraces between the wallplate and purlins.

The original rood-loft door still remains in the north wall of the nave. It is of oak and of 15th-century character, divided by four moulded stiles, the whole surmounted by solid carving, in the middle of which is a tracery circle formerly with eight cusps. The spandrels contain roses and leaves which are carved in the solid. There is no projection on the outside wall, but on the inside there is a staircase which ascends within the thickness of the wall to the former rood-loft.

The windows on the north side of the nave comprise a pair of two-light windows with cinquefoiled heads and labelled. The stained glass in the north-west window depicts the figure of St. Nicholas, the patron saint of children in the left-hand light and the figure of St. Thomas Aquinas, the medieval philosopher and theologian, in the right-hand light. At the top of the right-hand light an open book has the title *Summa Theologicae*, St. Thomas Aquinas' celebrated work. St. Thomas holds a book in his hands bearing the Latin Inscription 'Deus et se et alia amat' (God loves other things besides himself.) The window was erected in 1930 in memory of the Reverend William Franklen Evans, M.A., Fellow of Jesus College, Oxford, and the last clerical headmaster of Cowbridge Grammar School from 1890 to 1918. It was erected by Dr. Idris D. Evans and the Reverend John Robert Evans from a design prepared by Messrs. James Powell & Sons, Whitefriars, London. The nave is lit on the south side by a two-light cinquefoiled-headed window with square label.

The brass eagle lectern was placed in the church in 1907 as a memorial to R.

The interior *(above)* prior to restoration in 1896
and today *(below)*

Thurstan Bassett of 'Crossways' who was one of those responsible for the restoration of the church in 1896. The pulpit is of unique design. It is composed of Penarth alabaster, red Forest of Dean stone and Quarella stone from Bridgend and the marble shafts or columns are made from red Irish marble. The panels on each of the facets are richly carved with blind tracery on a marble background and each has two trefoil-headed arches beneath an ogee arch which extends into the square head. The spandrels are filled with rectilinear-style tracery. The two arches of each panel are separated by slender pillars on the muntins, each with a fillet along the leading edge. At the head of each in the hollowed marble cornice a bunch of wild foliage splays out from the top rail. Beneath the pulpit there is a pentagonal stem abutting the north wall and the bottom rail is supported by five small marble shafts with circular capitals decorated with flowers and fruit and round moulded bases. The inscription on the pulpit reads: 'To the Glory of God and in memory of Thomas Edmondes, M.A. Honorary Canon of Llandaff, vicar of this parish 1835 to 1883. This pulpit is erected A.D. 1896 by his surviving sons, F.W. and F.Q. Edmondes.' It was designed by C. B. Fowler, architect and carved by William Clarke of Llandaff.

Numerous memorial monuments line the walls of the nave including a benefactions board listing the church benefactors headed by the distinguished Sir Leoline Jenkins who donated the tenor bell to the church in 1685. On the north wall of the nave is a marble monument to his father, Jenkin Llewellyn (d. January 1667) and his mother, Elizabeth (d. November, 1667). Their gravestone was rescued and the details copied by the Principal and Fellows of Jesus College, Oxford in 1763. Although this tablet was ostensibly erected to the parents of Sir Leoline Jenkins, it gives nevertheless a lengthy account of the son's honours, but says little of his parents. Also on the north wall of the nave is a white marble memorial tablet to the memory of William Bruce of Llanblethian House (d. 1768), father of the Reverend Thomas Bruce (d. 1790), rector of St. Nicholas. This monument was erected in the nave by his grandson John Bruce Pryce of Dyffryn. At the base of the tablet is a tierced shield. In the centre:—'In pale or a saltire gules on a chief of the last a martlet of the first' (Bruce). On the dexter side, quarterly: 1st quarter—'Sable a lion rampant argent'; 2nd quarter—'A chevron between three spearheads azure, embrued gules'; 3rd quarter—'Sable a chevron between three fleurs-de-lys or'; 4th quarter—'Or on a quarter gules two lions passant—guardant' (Lewis). On the sinister side 'Chequy gules and or, a fesse erminois' (Turberville). The family crest is 'A dexter arm in armour in bend grasping a sceptre all proper'. The nave has an arch-braced roof with two tiers of curved windbraces between the principal rafters and the purlins which are in the lower two of the three panels, into which the purlins divide each side of the roof.

On the south wall of the nave is a fine hatchment which has remained an enigma to antiquarians and local historians for many years. The arms are quarterly: first and fourth quarters 'Argent a chevron gules between three lions rampant sable' (Bourne); second and third quarters 'Azure three bars or on a chief three mascles of the last or' (Spurling/Stanford). The motto below is

'Nosce te ipsum' (Know thyself). The person for whom this funeral hatchment was made was descended from the marriage of a male Bourne and a female Spurling/Stanford, the female being an heraldic heiress (i.e. a woman with no brothers, or else brothers who died childless). In the 19th century many families used arms in perfectly good faith believing themselves entitled to do so when in reality the arms belonged to another family of the same name or indeed a different family altogether, because sometimes it happened that arms were passed down through a female line. Because of this, although the hatchment ought to represent a Bourne-Spurling/Stanford match, it may in fact have been made incorrectly in commemoration of some other family, perhaps one descended through a female line from the Bournes.

One of the most interesting features of the church is the south chapel with its crypt below. During the restoration of the church in 1896 the crypt was discovered under the south chapel. It is approached by a flight of nine steps leading down from the chapel floor. The chamber is lit by three small openings which had been covered up with earth on the outside. Inside it is arched with stonework from east to west giving a height of about two metres to the crown of the arch. The whole of the chamber was found to be filled with about 200 human skeletons, together with portions of stone coffin lids of 13th-century date. Writing in her book *Annals of South Glamorgan* Marianne Spencer Robertson said that the skeletons found in the crypt may have been those of soldiers who took part in the battle in 1405 between Owen Glyndwr's troops and King Henry IV's army at Stalling Down three miles away. However, 'Morien' writing in the *Western Mail* in 1896 thought that the crypt in the south transept was the ancient charnel house which was used for depositing the bones of the dead which the sexton might happen to throw up in the course of digging fresh graves. The skeletons were reverently re-buried in a large common grave in the churchyard. A priest's grave was also discovered in the crypt. It was covered with a sepulchral slab placed face downwards and contained the remains of one of the early priests, for on closer examination of the wall of the grave, a small recess was found in the south side containing a pewter chalice of Romanesque or Norman character. Other incised sepulchral slabs were also discovered at this time and were placed around the inside walls of the tower. One of them, a sepulchral slab of a lady of the early 14th century with a floriated cross in the centre, bears the following Norman-French inscription in Lombardic characters around the edge of the slab:—

> DAME: EME-T: LA: FEMME: WATER: TORIG:
> GIST: ICI D(EV): (D)EL: AME: EIT: MERCI.
> (Dame Eme--t, the wife of Walter Torig lies here,
> God have mercy on her soul.)

The transept (as it was supposed to be over this crypt) proved to be a chapel, for when the plaster was removed and the old-fashioned pews taken out, the outline of an altar with a 14th-century window above was brought to light. Also an arched sepulchral recessed tomb and a piscina with cinquefoiled canopy were discovered in the south wall. One of its jambs is constructed out of a small coffin lid which once possibly covered a stone coffin of a child.

During excavations for the laying of a drain around the south-west corner of the tower a stone effigy was found acting as a foundation to support the south-west tower buttress when the tower was added to the church in the latter part of the 15th century. The effigy is of Sutton stone and of 13th-century character, very similar to the effigy in the nave of Llantrithyd church viz. a civilian recumbent with hands clasped in prayer with a greyhound at the feet. This effigy was replaced in the recessed arch in the south chapel from where it had probably been removed four centuries earlier. The consecration stone of the church was also found in the crypt—a square block of stone with a cross very deeply cut into each side.

The south window of the chapel is of three trefoiled lights with sexfoils and a trefoil in the head, all cusped. It is surmounted by a slender dripstone. It is a 19th-century window done in a 14th-century Decorated style. In the east wall of the chapel is a two-light ogee-foliated window. The south chapel now houses the organ loft. The two-manual organ, built by Messrs. Griffen and Stroud of Bath at a cost of £250, together with the organ loft and choir screen, was presented to the church in 1907 by Lord Aberdare, in memory of his ancestors who settled at Great House in the parish of Llanblethian soon after the 1745 Rebellion. The choir screen of Austrian oak, carved by William Clarke of Llandaff, is square-framed of eleven bays including the doorway near the chancel. There is a cornice with moulded fillet enclosing a combination of patera and Tudor decoration. Each bay contains three lights between slender mullions with cinquefoiled heads beneath ogee arches. The cusping in the tracery beneath ends in little multi-lobed flowers. There are mouchettes and typical 14th-century-style piercing in the spandrels. The lower stage of the screen is plain boarded. The other part of the south chapel is divided off by a pitch pine screen and acts as a choir and clergy vestry. Above the east window of the south chapel is a sundial inscribed with the date 1811 and below, the wall is reinforced by a massive buttress. On the west wall of the south chapel is a memorial monument to Hugh Robert Entwistle (d. 1867), J. P. and Deputy Lieutenant of Glamorgan. Below the tablet are the arms of the family 'Argent on a bend engrailed sable three mullets of the first with a mullet for difference'. Crest:—'A hand fesswise couped above the wrist proper holding a fleur-de-lys erect or' with the family motto 'Par ce signe à Agincourt' (By this sign at Agincourt).

The large south porch is built in the Perpendicular style and the outer pointed arch is surmounted by a dripstone and decorated with crockets and pinnacles. Grotesque gargoyles leer from either side of the porch. The inner south doorway is obtusely pointed and the inside walls of the porch display several interesting memorials above the stone benches. The wall of division between the south chapel and the porch has soffits of slightly-curved widespreading arches springing from three stone corbels on the eastern edge of the ceiling which may have been constructed to strengthen the wall at that point. The modern timber roof has a crenellated wallplate. On the arch of the south doorway are vertical grooves. Local tradition has it that these marks were the results of the gentry sharpening their swords as they entered or left the church. The more likely explanation is that these grooves were caused by workmen sharpening their scythes and tools on the freestone.

The tower opens to the nave by a plain pointed Perpendicular arch whose jambs continue from the floor without interruption. An inner arch springs in the head from the jambs of the other arch from which it is corbelled out on two grotesque 15th-century figures who appear to guard the entrance to the tower. Beneath the tower stands the Norman tub-shaped font carved from Sutton stone, which rests on a circular base on a square plinth. Around the walls of the tower are several interesting sepulchral slabs placed there in 1896 after their discovery in the crypt. One dating from the 13th century has a curious cross, the arms of which end in circles.

The tower is a massive Perpendicular structure some twenty-four metres in height and was built by Anne Neville, wife of Richard III in 1477. It consists of three main stages divided by stringcourses and reinforced by five stages of clasping buttresses. The belfry is lit on each face by a three-light window with pointed head, the mullions of which intersect as Y-tracery. This is repeated in miniature in the decorative stonework in the head of each light above the transoms. The spaces beneath are crossed by thin stonework strips of openwork forming quatrefoils. The battlement is surmounted with corner pinnacles and displays two grotesque gargoyles at the corners of its south face. The south wall of the tower is further lit by a window with pointed arch and above it is a small aperture. The staircase to the belfry now opens into the churchyard by a door in the north wall of the tower. The original doorway on the inside remains but is now built-in. The west window of the tower is a typical three-light Perpendicular window with rectilinear tracery lights. The round heads to the main lights within slightly-pointed tracery owe more to the 14th century. The window depicts the figures of St. David, St. George and St. Bleddian and was erected in 1920 from a design by Robert J. Newbery of London as a memorial to those men of the parish who fell in the Great War, 1914-1918. The names of the sixteen men are inscribed on a marble tablet on the west wall of the nave and adjacent to it is another tablet commemorating the three men of the parish who gave their lives in the last war. The west doorway has several concave mouldings but in appearance is earlier in date than the tower.

The tower contains a ring of six bells which were restored and rehung by Carr's of Smethwick when the tower was restored in 1907. The cost was borne by Mrs. Frances Ann Caroline Brereton as a memorial to her parents, Birt Wyndham Rous Jenner (d. 1863) and Ann Jenner. Prior to the restoration of the tower in 1907 the bells had not been rung for twenty-two years, because of their dangerous condition. The six bells bear the following inscriptions:—

No. 1 THE REV'D MR. WM MILES, VICAR TR 1769
CARR'S OF SMETHWICK
RECAST ME
1907.

No.2 MR. EVAN IENKINS BENEFACTOR T 🔔 R 1769

No. 3 WM THOMAS ESQR. IOHN WILLIAMS WARDENS
T 🔔 R 1769

No. 4 PEACE AND GOOD NEIGHBOURHOOD EE 🔔 WE 🔔
1726 o
(o is the imprint of the obverse of a William III crown)

No. 5 NOAH NEAL NEWCOME VICAR IOHN THOMAS CURATE
IOHN WILLIAMS & IOHN THOMAS CH: WARDENS
W 🔔 E 1746

Tenor THIS BELL WAS GIVEN (1) (1) (2) ANNO DOM 1685
BY SR LEOLINE JENKINS
(1 is obverse and (2) reverse of William III crown)
AND NOW MAINTAIN'D BY HIS BROTHER
EVAN. EVAN EVANS 🔔 🔔 (3);
((3) is obverse of Charles II half-crown)

(Firebell) probably a recast Sanctus bell has inscription in two lines:
EX DONO EV: IENKINS DE MAINDY (1)
GEN: QVI OB: 70 APRILIS 1702 (2)
(1) and (2) are the obverse and reverse of a Queen Anne shilling.

The tenor bell bears the date 1685, but Dr. Lemuel J. Hopkin-James, the clerical local historian, said that it must obviously be of a later date since the William III crown of which it bears the impression was first struck in 1695. The initials TR stand for Thomas Rudhall, bellfounder of Gloucester, who cast bells between 1760 and 1783, and the initials EE, WE stand for Evan Evans and William Evans, bellfounders of Chepstow, who cast bells between 1718 and 1727.

The church was restored in the years 1896-1897 when the many interesting discoveries in the south chapel described above were made. The work of restoration consisted of the removal of the old square pews and replacing them with new ones, laying down new floors, opening out the south chapel and the removal of plaster ceilings from the nave, south chapel and chancel exposing to view the original late medieval oak roofs which were carefully restored. The original low chancel arch was removed and replaced by the present one. The hatchment which hung on the south side of the chancel arch was removed to its present position on the south wall of the nave. A new doorway was opened up in the south chapel and the plaster was removed from the walls of the church. The old stonework was completely repointed. During the restoration some wall paintings were found on the north wall of the nave which represented cinquefoils, a scourge from which blood dripped, a curious saw and a sword. These emblems, which were probably symbolic of the Passion of Our Lord, were unfortunately destroyed when the plaster was removed. Three new stained glass windows were erected in the chancel and a new window was inserted in the north wall of the nave. The present stone pulpit was also placed in the church. The restoration was carried out at a cost of £1,200 by W. A. James of Cowbridge according to designs and specifications of C. B. Fowler, architect of Cardiff. The church was reopened for divine service after restoration on Wednesday, 5th May, 1897 by the Rt. Reverend Dr. Richard Lewis, Bishop of Llandaff.

In 1907 the tower was completely restored at a cost of £550. The buttresses were replaced, the four floors repaired and the foundations strengthened. As mentioned above, the peal of six bells was restored and rehung and the old second bell was recast into a new treble. A new pipe organ was installed in the south chapel and a new brass eagle lectern was erected in the nave.

On the green to the south-east of the church is the stump of the medieval churchyard cross which rests on a pedestal on three steps. David Jones of Wallington, (1834-1890), the antiquarian and genealogist, was born at Llanblethian. He copied all the older inscriptions in the churches and churchyards in Glamorgan and made sketches of many of the parish churches.

From 1917 to 1934 the vicar of Llanblethian was the Reverend Dr. Lemuel John Hopkin-James who did much valuable research into the history of Llanblethian and his other parishes of Cowbridge and Welsh St. Donat's, the results of which he published in his book entitled *Old Cowbridge* in 1922. In 1930 Dr. Hopkin-James was made Chancellor of Llandaff Cathedral.

Although the name of Evan Jenkins, brother of Sir Leoline Jenkins, is only mentioned on two bells he proved to be an even more generous benefactor of Llanblethian church than his brother. Income from the Evan Jenkins Charity Trust amounting to £30,000 has already funded extensive restoration work on the tower. The church building will therefore be maintained without any financial constraints or anxiety to the parishioners of Llanblethian in the foreseeable future.

The church plate includes a silver flagon whose lid is inscribed 'Lamblethian Parish' and round the base 'the gift of Hester Wilkins, widow, to the Parish of Lamblethian in the county of Glamorgan, 1739', hall-marked 1738. A silver paten is inscribed on the underside 'Ex dono a Bowens ux. T. Wilkins Gen. Ao. 1714'. The registers date from 1661.

Llancarfan Church

The parish church of Llancarfan is dedicated to St. Cadoc who founded a monastery here in the 6th century. The original Norman church was replaced by the present structure which was built during the 13th and 14th centuries. The church of Llancarfan was given to the Abbey of St. Peter, Gloucester, by Robert Fitz-Hamon circa 1107. In the years 1149-1188 the Abbey put the church and its appurtenances (except the tithes of Treguff which belonged to Tewkesbury) out to farm for £3 per annum, first to Urban, then to Radalph, Archdeacons of Llandaff. The former was expected to find chaplains to do the service.

In 1254 (Taxation of Norwich) the church was valued at £20. Since Llancarfan church was appropriated to Gloucester Abbey the Abbot of Gloucester was rector of the church and as rector was responsible for the repair of the chancel. Between 1284 and 1307 John, Abbot of Gloucester instructed Nicholas, who was Prior of the Gloucester dependency at Ewenny, to put in hand the repair of the chancel and arrange for 'any good workmen for the said work at piece work.' The earliest recorded incumbent of the church was Gilbert de Kyrlion (Caerleon) priest, who was presented to the church of Llancarfan on the 1st February, 1287. In 1291 (*Taxatio Ecclesiastica*) the church was worth £10 only but by this time the chaplains had been replaced by perpetual vicars and the vicarage was worth five marks. In 1535 (*Valor Ecclesiasticus*) the Rectory of Llancarfan (held by Gloucester Abbey) was valued at £12-6s-8d and the vicarage at £9-3s-0d per annum. At the Dissolution of the chantries under Edward VI (1547-1553) ¾ of an acre of meadow and ¼ acre of arable land, valued at 2s per annum, which had been left to the church for keeping the nave in repair, were alienated. In 1563 the vicar was resident. In 1603 the vicarage was worth £20 and the impropriation valued at £60 was held by Arnold Bassett, Esquire, from the Chapter of Gloucester. In 1771 (Bishop Barrington's *Llandaff Diocesan Book*) the living was worth £70; the Crown was the patron and the incumbent was the Reverend Richard Bassett. In 1835 it was a vicarage worth gross £185; the Crown was the patron and the Dean and Chapter were the Impropriators. Llancarfan church was joined with Llantrithyd church in 1972 to form one benefice.

The church consists of chancel, nave, south aisle, a chapel annexed to the south aisle (known as the Raglan Chapel), south porch and embattled western tower containing four bells. The chancel arch is Transitional Norman, pointed

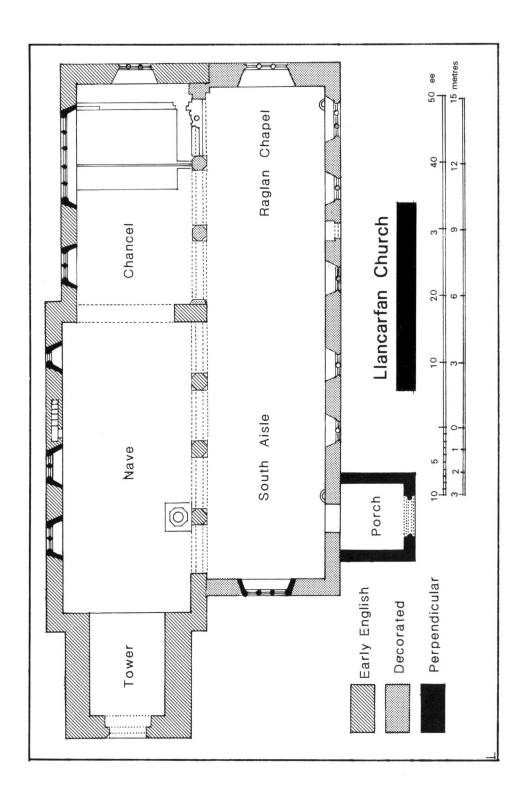

Llancarfan Church

Tower

Nave

Chancel

South Aisle

Raglan Chapel

Porch

Early English

Decorated

Perpendicular

10 5 0 10 20 3 40 50 ee

3 2 1 0 1 3 6 9 12 15 metres

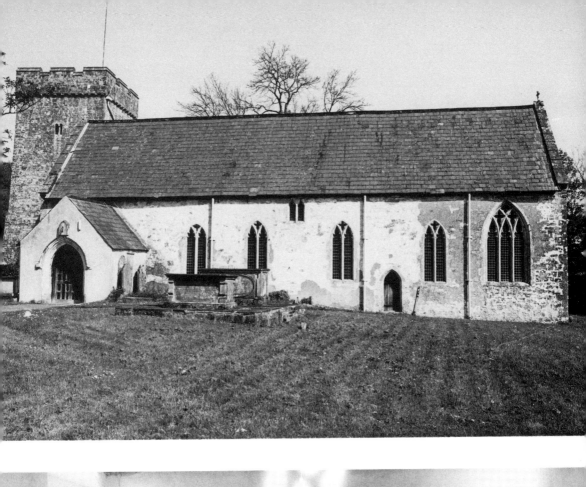

and very wide and the square imposts are decorated with an early form of dogtooth ornament in hollow squares. The east window is modern, of three pointed lights with intersecting tracery forming three quatrefoils above. The chancel is spacious and in the north wall are two windows, one Decorated of two cinquefoiled lights with a quatrefoil in the apex; the other is square-headed, of five lights beneath a depressed tracery arch in the head with quatrefoils and trefoils in the spandrels. Each light is cinquefoil-headed beneath a depressed arch and circular tracery lights enclosed within pointed arches. The mullions are continued straight through the head, with quatrefoils occupying the rather odd shapes resulting between this arrangement of tracery. The mullions and tracery of this window were partly damaged during the English Civil War in the 17th century when a fanatical Puritan farmer named Bush is said to have battered down the freestone of this window in an anti-papist outburst crying 'Down with the great whore of Babylon'.

Below this window is a smaller round-headed recess which may have once contained an effigy. Let into the wall under the arch is a tablet in the form of an open book with scrollwork and surmounted by a winged cherub-head inscribed:— 'Here lyeth the body of Thomas Morgan, Minister who dyed May the 20th, 1666.' Thomas Morgan was a noted pluralist. He was also vicar of Colwinston from 1644 to 1666, rector of Llandough-by-Cowbridge from 1616 to 1666, rector of Llandow from 1640 to 1660 and Canon of Fairwater in Llandaff Cathedral. He was ejected from his living under the Commonwealth but was later restored. In a recess in the north wall of the chancel is a marble memorial tablet surmounted by a winged cherub-head bearing the Latin inscription:— 'Infra inhumanatum corpus Milonis Willott de Lancadle obiit XVI Avgvst An Dom 1690.' (Below is buried the body of Miles Willott of Llancadle who died 16th August, 1690.) Beneath the Latin inscription is the text 'Blessed are the dead which die in the Lord' and beneath that is rudely inscribed the initials M.W. and the date 1695. A brass plaque on the north wall of the chancel commemorates Mary Catherine (d. 1891), wife of John Bilbie and eldest daughter of the Reverend Alfred Thomas Hughes, vicar of Llancarfan, who was interred in Highgate Cemetery, London. The chancel which was rebuilt in the 13th century, is divided from the Raglan Chapel by an arcade of three bays, a continuation of the nave arcade, but the arches are of wider span. The piers are octagonal with flared capitals of Decorated date. There is a fine carved oak screen in a decayed state now placed as a reredos near the east wall. It has nine spaces with canopies of delicate tabernacle work, undergroined and set on a modern stone base. Each canopy has a vaulted, ribbed head cut in the solid and shows traces of rich colour decoration. From this project three small canopies also vaulted and two-sided, having round arches with delicate drop tracery and above ogee-crocketed canopy heads or finials. It is of 15th-century date and appears to have been placed in its present position at the beginning of the 19th century. It is generally believed to have been either the screen of the rood-loft or to have been made out of the canopies of medieval choir-stalls imported into Llancarfan from a much larger church or cathedral. In the south side of the

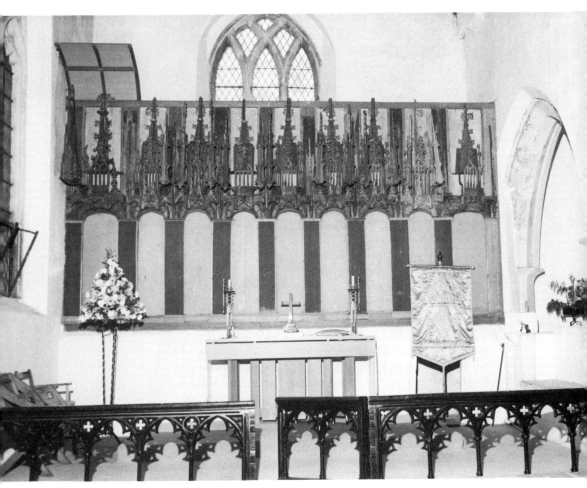

Wooden reredos in chancel

chancel is a stone bench or rude sedile and piscina with moulded circular bowl. The chancel has a cradle roof of 15th-century date which was restored in 1888. Part of the chancel roof between the chancel and the Raglan Chapel is supported on stone corbels.

The door and staircase to the rood-loft remain in the north wall, the staircase being lit by a diminutive square window. The corbels, which once supported the loft, remain, one each side of the chancel arch and a third corbel is still *in situ* on one of the pillars of the south arcade. In the north wall corresponding to the rood-loft place are two square-headed windows. The lower window is a single light, cinquefoiled and the other placed directly above it near the roof is of similar design but of two lights. These were obviously intended to light the rood screen and the rood gallery. The two westernmost windows of the nave are of peculiar construction and are probably early Perpendicular. They are of two lights, cinquefoil-headed with a cinquefoil in the apex. A black and white marble monument on the south side of the chancel arch commemorates Amelia (d. 1850), wife of the Reverend David Morgan, vicar of Llancarfan from 1837 to 1870, and their daughter, Amelia Alice (d. 1855).

Each manor had its respective seat in the church which was recorded on a metal plaque let into the wall by the side of the seat; thus the one allotted to Whitewell has this inscription on the plaque close to a certain seat on the north side of the nave: 'Whitewell seat O.R. 1691.' Apparently the Llanveithin seat was nearer the chancel arch on the same side but its plaque has been removed. The oak pulpit has a moulded cornice with a row of four-leaf flower decoration. Beneath are four square panels of linenfold pattern decoration and below a plain centre rail are another four rectangular panels of the same design, the whole resting on a stone base. The one-manual organ, built by P. G. Phipps, organ builder of Oxford, stands at the west end of the nave. A brass plaque on the organ records that Mrs. Doris Watts retired in 1978 'after 70 years of faithful and loyal service as church organist.'

The arcade of the nave to the south aisle has four sharply-pointed Early English arches springing from square pillars with broadly chamfered angles with stops at their lower extremities. The arches are plain without mouldings. The five columns supporting the arches are ornamented at the four corners of their respective square capitals with crude carvings (each divided into four scallops). The central pillar has four human heads, one at each corner. Two of these have crowned heads and cross-strapped face-pieces. The other two faces are clean-shaven. The fourth pillar has two round bunches of grapes at each corner, while the fifth is built into the west wall and shows only two corners which display two faces with leering expressions, slanting eyes and protruding tongues. The nave has a 15th-century cradle roof. The tower opens to the nave with a plain pointed arch upon corbels.

The Raglan Chapel, which adjoins the chancel has, like the rest of the building, a cradle roof plastered between the ribs and ornamented with bosses which extends the whole length of the south aisle. In the chapel lie buried the Raglans of Carnllwyd and on the wallplate high above the south-east window is a small wooden figure holding a shield bearing the arms of the Raglan family: 'Party per pale or and gules three lions counter-changed'. The east window is of three trefoiled lights surmounted by three quatrefoils shaped as daggers. The chapel has on the south side two windows of Decorated date. One is identical to the east window and the other is of two trefoiled lights surmounted by a quatrefoil similar to the windows of the south aisle. In the sill of the easternmost window is a piscina and in the south wall of the chapel is a priest's door with pointed arch. The chapel is divided from the chancel by a tombstone which at some time has been removed from its original position and placed so as to form the back of the sedile in the chancel. It bears the following inscription:— 'Here underneath this stone lyeth interred the body of Henry Jones, clerk, vicar of Lancarvan and rector of Porthkerrick who departed this life the Twentieth day of September, in the yeare of our Lord God 1686.' The south chapel was restored in 1961 in memory of Thomas Evans (d. 1953) vicar of Llancarfan (1937-1946) by his wife, Mary Elizabeth Evans.

The Raglan Chapel is separated from the south aisle by a carved oak Perpendicular screen now in a very decayed state. The ends look as if they have been cut to fit the present space and it was once clearly connected to something above, probably a rood-loft. The screen is square-framed, the opening in the centre and there are five lights on each side. The head beam is plain on the east side but on the west is well-moulded with ogees and half-rounds. Beneath the headbeam the arrangement is of three bays, with the heavier stiles each side of the opening and a multifoiled depressed ogee arch carved in the solid springing from little moulded corbels on the stiles with heavy crockets on the upper edge. Muntins and stiles are reeded and minutely decorated above the collars. There are cinquefoil-headed lights and above all minor openwork tracery lights in the head. The panels beneath the centre rail are plain to the east but have applied blind tracery to the west: cinquefoils beneath ogee arches with representation of flowing tracery in the spandrels. On the west face of each wainscot muntin is a small buttress planted on. This screen is believed to have been part of the original screen of the former rood-loft.

In the south aisle near the door is a medieval chest crudely fashioned in oak with iron bands which once held the church valuables and in the south face of one of the arcade pillars is a small modern safe which contains the reserved sacrament. The south aisle with its fine 15th-century cradle roof and splendid series of Decorated windows was widened in the 14th century and lengthened to form the Raglan Chapel. In the south wall are three fine windows of Decorated date each of two trefoiled lights surmounted by quatrefoils. A small two-light window with ogee-foliated trefoil head set high near the roof and opposite a similar window in the north wall of the nave suggests the presence of a rood-loft which traversed nave and south aisle or two rood-lofts, one to serve the nave and the other the south aisle. The window was obviously inserted to light the gallery of a rood-loft. In the sill of one of the windows of the south aisle is a fragment of Sutton stone of pre-Norman date which was found under the chancel during restoration. This stone has an interlaced ribbon pattern rudely carved. It is thought to be a fragment of a late 9th-century pillar-cross.

On the south wall is the only fresco which survives. It takes the form of a large painted panel which contains the text of the Apostles' Creed. Adjacent to the south door is a 12th-century tub-shaped holy-water stoup with roll-moulding. The font has an nonagonal bowl scalloped with crude five-leaved foliage on the underside and separated from the octagonal stem by a plain collar. It is set on a modern plinth. In the west wall of the south aisle is a Perpendicular window of three cinquefoiled lights with panel tracery in the head.

The south porch is of early Perpendicular date. The inner doorway is Early English and the round mouldings spring from the walls with the outer roll actually dying into the masonry. Over the inner doorway of the porch is a niche which once held a statuette of the patron saint of the church, St. Cadoc

(St. Cattwg). Each side of the doorway is a fluted conical feature shaped like a capital but the flat top suggests that these are pedestals. The outer doorway has a hood mould with square label stops with blank shields. The shield on the west side, retained until recently traces of the Raglan arms. The interior of the porch has an open ribbed roof with seven pairs of principals which are original but the woodwork between these has been replaced by modern timber. On either side of the porch is stone seating now covered with wood. Above the porch is a plain sundial, now much defaced.

The tower is square, broad and low with embattled parapet resting on small corbels. There are no buttresses or stringcourse. The north face has a single window ogee-headed and trefoiled and there is a single opening on the south face with a two-light round-headed window at a higher level. The west doorway has a pointed arch and above it is a modern two-light belfry window. Although the tower was constructed in the 14th century most of its present structure dates back only to 1877 when it was substantially rebuilt. The tower houses a ring of four bells, two of them were originally cast in 1646, one in 1664 and one in 1690. They were all recast in 1890 by Llewellins & James of Bristol and their original inscriptions were recast in facsimile. The bells bear the following inscriptions:–

Treble   G.D. I.H. 1646. T.S. A.T. HUGHES VICAR 1890
           LLEWELLINS & JAMES BRISTOL.

No. 2.   THOMAS BASSET GENT IOHN THOMAS GENT.
           CRESTOVER IENKINS C W'DENS.
           A.T. HUGHES VICAR 1890
           LLEWELLINS & JAMES BRISTOL.

No. 3.   SIR THOMAS LEWIS KNIGHT O IOHN THOMAS
           CHRISTOPHER IENKINS:C:W O 1664. I.P.
           RECAST IN MEMORY OF ANN PRICE CLARK LEWIS
           BY G.T.C. 1890 LLEWELLINS & JAMES BRISTOL.
           A.T. HUGHES VICAR.

No. 4.   IACOP GIBON GEORG MATHEW
           CHVRCH WARDENS + EE 🔔 🔔
           A.T. HUGHES VICAR
           LLEWELLINS & JAMES BRISTOL.

The treble bell was originally cast in 1646 by Thomas Stone, an itinerant bellfounder who cast bells in various churches from 1627 to 1655. Bells no. 2 and 3 were originally cast in 1664 by John Pennington of Monmouth whose trade mark was the obverse and reverse of a Jewish shekel and present on these bells. Bell no. 4 was cast between 1690 and 1695 by Evan Evans I (1686–1724) of Chepstow.

By the third quarter of the 19th century the interior of the parish church was in an advanced state of dilapidation. The neglect of the fabric over the years could partly be attributed to the absence of a resident gentry with sufficient resources to finance the repair work which was so badly needed. This was pointed out by the Reverend Alfred Hughes, the vicar who in 1875 made a general public appeal for funds to carry out a thorough restoration.

The church was restored in the years 1877-1878 at a cost of £690 and during this restoration all the colour-wash was removed from the inside of the church walls which were found to have been stencilled with stars. On the wall of the south aisle, just inside the south door, a large stencilled figure of the Virgin Mary was uncovered but was painted out with whitewash because it was considered to be Roman Catholic. The tower and bells were restored in 1890 at a cost of £570. There was yet another restoration of the church in 1907 involving the expenditure of over £300 on the tower roof and weather-proofing the building. Also a trench was dug around the church to lay down drain pipes to cure dampness in the church, and in digging the trench two beautiful arches in the south wall of the Raglan Chapel, one each side of the south doorway, were discovered. Although the object of these arches below ground level was obviously apparent, F. R. Kempson, the diocesan architect, who supervised the restoration of the church, was of the opinion that these arches had been built to strengthen the wall since the foundation at that spot was faulty. The church was reopened for divine service after restoration on Tuesday 5th November, 1907 by the Bishop of Llandaff, the Rt. Reverend Dr. Joshua Pritchard Hughes.

Like all the churches in the Vale of Glamorgan Llancarfan had a churchyard cross. It was probably broken by Cromwell's soldiers in the 17th century and the remains which stood on the south side of the church were removed entirely in 1815 to make room for a grave.

It is extraordinary that, with the exception of the stone of interlaced work in the south aisle, there are no early Christian inscribed stones or otherwise to be found at Llancarfan such as exist elsewhere in the Vale of Glamorgan on sites of early Christian foundations.

Edward Williams, whose bardic name was Iolo Morganwg, was born in Penon, a hamlet in the parish. He travelled the Principality collecting ancient manuscripts from castles, manor houses and farms. He left 70 volumes which are now in the London Library and the British Library. He died in Flemingston in 1826.

The church plate includes an Elizabethan silver chalice with its paten cover, now gilt with 'L.C.' 1576 engraved on the cover and on the foot of the cup are the letters E.W. and W.F. Also a silver paten or bread-dish of 18th-century type standing on three feet inscribed on the underside 'James Thomas, Francis Morgan, churchwardens.' The registers date from 1618.

Llandough-by-Cowbridge Church

The parish church of Llandough-by-Cowbridge is dedicated to St. Dochau (also known as St. Cyngar) who founded a small church or cell here in the 6th century. The church stands within the precincts of Llandough Castle, home of Le Waleis or Walsh family in the Middle Ages. The church dates from the early part of the 13th century and is built in the Early English style, but the architectural features of the interior are typically First Pointed Victorian Gothic, introduced during the restoration of the church in 1869.

The church was valued at 4 marks in 1254 (Taxation of Norwich). It defies identification in the *Taxatio Ecclesiastica* of 1291. In 1427 the manor of Llandough and St. Mary Church with the advowson of the churches was confirmed to Elizabeth, widow of Robert Walsh, late Lord thereof. This property passed by marriage in 1429 to the Van family who sold it to Sir William Thomas of Raglan in 1444 and in 1456 it was conveyed to Sir William Herbert. The church was a Rectory worth £5-7s-1d in 1535 (*Valor Ecclesiasticus*) and in 1536 the manor, lands and advowson of Llandough church were sold to Sir Edward Carne of Ewenny. It had a resident parson in 1563. In 1677 the manor, together with the advowson of the church, passed by marriage to the Mansel family of Margam, in whose possession they remained for over two centuries. In 1771 (Bishop Barrington's Primary Visitation of the Diocese) the living was worth £60. In 1797 at the instigation of Thomas Mansel Talbot of Margam Abbey, the then patron of the livings of Llandough and St. Mary Church, the two parishes were united by episcopal decree to form one benefice. In 1835 when C. R. M. Talbot was the patron, it was a Rectory which went with St. Mary Church, and was valued with it at gross £263. In 1966 the benefice of Llandough with St. Mary Church was joined with Llanblethian and Cowbridge to form a grouped benefice.

The church consists of chancel, nave, south porch and a western turret containing two bells. The chancel arch, which dates from 1869, is pointed and has heavy moulded bell caps resting on circular bases on octagonal plinths. The capitals have marble shafts decorated mid-way by triple-roll annulets. The east window has a depressed arch enclosing three trefoil-headed lights. The centre light, considerably taller than the flanking two, continues well into the head of the arch, and the spaces either side are pierced with quatrefoils giving the effect of plate tracery. The window is surmounted externally by a dripstone. The stained glass in the window shows Christ in Majesty.

The chancel is lit on the south side by three trefoil-headed lancets which depict the figures of St. Stephen, St. Christopher and St. Francis. In the south-east corner of the sanctuary is a trefoil-headed pillar piscina (although not free-standing) which includes a credence shelf and the feature below takes the form of an engaged shaft with simply-moulded capital and base. The sedilia provide double seating for the priest and clerk beneath little offset canopies whose arches are returned above quarter-round mouldings on the outside walls. The seats are stepped downwards towards the west and divided by a characteristically shaped upright.

Set into a slab of local limestone in the floor on the north side of the altar, still in an excellent state of preservation, is a sepulchral brass of Wenllian Walsche of Llandough Castle. The black letter inscription in Latin reads: 'Hic iacet Wenllan Walsche quonda uxor Walteri Moreton que obiit XXV° die Decembris Anno dni Millmo. CCCC°. XXVII°. cuius aie ppiciet deus. Amen.' (Here lies Wen-llian Walsche, formerly the wife of Walter Moreton, who died December 25th A.D. 1427, on whose soul may God have mercy. Amen.) Above the inscription is the figure of a woman wearing a horned head-dress, veil and a kirtle whose close-fitting sleeves are visible at the wrists. The gown laced below the neck has a large turned-down collar and high waist with full sleeves edged with fur at the wrists. On the left sleeve is a lightly-engraved graffito in the form of a figure-of-eight pattern, and on the skirt another figure-of-eight pattern combined with a knot pattern is discernible. Her hands are clasped in the attitude of prayer. The stone into which the brass is set is incised with an ogee crocketed canopy and has an indent for a shield.

The Walsche *alias* Walsh family settled in Glamorgan at the beginning of the 13th century, holding Llandough where they built a castle of which a fragment remains incorporated in a later house. Walter Moreton, husband of Wenllian Walsche, was Constable of Cardiff Castle in the 1420s.

Beneath the altar lie the remains of the Reverend Edward Williams, rector of Llandough (1708-1723). A door with pointed archway leads to the vestry built on the north side of the chancel. The vestry is divided from the chancel by a triple pointed open arcade above moulded bell caps, resting on a double arrangement of marble shafts. The moulding of the caps is continued across the walling between, but the feature is open below and the circular bases rest on octagonal plinths. This feature is coeval with the chancel arch and sedilia. The chancel has a wagon roof formed by a series of closely-set arch braces, the portion over the sanctuary is panelled. The chancel is divided from the nave by a low stone screen pierced by two apertures in the shape of quatrefoils and fitted with a pair of wrought iron gates.

The circular pulpit is an oddity even by Victorian standards. An arcade of trefoil-headed arches is sandwiched between a strongly-moulded rim and a central string. Beneath are bands of incised neo-Norman decoration—a double row of zig-zag between enclosed band of hollows. A door with pointed arch leads to the rood-loft staircase concealed in a projection in the north wall of the nave. Below the upper doorway of the rood-loft is a trefoil-headed window set quite low down and deeply splayed. A square-headed window high in the south-east corner of the nave presumably lit the rood-loft.

The other windows of the nave comprise a two-light trefoil-headed window and a single trefoil lancet on the south side and at the west end is a pair of trefoil-headed lights high in the west gable. There are no windows in the north wall of the nave. The trefoil lancet in the south-west wall is original and contains stained glass depicting Christ as the Good Shepherd. The stained glass in the south-east window depicts the figures of St. Mary and St. John and is a memorial to Francis Edmund Stacey (d. 1885) and his wife, Theodosia (d. 1893) of Llandough Castle. The window was erected 'in token of grateful love' by their nephews. The arms of the Stacey family are emblazoned on the brass plaques beneath the window. The one-manual organ on the south side of the nave, built by the 'Positive' Organ Co. Ltd., was installed in the church about 1912.

On the south wall of the nave is a remarkable and much quoted memorial to three young members of the Basset family. It is ingeniously set out and reads thus:–

Underneth the next adjoininge seat

Lyes

John	William	& Friswith	Basset
dyed 17	dyed 3	dyed 16	being 3 of
March	March	Aprill	Charles
1713	1713	1713	Basset's
Aged 23	Aged 18	Aged 12	children

William dyed first & lyes outmost of all

John lyes in ye middle & Friswith next ye wall

We are not told what calamity befell these grown children of the same family who died within weeks of each other. Also on the south wall is a Baroque marble memorial tablet surmounted with a winged skull signifying not death but the passage to immortality through death. It commemorates the Reverend William Lewis (d. 1715) chaplain for 30 years to the Mansel family of Margam Abbey.

The nave has an ancient cradle roof of solid oak timbers. The plain octagonal bowl and stem of the 14th-century font rests on a square base above a two-tier circular plinth with a projecting step. The underside of the bowl is chamfered to meet the stem where the only attempt at decoration is provided by triangular projections as exaggerated spurs on four of the sides. In the recess in the south wall near the door is a circular holy-water stoup. On the north wall of the nave is a framed rubbing of the memorial brass of Wenllian Walsche. There are several memorial monuments on the west wall of the nave to members of the family of Lynche-Blosse of Llandough Castle, and one to Richard Morgan, Esquire, of Llandough Castle (d. 1843), a former deputy-lieutenant and magistrate for the County of Glamorgan. The south porch has an obtuse arch to its outer doorway which is surmounted by a dripstone with mutilated carved

...derneth the next adjoininge seat
Ly e s
John william & frifwith Basset
dyed 17 | dyed 3 | dyed 16 | being 3 of
march | march | APRill | charles
1713 | 1713 | 1713 | Basset's
ed 23 | Aged 18 | Aged 12 | children

...lived first & lyes out...nost of all
... or in y middle of frifwith next y wall

Basset memorial

heads as stops and a grotesque carving. The inner south doorway of the church has a more rounded arch and the original woodwork in the roof displays floriated bosses and cornice and a central rib carved with the head of Christ. Stone benches line the sides of the porch. The western turret contains two bells which are devoid of any inscription or bellfounder's marks. They appear to be of 18th-century date and were rehung in 1912 by Llewellins & James of Bristol.

In 1862 during the incumbency of the Reverend Edward Powell Nicholl, plans were drawn up by Messrs. Prichard and Seddon, the diocesan architects, to reseat and improve the church. A grant of £40 was made in that year by the Incorporated Church Building Society towards the cost of the work and a Faculty for restoration was obtained from the Bishop of Llandaff in 1863. However, for some reason or other, probably lack of funds (St. Mary Church had only recently been restored in 1862 at a cost of £650) the work did not proceed. In 1867 the rector, the Reverend Stephen Nicholl, who had only recently been inducted to the living, set about restoring the church. But he was unaware that plans had already been drawn up to that effect and that a faculty had been granted. Also he was unaware of the grant of £40 from the Incorporated Church Building Society. Consequently he had forfeited this grant because the work had not been carried out within the prescribed period and was contrary in some respects to the directions laid down by the Society.

The church was eventually restored in 1869 by the architect Charles Buckeridge, a pupil of Sir George Gilbert Scott. Sir Stephen Glynne, that indefatigable church-crawler, visited Llandough church on the 18th August, 1869, while the church was undergoing restoration. He stated that the original chancel arch was small and narrow and had now been replaced by a new lofty, pointed one on marble shafts. A new stone screen had been placed across it. The chancel roof had been entirely replaced but the woodwork of the cradle roof of the nave was found to be in perfect condition and remained untouched in the restored church. Prior to the restoration of the church the nave was lit by a square-headed Perpendicular insertion which was replaced by the present two-light trefoil-headed light with rounded relieving arch. A new vestry had been added on the north side of the chancel and a modern pillar piscina and sedilia were placed in the sanctuary. The east window had been renewed and a new stone pulpit erected in the north-east corner of the nave. A large window in the south of the chancel was removed and replaced by three lancet windows. The cost of the restoration amounted to £862.

From 1759 until his death in 1797 the rector of Llandough was the famous Welsh lexicographer the Reverend John Walters. He was also vicar of St. Hilary, chaplain to the Mansel family at Margam and in 1795 he became a Prebendary of Llandaff. He was the author of the English-Welsh dictionary of which the first issue was printed at Llandovery but published in Cowbridge in April, 1770. Parts 1-14 (A-ST.) were printed at Cowbridge from 1770 to 1783 and the remainder was printed in London in 1794. It was in connection with this work that the first printing press was established in Glamorgan, Walters' printer Rhys Thomas, moving from Llandovery to Cowbridge, so as to be within a few miles of the compiler. Rhys Thomas and his family lie buried in Llandough churchyard; his son Caleb in 1780, his wife Esther in 1782 and Rhys himself in 1790. Walters' *Dissertation on the Welsh Language* was published at Cowbridge in 1771 and was probably the first book ever printed in Glamorgan.

Three members of the Nicholl family of Merthyr Mawr were rectors of Llandough and St. Mary Church in the 19th century; they were Edward Powell Nicholl (1858-64), his brother, Stephen Henry Fox Nicholl (1867-1898), and the latter's son, Henry Stephen Nicholl (1899-1917). The latter, known as Father Nicholl, who succeeded his father, was a prominent figure in the Catholic movement within the Anglican church in the diocese. In 1917 he became vicar of St. Martin's, Roath, then one of the leading Anglo-Catholic churches in Wales.

The Reverend William Bruce Knight, who was rector of Llandough in 1817, later became Chancellor, Archdeacon and Dean of Llandaff.

In the churchyard lies a pile of broken stones, all that remains of a mutilated effigy which was removed to the vestry after the restoration of the church. It apparently represented the figure of a knight and it must be assumed that it was an effigy of a male member of the Walsh family. In the north part of the churchyard is the grave of Sir Sidney Hutchinson Byass, the South Wales industrialist, who purchased Llandough Castle from the Margam estate in 1914 and lived at the Castle until his death in 1929. Another former tenant of Llandough Castle, the barrister, Francis Edmund Stacey, lies buried in the churchyard and his grave is marked by a marble cross upon which is carved in relief the head of the deceased.

The church plate includes a silver-gilt chalice set with amethysts and pearls and a silver paten and bread dish and two glass cruets silver mounted, which were presented by Theodore Mansel Talbot of Margam. Two silver chalices with their paten covers belonging respectively to Llandough and St. Mary Church together with other certain dishes were broken up and melted down to make the above-mentioned plate. These two cups with their covers were given to the above churches in 1552 by 'W' of Llanblethian, whose name was inscribed on the vessels. The registers date from 1585.

Llandow Church

The parish church of Llandow is dedicated to the Holy Trinity and its Welsh name was Llan-Dhuw meaning the 'church of God'. The church was built in the Early English style of architecture, although its foundation was originally Norman. The church was valued at 5 marks in 1254 (Taxation of Norwich),

197

£6-13s-4d in 1291 (*Taxatio Ecclesiastica*) and £7-10s-8d in 1535 (*Valor Ecclesiasticus*). The parson was resident in 1563. In 1771 (Bishop Barrington's Primary Visitation of the Diocese) the living was worth £20; the incumbent was the Reverend Hugh Evans and the patronage was held by Jesus College, Oxford. In 1835 the living was styled a Rectory worth gross £266 in the patronage of Jesus College, Oxford. The living of Llandow with Llysworney was joined with Colwinston in 1970 to form a grouped benefice.

The church consists of chancel, nave, south porch and low saddleback west tower containing one bell. The chancel arch is low and pointed upon imposts of crude Transitional Norman workmanship in Sutton stone. Above it is a broader and lofty outer arch also of Sutton stone protruding from the masonry of the chancel wall. On its north and south sides the walls have sagged a little giving the arch almost a horseshoe-like appearance. On each side of the arch are large apertures or hagioscopes probably of later date to give a view of the sanctuary. When the church was restored in 1889 the architect obviously preserved the lower part of the chancel wall with its interesting features, but had to rebuild the higher part of the structure. In addition he placed external buttresses of great solidity at the threatened points because the north and south walls were bulging outwards alarmingly. The only visible evidence of the existence of a former rood-loft are two rough stone corbels on the chancel wall and one on the south wall of the nave, which may have been displaced when a new three-light window was erected to the west of it.

The east window is of two cinquefoiled lights, with an elongated quatrefoil above and hood mould. The left-hand light depicts Christ on the Cross of Calvary with the inscription below:– 'It is finished'; and the right-hand light portrays the Risen Lord with the inscription:– 'I am the Resurrection', while in the quatrefoil above is the figure of God the Father. The reredos is very flamboyant with ogee heads within ogee heads. Two trefoil-headed panels flank a cinquefoil, their continuously-moulded arches springing from small marble shafts with little caps and bases. The pieces are surmounted by foliated crockets and topped by a finial.

The windows on the south side of the chancel comprise a single narrow Early English lancet depicting the Virgin and Child and a two-light round-headed window with square label of coloured patterned glass with red borders. Between these two windows on the south side of the chancel is a priest's door with rounded arch. In the south-east corner of the sanctuary is a pillar piscina with Norman cushion capital. Pinned against the north wall of the chancel is a large fragment of a mutilated effigy of a 14th-century lady. On the south wall of the chancel is an early 19th-century classical-style monument in black and white marble surmounted by a draped urn. It commemorates various members of the Jones family of Llandow including Louisa Jones (d.1836), the daughter of Whitlock Nicholl of the Ham, Llantwit Major. A square incised stone tablet on the west face of the chancel arch commemorates members of the Lewis family of Llandow who died in the 18th century. On the external wall of the chancel on the south side above the priest's door is a tablet with the following Latin inscription:— 'Hancorne R de Landon A.M. ab anno 1681 instauravit hanc Cancellarium ano 1712', which translated reads: 'Hancorne, rector of Landau A.M. from the year 1681, restored this chancel in the year 1712'.

The windows of the south side of the nave comprise a three-light and a two-light ogee-foliated window surmounted by square labels. The stained glass in the three-light window is a memorial to three men (out of twelve according to the roll of honour in the south porch) of the parish who fell in the Great War, 1914-1918, Trooper D. H. John, Lance-Corporal E. J. Nugent and Private E. R. Nugent. The centre light depicts a soldier being crowned and the outer lights represent Valour and Victory. The window was designed by Robert J. Newbery of London and was erected by relatives, friends and parishioners in 1919. On the window-sill below is a brass plaque to three men of the parish, William J. Allen, R.N., Brynley Amos, Army, and Douglas G. Johnson, R.A.F. 'who gave their lives in the Second Great War 1939-1945'. In the sill of this window is a drain piscina in the shape of a floriated cross.

The nave is lit on the north side by a single-light window with ogee-foliated head containing stained glass depicting the figure of Christ as the Good Shepherd. This window was erected in 1902 by relatives, parishioners and friends in memory of the Reverend William Joseph Edwards, a former rector of the parish for over 40 years. The window was designed by Messrs. Lavers, Barraud and Westlake of Bloomsbury, London.

The pulpit is a plain Victorian piece of stone blocks with a moulded cornice and flowers in the top rail. At the point where the two surfaces meet there is an inhabited niche, corbelled out and cinquefoil-headed beneath an ogee arch which is crocketed with a finial. The alabaster statuette depicts St. Paul, since he bears the two symbols associated with him: the sword pointing downwards to denote his former persecution of the Christian church, and in his left hand the book which represents the power which converted him.

In the centre aisle of the nave is an incised sepulchral slab with Calvary cross, around which is carved the Latin inscription:– 'HIC IACIT EDWARDES . . . VI . . . OBIT ANNO . . .' with the date 1587 at the base of the cross. On the south wall of the nave near the south door is a plaque to the memory of the Reverend George Morgan Llewellyn, Honorary Canon of Llandaff and rector of Llandow (1916-1950) with Llysworney (1921-1950) and his wife, Elizabeth.

The font is tub-shaped with roll-moulding and a fine example of Norman work in Sutton stone. The tower opens to the nave by a pointed arch and above it is a small square-headed opening or sanctum squint in the west wall of the nave. Above the tower arch on the west wall of the nave is a memorial tablet to the memory of Mary (d. 1789), the second wife of William Bruce, Esquire, of Llanblethian, and daughter of Edward Turberville of Ewenny. Below on either side of the tower arch are two other memorial tablets. One, on the south side, surmounted by a classical draped urn, is in memory of Edward Bowen (d.1809) of Colwinstone, Gent. The other, on the north side, commemorates Edward Rees (d.1800), son of the late William Rees of Sutton.

The south doorway is round-headed, severely Norman, and the outer arch of

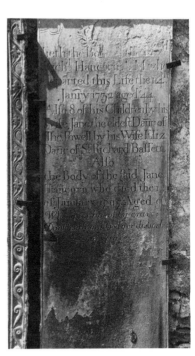

Tombstones outside church porch

the south porch is also semicircular. Over the front of the porch is a tablet bearing the following Latin inscription:— 'Sancta Trinitatis Ecclesia A.D. mdccclxxxix instaurata. Laus Deo in aeterna', which records the restoration of the church of Holy Trinity in 1889. Placed against the east wall of the porch are several interesting tombstones only recently removed from the floor of the sanctuary. Two of them bear incised Calvary crosses. One records the death of the above-mentioned Richard Hancorne A.M., a former rector (d. 1732). The inscription at the base of his tombstone was obviously overlooked, at its removal, for it reads:—

'Who does humbly crave
Don't touch my Body or disturb my Grave'.

The tower is square, battered at the base with a saddle-back roof, the gables running east and west. The belfry windows on each face at the top of the tower show the transition from Norman to Early English. At the base of the tower on the south wall is a square-headed window. The tower houses a single bell with the inscription:— 'MEARS & STAINBANK, FOUNDERS, LONDON RECAST 1923.' The chancel of the church was restored in 1712 and the whole of the church was renovated in 1889. In the churchyard is a cross base of Sutton stone much mutilated with its broken octagonal shaft in position.

The church plate consists of an Elizabethan silver chalice with a belt of floriated intersecting strap ornament round the bowl bearing no date, another silver chalice with a silver paten and flagon given by Miss A. E. Franklen, 1877 and a third silver chalice with its paten cover hall-marked 1721.

The register of baptisms and burials dates from 1688, marriages from 1754.

Llanfrynach Church

The parish church of Llanfrynach is dedicated to St. Brynach, a 6th-century Irish saint, who is reputed to have established the first Christian church on this site. Llanfrynach church is still the parish church of Llanfrynach with Penllyn but it fell into disuse at the end of the 17th century owing to its remoteness from the village. Regular services have long ceased to be performed at Llanfrynach church but occasional summer services are still held in the month of July to keep up the tradition of Christian worship. The chapel of Penllyn was rebuilt by the

Homfray family in 1850 as a memorial to the first Mrs. Homfray and has since been the church where more regular services are held.

That Llanfrynach did not become a complete ruin was due mainly to the efforts of a local antiquary Dr. William Salmon of 'Penlline Court' who had developed a strong personal interest in the old church and restored it mostly at his own expense in 1848. *The Cambrian* (1st September 1848) reported that:— 'The opening of Llanfrynach church took place according to announcement on Sunday last when the first regular service was performed after a period of nearly one hundred and fifty years. The ancient building has been restored through the liberality of William Salmon, Esq. Penlline Court.' It is interesting to note that the service was also performed for the first time in the English language.

Since Dr. Salmon's day, the Homfray family of Penllyn Castle took a great interest in the preservation of the building. In 1922 the church underwent a further restoration due to the efforts of Colonel J. Homfray and the vicar of Penllyn, the Reverend F. R. Williams, M.A. who as early as 1919 had set about collecting donations towards the church restoration fund.

The church is built in the Early English style and is of crude workmanship. The church was worth 4 marks in 1254 (Taxation of Norwich) and £6-13s-4d in 1291 (*Taxatio Ecclesiastica*). Between 1361 and 1382 Roger Cradock, Bishop of Llandaff with the consent of his Chapter 'by his ordinary authority for ever united, annexed and incorporated the parish church of Penllin with the Abbey of Margam.'

A Papal Bull and Royal Licence was obtained by the monks to confirm this act in 1384. Later, Cradock's successor, John Burghill, Bishop of Llandaff, confirmed the impropriation in 1397 with the following reservation:— 'saving a fit portion to be assigned for the sustenance of a perpetual vicar to be instituted by us in the same and a pension of 40s which the Abbot and Convent aforesaid are bound to pay annually to the Chapter of our church of Llandaff as an indemnity for the same church'. Although John de la Zouch, Bishop of Llandaff (1408-1425) disputed the Abbot's right to it in 1413, Margam still held the Rectory of Penllyn in 1535 (*Valor Ecclesiasticus*) when it was worth £6-13s-4d and the vicarage £5.

The living was styled a Rectory in 1563 and again in 1603 when it was worth £8 per annum. The impropriation worth £20 was held by Katherine Thomas, widow, by grant from the King. In 1660 the *Llandaff Records* state that 'David Williams of Penllyne was ordained priest on 3rd March. He was instituted to the perpetual vicarage of the parish church of Penllyne alias Llanfrynach on the presentation of Anthony Turberville, Gent. on the 24th September, 1662.' In 1771 (Bishop Barrington's Primary Visitation of the Diocese) the living was worth £40; the incumbent was the Reverend Leyson Morgan and the patronage was held by Lady Charlotte Edwin. It was styled 'the vicarage of Penlline or Pennclane or Llanfrynach' in 1780, 1819 and 1830 when it received grants from Queen Anne's Bounty amounting to £800. In 1835 it was referred to as 'Llanfrinach vicarage with Penllyne curacy' worth gross £140; the Earl of Dunraven was the impropriator and patron. Llanfrynach and Penllyn were

The chancel arch c. 1889

linked with Llansannor church in 1892 and these three churches were grouped with Ystradowen in 1973, the vicar residing at Llansannor.

The church consists of chancel, nave, south porch and embattled western tower containing one bell. The chancel arch is pointed, springing from plain impost blocks, and is Transitional Norman to Early English, probably 13th century. The east window has disappeared and is now blocked up but the roughly-formed jambs are still to be seen. Two plain square-headed windows, in the north wall and one in the south, provide the lighting in the chancel, while another in the south side has been blocked up.

In the south wall of the chancel is a trefoil-headed recess in which there is a piscina with octofoil drain. Above it is a small square recess, probably an aumbry. The chancel floor is on the same level as the nave but the sanctuary is raised a few inches by means of incised sepulchral slabs which date from the early 13th century. One in particular, which has an indecipherable inscription around the edges, has a cross head with a cinquefoil centre from which radiate four finely-executed floriated arms; this is enclosed in a quatrefoil which is in turn encompassed by a circle. The shaft is slender and from it springs a profusion of floral decoration.

In the south-east corner of the sanctuary beneath a sepulchral slab carved with a cross moline with fishtail base lie the bodies of Anthony Turberville (d. 1678), one-time patron of the church, and Christopher Turberville (d. 1709). Another sepulchral slab incised with a plain cross with Calvary base and billets on each side of the shaft bears the inscription:— 'Here lyeth ye bodies of William Sonne of Christopher Turberville ANO DOMI 1618 also Elinovre his wife'. The chancel has an arch-braced roof divided into two bays and supported by a single truss.

The nave is lit on the south side by a square-headed window (which at one time lit the rood-loft) and a three-light Perpendicular window with rounded heads. On the north side is a modern plain square-headed window which lights the pulpit. High up in the east wall of the nave north of the chancel arch is a sanctum squint looking apparently from the former rood-loft to the altar. The modern stone pulpit in the north-east corner of the nave was presented to the church by the Mayor of Cowbridge, Councillor Wybert Thomas, in 1922. It is an oddly-shaped piece insomuch as the sides are not of equal widths. It has a castellated cornice with plain mouldings and a deep hollow. It has no stiles or muntins, just a row of coffered square panels above a moulded centre rail and plain beneath. A doorway with a Tudor archway in the north wall of the nave leads to the rood-loft staircase which is still preserved in a projection on this side of the nave.

There are several memorial monuments in the nave near the chancel arch. On the north of the chancel arch is a tablet giving a résumé of the Lewis graves which lie below in a marked-off space on the floor. On the south side of the chancel wall are two marble monuments to the Deere family. The uppermost one is to the memory of Reynold Deere, Esq. (d. 1762) of Penlline Court and his brother, John Deere, clerk (d. 1765). Below is a tablet to Reynold Thomas Deere (d. 1815) erected by his grieving daughters. On either side are representative figures mourning over an altar on which is an appropriate verse of tribute. In the south-east corner of the nave is a memorial tablet to two infant children of Dr. William Salmon and his wife, Hester—Octavia Deere (d. 1828) and Spencer Fauconberg Deere (d. 1829). It also commemorates Susanna (d. 1830) daughter of Reynold Thomas Deere and sister of Hester Salmon. On the south wall of the nave are other memorial tablets to William Salmon, Esq. Senior (d. 1832) of Cowbridge, and another to Thomas Deere Salmon (d. 1882) second son of Dr. William and Hester Salmon of Penlline Court.

Llanfrynach church is one of the few churches in the diocese to retain the stone benches against the north and south walls of the nave, which, in most

The nave and chancel today

churches were destroyed by restoration and the installation of pews. In medieval times the congregation stood throughout the service except for the aged and the infirm, who sat on those benches and gave us the expression 'weakest to the wall'.

The nave has a fine 15th-century roof. It is of the open arch-braced collar truss type with carved windbraces between the purlins and the principal rafters and is divided into six bays. The wallplate is traceried and crenellated and the bases of the trusses are decorated with quatrefoil ornament. The principal rafters extend a short distance down the nave walls to rest on rough stone corbels. The centre of the nave is furnished with modern long wooden benches with ogee-shaped ends copied from some older benches in the east end of the nave. The tower opens to the nave by a pointed arch which springs from plain block imposts. It resembles the chancel arch but is somewhat narrower.

The outer doorway of the south porch has a depressed arch, and on the west side of the doorway is a tablet to Elizabeth Watkin, the wife of Thomas Richard (d. 1722) aged 29 years. The inner arch is pointed and is built over a tombstone with floriated cross which acts as a step. Over the inner arch is a niche containing a piece of window tracery. Inside the porch on each side are stone benches.

The font which stands under the tower has an octagonal bowl set on a slender stem which rests on three steps. Round the top of the rim is the inscription:— 'T.C. L.G. churchwardens 1745.'

The tower is a massive square structure with a saddleback roof within the parapet. Below the battlement is a prominent corbel table. The belfry has a two-light square-headed window on each face (except the northern one). Those on the east and west sides have been built up. A projection on the south side of the tower pierced by small apertures houses a spiral staircase leading to the belfry. It is approached by a doorway with four-centred arch at the base of the tower. The walls of the tower are of greater thickness than the remainder of the church. A stringcourse near the base of the tower is repeated at the foot of the belfry stage. The pointed west doorway has been built up and above it is a square-headed window, on either side of which is a tablet. That on the left bears the inscription:— 'A.Q. D.Q.1629. T.I.W. ALB.C. WARDENS'. The other reads '1932 A.Ll.J.v .H.R.H. H.C.R.H. WARDENS W.T.B.' (which are the initials of the Reverend A. Lloyd Jones, vicar, H. R. Homfray, Captain H. C. R. Homfray and William Thomas, builder (Llantwit Major).) Above the west window is another tablet which bears the inscription:— 'E.V. DODD, VICAR, SERENA HOMFRAY, ANTHONY J. POWELL, CHURCHWARDENS, 1968'. These inscriptions on the three stone tablets refer to various restorations of the church.

The tower originally housed four bells but now contains only one, which dates from the 15th century. It bears the inscription 'SCA MARIA' and was cast by the Bristol Medieval bellfoundry in 1430. It is now placed on a wooden frame on the floor of the belfry. In 1776 a faculty was granted by the Bishop of Llandaff to pull down the three other bells which were 'broken and quite useless'. The proceeds from the sale of the metal were used to restore the fabric of the church and also Penllyn church.

In front of the south porch are the stone steps and base of the churchyard cross, but the plinth of the cross is now surmounted by a re-used column with round mouldings and capped by a reeded capital. An interesting tombstone in the churchyard records the death of Thomas John of Penllyne (d. 1839) who died at the age of 71. He served as a soldier for 22 years in the time of Wellington and Picton. The Reverend David Williams ('Dafydd o'r Nant'), incumbent of the parish (1660-1694) was a celebrated bard who presided at the Beaupré Eisteddfod in 1681. To the east of the south porch several ledger stones have been resited. One is 'In memory of Rees Morgan of the Parish who died 7th August 1816 Aged 103'; another, surmounted by two crude cherubims, is to 'Jenet daughter of Rees Morgan of Lantrisant dyed November ye 11th 1746 aged 1 month.' Between these is a slab to one Rees Jenkins who died in 1743 aged 60 years; the rude skull and cross-bones (a symbol of death) carved at its foot gave rise to the mistaken local tradition of this being a 'pirate's' grave.

Since burials in the parish were carried out at Llanfrynach church, because there was no churchyard at Penllyn, the coffins had to be carried across fields along a footpath to the church. Consequently four coffin stiles were erected along the way to Llanfrynach church. These consisted of two ordinary stone slab stiles side by side with a central square-topped pillar on which a coffin could be rested while the bearers negotiated the stile without tipping the coffin. One of these coffin stiles can be seen in the north-east corner of the churchyard and another by the main road. The other two sets of double stiles are in the fields between the A48 and the church. These examples of coffin stiles at Llanfrynach are unique in the Vale of Glamorgan.

The church plate consists of a silver chalice inscribed on the underside 'Llanfrynach church and Penllyne chapel A.D. 1636', and a silver paten inscribed 'Deo et ecclesiae, presented to Llanfrynach church and Penllyne Chapel by Hester, wife of W. Salmon, Esq. of Penllyne Court June 1st, 1855.' The registers date from 1813.

Llangan Church

The parish church of Llangan is dedicated to a female saint, St. Canna, the mother of St. Crallo. Although the present building dates from the 12th century, it is a foundation of a much earlier date, as its pre-Norman cross bears witness. The church was valued at 4 marks in 1254 (Taxation of Norwich), £5 in 1291 (*Taxatio Ecclesiastica*) and £13-1s-0d in 1535 (*Valor Ecclesiasticus*). The parson was resident in 1563. The manor of Llangan belonged to a member of the Turberville family in 1525, 1546 and again in 1597 when a Turberville held a third turn in the advowson of the church of Llangan. In 1771 (Bishop Barrington's *Llandaff Diocesan Book*) when David Jones was the incumbent, the living was worth £80 and George Venables Vernon, Esq., and Lady Charlotte Edwin were the patrons. In 1835 the living was a Rectory worth gross £244 and Lords Clarendon and Dunraven were the patrons. The parishes of Llangan and St. Mary Hill were joined with Coychurch in 1966 to form a grouped benefice.

The church consists of chancel, nave, south porch, a large vestry north of the chancel and a western bellcote containing two bells. The chancel arch is pointed with continuous moulding and fairly wide. The east window, which is the only window in the chancel, is of three trefoiled lights beneath ogee arches surmounted by hood mould with foliated stops. Internally the arch springs from two engaged shafts with bell-shaped capitals. The stained glass in the window is a memorial to the Reverend David Jones (1735-1810). The centre light depicts the Ascension of Our Lord and the lights on either side contain a medallion portrait of the Reverend David Jones and of St. Canna, the patron saint of the church. David Jones was presented to the living of Llangan in 1768 by Lady Charlotte Edwin, wife of Charles Edwin of Llanmihangel and Member of Parliament for Glamorgan (1747-1756). She figures prominently in early Methodist history. David Jones wrote a number of hymns and although he remained in the Established church he was a strong supporter of the Methodist movement. He provided funds for the building of the first Methodist church in Wales, Salem at Pencoed in the neighbouring parish of Coychurch. He was a very popular preacher and large congregations used to come and hear him preach at Llangan and St. Mary Hill. The memorial window to him, which was designed by William Glasby of Kensington, London, was erected in September 1932 by public subscription at a cost of £105. Seven original brass lamps on weighted pulleys still hang above the altar rail in the sanctuary.

Statue of the blessed Virgin Mary above the south porch

Set into the external walls of the chancel are two fragments of two distinct headstones with a ring-cross dating from the 11th or 12th century. One fragment is embedded in the east wall and consists of a block of Rhaetic sandstone with one splayed arm of an incised cross within part of a double incised ring. The other fragment, which is in the south wall near the south-east corner, is of similar material and shows part of a cross with expanded terminals set in relief by sunk inter-arm spaces within a double incised ring.

In the south wall is a priest's door with pointed arch and prominent hood mould. Outside, on the same wall a tombstone is placed to the memory of the Reverend William Deere (d. 1746), vicar of Penlline and rector of the parish, aged 65 years, who (so the inscription reads) lies buried 'under the Communion Table'.

The only remains of the former rood-loft is the staircase doorway high in the north wall of the nave which is built-in. A door which formerly led to the rood-loft staircase on the north side of the nave is now the entrance to the vestry, built partly on the north side of the chancel. This door has a basically round arch with continuous and plain mouldings, one of which is concave. The keystone has dropped. The door tracery is of two bays of two cinquefoiled lights with foliage on the cusps. Foliage too appears as minor ornamentation in the head together with Perpendicular-style tracery lights. The large vestry which was probably used as a schoolroom in the late 19th century, was erected in 1881. On its south wall hangs a portrait of the Reverend David Jones.

The nave is lit by four windows, all of the same design, of two trefoiled lights, two on the south and two on the north. In the west wall of the nave is a single plain lancet window with trefoiled head and dripstone. On the north wall is a stone benefactions tablet. The pulpit is carved out of wood whose colour enhances its appearance. The posts which rest on radiating stretchers are carved above into the stiles of the pulpit where they end in a plain chamfer and roll or a trefoil—the top extending upwards as the flat front of the stile. It has a plainly-moulded cornice and bottom rail. The nave has a trussed-rafter roof with diagonal braces.

The font of Sutton stone has a round bowl with a flat string at the rim and a smaller one at the base. The bowl is quite plain with a pointed arcade on the underside. The stem is octagonal with stool stops dying on to a square base which stands on a hexagonal plinth. In 1869 Sir Stephen Glynne described it as being 'new in the Norman style' but it is more likely to be Early English in style. Over the west end is a bellcote for two bells. One bell has the inscription 'J. WARNER & SONS, LONDON, 1881.' and the other appears to be a late medieval bell.

The south doorway of the church has a four-centred arch and the outer doorway of the porch has a segmental pointed arch with its hood moulding ending in a large flower as label stop on one side and leaves on the other. The inhabited niche above is cinquefoil-headed beneath an ogee arch on little shafts with foliated caps and the piece is flanked by square pilasters which end in pinnacles with a large finial between. The statue of the Virgin Mary, placed there by the Reverend H. J. Humphreys in 1890 in memory of his two children, stands on an ornate pedestal developed with a decorative pointed trefoil in the stem.

Llangan church is famous for the two crosses in its churchyard. The oldest of the two stands near the west end of the church beneath a slated canopy to protect it from the weather. It is a 9th-century Celtic wheel cross with round head on which is carved a crude representation of the Crucifixion. The crucified Christ is depicted with a conical beard with his arms awkwardly extended wearing a short cloth or kilt around the lower part of a long body. At each side are two distorted crude figures representing a Roman soldier piercing the side of Christ while another stands ready with the sponge filled with vinegar. This grotesque mode of representing the persecutors of the Saviour was not uncommon in early art and indicates Irish influence. Below the figure of Christ is part of a smaller figure who holds a small cylindrical object in his right hand and a horn in his left. On the reverse side is a plain Greek cross with four circular bosses in the angles.

The other cross at Llangan is the beautiful 15th-century churchyard cross with its elaborate but weather-worn carvings of sacred persons and incidents. It is the most beautiful and perfect 15th-century churchyard cross in existence in the Vale apart from the only other surviving one at St. Donat's church. The broad faces have double canopies with a representation of the Crucifixion in high relief on one side and the Pietà (the Virgin with the dead body of Christ in her arms) on the other. The two narrow faces have single canopies with figures of saints or ecclesiastics. The upper part of the head is square in plan having four equal faces, each with a figure of a saint under a single canopy. Above the upper tier of sculptured faces there appears to be a small spire to complete the design. The church was restored about 1856 but unfortunately little is known of this restoration.

The church plate consists of an Elizabethan chalice with its paten cover. Round the bowl is the usual belt of interlaced strap ornament. The handle of the cover is dated 1576. Also a large silver bread-dish is inscribed 'The gift of Mrs. Mary Powell, 1837.' An entry in the register of baptisms records that John Prichard (1817-1886), the noted diocesan architect and son of the Reverend Richard Prichard, rector of Llangan from 1821 to 1856, was christened at St. Canna's church, Llangan on the 10th July, 1817. He died on the 13th October, 1886 and was buried in the churchyard on the south side of Llandaff Cathedral near the Lady Chapel in the same grave as his father, who was vicar-choral of Llandaff for 35 years. The register of baptisms dates from 1698, marriages 1716 and burials 1725.

Llanmaes Church

The parish church of Llanmaes is dedicated to St. Cadoc and although the present structure dates from the early part of the 13th century, it is obviously of a much earlier Celtic foundation. The church was valued at 5 marks in 1254 (Taxation of Norwich), £13-6s-8d in 1291 (*Taxatio Ecclesiastica*) and £10-10s-4d in 1535 (*Valor Ecclesiasticus*). Its parson was resident in 1563. The Earl of Pembroke held the advowson of the church in the 17th century. In 1771 (Bishop Barrington's *Llandaff Diocesan Book*) the living was worth £120; the incumbent was the Reverend Howell Edwards and the patrons were Thomas Edwards and Viscountess Windsor. In 1835 it was styled a Rectory worth gross £294 in the patronage of the Marquess of Bute. In 1920 Llanmaes was linked with the parish of Llanmihangel to form one benefice.

The church consists of chancel, nave, south porch and western tower containing three bells. The chancel arch is broad and pointed with jambs of Sutton stone which might have belonged to an earlier arch. The east window is a 19th-century insertion of three trefoiled lights with the mullions curving into the head to form lancet shapes enclosing dagger trefoils flanking a sexfoil circular light surmounted by a dripstone with crowned heads as label stops. The stained glass depicts in the centre light the Ascension of Our Lord, the left-hand light Jesus blessing little children and the right-hand light Christ giving Simon Peter the post-Resurrection commission. The window was erected as a memorial to the Reverend David Parry Thomas, rector of the parish for twenty-one years (1850-1871), Elizabeth, his wife and John Griffith Stuart Thomas, their only son.

The chancel is lit on the south side by three single, broad lancets with prominent dripstones terminating in carved heads as label stops. In a trefoiled arched recess in the south wall of the chancel is a square drain piscina of Sutton stone. In the sanctuary floor are several interesting tombstones. One is to the Reverend Illtyd Nicholl (d. 1732), rector of Llanmaes (1699-1732). Another tombstone with Latin inscription bears the coats of arms of Wilkins 'A Wyvern' impaling those of Swinglehurst 'An arrow in pale point downwards, a pair of wings conjoined in lure, in chief three pheons' and is a memorial to Elizabeth (d. 1671), daughter of Richard Swinglehurst and wife of Thomas Wilkins, rector of Llanmaes (1668-1699) and Prebendary of Llandaff. Next to her in the sanctuary floor is a memorial stone to her father, Richard Swinglehurst, rector of the parish (1642-1668). (He was ejected by the Parliamentarians

in 1650 but was restored to the living in 1660.) Among the well-worn memorial tombstones in the chancel floor is one to Margaret Towgood, the wife of William Towgood, gent. 'Practitioner of Physic and Chryrurgery', dating from the 16th century which is one of the earliest surviving tombstones in the Vale of Glamorgan. A doorway with pointed archway leads to a modern vestry on the north side of the chancel.

The chancel and nave are divided by a carved wooden screen, the surviving part of the original medieval rood screen. The screen is square-framed of five bays, of which four are each of three lights. The wider central bay is an opening which has lost its head tracery. The lights are divided by slender, chamfered muntins, the leading edge of which diverges into the tracery above. The heads are cinquefoiled beneath intersecting pointed arches with dagger quatrefoils above. The spandrels on either side are cut in the solid to represent a leafy design or in three cases two-headed, two-tailed serpents called amphisbaena. The west side of the beam is beautifully carved with vine leaf motif. The wainscot of the screen is modern and consists of tongue and groove boarding.

A doorway with four-centred arch in the north wall of the nave leads to a staircase within a projection on the north side of the nave to the former rood-loft. On the north of the chancel arch on the inside wall are the remains of a doorway, and the loft was originally illuminated by two small windows, one on either side of the nave, now blocked.

The windows on the south side of the nave consist of two three-light windows with rounded heads and square label. The south-east window depicts the figures of St. Illtyd, St. Cattwg and St. Teilo and was erected in memory of the Reverend H. Campbell-Davies, rector of the parish from 1927 to 1950 'by friends and parishioners in appreciation of the great kindness and devoted service' of the departed rector. The south-west window was erected as a memorial to the devoted life and service of Henry and Margaret Gertrude Campbell-Davies in 1964 by their children and grandchildren. The subject of the window comprises incidents from the Book of Ruth. The left-hand light depicts Naomi and Ruth in their bereavement, the centre light depicts the marriage of Ruth and Boaz and the right-hand light depicts the birth of a child to Ruth with Naomi present. Both windows were designed by Hubert Thomas of Celtic Studios, Swansea. A black and white marble monument surmounted by a plain, white sarcophagus on the south wall of the nave to the west of the south doorway was erected 'to perpetuate the memory of Colonel John Towgood (d.1754), son of William Towgood and Margaret, his wife' by his niece Margaret Bisse. Below is the touching epitaph:-

'His heart would melt to see another's woe
And as a man humanity could sham.'

The window in the north wall of the nave is of two lights with pointed heads and dripstone with carved heads as stops. The two single lights are separated internally by a single slender shaft with round moulded caps and astragal and a vertical fillet. The arches above, which are returned on half-caps set in the side wall, are decorated by continuous bands of 19th-century approximations of

Early English leaf forms. The window was erected in 1882 as a memorial to the Reverend Canon William Leigh Morgan (d. 1876) rector of the parish (1871-1876) and his wife, Elizabeth (d. 1878). The two lights depict David the King and Our Lord as the Good Shepherd and it was designed by John Prichard, diocesan architect.

A marble tablet on the north wall of the nave records that the brass lectern with eagle was given in memory of four men of the parish who made 'the supreme sacrifice' in the Great War, 1914-1918, and as a 'thankoffering for the providential return' of twenty-four others whose names are listed below. Also on the north wall of the nave is a marble monument to the memory of the Reverend Robert Carne (d.1849), of Dimlands House and Nash Manor, rector of the parish, who assumed the name and arms of Carne instead of Nicholl by Royal Mandate in 1842 on inheriting the Nash estates. The monument is surmounted by the Carne arms and crest and the Welsh motto 'Fy ngobaith sydd yn Nuw' (My hope is in God) and the second Carne motto 'En toute loyale' (Loyal in all things). Above the rood-loft doorway next to this monument is a memorial tablet to Robert Carne's youngest daughter, Frances Susanna Nicholl (d.1839) by Elizabeth, his second wife, daughter of Charles Loder Carne of Nash. The tablet also commemorates Robert Carne's second daughter, Anna Marie (d.1837), wife of Robert Kearsley Dawson, Captain in the Royal Engineers. The Carne family vault is located on the eastern side of the churchyard. The dark oak pulpit is very similar to the one in Flemingston church except for its condition. It has a moulded cornice and there are very heavy buttresses as stiles which are even deeper on the drum. The sunken panels have barely-carved trefoils and beneath is a moulded rail before the closed drum. The nave has a simple arch-braced roof similar to that in the chancel.

The western part of the north wall of the nave is covered with medieval wall paintings which are said to represent St. George and the Dragon with the Princess standing at the gate of the castle and what are thought to be three priests in eucharistic vestments, but unfortunately most of the details have faded. Near the south doorway is a holy-water stoup similar to that at Eglwys Brewis. Several interesting tombstones cover the floor of the nave, two of which have Calvary crosses with billets. One of these commemorates John Shirrey (d. 1624) aged 104 years and Edward Turberville (d. 1643). These names inscribed on the incised slabs were probably added years after the crosses were carved as the lettering of Edward Turberville sprawls across the top of the cross, and, like the other, the lettering is carved contrary to the standing of the cross, giving the idea of an ignorant misappropriation of an earlier monument. The massive Norman font is tub-shaped with roll-mouldings at the rim and near the base. It rests upon a circular plinth. On the west wall of the nave above the tower archway is a badly defaced marble monument which was erected to the memory of Mary (d.1799), first wife of the Reverend Robert Nicholl, M.A., rector of Llanmaes, and daughter of Daniel Woodward of Bristol. Below is an escutcheon with an acanthus leaf surround displaying the arms of Nicholl 'Sable three pheons argent' impaling those of Woodward 'Vert

Llancarfan church—south aisle ▶

three mulberry leaves or'. On the south side of this monument is a memorial tablet which commemorates several members of the Plaisteed family of Llanmaes; one of them, Alexander Plaisteed, whose name appears on one of the church bells, was churchwarden in 1777.

The south porch is a 19th-century addition. Both the inner and outer doorways have pointed arches and the outer one is surmounted by a moulded dripstone. The tall tower has a plain battlement and corbel table beneath. The belfry has two-light square-headed louvred windows on each face and small rectangular apertures on its south and north walls. The west doorway has a flat head and above it is a two-light square-headed window with square label. A Latin inscription above the west door of the tower (HOC CAPANARIVM PAROCHIALIUM ET BENEVOLORUM IMPENSIS ERECTVM FVIT EDVARDO LEN ET ELCVITO NICHOLL ECCLESIAE GARDIANIS ANNO DOMINI 1632) records that the tower was erected in 1632 at the cost of the parish and friends when Edward Llewellyn and Illtyd Nicholl were churchwardens. According to a contemporary note in the parish registers a ruined belfry had stood on the north side of the chancel and was possibly entered by the same door that led up to the rood-loft. The tower houses three large bells; the first is a pre-Reformation bell cast by the Bristol Medieval bellfoundry in the 14th century bearing the Latin inscription 'SANCTA MARIA ORA PRO NOBIS' (St. Mary pray for us.); the second bell carries the inscription 'EXULTEMUS NOMEN DOMINI (Let us praise the name of the Lord) GR/WR★W ★1637★TS' and was cast by Thomas Stone, an itinerant bellfounder. The third bell is dated 1777 and bears the inscription:– 'LET MY SOUND MOVE YE TO GODS GLORY' with the name 'ALEXANDER PLAISTEED CHURCHWARDEN' on the inscription band. It was cast by William Bilbie of Chewstoke, Somerset.

Llanmaes was once noted for the longevity of its inhabitants, and in the parish registers, which are some of the oldest in the Vale of Glamorgan (dating from 1583), there are several entries of persons having been buried upwards of 100 years of age. However, the following entry quoted verbatim from the burial register affirms that Ivan Yorath died at the age of 180 years:– 'Ivan Yorath buried a Saterdaye the xii day of July anno doni 1621 et anno regni regis vicissimo primo annoque aetatis circa 180. He was a Sowdiar in the fights at Bosworthe (1485) and lived at Lantwit Major and he lived muche by fishing.'

The churchyard cross has a modern metal spiral shaft and head set upon a circular stone and large square slab upon four steps. From 1600 to 1608 the living of Llanmaes was held by Andrew Vaen, one of the most notorious pluralists in the history of the Vale. He was a canon of Llandaff for over thirty years and held numerous livings as far afield as Christchurch, Newport and Coity near Bridgend.

On the east side of the church stands Great House, Llanmaes, the home of the Nicholl family during the 18th century. The Reverend Illtyd Nicholl occupied the house as rector of Llanmaes from 1699 until his death in 1732.

The church plate comprises a silver chalice and paten. The chalice, which was originally an Elizabethan drinking cup, is hall-marked 1569. Round the bowl is engraved a broad belt of loosely-interlaced foliated strap ornament forming four medallions in which are engraved four heads in profile, and round the lip is a band of beautifully-engraved foliated ornament. The paten is the only piece of pre-Reformation date in the diocese of Llandaff and G. E. Halliday, writing in his *Llandaff Church Plate* in 1905, assigned it the date 1495. It was restored by A. B. Basset of Llandaff and has been electro-gilded on the face only. The register of burials and baptisms dates from 1583, marriages from 1584.

Llanmihangel Church

The parish church of Llanmihangel is dedicated to St. Michael and All Angels from which the parish takes its name and points therefore to a Norman foundation. The church is built in the Early English style of architecture and dates from the 13th century. The church was worth 4 marks in 1254 (Taxation of Norwich), £5 in 1291 (*Taxatio Ecclesiastica*) and £5 in 1535 (*Valor Ecclesiasticus*). A parson was resident in 1563 and it is recorded that the services in the Roman rite were performed here much later than anywhere else in the district. In 1771 (Bishop Barrington's *Llandaff Diocesan Book*) the living was worth £30; the incumbent was the Reverend William Church and the patronage was held by Lady Charlotte Edwin. It was styled a Rectory in 1835 worth gross £150 when Lord Dunraven was the patron. Llanmihangel church was joined with Llanmaes church in 1920 to form one benefice.

The church consists of chancel, nave, south porch and western tower containing one bell. The chancel arch is plain and round-headed, larger than most chancel arches in this part of the Vale. The east window is Third Pointed Victorian Gothic of three cinquefoiled lights with rectilinear-style tracery above surmounted by a dripstone. The chancel is lit on the south side by a single light square-headed window and on the north side by a two-light round-headed window, which prior to 1889, was the east window of the church. Before the restoration of the church in 1889 the east window was flanked by two heavy, marble monuments fixed one on each side. These two large, marble monuments of the Edwin family who resided at one time at Llanmihangel Place are now on the north and south walls of the chancel. The monument on the south wall is finely executed in the classical style with urn, drapes, cherub-heads and fluted columns with composite Corinthian capitals surmounted by the family armorial achievement. It commemorates Sir Humphrey Edwin (d. 1707), (Lord Mayor of London in 1697), who was a Dissenter, and Dame Elizabeth, his wife (d. 1714). Also their eldest son, Samuel Edwin, Esq., (d. 1722), who married Lady Catherine Montague. The marble monument on the north wall also in the classical style surmounted by the ubiquitous urn is of inferior craftsmanship to that on the south wall. It commemorates Charles Edwin, the only son of Samuel Edwin and Lady Catherine Montague (d. 1756) and his wife, Lady Charlotte Edwin (daughter of the 4th Duke of Hamilton) (d. 1777). It was she who presented to the living of Llangan David Jones (1736-1810), who figures prominently in the early history of the Methodist movement.

The vault of the Edwins was known to be under the communion table and when a ladder was placed against the east end for the purposes of removing these mural monuments, the ladder, floor and all upon it disappeared into the vault. It transpired that a former rector, the Reverend Edward Evans, had had some sort of premonition that the flooring of the sanctuary was in an unsafe condition and, being a heavily-built person, he declined going into that part of the church at all, and the celebration of the Communion always took place outside the altar rails during his incumbency. After the accident referred to, the vault was filled in and concreted over. In this vault lies buried Sir Humphrey Edwin (d. 1707). In the window-sill of the south chancel window is a drain piscina. The piscina looks as though it was once a free-standing Norman pillar piscina with cushion capital now built into the wall. The chancel has a fine oak wagon roof.

The windows of the nave comprise on the south side a two-light cinquefoiled window with square label with square label stops carved with foliage and a square-headed light west of the porch. On the north side is a single cinquefoiled light, above which is a square-headed window which formerly lit the rood-loft, and towards the west end a trefoil-headed lancet. All the windows are glazed with lattice glass in pink, green and yellow. A round-headed doorway in the north wall of the nave leads to the rood-loft staircase which is concealed in the thickness of the north wall and the stone corbels which supported the former rood-loft are still *in situ* on the chancel wall.

The nave has an arch-braced roof with curved windbraces between the wallplate and the purlins and the principal rafters descend some distance down the wall to be supported on rudely-carved stone corbels. The corbels supporting the roof nearest the east end of the nave are lower than the others and this part of the roof is filled with panelwork with foliated bosses at the intersection of purlins and braces. On the north wall of the nave is a representation of a tomb-chest in low relief consisting of an effigy of the upper part of a three-quarter length figure of a layman with a ruff round the neck and the hands clasped in prayer over the breast, the lower part of the figure being replaced by a Calvary Cross. Around the latter is a row of letters '+ DEUS RESIPIT ANNIMOS ILLORVM IN MISERICORDIAM +' (God renews the souls of those in his mercy) outside of which on three sides of the stone runs the following inscription: 'Heare lyeth in grave the body of Grifithe Grante, sone to Richard Grant & Marget Ye 3 Rees Ab John deceased the X4 Daye of May, Anno Domini 1591. He lyved 67 Yeares in the end thereof departed his life and so departing hence left his wedded wife Blainch'. (Richard Grant married Margaret, the third child of Rees ap John and their son Griffith married Blainch Carne.) This effigy was once outside the east end of the chancel where it had been placed in 1707 when the church was restored by the Edwin family. However, in 1910, Sir Thomas Mansel Franklen, who was the last direct male descendant of Griffith Grant, obtained a faculty from the Bishop of Llandaff to bring the effigy back into the church. The work of removing and refixing the effigy was carried out by William Clarke of Llandaff and the position on the north wall was chosen because many of the Grants, an old family of Sigginstone nearby, are buried under the north side of the nave.

The stone pulpit on the north side of the nave has a moulded cornice and convex top rail. The panels beneath each have a large, pierced four-leafed flower with, at the centre of each, a typical Tudor-style flower decoration. The bottom rail is moulded and the stiles are cut to look like plain engaged shafts with capital at base. The stone desk surmounting the pulpit has a fillet on the leading moulded edge and is decorated on the convex underside by stiff-leaf foliage flanking a finely sculptured head of Christ. A brass candle-holder is attached to each side of the desk. The church is still (1987) lit by oil lamps which are an interesting feature of the church. On the right-hand side of the south doorway on entering the church is a holy-water stoup.

The font is massive and of very simple design. The basin is square with chamfered corners, the supporting stem is circular resting on a square plinth. The south porch which has stone benches inside, has an obtusely-pointed chamfered inner doorway and an acutely-pointed outer doorway surmounted by a dripstone. To the west of the south porch the wall of the nave is strengthened by a solid buttress.

The tower opens to the nave by a rude and narrow-pointed arch and above it is a doorway leading to the upper part of the tower. The tower, which has a distinctly military character, has a saddleback roof with corbel table below. The belfry has a square-headed louvred light on each face and instead of the more usual narrow slits in the middle stage of the tower there are exceedingly well-executed cross loopholes which gives it a quasi-military appearance. At the base of the tower is a heavy stringcourse. A projection on the north side of the tower houses the staircase to the belfry which is lit by a trefoil lancet and above by a cross loophole. This staircase was constructed in 1909 because the upper part of the tower could only be reached through a doorway by means of a ladder placed against the west wall of the nave. The turret staircase was designed by E. Jenkin Williams, architect of Cardiff, and the cost of the work amounted to £65. The west door of the tower has a rounded archway and above it is a Perpendicular west window of two cinquefoiled lights surmounted by a square label. The tower houses a single bell dated 1636 with the inscription 'EXUL-TEMUS NOMEN DOMINI' (Let us praise the name of the Lord), and the initials 'E.T.T.S.', which was cast by Thomas Stone, an itinerant bell founder who cast many bells in South Wales.

The church was restored in the years 1888-1889 and the work of restoration consisted of the laying of new floors in the nave and chancel, the erection of a new roof in the nave and reseating throughout. The reading desk, mural monuments and tombstones were rearranged and a new large Perpendicular-style window was inserted in the east wall of the chancel. The old east window was replaced in the north wall of the chancel and an old window was reopened in the south wall of the chancel. The windows were reglazed throughout. The Incorporated Church Building Society granted £15 towards the reseating and restoring the church. The work of restoration was carried out by John Morgan,

Llanmihangel church by Sir T. M. Franklen, 1887

Pontyglyn (Pontyclun) according to plans and specifications of F. R. Kempson, diocesan architect, and the cost of restoration amounted to £671 of which Lord Dunraven, the patron of the living, contributed £350. Sir Thomas M. Franklen and Colonel and Mrs. J. P. Turbervill also made large donations to the restoration fund. The church was reopened for divine service after restoration on Tuesday 7th May, 1889 by the Rt. Reverend Dr. Richard Lewis, Bishop of Llandaff.

To the west of the churchyard there was once a curious feature. It consisted of a well-developed woman's bust carved in stone through which breasts the water used to flow into the well below named St. Anne's well. It has now disappeared.

On the north side of the church is Llanmihangel Place, a Tudor mansion rebuilt by James Thomas in the early part of the 16th century. For many years it was the seat of the Thomas family until 1684 when it was purchased by Sir Humphrey Edwin. Llanmihangel Place descended from the Edwins to the Wyndham-Quins and later to the Dunravens.

The church possesses a silver chalice inscribed round the foot 'Ex dono samlis Edwin Armigeri 1705' (The gift of Samuel Edwin, Armiger, 1705.) On the bowl is engraved a coat of arms 'Four choughs between a cross through or, a cross of St. George on an oval'. A large silver paten has the same coat of arms and inscription. The arms, engraved on the church plate, resemble those on the Edwin memorial monuments in the chancel showing a cross of St. George, whereas all heraldic reference works give the arms of Edwin as 'Argent a saltire cross between four Cornish choughs sable'. The register of baptisms dates from 1755, burials from 1756 and marriages from 1759.

Llansannor Church

The parish church of Llansannor is dedicated to St. Senwyr, an obscure saint first mentioned in the 12th-century tract *Bonedd y Saint*. It is built in the Early English style of architecture. The church was first mentioned under the name 'Capella Sanctae Senwarae de la Thawa' in a document listing the possessions of Tewkesbury Abbey when it was a chapel attached to Llanblethian church. However, the Abbey did not retain it as it became a Rectory by the middle of the 13th century. The advowson of the church belonged to the Lord of Glamorgan in 1295 and 1317. The church was valued at £3 in 1254 (Taxation of Norwich) when it was referred to as 'Ecclesia de la Thawe' and (with the church of Rotheri) £4 in 1291 (*Taxatio Ecclesiastica*). It was valued at £5 in 1317 and £8 in 1535 (*Valor Ecclesiasticus*) when the name Llansannor first appeared in its present form (Llansannor alias Thawe). Its parson was non-resident in 1563. In 1771 (Bishop Barrington's *Llandaff Diocesan Book*) when the Reverend Combe Miller was the incumbent, the living was worth £40 and Francis Gwyn, Esq. was the patron. In 1835 the living was styled a rectory worth gross £130 and the patronage was held by J. F. Gwyn of Forde Abbey. The parish of Llansannor was grouped with that of Llanfrynach with Penllyn in 1892 and with Ystradowen in 1973 to form a grouped benefice.

The church consists of chancel, nave, south porch and western tower containing two bells. The chancel arch is pointed and springs immediately from the side walls. It is distinctly wide, evidently replacing an earlier arch. The east window is of two trefoiled lights under a pointed head. The beautifully-carved reredos decorated in English gold leaf is a memorial to Richard and Anne Louise Williams, the parents of the Reverend F. R. Williams, a former rector of Llansannor, and was erected in 1926 according to a design by F. E. Howard, architect of London. The central panel contains a representation of Our Lord upon the Cross with the attendant figures of the Blessed Virgin Mary and St. John on either side. Four panels on each side of the reredos contain shields bearing emblems of the Passion. On the right-hand side are the crown of thorns, the sponge on a reed and spear, the Cross and the ladder and spade; on the left-hand side are the scourge, pillar and binding cords, the seamless robe and three dice, the hammer and pincers and the thirty pieces of silver.

The chancel, whose roof was re-slated in 1986, is lit on the south side by a single square-headed light and a two-light round-headed window beneath an internal pointed head deeply splayed. Between these windows is a priest's door

with pointed arch. On the north side is a single square-headed light with deeply splayed embrasures. On the floor on the north side of the sanctuary is a stone recumbent effigy of a knight in armour with his hands clasped in the attitude of prayer with crossed legs which rest upon a lion symbolizing courage. This effigy, known locally as the 'King of Breigan', was once thought to represent Stephen Bauzan, the sheriff of Richard de Clare who died in 1258. However, an entry in the Pipe Rolls states that a sum of money was allowed to cover Bauzan's tomb at Carmarthen near where he fell in battle. Furthermore, the armour of the effigy, which includes a bascinet and camail, is clearly of a much later date, probably late 14th or early 15th century. The effigy is likely to mark the grave of Gronw ab Ifor, a prominent local Welsh landowner who held Llansannor and Alltgawddu near Llantrisant at the close of the 14th century. The chancel has a wagon roof panelled above the sanctuary with carved bosses on the braces at the intersections of the principal rafters and ridge and purlins.

The windows of the nave comprise on the south side two windows with cusped cinquefoils under ogee arches beneath a square head with label, one of three lights, the other of two. The north side of the nave is lit by a three-light window with cusped cinquefoils under a square head labelled. All windows are deeply splayed internally and are filled with coloured Victorian latticed glass with some coloured late 18th-century glass in the cinquefoils. These windows are 19th-century insertions done in a debased late Perpendicular style in Bath stone. A doorway with pointed arch in the north wall of the nave leads to the rood-loft staircase which is concealed in a projection outside the main line of building on the north side of the church and terminates at a doorway at the level of the original rood-loft. In the north wall of the nave is the outline of a stone archway which was once a north or 'devil's door'. This was exposed in the 1910 restoration of the church.

On the north wall of the nave are two memorial tablets to members of the Truman family of Pantylliwydd. The Truman memorial tablets display a coat of arms where Truman 'A chevron between three castles' is shown impaling the arms of Jenkins 'A chevron between three fleurs-de-lys'. The family motto in Latin is 'Aris et focis pugnare' which translated reads:— 'To fight for hearth and home'. The Truman family was descended from Trooper Thomas Truman, a Cromwellian soldier of fortune from Northampton who rose in the ranks of the Parliamentary Army and came to Glamorgan as a lieutenant under Colonel Philip Jones of Fonmon Castle and settled at Llantrisant. The most interesting member of this family was his great-grandson Thomas Truman (1713-1786), an antiquarian, who married Mary, daughter of William Llewelyn of Pantylliwydd, and settled there. Truman is regarded as the person who first aroused Iolo Morganwg's interest in the history of Glamorgan. Iolo described Truman as a 'learned antiquarian and skilful genealogist who is now in a better world than this, having left no equal behind him.'

The pulpit has panels of blind tracery. The stiles take the form of circular shafts and moulded bases on square plinth. The cornice has embattled cresting and Tudor-style floral decoration with wilder foliage as capitals of finials above the stiles. The blind tracery is a mixture of trefoils interrupting a semicircular arch, ogee arches and ultimately pointed trefoils in the spandrels. The centre cusps of the lower trefoil are each decorated with a small diamond-shaped flower. The stem beneath it all has plain sunken panels and there is a heavily-moulded plinth which is an attempt to represent the stone type in wood.

The nave has an arch-braced roof of four bays with three tiers of arched windbraces between the purlins and the crenellated wallplate. The principal rafters are supported on plain stone corbels. The font is octagonal in shape, the lower portion of the octagon being cut in hollows dying on to a bold square base. The tower opens to the nave by an obtusely-pointed arch which springs immediately from the side walls. Above it is a blocked up window which was the original window of the west wall of the church before the tower was added. In the floor near the tower is a sepulchral slab with Calvary cross and billets but no inscription. The small western tower has a four-gabled or crossed saddleback roof surmounted by a weather vane. The belfry has a square-headed louvred light on each face and a small aperture on its southern face above which is a stringcourse. The small west doorway has a pointed arch. The tower houses two bells of different sizes which are devoid of bellfounders' marks or inscriptions.

The church has a fine 16th-century porch with four-centred outer arch surmounted by a square label and pointed inner arch. Opposite the south door, which has the date 1674 carved on it, is a niche in which a holy-water stoup has been placed. A sundial which was placed above the entrance to the south porch in 1741 has recently been taken down and re-erected in the church. A replica of this sundial with Roman numerals and Latin inscription has been placed above the entrance to the south porch. The inscription, which is a facsimile copy of the original inscription, reads thus:— 'Sic transit gloria mundi T. Truman fecit, Mar. 10. 1741.' The Truman family vaults are beneath the chancel and in the east end of the churchyard. Inside the porch are the usual stone benches.

During repair work in the nave in the late 1960s parts of some early wall paintings were discovered under the plaster of the church wall. The wall painting opposite the south door is in the right position and of suitable shape to be a figure of St. Christopher, the patron saint of travellers. The nave of the church was reseated in 1850 and the chancel in 1875. The church was restored in 1910 when the work consisted of replacing the old pulpit, the choir-stalls and pews of deal with ones constructed of oak. The Truman tablets were taken down from their original position on the north-east wall of the nave and re-erected some four metres westwards on the same wall so that the entrance to the old rood-loft could be exposed. The outline of an ancient doorway in the north wall of the nave was also opened out. The restoration work was carried out under the supervision of William Clarke of Llandaff. An inscription on the steps of the churchyard cross records the fact that its base was restored and a new shaft added in 1937 as a memorial to Herbert Sarsfield Watson of Llansannor Court.

At the entrance to the church on the north side of the churchyard is a lychgate. Llansannor Court, an Elizabethan mansion which stands close by, was the residence of the Gwyns, a family which exerted a powerful influence on the affairs of the parish for several centuries. In 1816 John Fraunceis Gwyn of Forde Abbey, Devon appointed his nephew John Fraunceis Griffith to the living at Llansannor.

The Reverend William Thomas, who held the living in the 18th century, was a non-resident clergyman and lived at Abergavenny where he was head-master of the Grammar School. Another rector, the Reverend Combe Miller, a close relation of the second Francis Gwyn, resided at New College, Oxford, while the spiritual needs of the parish were provided by a curate who received a stipend of £12 per annum.

The church plate consists of a silver chalice inscribed round the foot 'Donum Ioannis Fraunceis Gwyn, De Combe Florry in Com. Somersett, Ford Abbey in Com. Devon, arm. eccl. et par. Llansannor Cal. Decembres, XVIII MDCCXCV (The gift of John Fraunceis Gwyn of Combe Florey in the County of Somerset and Forde Abbey in the county of Devon, armiger to the church and parish of Llansannor, 18. December, 1795).' A silver paten is engraved with the same inscription. The register of baptisms dates from 1726, marriages from 1726 and burials from 1727.

Llantrithyd Place and Church, 1830, by W. W. Young

By kind permission of the National Museum of Wales

Llantrithyd Church

The parish church of Llantrithyd is dedicated to St. Illtyd and probably dates from the latter part of the 12th century. The church was valued at 10 marks in 1254 (Taxation of Norwich), £5 in 1291 (*Taxatio Ecclesiastica*) and £9-0s-8d in 1535 (*Valor Ecclesiasticus*). The parson was resident in 1563. In 1771 (Bishop Barrington's Primary Visitation of the Diocese) the living was valued at £70; the incumbent was the Reverend Nehemiah Hopkins and the patrons were the heirs of Sir John Aubrey. The living was a rectory worth gross £165 in 1835 in the patronage of Sir Thomas Aubrey. The parish of Llantrithyd was joined with Llancarfan in 1972 to form one benefice.

The church consists of chancel, nave, south porch and embattled western tower containing five bells. The chancel arch is pointed with good continuous moulding. The east window of three lights with rounded heads and square label rising in the middle is Laudian bearing the date 1656. The stained glass in the window is divided into six panels and portrays the figures of Moses, Jesus, Elias, John, James and Peter, and was erected in the chancel in 1875 by Charles Aubrey Aubrey.

The chancel is lit on the south side by a two-light window with rounded heads and in the centre of the left-hand light is a roundel displaying the arms of Aubrey 'Azure a chevron between three eagles' heads erased or' impaling Lowther (Louther) 'Or, six annulets three, two and one, sable.' (Sir John Aubrey married Margaret, daughter of Sir John Lowther of Lowther Hall, Westmoreland). In the south wall of the chancel is a priest's door with four-centred arch and square label, which is coeval with the east window. In the floor of the chancel (now hidden by a red carpet) are several incised sepulchral slabs including one with a Calvary cross bearing the date 1586, and in the south-east corner of the sanctuary is a Norman bowl-shaped piscina. Above the chancel arch hangs a sanctus bell in an oak frame which was recast in 1677. On the walls of the chancel are several memorial tablets to former rectors of the parish. One of them is a memorial to the Reverend Roper Trevor Tyler, M.A. (d. 1885), rector of the parish for 47 years, and his wife, Isabel (d. 1859), daughter of John Bruce Pryce of Dyffryn, St. Nicholas. Another is to the memory of the Reverend Nehemiah Hopkins, B.D. (d. 1790), rector of the parish and Prebendary of Llandaff.

The outstanding feature of the church is an exceptionally fine tomb-chest with mural appendages and inscription. It fills the northern side of the chancel from floor to ceiling and projects nearly halfway across the chancel. The mural monument depicts John Basset and his wife, both dressed in black, kneeling in prayer before a reading desk, on the front of which are the words 'Elizabeth Mansel made this in 1597'. The whole of the upper part of the monument is in a rectangular recess surmounted by a complete Corinthian order of columns and entablature with corresponding pilasters. The lower part of the monument is of massive design supporting two recumbent effigies of Sir Anthony Mansel and his wife, Elizabeth, daughter of John Basset. Around this tomb as 'weepers' are the seven children of the younger pair (the Mansels) in Elizabethan costume (three boys and four girls) facing the centre in low relief, each kneeling on cushions. The girls are ruffed, the eldest boy collared and wearing a sword, while the younger boys are gowned and wear linen caps. All figures are dressed in black. A slate tablet inset in the north wall of the chancel records their names and some dates of death: 'Elizabeth, 1567, Edward 1573, Mary Aubre(y), Anne, 1570, Ryce, 1583, William, 1573, Cissil.' Two cartouches at the eastern end of the tomb below the feet of the Mansel figures bear the initials 'A.M. 66' and 'E.M. 64'. Behind the kneeling figures on the mural portion of the tomb is a panel bearing the following inscription in letters of gold on a black background: 'Here lyeth the bodyes of Iohn Basset, Esquier and Elizabeth his wife, a daughter to Andrew Norton of Bristow, Esquier who had issue by Elizabeth, his wife an only daughter named Elizabeth married to Anthony Mansel Esquier second sonne to Sir Reece Mansel of Margam, Knight at whose power bodyes are here intombed which Anthony had issue by the said Elizabeth three sonnes, fower daughters of al which two daughters survives, the elder married to Thomas Aubrey Esquier, the younger maryed to Rawleigh Bussye, Esquier'.

Below the inscription hangs a shield of arms with Basset impaling Norton. Alongside the Basset shield are the words 'Dyed anno 1554 aged 44 years' while near the Norton shield is 'She dyed anno 1596 aged 84 years'. Crowning the mural portion of the tomb on a circular frame is an imposing heraldic centrepiece surmounted by the Mansel crest—'A gold eagle rising'. The shield of arms consists of eighteen quarterings—Mansel (fourteen quarterings) impaling Basset (four quarterings).

The design of the tomb is carried out in the early Renaissance classical style. The architect is unknown, but the design is attributed to Richard Twrch, a native of Glamorgan. At one time the monument was enclosed by iron railings. It was restored and recoloured by the Reverend John Montgomery Traherne of Coedriglan in the last century. Formerly a bracket adjacent to the tomb held the helmet supposed to have been worn by John Basset. Today it is preserved in a safer place.

All traces of any rood-loft arrangements were swept away in the restoration in 1897 but Sir Stephen Glynne writing about the church in 1848, said that there was a rood-loft door in the north wall of the nave concealed by a monument and the beam of the loft was *in situ* twenty years earlier.

The rood screen is of Perpendicular date and is square-framed of three bays. The centre bay is the opening, the others are open above, with wainscot panels

Llantwit Major church—interior ▶

below and have openwork tracery in the head. This takes the form of double multi-foiled ogee arches with pendants between and typical 14th-century-style tracery above in the outer bays. The spandrels of the centre bay are filled with foliated decoration. The cornice includes patera and cresting above, both done evidently to conceal the disfigurement caused by the removal of the loft supports. The screen was restored in the latter part of the 19th century by William Clarke of Llandaff, and the west side of the screen was recoloured in pale blue and red with a lavish amount of gilt in 1941, in memory of Pilot Officer David Roy Watts killed in action.

In the south side of the chancel arch is a trefoil-headed niche containing a statuette of the Virgin and Child, which was presented to the church in the 1940s by a Dutch seaman. The windows on the south side of the nave comprise a pair of two-light windows surmounted by a quatrefoil in the apex and a single light window, all with cinquefoiled heads, and two single lancets and a two-light window with Y-tracery in the head on the north side. All windows are glazed with latticed glass having thin red borders and yellow fleur-de-lys motifs. Under an arched recess in the north wall of the nave is a recumbent effigy in low relief of a civilian or more probably a priest, with hands folded in prayer, the head being tonsured and at his feet a greyhound. Round the edge of the slab is a cornice of ball flower ornament with fleurs-de-lys. It appears to be of early 14th-century date. On the right of the south doorway is a Norman pillar stoup with a modern base. The stone pulpit was erected in 1897. The cornice is concave beneath the rim to admit rectangular patera, groups of fruit and foliage, then a plain moulded top rail. Beneath is a continuous trail of similar motifs. The central panel of the pulpit has a quatrefoil enclosing a marble cross fleurée.

The nave contains a number of monuments of great interest belonging to the Aubrey, Basset and Mansel families, many of whom lie buried in the family vault. The centre marble monument on the north wall of the nave commemorates Sir Thomas Aubrey, Bart. (d. 1786), and his wife, Dame Martha (née Carter), (d. 1788). The monument is surmounted by a draped urn below which is displayed the family achievement. The crest—'On a helm an eagle's head erased'. The arms—'A chevron between three eagles' heads erased or in chief a baronet's escutcheon' impaling those of Carter 'An eagle's head erased or' with the family motto below 'Solem fero' (I bear the sun). The mural monument on the left is to Richard Aubrey, Esq. of Ash Hall, near Ystradowen, Glamorganshire (d. 1808), youngest son of Sir Thomas Aubrey, and the monument on the right is to his wife, Frances (d. 1782), daughter of the Honourable Wriothesly Digby of Meriden, Warwickshire.

Opposite on the south wall is another fine marble monument to Sir John Aubrey (d. 1700), grandson of Sir Thomas Aubrey, who married first Margaret, daughter of Sir John Lowther of Lowther Hall, Westmoreland and secondly, Mary, daughter of William Lewis of the Van. The monument is surmounted by a tierced shield. In the centre the arms displayed are 'Azure a chevron between three eagles' heads erased or, on the fess point a baronet's escutcheon (Aubrey). On the dexter side 'Or six annulets, three, two and one sable' (Lowther) and on the sinister side 'Sable a lion rampant argent' (Lewis of the Van). Above the south doorway is a small oval panel under a cherub-head charged with the arms of Aubrey with a crescent for difference, framed by an oval cartouche that is surmounted by the Aubrey crest all set within a richly moulded surround.

On the west wall of the nave is a large cartouche enclosing an oval heraldic panel surmounted by a cherub-head flanked by two ravens' heads, the panel being charged quarterly of eight:—1st and 4th quarters: 'Azure a chevron charged with a crescent for cadency between three eagles' heads erased or' (Aubrey), 2nd and 3rd quarters: 'Sable a chevron between three spear heads their points imbrued argent' (Bleddyn ap Maenarch) impaling quarterly, 1st and 4th quarters 'Argent a chevron charged with a crescent for cadency between three maunches sable' (Mansel); 2nd and 3rd quarters 'Argent a chevron charged with a crescent for cadency between three hunting horns stringed sable' (Basset). The shield represents the marriage of Thomas Aubrey, Esq. to Mary, the daughter of Anthony Mansel and his wife, Elizabeth Basset. These last two mentioned escutcheons in veined marble came from Llantrithyd Place as they bear no reference to interment. The nave has an arch-braced roof with curved windbraces between the purlins and wallplate, and the principal rafters are supported on stone corbels. This fine open timber roof was placed over the nave in 1877 under the direction of John Prichard, diocesan architect. On the south wall of the nave near the doorway there is a marble tablet to the memory of George Eaton Tutton (d.1887), who was schoolmaster of Llantrithyd School for thirty years from 1845 to 1875. It was erected in 1911 'by those who were under his tuition as a slight tribute to his great ability and a sincere token of their respect and appreciation of the ennobling and enduring influence which he exercised over their lives.'

The font has an octagonal goblet-shaped bowl with moulded rim. The flat fillet which separates each panel, diverges into an arch beneath the rectangular head and returns again into the underside. The main decoration on each panel is a piece of scroll-edged strapwork, joined at the point of incline into the underside by typical Tudor floral decoration, circular and diamond-shaped. A moulded collar separates the bowl from the shaft which has triangular shapes on the angles of the base. The shaft rests on an octagonal base.

In the south-west corner of the nave is a built-in doorway which once gave access to a west gallery which was taken down in the 1897 restoration. The south porch does not appear to form any part of the original fabric except for one oak principal. It has a plain pointed inner doorway and the outer doorway has a depressed arch. The frieze of the porch roof is decorated with patera design and inside the porch are the usual stone benches.

The tower opens to the nave by a round-headed arch and is crudely vaulted. The tower is square and battlemented with a corbel table below. It has a louvred broad lancet belfry window on each face. The tower batters considerably at the base. The ground floor of the tower exhibits a two-light round-headed window on its south face. The west doorway is late 14th century with plain mouldings and dripstone with square label stops. The tower houses a ring of five bells. The treble bell is blank and devoid of any inscription or bell-founder's marks. The second bell bears the inscription 'CHARLES CARR, SMETHWICK,1897.' The third, fourth and fifth bells are inscribed 'T. MEARS OF LONDON FECIT,1814'.

The tower once displayed a weather vane with the date 1711 clearly visible from the churchyard. This was the date of an early restoration when the upper portion of the tower above the corbel course was entirely rebuilt. At this time a gallery was placed in the west end of the nave, access to which was obtained by an outside staircase. The doorway leading to this gallery can still be seen on the south side of the tower, but is now built-in.

The church was re-pewed in 1839 to provide additional seating with a grant from the Incorporated Society for Promoting the Enlargement of Churches. The church was restored in 1897 when new open benches of pitch pine were installed, new block floors laid down and the ground floor of the tower repaved. The west gallery was removed, the roof of the porch renewed and a new altar and pulpit were erected in the church. The bells in the belfry were rehung, a cracked bell recast and four louvred belfry windows were inserted in the tower. The rood-loft entrance doorway was removed from its proper place in the north wall of the nave and built into the tower wall. Finally the church was reglazed throughout. The cost of restoration amounted to £795 and the work was carried out by W. James of Fonmon under the direction of G. E. Halliday, diocesan architect. The church was reopened for divine service after restoration by the Rt. Reverend Dr. Richard Lewis, Bishop of Llandaff, on Wednesday, 25th August, 1897.

A gravestone on the south side of the churchyard records the notable fact that the deceased was the youngest daughter and thirty-sixth child of a former inhabitant of Neath. Also on the south side of the churchyard is the pedestal of what appears to be an old font with fine Norman arcading. The avenue of lime trees in the churchyard was planted by the Reverend Roper Trevor Tyler, rector of the parish in 1856, and the yew tree opposite the west corner of the tower was planted by John Howell in commemoration of Queen Victoria's Golden Jubilee in 1887. To the west of the church are the ruins of Llantrithyd Place, a large 16th-century house, the former seat of the Aubrey family. It fell into decay at the beginning of the 19th century.

Many of the incumbents of Llantrithyd were non-resident clergy and one of these was the Reverend William Bruce Knight, rector of Llantrithyd from 1815 to 1838. In 1817 he was presented by the trustees of C. R. M. Talbot to the living of Margam and the consolidated rectory of Llandough-by-Cowbridge and St. Mary Church. With the help of a curate he served these parishes from 1817 to 1843 living in the old vicarage Ty'n-y-caeau. In 1843 he moved to Llandaff as Archdeacon of Glamorgan becoming also Dean in the same year.

The church plate consists of an Elizabethan silver chalice and paten hall-marked 1576, also a large silver-gilt chalice with cover inscribed on the bowl

'Drink ye my bluid', given on 26th June, 1637, by Sir Thomas Aubrey 'with power to exchange it for one of another fashion when desirable'.

Llantrithyd, like Peterston-super-Ely church, is one of the few parishes in the Vale of Glamorgan which has a printed parish register. The register lists baptisms, 1579-1810, burials 1571-1810 and marriages 1571-1752, and was edited by H. Seymour Hughes in 1888.

Llantwit Major Church

The parish church of Llantwit Major (Llanilltud Fawr) is dedicated to St. Illtyd who, at the end of the 5th century or early in the 6th, founded a monastery on or near the site of the present church. Illtyd and his monastery are first mentioned in the early 7th-century *Life of St. Samson*. Although he is there described as a learned man 'of all the Britons the most accomplished in all the scriptures . . . and in those of philosophy of every kind', there is no evidence to support the view that Llantwit Major was a 6th-century university. But it was one of the most important monasteries in Glamorgan, a place where local kings and nobles were buried. The early buildings of the monastery have disappeared, but the foundations of the Western church may well incorporate masonry laid before the Norman Conquest of the area.

In 1080 the tithes and advowson of Llantwit Major were seized by Robert Fitz-Hamon and conferred on the newly-founded Abbey of Tewkesbury. The grant of the church of Llantwit Major to Tewkesbury was confirmed by the charters of 1106 and 1180. In accordance with the conditions imposed by the latter of these charters a vicarage had been fully established there before 1248, endowed with all the altar dues, the great and small tithes (except the tithe sheaf of hay) and the tithes of the chapel of Llysworney. In 1254 (Taxation of Norwich) the rectory was valued at £2 per annum and the vicarage at £5. In 1291 (*Taxatio Ecclesiastica*) the rectory was grouped with Llanblethian as belonging to Tewkesbury. The vicarage of Llantwit was valued separately at £6. In 1535 (*Valor Ecclesiasticus*) the living was classified as a vicarage worth £16. The Abbey drew some tithes and other receipts of the Rectory and in return supplied the parishioners with a bushel of corn to make the sacramental bread. At the Dissolution of the Monasteries the revenues of the church were granted by Henry VIII to the Dean and Chapter of Gloucester Cathedral, who until the Disestablishment and Disendowment of the Welsh Church in 1920 remained as patrons of the living and were responsible for appointing a vicar. In 1603 the living was a vicarage worth £13-3s-4d per annum: the impropriation worth £100 was held by Henry Doddington Esq., under the Chapter of Gloucester. In 1771 (Bishop Barrington's *Llandaff Diocesan Book*) the living was included in the same valuation as Llysworney, namely £90; the incumbent was the Reverend Noah Neal Newcombe and the patron was the Dean and Chapter of Gloucester. In 1835 it was styled a vicarage worth (with Llysworney) gross £370. The Dean and Chapter of Gloucester were the patrons and

Llantwit - Major.

J. H. Le Keux. Sc.

R. K. Penson. del.

impropriators. In 1982 Llantwit Major and St. Donat's church were grouped with the parishes of Marcross, Monknash and Wick to form a Rectorial benefice known as Llantwit Major.

The plan of Llantwit Major church must be unique among the churches of Wales. As it stands today it is a composite structure of very great length which consists of an Eastern church (known as the 'new church') comprising chancel, nave with north and south aisles, a central engaged tower embattled containing six bells, and a Western church (known as 'the old church') with an unusually large south porch and parvise above. At the west end of the church is a ruin now known as 'the Galilee chapel' and on the north side is a building called the sacristy.

G. E. Halliday, the diocesan architect, who restored a great part of the present church, found that local tradition was right in assigning these distinctive appellations to the several buildings which were described by Professor Edward Freeman, the noted historian, and Victorian ecclesiologist, as 'the elongated pile of the church.'

The earliest part of the present structure is to be found in the Western church which was originally a simple cruciform building of the late 12th century without a tower but built on foundations of pre-Norman date. The 13th century saw the major extension and enlargement of the church, when a low tower was added and later in the same century the transepts were removed. Other work accomplished at that time included the building of the north aisle as we see it today; the nave with chancel east of the tower without the chancel arch; the south aisle reaching two bays further east than at present; the construction of the south porch and parvise of the Western church; and the extension of the early nave westwards to form a chapel. At a later date a chantry was also provided in connection with this chapel.

In the late 14th century the south aisle, which originally reached to the east end of the chancel, was shortened by two bays and the east window of the chancel aisle was inserted at the east end of the south aisle of the nave. At the same time the chancel arch with a hagioscope on each side was inserted. The arcades were built up with stonework on either side to form a clerestory and two clerestory windows were inserted on the north side and one on the south. Two windows were inserted in the south wall of the chancel together with a priest's door in the space between the stone arches. A door was also placed in the south side of the south aisle in place of a window. The stone reredos belongs to this period of architecture.

The 15th century marks another active period in the architectural history of the church when the Western church was taken down and rebuilt, leaving the Norman south doorway and portions of the lower pre-Norman masonry in position, and re-roofed with the present oak roof. The east window of the chancel is probably of this date. Also the annexe adjoining the Lady Chapel on the north side appears to have been added at this time. The rebuilding of the Western church in the 15th century was attributed to the generosity of the Neville family, then Lords of the Manor. It was this rebuilding which confused

St. Illtyd's Church, Llantwit Major (Llanilltud Fawr)

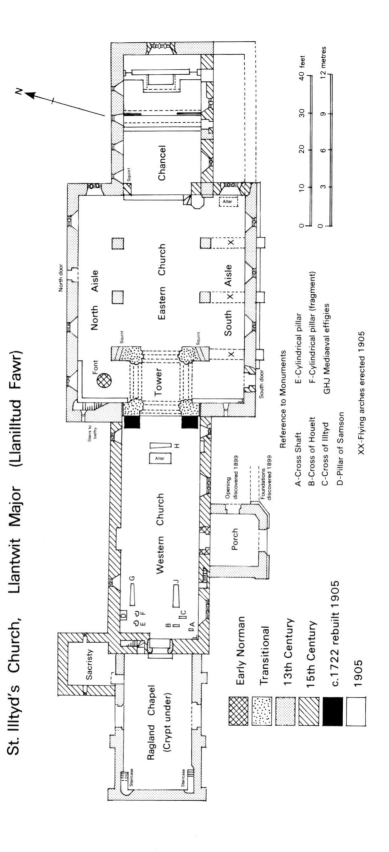

N

Chancel

North Aisle

Eastern Church

South Aisle

North door

South door

Squint

Squint

Squint

Altar

Font

Tower

Stairs to belfry

Western Church

Altar

H

G

D
E C
F

B
J
C
L A

Porch

Opening
discovered 1899

Foundations
discovered 1899

Sacristy

Ragland Chapel
(Crypt under)

Staircase

Staircase

Early Norman

Transitional

13th Century

15th Century

c.1722 rebuilt 1905

1905

Reference to Monuments

A - Cross Shaft   E - Cylindrical pillar
B - Cross of Houelt   F - Cylindrical pillar (fragment)
C - Cross of Illtyd   GHJ Mediaeval effigies
D - Pillar of Samson

XX - Flying arches erected 1905

0   10   20   30   40 feet

0   3   6   9   12 metres

19th-century antiquarians, since what was originally the oldest part of the church and referred to as 'the old church' is obviously the most recent architectural addition to this structure. In the early part of the 18th century two sloping buttresses were built in the Western church to support the failing piers of the tower.

The chancel arch is wide and crudely pointed. Above the chancel arch the chequer background of the rood with emblems of the Passion dates back to the late 15th century. The Cross was originally green with a wreath in black and green representing the crown of thorns, and the nails, scourge and spear were in black and yellow. The iron staples which steadied the original figures can still be seen *in situ*. The existing rood with Christ on the cross with the attendant figures of the Virgin Mary and St. John was erected in 1959 from a design by Alan Durst. The rood beam rests upon the original four stone corbels.

The east window is Perpendicular of four trefoiled lights. The centre mullion diverges in the head to form two pointed lights. There are transoms across the head of each pair of lights and above the pointed trefoil in the 'Y' square-shouldered tracery lights are similar to those below. It is surmounted by a plainly-moulded dripstone. The stained glass in the four main lights depicts the Annunciation, Crucifixion, Deposition and Resurrection of Our Lord, and in the panel tracery lights above are the four figures of Samson, St. Illtyd, King David and St. Patrick. The stained glass window was erected in 1905 under the supervision of W. D. Caröe, architect to the Ecclesiastical Commissioners (who were responsible at that time for restoring the chancel of the church as lay impropriators). The window is a memorial to Ernest Frederick de Winton Tanfield Vachell (d. 1903) of West House, Llantwit Major and was given to the church by his widow Joanna Phillips Vachell. It was designed by Messrs. Clayton & Bell, London.

One of the most notable features of the church is the magnificent stone reredos in the chancel which is constructed in the form of a wall a few feet from the east wall, through which pass a south and north door. The space behind was once used as a priest's vestry or sacristy. The stone reredos is of late 14th-century date and is a splendid example of the sculpture of that period. It was heavily restored in 1905 by the Ecclesiastical Commissioners under the supervision of their architect W. D. Caröe, and the new work can be distinguished by the colour of the stone. The reredos has a facade of twenty-two recessed and canopied niches from which the statues have long since been removed. Tradition states that the niches were once occupied by twelve golden statues of the Apostles. The piece is basically executed in five bays of unequal lengths. The central bay is a double tier of niches, five below and seven above. The lower row is quite shallow and the heads are multifoiled beneath ogee arches which are crocketed and end in a final just beneath a cornice of patera (square flowers typical of 14th-century decoration). They are separated by little shafts which end in pinnacles, also crocketed, and with finials. A taller central canopy in the row above is flanked by niches with similar-styled heads except that the outer arches include a small decorative motif. The finials are larger and more ornate

East window and stone reredos

than those done in relief below and there are square-sectioned foliated pinnacles between. In the centre of all this a wider, higher canopied niche between moulded shafts is vaulted internally. There is a cornice of embattled decoration beneath brattishing and the canopy has pinnacles and floral bosses. The finials above the arches include figurework.

On each side of the centrepiece is a two-tier niche canopied above with tabernacling similar to the feature already described and a lesser, but equally ornate, canopy below. The first and fifth bays of the reredos are again two-tier structures. The arrangement of the three niches is similar to those above on the centrepiece and below is a doorway beneath the many plain mouldings of a particularly deep ogee arch. The altar and sanctuary candlesticks were given in 1929 in memory of Marie Trevelyan, antiquarian and authoress of *Llantwit Major: its history and antiquities*. (1910).

In the south-east corner of the sanctuary is a piscina with cinquefoil drain, crocketed pinnacles and a foliated finial. The head of the piscina is a multifoil beneath an ogee arch with a gable above. All inclines have crockets and the arches are topped by finials. It is coeval with the reredos. The chancel is lit on the south side by a pair of two-light trefoil-headed lights under ogee arches with an elongated quatrefoil in the head, and on the north side by four single lancets deeply splayed. On the chancel walls are medieval wall paintings. The one on the north wall between two of the lancet windows is the figure of Mary Magdalene holding a jar of precious ointment in her right hand, with her left hand uplifted. She wears a red gown and has a flowing head-dress. It dates from the late 13th century. Next to it is a fragmentary figure of the Virgin Mary, also of late 13th-century date. On the south wall of the chancel is a decorative scroll with vine leaves, tendrils of fruit and cornice of chequer pattern below (late 15th century).

In the north and south aisles, each side of the archway leading into the chancel, are the remains of piscinas marking the position of the altars when these aisles were used as side chapels. The arcades of the nave consist of three bays with perfectly plain pointed arches springing from plain square pillars without capitals or any other decoration. The windows of the nave comprise three two-light trefoil-headed windows with plate tracery in the form of circles in the head on the south side, and by two similar 13th-century lights on the north side. The nave is also lit by three clerestory windows of 14th-century date, one on the south and two on the north. At the end of the south aisle is a south doorway with pointed arch of 14th-century character.

The hexagonal pulpit has an embattled moulded cornice and pierced sides. The angles have two-stage buttresses with caps, set-offs and bosses. The open-work tracery is varied but each side has an ogee arch with multifoils and floral decoration on the cusps. Above that there are various trefoils, quatrefoils, cinquefoils, mouchette shapes and tracery light shapes—all open with carved floral motifs between. Below, beneath another row of embattled moulding, are quatrefoils and pointed trefoils. The pulpit has an octagonal stem separated from the plinth by a single string. The pulpit was carved by William Clarke of

Llandaff and was the gift of Mrs. Rees Morgan, East Street, Llantwit Major in 1905. The massive spread-eagle lectern of solid brass was presented to the church in 1905 by Mrs. J. P. Vachell in memory of her parents, Mr. and Mrs. E. P. John of Ham Farm, Llantwit Major.

A notable feature of the nave is the many medieval wall paintings; the finest is that of St. Christopher, the patron saint of travellers, which occupies its usual position opposite the entrance where travellers could see him on the north wall of the nave. He is depicted crossing the stream with the Christ Child on his shoulders. The saint grasps a flowering staff, his attribute, in both hands and around his leg is entwined an eel. The mural dates from circa 1400. St. Christopher was a very popular figure in the Middle Ages when every journey was a potential hazard and he was often invoked for those setting out on a pilgrimage. To the east of St. Christopher is a much-faded painting of the Royal Arms of King James I with the inscription 'God save King James 1604', the date of his coronation. This is indeed a rare example of the Stuart Royal Arms, particularly in Wales. The pillars of the south arcade retain mural decorations with black letter texts. The most interesting one is that on the west face of the first pier of the south arcade. It is probably a late 15th-century or early 16th-century painted memorial according to Dr. E. Clive Rouse. The centre has an elaborate brocade pattern with a nebuly floral scroll frame. At the top is a crest of a goat's head erased and a black letter inscription which reads 'ORATE PRO ANIMA HE ... PROPICIET DEO' (Pray for the soul of He ... May God have mercy.) The wall paintings were completely uncovered, cleaned and restored in 1950 by Dr. E. Clive Rouse, O.B.E., F.S.A., in memory of Canon Richard David, vicar of this parish from 1912 to 1947.

Among the memorials in the church are several stones recording the burial there of a branch of the Westley family who lived at Letchmoor (Leechmoor) near Llantwit Major. Westley was the old way of spelling the surname of the Reverend John Wesley, the founder of Wesleyan Methodism, who, on entering Oxford University, signed himself John Benjamin Westley. On the 25th July, 1777 John Wesley visited Llantwit Major church and the following extract is taken from his diary:—'About eleven I read prayers and preached in Llantwit Major church to a very numerous congregation. I have not seen so large or so handsome a church since I left England. It was sixty yards long but one end of it is now in ruins. I suppose it has been abundantly the most beautiful as well as the most spacious church in Wales.'

The most remarkable piece of sculpture in the church is the Jesse niche which is now placed at the east end of the south aisle. The subject of the decoration of this niche is the family tree of Christ (the stem of Jesse's rod) as recorded in Matthew and Luke. On each side of the niche is a vine climbing and twisting round the heads of fourteen crowned personages (the heads of the kings of Judah of the House of David), seven on each side, some with beards, others without, and round a trefoiled arch at the central point of which is the head of Our Saviour with the crossed nimbus. In the lower portion of the niche we have Jesse lying down asleep with a stem proceeding from his left side and

The Jesse niche

branching off in two directions encircling five crowned heads. The niche is now devoid of its occupant but undoubtedly it once held the figure of the Virgin and Child. A silver crucifix with elongated shaft now stands in the niche. The whole of the decoration bears traces of painting and gilding all over the delicate scroll work. The niche dates back to the early part of the 13th century and is a very fine example of the work of that period. The niche is not *in situ* and was thought to have been the altar piece of the Transitional Church and much later found its way into the Galilee Chapel at the extreme west end of the church.

The east window of the south aisle is of 13th-century date and is of three trefoiled lights, the centre one being much taller than the side lights. It is surmounted by a plain dripstone. It depicts the Virgin Mary as the 'Madonna della Misericordia' (Mother of Mercy). The green cloak seems to be quite separate from the Madonna's own dress and she appears to be holding some articles (possibly bread with more in the basket presumably for distribution). All this reflects the usual presentations of the 'Corporal Acts of Mercy'—food, drink, and clothing for the needy. The window was designed by Clayton & Bell, London circa 1880/1890. The stained glass in the south-east window of the south aisle depicts the Crucifixion of Our Lord and the Crown of the Victor. It was erected in 1920 from a design by Messrs. Clayton & Bell, London, by parishioners of Llantwit Major 'in high praise and reverent memory' of those twenty-four men and one woman (whose names are inscribed on a brass plaque nearby) who sacrificed their lives for their country in the Great War, 1914-1918. The two-manual pipe organ, which stands at the eastern end of the north aisle, was presented to the church about 1910 by Alec Williams, a great lover of music and a close friend of Illtyd Nicholl of The Ham, Llantwit Major. It was built by C. H. Walker, master organ builder of Manchester Square, London about 1860. The manuals have a compass of fifty-six notes while the pedal-board, straight and flat, has twenty-nine. In 1959 the organ was provided with a 'chaire screen' in panelled oak by the architect, George G. Pace, thereby improving what would have otherwise been a rather plain front. On the north wall of the north aisle above the organ is a very early 17th-century monument with rectangular inscription tablet in Latin which commemorates Roger Seys, Esquire, bencher of Lincoln's Inn and Attorney-General for the Principality of Wales to Queen Elizabeth I. He married Elizabeth, the only daughter of Griffith Voss, by whom he had two sons, Richard and Alexander. The monument is surmounted by two classical urns, one on each side and in the centre by the Seys coat of arms which is blazoned as follows: 'Sable a chevron between three spearheads their points imbrued argent' (claiming descent from Bleddyn ap Maenarch.) It was erected in 1600 by his eldest son, Richard.

The font, in the north-west corner of the nave, is of Sutton stone and has a circular bowl of the Norman period according to Francis Bond (1908) with overlapping scallops known as 'scale pattern'. It has a moulding at the rim and another at the base of the bowl which rests on a circular stem and a similar base chamfered out and then inclined towards the square base. A slab with an incised cross in the floor of the church under the tower records the death of Matthew Voss in 1534 at the age of 129 years. Nearby another slab incised with a Calvary Cross marks the grave of a former vicar of the church, Stephen Slugge (1580-1662) whose name appears on the silver chalice. The Victorian stained glass in the west window of the north aisle is a memorial to John George Kibblewhite, founder's kin, St. John's College, Oxford (d. 1910) aged 19 years, and was erected by his parents. The window depicts John Kibblewhite dressed in plate armour, which suggests that he was a soldier.

The upper part of the central tower is of Welsh type, plain for the most part, without stringcourse or buttresses. The upper battlemented stage is corbelled out like so many of the churches in the Vale of Glamorgan. The central merlon of the battlements is however pierced with cross-eyelets. The belfry windows on each face are pairs of trefoil-headed lights. The tower was much lower than

Llantwit Major church bells, recast June 1908

at present since an earlier eastern belfry window is now visible below the roof of the nave inside the Eastern church. The arches beneath are pointed and narrow giving an exaggerated emphasis to the height but nonetheless are well-proportioned. The arches in each case are of two orders, the outer one flat with the surface of the wall, the inner one canted or chamfered. They spring above composite piers and whilst the shafts are similar in being alternatively wide and narrow (the former having a slight leading edge), the capitals with each engaged group are of two distinct types. Moulded abaci and necking string follow simple planes around the piers but the capitals are either of a plain 'lantern' type (i.e. slightly bulbous at the centre) or more conventionally shaped with typical 13th-century decoration which includes foliated scrolls and leaf forms.

The tower houses a ring of six bells originally cast in 1722 by Abraham Rudhall of Gloucester, and known locally as 'Moll, Poll, Doll, Prue, Sue and Bet'. The bells were recast and rehung in a new steel bellframe by Messrs. Mears & Stainbank of the Whitechapel Bell Foundry, London, in 1908. Before that time the bells were down in the churchyard for nearly 40 years, and it took a day to cut away the bushes, etc., that had grown up around them. The bells were rededicated by the Rt. Reverend Dr. Joshua Pritchard Hughes, Bishop of Llandaff on Monday, 29th June, 1908.

The inscriptions on the bells are as follows:—

Treble in D sharp.   ABR. RUDHALL CAST US ALL 1722.
HENRY MORRIS, VICAR, JOSEPH GASKELL, REES THOMAS CHURCHWARDENS. RECAST BY ILLTYD BOND NICHOLL OF HAM. A.D. 1908.

2nd in C sharp.   PROSPERITY TO THE CHVRCH OF ENGLAND.
   A ♗ R 1722.
   THIS BELL WAS RECAST BY JOHN WILLIAMS,
   COURT HOUSE, LLANTWIT MAJOR. A.D. 1908.

3rd in B.   PEACE AND GOOD NEIGHBOVRHOOD A ♗ R 1722.
   IN MEMORY OF EDWARD WILLIAM VAUGHAN, VICAR 1845-
   1901. RECAST BY PARISHIONERS AND FRIENDS A.D. 1908

4th in A sharp.   EVAN SEYS, ESQ. ILTYD NICHOLS, CLARK
   (i.e. Clerk in Holy Orders)
   CHURCHWARDENS, 1722 ROB'T POWELL, VICAR.
   RECAST BY THOMAS MANSELL FRANKLEN. A DESCENDANT
   OF THE ABOVE ROBERT POWELL.

5th in G sharp.   PROSPERITY TO THE CHVRCH OF ENGLAND 1722.
   TO THE MEMORY OF EDWARD WILLIAM VAUGHAN VICAR
   OF THIS PARISH 1845-1901 RECAST BY HIS CHILDREN AND
   GRANDCHILDREN A.D. 1908.

Tenor in F sharp.
   I TO THE CHURCH THE LIVING CALL
   AND TO THE GRAVE DO SVMMON ALL 1722.
   IN MEMORY OF ILLTYD NICHOLL DIED 1574 AGED 82,
   JOHN HIS SON, 1599, ILTYD HIS SON, 1651.
   ILTYD HIS SON 1670, ILTYD HIS SON 1700
   BY WHOSE DESCENDANTS THIS BELL WAS RECAST 1908
   ALSO OF DAVID NICHOLS, VICAR 1662-1720 AND MANY
   OTHERS OF THE NICHOLL FAMILY ALL BURIED WITHIN
   THIS CHURCH.

The Western church has an arch-braced roof with collar-beam trusses. The principal rafters, which are supported on wooden corbels carved in the form of human heads, have trenched purlins with a castellated moulding on their upper edges. The timber of the roof is Irish bog oak which is said to resist the infestation of the death-watch beetle. At the intersections of the lower purlins with the principal rafters are placed heavy square wooden bosses carved with various designs, some floriated, others representing coats of arms of noted families of the Vale. They include the families of Basset, Berkerolles, Boteler, Nicholl and Voss. Two bosses were replaced in 1899, that of the coat of arms of Voss which had fallen down and G. E. Halliday, the architect, thought it appropriate to add that of the coat of arms of the Nicholl family.

The windows of the Western church comprise on the south side a Perpendicular window of three cinquefoiled lights with panel tracery with trefoils above, surmounted externally by a dripstone with floriated square label stop on the west side; that on the east is damaged. In the recess of this window is placed a small figure of the Virgin and Child which was discovered during the 1899 restoration of the church amongst debris in the staircase leading to the upper

The Western church prior to restoration in 1899

chamber or parvise of the south porch. On the east side of the porch is a large window of three trefoiled lights with recticulated style-tracery above forming a double ogee neatly constrained into a row of trefoils beneath a square head. In the south-east corner is a pair of trefoiled lancets which were probably incorporated from the earlier building. In the south-east corner of the Western church is a broken piscina and an aumbry with little wooden doors let into the wall. These and the surrounding wall paintings displaying 15th-century 'perspective cube' decoration suggest that this was the site of the altar of the 15th-century church. The Western church is lit on the north side by a two-light trefoil-headed window with square label, and by a pair of trefoiled lancets with dogtooth ornament, probably incorporated from an earlier structure.

The free-standing stone altar of the Western church is the original pre-Reformation altar slab which was removed at the time of the Reformation when stone altars were forbidden, and replaced by wooden tables. This altar slab was used between 1559 and 1597 as a gravestone (as the inscription shows) for a certain 'Katherin Thomas of the Hame' but the five incised crosses are still visible. It was replaced in its present position in 1959 to the design of George Gaze Pace, architect of York.

On the east side of the altar is a sepulchral slab bearing the effigy of a medieval priest or layman dressed in a long loose tunic buttoned to the throat with apparently a collar of fur and with close sleeves. The left hand holds a glove and the right is raised and lies upon the breast; the head rests upon a square cushion set diagonally in a foliated recess. The slab, upon which the effigy is sculptured, is coffin-shaped, wider at the upper part than the lower, and probably formed the cover of the stone coffin in which the person commemorated was buried. This sepulchral slab dates from the middle of the 14th century and around its edges is the inscription in Norman-French in Lombardic characters:— WILLAM DE RAG ... SHAM ... GYT ICI DEU DE SA ALME EYT MERCI. AMEN (William de Rag ... sham ... lies here. May God have mercy on his soul. Amen.) In the centre of the north wall of the Western church is an empty niche.

Another effigy in the north-west corner of the Western church represents a lady of the late 16th century. She is dressed in a kirtle, intricately embroidered with long sleeves, a tasselled girdle, wide ruff, lace cap and high pleated hat with small feather. Her hands which are placed upon her breast, have three rings on the fingers of the right and one on the forefinger of the left hand. Above her right shoulder is the bust of a child, complete with ruff and cap. A fragment of the inscription as read many years ago, records it as being to the memory of a wife and child of Richard Hopkins. It has been suggested that this effigy may have been the work of a local sculptor since the ornamentation upon the lady's dress may have been copied from the interlaced work upon the early sculptured stones at Llantwit Major. Above this effigy on the north wall is a bracket for a monument now lost with a carved figure in Jacobean costume kneeling in prayer probably a weeper.

Set in the north-west corner of the Western church is one of the few funeral hatchments in the Vale of Glamorgan. Prior to 1959 this hatchment hung where the Rood once stood over the chancel arch. It commemorates the Reverend Robert Nicholl-Carne, M.A. of Nash Manor and Dimlands House, Llantwit Major, who died in 1849 aged 86 years. He inherited in right of his wife Elizabeth, daughter of Captain Charles Loder Carne and assumed the name of Carne by Royal Licence in 1842 in addition to his own name of Nicholl. On the hatchment is blazoned the arms of the Carne family which were granted in 1336, 'Gules a pelican in her piety proper'. Above the arms is the Carne crest 'A pelican displayed with two heads issuant from a Ducal coronet or'. The two Carne mottoes are displayed above the shield 'En toute loyale' (In all loyal) and under the arms 'Fy ngobaith sydd yn Nuw' (My hope is in God).

In the Western church are preserved a number of early Celtic stones and crosses which formerly stood in the churchyard and were re-erected in the Western church early in this century. The cross of Houelt is a slab cross with carved wheel head and stands about two metres high. It has panels of carved interlaced work on both sides. The Latin lettering in half-uncials reads:—
(I)N INOMINE DI PATRIS ET S/PERETUS SANTDI ANC/[C](?) RUCEM HOUELT PROPE[R]/ABIT PRO ANIMA RES PA[T]/RES EUS. (In the name of God, the Father and the Holy Spirit, Houelt prepared this cross for the soul of Res his father). Houelt is believed to be Hywel ap Rhys, king of Glywysing whose death is recorded in 886. The cross dates from the late 9th century.

The chancel arch c. 1899 with the Carne hatchment in its original position.

The pillar of Samson is a quadrangular cross shaft with decorated panels of carving. The Latin inscription in crude half-uncials is set horizontally over twenty-one lines with an overspill letter thus:— IN NOM/INE DI SU/MMI INCI/PIT CRU/X SAL/UATO/RIS QUA/E PREPA/RAUIT/SAMSO/NIS APA/ TI PRO/ANIMA /SUA:ET[P] RO ANI/MA IU/THAHE/LO REX: /ET ART/ MALI[ET]/TEC[A]/N. (In the name of God Most High begins the cross of the Saviour which Samson the Abbot prepared for his soul and for the soul of Iuthahelo the king, and(of)Artma(i)l (and) Tec(a)n'). The inscription is contained in a panel (defined) by a plain roll-moulding occupying the whole of the front of the stone. It is also of late 9th-century date.

The cross shaft of Samson commonly called the Illtud stone has no head, but both sides have decorated panels of interlaced work. Two panels on the face of the cross bear the following Latin inscriptions in rounded half-uncials:— + SAM/SON/POSUIT/HANC C[R]/UCEM+ (Samson erected this cross) (Left-hand panel). The right-hand panel, possibly in four lines originally, of which three survive, reads:— PRO A/NIMA EI/US: + (For his soul). The missing line might have read ORATE (Pray). The reverse side has four panels with the inscriptions ILTU/(TI) (Of Illtyd) SAM/SON//RE/GIS (Of Samson the King). The inner demi-panels have inscriptions on two lines above an incised Greek cross, that on the left reading SAM/UEL, the other EBI/SAR. The Samuel and Ebisar have not been identified but the latter is probably the same person recorded on the inscribed stones at Coychurch. The cross dates from the 10th century.

The cylindrical pillar stone is carved out of a single piece of local sandstone tapering from a flared base towards the head which has broken off and is missing. Its visible height is 2 metres with about 45 cm buried and the diameter measures 45 cm at the base decreasing to 35 cm at the top. A straight vertical groove runs the whole way down the back of the stone and the whole surface of the stone is decorated with carved sculpture divided into four panels by horizontal bead moulding. The three upper panels are decorated with various forms of double-beaded plaitwork but in the bottom panel an irregular pattern of double chevrons forms a base border. It dates from the 10th or 11th century.

A fragment of a pillar being the damaged base of a cylindrical pillar similar to the one mentioned above, is set beside it there. The block of local sandstone is 53 cm tall and is 48 cm in diameter at its widest point. The stone has indications of a similar V-shaped groove and horizontal bead moulding as described in the pillar stone above. It is presumed to be of 10th- or 11th-century date.

In the south-east corner of the Western church is a semi-effigial slab of blue limestone with a centre ridge decorated with a row of fifteen lozenge-shaped figures terminating above in a quatrefoil, within which is a bared head with large ears and closed eyes. On the left-hand side of the stone is a series of twenty-one interlaced rings, above which is a slight arabesque foliated decoration, and along the right-hand edge runs the following inscription in Lombardic capitals:— NE PETRA CALCETUR QUE SUBIACET ISTA TUETUR (Let not the stone be trodden on; let her who lies beneath be protected). The stone slab dates from the 13th century.

The west doorway of the Western church has a segmental arch but a very narrow moulding. The pointed opening above is very ornate by comparison. It has several mouldings with its dripstone firmly anchored to its contours. It belongs to the 14th century. The Western church at Llantwit Major is rich in its collection of 13th-century incised stones bearing floriated crosses, some with a circle and some without, all but two of which are let into the church floor.

The south porch is a delightful structure, so devoid of embellishment that it has almost a tithe barn appearance. The putlog holes give it an even more rural aspect (they were left in the walls so that workmen could erect their scaffolding; the name is derived from the crosspieces of the scaffolding called putlogs, on which the planks forming the floor are laid.) Built in rough courses of random stones the porch has an upper room lit by a single little trefoil-headed light to the south and a pointed one on the east and west sides. There is a short single-stage buttress at the south-west corner and the upper room is corbelled out on the south-east side. The base of the building has an outward splay to the south. Presumably the doorway, or rather arched opening, on the east side once separated the porch from another building. The niche in the north-east wall of the porch has an ogee arch and contains the remains of a holy-water stoup. The inner or south doorway of the church, which has a semicircular arch, is modern as is the door itself. It bears the inscription 'O go your way unto His gates with thanksgiving' which is taken from psalm 100, the *Jubilate Deo*. In the south wall of the church, west of the Norman entrance, is a pointed doorway opening on to the steps which lead to the upper chamber or parvise of the porch, the steps ascending in the thickness of the wall. On the north side of the chamber another pointed doorway opens into the church. It probably opened on to a corbelled gallery whose function can only be surmised. The upper chamber of the porch was probably used as a dwelling place for a priest, since the windows were originally fitted with shutters indicating something more than a store room.

The roof of the porch was restored in 1905 and on the east and west walls are carved castellated wallplates beneath the flat boarded roof with little double trefoil-headed openings with Tudor-style floral decoration between and below. The legend, which bears the last verses of the *Te Deum Laudamus*, is cut into a ribbon. The outer arch of the porch has a segmental pointed arch within an inner arch dying into the side walls and is of 13th-century date.

To the west of the Western church is the Lady Chapel or Galilee, now in ruins; the upper floor was used as a chapel with an altar and piscina, the lower floor or basement was a crypt. In the latter part of the 16th century a chantry chapel was founded by Thomas Ragland in connection with this chapel. The chantry priest lived in a house, now a ruin, on the south side of the churchyard. To the north of the Galilee is a building known as the sacristy, now the boiler house. Its upper floor, which may have been lived in, is reached by means of a stone staircase which also provided access to the chantry chapel.

Llantwit Major church was partially restored in 1888 at a cost of £1,000, in 1899 the restoration was recommenced and completed in 1905 at an outlay of nearly £3,000. The bells were restored in 1908. The work of restoration in 1888 included re-roofing of the Eastern church and the restoration of the walls of the nave, revealing the beautiful medieval wall paintings. The seats of the nave were rearranged and varnished and the belfry repaired. A temporary floor was laid down in the Western church and new seats were provided. The work of restoration was carried out by Richard Price, contractor of Llantwit Major, under the supervision of G. F. Lambert, architect of Bridgend. The church was reopened for divine service after restoration on Monday 4th June, 1888 by the Rt. Reverend Dr. Richard Lewis, Bishop of Llandaff.

In its report for 1888 the Society for the Protection of Ancient Buildings, which had taken great interest in Llantwit Major church, severely criticized the work of restoration carried out at the church because the architect had not heeded the advice or followed the recommendations given by the Society. For instance black mortar had been used to point the tower which made it appear smaller and less impressive. Roofs requiring recovering had not been dealt with in the way specified by the Society. The old stone tiles had been removed and substituted with poor quality slates. Deal or pitch pine had been mostly used for new roof timbers in the nave and aisles instead of oak, contrary to the advice of the Society.

In 1899, during the incumbency of the Reverend Edward William Vaughan, who at that time was 89 years of age, the Western church and south porch were restored. Since the Reverend John Wesley preached there in 1777 the Western church had not been used for worship except for the Llandaff Diocesan Church Choral Festival in 1884, and it bore more the appearance of a burial vault than a church. The west doorway and most of the windows had been walled up for many years and the tracery of the windows broken. The earthen floor was paved, the roof timbers repaired, the roof was re-boarded with oak boards and re-slated. The stonework of the windows was repaired and the windows re-glazed. The south porch was re-roofed and a new floor inserted in the parvise. The earth which had accumulated on the south side of the church, causing considerable dampness, was removed. All the walls were repointed internally and externally and all the pre-Norman stones were placed in the Western church.

The Reverend W. Wentworth Scott, curate of the parish at that time, initiated the work of restoration of the Western church in 1899. The work of restoration was carried out by William Clarke of Llandaff under the supervision of G. E. Halliday, diocesan architect. The church was reopened for divine service after restoration on Monday, 30th July, 1900 by the Bishop of Llandaff, the Rt. Reverend Dr. Richard Lewis.

In 1905 the Eastern church was restored. The arcade of the south aisle was found to be in a dangerous condition. This was remedied by rebuilding the foundations of the piers of the south arcade and supporting the arcade by means of four flying buttresses across the south side with external buttresses to take the thrust. The external buttresses are in the Early English style with gablets and offsets.

The chancel was restored by the Ecclesiastical Commissioners as lay impro-priators in 1905. The main structural work was covering the roof with oak boards and re-slating it. The 14th-century reredos was restored and a new stained glass window was erected in the east end of the chancel. When the restoration was undertaken at this time, the tower was found to be in a very critical condition. Early in the 18th century two buttresses had been built in the Western church to support the tower on its western side, which must have shown signs of weakness then. In 1899 when the Western church was restored it was discovered that the bases of the two western piers of the tower had been crushed and that the piers were very much out of the perpendicular. Between 1899 and 1904 movement was still taking place, threatening the imminent collapse of the whole tower. So serious was the condition of the tower that J. P. Seddon, architect of London, who examined it on behalf of the Llandaff Diocesan Church Building Society, advised the Building Committee to take it down and rebuild it from its foundations.

After due consideration the Reverend Henry Morris, vicar of Llantwit Major, and the Building Committee appointed G. E. Halliday, architect, to take charge of the restoration of the tower. The foundations of the piers were relieved of as much weight as possible by laying new concrete footings under each arch. The tower was shored up by massive square timber supports while new foundations of concrete, two metres deep in places, were laid down. Once the weight was relieved all loose stonework was removed and reset in cement. This difficult and painstaking task was carried out by William Clarke of Llandaff. The sacristy was also restored at this time by repairing the walls and re-roofing and re-glazing the windows. The walls were underpinned and a cellar formed to receive a heating apparatus.

The restoration of the Eastern church, the tower and sacristy was carried out under the superintendence of G. E. Halliday and John W. Rodger, architects of Cardiff. The restoration of the chancel in 1905 was carried out by W. D. Caröe, architect to the Ecclesiastical Commissioners. The church was reopened for divine service after restoration on Friday, 14th July, 1905 by the Rt. Reverend Dr. Joshua Pritchard Hughes, Bishop of Llandaff.

Before the restoration of the church there had been much speculation concerning the history of Llantwit Major church, and the opinions of antiquarians and archaeologists had been at variance as to which portion of the church occupied the site of the original church. The generally-accepted view was that what was known as the Eastern church was really the oldest building and that the Western church and chantry were additions. G. E. Halliday, who directed the work of restoration, had devoted considerable time to the study of the archaeological evidence and wrote two papers on the subject in *Archaeologica Cambrensis*. He now stated conclusively that local tradition had been correct in assigning the name 'Old church' to the Western church as this was probably the most ancient part of the building containing pre-Norman foundations.

In 1959 another programme of restoration was carried out by George Gaze Pace (whose work is as common in South Wales as it is in Yorkshire). Pace introduced the simple but elegant pews in the nave, and the attractive light fittings were designed by his associate, Ronald Sims. He restored the rood figures destroyed at the Reformation with replacements carved by Alan Durst. A chapel was erected at the east end of the south aisle. In the Western church Pace reintroduced the old medieval mensa or altar slab as part of the altar. The new altars were consecrated and the pews dedicated by the Bishop of Llandaff, the Rt. Reverend Dr. Glyn Simon, on the 31st May, 1959.

The churchyard cross, which stands upon six steps, was restored in 1919 by Colonel Joseph Gaskell, churchwarden, in memory of his son, Lieutenant-Colonel Frank Hill Gaskell who was killed in action at Merville, France in 1916 aged 37 years. The design for the top of the shaft and head was prepared by G. E. Halliday, architect of Cardiff, and the head contains on one side a representation of the Crucifixion and on the other the figure of St. Illtyd, the patron saint of the church.

The Reverend Edward William Vaughan was vicar of Llantwit Major church for a period of 55 years (1845-1901). Born in 1810 he saw the accession of four sovereigns and was present as a chorister from Merchant Taylor's School at the Coronation of George IV in 1820. He was also present as one of the clergy at the Coronation of Queen Victoria in 1837, and during his incumbency at Llantwit Major he buried over a thousand people—a number equal to the entire population of the village at that time. It was his wish to be buried in the churchyard at Llantwit Major beside the Cross of St. Illtyd and the tomb erected there by members of his family marks his grave on the north side of the church. In 1974 ecclesiastical history was made when a bishop became a curate with the arrival of the Rt. Reverend John Poole-Hughes. He had spent most of his clerical life with the Universities Mission to Central Africa and had been inducted in 1962 as Bishop of South West Tanganyika. When he returned to this country he acted as Assistant to the Bishop of Llandaff, but he also came to Llantwit Major, with special responsibility for the students of Atlantic College. However, in 1975 the Rt. Reverend John Poole-Hughes left Llantwit Major to become Bishop of Llandaff.

The church plate consists of a silver chalice with its paten cover, and round the bowl is inscribed: 'Edwin Powell ar. et Stephen Slugge cler. procuratores—Ecclesiae de Llantwit Major. Ano Do 1620'. It is hall-marked 1620. The Reverend Stephen Slugge was curate in 1620 and became vicar of Llantwit Major in 1629. The register of burials and baptisms dates from 1721, marriages from 1724.

Llysworney Church

The parish church of Llysworney is dedicated to St. Tydfil, a female Celtic saint of whom nothing is known for certain. The church is mentioned as a chapel of Llantwit Major in 1180 and it belonged to the Abbey of Tewkesbury. Llysworney had close ecclesiastical associations with Llantwit Major inasmuch as the incumbents of Llantwit Major from early times to the present century held the living of Llysworney. Nicholas of Llysworney was Dean of Groneath in 1246 but there is no further mention of the church until we come to 1535 (*Valor Ecclesiasticus*) when it was classified as a 'vicarage' worth £4-7s-5d; it is not mentioned by name in the Abbey Returns but is covered by the term 'Rectory of the church of Llantwit.' In 1771 (Bishop Barrington's *Llandaff Diocesan Book*) the value of the living was included in the same valuation as Llantwit Major amounting to £90; the church was served by the Reverend Mr. John Carne for Joshua Powell. In 1835 it was styled a Rectory but included in the same statement as Llantwit Major respecting the value, the patronage and the impropriation. Llysworney was joined with the parish of Llandow in 1921 and with Colwinston in 1970 to form a grouped benefice.

The church consists of chancel, central tower containing a single bell, nave, south porch and modern vestry on the north side of the chancel. Inside, the church has an unusual appearance, for the tower is not as wide as the nave, but is built flush with it on the north. The broad pointed arch from nave to tower is not on the same axis of the nave but considerably on the north side of it whilst the acutely-pointed arch from tower to chancel is still further to the north. Consequently this results in a very restricted view of the sanctuary from the nave. This irregularity of shape, being out of line, has been regarded by some authorities as a case of deviation where the placing of the chancel to the north or south of the nave is supposed to be symbolical of Christ's drooping head on the Cross of Calvary. As a result of the deviation a side squint under a pointed arch has been placed in the chancel wall. At one time, according to David Jones of Wallington, the noted antiquarian, there was a second squint now blocked up. It would appear that the unusual shape of the church was actually part of the original Norman design.

The east window is of three lights with trefoiled heads, the central one higher than the other two. The exterior of these lights is surmounted by a common hood mould. The window depicts the Resurrection of Our Lord and beneath in the centre panel is the coat of arms of the Nicholl-Carne family, a quartered

shield 1st and 4th quarters 'Gules, a pelican in her piety proper' (for Carne), 2nd and 3rd quarters 'Sable 3 pheons argent' (for Nicholl) surmounted by the Carne crest 'Out of a ducal coronet a pelican displayed with two heads' and the motto 'En toute loyale'. The window was erected in 1908 as a memorial to John Devereux Vann Loder Nicholl-Carne (d. 1905) by his widow, from a design prepared by A. L. Moore of London.

The chancel is lit on the south side by a narrow window with trefoiled head deeply splayed with external hood mould. In the south-east corner of the sanctuary is a pillar piscina with Norman cushion capital embedded in a recess in the south chancel wall. The open oak roof of the chancel rests on six massive stone corbels.

On each side of the crossing under the tower on the north and south walls is a two-light cinquefoiled headed window with square label. The flat roof of the crossing is panelled with oak. The square tower is massive with a corbel table just below the parapet. The tower has narrow slit-loopholes at various levels and the belfry has a two-light round-headed louvred window on its north and south faces. A doorway with pointed arch leads from the chancel to the modern vestry on the north side of the chancel to the modern vestry on the north side of the chancel and from there a doorway in its west wall leads to a turret-staircase on the north side of the tower which in turn leads to the upper chamber or belfry of the tower. The tower houses a large pre-Reformation bell which bears the inscription 'SANCTE PETRE ORA PRO NOBIS' (St. Peter pray for us) and was probably cast by John Gosselin of Bristol between 1449 and 1453. There were originally three bells in the tower.

On the south side of the arch between nave and tower is an inscription which records the death of Henry Williams in 1720. He was the grandfather of the Reverend Thomas Williams, M.A., B.D., headmaster of Cowbridge Grammar School from 1766 to 1783. He seemed to have possessed a strong affection for St. Tydvil's church for three of his children who died in infancy were buried there, and in his will he directed that his own body should be 'interred as deep as may be in the same grave as my three children in the church of Llysworney or in the chancel of Cowbridge at the discretion of my beloved wife'. Let into the north supporting arch of the tower is a picturesque stone carved with the symbols of birth, time passing (life) and death with the inscription 'underneath lyeth ye Body of Wenllian William who dyed ye 30 of June 1732 aged 100.'

The windows of the nave comprise on the north side a broad cinquefoil-headed single window with label and a two-light window with cinquefoiled heads with label. The latter depicts in one light Christ the King and in the other Christ the Good Shepherd and was designed by Frank Roper of Penarth; it is a memorial to Haydn Williams (d. 1971) and was erected in the church in 1972 by his wife and daughter. The nave is lit on the south side by a two-light round-headed window and a two-light cinquefoil-headed window, both labelled and of plain glass. The west window of the nave is of two round-headed lights and square label and represents 'Valour' in the left-hand light and a soldier receiving a crown in the right-hand light. The inscription reads:— 'Be thou faithful unto death and I will give thee a crown of life'. The window was erected as a memorial to those men of the parish killed in the Great War, 1914-1918, by relatives and friends. The stone pulpit has a moulded cornice with deep hollow, below which are six coffered panels with ogee heads. Beneath a castellated centre-rail is a row of six rectangular coffered panels with deeply moulded bottom-rail and solid base.

On the north wall of the nave are several memorial tablets to the Carne family of Nash Manor. One of them is to John Carne (d. 1762), who claims lineal descent from Iddyn, King of Gwent. The mural tablet is surmounted by the Carne arms 'Gules a pelican in her piety proper' and the Carne motto 'En toute loyale'. The font is octagonal of simple design, the base being very much smaller than the bowl. The inner door of the south porch has a pointed arch while the outer arch is semicircular and modern. Painted in black letters over the inside of the south doorway of the church are the words 'Peace be within thy walls' (Psalm no. 122, verse 7). On the exterior wall of the south side of the nave is a carved stone on which the design appears to include both chevron and dogtooth ornament. The nave has an arch-braced roof with trefoil lights as decoration above the collar beams. It is supported on ten massive stone corbels. The one-manual organ, built by W.E. Richardson & Sons of London, Manchester and Preston, was restored and fitted with an electric blower in 1950 in memory of Gilbert Stradling Nicholl-Carne of Nash Manor (d.1949). In 1960 the organ was renovated in memory of Margaret Ellen Jones (d.1959), organist of the church for 40 years.

In 1774 when the incumbent was the Reverend John Carne and David Jones the churchwarden a faculty was granted to Llysworney church to sell two bells which 'from time immemorial were broken and entirely useless' and to use the money received from the sale of the bells to provide new seats and pews in the parish church since the present pews were in 'a decayed and ruinous condition and unfit for the parishioners and inhabitants of the said parish to sit and kneel in to hear divine service.' The petition records that a considerable sum of money was spent on repairing the church and tower. A plan of the arrangement of the new seating attached to the petition showed how each pew was allocated and appropriated to families of the parish according to their social status.

The church was completely restored in the years 1893-1894 when new roofs were raised, new floors laid down and all defective walling was pulled down and rebuilt. The old-fashioned square pews were removed and entirely replaced with new seats of red deal. The old pulpit and reading desks were removed and a new pulpit erected. A new vestry was constructed on the north side of the chancel and a turret-staircase was built on the north side of the tower leading from the vestry to the belfry. The windows of the church were reglazed throughout. The cost of the restoration amounted to £1,000 and the work was carried out by Messrs. Hatherley and Carr of Bristol according to drawings and specifications prepared by the architects, Bruton and Williams of Cardiff. The church was reopened for divine service after restoration on the 6th June, 1894.

An entry in the marriage registers records that the parents of David Jones of

Wallington, Thomas John Jones of Llanblethian and Hannah Harries of Nash were married on the 30th April, 1832 in Llysworney church. The church plate includes a silver chalice hall-marked 1621. The register of baptisms and burials dates from 1665, marriages from 1813.

Marcross Church

The parish church of Marcross is dedicated to the Holy Trinity and was built in the early part of the 12th century. The church was a rectory worth 5 marks in 1254 (Taxation of Norwich) and £10 in 1291 (*Taxatio Ecclesiastica*). In the *Valor Ecclesiasticus* of 1535 it was valued at £10-12s-6d. It had a parson and a curate in 1563. In 1771 (Bishop Barrington's Primary Visitation of the Diocese) the living was worth £130; the incumbent was the Reverend Edward Carne and the patron was the Dean and Chapter of Llandaff. In 1835 it was a rectory worth gross £211; there was no impropriator and the patron was the Chapter of Llandaff. In 1950 the parishes of Marcross, Monknash and Wick were united to form one benefice and in 1983 the three parishes were joined with St. Donat's and Llantwit Major to form the Rectorial benefice of Llantwit Major.

The church consists of chancel, nave, south porch and western tower containing one bell. The chancel arch is Norman and semicircular and springs from square abaci. The roll-moulding on the western edge of the arch follows the curve of the arch, but at the top changes into five bold chevrons. The jambs are chamfered with ornamental stops, two of which are volutes and two vesica-shaped ornament. A low stone screen wall probably of 14th-century date, rebated for a door, reduces the width of the passage into the chancel.

The east window is a 19th-century insertion of three trefoiled lights which is filled with plain patterned glass with red and yellow diamond insets. It has an external dripstone with scrolled label stops. The two side lights are markedly less high than the middle one, above which is plate tracery in the form of two small trefoils which appear on either side. The chancel is lit on the north side by a deeply-splayed trefoil lancet and on the south side by two small trefoil lancets. One of these is divided by a transom, the lower half being shuttered thus forming one of the rare low-side or lepers' windows of the diocese. Just to the south of the centre of the chancel floor is an incised sepulchral slab probably in memory of an early 13th-century incumbent. On it is carved a beautiful Early English design of a cross, with the open Bible on the right hand and a chalice on the left hand side symbolizing word and sacrament. This slab of Sutton stone was unearthed by workmen when the church was being restored in 1893. The former rood-loft, of which only the corbels and the rood-loft doorway remain, was entered from the chancel (an uncommon entry which similarly existed at Eglwys Brewis and Monknash). To the north of the chancel arch stands the rood-loft doorway with four-centred arch and brattishing along the top of the

lintel of its partially-restored wooden frame. On the north wall of the chancel
there is a memorial tablet to the Reverend Pryce W. Jones (d. 1919) rector of
the parish for 37 years and perpetual curate of Monknash from 1896 to 1915.
Above it is another marble monument erected to the memory of the Reverend
John Williams, M.A. of Jesus College, Oxford (d.1869), rector of the parish for
nearly 37 years and vicar of St. Donat's for 26 years; the monument also
commemorates his wife, Ellen Louisa (d.1847), daughter of the Reverend
Robert Carne of Dimlands House, Llantwit Major and rector of Llanmaes.
Their remains lie interred outside beneath the east window of the chancel. The
chancel has a beautiful oak barrel roof which dates from 1893.

The nave is lit on the north side by two single-light windows and on the
south side by a pair of two-light windows, all trefoil-headed and glazed with
plain patterned glass edged in red. In the north wall of the nave is an arched
recess for a (missing) recumbent effigy with roll-mouldings dating from the
early part of the 14th century; the finial to the label is a man's head to the west,
that to the east is missing. In the recess is a slab of very dark limestone with a
floriated cross. This tomb, which had formerly been built up, was opened up
during the restoration of the church in 1893. The nave has an arch-braced roof
with two rows of curved windbraces between the purlins and wallplate. A
white marble tablet on the north wall of the nave is a memorial to three men of
the parish who gave their lives in the Second World War, 1939-1945.

The oak pulpit, erected in 1893, has a deep but plainly moulded cornice and
on each side a pair of trefoil-headed lights separated by a rail from a pair of
quatrefoils, all pierced. A thicker bottom rail divides it from a similarly-shaped
drum which also has openwork with trefoils. The stairway has a thick handrail
finely carved on the end with square-sectioned balusters formed as it were of
the sides of lancet windows. The pulpit retains a bracket for an hour glass.

The large Norman font of Sutton stone with its circular bowl has roll-
moulding on its rim and a fillet surrounds the bowl near the base. It is lined with
lead. It is positioned in the centre of the nave near the south door, a position
suggested by Miss Olive Talbot in the restoration of the church in 1893 for, in
her words, 'doctrinal and symbolical grounds'.

The south doorway is Norman and has a single arch which springs from
capitals decorated with leaf foliage. The hood mould, decorated with billet
moulding, has grotesque heads as label stops. The south porch is of 19th-
century date done in a 14th-century style with a little trefoil in the apex; the
outer doorway has a pointed arch surmounted by a dripstone with scrolled
stops. The apex of the gable is surmounted by a plain cross. In the porch, which
has stone benches on either side, is a mural tablet to the memory of the
Reverend Francis Gamage, (d. 1728), rector of the parish for 48 years and vicar
of Colwinston for 25 years, whose body is buried on the south side of the
chancel. This tombstone was removed from the south wall of the chancel
during the restoration of the church in 1893.

The tower opens to the nave by a round-headed arch. The 14th-century
tower is tall and sturdy with slightly battered base and saddleback roof whose

Merthyr Dyfan church—interior ▶

gables are surmounted by plain crosses. The west wall is pierced by slit-loopholes set high up and its base is lit by a small square window. On the north, south and east sides are single square-headed belfry lights, whose facing south and east being louvred. Below, halfway down the south wall of the tower is an additional slit-loophole. The tower houses a single bell which is blank and devoid of any inscription or bellfounder's marks. The whole building retains traces of the whitewash once so common on the Vale churches. In the churchyard is the base and fragment of the shaft of a medieval cross surmounted by a modern bronze sundial.

Marcross church was restored in 1893 and Miss Olive Talbot of Margam Abbey contributed generously to the restoration fund, as did Mrs. Mary Stradling-Carne and Mrs. Ella B. Pownall of St. Donat's. The work of restoration included new roofs on nave, and chancel; a new pulpit, lectern, holy table, altar rails and chancel seats were installed. The south porch was entirely rebuilt. The nave of the church was completely reseated with open benches. A new east window was inserted together with a new window on the north side of the nave, two new windows on the south side of the nave and an old window in the west end of the tower was opened out. Repairs were also carried out to the tower. The earth which had accumulated on the south side of the church above the floor level was removed and a new drain was laid down to keep the building dry. The cost of the restoration amounted to £875. The work was carried out by W. A. James of Cowbridge under the supervision of Messrs. Kempson and Fowler, architects of Cardiff. The church was reopened for divine service after restoration on Tuesday 16th January, 1894.

The church possesses an Elizabethan silver chalice, neither hall-marked nor dated. The bowl is conical and is decorated with a belt of intersecting foliated strap ornament. The stem and foot correspond in design with the paten cover inscribed, 'Marrcros, 1576'. Also a silver bread-dish inscribed 'Presented by the Reverend John Williams M.A. 1866' together with a plated alms-dish with the same inscription. The registers date from 1730.

◀ *Michaelston-le-Pit church—interior*

Merthyr Dyfan Church

The parish church of Merthyr Dyfan is dedicated to St. Dyfan, one of the early Christians who, an unreliable legend records, was sent with Fagan by Pope Eleutherius in 180 A.D., in the time of King Lleuwrg, King of Britain, to administer baptism to the nation of the Cymry. The place where he was killed by pagans, so it is claimed, took the name Merthyr Dyfan, meaning the burial place of Dyfan. The present church was built in the early part of the 13th century and was constructed plainly but strongly, for endurance rather than for beauty of architecture.

The church was valued at £3 in 1254 (Taxation of Norwich), 4 marks in 1291 (*Taxatio Ecclesiastica*) and £5-2s-4d in 1535 (*Valor Ecclesiasticus*), when it was classified with the Rectories. In 1553 the Commissioners of King Edward VI took from the church a cross of copper gilt worth 20s and a vestment of white fostian worth 6s-8d, a cape of white damask valued at 20s and a vestment of green damask valued at 33s-4d. The patron was resident in 1563. In 1771 (Bishop Barrington's Primary Visitation) the living was worth £50. In 1810 the Rectory received a grant of £200 from Queen Anne's Bounty. In 1834 the Reverend Gabriel Powell became the last rector to hold both the livings of Cadoxton-juxta-Barry and Merthyr Dyfan when he resigned the living of Merthyr Dyfan. In 1835 the Rectory was worth gross £126 when R. F. Jenner was the patron. Merthyr Dyfan church is now held with St. Paul's church, which was dedicated in 1893.

The church consists of chancel, nave, south porch and western tower containing three bells. The Tudor chancel arch is a drop arch which appears to be rusticated at least in part. The east window is set high in the east wall of the chancel and is of two cinquefoiled lights under a square head. The window depicts the Annunciation of the Blessed Virgin Mary and was erected in 1933 from a design prepared by Messrs. J. Wippell & Co. of Exeter in memory of David Davies (d. 1906), his wife, Mary Davies (d. 1906) by their son Thomas Davies of 'Seaforth', Barry.

The beautifully-carved and painted oak reredos on the east wall is panelled with applied tracery in flowing style in the head of each. It is bordered by a leaf trail in gold on a blue background beneath a row of brattishing. The central panel, beautifully coloured, depicts the Crucifixion scene with the attendant figures of the Blessed Virgin Mary and St. John on either side of the cross. The reredos was erected in 1933 in memory of George Beith of Pontypridd

(d. 1918) and his wife, Margaret Millwood Beith (d. 1933) by their daughter, Queenie Beith Davies of 'Seaforth', Barry. The oak altar table, which was coeval with this reredos, was replaced by the original medieval stone altar slab, supported on massive stone supports, in 1974. This altar slab, which has a groove along its side and some rough inscription on it, was used to cover a holy well in the churchyard for many years before it was taken inside the church for preservation. Local tradition has it that it was associated with the Druids and the groove was for the blood of human sacrifice.

The roof of the chancel has a simple arch-braced roof of 15th- or early 16th-century date plastered between the purlins and principal rafter. The chancel is lit on the south side by two pointed lancets deeply splayed and possibly original windows. In the south-east corner of the nave is a stone corbel which formerly supported the beam of the rood-loft, and opposite on the chancel wall, north of the chancel arch, is the rough outline of the former rood-loft doorway, now blocked up. A single trefoil-headed light set high in the north-east corner of the nave may well have illuminated the stairway to the low rood-loft.

The windows of the nave on the south side comprise a window of two cinquefoiled lights and two single cinquefoiled lights, all surmounted with square labels. The south-west window of the nave contains attractive, modern stained glass and was erected in 1986 by Mrs. D. C. Cotton in memory of her husband, Norman John Cotton (1920-1982), rector's warden for 25 years. The symbolism of the stained glass is as follows—the rainbow represents the Kingdom of Heaven from which the rays radiate outwards in groups of three representing the Trinity. Between the two angels the dove emerges to ascend just above the water (giving the design a focal point), out of which a further three emerge divided by bands of streaky ruby-yellow symbolizing the baptism of fire. The window was designed by Michael Gerald Lassen, a modern, stained glass artist of Bristol. Apart from the single lancet high in the north-east corner, the nave is lit on the north side by a window of two cinquefoiled lights under a square label. The stained glass in this window depicts the Holy Family with Jesus portrayed as an apprentice carpenter, and was erected in 1974, by Lilian Howarth in memory of her husband Tom James Howarth and her mother. It was designed by H. W. Harvey, a modern, traditional stained glass artist of York.

In the north-east corner of the nave stands a beautifully carved lectern on a single stem, circular at the top and chamfered below, on a square base. The desk which has drop pendants beneath, has a frieze of V-shaped decoration and is panelled with acorn leaf decoration enclosing the IHS monogram on the front. It is supported on small brackets which are decoratively shaped above a collar formed of a series of little columns. Next comes an octagonal piece of tabernacling done as a series of double lancet shapes each beneath a pointed arch. The stiles which separate each of these panels also have drop pendants. This feature bears the inscription 'We praise thee O God'. Immediately beneath this feature the stem has solid scroll brackets covered with leaf decoration. These are affixed to a base which is wider where it meets the plinth so that the deep sides are

Lectern or ambo

angled out towards the floor. The nave is lit by eight very attractive modern light clusters.

The 13th-century font near the south doorway has a plain cylindrical bowl with a single roll-moulding around the rim. The modern blocks which form the stem are chamfered on their upper edge to meet the flat underside of the bowl. It has an octagonal base set on a square plinth. Set into the floor of the west end of the nave, which is a metre or so higher than the rest of the church, are several 18th-century tombstones with interesting epitaphs. The nave has a modern arch-braced roof boarded between the rafters.

The south porch is modern but the trefoil in the apex of the porch and the style of gabled finial indicates a 14th-century-style Victorian restoration. The pointed outer arch has a hood mould with rectangular label stops and the inner south doorway is acutely pointed. Inside the porch are stone benches and in the south-east corner is an ancient square holy-water stoup resting on a modern stone corbel. In the east wall of the porch is a trefoiled lancet deeply splayed.

The tower opens to the nave by a four-centred arch, low and of a type which came in about the same time as the Perpendicular period began. It is infilled with beautiful modern black ironwork. The surfaces are flat and continue thus around the sides without interruption, but the blocks which form it are canted outwards. The west end of the nave is higher by about a metre than the rest of the church. The tower is square and has a corbel table under the battlement. It is of two storeys divided by a stringcourse. The belfry has a pointed louvred light on each face and on the south face there are three more openings, two of them below the stringcourse. There is no west doorway but instead there is a broad lancet in the west wall and above it is a slit-loophole. At the base of the tower is another stringcourse. An obtusely-pointed doorway in the north wall of the tower leads to a spiral stone staircase, contained in a projection on the north side of the tower. The staircase which is lit by a square-headed light, gives access to the belfry.

The tower houses three main bells and a smaller single bell. Two dated 1676, were cast by John Pennington of Monmouth and the other one, dated 1718, was cast by Evan Evans of the famous Chepstow bellfoundry. The inscriptions on the main bells are as follows:–

1. L:R:I:R:B:C:W:I 🔔 P: 76 ◇
2. L:R:I:R:B:C:W:I 🔔 P: 76 ◇
3. IOHN RICHARD CH. WARDEN EE 🔔 1718 O O.

The two circles on number 3 bell are the reverse and obverse of a Charles II half crown. The letters L.R. and I.R.B. on bells 1 and 2 are the initials of the churchwardens in 1676.

The church was restored in 1857 at a cost of £500 and the work of restoration included the raising of a new roof, the insertion of new windows and the construction of a new porch. In 1909 the tower was restored. In 1972 a faculty was granted to Merthyr Dyfan church to carry out an ambitious programme of restoration work in accordance with plans and specifications drawn up by the York architects, George G. Pace and Ronald G. Sims. Their aim was to blend the old with the new and the proposed work was to be carried out in stages and each stage had first to be approved by the Advisory Committee before the following stage was proceeded with.

The work carried out in 1974 included the re-roofing of the chancel, nave porch and tower. The Victorian plaster was hacked off the interior walls and the walls were re-plastered. It was the intention of the architects to restore the floor of the nave and the chancel to its original level but due to the fact that many human remains were found buried under the floor of the church it was impossible to restore the level completely. However, the floors of the eastern portion of the nave and the whole of the chancel were substantially lowered so that the greater part of the jambs of the chancel arch was uncovered. The original medieval stone altar, which had been brought into the church from the churchyard for preservation during the 1950s replaced the oak altar table which was transferred to St. Paul's church, Merthyr Dyfan. Modern furniture was installed throughout and attractive light clusters fitted. The base of the font was reconstructed and set upon three chamfered blocks. A new grille was placed at the west end of the nave under the tower arch to form a secure vestry and a similar black wrought-ironwork gate was placed in the porch.

In February 1987 a medieval aumbry was discovered in the north wall of the chancel when the exterior stonework was being repaired. It contained a skull and other human bones which have since been reverently re-interred in the churchyard. A drain hole, probably from a built-up ancient piscina, was also discovered on the south side of the chancel. The whole of the external stone-work of the church including the tower has now been repaired with new stone in places and completely re-pointed. Since 1974 over £25,000 has been spent carrying out this ongoing programme of restoration. All that remains of the medieval churchyard cross are two steps and a square base.

The church plate consists of a silver chalice, hall-marked 1748, and the sacred monogram IHC is engraved within a circle on the cup. The paten cover is hall-marked 1747. The register of marriages dates from 1754, baptisms and burials from 1813.

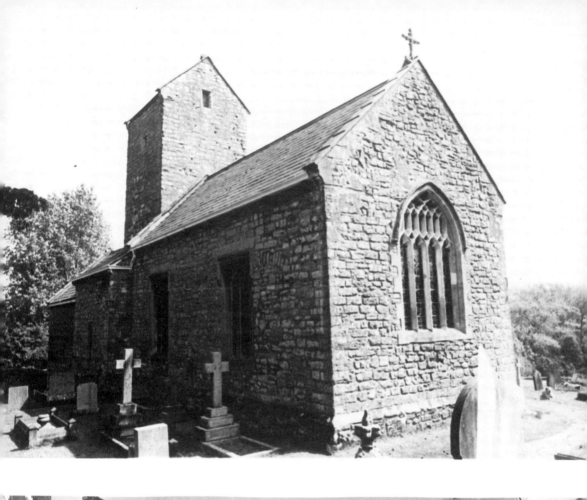

Michaelston-le-Pit Church

The parish church of Michaelston-le-Pit is dedicated to St. Michael and All Angels and is built in the Early English style of architecture with early Perpendicular insertions. It was probably built by a member of the Norman family of De Reigny who held Michaelston-le-Pit as a submanor of Dinas Powis, for in the 13th century the church was referred to as 'Sct. Michael de Renny'. The church was valued at 4 marks in 1254 (Taxation of Norwich) and in 1291 (*Taxatio Ecclesiastica*) and £4-19s-0d in 1535 (*Valor Ecclesiasticus*). The advowson of the church went with the manor in the 15th and 16th centuries. The parson was resident in 1563. In 1771 (Bishop Barrington's Primary Visitation of the Diocese) the living was worth £90; the incumbent was the Reverend Phillip Thomas and Robert Jones, Esq., of Fonmon Castle was the patron. The Rectory received grants from Queen Anne's Bounty amounting to £400 in 1779 and 1810. In 1810 the emoluments arising from 'Glebe lands and Rectorial tythes' amounted to £50. It was worth gross £65 in 1835 when Thomas Bates Rous was the patron. In 1954 Michaelston-le-Pit was joined with the parish of St. Andrew Major to form a grouped benefice.

The church consists of chancel, nave, short transepts, south porch and a central tower containing one bell. The east window is of three trefoiled lights with rectilinear tracery above. The pale Victorian stained glass depicts the Crucifixion of Our Lord with the Blessed Virgin Mary and St. John at each side of the cross, and was erected to the memory of Hely Hutchinson Keating Rickards, B.A. (d. 1881), rector of the parish for 42 years, and his wife, Katherine Diana (d. 1889).

The beautifully-coloured reredos has a greyish-blue painted background. A red painted concave moulding, which includes a gold running trail of leaves, flowers and berries, surrounds seven panels. These are alternately narrow (red) and wider (pale blue) with, in the latter, flowing tracery in the head above an ogee arch with multifoils, flowers and beads on the cusps. The slim panels have trefoil-headed arches similarly treated with what amounts to a crocketed finial in the head. All the tracery is picked out in gold. The reredos and panelling were erected in 1927 by parishioners and friends according to designs prepared by Messrs. J. Wippell of Exeter, in memory of the Reverend A. J. Holme-Russell, rector of the parish from 1882 to 1925. The altar table of oak has five consecration crosses carved on the top. Each side of the altar on the east wall is a stone tablet upon which is written the ten commandments from the Book of

Exodus, Chapter XX. On either side of the sanctuary are dark, oak chairs carved with scenes from the English Civil War, and the presence of these chairs is explained by the fact that the parish was one of the prizes awarded to Colonel Thomas Horton's victorious brigade after the battle of St. Fagans. The parish was purchased later by another Parliamentarian, Colonel Philip Jones of Fonmon, and his descendants were patrons of the living until the 19th century.

The chancel is almost equal in length to the nave on the other side of the crossing. On the south wall of the chancel are marble memorial tablets to Thomas Bates Rous of Court-yr-ala (d.1850) and his wife, Charlotte, (d.1861), daughter of Sir Robert Salusbury, Bart. of Llanwern, Monmouthshire. The memorial to Thomas Rous records that he served in Spain under Sir John Moore in the Grenadier Guards and was wounded at Corunna in 1809. The monument is surmounted by the family armorial achievement. The crest is 'A dove argent'. The arms are quarterly, 1st quarter—'Or an eagle displayed azure pruning the wing foot and beak gules' (Rous); 2nd quarter—'Gules two wings conjoined in lure or' (Seymour); 3rd quarter—'Argent three lions rampant gules within a bordure engrailed sable' (Kirkham); 4th quarter—'Azure three battle-axes or' (Dennis) impaling 'Gules a lion rampant argent ducally crowned or between three crescents or' (Salusbury). The family motto reads:- 'Vescitur Christo' (We feed on Christ). On the north wall of the chancel is a black and white marble monument erected by her grandchildren to the memory of Charlotte Rous, (d.1849), daughter of Dr. Hugh Thomas, Dean of Ely and wife of George Rous (d.1857, rector of Laverton, Somerset, who is himself commemorated on a white marble tablet on the opposite south wall. Set diagonally against the north wall of the chancel is a tombstone surmounted by a crude representation of the Matthew family crest in the form of a triangular mount charged with a lozenge. The supporters are on the dexter side 'A lion salient' and on the sinister side a 'Moorcock'. The motto reads:- 'Y fyno Dduw y fudd' (What God wills, will be.) The monument commemorates Thomas Matthew, Gent. of the parish of Leckwith (d.1772), and his wife, Ann, (d.1755). The chancel is lit on the south side by a two-light pointed window with trefoil-headed lights beneath ogee arches which continue straight into the head with an elongated quatrefoil between, surmounted by a hood mould. The window is too well preserved not to be a Victorian insertion and the whole piece is done in the 14th-century style.

The central tower is supported on four substantial plain pointed arches without chamfers, with ridge roof. A doorway with an Early English archway leads by way of a spiral stone staircase to a stone-floored cell where the priest who served the church once lived. From within this cell can be clearly seen the opening of a sanctum squint placed centrally across the crossing, which gave directly onto the sanctuary and altar, but is now blocked by a false ceiling put up in the 19th century. The tower has a saddleback roof and the tower staircase is lit by small square-headed windows, one under the east and one under the west gable and one each somewhat lower down the walls on the north and south sides. Below these are slit-loopholes lighting the priest's cell. The single bell in the tower bears the inscription 'Mikkleston le Pit John Jones Church W. 1698'. The bell is rung from the central crossing in the nave by a bell-rope passing through an aperture in the floor of the cell above. At one time it appears that there was a second bell, confirmed by the presence of a second opening in the roof of the central crossing. This bell was apparently stolen in 1769.

On either side of the crossing are diminutive transepts with lean-to roofs each housing two pews seating eight persons. From them the view of the altar is restricted except in the south transept where a hagioscope or squint has been cut through the wall to enable the worshippers to see the altar. In the corresponding wall of the north transept there is an empty niche, which before the Reformation probably housed the effigy of the patron saint of the church. This transept is lit by a trefoil-headed light with square label, while the south transept has an identical trefoil lancet. Clamped to the north wall of the crossing are two 18th-century tombstones dated 1761 and 1783, but the earliest inscribed stone in the church is a fragment of stone now placed in the squint of the south transept bearing the words 'David Harey, ioyner 1719'.

The windows of the nave on the south side comprise an original Tudor two-light window with square head and label on the west of the porch, and a large two-light Perpendicular window with cinquefoiled heads and rectilinear tracery in the head. The stained glass in this window depicts Christ as the Good Shepherd and St. John and was erected in memory of George Grey Rous (d. 1876) of Court-yr-ala. The nave is lit on the north side by two three-light windows with trefoiled heads under a square head and are 19th-century insertions. The north-east window depicts the figures of St. Agnes, St. Michael and St. Paul, and in the lower centre pane are the arms of the Rous family 'Or, an eagle displayed azure pruning the wing, foot and beak gules' together with the family motto 'Vescitur Christo' (We feed on Christ). The window was erected to the memory of Georgina Rous (d. 1907) of Court-yr-ala by her niece, Emma Brudenell Bruce. The north-west window depicts St. Francis of Assisi, and the modern stained glass shows the birds arranged formally in order to maintain an architectural structure. The window was erected in memory of Joseph Henry and Gertrude Helen Peacock of Dinas Powis by their three daughters according to a design by Frank Roper of Penarth and was dedicated by the Bishop of Llandaff in 1973. Joseph H. Peacock (d. 1969) was church-warden for over fifty years and he donated the lamps in the church which were converted to electricity in his memory by his grandchildren in 1970.

The west window is another of those 19th-century combination types which include the ogee arch in the same tracery as the more formal panel-style tracery, which were a feature of Perpendicular work. It is a four-light pointed window with trefoil-headed lights beneath ogee arches and the panel tracery diverges in the head to form a number of arch combinations in the form of four-centred arches. It has a plain hood mould with rectangular stops. It depicts the four Archangels of the Bible, St. Michael, St. Gabriel, St. Raphael and St. Uriel, and was erected in 1952 from a design by Sir Ninian Comper in memory of Norman Stuart Merrett, Flight-Lieutenant R.A.F., killed on active service in

'Three decker' pulpit

the Battle of Britain, August, 1940, by his father Sir Herbert Merrett of Court-yr-ala. On the north wall of the nave is a gilt bronze plaque to the Reverend Henry Holmes Stewart, rector of the parish from 1925 to 1934, which records that his friends and relatives purchased a cottage and plot of land to be used as the verger's residence in his memory.

A notable feature of the nave is the wooden pulpit, a version of the traditional 'three-decker' which has been skilfully adapted to meet local needs. Set on the south side of the nave between transept and south doorway it is in three stages; the lowest part forms the choir stalls, the centre the reading desk from which the lessons are read, and the topmost the pulpit proper. It is the only such pulpit in the Vale and probably dates from the 17th or 18th century. Across the aisle from the pulpit is a typical box pew of the 18th century, traditionally the seat of the Court-yr-ala family.

The nave has a simple arch-braced roof with crenellated wallplate. The font of Purbeck marble which belongs to the Early English period of architecture, has an octagonal bowl on a cylindrical shaft and angle spurs at the base. On the east side of the south doorway is an octagonal holy-water stoup. The south doorway has a pointed archway with two concave mouldings separated by a quirk with a half-pyramidal stop. The outer doorway of the porch has a depressed arch and the original 14th-century wooden trusses still support the beams and roof of the porch. The fine lychgate at the entrance to the churchyard was erected in June, 1920, in memory of those who fell and served in the Great War, 1914-1918.

Many of the rectors were pluralists and these absentee rectors installed curates as did Thomas Hancorne in the 18th and 19th centuries. From 1836 to 1839 the rector of Michaelston-le-Pit was the Reverend Henry Lynch-Blosse, successively Canon and Archdeacon of Llandaff who became Dean of Llandaff Cathedral in 1877, only to die a year later. The church plate includes a silver chalice and paten and inscribed on the latter is 'AMDG presented with chalice to the church of Michaelston-le-Pit by G. A. Rous A.D. 1894'. The registers date from 1783 and the first entry in the marriage section records the marriage of the Rector, Thomas Hancorne.

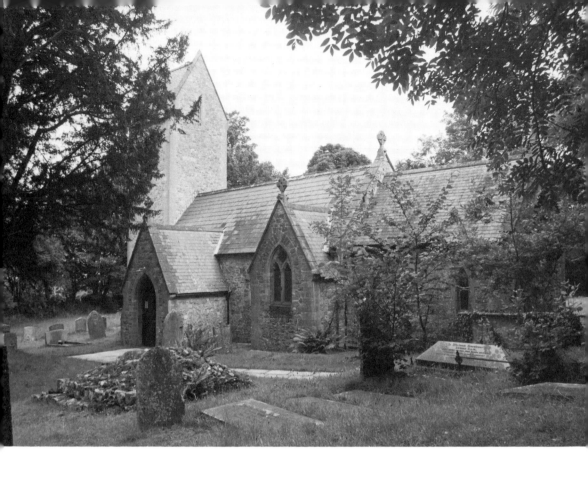

Michaelston-super-Ely Church

The parish church of Michaelston-super-Ely is dedicated to St. Michael the Archangel and was built in the latter part of the 12th century. The church is built in the Early English style of architecture. The site of the church slopes considerably to the east so that there are several different levels throughout the church, which gives the illusory impression that the chancel roof is much higher than it actually is. The church was valued at £2 in 1254 (Taxation of Norwich), 5 marks in 1291 (*Taxatio Ecclesiastica*) and £5 in 1535 (*Valor Ecclesiasticus*), when it was classified among the Rectories. The parson was resident in 1563. The Earl of Pembroke held the patronage of the church from the 16th century until 1690 when the advowson of the church passed to the Windsor family and later to the Trahernes. In 1771 (Bishop Barrington's *Llandaff Diocesan Book*) the living was included with the Rectories of St. Bride's-super-Ely and St. George's in the same valuation, namely £130. The incumbent was the Reverend William Llewellin and the patron was John Llewellin, Gent. According to the diocesan report in 1809 the annual value of the benefice arising from tithes and glebe was £117-7s-6d. In 1835 Michaelston-super-Ely was joined with the Rectory of St. Bride's-super-Ely and valued together at gross £95, Llewellyn Traherne was the patron of both livings. In 1950 the parish of St. George-super-Ely was linked with Michaelston-super-Ely and St. Bride's-super-Ely but in 1968 Michaelston was coupled with the parish of St. Fagans to form one benefice.

The church consists of chancel, nave, diminutive south transept, south porch and western tower containing one bell. The chancel arch is semicircular of Norman appearance and is of two orders; the inner arch is plain with square corners, the outer arch has chevron and bead moulding and springs from imposts decorated with a double row of star ornament. The pilasters supporting the outer arch are round with scalloped capitals. This chancel arch in the Norman style was constructed in the 1864 restoration of the church, replacing a Norman arch described by G. T. Clark in an account of his visit in about 1860. The east window, which is a 19th-century insertion, is of three trefoiled lights beneath a sexfoil encased by very heavy stonework. The stained glass in the window depicts the story of Christ with Martha and Mary, and in the sexfoil above is the Archangel Michael, the patron saint of the church. A brass plaque alongside the window records that this window was erected in 1864 to the memory of Mary Lewis (d. 1856) daughter of William and Elizabeth Lewis of

Llanmaes House, by her brother, Dr. James Lewis and Mrs. Charlotte Traherne of Coedriglan, her friend.

The chancel is lit on the south side by two modern single lancets and on the north side by a single lancet, all deeply splayed. On the north side of the chancel there is a walled-up stone arch which dates from 1908 when a decision to build a vestry was deferred due to lack of funds. Nevertheless, it was decided to breach the north wall and fill the space with brickwork within the confines of a stone arch in readiness for a future addition of a vestry. Built into the wall adjoining the south-west window of the chancel is a modern octagonal pillar piscina.

On the south wall of the chancel are two 18th-century memorial tablets, one to the children of Edward Lewis (1698-1767) and Catherine, his wife; the other to children of Richard and Jane Edmunds (née Lewis) which was originally on the north wall of the chancel. It was moved to the present position during the restoration of the church in 1908 when the north wall was breached. In the floor of the chancel under the priest's stall are other tombstones to the Lewis family.

On the south side of the chancel arch is a wooden plaque which records the 'estating' of a site probably for a tomb by the assigns of Edmund Malifant. It is dated 1546 and is carved with the arms of Iestyn ap Gwrgant 'Gules three chevrons argent with a crescent in the dexter canton for cadency' impaling the arms of Gibon 'Or, a wolf's head erased sable'. The shield is surmounted by the Paschal Lamb crest (which was used by the descendants of Iestyn ap Gwrgant) and below is the motto 'Duw ar fy rhan' (God for my portion). The person referred to on the plaque is George ap Morgan (d. 1546) who married Elizabeth, a daughter of Philip Gibon of Pentrepaen. Below a brass memorial plaque commemorates various members of the Lewis family of Michaelstone Court who died in the 18th century.

The diminutive south transept, which was restored in 1864, has a gabled roof with a modern two-light trefoil-headed window with a quatrefoil in the apex. On the south and west walls of the transept, which now serves as a vestry, are gravestones of members of the Lewis family who lie buried in the chancel where two gravestones commemorating other members of the same family remain. On the east wall of the transept is a monument in Penarth alabaster dating from the middle of the 17th century. It is surmounted by a shield on which are emblazoned the arms of Iestyn ap Gwrgant 'Gules three chevrons argent' impaling the arms of Basset 'Argent, a chevron between three hunting horns stringed sable'. The inscription is written partly in medieval Welsh in the form of an englyn (a Welsh poetical stanza) and Latin. The Latin, which is the obituary portion of the inscription, informs us that John died in 1630 aged 107 years and that his son, Richard, died in 1658 aged 77 years. Sir John Rhys, the Celtic scholar, translated the Welsh englyn as follows:

> 'To (our) grief for countryman to pursue from our part
> No mystery between us (is) the mark
> Richard is—here we have put him
> To be without noise (both) he and his father John'.

Penmark church—interior ▶

He found no hidden sense or cryptic message in it as a previous writer on the inscription, David Jones of Wallington, attempted to demonstrate (*Archaeologia Cambrensis* 1889, pp. 198-213). Richard ap John when anglicised becomes Richard Jones whom we recognise as a descendant of the George ap Morgan referred to on the wooden plaque on the south side of the chancel. Richard Jones married Jane daughter of Thomas Bassett of Bro Miskin. A copy of his will is extant as well as a copy of a Court Roll of 1650 in which both he and his son appear. On the south wall of the transept are two brass memorial plaques; one is a Roll of Honour of the nine men of the parish who served in the Great War, 1914-1918; the second commemorates Major A. C. Thomas of Persondy, who served in France 1914-1918 and died in London in 1918.

The windows of the nave comprise on the north side a single trefoil lancet and a two-light window with trefoil heads and hood mould which, prior to the restoration of the church in 1864, was in the south wall of the chancel. On the south side is a single trefoil lancet and a two-light trefoil-headed window under an ogee arch with label. All the window dressings of the church are in Bath stone. The oak pulpit has a continuous moulded cornice above a continuous moulded band of applied four-leafed flower decoration with cusps. Each of the panels is divided into two lights by applied Gothic tracery trefoil-headed and cusped beneath ogee shapes. These then continue into circles each containing quatrefoils enclosing decorative cusping. The base of each panel, beneath another moulded rail, is a repetition of what appears above but without the cusping.

The nave has a fine arch-braced roof which is boarded between the purlins and the common rafters. Like Llanfrynach church, Michaelston-super-Ely is one of the few churches to retain stone benches against the nave wall. The benches in the north-west corner are original but those in the south-west corner are replicas.

The tower opens to the nave by a pointed arch and above it high in the west wall of the nave is a pointed chamfered arch which once gave access to a gallery at the west end of the nave. Galleries were used either to house the church orchestra before the days of the harmonium and the organ or to provide additional seating. The font, which stands in the centre of the west part of the nave, has a plain octagonal bowl of 14th-century date. A plain moulding at the top of the circular stem is repeated again before the modern base which stands on a circular plinth. Near the south doorway stands an octagonal pillar stoup which is coeval with the font. The south porch was restored in Victorian times. There is an unusually low pointed arch from the porch into the church and the outer arch is trefoil-headed.

The tower is tall and slender with a saddleback roof and the west door has a pointed arch. There are slit-loopholes on the west and east faces and trefoil-headed louvred lights on the south and north faces. The tower houses a single bell which bears the inscription $^{V\&S}_{C}$ (standing for 'Vachell & Sons, Cardiff') and was installed in 1846 replacing an earlier bell sold to defray the cost.

The church was restored in 1864 and the work of restoration consisted of

◀ *St. Andrew's Major church—chancel*

removing a two-light trefoil-headed window from the south wall and inserting it in the north-east corner of the nave. Two modern lancets were inserted in its place. A large box-pew on each side of the nave and another in the transept were removed. The height of the tower was increased by some three metres and additional apertures were provided and a new west door fitted. The single bell was moved to the top floor of the tower and louvres were fitted to the north and south windows of the belfry. The roof of the transept was raised and a gabled south face with modern window added. The work of restoration was carried out according to plans and specifications drawn up by David Vaughan, architect. The cost of the restoration was defrayed by Mrs. Charlotte Traherne, who four years previously had restored St. Hilary's church in memory of her husband, the Reverend John Montgomery Traherne. The church was reopened for divine service after restoration on the 20th August, 1864.

In 1908 the church underwent a further restoration which included the removal of the soil from the exterior of the chancel which centuries of burial had brought about. This work necessitated the removal of six graves of the Lewis family from the south-east corner and also from the east end of the chancel exterior and their re-burial on the east side of the path. Two other graves on the south-east corner of the church were lowered including that of William Thomas. The 'Edmunds' memorial tablet was removed from its place on the north wall to its present position on the south wall. A new altar, communicants' desks, credence table and two seats and desks for the clergy together with a new pulpit and lectern, all constructed of oak, replaced the old furniture in the church. It was also intended to erect a vestry on the north side of the chancel but, as explained earlier, lack of funds prevented this. A simple wooden screen was fitted to the transept so that it could act as a vestry. The work of restoration was carried out according to plans drawn up by F. R. Kempson, diocesan architect.

In the churchyard on the south side of the chancel in a tomb-chest lies buried William Thomas (1727-1795) schoolmaster and diarist, who lived at Rough-brook, Michaelston-super-Ely. From 1750 he began keeping a diary which is now regarded as an invaluable source of information about life in this part of Glamorgan during the latter part of the 18th century. In 1888 the diary was in the possession of Dr. James Lewis of the Vale of Glamorgan and in that year considerable excerpts of it covering the years 1763-1794 were made by David Jones of Wallington (1834-1890) which are now in Cardiff Central Library.

Recent examination of the church by H. J. Thomas of the Royal Commission on Ancient and Historical Monuments in Wales has revealed the presence of Roman building materials in the 12th-century fabric near the base of the north wall of the nave, indicating that the church was partially built of material taken from the ruins of a Roman building. This is possibly the Roman villa, the remains of which lie just south of Cowbridge Road West.

The church plate consists of a handsome Elizabethan silver chalice decorated with intersecting foliated strap ornamentation, repeated on the paten cover. It bears the date 1576 on the paten cover. A separate paten is of plain silver, hall-marked London 1908. A silver alms–dish and silver ciborium have recently been presented to the church. The register of marriages dates from 1754, baptisms and burials from 1761.

Monknash Church

The parish church of Monknash is dedicated to St. Mary and is of early 12th-century foundation. The earlier form of the name of the village was Aissa, Essa or Ash and the prefix 'Monk' arose from the fact that it became a Grange of Neath Abbey in the 12th century. In 1129 Richard de Granville, who held the parish of Monknash, gave 'the whole fee of Aissa with the church and with it all its belongings to Neath Abbey'. At the Dissolution of the Monasteries this property passed first to Sir Richard Williams, then to Thomas Stradling, whose family held the Manor or Grange of Neath, alias Aysa and 'the chapel of Nash' in 1668. The church was evidently served by the Monks of the Grange of Neath Abbey or by a stipendiary chaplain, because it is not returned as a vicarage in the 13th- or 16th-century lists, nor is it mentioned in those of 1563 and 1603. In 1607 Francis Godwin, Bishop of Llandaff, granted a licence to the parishioners of the Grange of Nash to erect a baptistry for baptizing their infants in the nave of Nash chapel and to allow them to bury their dead within the chapel and in the adjoining cemetery. It had been demonstrated, the licence declared, that Edward Stradling and his predecessors had already been accustomed to provide at their own expense a monk for reading morning prayers on Sundays and feast days within the chapel of (Monk) Nash without any accusation of recusancy being made against him. In 1753 the curate William Savours, who was also vicar of St. Donat's from 1731 to 1758, was paid £20 per annum. In 1764, 1810 and 1827 the 'curacy' of Monknash received grants from Queen Anne's Bounty amounting to £600. In 1771 (Bishop Barrington's Primary Visitation of the Diocese) the living was worth £20; the incumbent was the Reverend Joshua Powell and the patron was John Richardson. In 1835 it was styled a perpetual curacy worth gross £67. The patron was William Booth Grey, but there was no impropriator. In 1838 the tithes were valued at £188; the curate received £46 (the value of the small tithes) and John Bruce Pryce, the lay rector, £142. Neath Abbey had impropriated the tithes of the church but had not appointed a vicar. The Stradlings continued to appoint perpetual curates so that Monknash remained one of the poorest livings in the Vale, without a resident priest for centuries. In 1950 the parishes of Monknash, Marcross and Wick were united to form one benefice and in 1983 the three parishes were joined with St. Donat's and Llantwit Major to form the Rectorial benefice of Llantwit Major.

The church consists of chancel, nave, south porch and western bellcote. The church has been much restored and the architecture is very varied, the windows

being examples of the Norman, Decorated Gothic and Perpendicular styles. The chancel arch is low, plain and semicircular with a primitive abacus. When Sir Stephen Glynne visited the church in 1869 he found a low, plain stone screen across the chancel arch which probably resembled the one remaining at Marcross. But now there is no trace of it.

The east window is Decorated, or Second Pointed, Victorian Gothic, of three trefoiled lights cusped with reticulated tracery in the head enclosed by ogee curves which blends elegantly into the window arch. The dripstone is set wide of the window arch clearly in order to show off the two colours of masonry blocks between. Internally there is another plain hood moulding and an equally plain inner arch which dies into the sides of the splay. Beneath on either side a little round shaft runs vertically down the angle which has been cut away to admit it, eventually dying into it with just the hint of a base.

On the north side of the altar in the sanctuary floor is a tombstone to the memory of the Reverend Thomas Hancorne, rector of St. Donat's and Llandow for nearly sixty years (1674-1731), who lies buried beneath. He was a Prebendary of Llandaff and he owned land in the parish of Monknash. With him lies his wife, Cecilia Hancorne, who predeceased him. She was related to the Stradlings of St. Donat's Castle and she also had family connections with the parish of Monknash.

The chancel is lit on the north side by a single plain round-headed Norman window with heavy moulding and on the south side by a two-light plain latticed window with pointed heads and square label. In the window-sill of the latter is a drain piscina. The floor of the chancel is covered with tombstones of local families. To the north of the chancel arch stands the rood-loft doorway. The stairs to the rood-loft were entered as at Marcross and Eglwys Brewis from within the chancel, but now they just lead to a solid stone pulpit which has been built into the north-east corner of the nave. The roofing of the chancel both inside and outside is typical of a 19th-century restoration.

The stone pulpit has a heavy roll at the top with a fillet developing into a concave moulding by a bulbous change in the line of the cornice, corbelled out with an ogee moulding below. The bottom rail has plain mouldings with what appears to be some representation of zig-zag decoration on the underside. On the centre panel is a motif of a cross within a circle which is purely decorative.

On the north wall of the nave is a stone corbel which evidently carried one end of the bressummer beam of the rood-loft. There is no sign of a corresponding corbel on the south side as the position is obscured by a memorial monument. The windows on the south side of the nave comprise two square-headed Perpendicular windows with square labels, both deeply splayed. The nave is lit on the north side by a small square-headed window which formerly illuminated the rood-loft. On the south side of the nave is a coffered memorial slab set into the wall in memory of Thomas William (d. 1752), 'late Bailiff of St. Donuts Castle.' inscribed with the following touching epitaph:—

> 'My loving wife and children dear
> weep not for me 'cause I lie here

> whilst I did live, I liv'd in pain
> and ease by death abliss to gain.'

The stone commemorates too Mary William (d. 1754), aged 13 years, daughter of Thomas William and Barbara his wife. Her epitaph reads:—

> 'Tender mother contented be
> Mourn not at all to much for me
> I lies upon my Fathers breast
> Belov'd on earth in love we rest.'

The memorial also records that her sister, Barbara, wife of Rees Thomas died in 1766, aged 23 years. To the east of this memorial is another stone which commemorates two other members of the same family, Edward William (d. 1736) aged 70 years and his wife, Elizabeth (d. 1738) aged 76 years. A small brass plaque on the wall of the nave between the William family memorials records that the chancel lights were given by Albert and Eirwen Morgan in memory of their daughter, Joan (d. 1951), aged 22 years. The arch-braced roof of the nave is most unusual; it has no inner covering and each stone tile is kept in place by a narrow strip of wood running across it. This roofing of raw, unstained and untreated timber with the underside of the stone tiles showing above the framework is used not only in the nave but also in the porch. Local tradition has it that the timber in the roof of the church was recovered from a wrecked galleon belonging to the Spanish Armada (1588), but it is probably of an earlier date than this.

In the north wall of the nave is a semicircular arch which may possibly have been taken from one of the monastic buildings of the nearby Grange. In the floor of the nave are several ledger tombstones marking the graves of members of the Prichard family of Monknash dating from the 17th and 18th centuries. The 13th-century font has an octagonal bowl scalloped on the underside and a square string separates it from a square stem with chamfered base. It rests upon a large square plinth. There is a square stone bellcote over the end of the church which is of similar proportions to those at Eglwys Brewis and Gileston, but, unlike those, it is not battlemented but what Sir Stephen Glynne describes as 'stepped', the steps forming a small surmounting pyramid. The single bell is inscribed IOHN STRADLING ◇ KNIGHT ◇ AND ◇ BAR ◇ 1637 and was brought from Merthyr Mawr church. It was probably cast by Thomas Stone, an itinerant bellfounder.

The large windowless porch is characteristic of the Vale of Glamorgan and inside are stone benches with wooden seats. The south doorway of the church has an obtusely-pointed arch, while within there is a much loftier Norman round-headed arch. The outer doorway of the porch is of slightly-pointed masonry. The cross on the porch gable bears the date 1628. Instead of using buttresses to reinforce the walls, the outside walls of the church are built at an angle.

The church was restored in the years 1890-1891. The work of restoration consisted of installing modern pews to replace the box-shaped pews and a wooden structure was built one and a half metres from the end of the west wall of the nave for use as a vestry. Before, there had only been a curtain across the west end. The font was removed from the middle of the aisle to its traditional position near the south door. New altar rails were installed and repairs were carried out to the roof of the chancel and the walls were replastered. In the churchyard are the graves of several shipwrecked mariners. One gravestone erected by public subscription commemorates members of the shipwrecked crew of the *Malleny* lost off Tusker Rock with all hands on the 16th October, 1886. Other members of the crew lie buried in St. Bride's Major and St. Donat's churchyards. Many ships were wrecked off Nash Point over the years.

The church plate consists of a silver chalice, neither marked nor dated. Also a silver paten and a silver-mounted glass cruet given by Miss A. E. Franklen of Southerndown in 1890, hall-marked 1890. In addition two pewter alms-dishes or collecting plates inscribed 'The gift of Willm. Savours, Clery to ye parish of Monk Nash, 1731'. The register of burials and baptisms dates from 1783, marriages from 1754.

Pendoylan Church

The parish church of Pendoylan is dedicated to St. Cadoc, a 6th-century Celtic saint, and although the foundations of the tower are Norman, the main structure of the church dates from the 14th century. The first known incumbent of Pendoylan church was Urban 'sacredos de Pendewelin' (Priest of Pendoylan) who sometime prior to the year 1205 gave 12 acres of land to the monks of Margam Abbey. His gift is recorded in a confirmatory charter of King John dated 1205. In 1254 (Taxation of Norwich) the church was worth £6 and was referred to as 'Eccl. de Pendeuloin.' In 1291 (*Taxatio Ecclesiastica*) it was valued at £4-13s-4d and assigned to the Chapter of Llandaff Cathedral. In 1535 (*Valor Ecclesiasticus*) the church was not classified among the vicarages in the diocese but placed in the schedule of property held by the Dean and Chapter of Llandaff, and valued at £3. There is nothing to show what was paid to the curate at Pendoylan. In 1603 it was styled a vicarage worth £25-13s-4d; the impropriation was worth £24 and held from the Cathedral Chapter by Nicholas Morgan, Gent. In 1771 (Bishop Barrington's Primary Visitation of the Diocese) the living was worth £59; the incumbent was the Reverend Edward Thomas and the patron was the Archdeacon of Llandaff. In 1835 it was a vicarage worth gross £120 per annum and the Chapter of Llandaff was patron and impropriator. In 1973 Pendoylan was joined with Welsh St. Donat's to form one benefice.

The church consists of chancel, nave, south porch and western embattled tower containing six bells. The chancel arch is pointed springing from a compound pier comprising three closely-arranged demi-shafts with castellated capitals displaying four-leaf decoration. The capitals here are separated by little decorative panels in the form of single lights. The east window is of three trefoiled lights cusped with mullions and vertical mouldings continuing straight into the head, except for the centre panel where they are curved to suggest panel tracery with typical tracery lights containing decorative panels of stained glass. Above all is a quatrefoil in a hexagon. It is surmounted by a dripstone with carved heads as label stops. Internally the head is so heavily done that it partly obscures some of the mouldings.

The external door with pointed archway beneath the east window of the chancel leads to the Hensol burial vault which was constructed in 1870 (following the granting of a faculty in 1867) by Rowland Fothergill of Hensol Castle for the benefit of himself and his immediate family. Its construction in 1870

293

resulted, so tradition says, in the collapse of one of the chancel walls. The east wall of the chancel is now strengthened by two-stage angle or clasping buttresses.

The chancel is lit on the south side by a single trefoil light under an ogee arch. In the south wall is a priest's door with pointed arch, which is walled up within. The brass cross and candlesticks on the altar were given in memory of two parishioners, Arthur Richmond Perkins and Ernest Edwards, who fell in the Great War, 1914-1918. On the north wall of the chancel is a simple memorial tablet to Rowland Fothergill (d. 1871) of Hensol Castle (who restored the church in 1855) and his two sisters, Elizabeth Forman (d. 1869) and Mary Fothergill (d. 1887), who lie buried beneath the chancel in the Hensol vault. Above the priest's door is a memorial tablet to Lady Isabella E. Price-Fothergill (d. 1918) of Hensol Castle, youngest daughter of John William Tarleton, Esq. of Killeigh Abbey, Kings County. The chancel has an arch-braced roof which is supported on four stone corbels. The decoration beneath the stone corbel is an extremely elaborate deeply-cut, elongated boss with strongly-developed leaf carvings. Each boss is different, one is clearly oak leaves and acorns, one is a thickly closely-knit vine with grapes, the other two represent luxuriant foliage (probably vines and acanthus).

On the north side of the chancel arch is a doorway with pointed arch leading to the vestry. Above this is another pointed doorway, access to which is gained by a spiral staircase (lit by a small lancet) between the nave and vestry, from which it was once possible to enter the rood-loft. The loft once extended across the chancel arch, but all traces of it were swept away in a thorough restoration of the church in 1855.

The pulpit, which was erected in 1893, has a heavily but plainly-moulded cornice and sunken panels beneath, divided horizontally into three unequal sections by flat mouldings, the top one of which is embattled. The upper panel has two ogee arches divided into a single moulding, the centre panel is plain and below are two quatrefoils in circles. The woodwork rests on a heavily-moulded stone base and is reached by five steps made of stone blocks. Above the pulpit on the north wall of the nave is a fine monument to members of the Williams family of Newton House, one of whom was the Reverend John Williams (d. 1818) rector of Flemingston and Llanmihangel. Beside the pulpit on the north side of the nave is the only stained glass window in the church, which depicts the figures of Ruth and Mary Magdalene. The window is of two trefoiled lights beneath ogee arches and is surmounted by a quatrefoil. It is a memorial to Mary Ann, the wife of James Harvey Insole of Llandaff and Tŷ Fry who donated one of the church bells in 1893. It was erected in 1884 from a design by W. F. Dixon of London. The other window in the north wall of the nave has a single trefoil-headed light beneath an ogee arch.

The nave is lit on the south side by a pair of two-light windows with trefoiled heads beneath ogee arches surmounted by a quatrefoil. Hardly any of the windows seem to be original, except the single lancet in the north wall to light the rood-loft staircase, and possibly the lower belfry window of two lights. On the south wall of the nave are memorial tablets erected to members of the Fortune family dating from the late 18th century and early 19th century, with distinctive shell ornamentation. The letter-cutting of these stones is of a high standard. On the same wall is a slate tablet, set in a decorated stone surround, commemorating Henry Jones of Hereford, Attorney-at-Law (d. 1787). On the north wall of the nave are two war memorials to those men of the parish who gave their lives in two World Wars, and a painted Benefactions Board which was erected in 1827 during the incumbency of the Reverend Dr. William Williams. A beautifully-carved memorial on the north-west wall of the nave depicts Jesus blessing little children and was erected to the memory of Miss Mary Fothergill, who, in her will dated 9th September 1887, bequeathed the sum of £2,000 to the vicar and churchwardens of the parish of Pendoylan for the National School.

The font is of typical 14th-century design, octagonal and relatively plain. The octagonal bowl is decorated with a sunken quatrefoil alternating with plain sides. Plain mouldings on the underside meet the short shaft and there is a single moulding again before the octagonal base which itself rests on an hexagonal base. The nave has an arch-braced roof and the principal rafters are supported on eight stone corbels, beneath which are elaborately carved bosses similar to those in the chancel, again representing oak leaves and acorns, vines and grapes but none are identical with the other. These bosses are indeed a striking feature of the church. The south doorway within the porch has an obtusely-pointed arch with moulding, but the outer door has an acutely-pointed arch. The south porch is strengthened by single-stage corner or clasping buttresses.

The tower opens to the nave by a pointed arch with inner arch with its flat soffit dying into the side walls below the point of spring. The inner arch is canted or chamfered. The tower screen, the upper part of which was erected in 1893, is square-framed of three bays below and pointed to fit the head of the arch with flat stylised tracery lights above, some trefoils, some cinquefoils. The left-hand bay is partly a door, boarded with arched panels above and rectangular panels below; a similar fixed panel to the right and centre, a door with a pointed head and mouldings over the vertical joints.

The tower is square and massive with a corbel table below the parapet. The belfry has on each face a broad square-headed two-light window with square label. There is a heavily-moulded stringcourse at the base of the tower which is repeated about halfway up, below which is a small pointed lancet. The west doorway has an acutely-pointed arch and consists of two stones set as a low triangle abutting each other in the centre. The window above is square-headed, its two lights almost round-headed, the points being so flat. The dripstone has a square label with square tops. On the internal south wall of the tower is a narrow doorway with pointed arch leading to the tower and to the lower platform from where the bells are now rung. The tower contains a ring of six bells. The first three bells were originally presented to the church in the latter part of the 17th century by Judge David Jenkins of Hensol (1582-1663), a staunch supporter of King Charles I, as a thank-offering for his safe return from the Tower of London where he had been imprisoned during the Cromwellian period. The fourth bell was given by the Lord of the Manor of Cottrell. These four bells were recast and rehung in 1892 by Charles S. Carr, bellfounder of Smethwick, Birmingham, and two new bells were presented to the church in 1893, one by Mr. & Mrs. J. H. Insole of Ely Court, Llandaff and the other by John S. Gibbon of Newton House.

The bells bear the following inscriptions:—

Treble.	GIVEN BY JOHN SAMUEL GIBBON, ESQ. OF NEWTON HOUSE. 1893 (CHARLES S. CARR, BELL FOUNDERS, SMETHWICK, BIRMINGHAM, GOLD MEDALLISTS FOR CHURCH BELLS, 1892)
No. 2.	GIVEN BY MR. & MRS. J.H. INSOLE OF ELY COURT, LLANDAFF, 1893 (CHARLES S. CARR, BELL FOUNDERS, SMETHWICK, BIRMINGHAM, GOLD MEDALLISTS FOR CHURCH BELLS, 1892)
No. 3.	CHARLES CARR, SMETHWICK, 1892.
No. 4.	CHARLES CARR, SMETHWICK, 1892.
No. 5.	THIS PEAL WAS RECONSTRUCTED & RECAST BY THE FIRM OF CHARLES CARR, SMETHWICK, SEPTEMBER 1892 GOLD MEDALLISTS FOR CHURCH BELLS AND DIPLOMAS OF HONOUR AT THREE PUBLIC EXHIBITIONS
Tenor.	CHARLES CARR, SMETHWICK, 1892.

In 1855 the church was thoroughly restored through the generosity of Rowland Fothergill of Hensol Castle, and the work included the refenestration of the church. In 1893 the church underwent a further restoration when the tower, which was in a very dilapidated condition, was rebuilt, the four bells recast and two new bells added. The seating was rearranged to secure additional accommodation for another forty worshippers and a new pulpit was erected on the north side of the nave. The tower screen was heightened to fill the tower arch completely. The work was carried out by Messrs. J. R. Haines, builders of Canton, Cardiff, under the superintendence of Messrs. Bruton and Williams, architects, of Cardiff and the cost of the restoration amounted to £800. The church was reopened for divine service after restoration on Tuesday, 13th June, 1893 and sermons were preached in English and Welsh.

In the 19th century Pendoylan church had close links with Cowbridge Grammar School since the vicar, the Reverend Dr. William Williams, who held the living from 1808 to 1847, was also headmaster of Cowbridge Grammar School. Between 1808 and 1814 he was assisted in the performance of his clerical duties by his curate the Reverend William Samuel. Two other noteworthy incumbents were the Reverend H. Lewis, vicar from 1874 to 1909, and the Reverend M. C. Gower Williams, vicar from 1909 to 1951.

The church plate includes a silver chalice standing on a baluster stem and splayed foot, hall-marked 1638. The registers date from 1727.

Penmark Church

The parish church of Penmark is dedicated to St. Mary and is one of the largest churches in the Vale of Glamorgan. It dates from the 12th century. In 1254 (Taxation of Norwich) the church was valued at £20 and in 1291 (*Taxatio Ecclesiastica*) it was worth 24 marks. A charter of 1370 confirmed the advowson of the church to Oliver St. John and others. In the *Valor Ecclesiasticus* of 1535 Penmark was classified among the vicarages and valued at £8-18s-8d. Its rectorial tithes were granted to Tewkesbury Abbey by Isabella, Countess of Gloucester, circa 1200 and the Abbey distributed 3s-4d of this to the poor of the parish annually 'according to the ordinance of the Bishop, Archdeacon and the Chapter of Llandaff.' In 1603 it was styled a 'Vicarage' worth £20: the impropriation worth £20 was held by Anthony Mansell under the Chapter of Gloucester. In 1771 (Bishop Barrington's *Llandaff Diocesan Book*) the living was worth £80; the incumbent was the Reverend Noah Neal Newcombe and the Dean and Chapter of Llandaff were the patrons. In 1835 it was a vicarage worth gross £242 and the patrons and impropriators were the Dean and Chapter of Gloucester. Penmark was joined with the parish of Porthkerry in 1972 to form one benefice.

The church consists of chancel, nave, south porch and embattled western tower containing six bells. The chancel arch is Transitional pointed Norman decorated with chevron mouldings on its face and springs from square imposts. Each of the chamfered corners of the impost blocks displays a small carved head of a monk or knight. The east window is of three cinquefoiled lights and is a 19th-century insertion, circa 1860, prior to which there was no east window. The mullions continue straight into the head with, in the spandrels of the centre light, two small quatrefoils beneath two cinquefoiled lights. The tracery of the two outer lights also branch in the head of the window forming irregular mouchette-like shapes. It is all typical 15th-century Perpendicular-style work. The stained glass window was erected in 1899 by Dr, George Neale, J.P. of Mount Sorrel, Barry in memory of his wife Sarah (née Mathews) (d. 1898) and her sister Maria Mathews (d. 1894), both being daughters of Thomas Mathews of Fontygary, who for the greater portion of their lives attended Penmark church. The window depicts the Crucifixion of Our Lord with Mary and St. John. In the base of the centre light is a scene representing the nativity. The chancel is lit on the south side by two large Perpendicular-style windows of two cinquefoiled lights with rectilinear tracery above. These windows were inserted

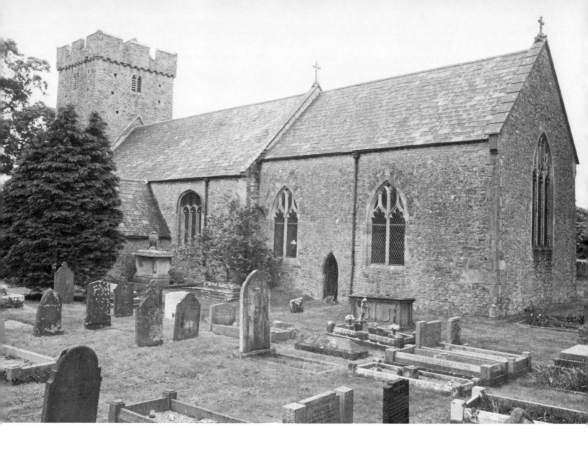

Monument to
Thomas Lewis, Esq.
(d. 1689)

about 1800 when the south wall was rebuilt. Between these windows is a priest's door with pointed arch. The chancel once had two north windows but they are now blocked up. In the window-sill of the one in the sanctuary is a statuette of the Madonna and Child, her foot on a serpent, which was given by Sir Hugo Boothby (1907-1986) at Easter 1949. A black and white marble tablet on the north wall of the chancel commemorates the Reverend Henry Jones, M.A., 'the benevolent and faithful vicar of the parish for twelve years' from 1783 to 1794. To the east of this mural tablet is a plain 17th-century memorial erected in memory of Catherine St. John (d. 1672), wife of William St. John of Highlight, Gent. In 1893 when the church was restored the level of the sanctuary floor was raised, and tombstones which were either broken or covered over, had their inscriptions copied onto brass lozenges which were set into the new floor. There are three of these lozenges; they are to the memory of Ann Kemmeys, the daughter of Edward Kemmeys (d. 1671), Catherine St. John, the wife of William St. John of Highlight (d. 1672), and Sir Thomas Lewis (d. 1669).

On the north wall of the chancel are two alabaster monuments to members of the Lewis family who once owned Penmark Place. It was the Lewis family who presented the silver alms-dish (1686) and the very remarkable chalice and flagon hall-marked 1708. One monument commemorates Thomas Lewis, Esq., (d. 1689), eldest son of Sir Thomas Lewis and grandson of Sir Edward Lewis of the Van, near Caerphilly, a house now in ruins. The monument records that he was 'a trew son of y church of England & a great example of vertve & piety.' The monument has twisting side columns with composite Ionic capitals and skulls supporting a broken pediment which admits the figure of a winged cherub. Above the oval inscription panel is the family achievement where the quarterly arms of Lewis impales Jeaffreson: 1st quarter (Lewis of the Van) 'Sable a lion rampant argent,' 2nd quarter (Einon ap Collwyn) 'Sable a chevron between three fleurs-de-lys argent'. 3rd quarter (Iestyn ap Gwrgant) 'Gules thre chevronels argent', 4th quarter (Bleddyn ap Maenarch 'Sable a chevron between three spear heads argent' impaling Jeaffreson 'Azure a fret argent on a chief of the last three leopards' faces gules'. The other monument is a memorial to Catharine Lewis (d. 1682), daughter of Thomas Tregonwell, Esq., of Anderston, Dorset and wife of Thomas Lewis of Penmark whose memorial is mentioned above. Surmounting the rectangular inscription panel is a broken pediment which contains a winged cherub-head, a skull, a symbol of death and a coat of arms showing Lewis 'Sable, a lion rampant argent' impaling Tregonwell 'Argent three roundels between two barrulets, the whole between three Cornish choughs, all sable.'.

In the floor on the south side of the chancel is a sepulchral slab with Calvary cross and billets bearing the inscription 'to the sacred memory of James Mathew of Rhoose (d. 1631) aged 31 years who was married to Elizabeth Van of Marcrosse who bore him three sons'. The organ, in its original case, is an attractively voiced one-manual instrument of early 19th-century date. It was brought to Penmark church in 1946 from Moriah Chapel, Abercynon. Before that time it was in a private house. It was the gift of Ernest Alexander Harbottle, churchwarden for many years.

On the south wall of the chancel is a monument to the Reverend John Thomas Casberd (d. 1843), vicar of Penmark for 44 years (1799-1843) who lies buried in the vault adjoining the south porch. He married Maria Charlotte, eldest daughter of Robert Jones of Fonmon Castle (1738-93). In *Yr Haul*, an unofficial monthly church magazine dated November 1881, this same clergyman was subjected to severe criticism for not administering the sacraments or praying at the sick bed in Welsh, the only language his parishioners understood. Nevertheless, he was a generous benefactor of St. John's College, Oxford (Casberd scholarship). The College restored his mural monument and tomb in 1973. He was also vicar of Llantwit Major and Llysworney and Canon of Llandaff and Wells. On the same wall another tablet commemorates the Reverend Percy Mortimer, (d. 1934), vicar of Penmark (1901-1923). On the south jamb of the chancel archway is a statuette of the Madonna with a Pelican in her piety at her feet made in cast bronze by Frank Roper of Penarth in 1977 in memory of Rollo (Robert Lonsdale) Charles (1916-1977), a former Keeper of Art at the National Museum of Wales, Cardiff who lies buried in the churchyard. The chancel has a wooden barrel roof with crenellated wallplate.

Apart from the brass lozenge memorial in the floor of the sanctuary to the memory of Ann Kemmeys there are other memorials to other members of the Kemeys family in the nave. A simple white marble tablet on the wall above the pulpit commemorates Mary Kemeys (d. 1753) and was erected by Sir Charles Kemeys-Tynte of Cefn Mably, who inherited her estate. A stone slab set in the floor of the nave near the pulpit is a memorial to Frances Kemeys (d. 1735), a sister of Mary Kemeys who is commemorated above. The Kemeys family pew was in the north-east corner of the nave.

On the north wall of the nave is a memorial to five men of the parish who gave their lives in the Great War, 1914-1918. Nearby in the north-east corner of the nave stands the Jacobean pulpit from which the Reverend John Wesley preached on Saturday, 26th July, 1777 about noon. He was then 74 years old and still travelling 6,000 miles a year on horseback preaching the Gospel of Salvation by grace through faith. He often stayed as a guest of the Jones family at Fonmon Castle. The pulpit was restored in 1970 in memory of Clara Margaret Boothby, the wife of Sir Seymour William Brooke Boothby, the 14th baronet by her children, Sir Hugo Boothby, the 15th baronet and Serena Margaret Boothby. The lectern commemorates the Reverend Frederick Charles Wood, M.A. (d. 1891), vicar of Penmark for 47 years (1843-1891). On the walls of the nave are memorials to members of the families of Savours, Hopkins and Spencer whose names recur throughout the parish registers.

The rood-loft staircase remains in a projection in the north wall of the nave, as does the upper doorway. Beneath this doorway is an original window—a fairly-wide cinquefoiled lancet with square label. The other windows on the north side of the nave comprise a large four-light Perpendicular window (inserted about 1860) and a two-light window, both cinquefoiled heads and panel tracery and external hood moulds. The two-light window in stained glass is a memorial to Robert Boteler of Llandough Castle (d. January 1866), and his wife, Mary Anne Boteler (d. January 1866), daughter of the Reverend J. T. Casberd, formerly vicar of the parish. Husband and wife died within days of each other and were buried the same day in the family vault in the churchyard immediately to the east of the south porch. The right-hand light depicts the Boteler coat of arms which is blazoned as a 'Gyronny of six, sable and argent a covered cup or between three talbots' heads (erased and counterchanged collared of the third'). The left-hand light depicts the shield of Robert Boteler which is blazoned as 'Argent three escutcheons sable charged with a covered cup or, with an inescutcheon or escutcheon of pretence' (which indicates marriage to an heiress whose descendants are entitled to bear the arms of those on the escutcheon as a quartering) with four quarterings, the first of which is the Casberd arms 'Per pale azure and gules a fess nebulée ermine between in chief two lions' heads erased and in base a falcon rising or'. The shield in each light is surmounted by the Boteler crest, 'A covered cup between two wings, the dexter argent, the sinister azure'. Each light displays the Boteler motto 'Do not for to repent'.

The south side of the nave is lit by a large three-light window with cinquefoiled heads and external hood mould and by an original 13th-century window of two lights with trefoil head with a sunk quatrefoil between the head minus hood mould. In the south-east corner of the nave is a side altar, the walnut table bears the date 1709 carved on its front together with the unidentifiable initials of the donors RA and TA. Before the restoration of the church in 1893 it served as the high altar. The brass cross and candlesticks came from the now closed church of St. Peter in Aberthaw.

The mural monuments around this side altar commemorate members of the Jones family of Fonmon Castle whose box pew at one time occupied this corner of the nave. On the south wall a Bath stone memorial commemorates two brothers, Robert Jones (1773-1834) and Major-General Oliver Jones of Fonmon Castle (d. 1815). The monument was erected by Robert Oliver Jones (1811-86) who inherited the Fonmon Estate. It is surmounted by an heraldic achievement with the quartered arms of Jones impaling Swinburne: 1st quarter (Bleddyn ap Maenarch) 'Sable a chevron argent between three spearheads proper, the points embrued'. 2nd quarter (King Pelinor) 'A wyvern's head erased vert, in the mouth a dexter hand gules'. 3rd quarter (Philip Gwys, Lord of Winston) 'Gules a chevron ermine'. 4th quarter (Matilda of Gower) 'Argent a stag couchant gules attired and unguled or, in its mouth a branch vert' impaling Swinburne 'Per fesse gules and argent, three cinquefoils counter-changed'. The painted stone medal at the base of the monument is a replica of the gold medal awarded to Major-General Oliver Thomas Jones who fought with Sir John Moore in the Peninsular War.

The monument in Bath stone below is divided into three panels surmounted by trefoil-headed arches with foliage in the spandrels below which hang three heraldic shields. The monument is to the memory of three members of the Jones family of Fonmon Castle who died in the latter part of the 19th century. They are as follows:— Alicia, second daughter of Evan Thomas Llwynmadoc, Breconshire (and Old Sully House, Sully) (d. 1851), first wife of Robert Oliver Jones; Maria Antonia Jones (née Swinburne) (d. 1860), second wife of Major-General Oliver Jones and mother of Robert Oliver Jones and Rosa Antonia Cholmely who erected the memorial; and lastly Rear-Admiral Oliver John Jones, second son of Major-General Oliver Jones and his second wife, Maria Antonia (d. 1878).

On the south-west wall of the chancel is a marble monument in Rococo style with crossed palm branches and at the sides beneath the urns are two cherub-heads with wings folded to frame the face, below which are short garland-like devices decorating the upper part of the frame which itself descends via a rather strongly pointed kink to the coils at the bottom. The monument displays at the top an heraldic cartouche of the Jones family of Fonmon Castle flanked by garlands of foliage and grape-vines with fruit. It commemorates Robert Jones of Fonmon Castle (1681-1715), who was Member of Parliament for Glamorgan in the last Parliament of Queen Anne and the first Parliament of George I. He married Mary, second daughter of Sir Humphrey Edwin of Llanmihangel Place (d. 1756). The monument traces his family genealogically and records that the first Robert Jones was the son of Oliver Jones and the grandson of Colonel Philip Jones of Fonmon and furthermore that his ancestors were descended lineally from Caradoc Vraychvas, Prince of Wales.

The monument immediately above the side altar commemorates Robert Oliver Jones (d. 1886), eldest son of Major-General Oliver Jones and Maria

Antonia, his second wife. He was Chairman of Glamorgan Quarter Sessions for twenty-two years. The memorial also records his two marriages, the first to Alicia, daughter of Evan Thomas of Llwynmadoc and secondly to Sarah Elizabeth, daughter of John Bruce Pryce, Esq. of Dyffryn, St. Nicholas. Above the inscription, which is framed by rope ornament, is the Jones coat of arms set above olive branches tied together by their stems threaded through a 19th-century revival of strapwork.

The nave has a high barrel roof, coved and plastered between the purlins and main braces with an arcade pattern on the wallplates. At the west end of the nave stands the 13th-century freestone font with circular bowl, cup-shaped with a damaged roll-moulding at the rim and a central moulding in the form of a single string. It has similar mouldings on the underside and the plinth is an elongated hexagon. On the right-hand of the south doorway on entering the church is a holy-water stoup set into a recess in the south wall of the nave.

The Perpendicular south porch is large with stone benches at the sides and its inner doorway in Bath stone has a plain pointed arch. Above it is a niche which probably once held a statuette of the Virgin Mary, the patron saint of the church. On the exterior south wall of the church at the south-west corner of the nave is a scratch dial, circular in form. A second dial can be seen above the first dial consisting of a series of concentric circles with a central hole but no radiating lines.

The tower opens to the nave by a Perpendicular arch of graceful proportions. The six bellringers can be seen in the ringing loft in full view of the congregation. The church has a lofty west tower and beneath the battlement is a corbel table of Welsh pattern. On each face it has a two-light belfry window and in the west face a three-light Perpendicular window, beneath which is a Decorated west doorway. About a metre from the base of the tower is a heavy string-course. A small pointed arched doorway in the south-west corner of the nave leads to the belfry. During the middle of the 19th century there was keen rivalry between the bellringers of Penmark and Coity, each claiming to have the best peal of bells. The Penmark ringers boasted that they could make their bells ring louder than those of the rival church. They struck the bells with sledge hammers taken from a nearby smithy, cracking three of them as a result. In 1899 these three cracked bells were recast by Charles Carr of Smethwick, Birmingham with their original inscriptions.

The ring of six bells in the tower was originally cast in 1721 by Abraham Rudhall of Gloucester. The bells were restored in 1899 by David Thomas Alexander of Bryneithan, Dinas Powis in memory of his parents and sister whose names appear on the bells. The second, fourth and tenor bells were recast by Charles Carr Ltd., of Smethwick and the bellframe and fittings were replaced. The third bell was rehung with all new fittings in October 1976 by F. White & Son of Appleton, Oxfordshire and the greater part of the cost was borne by Mrs. Joanna McKerrow and Dr. Malcolm McKerrow in memory of Colin McKerrow. The remainder of the cost was contributed by Welsh Brewers (whose Public House *The Six Bells* stands opposite the churchyard gate), and by the Penmark Ringers. The Tenor bell sounds G sharp and is thought to weigh about 9 cwt.

The bells carry the following inscriptions with Abraham Rudhall's elegant decorative motifs on the first, third and fifth bells and the inscription 'Restored by Charles Carr Ltd., Smethwick' on the second, fourth and tenor bells. To record the gift a fine brass plaque was erected on the north wall of the nave near the family pew of the Alexanders. The bells were rededicated by the Bishop of Llandaff, the Rt. Reverend Dr. Richard Lewis on the 14th March, 1899.

The inscriptions are as follows:—

Treble.   GOD SAVE THE CHVRCH AND KING A 🔔 R 1721.

No. 2.   OLIVER ST. JOHN
           RESTORED 1899 IN MEMORIAM JOHN ALEXANDER
           RESTORED BY CHARLES CARR LTD.
           SMETHWICK.

No. 3.   ABR. RVDHALL CAST VS ALL 1721.

No. 4.   MR. RICH'D GREGORY VICAR A 🔔 R 1721.
           RESTORED 1899 IN MEMORIAM MARY ALEXANDER
           RESTORED BY CHARLES CARR LTD
           SMETHWICK.

No. 5.   PEACE AND GOOD NEIGHBOVRHOOD A 🔔 R 1721.

Tenor.   THO: LOVE. THO: JAY (CHVRCH
                                (WARDENS 1721
           RESTORED 1899 IN MEMORIAM
           MARGARET ALEXANDER
           RESTORED BY CHARLES CARR LTD.
           SMETHWICK.

The church was restored in 1893 and the work of restoration was confined to a thorough structural repair of the tower and the reflooring and reseating of the nave and chancel. The nave was furnished with fine oak pews, every second pew supporting a three-branched candle-pole. The altar table dated 1709 was replaced by a new and larger one of oak, and new oak choir stalls, richly carved by William Clarke of Llandaff, were installed. In relaying the floors special care was taken to preserve the ancient monumental tombstones thereon. A ringing gallery was erected at the level of the sill of the Perpendicular west window which was approached by a wooden staircase from the vestry beneath through a trap-door in the floor. The space beneath the ringing gallery was enclosed to form a vestry. Plaster was stripped from part of the barrel roof to expose the principal rafters and the main braces. During the progress of the restoration a stone staircase was found leading to the former rood-loft in the north wall of the nave which was preserved. The work of restoration was carried out by J. S. Shepton of Penarth from plans and specifications of Messrs. Seddon and Carter, architects of Cardiff. The cost of the restoration amounted to £600. The church was reopened for divine service after restoration on Wednesday, 20th June, 1894, by the Rt. Reverend Dr. Richard Lewis, Bishop of Llandaff. The steps of the churchyard cross are medieval but the shaft and cross are late 19th century (circa 1888). An inscription on the base of the cross records that 'Alfred L. Wood, M.D. (d. 1888) of the City of Gloucester contributed largely to the restoration (of the cross) and his name is recorded on this stone in token of esteem and affection'. In the churchyard are old yew trees of considerable size. They were described as 'elegant specimens' in Iolo Morganwg's account of Penmark written about 1780. There were once two chapels of ease in the parish of Penmark—Rhoose chapel and East Aberthaw chapel but no trace remains of them today.

The church plate includes a silver Elizabethan chalice hall-marked 1602 with coeval paten cover. Also another silver chalice with its cover and a flagon with hinged lid. Both vessels are hall-marked 1708 and were made by Francis Garthone, a 17th century goldsmith. Both the chalice and flagon are inscribed 'The gift of Mrs. Anne Lewis to the Parish of Penmark, 1709' and are engraved with the arms of the Lewis family of The Van, near Caerphilly, Glamorgan, 'Sable, a lion rampant argent'. Also a bread-dish or salver on a foot decorated with a broad band of rope ornament round the edge, hall-marked 1686. The maker's mark is D.R. and in the centre of the paten are the arms of the Jeaffreson family of Dullingham, Cambridge, 'Azure a fret argent on a chief of the last three leopards' faces gules'. (The second wife of Thomas Lewis of Penmark Place was Mary, daughter of Colonel John Jeaffreson and was in all probability the donor of the dish). The registers date from 1751.

Peterston-super-Ely Church

The parish church of Peterston-super-Ely is dedicated to St. Peter and the present church is built in the Perpendicular style of the 15th century. At the time of the Taxation of Norwich (1254) the church had a chapel, Egloiswensen, and they were jointly valued at £6. In 1291 (*Taxatio Ecclesiastica*) it was valued at £6-13s-4d. The living was classified among the Rectories in the *Valor Ecclesiasticus* in 1535 and was worth £8. The parson was resident in 1563. In 1595 the fourth part of the manor and the advowson of the Rectory of Peterston-super-Ely, which was held under the Earl of Pembroke, of his castle at Cardiff with a net annual value of 12 shillings, belonged to Thomas Lewis of Van. In 1771 (Bishop Barrington's *Llandaff Diocesan Book*) the living was worth £90; the incumbent was the Reverend John Bassett and the patrons were the heirs of Sir John Aubrey, and Thomas Mathews. In 1835 the Rectory was worth £230 and Sir Thomas Aubrey and Colonel M. Wood were the patrons. In 1970 when the Reverend Cyril Edwards was instituted to the living, Peterston-super-Ely was joined with the living of St. Bride's-super-Ely to form one benefice.

The church consists of chancel, nave, south porch and western embattled tower containing six bells. The chancel arch has a segmental pointed outer arch and the inner arch springs immediately from the side walls. The east window is Decorated of three cinquefoiled lights under a sexfoil in the apex. The beautiful stained glass window depicts the Crucifixion of Our Lord in the centre light, St. Peter holding the church in the right-hand light and St. John (who normally appears in conjunction with St. Peter) with the Holy Spirit (the Dove) in the left-hand light. The window was erected in 1891 by Charles Waring as a memorial to his father, Alderman Thomas Waring, who took an active interest in the church and parish.

The beautifully-carved oak reredos decorated in English gold leaf depicts the Crucifixion of Our Lord with the Blessed Virgin Mary and St. John in the centre panel and the side panels bear the Latin inscription:— 'Ecce qui tollit peccata mundi' (Behold He who takes away the sins of the world.) The reredos was erected in 1935 by friends and parishioners as a memorial to Ada Brockett Grover (d. 1934), 'a devoted and generous benefactor of the church'. To the north of the altar is a very large round-headed niche which at one time probably held a statue but now contains a tabernacle for the Blessed Sacrament. A plaque on the north wall of the nave near the pulpit records that the tabernacle was given by the Horley family 'as a thank-offering for the privilege of worshipping and serving this church from 1902 to 1978.'

The chancel is lit on the south side by two windows of two cinquefoiled lights with square labels but of different sizes. The stained glass in the large Perpendicular-style south-east window depicts the figures of Abraham and his wife, Sarah. It was erected in 1891 by Elizabeth Turberville Llewellin in memory of her parents, Edward Turberville Llewellin (d. 1890) and Elizabeth Turberville Llewellin (d. 1879). In 1870 a faculty was granted for a vault and burial place in the chancel of the church for Edward Turberville Llewellin and his wife, where they now lie.

In the south wall of the chancel between the two windows is a priest's door with round-headed inner arch and pointed outer arch with dripstone. Above on the south wall is a monument to various members of the Llewellin family who claim their descent from Iestyn ap Gwrgant, last native ruler of Glamorgan in the 11th century. The monument is surmounted by an heraldic shield displaying a quartered coat of arms first and fourth quarters 'Gules three chevrons argent' (Llewellin) and second and third quarters 'Chequy or and gules a fess ermine' (Turberville). At the base of the shield is the family motto 'Vincit qui patitur' (He conquers who endures). On the north wall of the chancel is a brass plaque to the memory of the Reverend John Owen Evans M.A. (Oxon.) (d. 1912), rector of the parish (1890-98) 'during whose ministry this church was beautified and restored'. A doorway with pointed arch in the north wall of the chancel leads to a modern vestry. The two-manual organ, built by Alexander Young and Sons, Manchester, was installed in the church in 1893 in memory of Robert Francis Langley (d. 1892), youngest son of John Langley of Golding Hall, Salop and of Cardiff.

Across the chancel is placed a carved oak screen surmounted by a rood or wooden cross. The screen is of two bays, each of cinquefoiled lights, and the head of the doorway is cinquefoiled beneath an ogee arch. The cresting is embattled and the cornice includes four-leaf decoration. The chancel screen was erected at the restoration of the church in 1891 and the carving was executed by William Clarke of Llandaff. The entrance to the former rood-loft and its staircase is contained in the wall of the chancel arch and shares with the church of St. Cadoc at Cadoxton-juxta-Barry the unusual feature of having its entrance placed on the south side of the building.

The four windows of the nave comprise three cinquefoiled lights under a square head and labelled, two on the south and two on the north. At the south-east corner of the nave set high up in the wall is a square-headed two-light window which formerly lit the rood-loft. The stained glass in the large Perpendicular south-east window of the nave depicts Jesus in conversation with the Woman of Samaria who had come to draw water from Jacob's well, and below runs the biblical text 'Whosoever drinketh of this water shall thirst, but whosoever drinketh of the water that I shall give him shall never thirst' (John 1.4.13-14). Beneath is the quartered shield of the Turberville Llewellin family. The panel also displays the Turberville crest on the right—'An eagle displayed' and the Llewellin crest—'A lamb passant proper supporting a staff or, therefrom flows a banner gules charged with three chevrons argent'. The two mottoes below belong to the Turberville side of the family and are:— 'Vincit qui patitur' (He conquers who endures) and 'Avi numerantur avorum' (I follow a long train of ancestors). On the east jamb of this window is placed an attractive black and white memorial tablet with draped urn to several members of the William family of Allt Laes and Ty'n-y-caeau who lived in the parish during the 18th and 19th centuries. At the top left-hand corner of the tablet is a round inscription panel with an epitaph in Welsh:—

> 'Oddieithr geni
> Dyn drachefn ni
> ddichon efe
> weled teyrnas Dduw.'

which translated reads:—

> 'Only if man be born again
> May he see the Kingdom of God'.

The stained glass in the south-west window of the nave is a memorial to the Rt. Reverend Richard William Jones (d. 1953), Assistant Bishop in the Province of Wales, Archdeacon of Llandaff, and rector of the parish (1938-1953). It was designed by Alfred L. Wilkinson of London in 1957. The centre light depicts the figure of St. Michael slaying the dragon (a reference to the fact that Richard Jones attended St. Michael's College) and beneath is the coat of arms of the Bishop of Llandaff. His mitre and crozier are relegated to the sides of the coat of arms to show that he was an assistant bishop. The left-hand light depicts the figure of St. John the Divine with chalice and palm symbolizing martyrdom, and beneath, St. John is portrayed writing his letter to the seven churches of the Roman Province of Asia (symbolized by the seven-branched candlestick and the first and last letters of the Greek alphabet Alpha and Omega (Rev. 1.11-12). The right-hand light depicts the figure of St. Peter, to whom the church is dedicated, with his attributes, the church and the shepherd's crook. Beneath is the figure of St. Hubert who, while out hunting one day had a vision of a stag with a crucifix between the antlers and immediately repented of his sins and became first a priest and finally Bishop of Liège.

The stained glass in the window in the north-east wall of the nave portrays in its three lights the figure of Christ blessing little children, Christ as the Light of the World and Christ as the Good Shepherd. The window was erected in 1915 from a design by Messrs. Jones & Willis of London in memory of Rees and Sarah Radcliffe by their son, Charles. The nave has a simple arch-braced roof decorated with heraldic bosses but with only the purlins exposed. On the south wall of the nave are two marble memorials to the twelve men and one woman of the parish who lost their lives in two world wars.

The carved oak pulpit is a memorial to the Reverend Lewis Charles Lewis, rector of the parish (1855-1873) and his wife, Louisa, and was erected by their

children in 1891. The pulpit is well proportioned with plain mouldings in the
cornice and bottom rail and narrow two-stage buttresses as stiles. In the cornice
are representations of typical Tudor decorative motifs, the square-shaped four-
leafed flower and fleshy leaves. The main coffered panels are moulded and
rebated to produce a border which sets off the main decoration. In the side panel
these are almost a series of circles developing out of ogee arches, variously
formed and enclosing bisecting inner circles each of three quatrefoils. In fact
there are three different quatrefoil shapes within each segment of the pattern
and the whole thing can be viewed as a kaleidoscope which changes as you look
at it into several combinations of patterns. The straight lines and the rigid
format of the two-light windows above and the single lights below, immediately takes us away from any conformity to the 14th century which may have
been suggested by all these ogee arches and the detailed cusping throughout.
Below is a frieze of four-leafed flower in applied tracery; it mirrors in relief the
mouldings which are carved in the cornice of the pulpit. The panel with the
keys (symbolic of the dedication of the church to St. Peter) is much the same in
essence, except that the bisecting circles have become a series of round-headed
trefoils, whereas in the other panel they are all pointed. The single-light
windows below have given up their straight sides and have been slightly
retrospectively modified into a curved, almost mouchette shape. The whole
rests upon a moulded stone base and access to the pulpit is by way of four stone
steps. The font is of 15th-century type, octagonal with a plain bowl and similar
stem. Between the two there are a number of plain chamfered roll-mouldings.
The stem rests on a much older base which is octagonal ending with stops on a
square plinth. This present 15th-century font replaced an earlier 13th-century
font described and illustrated by C. B. Fowler in his *Rambling sketches from the
old churches in the Diocese of Llandaff* (1896) with the exception of the base and
plinth. This substitution must have taken place early in this century. The font
cover is in three stages. The highest is ribbed, has foliated crockets and is topped
by a similar finial. It is supported by little cinquefoil-headed niches below gables
which are themselves crocketed with finials and separated by pinnacles which
run through the middle stage. This stage includes little arches enclosing cinquefoiled lights with quatrefoils in the head. The lower stage which is angled out to
meet the top of the font comprises openwork panels of cusped quatrefoils and
long-lobed motifs representing flowing tracery. The south porch is large and
without windows. The inner doorway is acutely pointed but the outer doorway has a depressed arch. Inside are the customary stone benches.

   The tower opens to the nave by a continuous pointed arch of early Perpendicular date. The space beneath is screened off by enclosing the head in a series
of wooden panels with applied Gothic tracery—ogee arches and multifoils.
Between that and the doors below is a cornice of four-leaved flowers beneath a
finely-carved cresting which includes floral motifs, crowns and symbolic keys.
The screen was erected in memory of Walter Darwin Vaughan (rector's
warden 1930-1939) and his son, Montgomery Henry Walter Vaughan by Mrs.
Vaughan in 1947.

The massive Perpendicular west tower has a corbel table of Welsh pattern below the battlement and the tower is reinforced by four stages of clasping buttresses. Each corner of the battlement displays a fearsome gargoyle. A stringcourse at the base of the tower is repeated below the belfry stage. The belfry is lit on each face by a two-light trefoil-headed louvred window surmounted by a square label. Below on the south face is a square-headed aperture. The west door of the tower has an early Perpendicular arch and above it is a two-light cinquefoiled window with square label. The tower houses a ring of six bells which were originally cast by Evan Evans I of Chepstow in 1717 and recast by John Taylor of Loughborough in 1891 retaining the original inscriptions which are as follows:—

TREBLE— JOHN PERKINS ESQR. W^M NICHOLLS GENT.
        BENEFACTORS 1717 RECAST 1891.
        JOHN TAYLOR & CO. LTD.
        FOUNDERS LOUGHBOROUGH

No. 2.   PEACE AND GOODWILL. 1717 RECAST 1891.
        JOHN TAYLOR & CO. LTD.
        FOUNDERS LOUGHBOROUGH

No. 3.   PROSPERITY TO THIS PARISH 1717. RECAST 1891.
        JOHN TAYLOR & CO. LTD.
        FOUNDERS LOUGHBOROUGH

No. 4.   GOD PRESERVE THE CHURCH AND KING.
        RICHARD DEER, RECTOR 1717. RECAST 1891.
        JOHN TAYLOR & CO. LTD.
        FOUNDERS LOUGHBOROUGH

No. 5.   GOGONIANT I DDUW YN YR UCHELDER
        (Glory to God in the Highest) 1717. RECAST 1891.
        JOHN TAYLOR & CO. LTD.
        FOUNDERS LOUGHBOROUGH

TENOR— TI DDUW A FOLWYN (We praise thee, O God).
        THE GIFT OF MR W^M NICHOLLS 1717. RECAST 1891.
        JOHN TAYLOR & CO. LTD.
        FOUNDERS LOUGHBOROUGH

The lychgate was erected in 1922 in memory of those men of the parish who served their King and country in the Great War, 1914-1918.

The church was restored in 1855 when the structure was in such a state of dilapidation that the congregation could scarcely hear the sermon of the rector owing to the twittering of numerous birds which made their way through the decayed roof. However, in 1891 the church underwent a more thorough restoration. A new window was inserted in the south wall of the chancel to improve the light in that part of the church. A beautiful stained glass window was erected also in the chancel and new chancel seats and a holy table were provided. A fine oak screen was erected across the chancel arch and a carved oak pulpit was installed in the nave by the family of the Reverend L. C. Lewis. The vestry was extended westwards to make room for an organ chamber, leaving its east end with the old door and window in place. New floors were laid down throughout the church and the south door of the chancel and west door of the nave were renewed. The tower was re-faced, new buttresses put in and a new parapet was constructed. The peal of six bells in the belfry were recast and rehung by Taylors of Loughborough. The work of restoration was carried into effect by W. Morgan, builder of Canton, Cardiff, under the superintendence of Messrs. Kempson and Fowler, architects of Llandaff. The cost of the work amounted to £1,400 and the joint patrons of the living, Charles Aubrey and Colonel A. R. M. Lockwood, contributed £200 and £50 respectively, and the Reverend J. Owen Evans, rector of the parish, donated £100. The church was reopened for divine service after restoration on Thursday, 23rd July, 1891, by the Rt. Reverend Dr. Richard Lewis, Bishop of Llandaff.

Peterston-super-Ely church is one of the few parishes in Wales which can boast of a printed parish register. The earliest extant register covering the period 1749-1812 was edited in 1888 by Alfred F. C. Chichester Langley and a limited edition of only 50 copies was printed, so that this little volume is now an extremely rare work.

The church plate includes an Elizabethan silver chalice with a belt of interesting foliated strap ornament round the bowl. Also a paten cover with a narrow foliated band around it on the foot of which is engraved the date 1576.

The register of baptisms and burials dates from the year 1749, marriages from 1754.

Porthkerry Church

The parish church of Porthkerry is dedicated to St. Curig and is built in the Early English style of architecture of the 13th century. The church was valued at £6 in 1254 (Taxation of Norwich). In another 13th-century list it is returned as paying the highest sum in the scale of synodals, but curiously it is not mentioned in the *Taxatio Ecclesiastica* of 1291, although Barry is. It was classified as a Rectory worth £8-3s-0d in 1535 (*Valor Ecclesiasticus*). In 1563 it had a resident parson and is described as 'being a parochial church . . . having a chapel thereto annexed called Barry which hath both christening and burying.' The Lord of the Manor was the patron of the church in the 17th century. In 1771 (Bishop Barrington's *Llandaff Diocesan Book*) the living was worth £60; the incumbent was the Reverend Edward Thomas and the patronage was held by Robert Jones of Fonmon Castle. In 1835 it was styled a Rectory worth gross £190 and the heirs of Sir Samuel Romilly were the patrons. The living of Porthkerry had been linked with that of Barry since the 16th century, but in 1972 it was joined with Penmark to form the benefice of Penmark with Porthkerry.

The church consists of chancel, nave, south porch and an embattled western tower containing six bells. The restored chancel arch is plain and pointed. The east window is of two trefoiled lights with quatrefoil above surmounted by a hood mould with ogee-foliated head. The window depicts the figures of St. Paul and St. John and is in memory of Edmund Edward Allen, Honorary Canon of Llandaff, Rural Dean and rector of the parish (1865-1898). The chancel is lit on the south side by a broad round-headed lancet and a small square-headed light. Several tombstones cover the floor of the sanctuary: among them is one to the memory of John Richards, clerk, rector of the parish who was buried on the 14th May, 1757, aged 54 years.

Across the chancel arch is a square-framed oak screen of simple character. The west side of the headbeam is decorated with a small guilloche enrichment made of a series of concentric circles. The east side of the headbeam is devoid of ornamentation. The centre bay is the opening beneath an arch edged with interlacing cusping and it is evident that the now plain spandrels were originally decorated with additional carving planted on as at Llantrithyd church, since the holes by which it was affixed still exist. The bays on either side are separated by reeded muntins and have twin ogee-headed lights with standard tracery lights in the head and cusps beneath. The wainscot is decorated with linenfold panels on the west side only.

△ *Porthkerry church* in 1894   Interior today ▽

On the south side of the nave there is a square-headed rectangular window and a trefoil lancet, both with square labels, which J. Romilly Allen described as 'debased Perpendicular of the 19th century'. The stained glass in the easternmost window depicts the figure of St. Curig, the patron saint of the church, and was erected to the memory of Mary Jane Savours of Rhoose (d. 1934). The window was designed by Charles Powell, stained glass artist of London. A white marble tablet on the south wall of the nave between the two windows was erected in 1920 by Captain David Savours of Rhoose in memory of Arthur William Savours, Lieutenant, 6th Battalion Royal Fusiliers, youngest son of John Miles Savours, who was killed in action at Sailly Le Sec in August 1918. The tablet was designed by the Army and Navy Co-Operative Society. The stained glass window in the westernmost window depicts a pattern of butterflies, symbols of the Resurrection, as well as expressing the beauty and mystery of God's creation. The eye is led up to the sun symbol in the foliated head of the window, the Light of the World; below this, across the sky-blue background, are the words from St. Paul's epistle to the Romans, Ch. 6. verse 9, 'Death hath no more dominion.' The window, which was designed by John Petts, stained glass artist of Abergavenny, was erected to the memory of John Jickells, (1920-1985), a faithful member of St. Curig's church, by his widow, Mrs. Noreen Jickells on St. David's Day, 1987.

The one-manual organ built by Evans & Barr, Ltd. Belfast and placed in a recess in the north wall of the nave under a rounded arch, was installed in the church in 1921 as a memorial to those nine men of Porthkerry and Rhoose who gave their lives in the Great War, 1914-1918. Their names are inscribed on a brass plaque on the organ. A brass plaque records that the organ chamber was erected in 1925 in memory of Frank Lester Sadler, churchwarden. A pointed doorway in the north wall of the nave leads to a vestry built during the restoration of the church in 1867 and enlarged in 1925. In the north wall of the nave is a fine 17th-century monument in memory of Reynold Portrey (d. 1629). It consists of a slab having a raised cross and billets on it and is remarkable for the excellence of its lettering which reads as follows:— 'Heere lieth the bodie of Reynolde Portrey, Esquier decessed the 24 day of Februarii in Ao 1629 havinge lyved 63 yeeres who in his liefe time cured many of severalle infirmities without rewarde. He left livinge Johan his lovinge wieffe who caused this momment of her affeccon of soe lovinge a husbande to be set up and desires to be heire allso interred when she dieth. They had yssue on son Alexandur and two doughters.' Reynold Portrey was evidently some kind of physician for the tombstone records that he 'in his liefe time cured many of severalle infirmities without rewarde.' The tombstone also bears inscriptions to the memory of his wife Joan or Johan by whom the monument was erected, and also to later members of the family. Above his tombstone is a roll of honour of all the parishioners of Porthkerry and Rhoose who served in the Great War, 1914-1918. The pulpit on the south side of the nave has a moulded cornice and the three panels are decorated with linenfold design. It was erected in memory of Ivor Llewellin Lewis (1904-1938) by his wife, Gladys Rosalie Lewis.

On the south side of the nave near the south doorway is a holy-water stoup in the shape of a Norman cushion capital within a round-headed recess. The font is octagonal on a similar stem and base and is devoid of any ornamentation. The south porch is somewhat later than the main fabric of the church. The south doorway has a pointed arch, as does the outer doorway. In the porch are the usual stone benches.

The tower opens to the nave by a high rounded arch springing from chamfered imposts. The west doorway has been built up and a small square-headed lancet window has been inserted in its place. Above it is the west window of two cinquefoiled lights with square label. The tower is square and well-proportioned and is basically of 15th-century date despite a restoration in the 1950s. The upper portion of the tower was completely dismantled and rebuilt in 1958, the cost being borne by parishioners and friends of Porthkerry church.

Below the battlement is a corbel table and on each face a square-headed lancet lights the belfry. On the south face another square-headed aperture lights the belfry stairway. The tower contains a ring of six bells. Originally there were only four bells, but these four were rehung and two treble bells cast by Mears & Stainbank were added in 1950 in memory of Henry Gethin Lewis and Ann Lewis by their four children whose names appear on the bells. The bells bear the following inscriptions:—

Treble   (By Mears & Stainbank 1950)
          'TO THE GLORY OF GOD AND IN MEMORY OF
          HENRY GETHIN LEWIS AND ANN LEWIS
          HIS WIFE OF PORTHKERRY DIED 1945'.

Bell 2.   (By Mears & Stainbank 1950)
          'THE FOUR BELLS WERE REHUNG AND TWO
          TREBLE BELLS ADDED BY MARY GWENDA
          LANGMAN, MARGARET LLEWELLYN MEGGITT,
          HENRY GETHIN LEWIS, GODFREY LEWIS.'

Bell 3.   (By Evan Evans I of Chepstow 1695)
          'THOMAS HOPKIN, WILLIAM RICHARD,
          HENRY HAWKIN, MATHEW DEAR 1695. E.E.'

Bell 4.   (By Henry Gefferies (Jefferies) of Bristol c. 1550)
          'SANCTA MARIA ORA PRO NOBIS, hj.'

Bell 5.   (By Evan Evans I of Chepstow 1695)
          'JOHN MILES   MINISTER JOHN MAYO C.W.
          DAVID LEWIS E.E. 1695.'

Bell 6.   (By Llewellins & James, Bristol 1879)
          'TO LIVE TO DIE. BELL OF 14th CENTURY,
          RECAST BY LLEWELLINS & JAMES, BRISTOL, 1879.'

The treble bell is hung above the second and both are in a steel frame; the other four are in a wooden frame. At the 1950 restoration of the bells the fourth bell was quarter turned and a new headstock fitted to the fifth. New clappers were supplied and new rims fitted to the wheels. A steel girder was added to span the tower below the bell frame. The Llandaff and Monmouth Diocesan Association of Change Ringers rang the first peal on the bells on 13th January, 1952 in two hours and forty-six minutes which consisted of a peal of 5040 doubles (9 extents of St. Simons, 10 of South repps, 11 of Plain Bob and 12 of Grandsire.)

The church was restored in 1867 and when the wall between the chancel and nave was taken down a Tudor-shaped arch was discovered. A pewter chalice and a skeleton were also found beneath the floor. The church was re-roofed and a vestry added on the north side of the nave. The church was also furnished with open seats of pitch pine.

The original churchyard cross at Porthkerry was destroyed by a storm in December 1874. Only after the cross fell did the beauty of the carved figures become apparent. The pedestal holding the figures had four shields with a carved leaf between each. The central figure of the group of sculpture was the Virgin Mary sitting on a seat supporting the Holy Child on her right knee with her arm around his waist. There were other figures behind the Virgin Mary. Some of the heads of the figures had been broken off—probably the work of zealous Puritans who regarded them as symbols of idolatry. A fragment of the broken cross-head was carefully preserved at the rectory and was evidently replaced at a later date.

The lychgate, where the coffins were rested to await the arrival of the priest, was rebuilt after the 1914-1918 war in memory of the young men of the parish who gave their lives for their country. It was a frequent occurrence after a storm for the villagers of Porthkerry to find bodies of shipwrecked sailors lying on the seashore. In the 19th century the parishioners of Porthkerry erected a stone in the churchyard to a 'seafaring man found drowned 1868'.

The vicar of Porthkerry from 1728 to 1757 was the Reverend John Richards, a methodist sympathizer, who invited John Wesley to preach in Porthkerry church in 1741. Wesley's diary reads:— 'Tuesday, 6th October, 1741—I read prayers and preached in Porthkerry church. My text was: "By grace are ye saved through faith".'

The church plate includes a silver flagon, chalice and paten dated 1912, the gift of the Savours family. According to George E. Halliday writing in his *Llandaff Church Plate* in 1901 the church possessed a silver chalice, cast in 1871 from metal belonging to an Elizabethan cup, and paten cover dated 1575, all of which were either lost in a fire or robbery about the year 1905. The register of marriages dates from 1754, baptisms and burials from 1776.

St. Andrew's Major Church

The parish church of St. Andrew's Major is dedicated to St. Andrew and was probably built in the 13th century by a member of the Norman family of De Sumeri who held Dinas Powis Castle during the 12th and 13th centuries. The Abbey of Tewkesbury took 'two parts of the tithe of the Lordship of Roger de Sumerii' in 1180 which was confirmed by a charter dated between 1187 and 1202. The church was valued at £10 in 1254 (Taxation of Norwich), £13-6s-8d in 1291 ('Taxatio Ecclesiastica) and £16 in 1535 (Valor Ecclesiasticus) when Tewkesbury Abbey drew a portion of the tithes in the form of an annual pension of 5s paid by the Rector, but the church does not ever appear to have been appropriated. The parson was resident in 1563. In 1771 (Bishop Barrington's *Llandaff Diocesan Book*) the living was worth £90; the incumbent was the Reverend Nathaniel Wells and the patronage was held by the Crown. The Rectory was worth gross £400 in 1835 when the Crown was the patron. The advowson of the church came with the manor in 1485 and remained in its possession until the 19th century though subject to various conflicting claims ranging from the Earls of Warwick in the 17th century to the Hursts and Lees of 'The Mount' in the 19th century. In 1920 it was transferred to the Bishop of Llandaff on Disestablishment. St. Andrew's Major is the mother church of Dinas Powis and the parish has been grouped with Michaelston-le-Pit church since 1954.

The church consists of chancel, nave, north aisle with chapel, south porch and embattled western tower containing five bells. The chancel arch is a low pointed one of two orders which spring directly from the jambs and was reconstructed between 1860 and 1891. The east window is of two trefoiled lights with a quatrefoil in the apex and is a Victorian reconstruction of the original design. The stained glass window depicts the figures of St. Andrew and St. Peter and was erected as a memorial to Mrs. Constance Mary Lee by her husband Major-General Herbert Henry Lee of 'The Mount', Dinas Powis.

The beautifully-carved oak reredos which was erected in 1885 by Major-General and Mrs. H. H. Lee, is composed of three double panels surrounded by a concave border of patera with gold and colour-painted motifs. The whole is surmounted by brattishing and little shields containing 'IHC'—a monogram of the first letters of the Greek word IHCOYC (Jesus). The centre panel is extended upwards and at the point of intersection there is a rosette arranged as an heraldic device. The blank panels are of cusped and foliated tracery with

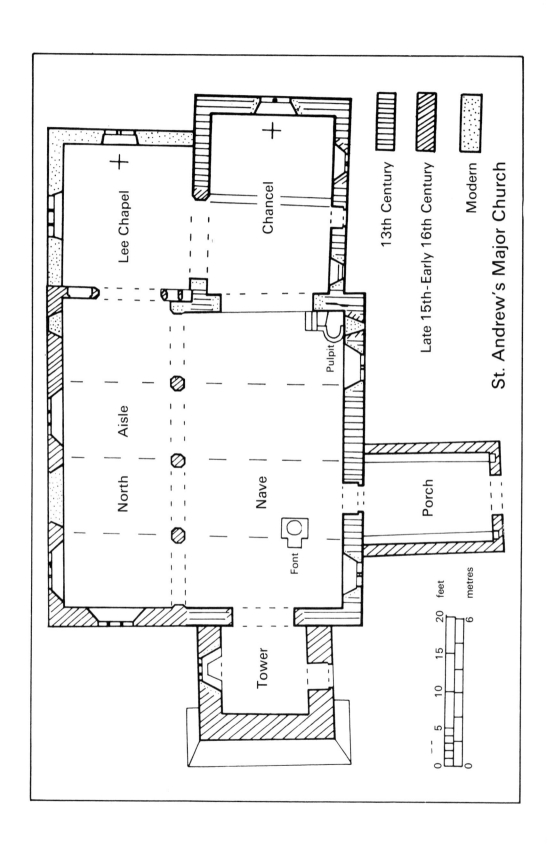

13th Century

Late 15th-Early 16th Century

Modern

Chancel

Lee Chapel

North   Aisle

Nave

Pulpit

Font

Porch

Tower

St. Andrew's Major Church

0   5   10   15   20 feet

0   6 metres

dagger-shaped or pointed trefoils and the spandrels into the centre are painted to provide a background for the shield in front. The central devices contain the instruments of the Passion which are the seamless robe and dice, the spear and sponge on reed and hammer and nails, the three-tailed scourges and the pillar and cords. The retable behind the altar has a carved front—a riot of fruit and foliage. The tapestries on each side of the altar, which were put up in 1885, have typical brattishing and a row of patera above the altar hanging in red, green and gold. Each panel is treated as a cinquefoil-headed light with various floral motifs in the spandrels. There are crowns and the monogram IHS.

The chancel, which was restored in 1878 in memory of the Reverend Henry T. Lee by his wife and children, was beautifully coloured inside in 1889. The chancel has a painted barrel roof with striped vaulting and floral bosses at the intersections. The panels themselves coloured in red, grey and gold leaf are somewhat overbearing and repetitive with the monogram IHC in each. The colouring on the walls of the chancel was spoiled by damp and was removed in the 1950s.

The chancel is lit on the south side by a two-light trefoil-headed window with label and a single cinquefoiled light also labelled. The south-east window depicts the parable of the Good Samaritan and is a memorial to William Wentworth (d. 1921) erected by his wife and children. The south-west window depicts the figure of St. Curig with a model of a ship in his arms and a replica of Porthkerry church at his feet and was erected by the Wentworths in memory of their son, Robert Jesse Wentworth (d. 1917), a chorister of the church who was washed overboard and drowned off Cape Horn. Between the south chancel windows is a priest's door with pointed arch. On the north wall of the chancel are three brass plaques in memory of former rectors; they are the Reverend Edward Windsor Richards (d. 1848) rector of St. Andrew's and St. Lythan's from 1828 to 1848 who is buried beneath the chancel; the Reverend Isaac Domer Jenkins, rector of the parish from 1875 to 1885, and the Reverend Edward Davies (d. 1942) rector of the parish from 1917 to 1942.

The chancel is divided from the Lee Chapel by a modern wooden screen which has a castellated cornice with little pommée crosses. The bottom rail is also castellated between open trefoil-headed arches. The mouldings of each arch spring above the bell caps of little shafts with annulets and bases, all with a 13th-century appearance. In the spandrels are various three-lobed stiff-leaf forms on a symmetrical trail. The floral motif sunk into a circle at each end is a stylised cross fleurée.

The windows on the south side of the nave comprise a pair of two-light Perpendicular windows with cinquefoiled heads and labels. The south-east one close to the pulpit illustrates the words of Our Lord, 'Suffer little children to come unto me'. This window was erected in 1952 to the memory of Lady Blanche Davies, who was well-known for her social work and the founder of Eastbrook and Dinas Powis Baby Clinic, the first of its kind in Wales. She was also the District Commissioner of the Girl Guides Association. The polished stone pulpit has a round drum with a crown and cross fleurée on the front and a band of little flowers and long-lobed leaves separating plain mouldings. At the side of the pulpit is a panelled pillar of elongated multi-lobed flowers. This pulpit was installed in 1835 and replaced the one from which Charles Wesley preached on his visit to the church on the 7th November, 1740. It was Nathaniel Wells, rector of the parish from 1734 to 1799 who was instrumental in bringing the Wesleys to South Wales. He was an ardent follower of their movement while it was still within the church itself, but abandoned the cause when it became clear that Methodism was becoming a separate institution outside the fold of the Anglican Church. Charles Wesley's visit to the church is commemorated on a brass plaque installed on the south wall near the pulpit to mark the centenary of Dinas Powis Wesleyan Methodist Church in 1976. The brass eagle lectern was presented to the church by his widow and children at Easter, 1888 in memory of John Humphrey England, Esq., (d. 1887), formerly of Eastbrook Hall.

The Norman font is tub-shaped with roll-moulding around the rim, but the step and plinth are modern. The tower opens to the nave by a segmental pointed arch formed of roughly-cut stones and is probably late Decorated in origin. The modern oak screen, erected in 1881 as a memorial to Barbara Stewart Craster (née Lee), is divided into four double-panelled bays beneath an inscription with the tracery decoration in the panels repeated as openwork in the head. These are basically trefoil-headed lights with an enclosed, three-lobed leaf or petal arrangement above, with a cluster of berries forming the intersection of the leaves at the centre.

The massive square tower has a corbel table beneath the battlement and the base batters considerably on the west face with slight returns on the north and south. An unusual feature of the tower is the south doorway with four-centred arch. On the centre merlon of the north face of the tower is a St. Andrew's cross, probably modern. The belfry has rectangular louvres on each face and the south wall of the tower is illuminated by three more rectangular apertures. The belfry or second stage of the tower contains a ring of five bells cast in 1747 by William Evans, bellfounder of Chepstow. The bells bear the following inscriptions:—

Treble.   COME LET US RING FOR CHURCH AND KING
          W ♦ E 1747

No. 2.   PEACE AND GOOD NEIGHBOVRHOOD.
          W ♦ E 1747

No. 3.   WILLIAM EVANS CAST VS ALL 1747

No. 4.   IOHN GWILLIM AND IOHN IENKINS,
          CH:WARDENS W ♦ E 1747

Tenor.   THE REVER'ND MR. NATHANIEL WELLS,
          RECTR. W ♦ E 1747

Because of decay in the beams the bells are no longer rung by hand but are operated by a chiming mechanism installed in 1950.

The Perpendicular south porch, which is unusually large in proportion to the rest of the building, has a depressed outer arch but the inner south doorway is plain pointed. Inside, the porch is lined with stone benches and on the west wall is a cluster of soldiers' memorials. One of them commemorates John Williams who served as a private in the Coldstream Guards during the Peninsular War from the battle of Busaco in 1810 to the siege of Bayonne in 1814. A wooden plaque in the porch records that the Incorporated Church Building Society granted £20 in 1865 towards reseating and restoring the church. The porch is now enclosed by wrought-iron gates, a memorial to Canon Hilary Jones, rector of the parish from 1943 to 1965.

The arcade of the nave to the north aisle has four pointed Perpendicular arches springing from octagonal pillars without capitals with octagonal bases on square plinths. The north aisle was added in the late 15th or early 16th century and was originally lit by four windows, each of three lights. Later one of these windows was blocked up and the remaining three were remodelled in the early part of the 17th century. Three Perpendicular windows light the aisle today. The two in the north wall are of three lights with rounded heads and flat top. The stained glass in the north-west window of the north aisle depicts the figures of St. Michael, St. George and St. Nicholas, and below these figures are the badges of the three armed services, the Royal Air Force, the Army and the Royal Navy. St. George and St. Michael are the warrior saints of the church, while St. Nicholas is the patron saint of sailors. The window was erected in 1945 to those men of the parish who gave their lives in the Second World War. The west window of the north aisle is of three lights with rounded heads under a square head and labelled. In the centre of the north wall is a memorial monument in white marble to those twenty-eight men of the parish who fell during the Great War, 1914-1918. Also on the north wall of the north aisle is a marble monument to three members of the Lee family of Dinas Powis. When Iolo Morganwg visited the church in 1761 he described some 'very fine painted glass (said to be the finest in Glamorgan) in the windows of the north aisle and throughout the church 'some good remains of split oaken board ceilings enriched with arms, fleurons, etc.' but on making a return visit there in 1789 he noted that 'these are like the fine windows to fall into ruin.'

The Lee Chapel has a blunt pointed arch made of irregularly-sized blocks of stone. Above and to the north of the chapel arch is the rood-loft doorway with four-centred arch which once gave access to a rood-loft built across both aisle and nave. A small window, now blocked, high in the south wall of the nave illuminated the former rood-loft while another built-up window low in the north wall of the north aisle probably lit the staircase leading to the rood-loft. The chapel screen consists of three bays. Each bay beneath the castellated central rail is divided into three panels of blind tracery with cinquefoiled heads. The bottom rail and the plinth are both plain. Slender muntins divide the openwork panels and the heads of the lights are cinquefoils beneath ogee arches with typical 14th-century-style tracery above. The cornice has a deep row of brattishing as cresting and a dense trail of leaves and flowers.

A brass plaque on the east wall of the north aisle records that the chapel, frequently referred to as the Lee Chapel, was restored in 1921 in memory of Major-General Henry Herbert Lee (d. 1920), Lord of the Manor, rector's warden and a generous benefactor of the church and parish. This work was carried out under the supervision of Brevet Colonel Cecil Locke Wilson, churchwarden and diocesan surveyor. Formerly, the chapel had been the burial place of the Howell family of Bouville until it fell into ruin. The two-manual organ, built by Evans and Barr of Belfast, was presented to the church in October, 1919 by surviving members of the Lee family in memory of Lieutenant James Robert Lee of the Indian Army, Rtd, (d. 1918), second son of the Reverend Henry Thomas Lee (1811-1877). It was removed from its former position in the east end of the north aisle to the chapel. In the chapel are the remains of a squint which originally gave the congregation a view of both altars but now the view from the squint towards the main altar is blocked by the organ. Numerous other brass plaques to members of the Lee family cover the west and north corner walls of the chapel.

The east window of the chapel is of two cinquefoiled lights surmounted by a quatrefoil and the chapel is lit on the north side by a three-light window with cinquefoil heads under a square head. Both windows are glazed with coloured patterned glass. The Victorian restoration of the church in 1875 swept away many of the old monuments but the place of burials beneath the floor of the sanctuary and chapel are marked by a series of encaustic tiles bearing the date of burial and initials of the deceased. The earliest of these in the sanctuary bears the inscription T.M. 1665 for Thomas Maddocks, rector of the parish from 1661 to 1665.

In 1887 the shaft of the churchyard cross was recovered from the common where it had lain for two hundred years and replaced in its original socket in the churchyard. The cross itself was never recovered but a new head was set on the ancient shaft in the same year. In the churchyard lies buried the local bard Dewi Wyn o Essyllt (1820-1891). Clamped against the outside of the north wall of the church is an inscribed tombstone (mentioned by Iolo Morganwg in his notes written in 1789) which was removed from the ruined Howell Chapel in 1921. The inscription has now faded but it once read:— 'Hear lyeth the body of John Gibbon James buried the 14th Aug., 1601 and Margaret Matthew, his wife, buried the 8th day of Jany., 1631, he aged 99—she aged 124'.

St. Andrew's Major Church has had a long and close connection with the Bishops of Llandaff. Hugh Lloyd was rector from 1616 until 1649 and on being appointed Bishop in 1660 his son-in-law, Canon Thomas Maddock became rector. From 1667 until 1718 four successive bishops of Llandaff held the living with their bishoprics, appointing curates to serve the church. The last Bishop to occupy the living was the Right Reverend Owen Lloyd Crossley, Assistant Bishop of Llandaff, who was rector from 1914 to 1917.

The church plate consists of an Elizabethan chalice with paten cover dated

1572, also a silver paten inscribed 'Parish of St. Andrews, the gift of Benj. Hall, D.D. Rector, 1819'. A second silver chalice and paten were given by Major-General H. H. Lee of Dinas Powis in 1897. The registers date from 1744.

St. Athan's Church

The parish church of St. Athan is dedicated to St. Tathan, a Celtic saint who founded a church here in the 6th century, and from this dedication the village takes its name. The present church is built in the Decorated style of architecture of the 14th century and its founder is reputed to be Philip de Nerber of Castleton. The church was valued at 12 marks in 1254 (Taxation of Norwich) and £13-6s-8d in 1291 (*Taxatio Ecclesiastica*). John de Nerber held the manor of Castleton and the advowson of St. Athan's church at his death in 1350. In the *Valor Ecclesiasticus* of 1535 it was referred to as 'Ecclesia Sancta Tathana' and was valued at £16-10s-6d. The vicar of Llancarfan held this rectory in 1563 and served both churches. In 1771 (Bishop Barrington's *Llandaff Diocesan Book*) the living was worth £140; the incumbent was John Deake and the patron was Charles Wyndham, Esq. In 1835 it was styled a Rectory worth gross £369 when William Rayer was the patron. St. Athan's church was joined with the living of Eglwys Brewis in 1912 and with the parishes of Flemingston and Gileston in 1978 to form a grouped benefice.

The church is built on the cruciform plan and consists of chancel, embattled central tower containing six bells, nave, north and south transepts and south porch. The east window is a 19th-century insertion of three cinquefoiled lights beneath pointed arches. There are quatrefoils in circles in the spandrels and a similar larger sexfoil above, which is typical of early Decorated tracery. The three main lights depict the Resurrection of Our Lord from the tomb with the Roman soldiers either shielding their eyes from the light or sleeping. The window was erected in 1905 from a design by A. L. Moore of London as a memorial to Hanmer Morgan-Stratford (1821-1902), rector of the parish for 47 years, and Mary, his wife, by their daughters. Outside on the east wall of the chancel is a tombstone to Edward Gamage (d. 1734) rector of the parish, who is buried in a vault below.

The reredos of oak panelling erected in 1890 has a plain moulded cornice above five panels with rounded corners. The centre one is interesting for the delicately-done patera which seems out of character with the rest of the piece. The edges of the panels are chamfered and beneath the sunken pointed arches there are circular floral motifs above sacred monograms in quatrefoils. These are, on the outside, IHC and IHS—the first letters of the Greek word IHCOYC (Jesus). To the left of the centre panel is XP- CHI RHO, the first two letters of XPICTOC (Christ) but here done more in keeping with the style of the other monograms than the usual ☧. To the right Alpha and Omega for the beginning and end of all things. The reredos also has boarded side pieces, narrow panels beneath a plain centre rail, wider ones above with three sunken quatrefoils on each side. The predella is pierced with holes.

In the south wall of the chancel is a piscina in a wide niche under an obtusely-pointed arch. The chancel is lit on the south side by four broad lancets in Bath stone which are supported by a half-round stringcourse. They depict the four Evangelists, Matthew, Mark, Luke and John and were erected to the memory of Hugh Hanmer Rayer Morgan-Stratford (1856-1888) and Helen Jane Essyllt Jenkins (1854-1903) by their sisters Mary Whiteside and Frances Newman. Below these windows in the south-west corner of the chancel is a priest's door with pointed arch. The chancel has a plain open roof of the cradle pattern. The north wall contains a sepulchral recess, round-headed with good Decorated mouldings which once contained an effigy of Philip de Nerber of Castleton, the reputed founder of the church. It now contains an 18th-century memorial tablet to Robert Corrock, the last member of an important family in the district, whose name appears on one of the church bells. On the north wall of the chancel is a memorial tablet to Thomas Holworthy Swymmer (d. 1827) and Diana, his wife, who lie buried in a vault beneath the chancel floor. The tablet is surmounted by the Swymmer crest 'A demi-lion gules holding in the paws a bell or'.

The massive central tower rests upon four very plain pointed arches without mouldings or imposts. The two openings into the north and south transepts are original and much narrower, but the other two openings into the nave and chancel have been restored. The tower is square with a corbel table below the battlement and the upper stages of the tower have light buttresses capping the angles. The belfry now contains six bells but originally the church had four bells, one of them dating back to 1653. In 1919 Alderman William Roberts, a former parishioner of St. Athan and Lord Mayor of Cardiff (1917-1918), paid for these bells to be recast with facsimiles of their original inscriptions, and he also donated the treble and tenor bells to celebrate the victory in the Great War, 1914-1918.

The inscriptions on the six bells are as follows:—

Treble: THE PEACE BELL
         THE GIFT OF ALDERMAN WILLIAM ROBERTS J.P.
         LORD MAYOR AND CHIEF MAGISTRATE OF CARDIFF
         1917-1918

No. 2:   THOS. SWEET. CHURCHWARDEN
         CHARLES CARN, RECTTOR
         THOMAS BAYLEY, BRIDGWATER BELLFOUNDER 1744
         PAX MUNDI

No. 3:   C. WALTER COTEN. D. IENKIN: C: WAR
         E.E. B. 1707.
         GLORIA IN EXCELSIS DEO

No. 4:   WILLIAM ROBERTS CH.W.
         THIS IN BAD TIMES ALLOW'D WAS CAST
         L. MORGAN CH.W. 1720
         YET HOPE GOOD DAYS TO COME AT LAST
         GEO. MORGANNWG JENKINS, RECTOR
         DAVID EVANS CHURCH WARDENS 1918-1919
         LIONEL ROBERTSON
         GOD IS LOVE

No. 5:   R. CORROCKE, H. SLADE, C. ROBERTS.
         1653
         OUR VOICES SHALL IN CONCERT RING
         TO HONOUR BOTH OF GOD AND KING
         THE VICTORY BELL.

Tenor: THE FOUR OLD BELLS WERE RECAST AND
         TWO NEW BELLS WERE ADDED TO
         COMMEMORATE THE VICTORY OF JUSTICE
         OVER MIGHT 1914-1919.
         THE GIFTS OF ALDERMAN WILLIAM ROBERTS J.P.
         A NATIVE OF ST. ATHANS
         I TRUST IN THE LORD.

The bells were recast and two new bells added by John Warner & Sons Ltd. London. Also in 1919 a new turret striking clock by Messrs. J. Smith, Clerkenwell, London, was installed in the tower. The entrance to the belfry is from the north transept by way of a wooden staircase. The one-manual 'Positive' organ which was originally installed in the north-west corner of the nave in 1911 is now located under the north arch of the crossing. It was fitted with an electrical blower about 1948 by the B.O.B. Co. Ltd. (British Organ Blowing Company Ltd.) of Derby.

The south transept or Berkerolles Chapel contains two fine tomb-chests of the 14th century. The two tombs represent the two penultimate generations of the Berkerolles family of East Orchard, Sir William (d. 1327) and Sir Roger Berkerolles (d. 1351) and their ladies. The finer of the two tombs is placed against the south wall of the transept under a canopied recess beneath a heavily-moulded ogee arch, with crockets and finial. There is a pinnacle on each side, the finials bursting above little gables. Beneath the ogee arch is a large pointed quatrefoil between arched multifoils cusped and supported in the middle by a bracket with a bearded human face. The side of the tomb is carved with blind arcading and beneath each of the four arches are weepers or mourners representing various orders of society; the eastern one is that of a civic dignitary and the western a soldier carrying shield and sword, both with scrolls in their hands. Between them are two monks kneeling on both knees; the others on one knee only. The heads of the arches are trefoils beneath ogee arches with crockets, finials and pinnacles between. In the spandrels are brightly-coloured heraldic

shields representing coats of arms showing the various matches of the Berkerolles.

1.   Berkerolles
2.   Berkerolles impaling De Vere
3.   De Vere
4.   Berkerolles impaling De Haia
5.   Talbot
6.   Berkerolles impaling Turberville
7.   Turberville
8.   Nerber.

Upon the tomb-chest repose the two recumbent effigies of Sir Roger Berkerolles (d. 1351) and his wife, Katherine Turberville of Coity, their hands
clasped in the attitude of prayer, resting on their breasts. The knight is cross-legged and wears a bascinet and camail of mail bearing a shield over the left
shoulder, emblazoned with the Berkerolles arms 'Azure a chevron between
three crescents or'. His head rests upon tasselled pillows while the feet are placed
upon a lion. The arms are protected by plate armour, the shoulders by circular
roundels. On the hands are gauntlets and the knees are protected by genouillères. In addition to the chausses which cover the legs and feet, shin plates or
greaves reach from the genouillères to just below the ankles, to which is
attached the spur. The sword has disappeared but the belt is ornamented with
lions' heads. The lady wears a wimple, veil and close-fitting bodice, over all a
super tunic or bliaus. The sleeves of the bodice fit round the wrists.

The shields surrounding the monuments were recoloured in 1932 by Major
and Mrs. Ridley of West Hoathley, Sussex, who claimed descent from the
Berkerolles family through the Stradlings of St. Donat's. A similar tomb lies
opposite the west wall of the transept which was placed there at the restoration
of 1934. Here the effigies represent Sir William Berkerolles and his wife, Phelice
de Vere, the parents of Sir Roger Berkerolles. The base of the tomb is of a later
period, but the effigies seem to be the work of the same hand as that of the tomb
against the south wall.

In the south wall of the transept, east of the tomb, is a piscina beneath a
trefoiled agee arch with finial and crocketed gable above, also with crockets and
finial. A pinnacle on either side are similarly treated. It points to the fact that this
was once a chantry chapel of members of the Berkerolles family. On the west
side of the tomb is a raised pedestal beneath a canopied niche which must have
once supported a substantial figure. The finial of the niche is defaced since the
top of the finial, which once rose above the little gables, is missing. The head of
the opening is a multifoil with decorative blind tracery, cusping and tiny
flowers. Ribs are cut in the underside of the canopy wih a central flower as a
boss. Roses appear also in the vertical mouldings—all typical 14th-century
work. The south window is surmounted by a dripstone with a little ogee
beneath the carved head of the apex. The dripstone has carved heads as stops,

the western one represents a woman's face looking across the window to the east, while the eastern one is a front-facing bearded male. There is a hagioscope or squint from the nave to the Berkerolles chapel and another from this chapel to the chancel.

The west window of the south transept is of three trefoiled lights beneath ogee arches with a single row of reticulated tracery above in the form of quatrefoils beneath a square label with crowned heads as label stops. The east window is of three trefoiled lights beneath ogee arches with two rows of reticulated tracery in the form of quatrefoils above under a square head.

The north transept was once referred to as the 'Castleton aisle' which suggests that this was the mortuary chapel of the Nerber family of Castleton. The east and west windows of the north transept have three trefoil-headed lights with two rows of reticulated tracery as quatrefoils under square heads. The north window is of three trefoiled lights with reticulated tracery as quatrefoils under a pointed arch surmounted by a dripstone.

A deeply-splayed broad lancet window high in the south-east corner of the nave indicates the existence at one time of a rood-loft which was reached through a doorway now concealed beneath the plaster on the north side of the east wall of the nave. In the 19th century a gallery was erected where the rood-loft stood, which housed the choir and church orchestra. On the east wall of the nave is a memorial tablet in Sicilian marble mounted on a grey marble slab with a marble inlaid cross at the top on a gold mosaic background surrounded by a bronze wreath. The tablet is a memorial to the ten men of the parish who gave their lives in the Great War, 1914-1918.

The stone pulpit has little vertical rows of nailhead decoration giving almost a serrated edge between the sides. Here the 20th-century designer has suggested almost a Transitional Norman/Early English feel with the nailhead decoration, the flat plain roundels on the bottom moulding, the cinquefoil-headed lancets, plain mouldings and crosses, trefoils and symbolism within the quatrefoils. These include the sacred monograms IHS derived from IHCOYC (the Anointed one—Jesus) the interwoven Alpha and Omega, CHI RHO—the first two letters of XPICTOC (Christ) and the Trinity star or Star of David. The pulpit was erected in 1934 by Mrs. Elizabeth A. Roberts in memory of her husband, William Roberts, J.P. (d. 1932).

The four windows of the nave, two on the south and two on the north side, are modern and are of two pointed lights with Y-tracery in the head. The south-east window depicts Jesus blessing little children and King David with the harp from a design by A. L. Moore, London, and was erected in 1918 as a memorial to Lewis Jones (d. 1910) by his widow. Lewis Jones was a schoolmaster at St. Athan for thirty years. The south-west window depicts the Epiphany and was erected by parishioners to commemorate the Coronation of King George VI in 1937. The north-east window depicts the laying on of hands by St. Peter and St. John (Acts 8) and was erected as a memorial to William Roberts, J.P. (d. 1932) by his widow in 1933. The north-west window depicts Anna and Simeon and was erected as a memorial to John Deere (d. 1885) rector of the parish, and his wife, Mary (d. 1870) by their grandson, William Roberts, J.P. in 1929, from a design by Robert J. Newbery, London.

The west window is a 14th-century window which was heavily restored in the 19th century. It is of three trefoiled lights beneath ogee arches. The mullions converge above to form pointed arches in the head enclosing mouchette shapes and quatrefoils. There are trefoils and dagger shapes in the spandrels and a quatrefoil at the apex, all cusped. The much-damaged dripstone has crisply-cut heads as stops. The window depicts the Ascension of Our Lord and was erected in 1936 as a memorial to the Reverend Miles Whiteside, M.A. (d. 1927). The west doorway has an obtusely-pointed arch with a single roll with fillet as dripstone and little eroded heads as stops. The blocks forming the arches are slightly offset with a concave moulding between. The west door of the church, which was formerly blocked up, was reopened in 1919 as a memorial to Lewis Jones (d. 1910), a native of Gelligaer, who was schoolmaster at St. Athan for thirty years. The expense of the work was defrayed by W. A. H. Fisher. However, the west door is only used today for weddings, funerals and other occasional processions. The nave has a barrel roof of oak.

The font is of Sutton stone and probably late Norman. It has a plain cup-shaped bowl, bulbous before the double string and the slightly concave stem, all done of one piece. It rests on a square plinth. The font has a twelve-sided pyramidal cover of oak with ribs down each angle and is surmounted by a finial. The bowl is lined with lead.

The south porch is large with a ribbed oak roof having a boss which displays the Berkerolles arms. The south doorway has a segmental pointed arch of three orders with the inner arch dying into the sides. The voussoirs are of different sizes and the result is very heavy for the opening beneath. The outer doorway has an obtusely-pointed arch. Across the floor of the outer entrance is a stone coffin lid and another across the inner entrance. The freestone jambs of the outer door of the porch have some perpendicular grooves where workmen probably sharpened their scythes or tools. On the outside south wall of the nave near the porch is a memorial in Welsh to John Williams (1728-1806), the famous hymn writer.

The church was restored in 1888 when the tower was re-roofed and re-pointed. The tower arches opening to the chancel and nave were groined in Bath stone. The old pews in the church were removed and replaced with open seats and the whole of the nave was refloored. The old windows in the north transept were replaced by new ones and the roof was entirely renewed. Three new windows were inserted in the nave. A new vestry was built on the north side of the church. During the restoration of the church, wall paintings, which were discovered under the lime-wash in the nave and chancel, were unfortu-nately destroyed. In 1890 the chancel was restored when the two-light east window was removed and replaced by the present three-light window from a design by the architect, W. Martin. Four windows in the south chancel wall were restored with Bath stone dressings according to their original design. The sanctuary within the communion rails was refloored with encaustic tiles and the altar steps renewed. The chancel was reseated with open seats and the walls were relined with oak panelling. An oak reredos was also erected in the sanctuary. The total cost of the restoration work amounted to £1,105.

The living of St. Athan's has often been held in plurality and from 1572-1611 the rector was Gervase Babington who was Bishop of Llandaff from 1591 to 1595 and then Bishop of Exeter, though he continued to hold the rectory of St. Athan for 54 years from 1775 until his death in 1829.

The church plate consists of two silver chalices, a silver paten, a large silver flagon and two silver alms-dishes which were given, circa 1847, by the Reverend William Rayer, the then patron of the living. A pewter flagon is dated 1729. The register of burials dates from 1663, baptisms from 1679 and marriages from 1683.

St. Bride's Major Church

The parish church of St. Bride's Major is dedicated to St. Bride (an abbreviated form of St. Bridget) a 5th-century Irish Saint to whom several churches are dedicated in South Wales. The church was built in the early part of the 12th century but most of the remaining architectural features are either 14th-century Decorated or Second Pointed Victorian. The chapel of Lampha was apparently attached to St. Bride's Major church in 1141 and with it given to Ewenny Priory by the Lord of Ogmore. In the Taxation of Norwich (1254) it was not mentioned and was probably included in the valuation of Ewenny as it is by name in 1291 (Taxatio Ecclesiastica) when the vicarage was valued separately at 4 marks. In 1535 the Priory drew £23-13s-4d from the Rectory besides a pension of £1 from the vicar whose income was gross £12-0s-4d per annum. In 1563 it was styled a vicarage as it was again in 1603 when the vicar's income was £20 and the impropriation, held by John Carne, Esquire in fee from the King, was worth £20. In 1771 (Bishop Barrington's Primary Visitation of the Diocese) St. Bride's Major church with Wick was valued at £80; the incumbent was the Reverend Edmund Williams. In 1835 it was a vicarage held with the curacy of Wick, worth gross £200; Richard Turbervill was the patron and C. R. M. Talbot was the impropriator. St. Bride's Major was a vicarage with Wick annexed until 1950 when the parishes of Marcross, Monknash and Wick were united to form a grouped benefice.

The church consists of chancel, nave, north porch and embattled western tower containing six bells. The chancel arch is a plain semicircular one of Norman date and springs from square impost blocks with regular mouldings. On each side of the chancel arch is a squint or hagioscope with depressed arch of a much later date and in the right-hand squint is a stone statuette of St. Bridget, the patron saint of the church. The Decorated Gothic east window is a 19th-century insertion of two trefoiled lights under ogee heads with a quatrefoil with cusps in the apex, together with mouchettes surmounted by a slender dripstone. The stained glass in the window depicts Christ uttering the comforting words 'Come unto me all ye that labour and are heavy laden and I will give you rest' which forms the inscription at the base of the window. It was erected in 1926 as a memorial to Isaiah Verity (d. 1912) and his daughter, Enid Verity (d. 1921) by wife and mother from a design by William Glasby, South Kensington, London. In the north-east corner of the sanctuary floor is a sepulchral slab, in the two upper spaces of which are crosses within circles. The rude stone tapers and is

The Butler tomb (c. 1540)

probably of early 13th-century date. It marks the burial place of a former priest of St. Bride's. In the south wall of the chancel is a small piscina beneath a small niche with rounded arch. The chancel roof has cove vaulting which resembles barrel vaulting.

The most interesting feature of the church is an incised sepulchral slab or coffin-lid which lies beneath the altar where it was placed in 1854. The engraving shows Johan le Botiler (Butler) of Dunraven in the cross-legged attitude with hauberk and chausses wearing a long surcoat open in front. On his head, over his "coif de mailles", he wears a cervellière or skull-cap of plate with a fleur-de-lys in the centre between two covered cups. The shield which hangs over the left arm is emblazoned with three covered cups, the arms of the Botiler family. In his right hand he holds his sword drawn and upraised and there appears to be a wavy line or ridge along the middle of the blade. The handle of the sword has a three-lobed pommel. His spurs have rowels and the feet rest upon a wyvern (a winged two-legged dragon with barbed tail). The inscription which runs around three edges of the slab is in Norman-French and reads as follows:— + JOHAN: LE: BOTILER: GIT: ICI: DEU: DE: SA: ALME: EIT: MERCI: AMEN (John le Botiler lies here. May God have mercy on his soul. Amen).

This effigy is regarded today as a valuable example of military costume of the 13th century. Its excellent state of preservation is due to the fact that it was buried together with its coffin in the churchyard until it was discovered in 1845. It has been assigned a date at the latter part of the 13th century (c. 1285). The coffin was kept for several years after its discovery under the tower but in 1854 it was placed on the south side of the chancel. On the north wall of the chancel hangs a framed rubbing (1935) of the incised slab made by F. A. Greenhill, author of *Incised Effigial Slabs*, 1976. Beneath this rubbing stands an old Norman font, tub-shaped and very worn. In the sanctuary floor beneath the altar is another sepulchral slab inscribed with Calvary cross and billets. At the base of the slab are the letters EDW . . . RE, at the top, OD . . . 25 and on the shaft of the cross the letters ET . . . A doorway with flat-headed arch leads on the north side of the church to a vestry which was erected in 1854.

The chancel is lit on the south side by three plain trefoiled lancets and on the north side by a four-light square-headed Tudor window. Under this window is a recess containing a fine tomb-chest. It stands beneath a canopy which has a depressed ogee arch with motifs in the spandrels surmounted by a coat of arms. The head is foliated and there are minor decorative motifs in the concave moulding which appear to include leaves, birds and a winged cherub-head. The side of the tomb-chest on which the two effigies lay is carved with very elaborate double canopies and pinnacles between, all with finials which have foliated crockets against a background of small tracery lights. The underside of the canopies are carved to represent ribs and bosses. Beneath each set of canopies is a weeper kneeling in prayer, four children in all, two sons and two daughters against a panelled background. Each is separated by a pillar and there is a standing figure on a pillar at each end. Some of the figurework is mutilated.

The recumbent effigies represent John Butler (d. 1540) and his wife, Jane Basset of Beaupré. The hair and style of dress indicate a date between 1480 and 1550. John Butler is bare-headed and dressed in plate armour with his legs crossed which is an uncommon feature for this period. The lady wears a pedimental head-dress and loose-hanging sleeves which is typical of the 16th century. Both figures wear chains around their necks. Above the tomb, finely sculptured, is a shield bearing a quartered coat of arms, first and fourth quarters 'Azure three covered cups or' (Butler), second quarter 'Gules a fret argent overall a fess azure' (Fleming), third quarter 'Azure on a fess argent three ravens beaked and claws gules' (Bawdrip). The supporters appear to be lizards. In the floor of the chancel in front of the tomb-chest is a stone slab bearing the same quartered coat of arms which probably marks the entrance to the Butler vault.

On the north wall of the chancel adjacent to the tomb-chest is an elegant monument to the memory of John Wyndham, Esq. (d. 1697) Serjeant-at-Law and Jane (née Strode) (d. 1698), his wife. (His father was Humphrey Wyndham and his mother Jane, daughter of Sir John Carne of Ewenny; his wife was a daughter of William Strode of Barrington, Somerset.) The Wyndham arms, 'Azure a chevron between three lions' heads erased or' stand between decorative swags which descend to the cornice beneath an open scrolled pediment. Beneath the cornice on each side of the effigies and tablet, free-standing Corinthian columns are encased in drapery. The columns have deep bases and rest on plinths above consoles in the form of lions' heads. The two demi-figures of John Wyndham and his wife face each other, the husband in his wig and gown and his wife in the dress of the period. Beneath is a scroll-like apron with the arms of Wyndham "Azure a chevron between three lions' heads erased or" impaling those of Strode "Ermine on a canton sable a crescent argent". On the south side of the sanctuary is a mural monument to William Turbill (Turberville) of Ogmore, Gent. (d. 1666) who lies buried beneath the floor of the sanctuary.

On the south wall of the chancel is a monument, beautifully executed in white marble by Sebastian Gahagan of Bath to the memory of Thomas Wyndham, Esq. (1763-1814) of Dunraven Castle and Clearwell Court, Gloucestershire, on which are carved the effigies, in Greek Revival style, of himself and his two sons, who died in infancy. He represented the County of Glamorgan in eight successive parliaments from 1790 until his death in 1814. His genial disposition and open-hearted benevolence together with his generous hospitality made him extremely popular throughout the county, especially among his poorer neighbours. According to a contemporary newspaper account his funeral, which took place at St. Bride's Major church on the 8th November, 1814, was the largest ever known in the area and more than a thousand mourning bands were distributed to the country people who attended it.

The floor and walls of the chancel are covered with memorials to various clergy of the district who lie buried beneath; they include the Reverend A. Butler (d. 1678), vicar of the parish, a descendant of Sir Arnold Butler of Dunraven Castle; the Reverend William Jones (d. 1682) vicar of St. Bride's; the

Reverend Thomas Lloyd (d. 1706), vicar of the parish; the Reverend Charles Gally (d. 1821) and the Reverend John Richards (d. 1843), rector of St. Bride's Minor and Lecturer of Llantwit Major.

A small niche on the east side of the chancel could possibly have been the position of the original entrance to the rood staircase. No corbels remain and the renewal of the windows to the north and south of the chancel arch may have been responsible for their destruction on these walls. A trefoil lancet in the north-west wall of the chancel looks into the vestry. Painted on the wall above the chancel arch there was once a beautiful coloured scroll, in the centre of which was an Iona cross with the sacred monogram IHS. It bore the inscription:— 'Holy, Holy, Holy, Lord God Almighty'. Part of it was obliterated in the 1920s leaving only the cross, which was itself removed in the 1950s.

The nave is lit on the south side by three windows of two cinquefoiled lights with a quatrefoil, a cinquefoil and a sexfoil in the apices. They are all 19th-century insertions done in a 14th-century style. Two of these windows contain stained glass; the one nearest the chancel arch depicts the figures of Faith, Hope and Charity and was erected in memory of Caroline Emily Booker (d. 1925) by her daughters from a design prepared by Messrs. Burlison & Grylls, London. The other stained glass window in the middle of the south wall of the nave depicts the figures of St. Francis and St. Helena. It was erected in 1980, from a design by James A. Crombie of Bristol, in memory of John Francis Powell (d. 1968) and Florence Helena Powell (d. 1977) by their son, Colin James Powell.

The three windows on the north side of the nave are 19th-century insertions also done in a 14th century style. The window on the west side of the north porch is of three trefoiled lights; the centre mullions arched in the head to enclose trefoils. Between them is a circle enclosing a sexfoil. The hood mould has carved heads as label stops. It is a 19th-century window in a Geometrical style with plate and bar tracery. On the east side of the porch there are two windows, one of two lights, the other of three lights. The window to the east is of two trefoiled lights with the mullion continued as a Y-shape into the head. The central tracery light is dagger-shaped and there are trefoils in the spandrels. The western window is of three trefoiled lights with intersecting tracery above enclosing trefoils. There are dagger-shaped lights in the head. They both have hood moulds with carved heads as label stops. The latter window depicts the figures of Christ as the Good Shepherd, St. Paul and St. Elizabeth. It was erected as a memorial to the Reverend Thomas Jones, vicar of the parish (1863-1897) and Elizabeth his wife, by their sons, from a design by Charles Powell of London.

The stone pulpit has an embattled and moulded cornice and is decorated with a row of leaf forms with berries. The stiles are plain and the panels between are treated as two-light windows with cinquefoils or trefoils. Other than that they variously represent reticulated tracery, ogee arches (one beneath a pointed arch in the head) and trefoils and quatrefoils in the spandrels. The underside into the stem is more heavily moulded with pointed trefoils in panels developing through yet more mouldings into an octagonal plinth.

The font has a plain octagonal bowl with a moulded rim and again just before the underside the bowl is angled out to meet yet another plain moulding and flat collar at the top of the octagonal stem. Stool stops break the octagon into a square base.

The two-manual organ, built by Albert E. Pease of Stoke Newington, was presented to the church in October 1980, in memory of William Howell Yorath (d. 1977) who was organist of St. Bride's Major church for 42 years. The organ came from the parish church of St. John the Baptist, Ystradyfodwg (Rhondda) which was closed through subsidence. It replaced an older organ which was riddled with woodworm. On the south wall of the nave is a memorial tablet in Sutton stone to the ten men of the parish of St. Bride's Major with Wick, who fell in the Second World War, 1939-1945. It is interesting to note that Colin Lewis Dillwyn, who fell at Dunkirk in 1940, the last male member of that distinguished Swansea family, heads the list. The nave has a cradle roof.

The north porch which is a large structure was restored in the Decorated Gothic style in 1854. The outer doorway has an acutely-pointed arch with several concave mouldings and is surmounted by a hood mould with carved heads as label stops. The head of the inner doorway is a kind of flattened trefoil under a semicircular tympanum. It lacks the customary stone benches. Over the doorway leading out into the porch was another scroll of similar design to that above the chancel arch, which bore the inscription "Remember Thy Creator In The Days Of Thy Youth". The scroll was also obliterated in the 1920s.

The tower opens to the nave by a pointed Perpendicular arch with continuous moulding. The massive Perpendicular west tower consists of three main stages divided by stringcourses reinforced by three-stage clasping buttresses with intermediate set-offs formed by single chamfered wall blocks. Below the pinnacled battlement is a corbel table of Welsh pattern with grotesque gargoyles protruding from the corners. The belfry is lit by a pair of cinquefoiled lights with square label on each face. The west doorway with window above is entirely Victorian done in poor quality sandstone, weathered so as to present a medieval appearance. They occupy the site of a medieval opening as is indicated by the relieving arch which is off centre. The west doorway is acutely pointed and deeply moulded beneath a square head and label which terminates in carved heads as label stops. The spandrels contain sexfoils and mouchettes—standard 14th-century-style decoration. The window above is of three lights, the mullions being carried into the head as Y-tracery since they diverge but do not intersect. The arrowhead-shaped lights between are long-lobed trefoils. A projection on the south side of the tower with cross loopholes contains a staircase leading to the ringing chamber which is lit by a three-light modern square-headed window.

In 1770 the tower housed four bells which were cracked, and a faculty was obtained at that time to sell the four bells and replace them with two new bells. The additional money received from the sale of bells was used to reseat the church. The tower now houses a ring of six bells (originally five) presented by

Caroline, Countess of Dunraven in 1852 in memory of her parents, Thomas Wyndham (d. 1814) and Anna Maria Charlotte Bennett, who lie buried in the church (see brass plaque in porch). In 1939 the present ring of six bells was recast from the original five bells cast by J. Warner & Sons, London in 1851 and hung in a new bell frame by John Taylor, bellfounders of Loughborough. The inscriptions on the bells are as follows:—

Treble   E.   TAYLOR LOUGHBORO 1939

No. 2   D.   ANNA MARIA BENNETT
               CAST 1851
               TAYLOR LOUGHBORO
               RECAST 1939

No. 3   C.   THOMAS WYNDHAM
               CAST 1851
               TAYLOR LOUGHBORO
               RECAST 1939

No. 4   B.   CAST 1851
               TAYLOR LOUGHBORO
               RECAST 1939

No. 5   A.   CAST 1851
               TAYLOR LOUGHBORO
               RECAST 1939

TENOR   5 BELLS RECAST INTO 6 AND
               BELFRY RESTORED 1939
               TAYLOR LOUGHBORO
               PROMOTED BY SUBSCRIPTIONS
               DAVID J. WILLS. VICAR
               JOHN EVANS
               HUBERT E. TAYLOR   CHURCHWARDENS
               CAST 1851
               RECAST 1939

The church clock on the east face of the tower made by Gillett and Johnston was dedicated on Sunday 9th November 1919 as a memorial to those twenty-three men of the parish of St. Bride's Major and Wick (see stone tablet on south wall of the nave) who gave their lives during the Great War, 1914-1918. The quarters are struck on the 3rd and 5th bells, hours on the tenor.

    The church was thoroughly restored in 1854 at a cost of £1,000 when the windows of the nave were renewed in the Decorated Gothic style. A new vestry was added on the north side of the chancel. The incised sepulchral slab of Johan Le Botiler was placed in the sanctuary floor beneath the altar, and its coffin was removed from beneath the tower arch to its present position on the south side of the chancel. A new stone pulpit was erected in the nave and the north porch was restored. It was probably at this time that all traces of the former rood-loft were destroyed. The work of restoration was carried out according to plans and specifications drawn up by the architect, Egbert Moxham of Neath and a grant of £75 was obtained from the Incorporated Church Building Society towards reseating the church.

The shaft of the churchyard cross rests on a pedestal on five steps which are indented and worn, caused, it is said, by pilgrims kneeling in prayer. St. Bride's Major church is said to have been the last place in which Lt.-General Sir Thomas Picton worshipped before leaving for Waterloo, where he fell at the head of his troops. Having a premonition that he would be killed in battle, he visited all his relatives in the area staying with his brother, the Reverend Edward Picton, vicar of St. Bride's, at Ty'n-y-caeau. A gravestone with an anchor for emblem was erected in St. Bride's Major churchyard by voluntary subscription 'To the memory of the shipwrecked crew of the *Malleny*, lost on Tusker Rock 15 Octr. 1886.'

The church plate consists of a silver chalice and paten, a plated flagon and bread-dish which were given by the then Earl of Dunraven in 1850. The registers date from 1723.

St. Bride's-super-Ely Church

The parish church of St. Bride's-super-Ely is dedicated to St. Bride (St. Bridget) and was built in the early part of the 13th century. The church was valued at £2 in 1254 (Taxation of Norwich) and in 1291 (*Taxatio Ecclesiastica*) it may well have been one of the unnamed chapels of Peterston which at that date was valued at £6-13s-4d. In 1535 (*Valor Ecclesiasticus*) the living was classified among the Rectories and valued at £3-19s-0d. Its patron was resident in 1563. Over the years St. Bride's has been frequently linked with the neighbouring parishes of Michaelston-super-Ely and St. George's. In 1771 (Bishop Barrington's *Llandaff Diocesan Book*) the living was included with the Rectories of Michaelston-super-Ely and St. George's in the same valuation, namely £130; the incumbent was the Reverend William Llewellin and the patron was John Llewellin, Gent. In 1785 the Reverend Morgan Deere was rector of St. Bride's, Michaelston-super-Ely and St. George's. In 1835 the Rectory was coupled with the Rectory of Michaelston-super-Ely in the same valuation, namely £95 gross, and Llewellyn Traherne was patron of both livings. In 1950 the Reverend Harold George Rew became rector. In 1970 St. Bride's was linked with Peterston-super-Ely to form one benefice.

The church consists of chancel, nave, south porch and western tower containing one bell. The chancel arch is a replica of the original Norman work and was placed in the church in the restoration of 1849. It is a plain semicircular arch of two orders with simple square stops beneath a plain moulding to the edge of the outer arch. The square abacus from which the arch springs has a continuous band of star ornament—a widely-used 12th-century motif. On either side an engaged column is let into the wall; it has barely scalloped capitals above a single roll.

The east window is Perpendicular of three lights with round trefoil heads which are repeated in the two panels in the head. This window, together with the canopy and niche, was brought from the chapel of Llanfair Vawr (i.e. chapel of St. Mary) at St.-y-Nyll when it was demolished in 1849. The foundation of this interesting chapel (of which substantial remains existed before its demolition) may well have pre-dated that of the parish church on which it once depended. It is mentioned as the church of Llan Tilull in a 9th-century charter copied into the *Book of Llandaff*. It then served a village called Penn Onn which is probably represented by the present-day hamlet of St.-y-Nyll. The stained glass ornamentation in the window was placed there in 1956

in memory of Allan Everett Renwick and David and Ada Llewellin-Evans in accordance with a design by George G. Pace, architect of York. The stained glass consists of ten roundels and two panels of 14th- and 15th-century glass set in a clear background. The subjects are, from left to right:—

1. Flowers.
2. Good and evil.
3. St. William of York.
4. Censing angels.
5. and 6. Angels.
7. Salome dancing.
8. Beheading of John the Baptist.
9. Tobias and Angel.
10. Return of Tobias.
11. Descent from the cross.
12. The Resurrection of Our Lord.

The niche, which has all the hallmarks of 14th-century workmanship, has three little ogee arches, foliated crockets and finials. The Madonna and Child, which now occupies the niche, is seated on a throne and is a very good specimen in carved wood with old colour and gilding. The piece is in the style of the 17th-century Venetian school and was formerly in the celebrated Strogonoff collection. It was purchased by the church in 1950 at a cost of £78 from S. W. Wolsey Ltd. of London, to replace a medieval figure, probably destroyed at the Reformation. It rests on a modern plinth which bears the inscription 'John Cory in piam memoriam obit 17.5.[19]39'. Local tradition has it that several men of the parish, killed at the Battle of St. Fagans in 1648, lie buried beneath the chancel floor.

The chancel is lit on the south side by a single light with cinquefoiled head. The window depicts the figure of St. Brigid, (St. Bridget), the patron saint of the church, holding a crozier in her hand. It was erected as a memorial to the Reverend David Jenkins, rector of the parish (1909-1949) and his wife, Minnie Jenkins, by their daughters in 1954, in accordance with a design by Hubert Thomas of Celtic Studios, Swansea. In the south wall of the chancel is a priest's door with four-centred arch. On the south wall is a memorial tablet in Penarth alabaster surmounted by a coat of arms with four quarterings, each containing a lion rampant. The tablet (now largely obscured) commemorates Captain William Jones (d. 1658) and his sons William (d. 1648) and Robert (d. 1650). On the north wall of the chancel is a brass memorial plaque to those men of the parish who fell in the Great War, 1914-1918. A doorway with four-centred arch leads to a modern vestry on the north side of the chancel.

The nave is lit on the north side by a pair of two-light windows, one with ogee-foliated head, the other cinquefoiled, both under square heads, labelled. On the south side are two windows, the south-east window is a 19th-century insertion of three pointed lights, square-headed with label. Internally the heads of the lights are ogee-shaped, trefoiled with cusps. The south-west window of the nave is of two trefoil lights under ogee arches with label and square-headed. The modern stone pulpit has an hexagonal drum and a castellated cornice. The panels are arranged as single lights between the muntins, cinquefoiled with rectilinear tracery in the head. The nave has a trussed-rafter roof.

The font is a typical plain 14th-century design, even if the bowl is misshapen. It is octagonal throughout (the favourite shape of the period) with a moulded rim and underside and again at either end of the stem. The base is simply a continuation of the piece above splayed out to meet the floor. The decoration of the outer doorway of the south porch is a splendid specimen of Norman workmanship. It was brought there from Margam Abbey in 1849 by Mrs. Charlotte Traherne, wife of the then rector of the parish, and sister to C. R. M. Talbot, who then occupied Margam Abbey. A manuscript account of Margam Abbey written in 1787 by the Reverend William Thomas of Baglan, has a marginal note in the hand of the Reverend John Montgomery Traherne who stated that 'a Romanesque arch was discovered when a stable abutting on the south side of the old building east of the almshouses was taken down in March 1840'. Presumably the arch was part of the fabric of the building. The inner arch is adorned by chevron or zig-zag decoration above little scalloped capitals. The chamfered outer arch which springs from square abaci above trumpet capitals—the western one with a hint of volute—is surmounted by a row of chevron ornament at right angles to the surface of the wall. To the west is an inscribed consecration cross, a smaller one to the east of the doorway and another let in at the head. The inner arch of the porch has a Norman rounded arch around which there is herringbone decoration. Inside the porch are stone benches, and resting on the western one is a stone memorial to three men of the parish who fell in the Great War, 1914-1918. The tower opens to the nave by an obtusely-pointed arch.

The tower is tall and slender with saddleback roof surmounted by two crosses. The belfry is lit on each face by a single trefoil-headed louvred lancet and on its north, south and west faces are slit-loopholes at various levels. The west doorway has a pointed arch with hood moulding, and above it a small pointed lancet surmounted by a rare ancient bishop's consecration cross.

On the south side of the west doorway is a memorial tablet set into the west wall of the tower, but unfortunately the inscription has faded completely. It was placed there in 1764 as a memorial to William Gyles, an infant who, having thrown down a beehive, was stung repeatedly in the head and neck, which occasioned strong convulsive fits, from which he died. The tower houses a single bell inscribed LLEWELLINS & JAMES, BRISTOL, 1871.

The church was restored in 1849 when the Norman outer arch of the south porch and the pseudo-Norman chancel arch was installed, together with the east window. The church was reopened for divine service after restoration on the 6th September, 1849. The church underwent further restoration in 1902 when the work of restoration included repairs to the tower, the addition of a vestry on the north side of the chancel, the laying down of wood-block flooring, reseating the nave, erecting a glazed screen to the tower arch, the insertion of a new three-light window in the south wall of the nave and general repairs to the whole fabric of the church. The cost of restoration amounted to £350. The contractors were Messrs. Harries and Davies of Cardiff, and the architect was George E. Halliday of Cardiff, the diocesan architect. The church was reopened for divine service after restoration on Thursday 6th March, 1902 by the Venerable F. W. Edmondes, Archdeacon of Llandaff, a former rector of St. Bride's (1867-1873). The old yew tree in the churchyard is one of the largest in South Wales.

The church plate consists of a silver chalice with trumpet-shaped stem with its paten cover, hall-marked 1640. The registers date from the year 1757.

ST DONAT'S CASTLE AND CHURCH, GLAMORGANSHIRE.

(From the *Gentleman's Magazine*, June, 1821)

St. Donat's Church

The parish church of St. Donat's is dedicated to St. Dunwyd (St. Donat) and the present building dates from the 12th century with additions in the 14th and 15th centuries. The church was valued at 5 marks in 1254 (Taxation of Norwich) and at £13-6s-8d in 1291 (*Taxatio Ecclesiastica*). The earliest recorded vicar of St. Donat's was 'William de Sancto Donato, Presbyter of St. Donat's 1201'. Shortly before 1341 Edward Stradling gave the advowson of the church and one acre of land there to Neath Abbey. The monks established a vicarage of 8 marks per annum; the Bishop sanctioned the appropriation in 1343. This grant was confirmed by the Lord of Glamorgan in 1468. In 1535 (*Valor Ecclesiasticus*) the Abbey drew 15 shillings from St. Donat's wheat; the living was classified among the vicarages as worth £3-14s-4d. It had a vicar resident in 1563 (Reverend John Cauntlow or Cantelupe). In 1603 it was styled a vicarage worth £6-13s-3d; the impropriation worth £6 was held by Sir Edward Stradling, knight in fee. In 1668 the Rectory of St. Donat's and the advowson of its vicarage went with the castle and manor of St. Donat's. In 1771 (Bishop Barrington's *Llandaff Diocesan Book*) the living was worth £50; the incumbent was the Reverend Thomas Williams and the patrons were the heirs of Sir John Tyrwhitt. It was styled a vicarage worth gross £131 in 1835; the patron and impropriator was Thomas Tyrwhitt Drake. St. Donat's church was linked with Llantwit Major in 1954 and in 1983 the two parishes together with Marcross, Monknash and Wick became a Rectorial benefice known as Llantwit Major.

The church consists of chancel with Lady Chapel on the north side, a nave, north porch and western tower containing six bells. Originally the church had an apse and the present chancel reached by three steps is a 15th-century extension. The semicircular stilted Norman chancel arch is composed of large blocks, resting on flat imposts which are chamfered into the jambs. The angles beneath carry engaged shafts surmounted by caps with a single volute as decoration. The east window is Perpendicular of three cinquefoiled lights with panel tracery of trefoils in the head and surmounted by a hood mould. The beautiful Victorian stained glass in the window is a memorial to Edward Stradling Nicholl-Carne who died at Malvern in 1862. The centre light depicts St. Donat as a bishop and in the panel below he is portrayed as the patron saint of shipwrecked sailors. The left-hand light depicts the crest of the Stradling family 'A stag courant on his neck a scarf argent' with the Stradling motto in Welsh 'Heb dhyw heb dhym dyw a dygon' (Without God, without anything,

God is enough) followed by the Stradling arms 'Paly of 6, argent and azure on a bend gules 3 cinquefoils or' and below the initials E.S. The right-hand light portrays the crest of the Carne family 'A pelican displayed with two heads issuant from a Ducal coronet or' with the Carne motto 'En tout loyale' (Loyal in all things) followed by the Carne arms 'Gules, a pelican in her piety proper' and below the initials N.C.

The stone altar or mensa is of pre-Reformation date (circa 1470) and bears the five incised crosses representing the five wounds of Christ while on its front edge is the consecration cross of the bishop. This stone altar was removed at the Reformation and placed in the floor of the sanctuary from where it was recovered during the restoration of the church at the beginning of this century. On the east wall of the sanctuary north of the altar is a vacant ledge upon which once stood a statuette of the patron saint.

The altar cross is the upper portion of a gilded latten processional cross dating from the latter part of the 15th century, which was found blocked up in debris about 1870. It was restored in 1907 in the form of an altar cross according to a design by G. E. Halliday. It bears the symbolical representation of the four evangelists, three of which are original. On the reverse side a Tudor rose is engraved behind each of the emblems. In the south wall of the sanctuary is a 14th-century piscina under a trefoiled ogee arch.

The chancel is lit on the south side by two large Perpendicular windows of two cinquefoiled lights with panel tracery of trefoils in the head surmounted by hood moulds. The beautiful Victorian stained glass in the south-west window is in memory of John Whitlock Stradling-Carne (d. 1889) (who assumed the name of Stradling-Carne in lieu of Nicholl-Carne in 1877), the father of Edward Stradling Nicholl-Carne commemorated in the east window. The two lights depict the miracle of Jesus feeding the multitude with five barley loaves and two small fish. The window was erected by his widow, Mary Salusbury Stradling-Carne. The glass in the south-east window, which depicts the figures of St. Peter and St. Elizabeth, is in memory of Peter Whitfield Brancker (d. 1864) and his wife, Elizabeth (née Houghton) (d. 1853), the father and mother-in-law of John Whitlock Stradling-Carne. Between these two windows is a priest's door with pointed arch surmounted by a dripstone with floriated label stops. In the north wall of the chancel is a single-light window with cinquefoiled head and square label, with patera decoration. On the north wall of the chancel is a memorial plaque to Morgan Stuart Williams (1846-1909) who restored the castle and church of St. Donat's and as Lord of the Manor conferred many benefits upon the parish and neighbourhood. The lectern which is in fact an ambo was given to the church as a genuine Breton medieval piece in 1913. On the desk faces are coats of arms. Supporting the desk is the figure of St. John the Evangelist bearing in his arms a tablet upon which is inscribed the word 'Evangel' at the top.

On the north side of the chancel stands the 14th-century Lady Chapel or Stradling Chapel which was rebuilt by Sir Thomas Stradling (d. 1571) circa 1540 when it became the burial place of the Stradling family. It was probably at this time that the chapel was stripped of its altar and furnishings. It was dedicated to St. Mary, probably in honour of the Abbey of St. Mary, Neath, to which the church was attached from 1341 to 1539. There are two entrances, one from the churchyard on the north side, and another from the chancel directly opposite. Both doorways have four-centred archways, the inner arch being of Quarella stone, the outer modern. Near the north door is a trefoiled niche under an ogee arch which once housed a holy-water stoup. There is not a vestige of an altar remaining.

The chapel has in its east wall a square-headed Decorated window of three-trefoiled lights with reticulated tracery above as quatrefoils in the head with trefoils above all cusped with square label. It bears a striking resemblance to the tracery in the windows of the south transept of St. Athan's church. On the west wall of the chapel hang three painted panels on which are portrayed members of the Stradling family whose remains repose there. The paintings show the costume of the period as well as the family armorial achievements. The first one is a memorial to Sir Edward Stradling (1529-1609) and his wife Agnes, daughter of Sir Edward Gage of Firle, Sussex, who are also commemorated by the Jacobean monument on the north wall. He is dressed in a black doublet and hose with white cuffs and an elaborate ruff. Lady Agnes is richly dressed with a beautiful ruff and head-dress. The sleeves of her black and gold dress are puffed and ornamented with a floral design. Both figures are kneeling holding open books on which are the versicles 'God have mercie upon us' and 'Christ have mercie upon us.' There are no children. At the top of the panel is Sir Edward's motto:—'Vertues hole praise consisteth in doing,' and the date 1590 below. The second painting commemorates Thomas Stradling (d. 1480) whose widow Jenet, the daughter of Thomas Mathew of Radyr, married Sir Rhys ap Thomas the leader of the Welsh levies at Bosworth field. Kneeling in the background are two boys and a girl. At the back of Thomas Stradling is painted the inscription: 'He died before he was 26 years of age,' while in a similar position behind Lady Jenet is 'Anno aeta sue 24'. Both Thomas Stradling and his wife hold open books inscribed respectively 'Iesu have mercy upon me' and 'Blessed be thou O Lorde.' He is dressed in a black belted coat with red sleeves which are richly damasked with a black floral design. She wears a mantilla head-dress with a gold and jewelled border. Her cloak is black with red sleeves. The third painting is a memorial to Sir Edward Stradling (d. 1535) and his wife, Elizabeth, daughter of Thomas Arundell of Lanherne, Cornwall. Sir Edward, son of the above-mentioned Thomas Stradling, was the famous soldier knighted by Henry VIII and he kneels before a table wearing a suit of shining armour with sword and spurs. He holds in his hand an open book which is inscribed 'Lord have mercie upon us'. Behind him kneel five boys—four dressed in red and brown doublets and one in a dress of lighter colour. Lady Elizabeth wears a black head-dress edged with gold which falls to her shoulders; her dress is red and black with gold braiding and five girls variously dressed kneel behind her. These paintings were commissioned by Sir Edward Stradling (1529-1609) and were executed by an artist named Byrd about the year 1590.

On the north wall of the chapel is a fine early 17th-century marble monument which resembles the Basset-Mansel tomb in the chancel of Llantrithyd church. The figures of Sir Edward Stradling (d. 1609) and his wife, Agnes, daughter of Sir Edward Gage of Firle, Sussex, are shown kneeling on cushions on opposite sides of a centre altar on which rests a front-facing helmet. Sir Edward is shown bare-headed, bearded and ruffed. He is wearing armour and his hands are clasped in an attitude of prayer. Lady Agnes wears a ruff and head-dress which falls to her heels. There are two inscriptions on the tomb, both in Latin. The design is of English Renaissance type with full entablature and columns of the Corinthian order supporting the Stradling armorial achievement. It consists of the eight quarterings adopted by the Stradling family since 1411, surmounted by a helmet and wreath over which is the crest—'A stag courant, scarfed round neck' bearing the family motto 'Duw a Digon' (God is enough). The eight quarterings are blazoned as follows:— 1st quarter—'Paly of 6, argent and azure on a bend gules 3 cinquefoils or' (Stradling); 2nd—'Argent a chevron between 10 crosses pattée gules' (Hawey); 3rd—'Azure, 3 crosses pattée or, a file of 3 points ermine' (Strongbow); 4th—'Argent, a fess between 3 crosses pattée sable' (Garnon); 5th—'Sable, a cross quarterly pierced argent' (St. Barbe); 6th—'Gules 3 chevronels argent' (Iestyn ap Gwrgant); 7th—'Chequy, or and gules a fess ermine (Turberville); and 8th—'Azure a chevron between 3 crescents or' (Berkerolles). The achievement is flanked at either corner by shields surrounded by scrollwork ornamented with roses displaying the Stradling arms impaled with those of Gage. Under the arcading behind the two figures are two fine heraldic panels. That behind Sir Edward shows the eight quarterings of the Stradling family mentioned above. The other shield displays the Gage quarterings—quarterly of four, 1st and 4th quarters—'Quarterly argent and azure, a saltire gules' (Gage), 2nd and 3rd quarters—'Azure a sun in splendor or' (St. Clere).

The centre of the chapel is taken up by a magnificent rectangular tomb-chest of polished white marble mounted on a black marble base. The tomb is richly carved having oval panels on the north and south sides, on which are inscribed the names of the last two Stradlings, Sir Edward who died in 1726 and Sir Thomas who died in 1738 and was buried there in 1739.

A doorway with Tudor arch in the north wall of the nave leads to the rood-loft staircase which terminates in an upper doorway at rood-loft level. The corbels which once supported the loft remain on each side of the chancel arch and on the north and south walls of the nave. The rood-loft was lit by a two-light cinquefoiled-headed window which still remains high in the south wall of the nave. The nave is lit on the south side by two three-light Perpendicular windows with cinquefoiled heads and square labels. On the exterior wall of the nave below the south-east rood-loft window is a large memorial slab to Morgan S. Williams (d. 1909) who restored the castle and church.

The nave wall is pierced on the north side of the chancel arch to accommodate a modern stone pulpit which projects into the nave, the access to which is from the chancel. The pulpit has an embattled cornice and moulded top rail with plain stiles and panels between, all in stone with moulded bottom rail and ribbed triangular drum. The north side of the nave is lit by a two-light window with cinquefoiled head surmounted by square label with a grotesque head as one of the label stops. Near the north doorway is an octagonal holy-water stoup, and above the north door hangs a Victorian imitation of the Stradling Tudor wooden memorials. On the north wall of the nave is a monument to the Reverend John Thomas (d. 1832), vicar of the parish for 27 years and perpetual curate of Monknash for 35 years.

In the floor of the nave lies buried William Savours (d. 1727), father of the Reverend William Savours, vicar of the parish (1731-1758). In the south wall of the nave (now blocked up internally) is a doorway with Tudor arch known as the 'soldiers' door' which local tradition states as having been the door through which the Cromwellian soldiers entered the church during their occupation of St. Donat's castle. The upper parts of the south and north walls of the nave are corbelled out. On the north-west wall of the nave is an unusual monument whose borders are decorated with symbolic cross-bones as *memento mori* and crossed torches of life. Its base is adorned with a winged cherub-head symbolizing immortality. It commemorates Edward Hyett (d. 1735) 'Practinoner [*sic*] of Surgery at St. George's Hospitall in London,' son of Richard Hyett and Catherine Thomas of St. Donat's. The north doorway of the church displays a Tudor arch and in the porch which has stone benches, is a mural tablet erected to two centenarians of the parish, Francis Stych (d. 1671) aged 108 years and John Harry (d. 1792) aged 110 years.

The tower arch is pointed and consists of stone blocks of varying sizes, the outer arch is inclined inwards and the inner arch has a deep but slight chamfer. In the middle of the tower space stands the Norman font, the bowl of which is circular, decorated at the top with two rows of fish-scale ornament set on a square base and plinth. The tower has no west doorway and is lit at the base by a single modern cinquefoiled window with Bath stone dressings deeply splayed internally under a circular arch. The stained glass in the window depicts a golden chalice on a lozenge-shaped background.

The tower is square and lofty and has four small corner pinnacles. It is strengthened at its western end by small buttresses. Below the parapet is a corbel table and the tower is pierced with slit-loopholes. The tower contains a chime of six hemispherical bells which were recast in 1913 from the single bell in the church and two other bells from the castle by the Whitechapel Bell Foundry. The new bells were the gift of Godfrey H. J. Williams of St. Donat's Castle. One of the bells bears the inscription:— 'St. Donat's church, 1913'.

In the churchyard are two Calvary crosses. One is modern and records the restoration of the church in 1878. The other on the south side of the churchyard is a fine 15th-century churchyard cross with its original head, one of the few remaining in the diocese. One side has a representation of the Crucifixion and the other has a figure of the Virgin Mary crowned. It is built of three different types of stone. The head is Sutton stone, the shaft and socket of Quarella and the base and steps are of blue lias limestone. Like that at Llangan this cross was

thankfully spared in the general destruction of crosses ordered by the Parlia-
mentarians. The churchyard cross was restored in 1928 by Messrs. Raines &
Porter Ltd of Park Lane London, under the personal direction of Mr. Arthur R.
Warnes following a visit to the church earlier that year by the Cambrian
Archaeological Society.

William Stradling who visited the church in 1838 gives us the following
account of the building:— 'The church is in a most wretched condition—the
windows closed with wood and most of the fine old glass broken, although it is
so full of curious monuments, as to induce my late worthy friend, Sir R. C.
Hoare, to send an artist twice to copy them. He several times visited what he
calls classic ground.' Dr. John Whitlock Nicholl-Carne (1816-1889), who
changed his name to Stradling-Carne in 1877, purchased St. Donat's Castle
from Thomas Tyrwhitt Drake in 1862. In 1878 he restored the church and over
the years he also restored the Castle taking exceptional care to preserve the
ancient character of the building. On his tombstone which forms the base of the
modern churchyard cross on the north-west side of the church is the inscription:—

> 'A church revived
> A castle restored
> The surrounding wilderness
> Made to blossom.'

The base of the churchyard cross also bears a memorial inscription to his first
wife, Mary Jane Nicholl-Carne (d. 1874) and below is a Latin epitaph (which is
a combination of two famous epitaphs, the first to Oliver Goldsmith by Dr.
Johnson and the second to Sir Christopher Wren (1632-1723) by his son
Christopher.) 'Nihil tetigit quod non ornavit; si monumentum quaeris
circumspice.' (She touched nothing she did not adorn; if you want her
monument—just look around you.) Other memorial inscriptions on the base of
the churchyard cross commemorate Mary Salusbury Stradling-Carne, (d. 1935)
second wife of John Whitlock Stradling-Carne and their son, Caradoc
Stradling-Carne (d. 1912).

The church was restored to a certain extent during 1907 by the then owner of
St. Donat's castle, Morgan Stuart Williams. He did this in return for some
concessions made to him on the estate regarding the access road to the church
by the church authorities. The work of restoration included the reflooring of
the nave with wooden blocks and the restoration of the high altar slab from the
sanctuary pavement. The parapets of the tower were rebuilt and the external
walls were repointed. Morgan Stuart Williams, the patron of the living, bore
the entire cost of the work himself and he presented a handsome stone pulpit
and constructed a pseudo-Norman arch to provide access to it from the chancel.
G. E. Halliday, the diocesan architect, acted in the capacity of consulting
architect for the restoration of the church. The church was reopened for divine
service after restoration on the 23rd April, 1907 by the Venerable Archdeacon
F. W. Edmondes of Llandaff.

The church plate includes an Elizabethan silver chalice decorated with intersecting foliated strap ornament round the upper part of the bowl, below which is a plain line band. Also a silver paten inscribed 'An offering to the church of St. Donat's E.S. (Evan Seys) 1706'. An entry in the burials register of St. Donat's church records that 'William John of Wick—an idiot who rode a blind horse over the cliffs—a tremendous death' was buried in the churchyard on the 5th October, 1817 aged 21 years.

The registers, which include some of the earliest and most perfect in the diocese, date from 1570.

St. Fagans Church

The parish church of St. Fagans is dedicated to St. Mary, the reason for which is explained by John Leland (1506-1552) in his *Itinerary of England and Wales* who says:— 'The Paroch church of S. Fagan is now of our Lady; but ther is yet by the village a Chapelle of S. Fagan sumtime the Paroch Church.' The original church of St. Fagans stood at the foot of a declivity in the Castle grounds. It was dedicated to St. Fagan, one of the early Christians who, an unreliable legend records, came to Britain with Dyfan, Medwy and Elfan in A.D. 180 at the request of King Lleuwrg to preach the gospel and baptize the people. The present church was built in the 12th century probably by Robert Le Sore, one of Fitz-Hamon's knights who owned land in St. Fagans and Peterston-super-Ely. However, much of the architecture of the church is in the Decorated style of the 14th century.

At one period the church was appropriated to Tewkesbury Abbey, for not only was 'half the tithe of the Lordship of St. Fagan' confirmed to it by the charter of 1180 but its 'vicarage' was mentioned expressly in the Norwich Taxation of 1254 when the church with its vicarage and the chapel of Llaniltern were together worth £8. In 1291 (*Taxatio Ecclesiastica*) its value was £13-6s-8d. The impropriation had ceased before the 16th century and survived only in a pension of 3s-4d paid to the Abbey annually by the 'Rector' whose income in 1535 (*Valor Ecclesiasticus*) was £15-12s-4d. The parson was resident in 1563. In 1741 the Lewis of Van family held the advowson of the church. In 1771 (Bishop Barrington's Primary Visitation of the Diocese) the living was worth £160; the incumbent was the Reverend Thomas Bowen and the Earl of Plymouth was the patron. In 1835 the Rectory including the curacy of Llaniltern was worth gross £420 and the patronage was held by the Earl of Plymouth. In 1968 St. Fagans was linked with the parish of Michaelston-super-Ely.

The church consists of chancel, nave, north aisle, north vestry, south porch and embattled western tower containing two bells. The chancel arch is acutely pointed and lofty and springs from a composite pier of three engaged shafts with typical 13th-century capitals. The east window is a mixture of 13th- and 14th-century Geometrical and Curvilinear forms. It is a three-light cinquefoil-headed window with the centre mullions curving outwards in the head to form arches enclosing pointed cinquefoils. In the space between is a circle enclosing trefoils and sexfoils with cusping throughout. The whole is surmounted by a hood mould with carved heads as label stops. Internally the arch springs above

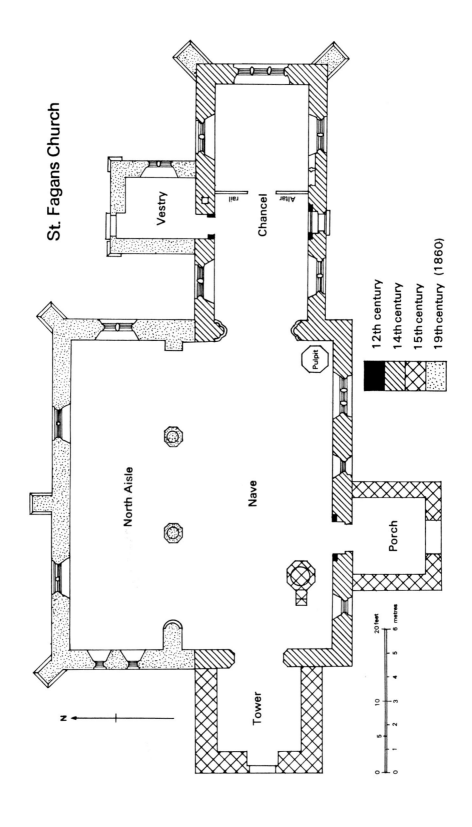

St. Fagans Church

Vestry

Chancel

rail

Altar

North Aisle

Nave

Pulpit

Porch

Tower

N

12th century
14th century
15th century
19th century (1860)

20 feet
6 metres

0 5 10
0 1 2 3 4 5 6

two engaged shafts, one with a typical 13th-century capital, the other foliated. The stained glass depicts the Crucifixion in the centre light and Jesus blessing little children and the Last Supper in the other lights. The window was erected in 1859 in memory of the Honourable Robert Windsor Clive (d. 1859) M.P. for Ludlow and Salop, by the tenantry on the family estates in Glamorgan as a token of their respect for him. This window and the other beautiful stained glass windows in the church were designed by Messrs. John Hardman & Co. of Birmingham.

When Richard Symonds, who accompanied Charles I to St. Fagans on the 29th July, 1645, visited the church he made the following note in his diary which is preserved in the British Library:— 'St. Faggin's church at com. Glamorgan two myle from Landaffe. East window of the church this twice— 'Or, three chevronels Gules' (Clare) (the arms of the De Clares who were Lords of Glamorgan until 1314)'. In the east wall of the sanctuary is a square aumbry. On the south side of the chancel the fine piscina and sedilia is a particularly harmonious piece done in the 14th century almost as a panel and stepped downwards from the east. It is of four bays, the bottom of the most westerly two on the same level, with cinquefoils and caps. The labels of the arches terminate in carved heads, the middle ones those of kings, the westernmost in a close-fitting cap like those at St. George's. In the spandrels are large leaf forms and a tailed and winged monster in the westernmost one. The piscina has a credence shelf, a quatrefoil drain hole and a sculpted leaf on the front.

The chancel is lit by four 19th-century windows done in a 14th-century style with two-light trefoil heads with the centre mullion curving into a Y in the head to enclose trefoils within the arches with a quatrefoil between. Externally the hood moulds terminate in carved heads as stops and internally the arch is corbelled out on grotesque heads. The south-east window depicts the Presentation in the Temple and Mary with Elizabeth and Zacharias, and the north-east window depicts Mary Magdalene with the risen Christ on Easter Sunday and the raising of Lazarus from the dead. These two windows were erected in 1864 by Lady Mary Windsor Clive in memory of her husband, the Honourable Robert Windsor Clive.

The north-west window depicts St. Matthew and St. Mark and the opposite window St. Luke and St. John, the four Evangelists. These windows were erected in memory of Baroness Harriet Windsor in 1870 by a nephew and three nieces. In the south wall of the chancel is a priest's door with external dripstone and mutilated heads as label stops. Inside the outline of a round arch beneath the plaster, carefully preserved by the restorer, still tells of the 12th-century Norman church. A door with pointed archway on the north side of the chancel leads to the large vestry built in 1860 when the church was restored and enlarged. Fragments of the Norman arches occur also above the vestry door. In the vestry is a small stained glass window showing the man (St. Matthew), the lion (St. Mark), the ox (St. Luke), and the eagle (St. John). In the south wall of the chancel near the chancel arch is an arched recess probably an aumbry. The chancel has a fine wagon roof. Corner or clasping buttresses of two stages were added to the east wall of the chancel by the restorer in 1860 but they are a purely decorative feature.

The south-east window of the nave is Perpendicular of three cinquefoiled lights with rectilinear tracery in the head, surmounted by a dripstone with carved heads as stops. A curious feature of the inside of this window is a bracket with carved head against the jamb of the window nearest the chancel arch which is believed to have supported the beam of the rood loft. This window illustrates in each light the subject of Christ's raising of the widow's son from the dead (St. Luke, Ch. 7, verses 11-17), and was erected in 1859 by Baroness Windsor as a memorial to her son the Honourable William Windsor Clive who was killed in a railway accident near Tuxford on the 24th September, 1857. The window is placed immediately above the seats set apart for the Castle family. The design for the window was prepared by the Honourable Robert Windsor Clive in 1859, but due to his own death in that year the window was completed by his widow, Lady Mary Windsor Clive. In the centre of the south wall of the nave is a brass memorial tablet set under a trefoiled arch springing from diminutive marble capitals with pillars and bases. It commemorates Flora (d. 1887), wife of Robert Forrest, Esq., Lord Windsor's agent and was erected by the Glamorgan Tenantry of the Windsor Estate. Each side of the south porch is a broad trefoil lancet with a trefoil in the apex surmounted by a dripstone. The west one is original 14th century and has the peculiarity that the second recess member is carried round or following the top of the trefoil in the tracery head. The window depicts John the Baptist baptizing Jesus in the river Jordan and was erected in 1874. The other one is an excellent copy of the original inserted by G. E. Street in 1860. It depicts the figure of Christ as the Good Shepherd and was erected in April, 1986 by Mr. & Mrs. Derrick Strong in memory of their son Mark (d. 1983) aged 27 years. The window was designed by Colwyn Morris, a traditional, stained glass artist of Glantawe Studios, Morriston, Swansea. Between this window and the south doorway is a memorial tablet erected by the Tenantry and villagers of St. Fagans 'as a mark of their esteem and respect' for Robert Forrest, J.P., D.L., (d. 1910), who was chief agent of the Plymouth Estates for 36 years and also rector's warden for as many years. On the west wall of the nave is a marble monument to Ivor Miles (d. 1943) 2nd earl of Plymouth and Lord Lieutenant of the County of Glamorgan 1923-1943 which was erected 'by the tenantry of the Glamorgan estate, the villagers of St. Fagans and other friends in affection and gratitude.'

The pulpit has a plain cornice with a single row of bead decoration and the rest is quite plain except for the sunken panels, each representing a two-light trefoil-headed window with a quatrefoil above—made in the likeness of 13th-century plate tracery. The brass candleholders on each side of the pulpit are indeed rare fittings nowadays. The two-manual organ built by J. W. Walker & Sons of Brandon, Suffolk at a total cost of £539 raised by public subscription was installed in 1881 in the north-east corner of the nave near the chancel wall where the pulpit and reading desk had stood prior to the restoration of the church in 1860.

The tower arch is high and segmental, the inner arch springing from the jambs. The whole space beneath is occupied by an oak screen of four bays below and corresponding to four lights above. The two centre bays are doors and each is treated as a two-light trefoil-headed window beneath a pointed arch enclosing a quatrefoil with little trefoils in the spandrels. Beneath are blind plain panels. The screen is extended upwards into a 14th-century-style window of four trefoil-headed lights, the arches in the head springing from little caps above slender shafts with corresponding similar features below. The mullions of the two centre lights are continued as an arch into the head enclosing a circle with trefoils, circles and ovals in the spaces between. In the two centre lights are depicted St. Lleuwrg and St. Fagan with the date A.D. 180, the year when legend records that King Lleuwrg dispatched two messengers to Eleutherius, Bishop of Rome, entreating him to send missionaries to Britain to baptize himself and his people. The glass screen was erected in the tower archway in 1889 in memory of Lady Mary Windsor Clive who died in that year.

From the nature of its masonry the tower was built at a later period than the nave and chancel of the church, probably in the 15th century. It was restored and refaced in the 18th and 19th centuries. The battlemented tower has grotesque gargoyles at the corners of a simple moulded stringcourse below the parapet. The stringcourse is repeated a metre or so from the base of the tower. Just below the parapet on the west wall of the tower is a stone plaque with what appears to be the arms of the Lewis family: 'A lion rampant' and below this is inscribed the date 1730, the year in which Thomas Lewis' daughter, Elizabeth, married Other Windsor, Earl of Plymouth.

The tower has a two-light round-headed belfry window on each face and a small square aperture halfway up the south wall. Above the 15th-century west doorway are two single elongated trefoil lancets. Until recently the tower housed a ring of six bells and four of these bells were recast in 1860, when the church was restored, by George Mears of the Whitechapel bellfoundry, the cost being defrayed by Baroness Windsor. The treble bell was recast in 1875 by Mears & Stainbank, London. The Tenor bell originally bore the inscription 'GIFT OF THE HONBLE THOMAS LEWIS. W.E. (William Evans, Chepstow) 1737' but in 1860 this bell was recast and inscribed 'THE GIFT OF HARRIET BARONESS WINDSOR 1860'. The second bell bore the inscription 'IOSHVA WARD IOHN ROSER, C. WARDENS. E.E. (Evan Evans, Chepstow) 1707'. Unfortunately the bells have remained silent for many years due to the unstable condition of the tower. In January 1986 the bells were taken down and sold to pay for urgent repairs to be carried out on the tower and north aisle. Two smaller bells from St. James' church, Leckwith, now closed, were installed in the tower in place of the former ring of six bells. The new bells have indecipherable inscriptions.

The font has an octagonal bowl with a Perpendicular quatrefoil design on each face, while that on the faces of the octagonal base is a linked-trefoiled window. The plinth is modern. Inside the south door of the nave is a mutilated holy-water stoup. The outer doorway of the south porch is 15th century, which is borne out by the little trefoil in the apex and the style of the 19th-century foliated cross in Bath stone immediately above, which is sitting on a stump of something much older. Above the doorway are the remains of a sundial which once bore the date 1622. The 15th-century inner doorway of the porch has a moulded pointed archway but the original Norman arch of the south doorway which is visible inside the church attests unmistakably a 12th-century date for the first church. The nave has a cradle or wagon roof and the intersection of the braces and purlins are covered by floriated bosses.

The arcade which separates the nave from the north aisle has three pointed arches springing from simple moulded capitals on circular piers with octagonal bases. The north aisle which extends the whole length of the nave was added in 1860 by G. E. Street when he restored and enlarged the church. The windows of the north aisle are all in the Decorated style of architecture. The east window is of two trefoil-headed lights with a quatrefoil in the apex and mouchettes. The stained glass depicts the Descent from the Cross and the three Marys at the Sepulchre. In the quatrefoil above, Jesus, now risen from the dead, breaks bread with two of his disciples he met on the road to Emmaus. The window was erected in 1871 in memory of the Rt. Honourable Harriet Baroness Windsor by the tenantry of the Windsor estates. The two windows in the north wall of the aisle are of two trefoiled lights with a trefoil in the apex. The north-east window depicts Our Lord meeting the Blessed Virgin Mary and the Holy women on the way to Calvary and in the trefoil above is Mary at the marriage at Cana in Galilee. This window was erected in 1891 in memory of Lady Mary Windsor Clive (d. 1889) by Lord Windsor and Miss Clive in memory of their beloved mother. The north-west window depicts the Nativity and Jesus with the Doctors in the temple and in the trefoil above is Repose in Egypt. It was erected in 1876 to the memory of Thomas Goddard (d. 1874) by some close friends and the tenantry of Lord Windsor and other estates under his management. Between these two windows on the north wall of the aisle is a memorial tablet surmounted by the Windsor-Clive arms 'Quarterly 1st and 4th quarters 'Argent on a fesse sable three mullets or (Clive)', 2nd and 3rd quarters 'Gules a saltire argent between twelve cross crosslets or (Windsor)'. It was erected to the memory of Robert George Windsor-Clive (d. 1923) 1st Earl of Plymouth, Lord Lieutenant of the County of Glamorgan, 1890-1923, by 'the tenantry of the Glamorgan estate, the villagers of St. Fagans and other friends in affection and gratitude'.

The west end of the north aisle is lit by two rather lofty trefoils lancets which were erected by Lady Mary Windsor Clive in 1878. The lights depict the Annunciation of the Blessed Virgin Mary and Elizabeth with the Virgin Mary (Visitation of Our Lady). The biblical text is taken from the Latin Vulgate.

In 1860 the church was thoroughly restored and considerably enlarged by the addition of a new north aisle containing five windows in the Decorated style at the cost of nearly £2,000 which was chiefly defrayed by the generosity of Baroness Windsor. Other work included the insertion of the Decorated-style windows of the chancel. A new screen was placed at the base of the tower to

St. Athan's church—Berkerolles tomb in south chapel ▶

divide it from the nave and three broken bells were recast by George Mears of London. A new lancet window, an exact copy of the one to the west of the porch, was inserted in the south wall of the nave. During the restoration some of the tombstones of the Gibbon family were found under the Castle pew. They were carefully buried beneath the tower floor for preservation, their position recorded on a leaf in one of the Parish Registers. When the whitewash was removed from the walls inside the church the Lord's Prayer was found written in black letters on the south side of the chancel arch and several Norman arches were discovered confirming that a church of much earlier date stood upon the same site. The work of restoration was carried out by Thomas Williams, contractor of Canton, Cardiff, under the supervision and according to plans drawn up by George Edmund Street, architect of London. The church was reopened for divine service after restoration on Tuesday, 4th September, 1860 by the Rt. Reverend Dr. Alfred Ollivant, Bishop of Llandaff.

The churchyard is entered from the west through a lychgate given in 1885 in memory of his four-year old son by Robert Forrest, the agent for the Plymouth estate and rector's warden at St. Fagans church from 1874 until his death in 1910. It is interesting to note that from 1792 to 1897 there were only two rectors—the Reverend Dr. William Berkin Meackham Lisle, Prebendary of Llandaff, from 1792 to 1857 and the Reverend William David from 1857 to 1897.

The church plate consists of a silver bell-shaped chalice hall-marked 1722 by Gabriel Sleath of London, a silver flagon, two silver patens and a metal alms-dish. The registers date from 1689 with a gap from 1692 to 1729.

◀ *St. Donat's church*—interior

St. George-super-Ely Church

The parish church of St. George-super-Ely is dedicated to St. George and is built in the form of a Greek or St. George's cross. It is one of the smallest cruciform churches in the diocese if not in Wales and is in the Decorated style of architecture of the 14th century. The original church was built here in pre-Norman times. The church was worth 6 marks in 1254 (Taxation of Norwich), £10 in 1291 (*Taxatio Ecclesiastica*) and £7-13s-0d in 1535 (*Valor Ecclesiasticus*) when it was classified with the Rectories. The parson in 1563 held Bedwas where he resided but kept a curate at St. George's. The Earl of Pembroke was the patron of the living in the 17th century. In 1771 (Bishop Barrington's *Llandaff Diocesan Book*) the living was included with the Rectories of Michaelston-super-Ely and St. Bride's-super-Ely in the same valuation, namely £130; the incumbent was the Reverend William Llewellin and the patron was John Llewellin, Gent. In 1835 the Rectory was worth gross £143 and Llewellyn Traherne was the patron. According to the diocesan report in 1809 the yearly value of the benefice arising from tithes and glebe was £105-17s-0d. In 1950 St. George's was joined with St. Bride's-super-Ely and Michaelston-super-Ely to form one benefice. Three years before that St. George's was served by the staff and students of St. Michael's Theological College at Llandaff. St. George's was grouped with St. Nicholas and Bonvilston in 1970.

The church consists of chancel, nave, central tower containing two bells, transepts and south porch. The east window, which is a 19th-century insertion, consists of three large lancets, the two side ones trefoils, the centre one which is somewhat higher is not foiled but pointed. They are surmounted by three quatrefoils which give the effect of Geometrical plate tracery. The centre light depicts the armorial bearings of Bishop Edward Copleston with the arms of Llandaff 'Sable two croziers in saltire one or, the other argent, three mitres with labels of the second' impaling the arms of Copleston 'Or, chevron engrailed gules between three leopards' faces azure'. In the three quatrefoils above are the arms of the Llewellyn family (who claim descent from Iestyn ap Gwrgant) 'Gules three chevrons argent'; the arms of Llewellin Traherne 'Argent a chevron sable between three choughs proper on a canton barry of six of the first and azure a lion rampant gules' impaling Sinclair 'Gules a lion rampant or' and the arms of Dive of Stafford 'Gules a fesse dancetée between three escallops ermine'.

A painting on the front of the altar is a representation of the patron saint of the church, St. George, slaying the dragon. The altar consists of a massive block of stone so heavy that six strong men were required to carry it into the church. The oak reredos has castellated cresting and moulded cornice which includes typical Tudor-style square flower ornament continued as a surround to the central panel which is unusually plain. The side panels are treated as three-light cinquefoiled square-headed windows with semicircular arcs above enclosing a quatrefoil with central flower and mouchette shapes.

In the north wall of the chancel are two large arched recesses which formerly held the effigies of the founder of the church and his wife and which were removed at the end of the 19th century. The arch at the extreme east of the church has scroll-moulding and the finial to the labels are men's heads in tightly-fitting skull caps which show the faces but cover the rest of the heads. The other recess springs from the ground and is higher than its partner. The whole of the arch is formed into a cinquefoil, each of the five foils being in turn a trefoil. Corner buttresses reinforce the east and west walls of the church and the north wall of the chancel is strengthened by a two-stage buttress. The chancel is lit on the south side by a two-light trefoil-headed window labelled and a single trefoil lancet. Between these two windows is a priest's door with pointed arch but it is blocked internally. Cut out of the sill of the window in the south-east corner of the chancel is a floriated drain piscina. Under the piscina is a brass plaque erected to the memory of a former rector of the parish which reads:— 'Pray for the soul of my dear husband W. Howard Leeds sometime rector of this parish. Born 1853 died 1893. Loving and beloved. His life is hid with Christ in God.' The chancel has a simple arch-braced roof with the space between the common rafters and the purlins plastered. The roof is supported by a single corbel on each side of the chancel which is shaped like an octagonal capital half-embedded in the wall. The corbel is in the 14th-century style and is arranged in a number of decreasing stages towards the little curved step which returns it into the wall. The wallplate is castellated. Some beautifully-carved old seats in the chancel are said to have been brought from Margam Abbey in the 1840s when the rector was the Reverend J. M. Traherne, the brother-in-law of C. R. M. Talbot of Margam Park.

The central tower which rises on four very plain pointed arches opening to the chancel, nave and transepts, exhibits a quadripartite vaulted roof. At the intersection where the tower rises there are four very ancient coats of arms which were the armorial bearings of the early lords of the manor, Le Fleming, Malefant, Jasper Tudor and William Herbert, Earl of Pembroke. The central boss of the crossing, which is ornately embellished, bears a shield displaying the arms of Iestyn ap Gwrgant. The tower has a four-gabled saddleback roof and is built in the Rhenish-Romanesque style used in these four-gabled forms of tower. The upper stage of the tower has an eccentrically-shaped blind parapet in the appearance of a gable on each face, the apex in each case surmounted by a foliated finial. The gilded copper weathervane depicts St. George and the dragon. On the south face the opening into the belfry stage is of two cinque-foiled lights above louvres surmounted by a hood mould. There are slit-loopholes on the south and north faces of the tower and the belfry stage has trefoil-headed lights on its north and east faces. The belfry is approached on the north side by an external stair turret. The tower houses two bells, one small bell with the inscription $^{J\ \&\ P}_{\quad B}$ which stands for Jefferies and Price, bellfounders of Bristol who cast bells between 1839 and 1854. The other much larger bell bears the inscription:— 'Exchanged by Edwd. Bird, Ironmonger, Cardiff 1st Jan. 1819'.

The transepts are exceedingly small, the south one is lit by two well-splayed lancet windows, the eastern one single, the southern one double with square label. This is filled with stained glass depicting the figures of St. Teilo and St. Margaret of Scotland. The window is a memorial to Commander Llewellyn Edmund Traherne (d. 1914) and Dorothy Emma Olivia Traherne (née Sinclair) (d. 1957). Beneath the figure of St. Teilo is emblazoned the coat of arms of the Traherne family 'Argent a chevron sable between three choughs proper, on a canton barry of six, of the first and azure a lion rampant gules' together with the family crest 'A goat's head erased surmounting a wreath' and motto 'Ofna Dduw a'r Brenhin' (Fear God and the King). Beneath the figure of St. Margaret of Scotland is blazoned the coat of arms of the Sinclair family of Ulbster, Caithnessshire 'Quarterly, 1st quarter Azure, a ship at anchor, her oars erected in saltire, within the royal tressure or', 2nd and 3rd quarters 'Or a lion rampant gules', 4th quarter 'Azure, a ship under sail or; over all dividing the quarters, a cross engrailed quarterly argent and sable, all within a bordure quartered or and gules the last charged with three stars of the first'. The window was designed by Hubert Thomas of Celtic Studios, Swansea. The north transept is lit on the north side by three linked trefoil lancets of equal height with label.

The three-light window in the south wall of the nave is a 19th-century insertion and has trefoils under ogee-shaped heads labelled. The nave has a cradle roof formed by a series of closely-set rafters and arch braces with carved bosses at the intersections of the purlins and braces. The only evidence of a former rood-loft is the doorway in the north wall of the nave which is now built in. The pulpit has a plain top, centre and bottom rail. The sides have panels of applied tracery. Between the sides are representations of buttresses, the bases of which develop out of the bottom rail with the centre rail suggesting a set-off. The carving above suggests a trefoil-headed niche with a finial above. The west window of the nave consists of two trefoil lancets and below is a 14th-century west doorway which is now built in internally. The west wall of the nave is reinforced by two corner buttresses similar to those at the east end of the church.

The font which stands near the south doorway is octagonal and appears to be of 15th-century date. The rim of the bowl has a double moulding and each panel includes a quatrefoil in a circle with a flat fillet at the top and base of the bowl proper. The bowl is chamfered out on the underside onto an octagonal stem which is splayed at the bottom to meet the plinth. On the north wall of the nave are two marble memorials to those fourteen men of the parish who lost their lives in two world wars. Alongside these is a mural monument to 'Mary,

Relict of John Llewellin, Esquire of Coedriglan and daughter of Llewellin Traherne' (d. 1812). This monument was erected by her great-nephew John Montgomery Traherne in 1838 when he rebuilt the tower and north transept and restored the whole fabric of the church. Also on the north wall of the nave and immediately facing the south door is a brass tablet erected by parishioners to the memory of the Reverend Robert Evan Rowlands, M.A., rector of the parish from 1894 to 1928.

The outer doorway of the large south porch has a typical depressed arch of the 14th century with a plainly moulded label and rectangular stops. Above it is the inscription 'Lord, I have loved the habitation of thy house and the place where thine honour dwelleth'. The inner south doorway has a plain pointed arch and there are stone seats in the porch. The church was restored in 1838 when the tower and north transept were rebuilt, the roof of the chancel renewed, the old pews of the church replaced and the whole of the fabric repaired. The cost of the restoration was defrayed by the Reverend J. M. Traherne. The church was again restored in 1857 and 1886 when a massive stone altar slab was placed in the chancel. The cross in the churchyard is square at the base but is chamfered at the top to an octagon. The cross and shaft are modern but the base consisting of three Calvary steps is old. Once there was a charnel or bone-house in the churchyard where any bones that were unearthed in the process of digging new graves were reverently placed.

One rector, the Reverend Henry Llewellyn, was rector of the parish for nearly fifty years from 1789 to 1837. He was also rector of St. Bride's-super-Ely and Michaelston-super-Ely. His mother was Elizabeth Turberville of Hendre-sgythan. At one time services were regularly conducted in the Welsh language. In November, 1746 Leyson Morgan was licensed to the curacy of Pentyrch and to serve the livings of St. George's, St. Bride's and Michaelston-super-Ely in the Welsh tongue.

The church plate comprises an Elizabethan silver chalice with a belt of intersecting foliated strap ornament round the bowl and foliated band round the cover, on the handle of which is inscribed '1576'. Also a paten standing on a foot hall-marked 1710 inscribed 'The gift of Theodorett Bassett' (one time rector of the parish). The register of baptisms dates from 1693, marriages from 1697 and burials from 1695.

St. Hilary's Church

The parish church of St. Hilary is dedicated to St. Hilary (St. Hilarius, Bishop of Poitiers in the 4th century) and was built in the latter part of the 12th century. The church was valued at £5 in 1254 (Taxation of Norwich) and at the same value when it was recorded as belonging to the Chapter of Llandaff in 1291 (*Taxatio Ecclesiastica*). In 1535 (*Valor Ecclesiasticus*) it was classified among the vicarages and was worth £5-14s-3d of which £2 came from the Chapter as an augmentation. The rectorial tithes brought £5-6s-8d to the Cathedral funds. In 1603 it was styled a 'curacy', the impropriation was worth £10 then and held from the Chapter of Llandaff by Mrs. Basset, widow and John Mathew, Gent. In 1771 (Bishop Barrington's Primary Visitation of the Diocese) the living was worth £20 and the incumbent was the Reverend John Walters. It was styled a vicarage worth gross £67 in 1835 and the Chapter of Llandaff was patron and impropriator. In 1962 the living of St. Hilary's was attached to the Rectory of Flemingston with Gileston, but in 1978 St. Hilary became a suspended benefice. The priest-in-charge of St. Hilary's church is the rector of Llanblethian with Cowbridge and Llandough-by-Cowbridge with St. Mary Church, the Reverend Gwilym E. Williams.

The church consists of chancel, nave with south aisle, western tower and south porch. The chancel arch is Transitional Norman obtusely pointed with square-stepped arch mouldings and simple abacus. The east window is a 19th-century approximation of flowing Decorated architecture and the Geometrical tracery in the head has a hint of reticulated tracery in the quatrefoils. It is a window of five trefoil-headed lights in a 2:1:2 arrangement; the two principal centre mullions are arched and carried through the head to admit typical tracery within a circle. The hood mould has foliated stops. The window was designed by Sir George Gilbert Scott during the restoration of the church in 1862. The beautiful stained glass in the window was presented to the church in 1873 by George Montgomery Traherne as a memorial to his sister, Frances Elizabeth Traherne (d.1872). The window depicts scenes from the Passion, Crucifixion, Resurrection and Ascension of Our Lord according to designs prepared by Messrs. Clayton & Bell of London under the supervision of Sir George Gilbert Scott.

The beautiful reredos beneath the east window is very ornate with its side panels and done of a piece of various polished marbles inlaid with minor decorative motifs. The centre panel is a representation of the Last Supper after

Leonardo da Vinci. It depicts the varied emotions and expressions of the twelve Apostles just after Jesus has told them that one of them will betray Him. The central panel has a castellated cresting and cornice of plain mouldings, fruit and leaf trails and is framed with unconnected floral motifs carved in the angles. These are formed by the central area being offset against the side panels with little marble pillars carrying stiff-leaf forms on the caps and plain moulded abaci in 13th-century style. The side panels are each a double arrangement with similar shafts and caps supporting square-headed arches and leaf trails in the mouldings above. There is feathering between the bases of the shafts and the background to each panel is diagonal diaper work and square diaper below. The reredos was erected by Mary Ellen Penrose in memory of her husband Samuel Devonsher Penrose (d. 1872).

In the north wall of the chancel is a small lancet window with rounded head inside running externally into a slight ogee-head. The chancel is lit on the south side by a single square-headed plain lancet and a square-headed, three-light cinquefoil window under ogee arches above which is a horizontal row of medieval consecration crosses. Between these two windows is a flat-headed priest's door.

Only five steps remain in the thickness of the north wall of the nave which once led to the rood-loft. There are two windows, one above the other, which were once connected with the rood-loft, one square and set quite low, the upper one of two lights with trefoiled heads under a square head with label which once illuminated the rood-loft. In the south-east corner of the nave on the east wall is a memorial to Daniel Jones of Beaupré (d. 1841), Deputy Lieutenant of the County of Glamorgan and founder of Cardiff Infirmary. The tablet shows his head encircled by a serpent devouring its own tail (the uroboros) which is an ancient symbol of eternity and also symbolic of the Greek God of medicine, Aesculapius. It was carved by the sculptor, John Evan Thomas of London (1810-1873).

The pulpit is a modern wooden structure, its panel full of Early English forms and treated as a two-light trefoil-headed window with a quatrefoil above and various leaves and fruit in the spandrels. The splendid, oak reading desk is double-sided with each side pierced with three trefoil-headed openings above square panels. It has a plain moulded cornice and upper rail with projecting stiles almost as buttresses but overpowering and entirely for decoration continued above into curved finials with roundels. The stiles have slender engaged columns with little bell caps and bases. Under the most easterly arch of the arcade of the south aisle is a tomb-chest upon which lies the recumbent effigy of Thomas Basset (d. 1423) in an attitude of prayer. The head, which rests on a square cushion placed diagonally on another square cushion with tassels, is covered by a bascinet of ovoid shape. He is dressed in a complete suit of plate armour, wearing a jupon or tightly-fitting surcoat upon which the Basset arms are emblazoned 'Argent, a chevron, between three hunting horns stringed sable'. Round the waist is a handsome swordbelt. The thighs are covered with cuisses and the legs with greaves or jambs; the knees are protected by genouil-

East window with reredos below

lères with ornamental circular plates on the outside and the feet, which rest on a lion couchant, are covered with pointed sollerets of overlapping plate. The arms have been broken off above the elbows and the face has been mutilated. The effigy, which formerly stood in the sanctuary, was probably defaced by Cromwell's soldiers after the defeat of the Royalists (who included the descendants of the Bassets) at the Battle of St. Fagans in 1648. The inscription which is incised in black letters along one side and round the end reads thus:- 'HIC IACET THOMAS BASSET QUI OBIIT XIII^mo DIE ME'SIS DEC'BRIS A°D° NI M° iiii° xxiii° CU' A'IE PRO (PICI) ETUR DEUS AMEN'. (Here lies Thomas Basset who died 13th December, 1423. May God have mercy on his soul. Amen.)

Under a sepulchral recess in the north wall of the nave within a segmental arch with ornate mouldings rests the recumbent effigy of a layman. It is of a young man, dressed in a long tunic with close-fitting sleeves and traces of wrist bands; perfectly plain without a girdle or any ornament and fitting close to the neck and chest. The head rests on a plain square cushion. The hair is worn long and curls inwards over the ears descending over the neck behind them and is tied round the forehead by a fillet or garland. The right arm rests upon the hip, and holds a pair of long gloves or gauntlets, the left hand resting upon the breast. On the feet are 'hautes de chausses' covering ankles. The lower portion of the stone has been broken off but the right foot remains and shows the curious round-toed and slightly peaked shoe which was worn in the early part of the 13th century. The figure is thought to represent the son of one of the lords of St. Hilary, of the De Cardiff family in the 13th century, who died in his youth.

The north wall of the nave is covered with numerous memorial monuments. Among them is a marble tablet to Llewellyn Traherne, Esq. J.P. (d. 1841), the father of the Reverend John Montgomery Traherne of Coedriglan (d. 1860), who is also commemorated by a brass plaque as is the latter's nephew, George Montgomery Traherne (d. 1896). A fine marble monument with bust portrait inside a laurel wreath carved in relief depicts Major William West James Basset of Beaupré (d. 1871), son of Isabella Basset and Lieutenant-Colonel William Bruce. He assumed the name and arms of Basset by Royal Licence in 1865. The monument is surmounted by the armorial achievement of the Basset family with the crest 'A stag's head cabossed between the attires a cross formée fitchée argent', and the Basset motto 'Gwell angau na chwilydd' (Better death than dishonour). The arms are quarterly of eight: 1st and 8th quarters—'Argent a chevron between three hunting horns stringed sable' (Basset), 2nd quarter—'Azure a bend cotised or between six martlets of the second' (De la Bere), 3rd quarter—'Chequy or and gules a fess ermine' (Turberville), 4th quarter—'Gules three chevrons argent' (Bowen), 5th quarter—'Argent a chevron sable between three crows close proper' (Ap Rhys or Rice), 6th quarter—'Sable a lion rampant argent' (Dowell), 7th quarter—'Argent a fess embattled between three battle-axes sable' (Bainbridge). Other memorials are to Captain George Gilbert Traherne, Lieutenant Hugh Thomas Ackland-Allen and Sergeant

George Rees who fell in the Great War, 1914-1918. In the north wall of the nave is a three-light trefoil-headed window with sharply-cusped reticulated-style tracery in the shape of two quatrefoils above under a square-head. Around the window is a concave moulding decorated with ballflower ornamentation and the label stops are foliated or animal heads. The window depicts angels worshipping Christ carrying the Cross of Calvary and was erected in memory of the Reverend George Traherne, M.A., rector of St. George's and vicar of St. Hilary's (d. 1853). The Norman font, which is placed opposite the south door near the north wall of the nave, is of Sutton stone. It has a cylindrical bowl with bulging sides with a bold roll-moulding round its rim and stands on a small stone plinth. The roof of the nave has a king-post arrangement with cambered tie-beams and curved braces.

The slender arcade of the nave to the south aisle (which was built in the 14th century and was once known as the Edmondes aisle) has four pointed arches with concave mouldings in the Decorated style which continue uninterrupted from floor to apex without capitals. The windows of the south aisle are mostly 19th-century insertions in the Decorated style except for the east window which is Perpendicular in style, of four cinquefoiled lights with typical Perpendicular panel tracery lights above with pointed quatrefoils in the head. The panel tracery contains stained glass bearing the text of the *Agnus Dei*. The south-east window is a three-light, cinquefoil arrangement with sharply-cusped reticulated-style tracery above. The window is square-headed with a row of fourteen medieval consecration crosses cut horizontally above. The window depicts the appearance of the risen Lord to Mary Magdalene, the Ascension and Christ in Majesty and was erected by Isabella Bruce in memory of her brother Richard Basset, her son, William West James Basset and her sister, Georgiana Anne Mansell Basset of Beaupré. The south-west window is plain of three lights with trefoil heads and sharply-cusped reticulated-style tracery above with hood mould. The west window of the south aisle was designed by Sir George Gilbert Scott in 1862 and is square-headed of three cinquefoiled lights under ogee arches with sharply-cusped cinquefoils above, surmounted by a row of medieval consecration crosses. The three lights portray the figures of St. Hilary, St. Anne and St. John. Below is a memorial tablet to Charlotte Traherne (d. 1796) and her sister, Anna Maria Edmondes (d. 1797). Adjacent to the window is a fine brass memorial plaque to Charlotte, first wife of John Edmondes (d. 1770). On the right of the south doorway on entering the church is a crude hexagonal holy-water stoup in a recess. The roof of the south aisle has a king-post arrangement similar to that of the nave.

The south porch dates from the restoration of the church in 1862 and was designed by Sir George Gilbert Scott. Over the south doorway, which has an obtuse arch with continuous moulding, is a semi-octagonal bracket for an image enriched with flowers and bearing the Basset arms. The porch has conspicuous single-stage buttresses on the south side which are purely decorative. Above the pointed outer doorway is an inset IHS monogram and on the interior and exterior of the jambs is a touch of abbreviated zig-zag or chevron decoration. The hood mould of the porch has foliated stops. The little round-headed windows with their circular holes as peepholes each side of the porch are reminiscent of the outside squints which were sometimes built in porches of medieval churches so that the priest could keep an eye out for the approach of the burial party.

The tower opens to the nave by a continuous moulded pointed arch and a door with rounded arch in the south-east corner of the nave leads to the belfry. The oak tower screen at the west end of the nave has a cornice of castellated cresting and a row of Tudor-style ornament as patera and running trail which includes Tudor roses. The double bays of the screen separated by slender two-stage buttresses with double set-offs each have two square-headed panels, cinquefoils below and typical Perpendicular-style tracery lights above. The tower screen was erected by parishioners and friends from a design by William Clarke of Llandaff in 1913 in memory of the Reverend Henry Charles Davies, M.A., rector of St. Hilary's (1892-1911).

The square tower has an embattled parapet with four gargoyles at each corner below which is a corbel table. The tower, which has two stringcourses, is strengthened by four stages of angle buttresses. The west doorway has a pointed arch above which is a Perpendicular window of three lights with cinquefoiled heads and square label. The window depicts Christ as the Good Shepherd and was erected to the memory of Louisa Traherne (d. 1870). The belfry windows are square-headed and labelled. The tower contains a ring of five bells of which four were originally cast in 1734 by Abraham Rudhall of Gloucester. In 1906 a new bell was added and two of the original four bells were recast by Taylors of Loughborough. At this time the bells were refitted and rehung in a strong steel frame. The bells bear the following inscriptions:-

Treble   WE WERE ALL CAST AT GLOCESTER BY A. RUDHALL. 1734.

No.2.   PEACE AND GOOD NEIGHBOURHOOD A ♣ R.1734. RECAST 1906 BY TAYLOR, LOUGHBOROUGH.

No.3.   PROSPERITY TO THIS PARISH A ♣ R. 1734. RECAST 1906 BY TAYLOR, LOUGHBOROUGH.

No.4.   HENRY CHARLES DAVIES, RECTOR, THOMAS MANSEL FRANKLEN, CHURCHWARDEN. 1906.

Tenor   THOMAS BASSET & LEWIS THOMAS, CHURCHWARDENS. 1734.

The church was restored in 1862 under the supervision of Sir George Gilbert Scott, the famous Victorian church architect, whose best work in Wales can be seen in St. David's Cathedral. As in all the restorations in which he was engaged, he showed a reverential regard for the preservation of all the ancient features of the building. The restoration of the church was entirely due to Mrs. Charlotte Louisa Traherne of Coedriglan who carried out the last wishes of her husband, the Reverend John Montgomery Traherne as a memorial to him. The work consisted of renewing the fenestration of the main body of the church which included the new east window and the south-east window of the chancel, a new window in the north of the nave and new windows in the east, west and south-east of the south aisle. All the old walls were retained but securely underpinned and drained. The arcade between the south aisle and the nave which was formerly very much out of the perpendicular was forced up into its place without dismantling. The whole of the walls were repointed outside including the tower, and all the dressed stonework inside had the whitewash removed from it by an application of an acid and was pointed. A new south porch was added. During the restoration the remains of the old rood-loft consisting of some steps of the stairs were discovered. These were preserved within the north wall of the nave. The roofs of the nave and the south aisle were renewed with ones consisting of tie-beams and king-posts and made of pitch pine with coats of varnish. The Basset tomb was moved at this time from the chancel to its present position between the nave and south aisle under the arcade. The contractors employed were Messrs. James and Price of Cardiff, who carried out the important work entrusted to them to the entire satisfaction of the architect and Mrs. Traherne. The church was reopened for divine service after restoration by the Bishop of Llandaff, the Rt. Reverend Alfred Ollivant on Friday 2nd May, 1862. The church was repaired in 1900 under the direction of the architect, William Weir, on behalf of the Society for the Protection of Ancient Buildings.

The lychgate, constructed of stone and teak, from a design by Edwin Seward, architect of Cardiff, was erected in 1900 on the east side of the churchyard as a memorial to George Montgomery Traherne of St. Hilary and Coedriglan (d.1896), by his widow, Mrs. Harriet Traherne. Affixed to the lychgate is a marble tablet recording the safe return of fifteen men from the parish who served in the Great War, 1914-1918.

At the east end of the churchyard stands the gravestone of Richard Basset which is enclosed by iron railings. The inscription reads:- 'Richard Basset, Esq., of Beaupré died Nov. 8, 1849 aged 51 years, last male heir of the ancient family of Basset of Beaupré. Also Frances Basset, his relict, who died at Nice 2 May, 1864, aged 64.' The armorial achievement of the family is displayed on the tomb with the family motto 'Gwell angau na chwilydd' (Better death than dishonour).

The base of the churchyard cross with its four high steps formerly stood in the village. It was removed from there to the churchyard and a new cross was erected on the old base. The parish of St. Hilary can boast the best record of long and faithful service among its clergy in the Vale of Glamorgan. In the 17th century the Reverend Rowland Williams was vicar there for 68 years and his successor the Reverend Joseph Merrick for 41 years. In the 19th century the Reverend Thomas Thomas held the living for 55 years and in 1962 the Reverend Lewis Crockett retired after an incumbency of 48 years. The communion plate consists of an Elizabethan chalice and cover dated 1577 and a silver paten dated 1818. The registers date from 1690.

St. Lythan's Church

The parish church of St. Lythan's is dedicated to St. Bleddian according to the Llandaff Diocesan handbook, but Professor Gwynedd Pierce has outlined a number of theories to explain its true dedication. Eliddon, the main element in the name of this parish, is the saint to whom the parish was originally dedicated. A charter copied into the *Book of Llandaff* records that the church of Elidon was granted to Bishop Euddogwy by King Ithel ap Athrwys in the last quarter of the 7th century. It is one of the few Glamorgan churches whose existence as a place of worship is therefore securely attested by a document drawn up well before the Norman Conquest of the area. The church is built in the Early English style of architecture and dates from the late 12th century. From a very early date the advowson of the church was vested in the Archdeacon of Llandaff and was held by successive Archdeacons until the Disestablishment of the Welsh Church in 1920.

In the Taxation of Norwich (1254) it is not mentioned among the parishes and had already doubtless been attached to the Archdeaconry as we find to be the case in the *Taxatio Ecclesiastica* of 1291, when its value was £5. Then it was referred to as 'Ecclesia de Sancto Lychano'. A vicarage was established by 1535 (*Valor Ecclesiasticus*) valued at £7-9s-10d but there was a large payment to the Bishop and Archdeacon of 28s-8d per annum of which the Archdeacon took 26s-8d as a pension. In 1603 it was styled a vicarage, 'The parsonage belongeth to the Archdeacon of Llandaff and is held with the vicarage by the grant of the Archdeacon'. The parsonage and vicarage together were then valued at 20 marks. In 1771 (Bishop Barrington's Primary Visitation of the Diocese) the living was worth £63. In 1835 it was valued at gross £200 and declared to be a vicarage endowed with the great tithes in the patronage of the Archdeacon. In 1925 St. Lythan's church was joined with the parish of Wenvoe.

The church consists of chancel with south chapel, nave, south porch and a western tower containing one bell. The chancel arch is fairly wide and plain pointed. The east window is a 19th-century insertion of three trefoiled lights with 14th-century-style reticulated tracery in the head surmounted by a dripstone with foliated label stops. The interior of the window has a simple round moulded arch with a fillet. It springs from engaged bell caps above shafts which run the length of the jambs, ending in little engaged moulded bases. The outer moulding of the arch is a single roll ending in a circular stop comprising three five-lobed leaves. The altar table has inlaid work of various coloured woods. The centre panel shows the chalice with the words 'Do this' and the flanking

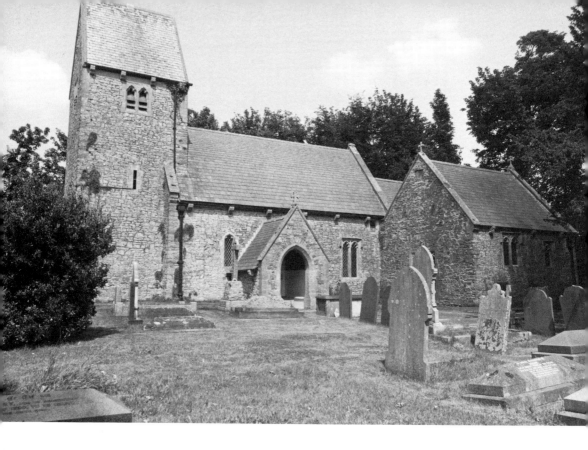

St. George's church—interior ▶

The unique chancel arcade

panels have representations of ears of corn and a vine with leaves and grapes symbolizing bread and wine, the elements of the Holy Eucharist. The side panels are carved with the sacred monogram IHS and the Trinity Star or Star of David. On the north side of the altar is a round-headed niche and on the opposite side a low bracket probably for a statue. The chancel has a modern wagon roof with carved bosses and around the wallplate are eight shields on which are engraved the symbols of the four Evangelists and the instruments of the Passion of Our Lord.

The Button Chapel, built in the Perpendicular style of architecture on the south side of the chancel, is quite out of proportion to the rest of the church. It is divided from the chancel by an arcade of two flat segmental arches springing from a massive central circular pier with similar enormous responds. C. B. Fowler, the noted architect, described it as 'one of the most crude arcades' he had come across in the diocese. He was of the opinion that at one time it was a solid wall cut through to form an entrance to the south chapel at a later period, and the piers were shaped so as to resemble 12th-century Norman workmanship. It is an architectural feature which is unique in the Vale of Glamorgan. The Button Chapel has an alternative means of entry by a large Tudor door leading from the exterior on its western side. Externally the head of the door, which has a four-centred arch, is surmounted by a winged cherub holding a defaced coat of arms, and the spandrels enclose two small shields bearing the letters R and B (Robert Button). The chapel was erected as the burial place of

◀ *St. Hilary's church* (chancel and east window)

members of the Button family of Dyffryn House, among them Sir Thomas Button, the gallant admiral. However, despite the fact that members of the Button family lie buried below the chapel, there are no monuments or inscriptions recording the fact. But there are memorials to members of the Sprosson family of London and the Fisher family of Warwickshire.

The chapel is lit on the south side by a single trefoil-headed window and a two-light trefoil-headed window, both labelled. The east window of the chapel is of three cinquefoiled lights with rectilinear tracery under a flat top and square label. The south chapel has a wagon roof formed by a series of closely-set arched braces with crenellated wallplate.

Above the chancel arch are two stone corbels which once supported the rood-loft. All other traces of a rood-loft were swept away during a Victorian restoration. Set into the south side of the chancel arch is a stone memorial to Cecily (d. 1738), aged 14 years, daughter of John Rees and his wife, Elizabeth. There were originally no windows on the north side of the nave but two windows were inserted in the 19th century. They comprise a trefoil-headed lancet and a two-light trefoil-headed window with 14th-century-style reticulated tracery in the head surmounted by a dripstone with foliated label stops. The latter is more or less identical to the style of the larger east window and they are probably coeval. The south side of the nave is lit by a window of two cinquefoiled lights and square label and a single trefoil lancet. High in the south wall of the nave is a small built-in window which formerly illuminated the rood-loft. The nave has a simple open arch-braced roof.

The pulpit is of oak with diagonal arched members as it were, corbelling out the plain moulded cornice from the stiles. The underside of the cornice is treated as panels with some elegantly carved stiff-leaf forms. Beneath the moulded top rail the panels are treated as blind window tracery, trefoil-headed with foliated lobes on the cusping beneath a pointed arch with trefoils in the spandrels. The handrail is affixed to the pulpit by means of a black wrought iron decorative bracket.

The walls of the nave display several elegant but diminutive memorial tablets of 18th- and 19th-century date. One of these on the north wall in black and white marble surmounted by a classical urn above a plain sarcophagus commemorates Robert Thomas, (d. 1794), Gent. of the parish, his wife, Ann (d. 1786) and their daughter Susanna Williams (d. 1844), widow of Henry Williams of the parish of St. Nicholas. Directly opposite the south doorway on the north wall of the nave is a marble memorial tablet to those twelve men of the parish who served their country in the Great War, 1914-1918. A brass plaque on the south wall was erected to the memory of Samuel Charles Hague (d. 1911), husband of Mary Elizabeth Hague, youngest daughter of Joseph Jones, rector of the parish. The Victorian oil drop-lamps remain, now skilfully converted to electricity. The Norman font is barrel-shaped and decorated with six rows of large chevron moulding in a continuous pattern. There is no base or stem and the font rests upon some modern stonework. Its size provides ample evidence for the practice of total immersion of the infant at the administration of Holy Baptism, which was not uncommon at the period when the font was constructed. Near the south doorway is an hexagonal holy-water stoup. The south porch is a Victorian structure; the inner doorway is plain pointed as is its outer doorway and on the east and west sides are the customary stone benches.

The tower opens to the nave by a plain pointed arch similar to the chancel arch. The archway is filled with a panelled oak partition with a trefoil-headed light, which still contains some medieval stained glass. The west tower has a saddleback roof and on the exterior of the south wall are two grotesquely-carved gargoyles with ape-faced heads. The belfry has a two-light ogee-foliated trefoiled window on each face, each of which is a 19th-century insertion. There are slit-loopholes on each face. St. Lythan's is one of the few Vale churches which possesses no west door in the tower and there is no trace of one ever having been provided. In the north-east corner of the tower is the remains of an oven which was used to bake wafers for Holy Communion and to heat the charcoal for the incense burner. High on the north wall of the tower below the eaves is a circular orifice with a small canopy or pent roof which was originally the outlet for the flue of the oven referred to above. A similar oven once existed at St. Mary's church, Caerau, now closed. The tower houses a single bell completely devoid of any inscription or bellfounder's marks and was probably cast in the churchyard by an itinerant bellfounder.

Although the small living of St. Lythan's suffered from persistent pluralism, three former vicars, Reverend Thomas Maddocks (d. 1665), Reverend Walter Evans (1865-1874) and Reverend Joseph Jones (1886-1914) are, however, buried here, the grave of Prebendary Maddocks being in the chancel.

In an article in the *Archaeologia Cambrensis* for 1862 George T. Clark and Robert Oliver Jones stated that the church was 'recently repaired in excellent taste by a happy combination between the squire and the vicar'. The squire referred to was John Bruce Pryce, Esq. of Dyffryn (1784-1872) and the incumbent was the Reverend William Bruce, vicar of the parish from 1848 to 1863. Although there is no firm documentary evidence it is fairly certain that the restoration of the church was carried out according to plans and specifications drawn up by Messrs Prichard and Seddon, the diocesan architects in or about the year 1861. The work of restoration consisted of the insertion of a new east window and new windows in the north wall of the nave. New ogee-foliated trefoil-headed belfry lights replaced the former narrow apertures in the tower. The chancel arch which Sir Stephen Glynne described in 1849 when he visited the church as 'very small and rude pointed', was enlarged and a new south porch with wagon roof was constructed. New roofs were raised in the nave and south chapel and the boarding and ribs of the chancel roof were renewed. A new carved altar table and pulpit displaying similar inlaid work were installed in the church.

The church plate consists of an unusually large Elizabethan silver chalice and cover with a belt of intersecting foliated strap ornament round the bowl. On the handle of the cover is inscribed 'Saincte Lethyans 1577'. The registers date from 1748.

St. Mary Church

The parish church of St. Mary Church is dedicated to the Annunciation of the Blessed Virgin Mary. The church dates almost entirely from 1862 when the original 13th-century church underwent a drastic Victorian restoration. Apart from the medieval tower the church as it stands today is an example of First Pointed Victorian Gothic ecclesiastical architecture. The restoration was carried out under the superintendence of Messrs. Prichard and Seddon, diocesan architects and the church was reopened after restoration on the 29th May, 1862, the feast of the Ascension. The patron of the living at that time, C. R. M. Talbot of Margam Abbey, contributed £300 towards the cost of the restoration.

The church was known in early records as 'St. Mary's on the Mountain' to distinguish it from St. Mary Hill then referred to as 'St. Mary's-by-Gelligarn'. In 1254 (Taxation of Norwich) it was worth 4 marks, in 1291 (*Taxatio Ecclesiastica*) £5, and in 1535 (*Valor Ecclesiasticus*) it was valued at £6. In 1427 the advowson of St. Mary Church and Llandough passed by marriage to the De Ann or Van family and later to the Earl of Pembroke, the Carnes and Bassetts and finally to the Mansels and Talbots in the 19th century. In 1563 the parson was resident. In 1771 (Bishop Barrington's *Llandaff Diocesan Book*) the living was worth £50; the incumbent was the Reverend John Williams and the patron was Mansel Talbot. In 1797 during the incumbency of the Reverend John Walters, the parishes of Llandough and St. Mary Church were united to form one benefice by episcopal decree. In 1835 the Rectory of St. Mary Church was included in the same valuation as Llandough which was valued at gross £263. In 1966 the benefice of St. Mary Church with Llandough was grouped with Llanblethian and Cowbridge.

The church consists of chancel, nave, south porch and western embattled tower containing four bells. The chancel is not in direct line with the nave but is inclined to the south. The so-called 'weeping chancel' is attributed to the fact that the church was built like this to remind worshippers that when Jesus Christ was crucified on the Cross of Calvary His head drooped to one side. The chancel arch is pointed springing from the side walls. Above the chancel arch painted on brass plates which follow the contour of the arch is part of a verse from the *Benedicite omnia opera*:— 'O ye servants of the Lord, bless ye the Lord, praise him and magnify him forever.' The east window is of three widely-spaced trefoil-headed lights deeply recessed and separated internally by three continuous pointed arches which spring from square abaci above slender capitals decorated with stiff-leaf foliage and shafts on square bases. The outer moulding ends in floriated stops above square abaci in the surface of the east wall. The three broad lancets are surmounted externally by hood mouldings terminating in foliated stops. The stained glass in the centre light depicts the presentation of Jesus in the Temple with the old priest Simeon uttering the words of the Song of Solomon, known to us today as the *Nunc Dimittis*. Beneath is the Agnus Dei with the banner of victory. The left-hand light depicts a scene from the Nativity showing Mary and Joseph with the baby Jesus wrapped in swaddling clothes and in a panel below is a gold chalice. The right-hand light depicts the flight into Egypt of the Holy family and in the panel below is an open book with the Latin text 'Verbum Dei manet in eternum' (The word of God endures forever). A brass plaque on the north wall of the chancel informs us that the super altar was given by parishioners of St. Mary Church and Llandough to the Glory of God and to the memory of Sir Sidney Hutchinson Byass (d. 1829) of Llandough Castle.

In the north wall of the chancel is a modern trefoil-headed aumbry decorated with stiff-leaf foliage, the inner arches of which die into the jambs. The moulded base shelf has a band of dogtooth work and an amount of stiff-leaf foliage where it inclines into the wall below. The text 'Do this in remembrance of me' is in keeping with its intended use as a recess for the safe-keeping of the eucharistic vessels.

The chancel is lit on the south side by two deeply-recessed trefoil-headed windows separated internally by a single slender shaft with a capital of rounds and hollows and a vertical fillet. The two moulded arches which spring from above the shaft end in decorative stops of bunched stiff-leaf foliage whilst internally they are returned into the outer walls of the window splay. The stained glass in these windows depicts the Annunciation of the Blessed Virgin Mary with the Archangel Gabriel in one light and the Virgin Mary in the other. In the south-east corner of the sanctuary is an ancient piscina on a twisted and fluted pillar. The chancel has an arch-braced roof with a continuous internal curve and curved windbraces between the purlins. The part of the roof over the east end of the chancel is boarded.

A low stone screen with a horizontal band of continuous three-lobed leaf decoration divides the chancel from the nave. The windows of the nave comprise a single lancet deeply splayed on the north side and on the south side a three-light trefoil-headed window in the south-west corner of the nave. The stained glass in the south-east window depicts the figures of St. Francesca and St. Stephen. The centre light which consists of two panels, depicts Jesus uttering the comforting words and below blessing little children. The figures of St. Stephen and St. Francesca represent the Reverend Stephen H. F. Nicholl, rector of St. Mary Church and Llandough (1867-1898), and his wife, Sarah Frances Nicholl, since the window is referred to in church records as the Nicholl memorial window. The south-west window depicts Jesus as the Good Shepherd with Simon Peter receiving the post-Resurrection commission 'Feed my sheep'. All three stained glass windows on the south side of the church were erected 'To the glory of God, Easter, 1905' probably by members of the Talbot family. The one-manual organ, built by the 'Positive' Organ Co. Ltd., London about 1912, is located on the south side of the nave.

In the north wall of the nave a doorway with four-centred arch leads to the rood-loft staircase which is built within a projection of the north wall. The stone pulpit is an odd Victorian monstrosity. It is clearly something created for its decorative value and therefore defies any 'architectural' description. The decoration with its multi-coloured banding and general appearance from the heavy buttress to the part demi-column, decorated with a line of stiff-leaf foliage below, are all testimony to the architect's eccentricity. The rim is at once the upper moulding of the pulpit proper and again a little capital for the half shaft. The leaves which boldly tumble about the upper frieze are matched by those in the stem below where the drum of the pulpit is returned into the wall. The front panel is topped with a band of open four-leafed decoration. The nave has an arch-braced roof similar to the chancel with curved windbraces between the purlins.

The Norman font has a plain cylindrical bowl and is barrel-shaped. It has a lower plain circular roll-moulding and is set on an ugly overpowering base, circular at the junction with the bowl, then angled out at the corners to meet the heavy square step and plinth.

Above the south porch a trefoiled niche contains the sculptured figures of the kneeling Archangel Gabriel and the Virgin Mary, a representation of the Annunciation illustrating the dedication of the church. The porch has a pointed outer arch and a similar inner arch which is surmounted by a corbel which once supported a niche for a statuette. On the right of the south doorway is a holy-water stoup.

The tower opens to the nave by an obtuse arch with continuous jambs devoid of impost or any other feature to mark the points from which the arch springs. An inner arch, rising directly from the jambs in its head, is a trefoil shape. The tower is lofty and plain with a battlement and below the parapet is a small corbel table. A projection on the south side of the tower houses the belfry staircase which is lit by two square-headed lights. The louvred belfry windows on each face are square-headed and divided by a mullion. Below on the south face are two other square-headed openings. The west doorway has an obtuse arch and above it is a three-light square-headed window deeply splayed internally. At a height of one metre is a heavily-moulded stringcourse. The tower houses a ring of four bells. The first bell bears the inscription 'AVE MARIA GRACIA dLENA' tg (Hail Mary full of grace—a reference to the Annunciation) and was cast by Thomas Gefferies from the Bristol Medieval foundry. The second bell comes from the same foundry and was also cast by Thomas Gefferies ('tg' being his mark) and bears the inscription 'Sancta Maria tg'. The third bell has the inscription:— 'BLESSED BEE GOD' R.D. T.L. WAR 16 and around the rim is a further inscription:— IT IS NOT MY SOUND THAT SOVLE CAN SAVE TO PLEASE THE EARE IS ALL I CRAVE THO:STONE BELL. This bell was cast by Thomas Stone, an itinerant bellfounder who cast many bells in South Wales during the years 1627-1655. R.D. and T.L. are almost certainly the initials of the churchwardens. The fourth bell was recast in 1885 by Llewellins & James of Bristol and bears the inscription 'STEPHEN H.F. NICHOLL, RECTOR. LLEWELLINS & JAMES, BRISTOL 1885'. All the four bells were rehung in 1885. In the churchyard the steps to the cross still remain.

During the 17th century Thomas Wilkyn (d. 1623), his son, Roger Wilkins (d. 1648), and his grandson Thomas Wilkins (1626-1699) were successively rectors of St. Mary Church. The last named Thomas Wilkins went to Jesus College, Oxford, in 1641 and took a degree in law. In addition to St. Mary Church, he also held the rectories of Gelligaer (1666) and Llanmaes (1688) and was a Prebendary of Llandaff. Wilkins was a very important figure in the history of Welsh literature as he was one of the finest antiquarians and collectors of manuscripts in 17th-century Wales. Some of the most important medieval Welsh manuscripts found their way into his possession, notably the *Red Book of Hergest* which was generally acknowledged to be the richest single manuscript compilation of medieval Welsh literature and which his eldest son presented to Jesus College, Oxford, in 1701.

On the 18th July 1781 an entry in the marriage registers of the parish of St. Mary Church records the marriage of Iolo Morganwg (Edward Williams (1747-1826)) to his bride, Margaret 'Peggy' Roberts. During the 19th century three members of the Nicholl family of Merthyr Mawr were rectors of St. Mary Church and Llandough. They were Edward Powell Nicholl (1858-1864), his brother Stephen Henry Fox Nicholl (1867-1898) and the latter's son, Henry Stephen Nicholl (1899-1917).

The church plate consists of a silver chalice, a silver flagon and paten which were given as a sign of appreciation and affection by parishioners and pupils in memory of Albert Bown, churchwarden (1885-1940), and schoolmaster (1883-1922). The registers date from 1584.

St. Mary Hill Church

The parish church of St. Mary Hill is dedicated to St. Mary and was built in the latter part of the 12th century. The church was formerly referred to as 'St. Mary's by Gelligarn' to distinguish it from St. Mary Church in the valuations of the 13th century. Its Welsh name was 'Eglwys Fair y Mynydd', so called also to distinguish it from St. Mary Church (Llanfair) in the heart of the Vale. In 1254 (Taxation of Norwich) the church of St. Mary Hill was valued at one mark and in 1291 (*Taxatio Ecclesiastica*) £1, and assigned to the Abbot of Neath. By 1291 a separate vicarage had been established worth £2. In 1535 (*Valor Ecclesiasticus*) the tithing barn there brought 10 shillings to the Abbey which paid the synodals and procurations due thereon to the Bishop and Archdeacon. At the Dissolution of the Monasteries the rectory of this parish was in the hands of John See of Comsbury in the county of Somerset, who farmed it in 1546 to the perpetual vicar. In 1563 there was a vicar resident there. In 1603 it was styled a vicarage worth £10 per annum; the impropriation worth £1 was held by Anthony Mansel, Esquire, in fee from the King. In 1771 (Bishop Barrington's Primary Visitation of the Diocese) the living was worth £20; the incumbent was the Reverend Edward Thomas and the patrons were the heirs of Sir John Aubrey. In 1772 the vicarage of St. Mary Hill received £200 from Queen Anne's Bounty. In 1835 it was styled a vicarage worth gross £90 and Sir Thomas Aubrey was the patron and impropriator. The parishes of St. Mary Hill and Llangan were grouped with Coychurch in 1966 to form one benefice.

The church consists of chancel, nave, south porch and western embattled tower containing four bells. The restored chancel arch is broad and pointed, springing directly from the side walls. The original Norman chancel arch, a plain round one, was removed bodily into the north wall of the nave round the embrasure of the window. It is a striking example of the Vale type of contracted chancel arch. The east window is of two lights with pointed heads surmounted by a quatrefoil with hood mould and carved heads as label stops. It is a 19th-century insertion in the early Decorated style of the 14th century.

A small tablet above the east window records the fact that the chancel was restored in 1803 by Sir John Aubrey, the then patron of the living. In the east wall of the chancel, on the north side of the altar, is a trefoiled niche with fleurs-de-lys motifs carved in low relief, probably an aumbry. In the south wall of the chancel is a crude double-drain piscina beneath a small rounded arched recess which probably dates from the late 13th century. There are no other windows

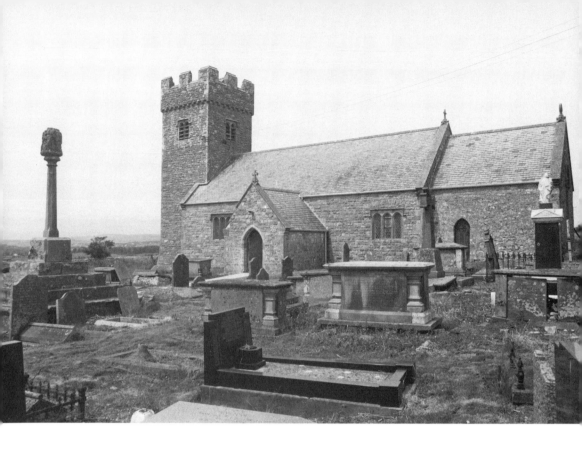

in the chancel but in the south wall is a priest's door with pointed arch and prominent hood mould. The chancel has a cradle roof and the area over the sanctuary is filled with oak panel work. The chancel is divided from the nave by a low stone wall on each side of the church. On the north side of this wall, directly under the chancel arch, is a distempered, life-like bust of the Reverend John Griffiths, a former vicar of the parish from 1847 to 1855 and Archdeacon of Llandaff from 1877 to 1897. It was presented to the church by the daughter of his first wife, Mary (née) Lewis, daughter of Caleb Lewis of Cardigan.

The pitch pine pulpit has a plain moulded cornice bracketed out from the flat stiles and a top rail between, decorated with a trail of oak leaves and acorns. There is a little row of zigzag above each panel and the narrow panels themselves have trefoils beneath pointed arches with fleurs-de-lys on cusps and pointed trefoils in the spandrels. The base is merely a continuation of the thick stiles as legs, open beneath with small brackets. A tablet above the pulpit dated 1829, when the Reverend William Leigh was the incumbent, lists the names of the donors of benefactions given to the poor of the parish.

The windows of the nave comprise a pair of two-light windows with pointed heads on the north side and two three-light windows with similar heads on the south. All the windows are filled with latticed glass and have square labels. An arched recess in the north wall of the nave, now built-in, was originally the fireplace before the installation of the present heating system. It has been mistaken by previous writers for a built-in rood-loft doorway.

The most notable feature of the church is the number of memorial tablets on the walls, many of which bear curious and interesting inscriptions. An example of this is the memorial over the pulpit on the north side of the chancel arch to Thomas Stradling (d. 1708) which reads:—

'Underneath lyeth the body of
Thomas Stradling died 13th January
1708 Aged 67.
This beuring plase belongeth unto
this family this hundred years and more'

Another example on the south wall of the nave more serious in tone, is to the memory of Watkin Hopkin, (d. 1699) and his only son, also Watkin Hopkin, (d. 1702) which was erected by 'the disconsolate widow and mother.'

'A loveng youth beneath doth lye
That calls to all prepare to dye
I was soone nipd and called away
And so mayst thou repent too day
I while alive this caution gave
And do the same hold in my grave
Leave of thy sins make God thy dread
Slight not the counsell of the dead.'

On the north wall of the nave there is a sad memorial to various members of the Bassett family including five children who died between 1793 and 1812 aged 4 years, 1 year, 3 days, 2 years and 9 days.

The nave has an arch-braced roof with crenellated wallplate. The tower opens to the nave by a pointed arch. In the base of the tower are stored two tombstones with foliated crosses. One of them has been turned upside down and used a second time and thus bears two inscriptions with widely-separated dates. Near the door is the Norman font which is tub-shaped with a bold roll-moulding round the rim. The embattled west tower, which has a corbel table beneath the parapet was mostly rebuilt in the 1803 restoration. The tower has a pair of round-headed louvred belfry lights with square label on each face, but there is no west doorway. On the north wall of the tower is a circular orifice with a small modern canopy like the one at Wick church. This was the outlet for the chimney flue when there was a chimney place at the base of the tower in the 19th century. There are now four bells in the tower where originally there was a full ring of eight bells. They were cast by William Evans, bellfounder of Chepstow in 1746 and bear the following inscriptions:—

Treble   Wm LEWIS THO'S IENKIN CH:WDNS W🔔E 1746

No. 2.   IENKIN IONES Wm MEIRICK W🔔E 1746

No. 3.   Wm EDWARD   THO'S EDWARD W🔔E 1746

Tenor   HOPKIN REES ESQR Wm EVANS FECIT 1746

The south porch is large with stone benches and probably dates from the 14th century. Its inner doorway has a pointed arch with plain mouldings. The outer doorway is also plain pointed.

On the south side of the church stands a 15th-century churchyard cross with its original head but much less well preserved than the one at Llangan. The head which is canopied and sculptured in exquisite tracery, bears a representation of the Crucifixion upon one side, the Embalming on the other and figures of saints on the two remaining sides. In 1887 this fine medieval cross lay in ruins with its head placed on four courses of dilapidated steps without a shaft. However, Sir Thomas Mansel Franklen of St. Hilary noticed its abject state on visiting the churchyard one day and decided to restore it to its original condition as a Jubilee memorial. The work was carried out by local masons; a new base and capital were hewn from adjacent sandstone quarries. A new shaft was brought from St. Hilary and the steps were entirely reset. The Reverend H. J. Humphreys presented Lady Florence Franklen with a handsome inkstand and candlesticks on behalf of the grateful parishioners of St. Mary Hill once the work was completed.

The church was restored to some extent in 1803 when the chancel and tower were repaired, but a more thorough restoration was carried out in the years 1884-1885. The existing Norman chancel arch which was replaced by a new one of larger span (so as to improve the view from the nave into the chancel), was built into the north wall of the nave. New roofs were placed on the nave and porch and a new window was inserted in the north wall of the nave. Two memorial tablets on the north wall were placed in new positions to allow for the construction of this new window. New floors were also laid down in the nave and the porch. The work was carried out according to plans and specifications prepared by John Prichard, diocesan architect. The total cost of the restoration amounted to £800 and the patron of the living, Charles Aubrey Aubrey, contributed generously to this work.

The church plate consists of a silver Elizabethan chalice with its cover dated 1576, similar in design to the Llangan cup. Also a silver bread-dish standing on a foot, was given by Mr. Aubrey.

The registers date from 1751.

St. Nicholas' Church

The parish church of St. Nicholas was probably established in pre-Norman times but cannot be traced with much certainty in the *Book of Llandaff*. It is probable therefore that it acquired its present dedication to St. Nicholas, a favourite Norman saint, after the Conquest of Glamorgan. Of the early structure there is now no trace, the present structure being built in the Decorated style with Perpendicular insertions. The church was valued at £10 in 1254 (Taxation of Norwich) and at £13-6s-8d in 1291 (*Taxatio Ecclesiastica*). The living was a Rectory worth £11-5s-4d in 1535 (*Valor Ecclesiasticus*) and had a resident parson in 1563. In the 17th century the patronage of the church belonged to the three holders of the Lordship in turn. In 1771 (Bishop Barrington's Primary Visitation of the Diocese) the living was worth £120; the incumbent was the Reverend John Bassett and the patron was Thomas Pryce. In 1835 the Rectory was worth gross £220 and the patron was the Honourable William Booth Grey. The benefice of St. Nicholas was linked with Bonvilston in 1953 and with St. George-super-Ely in 1970 to form a grouped benefice.

The church consists of chancel, nave, south chapel, south porch and an embattled western tower containing five bells. The chancel arch has a segmental pointed outer arch and the inner arch springs immediately from the side walls on each side. The east window is a modern insertion of the Decorated or early Perpendicular style of three cinquefoiled lights. Vertical tracery bars continue from the apex of the lights beneath circles enclosing quatrefoils with a pointed quatrefoil between. It is surmounted by a dripstone with rectangular label stops. The centre light depicts the Crucifixion of Our Lord. In the left-hand light are the three maidens receiving their dowries secretly at night from St. Nicholas, and in the right-hand light is the figure of St. Nicholas with St. Martin and the beggar, to whom St. Martin gave his cloak. Beneath are three smaller panes portraying in the centre the Resurrection of Our Lord, on one side the three women going to the tomb on Easter morning to embalm the body of their Lord, and on the other St. John and St. Peter. At the top of the window in four small panes are the symbols of the four Evangelists: a man to represent St. Matthew, a lion, St. Mark, an ox, St. Luke and an eagle, St. John. The window was erected as a memorial to Sarah (d. 1842), wife of John Bruce Pryce, Esq., of Dyffryn in 1860 from a design by Messrs. Clayton & Bell, London. The chancel is lit on the north side by a modern two-light trefoil-headed window beneath a square head. On the north wall of the sanctuary is a black and white marble monument surmounted by a classical urn in memory of Thomas Pryce, Esq., of Dyffryn (d. 1789). The monument also commemorates his first wife, Elizabeth, (d. 1777), daughter of Sir William Owen, Bart. of Orielton, Pembrokeshire and his second wife, Frances, (d. 1782), daughter of the Reverend William Pigot of Edgmond, Salop. On the south side the chancel opens to the south chapel by a modern drop arch. Just below the roof on the south side of the sanctuary hangs the sanctuary bell in an oak frame. In pre-Reformation times the bell was rung at the elevation of the consecrated host. The two-manual organ, built by J. S. Dane & Sons, organ builders of Swansea in 1875, now occupies part of the south chapel inside the drop arch. On the north wall of the chancel is a memorial tablet to Frances Anne (d. 1837), wife of the Honourable William Booth Grey, one time patron of the living. The chancel has a barrel roof with embattled wallplate.

The south chapel, which may have been formerly a chantry attached to Cottrell, the ancient seat of the Merrick family, is on the south side of the chancel and extends from opposite the middle of the nave near the south porch as far as the east end of the chancel. The south wall of the chapel was rebuilt in 1803 when 'ugly Italian windows' were inserted. A benefactor replaced these windows with the present ones which are in the early Decorated style and consist of two cinquefoiled lights with a quatrefoil in the apex surmounted by prominent dripstones. The centre light replaced a small priest's door. Two of these three windows contain stained glass depicting St. Philip and St. Michael, St. Nicholas and St. David from a design by E. Liddall Armitage of Notting Hill, London. Between these two windows are two mural tablets surmounted by two swords, memorials to eminent members of the Tyler family of Cottrell. A third tablet on the south wall records that these stained glass windows and tablets were erected to the memory of Major-General Trevor Bruce Tyler (d. 1923) and his son, Lieutenant-Colonel Roper Maxwell Tyler (d. 1919) by Ada Tyler, wife and mother in 1924.

The east window of the chapel is also a modern insertion of three cinque-foiled lights with panel tracery of trefoils in the head. It is in the Perpendicular style of the 15th century. The west window, also of three cinquefoiled lights with two elongated quatrefoils in the head, is placed high up in the west wall of the chapel above the south porch. The floor of the chapel is covered with ledger tombstones, some of which are covered over and some worn and defaced. On the north wall of the chapel is a white marble tablet to the memory of Sir Charles Tyler of Cottrell (d. 1835), Admiral of the White and Knight Grand Cross of the Most Honourable Order of the Bath, who commanded H.M.S. *Tonnant*, a ship of 80 guns at the Battle of Trafalgar in 1805 under Lord Nelson. The monument is surmounted by a draped urn and below is the family achievement of Sir Charles Tyler. Two escutcheons are displayed, the dexter emblazoning the arms of Tyler, 'Sable on a fess wavy or between three tigers passant guardant erminois a cross pattée of the first between two crescents gules, in centre chief a medal or for Trafalgar'. This escutcheon is surrounded by a circlet bearing the motto of the Order of the Bath 'Tria juncto in uno' (Three joined in one), which is balanced on the sinister side by an escutcheon, enclosed in a laurel wreath on which are emblazoned the arms of Tyler impaling those of Leach 'Gules a chevron between three swans argent.' Pendant from the dexter shield is the badge of the Order of the Bath with the motto 'Ich dien' (I serve). The supporters are 'Two tigers rampant guardant proper navally crowned or, each gorged with a laurel wreath vert pendant from which is a gold medal, each bearing a banner, the dexter inscribed Algeziras and the sinister Ildefonso.' The crest is 'A tiger rampant guardant proper navally crowned or holding in the dexter paw a flagstaff therefrom flying the French tricolor depressed and reversed.' The motto is 'My King and Country.' There are tombstones bearing only initials and dates:— F.A.G. 1837, E.L. 1829, which the parish registers tell us refer to Frances Anne Grey of Dyffryn buried 7th August, 1837, and Elizabeth Leach of St. Mary, Pembroke, buried 9th December, 1829.

The nave opens to the south chapel by a pointed arch with continuous mouldings of 14th-century character springing from plain capitals on clustered shafts. In the north wall of the nave are two old Perpendicular windows of three cinquefoiled lights with panel tracery in the head surmounted by a hood mould with carved heads as label stops. A small door with pointed arch leads to the vestry. The north wall of the nave is reinforced by two slender buttresses. The south-west window of the nave is early Perpendicular of three cinquefoiled lights beneath ogee arches and the tracery lights are in the form of blank shields with trefoils within the basic panels. It is surmounted by a hood mould with carved heads as label stops.

The stone and marble pulpit, the gift of Mrs. Ella Mackintosh of Mackintosh of Cottrell in 1880, was placed on the south side of the nave as it was found to be too large to go in the place of the old pulpit on the north side. The pulpit has a narrow moulded rim which gives way to an ornate cornice comprising a double row of leaf trails and mouldings. These follow the line of panels and the ornate foliated capitals above slender shafts arranged as muntins with bases. They run between the cornice and the leaf trail and plain mouldings which make up the bottom rail. The panels between each have representations of two-light trefoil-headed tracery beneath ogee arches with a pointed arch above and quatrefoils in the head. The lights are separated by little shafts with round moulded caps and bases and the arch is decorated with foliated crockets ending up in a similar finial within the cornice. The substantial stem has short marble shafts alternating with columns. The plinth is heavily moulded. The most aesthetically pleasing aspect of this pulpit is the way the little stairway treads curve so nicely with trefoils beneath pointed arches in square-headed panels in the side.

On the north wall of the nave are two black and white marble monuments. One is to the memory of the Reverend Thomas Bruce (d. 1790), rector of the parish from 1779 to 1790 and only son of William Bruce of Llanblethian. It was erected in the church by his nephew, John Bruce Pryce, Esq. of Dyffryn. The monument is surmounted by the Bruce coat of arms 'Or a saltire gules on a chief of the last, a martlet of the first' with the family crest 'A dexter arm in armour in bend, grasping a sceptre all proper'. Beneath is the family motto 'Fuimus' (We have been). The other monument was also erected by John Bruce Pryce, Esq. to the memory of his wife, Sarah (d. 1842). At the base of the monument is the crest of Bruce Pryce 'A paschal lamb proper'. Opposite on the south wall of the nave is a brass plaque in memory of Anne Maria Tyler of Cottrell (d. 1886).

The south porch is large with stone benches inside. The south doorway of the church is Perpendicular with four-centred arch and the outer door of the porch has a good segmental pointed outer arch and inner arch dying into the sides. Over it was a niche which once contained an effigy of the patron saint, but this niche was blocked up at some time in the past and a sundial placed there instead. The 13th-century font has a plain octagonal shallow bowl with typical strings of the period. The octagonal stem splays at the bottom to rest on a modern octagonal plinth.

The tower opens to the nave by a segmental pointed outer arch and the inner arch springs immediately from the walls on each side. The tower arch matches that of the chancel in width and style but is less acutely pointed. The tower is square and lofty, well-proportioned with a parapet thrown slightly out upon corbels in the Welsh fashion. At the base space of the tower is a plinth surmounted by a stringcourse of white honeycombed limestone. The west doorway is a drop arch of ashlar blocks and above it is a two-light square-headed window of two cinquefoiled lights beneath ogee arches. It is a 19th-century insertion and looks very much out of place on this wall. The tracery bars become circles in the head enclosing a quatrefoil with only trefoils possible in the remaining spaces. The stained glass depicts the figures of St. Peter and St. John and was erected as a memorial to John Bruce Pryce of Dyffryn (d. 1872), who restored the church in 1860. A small door with pointed arch in the south-west corner of the nave leads to the belfry staircase. The belfry windows are of two lights with pointed heads and on the south side there are two smaller apertures at a lower level. The tower houses a ring of five bells, of which three were rehung and two added in 1881 through the generosity of Mrs. E. Mackintosh of Mackintosh of Cottrell. The bells bear the following inscriptions:—

Treble   PRESENTED BY ELLA MACKINTOSH OF MACKINTOSH
         ONE SIDE
         WILLIAMS EVANS
         WILLIAM MOORE   CHURCHWARDENS
         OTHER SIDE
         (ROYAL ARMS)
         LLEWELLINS & JAMES
         BRISTOL 1881

No. 2.   PRESENTED BY ELLA MACKINTOSH OF MACKINTOSH
         ONE SIDE
         WILLIAM CONYBEARE BRUCE, RECTOR
         COME TO THY GOD IN TIME

SO PEALS OUR WARNING CHIME
YOUTH MANHOOD OLD AGE PAST
COME TO THY GOD AT LAST
OTHER SIDE
LLEWELLINS & JAMES
BRISTOL 1881

No. 3.   LLEWELLINS & JAMES
RECAST 1870

No. 4.   DAVID RICHARD, IOHN REES CHURCHWARDENS
EE 🔔 1717

No. 5.   PEACE AND GOOD NEIGHBOURHOOD
IOHN THOMAS RECTR 1717
E 🔔 E

A fine war memorial in the form of a Celtic cross constructed from Portland stone was erected on the village green to the memory of the ten officers and men of the parish who fell in the Great War, 1914-1918. The memorial was unveiled by the Mackintosh of Mackintosh and Mrs. Charlotte Traherne in 1920. Among the tombstones in the north-west part of the churchyard is one notable for the fact that on it is engraved the opening bar of Chopin's 20th Prelude which the White family called 'God's Answer'.

The church was restored in the years 1859-1860 and the patron of the living John Bruce Pryce, Esq. of Dyffryn contributed £1,000 towards the cost of the restoration. The work consisted of completely renewing the roofs with Memel timber, reflooring the centre area of the church and erecting a new pulpit, installing new altar rails, new seating of pitch pine and new teak wood doors. All the windows were restored or renewed with Decorated and Perpendicular-style tracery. In the restoration of the church the architect, John Prichard, regarded the prevailing architectural style of the building as late Decorated passing into Perpendicular and judiciously worked in that style. The work was carried out by the firm of Messrs. Parry, contractors of Llandaff from designs by and under the superintendence of Messrs. Prichard and Seddon, diocesan architects. The church was reopened for divine service after restoration on Thursday 24th May, 1860.

Rice Merrick (c. 1520-1587), genealogist and historian, lived at Cottrell in the parish of St. Nicholas. His major work on the history of Glamorgan, entitled *A book of Glamorganshire's antiquities* was published in two editions in the 19th century, one in 1825, the other in 1887, both based on a manuscript in the Library of Queen's College, Oxford. In a recent edition of the work *Morganiae Archaiographia: a book of the antiquities of Glamorgan* (1983) the editor, Brian Ll. James, rightly asserts that Merrick, who died on the 1st March, 1587 (new style), was buried in St. Nicholas' church (of which he was one of the patrons) and not in Cowbridge church, an error perpetuated by recent historians through confusion in Dineley's manuscript. Brian James states that according to Thomas Dineley in his *Account of the official progress by his Grace Henry first Duke of Beaufort . . . through Wales in 1684,* Dineley saw the tombstone and copied the inscription which reads as follows:— 'Hieere lyethe the bodYe of Rice Miricke disceseD the first day of Marche in the yeare of ovre Lorde One thovsand fieve hundred eighty six.' The stone has since disappeared although it still existed with a partially decipherable inscription in about 1860. Since the church was restored in that year it is probable that the stone was irretrievably damaged at that time.

From 1625 to 1649 and 1660 to 1663 the rector of St. Nicholas was the Reverend Hugh Lloyd who was also rector of St. Andrew's Major and vicar of Denbigh. He was dispossessed of his livings during the period of the Common-wealth and rule of Oliver Cromwell, but served from 1649 to 1660 as Arch-deacon of St. David's. At the restoration of Charles II he was consecrated Bishop of Llandaff although he was 74 years of age and he regained his livings, though he resigned St. Nicholas in 1663. During his long incumbency it is recorded that Bishop Lloyd was well loved at St. Nicholas. He died in 1667 at the age of 81.

At the south entrance of the churchyard is a well-designed modern lychgate which was erected soon after the restoration of the church. The church plate includes a silver chalice and silver paten, both inscribed 'St. Nicholas 1698' and another large silver paten inscribed 'St. Nicholas Parish—the gift of Mrs. B. Button', and a silver flagon. The register of baptisms and burials dates from 1762 and marriages from 1755.

Sully Church

The parish church of Sully is dedicated to St. John the Baptist. This dedication may be due to the fact that the De Sully family who founded the church probably belonged to the medieval Order of the Knights Hospitallers of St. John of Jerusalem, who regarded St. John as their patron saint. The church is built in the Early English style of architecture of the 13th century with Perpendicular insertions. The first recorded incumbent of Sully was Thomas de Sully in 1242.

The church was valued at £10 in 1254 (Taxation of Norwich) and in 1291 (*Taxatio Ecclesiastica*) and £12-3s-4d in 1535 (*Valor Ecclesiasticus*). The parson was resident in 1563. In 1668 the rectory and advowson of Sully belonged to the Stradling family of St. Donat's. In 1771 (Bishop Barrington's *Llandaff Diocesan Book*) the living was worth £60; the incumbent was the Reverend Thomas Bassett and the patron was George Venables Vernon, Esq. of Briton Ferry. According to the diocesan report in 1809 the annual value of the benefice arising from tithes and glebe was £133-9s-6d. In 1835 the Rectory was worth gross £250 and the patron was Mrs. Alicia Thomas of Llwynmadoc and Sully.

The church consists of chancel, nave and embattled western tower containing six bells; the lower stage of the tower forms a porch with entrance on the south side. The chancel arch is of 14th-century style; the inner arch springs immediately from the side walls and a single mould continues all around the outer arch to the floor. The 15th-century-style east window is of three cinquefoiled lights with standard Perpendicular tracery lights and a label simply returned at right angles to form stops. Internally the considerable thickness of wall allows a small inner arch to be formed as it were out of a chamfer on the outer one dying into the side wall at the point of spring. There is an internal label similar to the one on the outside. The window depicts the figures of St. John the Baptist and St. Paul, and in the centre light the risen Christ standing on the whole world. In the tracery lights are the badges of the Royal Navy, the Army, the Royal Air Force and the Merchant Navy. The window was erected in 1949 from a design by Alfred L. Wilkinson, stained glass artist of Barnet, Hertfordshire, in memory of the men of the parish who gave their lives in the Second World War, 1939-1945.

The chancel is lit on the south side by a window of two cinquefoiled lights under a square head and labelled. The window depicts the figures of Dorcas and Christ as the Good Shepherd and was erected in 1953 in memory of Christmas

Sully Church from a sketch
by Mifs Emily Woods (about 1

Jonathan Page (d. 1953) from a design by Bristow, Wadley and Co. A doorway with pointed archway and hood mould with rectangular stops leads to a modern vestry on the north side of the chancel, built in 1955. Opposite, on the south wall, is a priest's door with pointed arch and dripstone with battered heads as label stops. Set into the south wall is a 13th-century piscina with a deep basin beneath a simple trefoil canopied niche made of three orders to add visual depth. The surface containing the drain projects considerably from the wall, which is uncommon and poses the question whether the piscina is *in situ* or was moved there at some time in the past.

The heads of the choir stalls in the chancel are shaped like fishes, which was a symbol of Christianity in the early years of Christian persecution and derived from the acronym of the Greek word IXΘYC (fish) for Jesus Christ, Son of God, Saviour. The altar is a plain modern stone slab set on two stone pillars. The chancel has a trussed-rafter roof, but the eastern part of it over the sanctuary is boarded.

The windows of the nave on the south side comprise two Perpendicular windows of three trefoiled lights with rectilinear tracery under a square head with label. The south-east window depicts Christ (centre) with a soldier in plate armour kneeling with the banner of St. George, with a winged Satanic figure holding a flail symbolizing the horror of war (left) and a dead soldier in armour with the heavenly host, one bearing a crown above his head (right). The text reads:— 'Be thou faithful unto death and I will give thee a crown of life.' The window was erected by Alfred T. Yeld Stephens of De Sully Grange in memory of the men of the parish who lost their lives in the Great War, 1914-1918. At the top of the centre light are the arms of the Stephens family 'Party per chevron azure and argent, in chief two falcons, wings expanded or' and the family motto 'Deus intersit' (May God attend).

The south-west window depicts St. John (left) and St. Luke (right) and in the centre St. Ann, the Virgin Mary and Jesus and John the Baptist as children. This window was designed and erected in 1933 by Isaac John Williams, Keeper of the Department of Art in the National Museum of Wales, in memory of his wife, Annie (d. 1932), who lies buried in the churchyard. Mr. & Mrs. I. J. Williams were married in Sully church on the 26th December, 1903.

The nave is lit on the north side by two Perpendicular-style windows of three trefoiled lights under a square head with label. These windows were inserted in 1927 to provide additional light in the nave and were designed and constructed by Vickery Brothers of Barry Dock, to conform with the style of the other windows of the nave. The brass eagle lectern was given by Alfred T. Stephens of De Sully Grange in 1904.

The Victorian stone pulpit was erected in 1895 and the reading desk is a piece of the heavy mouldings of the cornice containing square floral decoration which in part masks the fleur-de-lys and stiff-leaf forms. The stiles are cut into the stone and the main decoration on the rectangular panels are openwork quatrefoils with diamond-shaped ornamentation at the centre. Similarly two small squares with similar motifs act as blind panels below. Behind the pulpit is

Interior view c. 1895

a plain cross in memory of the Reverend Trevor Owen Thomas, rector of the parish (1930-1944). The Litany desk was given by him in 1931 in memory of his sister.

On the north wall of the nave are two memorial monuments, one to the memory of William Daniel Conybeare, D.D., F.R.S. (d. 1857) rector of the parish (1822-1836) and Dean of Llandaff during the restoration of the Cathedral Church (1845-1857). The tablet records that he was a pioneer in the study of geology and structure of the South Wales Coalfield. It was the Reverend W. D. Conybeare who was responsible for substituting the English language for Welsh in the services, for until 1824 the predominant language of the parish was Welsh. Charles Kingsley, the novelist, was a friend of the rector Conybeare, and his family used to stay at Sully rectory. His name is engraved on a window in the old rectory. It was in June 1841 while staying with Sir J. J. Guest and his wife at Old Sully House that Charles Kingsley was called to the Ministry of God and made the decision to take up Holy Orders.

The other memorial monument is to Evan Thomas of Llwynmadoc, Breconshire and Old Sully House (d. 1832) 'resident proprietor of the parish' for twenty years and Chairman of Glamorgan Quarter Sessions. The monument displays the family coat of arms 'Per pale argent and gules on a chevron engrailed, two griffins passant combatant counterchanged on a chief wavy azure three cinquefoils of the first'. The crest is 'Out of a mural crown argent a demi-seahorse gules crined or, charged on the shoulder with a cinquefoil argent and in his paws an anchor erect sable resting on the mural crown.'

The goblet-shaped font, beautifully and elaborately carved, has a slightly moulded rim which gives way to a trail of foliage and fruit. The curve into the underside of the bowl and the stem is emphasized not only by the particularly good line of the angels' bodies into the ribbing below, but also by the shape of the wings which flow into the stems of the leaf trails beneath. The ribs have little moulded bases which die into an octagonal moulded plinth. The font was erected circa 1870 in memory of members of the Evans family of Old Sully House by their daughter, Mrs. Catherine Deakin. The font cover was presented as a Lenten offering in 1931.

The nave has a simple arch-braced roof with the spaces between the purlins, principal and intermediate rafters plastered. In the south-west corner of the nave stands a 16th-century wooden capstan font. On the west wall of the nave is a plaque designed by Messrs Caröe and Partners, Westminster, a memorial to the fifteen men of the parish who lost their lives in the Second World War, 1939-1945. The tower opens to the nave by a plain low archway. Above it are the pipes of the modern organ the console of which is placed in the south-east corner of the nave. The instrument, built by J. W. Walker & Sons of Brandon, Suffolk, was installed in the church in December 1965. Inside the south-east wall of the tower can be seen the outline of a stairway which once either led to the tower or to a west gallery.

The tower is square and beneath the battlement is a corbel table of Welsh pattern. The belfry has square-headed loopholes on each face and additional slit windows on its north and south walls at a lower level. The tower batters considerably at the base under a stringcourse and in its west wall is a plain pointed broad lancet. The lower part of the tower forms a porch with entrance through a pointed doorway on the south side. On one of the stones on the south wall of the tower is inscribed the letters R.M. and the date 1701, when it was rebuilt to house the bells. The tower houses a ring of six bells, three of which were recast in 1880 by Llewellins & James of Bristol. In 1961 a new treble bell was added which was cast by John Taylor, bellfounder of Loughborough.

The inscriptions on the bells are as follows:—

Treble   JOHN TAYLOR & CO ★ BELLFOUNDERS ★
          LOUGHBOROUGH ★ LEICESTERSHIRE ★ 1961 ★

No. 2.   VENITE EXULTEMUS DOMINE
          LLEWELLINS & JAMES, BRISTOL, 1880

No. 3.   GLORIA IN EXCELSIS DEO
          LLEWELLINS & JAMES, BRISTOL, 1880

No. 4.   TE DEUM LAUDAMUS GEORGE WOODS RECTOR
          LLEWELLINS & JAMES, BRISTOL, 1880

No. 5.   PEACE AND GOOD NEIGHBOURHOOD
          W. EVANS 1758

No. 6.   EVAN LLOYD CHURCHWARDEN
          WM EVANS FECIT 1758.

During the incumbency of the Reverend W. D. Conybeare in the early 19th century, a south aisle, built in the 15th century probably as a chantry chapel, was removed and the window frames re-used in the south wall of the nave. A south porch was also demolished. Several early tombstones from the south aisle were incorporated in the churchyard path. The old Norman chancel arch was taken down and the present one erected.

In 1848 the Reverend George Woods became rector of Sully. He had the chancel restored to its original dimensions and repaired the choir. In 1874 the church underwent a thorough restoration when the three-decker pulpit and the old high pews were removed and new pews, a pulpit and a font installed. The church was reopened for divine service after restoration by the Rt. Reverend Dr. Alfred Ollivant, Bishop of Llandaff on the 31st August 1876.

In 1895 the church was restored again when the flat plaster ceiling was removed and a new open timber roof of red deal with deal cornices was raised. New choir stalls were erected in the chancel, the pews were replaced by open benches of deal and a new stone pulpit was erected on the north side of the nave. New stone arches were placed internally over the two Perpendicular windows on the south side of the nave in place of the wooden lintels. New stonework dressings were put to the modernised south doorway of the tower. The work of restoration was carried out according to plans and specifications of Messrs. Seddon and Carter, architects of Cardiff, and the cost of the restoration amounted to £550, of which Lord Wimbourne, Lord of the Manor and patron of the living, generously contributed £100. The church was reopened for divine service after restoration by the Rt. Reverend Dr. Richard Lewis, Bishop of Llandaff, on Thursday, 17th October, 1895.

Under the east window are the graves of the Reverend E. Combs and his wife who died in 1887 after drinking contaminated water from a well in the pump field near the Rectory. In the churchyard are the original Calvary steps of the churchyard cross, which now has a modern cross placed upon them. It was restored in 1927 during the incumbency of the Reverend John Williams. The lychgate at the entrance to the churchyard was given by the Yeld Stephens family of De Sully Grange in 1920 to commemorate peace after the Great War, 1914-1918. It bears the arms and motto of the Stephens family.

The church plate includes an Elizabethan silver chalice with its paten cover. Round the bowl is a band of intersecting foliated strap ornament. The foot of the chalice and handle of the cover are dated 1576, but the hall-mark date is for 1566 which is the earliest hall-marked and dated chalice in the diocese of Llandaff. A more modern silver bread-dish is inscribed 'Sully church 1860'. The register of marriages dates from 1754, baptisms and burials from 1759.

Welsh St. Donat's Church

The parish church of Welsh St. Donat's is dedicated to St. Donat and is built in the Early English style of architecture. As one of the chapels attached to Llanblethian church under the name 'Capella Sancti Donati' Welsh St. Donat's was specifically confirmed to Tewkesbury Abbey in 1180. In the Taxation of Norwich (1254) the church of Llanblethian with its chapels (which included Welsh St. Donat's) was valued at 18 marks (£2). The earliest recorded instance of the name 'Welsh St. Donat's' is to be found in a document dated 1482. The church was called Eglwys Llanddunwyd or Welsh St. Donat's to distinguish it from St. Donat's on the coast called English St. Donat's or 'Sancto Donato Anglicana'.

In the *Valor Ecclesiasticus* of 1535 Tewkesbury Abbey drew the tithes of corn and hay from this chapel. In 1563 it was said to have 'christening and burying and other divine service as a parish church.' In 1603 it was styled a 'chapel' of Llanblethian and it was designated a 'curacy' in 1764, when it received £200 from Queen Anne's Bounty and likewise in 1835. In 1771 (Bishop Barrington's Primary Visitation of the Diocese) it was included in the same valuation as Llanblethian which amounted to £90. Welsh St. Donat's remained attached to Llanblethian until the Disestablishment of the Welsh Church in 1920 when it was joined with Ystradowen. In 1973 Welsh St. Donat's was joined with the parish of Pendoylan to form one benefice.

The church consists of chancel, nave, south porch and embattled western tower containing a single bell. The chancel arch is broad and slightly pointed. The Perpendicular east window which is not in the centre of the east wall, is of two cinquefoiled lights surmounted by a square label. To the north of the east window is a niche with ogee-headed trefoil arch which formerly held a statue. The chancel is lit on the south side by a two-light cinquefoiled window with square label. Cut into the sill of this window is a square drain piscina. To the west of this window is a priest's door with pointed arch. In the north wall of the sanctuary is a recess to house a tomb of a distinguished parishioner, but the effigy is missing. On the north wall of the chancel is a memorial tablet to the Reverend William Jenkins (d. 1777) Rector of Merthyr Dyfan and Cadoxton from 1766 to 1777 and other members of his family. The main feature of interest in the church is the pre-Reformation sanctus bell which still hangs in its original position suspended from a yew beam near the roof on the eastern side of the chancel arch. It is cast in bronze and is devoid of any inscription. It has a hemispherical haunch and has three parallel lines on its shoulder and four near the rim. It was rung at certain times during the mass, principally at the *Sanctus* and at the elevation of the consecrated host. It is one of the very few pre-Reformation bells still in existence in the Vale of Glamorgan. A doorway with Tudor arch in the north wall of the chancel leads to a staircase which once led to the rood-loft. The chancel has an arch-braced roof with foliage bosses at the intersections of the principal rafters and collar purlin.

The windows of the nave comprise on the south side a three-light and a two-light trefoil-headed window and on the north side a pair of two-light windows, one with trefoiled heads, the other with rounded heads. All the windows of the nave are filled with latticed glass decorated with a red border. On the north side of the chancel arch is the outline of the doorway, now built-in, to the former rood-loft, the entrance to which was from the chancel, not from the nave as is usually the case.

The most interesting feature of the nave is the 15th-century oak roof which is of the open arch-braced collar-truss type with two tiers of curved windbraces between the purlins and the wallplate. It is boarded between the common rafters. The principal rafters are cut out of large oak scantlings which rest on wallposts supported on stone corbels. The pulpit, erected in 1891, is a simple wooden structure on a plain masonry drum. The cornice is plainly moulded, the stiles reeded and the decoration pierced through the panels. Above the flat centre rail in each case are two trefoil-headed openings with a little trefoil between. In the centre of each sunken panel below is a fleur-de-lys.

On the east and south walls of the nave are memorial tablets in white marble to members of the Jenkins family who lived at Caercady House and were the principal landowners in the parish for many generations. They include the Reverend John Thomas Jones (d. 1827) and his wife, Mary Jones (d. 1824), daughter of William Jenkins, Esquire of Caercady House. Another memorial commemorates members of the Thomas family who resided at Caercady House in the 19th century, among them John Thomas, Esq., R.N. (d. 1875). On the south wall near the south door is an unusual lozenge-shaped inscription tablet in memory of William Thomas (d. 1802), aged 89 years. The tablet bears an epitaph in Welsh which runs as follows:—

> 'Gofidiwch ddim na fyddwch drist
> Achos fy wedi huno yng Nghrist
> Does yma ond y corph o glai
> Mae'r enaid fry yn llawenhau.'

which translated reads:—

> 'Do not worry, do not be sad
> Because I have gone to sleep in Christ
> There is only here the body of clay
> The spirit is on high rejoicing.'

On the north wall of the nave are several memorial monuments, one of those near the pulpit is in the Welsh language. It is in memory of Gomer Waite (1887-1918) who was assistant overseer of the poor of the parish from 1914 to 1918 and was erected by his relatives E. J. and Margaret Bassett. Also on the north wall is a stone tablet erected in 1830 and recording two benefactions. Just inside the south doorway is a rectangular holy-water stoup. The absence of pews in the church creates an impression of spaciousness in marked contrast to most of the Vale churches.

The massive font of 13th-century date has a circular bowl with scalloped underside. The short stem is separated at either end from the base and stem by a single roll-moulding. The base has two heavy rolls, one upon the other, and a deep indentation where it meets the stem. The floor of the nave is lined with gravestones dating back to the 17th and 18th centuries. One of them, dated 1673, bears the inscription:—

> 'Underneath this stone i ly in dust
> Untill the Resurection of the Just'.

The south porch is large and inside are stone benches with wooden seats. On one of the seats is carved the date 1723. The inner doorway has a pointed arch and the outer doorway has a depressed arch. On the floor just inside the doorway is placed what appears to be part of a large 15th-century octagonal pillar stoup which was recently discovered in the purlieus of the churchyard.

The tower opens to the nave by a slightly-rounded modern arch. The tower is a massive square structure with a small corbel table beneath the battlement. The belfry has on its north and south faces a two-light square-headed window and a small square-headed light on its east and west faces. A stringcourse halfway up the tower divides it into two portions. The lower stage of the tower is of late 13th-century date and the west doorway has a horseshoe arch which is quite a rare feature. In the south wall of the tower at ground level, is a trefoil lancet which was opened out during the restoration in 1891. The tower houses a large bell which bears the date 1836 and was probably cast by Thomas Mears & Son of London.

Outside the church, affixed to the south wall of the nave, is a memorial tablet, now badly weathered, with an inscription which once read:—

> 'Short was the notice
> Death me gave
> When I was summoned
> To my grave'.

The church was restored in 1891 and the work of restoration included the repair of the roofs of the chancel, nave, south porch and tower. A new window was inserted in the south-west wall of the nave and a small lancet window was opened out in the base of the tower. The windows were reglazed throughout the church. A new pulpit, lectern, holy table and chancel seats were provided and the priest's door was opened out in the chancel. The west door of the tower was renewed and the bell was rehung in a new bellframe. The work of

restoration was carried out according to plans and specifications prepared by
Messrs. Kempson and Fowler, architects, of Cardiff, at a cost of £800.

A very ancient custom practised in the churchyard of Welsh St. Donat's and
some neighbouring parishes, was that of 'raising the summer birch'. A birch
bough was bedecked with ribbons by the ladies of the parish and on Easter Day
their menfolk assisted them in lifting it up upon the cross in the churchyard.
The birch was guarded for four days and nights for it was a disgrace for a parish
to lose its birch, while a parish that succeeded in stealing a bedecked bough and
retaining its own was held in great esteem.

Until the end of the 19th century Welsh St. Donat's church was particularly
noteworthy as being the only church in the Vale of Glamorgan to hold regular
services in the Welsh language. The church plate consists of a silver chalice and
cover. The paten is inscribed W.S.D. 1610. The register of baptisms dates from
1725, marriages and burials from 1726.

Wenvoe Church

The parish church of Wenvoe is dedicated to St. Mary and is built in the early Decorated style of architecture. Wenvoe bears the aspect of a well-cared for, thoroughly renovated church. The church was worth £10 in 1254 (Taxation of Norwich) and in 1291 (*Taxatio Ecclesiastica*) and £13-6s-8d in 1535 (*Valor Ecclesiasticus*) when it was classified with the rectories. In 1561 the rector was resident at his rectory at Peterston-super-Ely. In 1563 it had a resident parson and curate. In 1771 (Bishop Barrington's Primary Visitation of the Diocese) the living was worth £100; the incumbent was the Reverend John Hodges and the patron was Sir Edmond Thomas. It was styled a Rectory in 1835 worth gross £380 and R. F. Jenner was the patron. Wenvoe was linked to the parish of St. Lythan's in 1925.

The church consists of chancel, nave, south porch and embattled western tower containing three bells. The chancel arch is pointed with continuous jambs from floor to apex. The inner chancel arch is corbelled out from the wall at the point of spring by an elaborately-carved 19th-century corbel in the form of a capital decorated with three-lobed stalks in 14th-century style. The east window is a 19th-century insertion of three trefoiled lights, the outer two more slender than the one in the centre. The head comprises two intersecting ogee arches which bisect above to form a quatrefoil within an ogival. In the spandrels there are quatrefoils and the other tracery lights are mouchettes. The centre light depicts the Crucifixion of Our Lord above an Epiphany scene. The right-hand light depicts the taking down (Deposition) of Jesus from the cross above a scene showing the flight into Egypt and the left-hand light portrays Jesus carrying the Cross of Calvary greeting Mary above a Nativity scene. The window is a memorial to Edward and Elizabeth Lewis and Edward their son. The beautifully carved reredos by Sir Ninian Comper has ogee arches with foliated crockets and finials with pinnacles between, which end in bosses with tracery lights and window heads below in the backdrop. The seven carved statuettes include the Virgin Mary and Child (centre figure); next to her, St. George slaying the dragon and at each extremity St. Peter and St. Paul. The other three are unidentified bishops. A brass plaque records that the reredos and altar table were given by William Walter Nell, churchwarden for 28 years. A marble slab in front of the altar table is incised with the initials of members of the Birt and Jenner families and is presumably the entrance to the family vault.

The chancel is lit on the south side by two broad trefoil-headed lancets. The

south-east window which is somewhat shorter than its partner depicts Christ's agony in the Garden of Gethsemane and is a memorial to Alfred Herbert Jenner, erected by his widow. The south-west window depicts Christ's entry into Jerusalem on Palm Sunday. Between these two windows is the priest's door which has plain glass in its upper panels to enable more light to penetrate a rather dark chancel. The doorway has a pointed arch surmounted by a drip-stone with rectangular label stops. Opposite the priest's door is the vestry which was constructed in 1930. The vestry screen was erected in 1981 'with thanks to God for the Ministry of W. J. Christopher (rector of Wenvoe and St. Lythan's from 1957 to 1976) and in memory of generous benefactors.' To the west of the vestry is an organ chamber which opens to the choir part of the chancel by a low pointed arch, so that space is provided for a small, modern Hammond electric organ. The chancel has a simple wagon roof plastered between the rafters and is markedly lower than the lofty roof of the nave. On the north wall of the sanctuary is a marble monument surmounted by a draped classical urn to the memory of Peter Birt (d. 1791) of Wenvoe Castle, his wife, Ann (d. 1797) and his son, Peter (d. 1788) and two members of the Jenner family who were related by marriage to the Birts. Opposite on the south wall of the sanctuary is a black and white marble tablet in memory of Gilb Birt Price Jenner, Esq. (d. 1830), third son of Robert Jenner, Esq., of Wenvoe Castle. Inset into the south wall of the chancel is a memorial stone to Mary Powel (d. 1724), aged 7 years and 14 weeks, daughter of Edward Powel of Brinhil and Mary, his wife, and granddaughter of the Reverend Philip Hawkins, former rector of Wenvoe. On the north wall near the chancel arch is a brass plaque with Latin inscription which records that William Walter Nell (1804-1871) and Elizabeth, his wife (1809-1868), who were generous benefactors of the church, are buried in the chancel.

The chancel screen is square-framed of three bays with a plain moulded cornice and top rail. Each bay has two lights separated, but for the one in the centre, by slim muntins with little caps, bases and annulets. The lights are trefoil-headed, cusped beneath ogee arches, all slender openwork. The screen is surmounted by an actual rood carved in London with the attendant figures all well-designed and carved by Zwink of Oberammergau. The screen was de-signed by E. P. Warren, a pupil of G. F. Bodley, and was executed by William Clarke of Llandaff. It was placed in the church in the early part of this century during the incumbency of the Reverend G. H. Jenner, rector of the parish from 1882 to 1924.

The beautifully-carved pulpit, which is also attributed to Sir Ninian Comper, has a plain moulded cornice and three sculpted inhabited panels separated by slender two-stage buttresses with set-offs and plinth. The head of each panel is a double ogee arch with foliated crockets and a finial separated by foliated pinnacles which extend into the cornice. Each pinnacle ends in a square boss. The central figure is presumably Christ with the right hand raised in benediction. The figure on the right is St. Andrew with saltirewise cross and the other figure is St. Peter holding his attribute, a key. The pulpit was placed in the church in the early part of this century to the memory of William Walter Nell (d. 1902), churchwarden of the parish for 28 years.

The windows of the nave, which all have dressings of Bath stone, comprise five single trefoil lancets all in stained glass, three on the south side and two on the north. The south-east window depicts the Ascension of Our Lord and is a memorial to Lucy Elizabeth Marriott (d. 1896); the centre window in the south wall depicts Christ as the Good Shepherd and is a memorial to the Mission of 1895, and the south-west window represents the Baptism of Jesus by John the Baptist and is in memory of Robert Francis Lascelles Jenner (d. 1883). The north-east window portrays the Annunciation of the Blessed Virgin Mary and is a memorial window to Charlotte Anne Jenner (d. 1911); and the north-west window, designed by Percy Bacon, stained glass artist of London, depicts the presentation of the Baby Jesus in the Temple and is in memory of Charles Herbert and Fanny Jenner, also Henry Augustus and Edwin Arthur Jenner.

On the north wall of the nave are two fine marble monuments to members of the Thomas family of Wenvoe Castle who were principal landowners in the parish during the 17th and 18th centuries. The one on the west side bears an oval tablet with a Latin inscription which records that William Thomas, son and heir of Edmond Thomas predeceased his father in 1636 aged 25 years and was married to Jane (d. 1688) daughter of Sir John Stradling, who erected this monument in the nave to her husband. The inscription tablet is on a rectangular panel flanked by black marble free-standing Corinthian columns supporting a moulded cornice. The columns have pink and black-veined marble caps and bases supported by black brackets. Above it all the triangular pediment has a broken arch to admit the standing figure of a female with her two children on a pedestal between two reclining figures, all in Classical clothing. The inscription oval is edged in red with a grey superimposed cross giving the appearance of a nimbus. The spandrels include figurework in low relief. The apron between the brackets has swags of fruit issuing from above an achievement with festoons beneath. The heraldic shield or achievement displays the arms of Thomas of Wenvoe 'Sable, a chevron and canton ermine' impaling those of Stradling 'Paly of six, argent and azure, on a bend gules three cinquefoils or'.

The other mural monument commemorates Sir Edmond Thomas (d. 1723), 2nd baronet 'a person of great integrity, piety and charity' and his wife Mary, daughter of the Rt. Honourable John Howe of Stowell, Gloucestershire (d. 1746); also Sir Edmond Thomas, 3rd baronet and Member of Parliament for Glamorgan. The monument has two rectangular inscription tablets on a border enclosed above and to the side by swags as drapery and surmounted by three cherubic angels' heads. The piece is framed by pilasters beneath a moulded cornice and segmental pediment with both this and the tympanum broken to admit a painted achievement displaying the arms of Thomas of Wenvoe 'Sable, a chevron and canton ermine'. Reclining figures on top of the pediment are cherubs. The apron is flanked by floral wings and includes a plain cartouche on a rectangular panel against a background with tapering wings. On the south wall of the nave to the west of the south door is a brass memorial plaque to the memory of Trooper Cyril Llewellyn Nell of the Imperial Yeomanry who was killed on active service near Winburgh, South Africa in the Transvaal War in 1900, aged 21 years. Opposite on the north wall is a marble tablet recording the twelve names of the men from the parish who served their country in the Great War, 1914-1918. The nave has a simple open arch-braced roof which replaced an earlier, and lower wagon-truss roof in 1887.

The font is Victorian and has an octagonal bowl on a short circular stem of red marble. The bowl has a moulded rim above a plain frieze and again beneath. The top of the stem has several mouldings and a large roll-moulding connects it with a plain octagonal base which rests on a plain square plinth.

The tower opens to the nave by a crudely-pointed arch with glazed doors and the space above the doorway is filled with modern stained glass depicting an attractive representation of a Jesse tree with the Virgin and Child framed within the tree. The grapes and vine leaves are arranged as a spot pattern with two crowns of David and Solomon. The window was designed by Frank Roper of Penarth and was erected in 1981 in memory of the Reverend W. J. Christopher, rector of the parish from 1957 to 1976 and several generous benefactors of the church. The south doorway of the church is pointed and was reconstructed in Bath stone in 1876. The outer doorway of the south porch has an obtusely-pointed arch and above it is a round-headed niche containing an attractive statuette of the Blessed Virgin Mary, the patron saint of the church.

An inscribed stone above the west door of the tower records that the whole tower was removed from the north side of the chancel to its present position at the west end in 1699 when Wil. Morgan and Wil. Wade were churchwardens. The tower has a plain battlement and below is the usual corbel table of Welsh pattern and, unusual for a Vale church, a clock, the single face of which is in the east wall. The clock, made by John Smith of Derby, was placed in the church in 1884 by parishioners and friends in memory of Captain Robert Lascelles Jenner (d. 1883). The belfry windows are plain rectangular openings with louvres. The tower houses three large bells recast in 1882 by John Taylor of Loughborough from the original bells cast by T. Pyke and J. Kingston of Bridgwater in 1806. The churchyard cross to the south of the church has a restored cross (1930) but the original base and five steps remain underneath the three restored steps. The massive convoluted yew tree in the churchyard is reputed to be over 800 years old.

The church was restored in 1876. A gallery at the west end of the nave was removed, flagstones in the porch were replaced by encaustic tiles and wood block floors were laid down in the nave. New open benches of pitch pine replaced the old-fashioned pews and a new font was also erected. The Queen Anne windows in the nave were replaced by the present lancets and new doorways to the porch and tower reconstructed in Bath stone. It was intended to renew the roof of the nave but this work was deferred until 1887 due to lack of funds.

It was during the 19th century that Wenvoe church came into some prominence through the Jenner family. Apart from the years 1849-1853, four members of the Jenner family were rectors between 1834 and 1924, the most famous of whom was the last, the Reverend George Herbert Jenner, rector for 42 years (1882-1924). Father Jenner, as he was known, was one of the leaders of the Anglo-Catholic (High Church) Movement in the diocese and Wenvoe church contains memorials of his incumbency, the most notable being the rood screen between nave and chancel and the sanctuary lamps above the altar.

John Wesley, during his visits to the Vale, preached at St. Mary's Church, Wenvoe, on three occasions, in 1743, 1746 and 1763. The Reverend John Hodges, vicar of Wenvoe (1725-1777) was an intimate friend of John Wesley and was one of the clergy who supported him in his early campaign.

The church plate consists of an Elizabethan silver chalice and cover dated 1576. The registers date from 1588.

Wick Church

The parish church of Wick is dedicated to St. James and dates from the early part of the 12th century. It originated as a chapel and was given to Ewenny Priory in the latter half of the 12th century 'on condition that the Prior should provide for three services weekly' in it. In 1575 we find that the 'Rectory and Parsonage impropriate' of Wick belonged to Thomas Carne who transferred them to Humphrey Wyndham and John Turberville. Wick was probably 'the chapel annexed (to St. Brides Major) called the Noige which hath burying and christening in it as a parish church' mentioned as served by the vicar of St. Bride's in 1563. It was not recorded in 1603 but in 1771 (Bishop Barrington's *Llandaff Diocesan Book*) it was a curacy annexed to St. Bride's Major and was valued jointly with the latter living, at £80. Again in 1835 it was styled a curacy attached to St. Bride's. The church of Wick was served by the vicars of St. Bride's Major until 1950 when Marcross, Monknash and Wick were grouped together to form one benefice. In 1983 these three parishes were joined with St. Donat's and Llantwit Major church to form the Rectorial Benefice of Llantwit Major.

The church consists of chancel, nave, south porch and western tower containing one bell. The church is built in the Early English style although the oldest parts of the structure—the chancel arch, the inner south doorway and a small window in the chancel—date from the 12th century. The chancel arch is Norman and semicircular with square corners without mouldings and a primitive abacus. Two large squints or hagioscopes which pierce the chancel wall on either side increase the view of the altar from the nave; each of these apertures is crowned by a round-headed arch. The Laudian east window is of three lights with rounded heads and square label with floriated square label stops. It is the only stained glass window in the church and is a memorial to three parishioners belonging to the same family. The centre light portrays Our Lord as the Good Shepherd and is in memory of Edward Williams (Sealand) (d. 1940); the right-hand light depicts the figure of St. Elizabeth and commemorates Elizabeth Williams (Sealand) (d. 1971); the left-hand light contains a representation of the Blessed Virgin Mary and is to the memory of Mary James (The Grange) (d. 1979). This stained glass window was designed by Messrs. G. Maile & Sons Ltd. of Regents Park, London, and was erected in the church in 1940 but the inscriptions in the outer lights were inserted in the 1970s.

There are unusual niches in the east wall on either side of the altar. The niche

on the north side has an Early English trefoil head but above this is a kind of miniature pediment of steep form appropriately decorated. On the bevelled sides of the niche fleurs-de-lys and other ornaments protrude in high relief; this niche, now empty, would probably have contained a statue of St. James, the patron saint of the church. The niche to the south is wider and has a flattened round head within the curve of which is an open scroll of Early English work.

The windows on the south wall of the chancel comprise a broad single light window pointed and deeply splayed within and labelled without, and a small Norman round-headed lancet. Between these windows is a priest's door with obtusely-pointed arch. The altar has a pre-Reformation mensa or altar slab incised with a central consecration cross. On the north wall of the sanctuary is a memorial to Frances Hewett (née Prichard) (d. 1828) aged 30 years who lies buried in the chancel. The memorial takes the form of a figure in loose classical dress seemingly distraught leaning against the ubiquitous urn, a symbol of death derived from antiquity. The urn has a frieze of Greek key decoration and the memorial inscription below in Roman lettering is topped by a band of acanthus leaves. The memorial was erected by her husband, John Hewett, an officer in the Royal Marines, and her brother, the Reverend John Prichard.

On the north side of the chancel a doorway with pointed archway leads to a modern vestry. Above this doorway is a brass memorial to Frances (d. 1865) daughter of Thomas Thornewill, Esq. of Dove Cliff, Staffordshire, and her husband Colonel John Hewett, J.P., D.L., of Tyr Mab Ellis (d. 1868). They both lie buried in a vault below the floor of the chancel. At the base of the plaque are two coats of arms; one for Hewett 'Gules a chevron engrailed between three horned owls argent' with the crest 'The stump of a tree sprouting proper thereon a falcon close, argent, legged and belled or'. The motto is 'Une pure foy' (A pure faith). The other shield is for Thornewill 'Argent a bend vert fimbriated throughout between two cross crosslets vert' with the crest 'A tree eradicated proper'. The motto is 'Fidelitas' (Fidelity).

The chancel has an arch-braced roof supported on stone corbels. No details of the rood-loft remain. The chancel rises by two steps and there is a third at the altar rail. On the north side of the chancel arch is an 18th-century memorial monument with rectangular inscription panel flanked by columns supported by an entablature and broken pediment. It is to the memory of members of the Lloyd family of Westard, among them the Reverend Jenkin Lloyd, rector of Coychurch from 1705 to 1708 and Watkin Lloyd Jenkin sometime Town Clerk of Cardiff.

The nave is lit by five 19th-century windows, all of the same design; the two on the north are probably insertions and the three on the south wall are most likely replacements. Each window consists of two broad trefoiled lights with an obtusely-pointed arch over the embrasure of the internal splay. The thickness of the walls makes the interior splaying of the windows a conspicuous feature throughout the church. From the nave a doorway with straight sides and pointed head leads to the space beneath the tower. The nave has an arch-braced roof with a crenellated purlin. The Norman font of Sutton stone is tub-shaped and ornamented with cable moulding around the rim and roll-moulding around the base. It rests on a modern stone plinth and is placed near the south doorway. These large-sized fonts were used in the Middle Ages for the complete immersion of the infant during the service of Holy Baptism. The south porch, which has stone benches within, is a modern addition to the original structure. The inner doorway of the church has a round-headed Norman arch while the south doorway has a four-centred arch. The outer doorway of the porch is plain pointed.

The tower is tall and slender with a saddleback roof. In the upper part of the tower there is a long slit window on the south and two others, perhaps double the length, on its east and west faces which enable the bell to be heard. On the north wall of the tower is a circular orifice with a small modern canopy like the one at St. Mary Hill church. This was the former outlet for the chimney flue when the church had a chimney place at the base of the tower. The tower houses a single bell without inscription or bellfounders' marks which came from St. Michael's church, Bilston, Staffordshire. It is a tenor bell in C weighing 75 lbs. including the clapper. The former bell, which was removed due to a crack, bore the inscription 'George Thomas churchwarden 1807'. At the base of the tower is a small gravestone to John Deere (d. 1681) son of John Deere.

In 1765 the seats or pews in the church were in such a decayed and dilapidated condition that they were unfit for the parishioners to kneel or sit in. Consequently new seats or pews had to be erected in their stead. The church underwent a thorough Victorian restoration about 1871 so that the present structure has the aspect of a new building. Most of the walls were rebuilt, new roofs raised and modern windows inserted. A new porch and vestry were also added. The tower was also partially rebuilt at this time. The cost of the restoration amounted to over £900 and the work was carried out according to plans and specifications drawn up by John Prichard, the diocesan architect. A grant of £25 was obtained from the Incorporated Church Building Society towards reseating and restoring the church.

In the churchyard to the south of the church is the stump and pedestal of the churchyard cross resting on three steps. At the entrance to the churchyard is a modern lychgate. The church plate consists of a silver chalice dated 1637. The cover of the cup when turned back forms the paten. Round the lip is the inscription 'The Communion Cup of the parish of Wick, Edward Lloyd 1637'. The registers date from 1813.

Glossaries
Bibliography
and
Indexes

Glossary of Architectural and Ecclesiastical Terms used in this Work

ABACUS—the uppermost member of a capital. It takes the thrust at the point of spring of an arch.

ABBEY—a monastic community of monks under an abbot.

ABBOT—the title of the head of a large religious house following the rule of St. Benedict, including Cistercians.

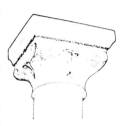

ABACUS

ACANTHUS—in Classical or Renaissance architecture stylised leaf form of the acanthus plant, called in English 'Bears breech', the leaves of which are often imitated in decorating the Corinthian and Composite capitals of columns.

ACROTERIA—Quadrant-like bodies projecting upwards at the apex and ends of the pediment on hanging wall-monuments.

ACANTHUS

ACT OF UNIFORMITY 1661—this act ordered the exclusive use of the 1662 Prayer Book in all places of worship from St. Bartholomew's Day (24th August, 1662). Ministers failing to observe the Act were deprived of their livings.

ACUTE ARCH—a two-centred arch higher than equilateral.

ADVOWSON—right of presentation to a living or benefice.

ACROTERIA

AGNUS DEI—the figure of a lamb passant carrying a pennon adorned with a cross symbolizing Christ. The attribute of John the Baptist. Also name given to the wafer stamped with this emblem and to the musical setting of part of the eucharist.

AISLE—wing of a church separated from the central part by a row of columns. Sometimes the whole or part of an aisle was used almost as a private pew by some notable local family and was called by their name.

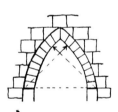

ACUTE ARCH

ALABASTER—soft, slightly translucent limestone used for sculpture.

ALMONRY—in any medieval monastic or other church a room or place where alms were distributed.

ALPHA AND OMEGA—the names of the first (Λ) and last (Ω) letters of the Greek alphabet which form the sacred monogram Λ-Ω.

ALTAR—table in Christian churches for the celebration of the Holy Eucharist.

AGNUS DEI

ALTAR RAILS—a low railing of wood or metal separating the sanctuary from the rest of the chancel. In 1610 Archbishop Laud directed that altar rails should be erected in the sanctuary to stop stray dogs defiling it.

AMBO—a reading-desk or lectern which was raised on two steps for the reading of the Epistle and the Gospel.

AMDG—the initial letters of the Latin Ad Majorem Dei gloriam 'To the greater glory of God'.

AMPHISBAENA—a fabulous two-headed, two-tailed serpent.

ANGLE BUTTRESS—two buttresses meeting at right angles at the corner of a building.

ANGLO-CATHOLIC—a lay member or priest of the Church of England, heir of the Oxford movement which emphasizes Catholic tradition and ceremonial.

ANNATES—the first year's revenue of any ecclesiastical benefice paid to the Pope. Conditionally restrained in England in 1532, transferred to the Crown in 1534, became Queen Anne's Bounty in 1704.

ANNULET—a shaft-ring, a motif of 12th and 13th centuries.

APEX—the top or highest point of a pyramid, pediment, roof or window.

APOSTLES' CREED—a concise statement of faith used in the liturgy and frequently set to music. It derives its name from the legend that, before departing on their respective missions, each of the Apostles contributed a clause.

APPROPRIATION—a benefice was said to be appropriated when it was annexed to the perpetual ownership and use of some religious body, especially to a monastery which thereby became perpetual incumbent and so was bound to provide for the care of souls in that benefice. After the dissolution all the appropriated benefices came into the hands of the Crown and many of them were granted or sold to laymen who thereby became lay rectors or impropriators.

APRON—a panel below a hanging wall-monument sometimes shaped and decorated.

APSE—a semicircular or polygonal eastern end to a chancel.

ARABESQUE—decoration used for enriching flat surfaces either inlaid in mosaic or carved in low relief using flowing lines, tendrils and foliage.

ARCADE—row of arches supported on columns.

ARCADING—rows of small arches forming arcades but used solely as decoration in Norman architecture.

ANNULET

APSE

APRON

ARABESQUE

ARCADING

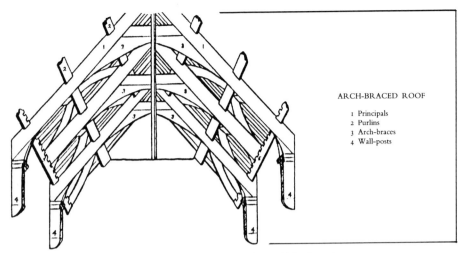

ARCH-BRACED ROOF

1 Principals
2 Purlins
3 Arch-braces
4 Wall-posts

ARCH—a curved structure formed of wedge-shaped blocks of stone (voussoirs) held together by mutual pressure and supported only at the sides.

ARCH-BRACE—a carved piece of timber used to strengthen a principal or rafter.

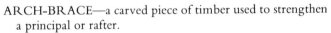

ASTRAGAL

ARCHDEACON—a cleric having a defined administrative authority delegated to him by the bishop in the whole or part of the diocese. The territory assigned to him is known as an archdeaconry and gives him a territorial title, e.g. Archdeacon of Llandaff.

ARCHITRAVE—lower part of the entablature.

ARTS AND CRAFTS MOVEMENT—the Arts and Crafts Movement originated in the late 19th century in an attempt to revive handicrafts and improve standards of decorative design in Victorian England.

AUMBRY

ASHLAR—regularly laid stone blocks with squared edges and smooth faces.

ASTRAGAL—a small semicircular moulding usually encircling a column.

AUMBRY—recess built into the north or south wall of the church near the altar to hold sacred vessels used at communion.

AVE MARIA—the opening words in Latin of the invocation addressed to St. Mary the Virgin known as the 'Hail Mary', or the angelic salutation because it is derived from the Archangel Gabriel's greeting at the Annunciation.

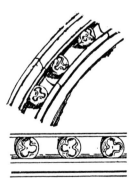

BALLFLOWER—a characteristic enrichment of the early 14th century consisting of a globular ball carved with the appearance of an outer skin pierced and folded back in petals.

BALLFLOWER

BALUSTER—small column, the shaft of which is characterized by a pear-shaped swelling at the lower part.

BALUSTRADE—a protective rail or cornice supported by balusters or ornamental uprights.

BALUSTRADE

BAR TRACERY—a development of plate tracery using slender shafts and shaped members branching out from the mullions to form a decorative pattern in the window head.

BAR TRACERY

BAROQUE ARCHITECTURE—a phase of architecture specially prevalent in the Catholic countries of Europe during the 17th and 18th centuries.

BARREL ROOF—semicircular or curved roof.

BARREL VAULT—a continuous semicircular arch or tunnel of stone used from very early times in Romanesque architecture.

BARREL VAULT

BASE—the projecting member between the shaft of a column and the plinth.

BATH STONE—a yellow-coloured building stone quarried at Bath.

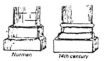

Norman   14th century

BASE

BATTER—a slight inward inclination of a wall from its base upwards.

BATTLEMENT—a form of parapet cut with regular indentures as in a castle.

BAY—the vertical compartment between two columns, or roof-trusses or transverse vaulting-ribs and their supporting buttresses.

BELFRY—part of the tower in which the bells are hung.

BELL-CAPITAL—a form of capital of which the chief characteristic is a reversed bell between the neck moulding and upper moulding.

BELLCOTE—a small arch which contains a bell.

BELLCOTE

BENCH ENDS—the end of a bench or seat in a church often carved with great imagination and beauty in English churches of late Gothic date.

BENEDICTINES—monks of the Order of St. Benedict called the Black Monks after the colour of their habit. They follow the Rule of St. Benedict and trace their origin to the monastery which he established at Monte Cassino, Italy, circa 529.

BENEFICE—a term originally used for a grant of land for life as a reward (beneficium) for services. Parochial benefices in the Church of England are of three kinds—rectories, vicarages and perpetual curacies.

BENCH ENDS

BILLET—ornamental moulding of regular raised rectangles used in Norman architecture.

BLACK LETTER—the Gothic script that replaced Lombardic script towards the end of the 14th century.

BLIND TRACERY—in Gothic architecture an imitation of actual window tracery on a flat surface carved in solid wood or stone on chancel screens or pulpits. Tracery sunk in the solid not perforated or open.

BLIND TRACERY

BONEDD Y SAINT—a 12th-century tract outlining the lineage of the Celtic saints.

BOOK OF LLANDAFF—the Book of Llandaff (Liber Landavensis) was compiled between 1120 and 1140 to justify the claims of Bishop Urban (d. 1134) to churches dedicated to the three patron saints of Llandaff (Dyfrig, Teilo and Euddogwy) which lay outside the diocese.

BOSS

BOSS—projecting ornament placed at intersection of ribs in a roof to disguise the joint. It is eventually carved with foliage, faces or heraldic shields.

BOSS

BOX-PEW—a box pew is one with a high wooden enclosure all round and a small door; it is essentially a Georgian type.

BRACE—in a roof-truss or timber framing an inclined member to support an horizontal member.

BRACKET—an ornamental projection from the face of a wall to support a statue, especially at the east end of the chancel and aisles where they supported statues which were placed near the altar.

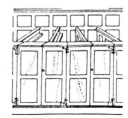

BOX PEW

BRASS—monumental plates of brass or alloy called latten inlaid on large slabs of stone or marble set into the floor of the church and engraved with the figure of the deceased. Finest brass dates from the 14th century.

BRATTISHING—a form of ornamental cresting on top of a screen or cornice in English late Gothic architecture and composed of Tudor flowers.

BRESSUMMER—the main beam supporting a rood-loft.

BRATTISHING

BROACH STOP—a stop with two sloping facets like a half-pyramid.

BROKEN PEDIMENT—when the base of the triangular pediment is left open.

BULL—a formal proclamation or letter on a subject of major importance, that is issued by the pope and is sealed with a bulla, a lead seal.

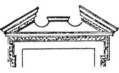

BROKEN PEDIMENT

BUTTRESS—mass of masonry built against and so supporting a wall.

CABLE MOULDING—a convex Norman moulding carved spirally to imitate a cable or rope.

CADW—Welsh Historic Monuments—carries out the statutory responsibilities of the Secretary of State for Wales for protecting, conserving and presenting monuments and historic buildings in Wales.

CAMBER—the slight curved rise given to a beam of wide span or to the underside of a flat arch to avoid sagging or the appearance of sagging.

CANT—an oblique line cutting off the corner of a rectangle usually at forty-five degrees.

CAP—an abbreviation of capital.

CAPITAL—the uppermost part of a column or pilaster in Romanesque or Gothic architecture often ornamented and carved with figures and designs.

CARTOUCHE—in architectural ornament of the Renaissance period a carved panel resembling a sheet of paper with the edges turned over, or a scroll.

CASTELLATED—decorated with battlements.

CAVETTO—a bold concave moulding usually a quadrant in section.

CELL—a room in which a member of a religious community lives.

CHALICE—a cup with bowl, stem and base usually of precious metal in which the wine is consecrated at the Eucharist. The chalice represents the cup used at the Last Supper and is a symbol of Christ's agony.

CHAMFER—the surface formed when an angle is cut away obliquely.

CHANCEL—that part of the church beyond the nave which contains the sanctuary and the choir.

CHANCEL ARCH—single span at the west end of the chancel separating it from the nave.

CHANTRY CHAPEL—a small chapel (attached to a church) in which masses were sung for the soul of the person who had originally endowed the chapel.

CHAPEL—small church or sub-division of larger church with its own altar.

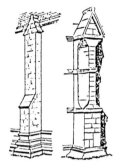

BUTTRESS

CABLE MOULDING

CARTOUCHE

CAVETTO

CHALICE

CHAMFER

CHAPTER—the governing body of a monastery or a cathedral presided over, in the case of an Anglican cathedral, by the Dean.

CHARNEL HOUSE—a vaulted room under or adjoining a church to receive the human bones disinterred by the grave-digger.

CHASUBLE—an outer garment, a vestment made of silk, often ornamented with floral or other symbolic motifs, worn by the priest during the celebration of the Eucharist.

CHASUBLE

CHERUB—a winged head which appears on monuments and gravestones.

CHEVRON—a Norman decoration formed by zigzags deeply cut.

CHERUB

CHI-RHO MONOGRAM—the symbolic monogram composed by the imposition of the first two Greek letters of Christos 'Christ', Chi(X) on rho(P).

CHEVRON

CHOIR—that portion of a church which is specially reserved for choristers. It usually occupies the western part of the chancel.

CHRISM—a special oil, made of olive-oil and balsam used liturgically especially in the consecration of Bishops and Kings and in baptism and confirmation.

CHI RHO

CHURCHWARDENS—men acting as the chief lay officers of a parish. The office has been in existence at least since 1127. There are normally two wardens, the Rector's (or vicar's) warden and the People's Warden.

CIBORIUM—a vessel to contain the element of bread at the Eucharist usually shaped like a chalice with a lid.

CINQUEFOIL—five cusped ornamental filling for a circle or arch.

CINQUEFOIL

CISTERCIAN ORDER—the order of white monks so called from the mother house of Citeaux which was founded in 1098 by St. Robert of Molesme who sought to establish a form of Benedictinism stricter and more primitive than any then existing.

CLAS, CLASAU—a monastery of the Celtic church consisting of a body of hereditary canons, often headed by a layman. The Normans did their utmost to suppress the Celtic church and the clasau were replaced by cathedral chapters or collegiate churches.

CLASPING BUTTRESS—formed when a solid pier of masonry literally encloses or 'clasps' the external angle of two walls.

CLASPING BUTTRESS

CLERESTORY—the upper storey of the nave above the aisle roofs pierced with a series of windows illuminating the interior.

CLERK—a term applied loosely to all clergy. 'Clerk in holy orders' is now in the Church of England a term for those who are ordained bishop, priest or deacon. In the Middle Ages the term 'clerk' was applied to all clergy in minor orders.

CLOISTER—a covered walk or arcade in a monastery or priory.

CLUSTERED COLUMN—an apparently single column formed of several stone shafts or pillars attached to each other.

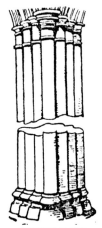

COMPOUND PIER
(CLUSTERED SHAFT)

COFFERING—a series of sunken panels in the surface of a wooden screen or ceiling.

COLLAR-BEAM—in a roof a horizontal beam framed to and serving to tie a pair of rafters together some distance above the wallplate level.

COMMON RAFTERS—the sloping rafters carrying slates or tiles in any type of sloping roof.

COMMUNION TABLE—a piece of church furniture usually placed near the wall at the east end of the chancel where the priest stands to administer the sacrament. The communion table was substituted for the stone altar at the time of the Reformation.

COMPOUND PIER—a pier with several shafts attached or detached, also called a 'clustered shaft'.

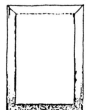

COFFERING

COLLAR BEAM

CONSOLE—in Classical architecture an ornamental bracket of slight projection but of much greater height with two reversed volutes.

CONTINUOUS MOULDING—a term applied to the mouldings of an arch which are continued without interruption down the uprights to the ground or base.

COPING—a protective capping or covering of stone on the top of a wall.

CORBEL—short block of stone projecting from wall and supporting a weight, often carved or moulded.

CORBEL TABLE—series of corbels supporting a parapet.

CORBELLING—masonry courses each built out beyond the one below like a series of corbels to support a turret, etc.

CORINTHIAN ORDER—a type of column in Classical architecture named after the region of Greece—Corinthos— in which it originated.

CONSOLE

CORBEL
(*Llancarvan*)

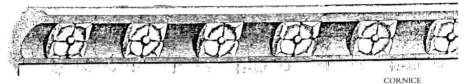

CORNICE

CORNICE—projecting upper portion of an entablature or any projecting top course.

CRADLE ROOF—see WAGON ROOF.

CREDENCE—a small table or shelf near the altar on which bread, wine and water are placed for the celebration of the Eucharist.

CREDO—Latin for 'I believe' the part of the Mass at which the Nicene Creed is said or sung.

CRENELLATION—a battlement.

CRENELLATION

CRESTING—a line of ornament on the ridge of a roof or on the top of a screen or reredos.

CRESTING

CROCKET—in Gothic architecture a little hook, or a hook-shaped bunch of foliage placed at intervals on a canopy or coping of gable.

CROSIER—the pastoral staff of a bishop whose head resembles a shepherd's crook.

CROCKET

CROWN—the highest point of a semicircular arch or vault.

CRYPT—a chamber under a building either wholly or partly underground.

CURATE—until the 17th century the term 'curate' was often synonymous with 'incumbent' but latterly it has been applied almost exclusively to an assistant parish priest paid a salary or stipend and removable by the incumbent or bishop.

CURVILINEAR TRACERY—window tracery consisting of curved lines.

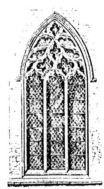

CURVILINEAR TRACERY

CUSHION CAPITAL—in Romanesque architecture a cubical capital with its lower corners cut away and rounded to resemble a cushion.

CUSP—point between the small arcs of trefoil and quatrefoil tracery.

CUSHION CAPITAL

DAGGER—a form of tracery-light cusped and pointed at both ends resembling in outline a dagger.

DEAN—the head of a cathedral 'primus inter pares' of the canons. He is president of the chapter and controls the services, the fabric and administration of the cathedral largely independent of the bishop, to whom he ranks next.

CUSP

DECORATED STYLE—period of English architecture from about 1300 to 1377 also called Middle-Pointed or Mid-Gothic.

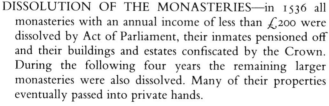

DECORATED STYLE

DEMI-SHAFT—a shaft or column half-sunk into a wall.

DENTIL—a small block used in rows in the cornices of Classical buildings for purely ornamental purposes.

DENTIL

DEPOSITION—the taking down of the body of Christ from the cross and laying it in the sepulchre.

DEVIL'S DOOR—door on north side of nave which was supposed to be left open at baptism for the escape of the exorcised devil.

DIAPER—decoration of surfaces with squares, diamonds and other patterns.

DIOCESE—the area of jurisdiction of a bishop. Each diocese includes one or more archdeaconries, each archdeaconry several rural deaneries, each rural deanery several parishes

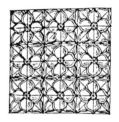

DIAPER

DISESTABLISHMENT OF THE WELSH CHURCH—by the Welsh Church Act of 1914, which took effect on 31st March, 1920, the four Welsh dioceses ceased to be part of the Province of Canterbury. In the reorganization which followed, two new dioceses were created: Monmouth on 29th September, 1921 and Swansea and Brecon on 4th April, 1923.

DISSOLUTION OF THE MONASTERIES—in 1536 all monasteries with an annual income of less than £200 were dissolved by Act of Parliament, their inmates pensioned off and their buildings and estates confiscated by the Crown. During the following four years the remaining larger monasteries were also dissolved. Many of their properties eventually passed into private hands.

DOGTOOTH

DOGTOOTH—late Norman and Early English ornament consisting of a series of four-cornered stars placed diagonally and raised pyramidly. Used to cover hollow mouldings.

DONATIVE—a spiritual preferment, church or vicarage which is in the free gift or collation of the patron without presentation to the bishop and without admission, institution or induction of the donee.

DROP ARCH

DORSAL—a curtain or hanging often embroidered, hung at the back of an altar instead of a reredos.

DRESSINGS—the stones used about an angle, window or other feature when worked to a finished face whether smoothed, moulded or sculptured.

DRIPSTONE—see HOOD MOULD.

DROP ARCH—an arch whose span is greater than its radii.

DRUM—the cylindrical part of a pulpit.

EARLY ENGLISH STYLE—period of English architecture from 1200 to 1300.

EAST WINDOW—usually the largest window in the church behind the altar.

EARLY ENGLISH STYLE

EAVES—the underpart of a sloping roof overhanging a wall.

ECCLESIASTICAL COMMISSIONERS—a body appointed in 1835 to consider reforms in the management of church revenues. This body made permanent by Act of Parliament in 1836, continued until 1948 when it was combined with Queen Anne's Bounty as the Church Commissioners for England.

EFFIGY

ECCLESIASTICAL DUTIES AND REVENUES ACT 1840—the main object of this measure was to effect the most radical proposals of the Ecclesiastical Commission by abolishing all non-resident prebends and sinecure rectories attached to cathedrals and resident canonries above the number of four to each cathedral. There were certain exceptions to this Act. The money saved was used to augment poor livings and create new parishes.

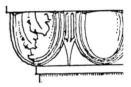

EGG AND TONGUE MOULDING

ECCLESIOLOGIST—periodical first published in November 1841 by the Cambridge Camden Society for those interested in the study of ecclesiastical architecture and church-building. It produced critical accounts of contemporary church building and enlargement. Ceased publication 1868.

ELLIPTICAL ARCH

EFFIGY—sculptured likeness of a person carved in stone.

EGG AND TONGUE MOULDING—patterns of alternating oval and pointed motifs used to enrich ovolo mouldings.

ELLIPTICAL ARCH—a half ellipse from a centre on the springing line.

EMBATTLED—furnished with battlements.

EMBRASURE—open portion of a battlement.

ENCAUSTIC TILES—glazed clay tiles of different colours used on the floor of the church.

ENGAGED COLUMN—a column built into a wall.

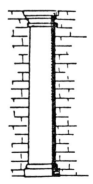

ENGAGED COLUMN

ENTABLATURE—horizontal members above the columns consisting of architrave, frieze and cornice in Classical building.

ENTASIS—the swelling in the middle of a baluster or of the shaft of a column.

EPITAPH—an inscription to the memory of a deceased person on a tomb or monument.

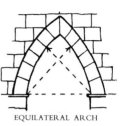

EQUILATERAL ARCH

EQUILATERAL ARCH—an arch produced by two curves each with a radius equal to the span and meeting in a point at the top. Also called a pointed arch.

ESTABLISHED CHURCH ACT 1836—carried into effect the reports of the Ecclesiastical Commissioners so far as they related to dioceses and episcopal revenues.

EXTRADOS—the outer curved face of an arch or vault.

EYELET—a small aperture in a merlon of a tower.

FACULTY—authorization or licence from the Bishop of the diocese to carry out additions or alterations to church fabrics and churchyards. The issue of a faculty is preceded by the citation of persons with a proper reason for objection.

FENESTRATION—a general term applied to the arrangement of windows in a building.

FINIAL
(*Llancarvan*)

FESTOON

FESTOON—Classical decoration of drapery or garlands of fruit and flowers suspended at the ends or bases of hanging wall-monuments.

FIELDED PANEL—a panel with a raised central area.

FILLET—a narrow flat band used to separate two mouldings.

FINIAL—ornament on top of a spire, pinnacle, gable.

FIRST POINTED—Victorian Gothic term for Early English-style architecture.

FLAMBOYANT TRACERY—originally a French form of tracery but also found in this country. It is a further development of flowing tracery but has an upward tendency giving a flame-like form.

FLAT ARCH—an arch which is almost flat but given a slight camber to avoid sagging.

FLEUR-DE-LYS—a variety of lily, symbol of purity and in particular of the purity of St. Mary the Virgin.

FLAMBOYANT TRACERY

FLEUR-DE-LYS

FLOWING TRACERY (OR CURVILINEAR TRACERY)—a 14th-century form sometimes in conjunction with Geometrical tracery consisting of sinuous lines with circles drawn at top and bottom into ogee shapes.

FLOWING TRACERY

FLUTING—vertical channelling on the shaft of a column or pillar.

FLUTING

FLYING BUTTRESS—a stone buttress in the form of an arch prop, supported at one end by the main wall of a building and at the other by a pier, in order to resist a lateral thrust.

FOIL—area between projecting points in tracery.

FOLIAGE—a carved or sculptured representation of an ornamental assemblage of leaves of plants and flowers.

FOLIATED—any surface covered with leaf ornament.

FONT—structure designed to hold the holy water for baptism.

FOUR-CENTRED ARCH

FOUR-CENTRED ARCH—a pointed arch of four arcs, the two outer and lower ones springing from centres on the springing line, the two inner and upper arcs from centres below the springing line. Also known as a depressed or Tudor arch.

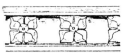

FOUR LEAF DECORATION

FOUR-LEAF DECORATION—a very favourite ornament in the Decorated and Perpendicular styles.

FREESTONE—fine-grained stone which can be cut in any direction. Usually limestone or red sandstone.

FRET

FRET—an ornamental pattern of repeated combinations of straight, vertical and horizontal lines.

FRIEZE—the middle division in an entablature between the architrave and the cornice; generally any band of ornament immediately below a cornice.

FRIEZE

FRONTAL—a hanging of silk often richly embroidered or patterned, placed over the front of an altar. In most cases its main colour is the liturgical colour of the season or feast.

GABLE—end of roof of triangular or other form.

GABLET—small ornamental gable or canopy formed over buttresses, niches, etc.

GABLET

GALILEE—a term applied to the west end of the nave. It was considered to be somewhat less sacred than the other portion of the building.

GALLERY—upper storey at the west end of the nave.

GARGOYLE—spout in form of a carved grotesque human or animal head projecting from the top of a wall to throw off rainwater.

GARGOYLE
(*St. Lythans*)

GEOMETRICAL TRACERY—consists of simple symmetrical shapes such as circles, trefoils, etc.

GEORGIAN STYLE—the architecture during the period of the reign of the 'four Georges' 1714-1830. Its earliest phase was mainly 'Palladian' and its last phase 'Regency'.

GLEBE—a portion of farmland once set aside for the maintenance of a parish priest who lived in the glebe-house or parsonage.

GLORIA IN EXCELSIS DEO—the Latin for 'Glory to God in the highest', the opening words of the angels at the Annunciation of the shepherds incorporated into a hymn of praise which is sung on Sundays and festivals except in Advent and Lent.

GNOMON—pin of sundial or scratch dial showing time by its shadow on marked surface.

GOTHIC ARCHITECTURE—the style of architecture in use from the latter part of the 12th century to the middle of the 16th century.

GOTHIC ARCHITECTURE—the style of architecture in use from the latter part of the 12th century to the end of the 15th century.

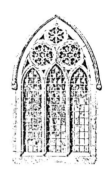

GRADINE—a shelf or ledge above and behind the altar on which the cross, candle-sticks, etc. may be placed rather than on the altar itself.

GRAFFITO—mural scribbling or drawing.

GRANGE—a farmhouse belonging to a monastery worked by lay tenants of the monastery.

GREAT TITHES—the tithe of the greater crops such as wheat, barley and oats was usually the prerogative of the rector as distinct from the smaller tithes taken by the vicar.

GREEK CROSS—cross with all four arms of equal length.

GREEK KEY DECORATION—an ornamental pattern of repeated combination of straight vertical and horizontal lines. Also called fret.

GREEK REVIVAL—a movement which arose from the interest in Greece as a source for architectural style. The Greek Revival lasted till about 1840 in England alongside the Gothic Revival.

GRID TRACERY—a series of narrow lancet lights with cusped heads of upright character in tracery usually divided by a transome.

GROIN—the angle formed by an intersection of vaults.

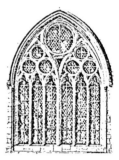

GEOMETRICAL TRACERY

GREEK KEY DECORATION

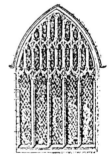

GRID TRACERY

GUILLOCHE

GROUTING—thin semi-liquid cement or mortar poured into the internal joints of masonry or rubble-work.

GUILLOCHE—an ornament of two regularly interlacing bands forming a series of circles.

HAGIOSCOPE—an opening usually diagonal in the walls of a chancel especially the dividing wall between nave and chancel.

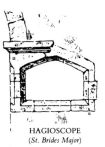

HAGIOSCOPE
(*St. Brides Major*)

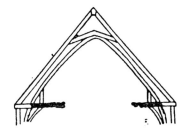

HAMMERBEAM ROOF

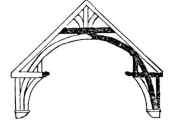

15th CENTURY HAMMERBEAM TRUSS

HAMMERBEAM—bracket forming part of the principal truss of an open timber roof.

HATCHMENT—a lozenge-shaped armorial board formerly exhibited at funerals then hung up in the church.

HAUNCH—the part of an arch between the crown and the springing.

HELM ROOF—a helm roof has four inclined faces joined at the top with a gable at the foot of each.

HERRINGBONE WORK—an arrangement of stones or tiles laid diagonally to form a zig-zag pattern on a floor or wall.

HEXAGON—a figure with six sides and six angles.

HIP—the external angle formed by the intersection of the sloping sides of a roof.

HOOD MOULD—projecting moulding to throw off the rain on the face of a wall, above an arch, doorway or window. Also called label or dripstone.

HORSESHOE ARCH—a stilted arch with the masonry between the springing line and imposts inclined towards.

HOUR-GLASS STAND—a bracket or frame of iron for receiving the hour-glass which was often placed near the pulpit.

IMPOST—flat horizontal projecting stone placed at the springing of an arch.

HELM ROOF

HERRINGBONE WORK

HOOD MOULD

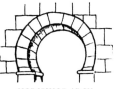

HORSESHOE ARCH

IMPOST

IMPROPRIATION—the transfer or annexation of some form of ecclesiastical benefice to a lay holder. After the Dissolution the majority of these appropriated benefices passed into the hands of impropriators and lay rectors who appointed perpetual curates as incumbents.

INCISED SLABS—stone or alabaster slabs with figures engraved on them used as sepulchral memorials.

INCORPORATED CHURCH BUILDING SOCIETY— founded in 1818 and incorporated in 1828, the Society took an important and continuous part in furthering the construction and repair of Anglican churches in England and Wales.

INCUMBENT—the holder of a benefice in the church of England whether as rector, vicar or curate.

INDENT—a shape chiselled out in a stone slab to receive a brass effigy.

INDUCTION—the stage in the appointment of a new incumbent of a parish in the Church of England when he is admitted to legal possession of the temporalities of the benefice and given control of his parish.

INRI—the initial letters of 'Iesus Nazarenus Rex Iudaeorum'—Jesus of Nazareth, King of the Jews'—the Latin phrase which Pilate caused to be placed on the cross at the Crucifixion.

INSTITUTION—the act of admission of a new incumbent into the spiritual care of his parish, distinct from and usually following into the temporalities.

INCISED SLABS

Scourges · Nails · Hammer and Tongs · Crown of Thorns

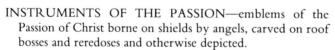

INSTRUMENTS OF THE PASSION—emblems of the Passion of Christ borne on shields by angels, carved on roof bosses and reredoses and otherwise depicted.

INSTRUMENTS OF THE PASSION

INTERSECTING TRACERY—a development of Y-tracery in which each mullion branches out into two curved bars intersecting the adjacent bars.

INTRADOS—the inner curve or underside or soffit of an arch.

IONIC ORDER—a type of column in Classical architecture named after the region of Greece—Ionia—in which it originated.

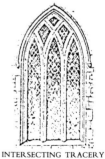

INTERSECTING TRACERY

JACOBEAN—a style of architecture predominant during the reign of James I (1603-25) characterized by an increasing awareness of purer classical forms.

JAMB—the vertical side of a doorway, window or archway.

JESSE, TREE OF—a representation usually in glass but sometimes in stone of the descent of Jesus from Jesse the father of David. Jesse is shown recumbent and asleep as the root of the tree with Jesus or the Virgin and Child as the topmost shoot of the main stem. Intermediate generations are shown as foliage or fruit on the main stock or branches.

JESSE (TREE OF)

KEY PATTERN—an ornamental pattern in classical architecture composed of combinations of straight lines usually on a flat surface.

KEYSTONE—the central wedge-shaped stone or voussoir at the top of an arch which locks the whole together.

KING POST TRUSS—a roof truss consisting of a central vertical member joining the tie-beam to the ridge beam.

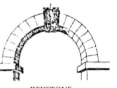

KEYSTONE

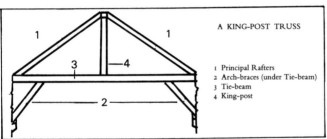

A KING-POST TRUSS

1 Principal Rafters
2 Arch-braces (under Tie-beam)
3 Tie-beam
4 King-post

KING'S BOOKS (LIBER REGIS)—a term often used for the 'Valor Ecclesiasticus' of 1535.

KYRIE ELEISON—the Greek for 'Lord have mercy' the opening words of the liturgical petition 'Lord have mercy, Christ have mercy/Christe eleison/Lord have mercy' which is either recited or sung alternatively by celebrant and server or congregation at the Eucharist.

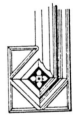

LABEL STOP

LABEL—see HOOD MOULD.

LABEL STOP—an ornamental boss terminating a label or hood mould.

LADY CHAPEL—a chapel dedicated to the Blessed Virgin Mary.

LANCET—tall, narrow window with a sharply-pointed head.

LANTERN—tower of which the whole is open to and visible from the floor.

LATTEN—copper alloy used for memorial brasses.

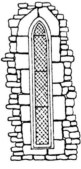

LANCET

LATTICE WINDOW—a window divided into small panes by lead bars, usually arranged diagonally.

LAUDIAN RAILS—railings placed around the altar area by Archbishop Laud in the 17th century.

LAY RECTOR—after the Dissolution many benefices came into the hands of lay rectors especially in churches appropriated to monasteries; the lay rector was responsible for providing a vicar or curate and was responsible for the repair and maintenance of the chancel.

LEAN-TO—a roof with a single slope built against a vertical wall.

LECTURER—a minister appointed to parishes by Parliament during the Commonwealth period who was not ordained but was to lecture in church on the Christian faith. The lecturer was maintained by voluntary contributions from the parishioners.

LEDGER—horizontal memorial slab, incised in low relief.

LIAS LIMESTONE—the characteristic stone of the Vale of Glamorgan of varying quality but normally a brittle light blue-grey stone.

LIGHT—part of a window between two mullions.

LIGHTS—the openings between the mullions of a screen or window, sometimes named bays in a screen.

LINENFOLD PANELLING—a form of panelling popular in England during the Tudor period in which the panels are carved with vertical grooves to resemble folded linen.

LINTEL—the horizontal member that spans an opening.

LLANDAFF CHURCH EXTENSION SOCIETY—the Society was founded in 1850 and its aim was not only to build churches but also to give grants towards the maintenance of clergy in new districts and parishes.

LOMBARDIC SCRIPT—the earlier form of lettering used on tombs before 1375.

LOOP-HOLE—arrow-slit in fortification.

LORD'S TABLE—a Protestant name for an altar.

LOUVRE (OR LUFFER BOARD)—one of a series of overlapping boards used in church belfries to admit air and let the bells be heard.

LOWSIDE WINDOW—a window usually in the south wall of the chancel of medieval churches generally with the lower part of the window unglazed but fitted with shutters. For the use of outside communicants and for a sanctus bell.

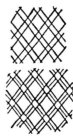
LATTICE WINDOW

LAUDIAN RAILS

LINENFOLD PANEL

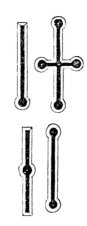
LOOP HOLES

LOZENGE—a diamond-shaped panel or figure with four equal sides.

LYCHGATE—churchyard gateway with a roof over it, under which the bier or coffin might be rested at a funeral.

LYCHGATE

MABSANT—in Wales a festival associated with the patron saint of the parish church. The patronal feast lost much of its religious significance after the Reformation and by the 19th century it had become a mainly secular festival.

MARBLE—a term applied to the finer varieties of limestone of hard and compact substance and capable of a high degree of polish.

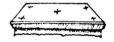

MENSA

MARQUETRY—a kind of mosaic or inlaid work formed of small pieces of wood.

MENHIR—literally a long stone; an upright prehistoric monolith.

MENSA—the flat stone slab forming the top of an altar marked with five consecration crosses.

MERLON

MERLON—the solid part of an embattled parapet between the embrasures (openings).

MIDDLE-POINTED—see DECORATED STYLE.

MOIETY—a half or one of two parts or divisions.

MONASTERY—a general term for a house of a religious community including seculars, male or female.

MONK—a member of a religious community for men living professed under monastic vows of poverty, chastity and obedience.

MONOLITH—a pillar or column of a single stone.

MOSAIC—a form of inlaying with small pieces of coloured glass, wood, enamel or other materials so as to form various ornamental patterns.

MOUCHETTE

MOUCHETTE—a curved dagger-shaped opening in tracery characteristic of the Decorated period.

MOULDING—contoured outline to projections, cornices, pillars, windows, etc.

MULLION—a vertical post or upright dividing an opening into lights.

MUNTIN—an intermediate upright in the framing of a screen or panel, set between the horizontal rails.

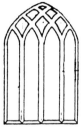

MULLION

MURAL PAINTING—wall decoration depicting religious scenes and events in medieval churches.

NAILHEAD—a moulding of the Early English style consisting of a band resembling a series of pyramidal nailheads.

NAVE—the central part of the church.

NECK, NECKING—the small convex moulding near the top of the shaft of a column and below the capital.

NAIL HEAD

NEO-CLASSICAL—the style of architecture and decoration which dominated virtually all of Europe from about 1760-1790.

NEW PARISHES ACT 1843—Sir Robert Peel's New Parishes Act of 1843 allowed the Ecclesiastical Commission to form, on the authority of an Order in Council, new parochial districts in heavily-populated areas.

NICENE CREED—the creed recited at Mass or Eucharist which came into use after the Council of Constantinople (381) replacing the earlier creed issued in 325 by the Council of Nicaea hence its (not strictly correct) name.

NIMBUS

NICHE—ornamental recess in a wall usually intended to contain an effigy.

NIMBUS—a bright disc, aureole or halo surrounding the head of saints.

NOOK SHAFT—shaft in the nook or recess of a jamb.

NORMAN ARCHITECTURE—phase of English architecture from 1066 to 1189.

NOTITIA EPISCOPATUM—a manuscript that comprises lists of benefices arranged by dioceses giving details of their values in the Liber Regis (King's Books) and the reputed contemporary value, the names of both incumbent and patron and the amount of the subsidy at the rate of 4 shillings per pound. The manuscript dates to 1664-1665 and is deposited at Lambeth Palace Library (MS.932).

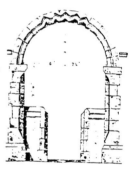

NORMAN ARCH
(Marcross)

NUNC DIMITTIS—the Latin opening words in the Vulgate version 'Nunc dimittis servuum tuum Domine' of the Song of Simeon 'Now lettest thou thy servant depart in peace for mine eyes have seen thy salvation'.

OBELISK—tapering shaft of stone, square in section with pyramidal top, Egyptian in origin but adopted in post-Reformation period as a monumental feature.

OCTAGON—a plane figure having eight sides and eight angles.

OCULUS—a central opening at the head of a traceried window larger than an eyelet.

OBELISK

OFF-SET or SET-OFF—the part of a buttress left exposed upwards when the part above is reduced in thickness.

OGEE—compound curve partly convex and partly concave.

OGEE ARCH—a pointed arch of double curvature, the lower curve being convex and the upper curve concave, used in late Gothic architecture.

OGEE ARCH

OGIVAL ARCH—an arch having a double or ogee curve but the term is often loosely applied to any pointed arch.

OPEN PEDIMENT—when the top of the pediment is opened.

OPEN PEDIMENT

ORATORY—a small chapel or room for private devotions and prayer.

ORDER—in classical architecture a column with base, shaft, capital and entablature decorated according to one of the accepted modes—Doric, Ionic and Corinthian.

OVIFORM—egg-shaped.

OVOLO MOULDING—a convex moulding used in all periods of architecture, usually a quarter of a circle.

OVOLO MOULDING

OXFORD MOVEMENT—the movement in the Church of England to reassert the Catholic tradition dating from 1833 when John Keble (1792-1866) preached his controversial sermon at Oxford. The principles were set out in a series of 'Tracts for the Times' (1833-41), hence the name Tractarians for members of the movement.

PANEL TRACERY—a form of tracery belonging to the Perpendicular style introduced in the 15th century.

PARAPET—a low wall sometimes battlemented, placed to protect any spot where there is a sudden drop.

PARISH—the general name in England and Wales for the area which forms the separate spiritual charge of a priest known as the incumbent or curate, that is, the person in charge or with 'cure' of souls.

PANEL TRACERY

PARSON—a rector is called parson or 'persona ecclesie' because he is the local personification of the church.

PARVISE—a room or chamber above a church porch.

PATERA—a circular or oval disc-like ornament usually rendered in a low relief; the term is also applied to flowers on Gothic cornices, etc.

PATRON, PATRONAGE—the right to fill a church or benefice by presentation or collation is called the advowson or right of patronage and the owner of the right is called the patron.

PATERA

PATRON SAINT—a patron saint of a church is the spiritual protector and advocate and spiritual patron of the church.

PEDESTAL—base of a column or statue.

PELICAN IN HER PIETY—a symbolic figure of a pelican on her nest wounding her breast in order to feed her young with her own blood. Used typically to represent the redeeming work of Christ.

PELICAN IN HER PIETY

PENDANT—a hanging ornament of 15th century date intended for the enrichment of a roof or screen.

PERPENDICULAR STYLE—style of English architecture from about 1377 to 1485.

PERPETUAL CURATE—the name given before the passing of the Pastoral Measure 1968 to a clerk who officiated in a parish to which he had been nominated by the Impropriator and licensed by the Bishop.

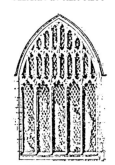

PERPENDICULAR

PEW—bench seat in a church, sometimes with a door.

PIETÀ—a sculpture or a picture representing the dead Christ after the Crucifixion lying on the knees of his mother.

PILASTER—a flat column against the face of a wall, usually engaged (i.e. built into it).

PILE—a large building or mass of buildings.

PILLAR—the column supporting the arch.

PINNACLE—an ornamental feature terminating either in pyramidal or conical form on the top of a Gothic buttress.

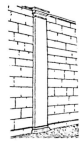

PILASTER

PISCINA—a niche containing a stone bowl or drain through which the water used by the priest was drained.

PITCH—inclination of a roof.

PLAQUE—an ornamental or commemorative tablet affixed to a wall.

PLATE TRACERY—early Gothic tracery formed by the grouping of separate lancets and an oculus beneath an arch, as if pierced through a solid plate of masonry.

PLINTH—the lowest projecting member of the base of a column or font.

PLURALITIES ACT 1836—an act forbidding any clergyman in the Church of England to hold simultaneously more than one ecclesiastical benefice with cure of souls except by dispensation of the Archbishop of Canterbury. The Act also provided more stringent regulations for residence.

PINNACLE

PISCINA
(*Llanfrynach*)

PLURALITY—the holding of two or more benefices at once by the same incumbent. Always discouraged by the church on account of the difficulty of exercising equally the cure of souls in all places at once.

POINTING—in masonry the finishing of rough mortar joints with fine mortar after the wall is complete.

POPPYHEAD—ornament often carved on the wooden ends of benches.

PORCH—covered entrance to the church to protect the south doorway.

PORTLAND STONE—an oolite building stone which is quarried in the Isle of Portland.

PLATE TRACERY

PREDELLA—the lowest part of a reredos immediately above the altar. Also the step or platform upon which an altar stands.

PRESBYTERY—that part in the eastern arm of the church between the choir and the sanctuary (i.e. high altar) reserved for the clergy.

PRESENTATION—the formal offering of a clerk by the patron of a church to the bishop as incumbent-to-be duly nominated and with suitable testimonies for institution and induction to the cure of a parish.

PRIEST'S DOOR—small entrance for the use of the priest located in the south wall of the chancel.

PRINCIPALS—the main trusses of a roof or the main rafters, posts, or braces in the wooden framework of a building.

PRIOR—in a priory the head of the convent. Often used also in later medieval times for the head of a cell or smaller house dependent on an abbey or priory.

PRIORY—a building occupied by a society of religious persons, the chief of whom was termed as prior or prioress.

POPPY HEADS

PULPIT—a pulpit is a raised stand of wood or stone surrounded by a parapet from which sermons are preached. Usually placed on the north side of the nave.

PURBECK MARBLE—a dark conglomerate from the Isle of Purbeck capable of receiving a high polish. Used for effigies particularly in the 13th century and for font bowls.

PURLIN—an horizontal timber resting on the principal rafters, posts or braces in the wooden framework of a building.

PURLIN

PUTLOG—in timber scaffolding a short horizontal member built at one end into the wall under repair and secured to the scaffold poles at the other end. The putlogs supported temporary platforms of boarding.

PYX—a small box or shrine sometimes called a 'tabernacle' intended to contain the reserved sacrament.

QUADRIPARTITE VAULT—one bay of vaulting divided into four quarters or compartments is termed quadripartite.

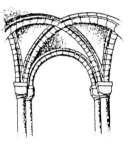

QUADRIPARTITE VAULT

QUARELLA STONE—formerly quarried immediately north of Bridgend became the best-known variety of Rhaetic sandstone.

QUARTER-ROUND MOULDING—an ovolo moulding which is one quarter of a circle in section.

QUATREFOIL—circular or square opening having four foils separated by cusps.

QUATREFOIL

QUEEN ANNE STYLE—English Renaissance domestic architecture of Queen Anne's reign 1702-14.

QUEEN ANNE'S BOUNTY—the annates and tenths diverted by Henry VIII were surrendered by Queen Anne in 1704 for the benefit of the church to form a fund which might be used to augment poor livings by grants of capital, not income, or by loans and payments for repairs of parsonage houses.

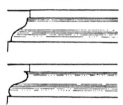

QUIRK

QUIRK—a sharp-edged groove or hollow moulding between two other mouldings mainly used in Gothic architecture.

QUOINS—stone dressings or ashlar at the angles of a building.

RAFTER or COMMON RAFTER—a member sloping from the wallplate to the ridge.

QUOINS

REBATE—a continuous rectangular notch or groove cut as an edge so that a door etc. may be fitted.

RECTILINEAR TRACERY—introduced in the 15th century, the mullions pass uninterrupted to the head of the arch. The tracery consists of upright straight-sided panels above the window lights.

RECTOR—in the Church of England a rector as distinguished from a vicar, is a parish incumbent whose tithes are not impropriate.

RECUSANT—one who refuses. One, either of the clergy or the laity, who refused to accept the religious changes of the Reformation to acknowledge the supremacy of the Crown, to conform to the Book of Common Prayer or to attend the services of the Church of England.

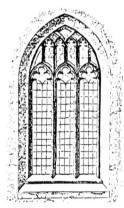

RECTILINEAR TRACERY

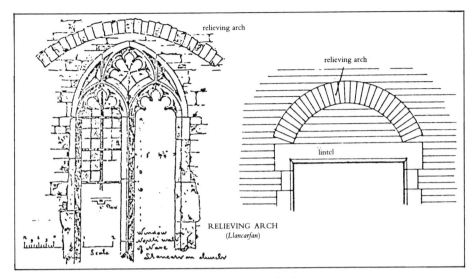

relieving arch

relieving arch

lintel

RELIEVING ARCH
(*Llancarfan*)

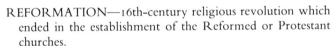

RED BOOK OF HERGEST, THE—one of the most important Welsh manuscripts of the Middle Ages containing examples of almost every kind of Welsh literature of the period now in the Bodleian Library.

REEDING—a band of decoration consisting of shallow parallel grooves.

REFORMATION—16th-century religious revolution which ended in the establishment of the Reformed or Protestant churches.

RELIEVING ARCH—usually of rough construction placed in a wall above an arch or opening to relieve it of much of the superincumbent weight.

REREDOS—a decoration of any kind put up behind and above a high altar, usually the painting of scenes or figures, a rich hanging or curtain, painted wooden panels, a group of carved figures.

RESPOND—the half-pillar or pier at the end of an arcade or abutting a single arch.

RESTORATION–rebuilding or renovation of a church in a dilapidated condition. The late 19th century was the period when most churches were restored.

RETABLE—a structure behind and above an altar which may be either a ledge on which ornaments may be set, a 'gradine', or a frame for the panels of a reredos.

RETICULATED TRACERY—stone tracery of the mid-Gothic periods with openings repeated in rows, thus resembling the meshes of a net.

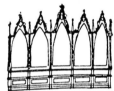

REREDOS

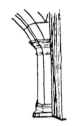

RESPOND

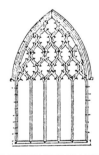

RECTICULATED TRACERY

RETURN—the terminating of the dripstone or hood-mould of a window or door.

REVEAL—the inner vertical side of an opening, as of a doorway or window behind the frame.

RHAETIC SANDSTONE—a late Triassic sandstone occurring in the area between Pyle and Cowbridge easily worked for dressings and ashlar.

RIDGE—a member laid longitudinally at the apex of a roof and against which the upper ends of the rafters pitch or meet.

ROCOCO ARCHITECTURE—latest phase of Baroque-style mid-18th century in England, a hybrid ornament with quasi-Chinese and Gothic motifs.

ROLL-MOULDING—a continuous convex moulding cut upon the edges of stone and woodwork.

ROLL MOULDING
(*Marcross*)

ROMANESQUE—style of architecture prevalent in Romanized Europe between the Classical and Gothic periods, especially in the period 1066-1189 with massive vaulting and round arches. Usually referred to as Norman.

ROOD—cross of Christ, the crucifix.

ROOD BEAM—beam across front of chancel arch to support great rood and rood-loft.

ROOD-LOFT—platform or singing gallery above rood-screen.

ROOD-SCREEN—screen below the rood, set across the east end of the nave shutting off the chancel.

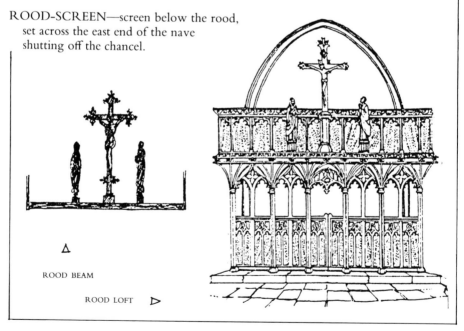

ROOD BEAM

ROOD LOFT

ROOF-TRUSS—a triangulated frame of timber usually placed of 3 to 4 metres apart to carry the purlin and rafters.

ROSE WINDOW—a circular window with concentric or radiating tracery patterns.

ROSETTE—a circular ornament carved or moulded resembling a formalised rose.

ROUNDEL—a circular panel or medallion—also a similarly shaped panel in a stained glass window.

ROYAL ARMS—symbol of assertion of Royal Supremacy over the Church in England at the Reformation. At the Restoration of Charles II it became mandatory for the Royal Arms to be displayed in churches.

ROYAL COMMISSION ON ANCIENT AND HISTORICAL MONUMENTS IN WALES—originally appointed in 1908 to make an inventory of the Ancient and Historical Monuments in Wales and Monmouthshire, the Commission now includes the National Monuments Record for Wales.

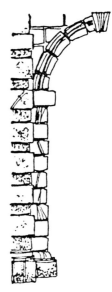

RUSTICATION

RUBBLE MASONRY—walls of rough uncut stones.

RURAL DEAN—in the Church of England the head of a group of parishes in a given area (Rural Deanery). He is appointed by the Bishop of the diocese usually from among the beneficed clergy of the Deanery.

RUSTICATION—a mode of building masonry in which the individual blocks or courses of stone are emphasized by deeply recessed joints and often by a roughened surface.

SACRISTY—repository of vestments or vessels of a church.

SADDLEBACK ROOF—the roof of a tower which has a ridge and terminates in gables instead of being the usual pyramidal form.

SALTIRE—a cross in the form of the Greek letter X-chi symbolizing Christ. It is the attribute of St. Andrew who was said to have been crucified on a cross of this design.

SADDLEBACK ROOF
(*Llanmihangel*)

SANCTUARY—the east end of a church containing the high altar and reserved for the clergy.

SANCTUS BELL—a small bell rung at the elevation of the host in the communion service.

SARCOPHAGUS—a stone or terracotta coffin, often elaborately carved and inscribed.

SCALLOP—an ornament carved or moulded in the form of a shell.

SANCTUS BELL
(*Welsh St. Donats*)

SCALLOPED CAPITAL—a Romanesque cushion capital in which the four sides are shaped in a series of curves or scallops.

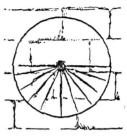

SCANTLING—the size of a piece of timber in cross-section.

SCRATCH DIAL—sundial scratched on the exterior wall of the church to tell time of masses.

SCROLL MOULDING—a moulding of two rounded parts, the upper projecting beyond the lower thus resembling a scroll of parchment.

SCRATCH DIAL

SECOND POINTED—Victorian Gothic term for Decorated style architecture. Also referred to as Middle Pointed, or Mid-Gothic.

SEDILIA—the seats on the south side of the chancel near the altar for the use of the clergy.

SEE—the 'seat' (Latin sedes) 'chair' or 'throne' on which a bishop sits in his cathedral and, by extension, the diocese where the church is located.

SEDILIA
(St. Fagans)

SEGMENTAL ARCH—a segment of a circle drawn from a centre below the springing line.

SEGMENTAL ARCH

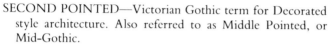

SEMI-EFFIGIAL
(Llantwit Major)

SEMI-EFFIGIAL—type of memorial in which an effigy appears to be enclosed in a coffin partly cut away to reveal portions of the figure.

SENTENCES—proverbs and biblical texts painted on the walls and other parts of ecclesiastical buildings.

SERRATED—notched along the edge or rippled upon the surface.

SET-OFF—see OFF-SET

SHAFT—the body of a column between the base and capital.

SPANDREL
(St. Fagans)

SLOTTED—a groove or mortice into which the end of a panel is inserted for framing.

SOCIETY FOR THE PROTECTION OF ANCIENT BUILDINGS (SPAB)—founded in 1877 by William Morris (1834-1896) a trained architect turned painter and poet in an attempt to combat the drastic methods of restorations then being carried out in the parish churches of Great Britain.

SPUR

SOFFIT—the underside of any architectural feature e.g. an arch, window or door head.

SPANDREL—space enclosed between the extrados of an arch or between arch and its foliation.

SPIRE—tapering roof of a tower, turret or pinnacle as distinct from the tower itself.

SQUINT

SPLAY—chamfer usually of the reveal of a window.

SPRINGING LINE—the level at which an arch springs from its supports.

SPUR—a spray of foliage which fills the gap when a circular base of a column stands on a square or octagonal plinth.

STIFF-LEAF FOLIAGE

SQUINT—an obliquely-cut opening in a wall to allow a view of the high altar of a church whence it could not otherwise be seen.

STANDARD—the posts of a screen running through from wall to the head.

STATIONS OF THE CROSS—a series of paintings or carvings depicting incidents of Good Friday. In the modern form they offer fourteen incidents for prayer and meditation.

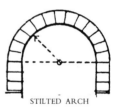

STILTED ARCH

STIFF-LEAF FOLIAGE—13th-century ornamental foliage with multi-lobed leaves and rhythmic stems.

STILE—the vertical member of a frame into which the ends of the rails or horizontal members are tenoned.

STILTED ARCH—an arch sprung from a point above the imposts; the vertical masonry between the imposts and springing line resembling stilts.

STOUP
(*St. Donats*)

STOUP—vessel to contain holy water in a church usually placed in the porch.

STRAPWORK—in Elizabethan architecture a form of ornament composed of interlacing bands, resembling straps with rivets at their intersections.

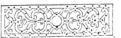

STRAPWORK

STRING, STRINGCOURSE—a moulding or projecting band running horizontally across a building.

SUTTON STONE—a conglomerate limestone quarried between Ogmore and Southerndown.

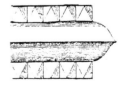

STRINGCOURSE

SWAG—an ornamental festoon of flowers, fruit and foliage often tied with ribbons carved in wood or modelled in plaster, suspended at each end and hanging down in the middle.

SYNODAL—payments to a bishop by his clergy by reason of holding a synod. The sum which a bishop originally had the right to demand was two shillings.

TABERNACLE—a receptacle for the pyx or other vessel containing the reserved sacrament in the church. Usually some form of box set in the middle of the altar on the gradine and covered with white silk and a veil.

TABERNACLE WORK—the elaborate carved work on canopies over niches, stalls, pulpits and church screens.

TAXATIO ECCLESIASTICA—an assessment made in 1291 during the papacy of Pope Nicholas IV for the purpose of levying a tax granted to Edward I on taking the Cross. The full title is *Taxatio Ecclesiastica Angliae et Walliae auctoritate P. Nicolai IV 1291* and was first printed by the Records Commission in 1802.

TABERNACLE WORK

TAXATION OF NORWICH, 1254—a 13th-century taxation assessment called the Taxation of Norwich after a bishop of that city who was one of the assessors. Its purpose was to levy a tenth of the value of each benefice to provide money for the crusade of Henry III.

TE DEUM—the opening words *Te Deum laudamus* (We praise thee, O God) of the ancient Latin hymn of praise and thanksgiving sung at Matins on Sundays.

THIRD POINTED—Victorian Gothic term for Perpendicular-style architecture.

TIE-BEAM TRUSS

THOMAS AQUINAS, ST.—the Angelic Doctor (1226-74) renowned for his immense learning and his theological and philosophical writings, and patron saint of universities and seats of learning.

THRUST—the downward and outward pressure or force exerted by a vault, arch, roof-truss or other structural member upon its supporting walls or piers.

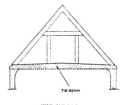

TIE-BEAM

TIE-BEAM—the horizontal transverse beam in a roof, tying together the feet of the rafters to counteract the thrust.

TITHE—originally tithe was the tenth part of the yearly produce of land due to the rector of the parish. In 1836 the Tithe Commutation Act abolished all tithes in kind converting them into tithe rent-charge.

TOMB-CHEST

ALTAR TOMB

TITHE COMMUTATION ACT 1836—in 1836 the Tithe Commutation Act abolished all tithes in kind converting them into tithe rent-charge—an annual money payment to be calculated year by year on the average price of corn of the preceding seven years.

TOMB-CHEST—a raised monument resembling a chest. A chest-shaped stone coffin, the most usual medieval form of funerary monument. Also referred to as Altar tomb.

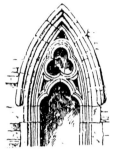

TREFOIL
(*St. Fagans*)

TOWER—square structure rising above the roof of the church, usually placed either centrally or at the west end.

TRACERY—the ornamental perforated filling placed in the head of a light of a screen or in a window.

TRAIL—a form of plant life growing upon an undulating stem filling in the hollow of the beam of a screen.

TUDOR ARCH

TRANSEPT—transverse arm of a cruciform church.

TRANSITIONAL ARCHITECTURE—a term usually referring to the period of transition from the Romanesque to the Gothic or in Britain from the Northern to the Early English style, circa. 1150-1200.

TRANSOM—the horizontal cross-bar to the mullions of a window or the tracery of a screen.

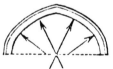

TUDOR ARCH

TREFOIL—three-lobed panel or tracery light.

TRUSS—main frame in a timber structure supporting a roof.

TUDOR ARCH—a depressed four-centred arch used in Tudor architecture.

TUDOR FLOWER—diamond-shaped leaf ornament used in screen of the Tudor period, etc.

TUDOR ROSE—a conventionalized rose much used in Tudor architecture.

TUDOR STYLE—the period (1485-1603) and style extending from the late Perpendicular to the end of Queen Elizabeth I's reign.

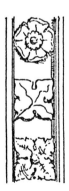

TUDOR FLOWER

TURRET—a small tower.

TYMPANUM—in medieval architecture the vertical triangular or segmental space over a doorway between the lintel.

UNCIALS—a form of writing in usually large somewhat rounded characters used in ancient manuscripts.

UNDERPINNING—the strengthening of an existing wall by removing and renewing its lower portions in short lengths at a time.

UROBOROS (OUROBOROS)—a serpent devouring its own tail, a symbol of eternity.

UROBOROS

VALOR ECCLESIASTICUS—the official valuation of ecclesiastical and monastic revenues made in 1535 by Henry VIII. It became popularly known as the 'King's Books', (Liber Regis)

VAULTING—an arched ceiling or roof of stone sometimes imitated in wood or plaster.

VESICA-SHAPED—oval with pointed head and foot.

VESICA

VESTRY—room in the church used by the clergy to store vestments and sacred vessels.

VICAR—from Latin 'vicarius' meaning 'a substitute'. In the Anglican church the priest of a parish where the tithes have been appropriated. As a parish priest a vicar has exactly the same spiritual status as a rector and the forms of institution and induction are identical since in both cases he holds his full spiritual jurisdiction from the bishop.

VOLUTE

VISITATION, EPISCOPAL—periodic inspections of those temporal and spiritual affairs of a diocese under the bishop's control. A bishop is enjoined by the Anglican canons to observe the medieval custom of a visitation every three years.

VOLUTE—a spiral scroll, the distinctive feature of the Ionic capital and also used in a modified form in Corinthian and composite capitals and in consoles and brackets.

VOUSSOIR—one of a series of wedge-shaped stones used to form an arch.

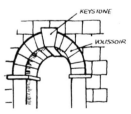

VOUSSOIR

VULGATE—the Latin version of the Bible which was first printed in the Gutenberg Bible of 1456 revised and declared by the Council of Trent to be the only authentic Latin text.

WAGON ROOF—so called because of its resemblance to the stretched canvas roof of a wagon. Formed by closely-set rafters with arch-braces and often panelled or plastered. Sometimes known as a Cradle roof.

WAGON ROOF

WAINSCOT—wooden panelling used in the lower part of a screen.

WALLPLATE—a timber laid lengthwise on the wall to receive the ends of the rafters and other joists.

WEEPERS—small figures usually children placed in front of medieval tombs. Also called mourners.

WINDBRACE—short struts either curved or straight used between the purlins and principals of a roof to strengthen the framework. These are placed at the intersections.

WINDBRACE

Y-TRACERY—divergent tracery where a single mullion is divided into two beneath the main arch.

YEW TREE—tree found on the south side of the churchyard. Common object of pre-Christian worship.

ZIG-ZAG—see CHEVRON.

Y-TRACERY

WAINSCOT

Glossary of Heraldic and Related Terms used in this Work

ACHIEVEMENT—the coat of arms (helmet, crest, mantling, motto) fully emblazoned according to the rules of heraldry (*see* 'armorial bearings').

AFFRONTÉ—showing full face or front.

AGNUS DEI—a lamb passant with a nimbus about its head, supporting on the dexter shoulder a cross-staff from which flies a pennon argent charged with a cross gules.

AGNUS DEI

ANNULET—a small circle or ring borne as a charge in coats of arms. Also in English heraldry the cadency mark for the fifth son.

ARGENT—the French word for silver, usually represented by the colour white.

ARMED—a word used to describe the horns, beak, teeth or talons of any beast or bird of prey when of a different tincture from the body.

ANNULET

ARMIGER—a person legally entitled to bear arms. Also an esquire.

ARMORIAL BEARINGS—a term referring not only to arms displayed on a shield or banner but also crests, supporters, badges, etc. A complete display of armorial bearings is termed 'an achievement of arms' or 'achievement'.

ATTIRED—when the horns of a stag are of a different tincture to its head, it is said to be attired of that tincture.

AZURE—the colour blue.

BARS

BAR—a diminutive of the fess occupying one-fifth of the shield. It is seldom borne singly and consequently is not confined to the middle of the shield.

BARRULET—the smallest diminutive of the bar.

BARRY—when the field is divided into an equal number of bars of alternating tinctures.

BARRY

BASCINET—a basin-shaped helmet used at the end of the 14th century.

BEAKED—the beak of a bird when of a different tint from the body is said to be beaked of a tincture or metal.

BELLED—having a bell or bells attached e.g. a falcon.

BEND—a diagonal band from the top left (dexter) to the bottom right (sinister) base of the shield.

BEND

457

BILLET—a rectangular block of any tincture set upright.

BILLETÉE—when the field is strewn with billets.

BILLETEE

BLAZON—to describe in proper heraldic language and colours all that belongs to coats of arms.

BORDURE—the heraldic name for border. It is a border round the edge of the shield. Its position is always the same.

BOWEN'S KNOT—a continuous piece of rope set out in a square with a loop at each corner.

CABOSHED—beasts' heads displayed without any part of the neck and full face.

CABOSHED
CANTON

CADENCY—a system of differencing arms to show the position of younger members or cadet branches of the family in relation to the head of the family. In England the cadency marks are as follows:— the eldest son a label during his father's lifetime; second son a crescent; third son a molet; fourth son a martlet; fifth son an annulet; sixth son a fleur-de-lys; seventh son a rose; eighth son a cross moline; ninth son a double quatrefoil. All cadency marks are small and placed unobtrusively at some convenient point at the top or middle of the shield.

CAMAIL—a form of mail cape which was suspended from the bottom of the helmet to protect the chin, neck and shoulders.

CHEQUY

CANTON—the French word for corner—it is a small square figure generally placed at the dexter chief of the shield.

CERVEILLIÈRE—steel skull cap.

CHAINED—when animals are fixed with chains by the collar.

CHARGE—anything borne on an escutcheon, whether upon the field or upon an ordinary.

CHAUSSES—strips of mail introduced circa 1150 for the protection of the front of the leg for mounted men.

CHEVRON

CHEQUEY (CHEQUY)—a field covered with alternate squares of metal or colour or fur.

CHEVRON—One of the major ordinaries, like an inverted V.

CHEVRONEL—a narrow chevron, usually used when there are more than three shown on a shield.

CHIEF—the upper part of the shield (⅓-¼ deep).

CINQUEFOIL—a conventionalised flower of five equal petals, probably in the early days of heraldry based on the wild rose.

CLOSE—of a bird when the wings lie close to the body.

COIF DE MAILLES—a close-fitting skull cap of mail.

CINQUEFOIL

COLLARED—having a collar.

COMBATANT—describes two animals rampant facing each other on a shield as if in battle. It is the French word for fighting.

CONJOINED—joined together.

CONJOINED IN LURE—two wings joined in the centre with the tips inverted.

COOPED—cut off in a straight line.

CORNISH CHOUGH—a crow with red and orange legs.

COUCHANT—the French word for lying down, usually a term applied to an animal lying down, e.g. lion couchant.

COUNTER-CHANGED—the division of a shield into two parts one colour and one metal.

COUPED—indicates a head or limb of a person or creature cut off straight at the neck.

COURANT—running.

CRESCENT—the crescent moon with its horns turned upwards. Also used as a cadency mark for the second son.

CREST—the ornament on the upper part of the helmet in heraldry placed over the arms. Crests are usually displayed upon a wreath.

CRINED—of an animal whose hair is of a different tincture from its body.

CROSS BOTONNÉ (BOTONNY)—an ordinary cooped cross with three rounded knobs at the end of each arm.

CROSS CROSSLET—an ordinary cross cooped with a small additional bar placed across each arm towards its end, thus making four passion crosses conjoined in the centre.

CROSS FITCHÉE (FITCHY)—a cross pointed at the lower part, generally applied to crosses when the lower arm is pointed as if for sticking into the ground.

CROSS FLEURÉE (FLEURY)—a cross with the limbs ending in fleurs-de-lys.

CROSS FORMÉE (FORMY)—describes a cross the arms of which are splayed out by straight lines.

CROSS MOLINE—is usually emblazoned as a couped cross with the end of each arm splayed out to two points.

CROSS PATTÉE (PATY)—a cross small in the centre, wide at the ends.

CROSS POMMÉE—a cross having each limb ending in a ball.

COMBATANT

CONJOINED IN LURE

COUNTER-CHANGED

CRESCENT

CREST

CROSS BOTTONY

1. CROSS CROSSLET.
2. CROSS FITCHY.
3. CROSS FLEURY.
4. CROSS MOLINE.

CROSS POTENT—so called because its arms terminate in potents (a capital H lying on its side).

CUISSE—an extra protection designed to cover the weakest point of the mounted man-at-arms which was his thigh.

DANCETTÉ (DANCETTY)—a zig-zag or indented line.

DEMI—when an animal is referred to, its upper or fore half is always intended e.g. demi-lion.

DEXTER—the right hand side of the shield from the point of view of the man behind it, that is the left hand side to the viewer.

DIFFERENCE—the term given to a certain figure added to coats of arms to distinguish one cadet branch of the family from another. *See also* 'Cadency'.

DISPLAYED—a bird whose wings are expanded and legs spread is said to be displayed.

DUCAL CORONET (DUCAL CREST-CORONET)—the crest-coronet is misleadingly blazoned as a ducal coronet. It has no relationship to ducal rank and little resemblance to the coronet worn by a duke. The ducal crest-coronet has four strawberry leaves, three being visible in the flat.

EAGLE—the eagle is the principal charge amongst birds. The position most commonly found for the eagle is 'displayed' when the body is affronté with the wings and legs spread out on either side, the wing tips upwards and the head turned to the dexter.

EMBLAZON—the act of translating a blazon to paper or other material in full colour.

EMBRUED—a weapon depicted with blood upon it.

ENDORSED—of animals back to back.

ENGRAILED—the edge of a field or a charge when made up of curved indents.

ERADICATED—torn up by the roots.

ERASED—signifies anything torn or plucked off with a ragged edge generally applied to the head and limbs of man or animal.

ERECT—in an upright position.

ERMINE—a white fur with black spots.

ERMINOIS—a fur, the field or, the spots or tufts sable.

ESCALLOP—the scallop shell used to decorate the palmers on their way to and from Palestine.

ESCUTCHEON—a shield on which a coat of arms is represented; an heraldic shield.

1. CROSS PATY.
2. CROSS POMMEE.
3. CROSS POTENT.

DEMI LION

DUCAL CORONET

DANCETTY

BORDURE ENGRAILED
TREE ERADICATED
ESCALLOP

ERMINE
BEND ENGRAILED

ESCUTCHEON OF PRETENCE—a small shield of the wife's arms placed in the centre of the man's shield and thus indicating a marriage to an heraldic heiress.

FALCON—a bird of the hawk family which is almost invariably represented with bells and jesses.

FESS—a broad horizontal band across the middle of the shield.

FIELD—the whole surface of the shield or escutcheon; it is the ground upon which the tinctures, furs, ordinaries and charges are represented.

FIMBRIATED—having a narrow edging of a different tincture from the rest of the charge.

FLEUR-DE-LYS—supposed to represent the garden lily. It is the bearing of the Bourbons of France.

FRET—consisting of two long pieces in saltire, extending to the extremities of the field, and interlaced within a mascle.

FRETTY—denotes a field covered with fretwork or laths crossing each other diagonally and interlacing each other.

FURS—furs are used in heraldry not only for the lining of mantles of sovereigns and peers but also as tinctures on escutcheons. The two most common furs are ermine and vair.

GAUNTLET—an iron glove of armour formerly thrown down in challenge and taken up in acceptance.

GENOUILLIÈRES—a general term covering armour for the knee caps.

GORGED—any animal or bird having its neck encircled with crown, coronet, etc.

GRAND QUARTERS—often found in Royal Arms when a quarter is itself quartered.

GREAVES—armour for the leg from knee to ankle.

GRIFFIN (GRYPHON)—an animal that has the head, breast, fore-feet and wings of an eagle, the only difference being that it has ears and the hind quarters and tail of a lion.

GUARDANT—refers to an animal, usually a lion, depicted with the body sideways but the head toward the spectator.

GULES—the colour red.

GUTTÉE DE SANG—dripping with blood.

GYRONNY—when the field is divided per cross and per saltire, thus forming eight wedge-shaped divisions of alternating colours.

GRIFFIN'S HEAD ERASED

FESS FIMBRIATED
ESCUTCHEON OF PRETENCE
FLEUR DE LIS

FRET IMPALED
FRETTY

GRIFFIN

(LION RAMPANT)
GUARDANT

GYRONNY

HATCHMENT—a lozenge-shaped canvas and wooden panel emblazoned with the coat of arms of a deceased armiger which was hung on the front of his house for a period of mourning. It was then hung inside the church where he worshipped or held land.

HAUBERK—a garment of mail which fitted over the whole body.

HELM—a helmet usually placed on top of an achievement.

HORNED—an expression used when referring to the horns of animals.

HUNTING HORN STRINGED—a hunting horn—a curved or bugle horn with the mouth-piece to the sinister generally shown suspended by ribbons or strings which are tied in a knot above.

IMPALED—two coats of arms placed side by side on the one shield. For example, the arms of husband and wife, or a Bishop and his see.

IMPERIALLY CROWNED—when any charge in arms, crest or supporters, is crowned with a regal crown.

IN BEND—figures placed in a slanting direction from the dexter chief to the sinister base are said to be in bend.

INESCUTCHEON—a small shield used as a charge and placed in the centre of another shield.

ISSUANT OR ISSUING—a term which signifies proceeding from or coming out of.

JAMBS—armour protecting the shins.

JESSANT-DE-LIS—an expression used generally in connection with a leopard who has the lower half of a fleur-de-lys protruding from his mouth like a tongue and the upper part issuing from the top of his head.

JESSES—the thongs by which bells are fastened to the legs of a hawk or falcon.

JUPON—an alternative name for the surcoat when reduced in size to thigh length.

KNOWED—knotted.

LABEL—a label of three points of a suitable tincture is used as a mark of cadency of an eldest during his father's lifetime, and then removed when the heir succeeds.

LION—the lion is the principal charge amongst beasts. It was appropriated by sovereigns and leading nobles for their arms.

HATCHMENT

HUNTING HORN
STRINGED

INESCUTCHEON

JESSANT-DE-LIS
LABEL
MURAL CROWN

MARTLET—an imaginary bird like a swallow with fished tail shown without legs. Used as a mark of cadency for a fourth son.

MASCLE—a voided lozenge-shaped figure.

MAUNCH—a medieval lady's sleeve.

METAL—the two metals used in heraldry are gold and silver, called 'or' and 'argent'.

MITRE—one of the principal insignia of the episcopal office. It is usually found surmounting the shield instead of the helm, torso and crest as used by non-ecclesiastical armigers.

MOTTO—a word or short sentence inserted in a scroll generally placed beneath the escutcheon. The motto is regarded as a significant indication of the attitude of the family to which it belongs.

MULLET (MOLET)—a star of five points from a French word 'molette' meaning the rowel of a spur. Also used as a cadency mark by the third son.

MURAL CROWN—an embattled crown.

NEBULÉ (NEBULY)—a French word signifying cloudy, represented by a curved line—usually used horizontally.

NOWED—knotted.

OR—the French word for gold, usually represented by the colour yellow.

ORDINARY—in the early practice of painting a band or bands of colour across a shield for the purpose of distinction, certain simple forms originated and, on account of their common usage, these have come to be called ordinaries. They are the chief, bar, bend, chevron, pile, cross and saltire.

ORLE—a band set a little way inside the shield and following its edge all the way around.

PALE—a vertical stripe in the middle of a field.

PALY—a field divided into an equal number of vertical parts of metal and tincture interchangeably disposed.

PARTY or PARTED—signifies divided and is used when a shield is divided as party per chevron, party per fess.

PASCHAL LAMB—the badge of the Knights Templars—the Holy Lamb which is always emblazoned facing the dexter and holding a flag bearing the cross of St. George.

PASSANT—a word used to express the position of a beast walking to the dexter. His dexter paw is raised but the other three are firmly placed on the ground.

MITRE, MARTLET,
MASCLE, MOTTO,
MULLET & MAUNCH

NEBULY

PALY
PASSANT

PELICAN IN HER PIETY—a pelican is said to be 'in her piety' when seated on her nest and vulning (wounding) her breast to feed her young.

PER—by means of—used in conjunction with a dividing line e.g. per fess, per pale.

PER CHEVRON—chevronwise (a way of dividing the shield).

PHEON—the head of an arrow or dart (from a crossbow) which is barbed or engrailed on the inner side.

PILE—a wedge-shaped figure normally issuing downwards from the top edge of the shield. It can, however, issue from elsewhere. More than one are blazoned 'two piles' or 'three piles', etc.

POMMEL—the circular knob on the handle of the sword.

PROPER—an expression used to denote that charges in an escutcheon appear in their natural colour.

QUARTER—where a number of coats of arms (more than two) are marshalled on one shield, each is known as a quarter.

QUARTERINGS—an escutcheon divided into any number of squares is said to contain as many quarterings; they may be as numerous as the arms required.

QUARTERLY—signifies that the shield is quartered i.e. divided into four equal parts by a cross.

RAMPANT—an animal standing on its hind legs.

REGUARDANT—having the head turned so as to look backwards over the shoulder.

RISING—applied to a bird about to take flight.

ROUNDEL—a circular charge.

ROWEL—a spiked wheel or disc on a spur.

SABLE—the term used in heraldry for black.

SALTIRE—the cross of St. Andrew which may be found used as an ordinary or a charge.

SCROLL—a scroll or ribbon, especially the scroll bearing the motto.

SHIELD—contains the field or ground whereon are represented the charges or figures that form a coat of arms.

SINISTER—signifies the left side of any object, that is the side on the right of the viewer.

SOLLERETS—jointed flexible plates of armour protecting the foot.

PELICAN IN
HER PIETY

PER CHEVRON
PHEONS

PILE, SPUR, ROWEL,
QUARTERINGS

QUATREFOIL
SALTIRE

LION
RAMPANT
REGUARDANT

SUB-ORDINARY—considered as a lesser charge than the ordinary but of frequent appearance in heraldry. They consist of the bordure, the escutcheon, the orle, the double tressure, the canton, the gyron, the mascle, the lozenge, the billet, the label and the fret.

TIERCED WAVY

SUPPORTERS—these are the figures flanking the shield and supporting it, such as the lion and unicorn of the Royal Arms.

SURCOAT—the light linen coat worn over the armour.

TALBOT—a dog with long drooping ears formerly used for hunting. It is formed something between a hound and a beagle.

TALBOT'S HEAD ERASED

TASSET—in plate armour, one of a series of overlapping pieces forming a skirt.

TIERCED—when the field of the shield is divided into three equal parts.

TINCTURE—any metal, colour or fur used in heraldry.

TRESSURE—an ordinary not so broad as an orle. The tressure is always double and occasionally ornamented with fleurs-de-lys.

TRESSURE CROSS VOIDED

TUILLE—in medieval armour one or two or more plates of steel hanging below or forming the lowest part of the tassets and covering the front of the thighs.

UNGULED—when hoofs, nails, claws or talons are of a different tincture from the principal charge.

VAIR—one of the furs used in heraldry, and much favoured in the Middle Ages by the nobles.

VAIR

VERT—the tincture green.

VOIDED—of a charge with the middle removed leaving little more than the outline.

VULNING—any creature in the act of wounding itself.

WAVY—an undulating or wavy line or edge.

WIMPLE—a woman's headdress, often of fine white linen, covering the head, neck, cheeks and chin worn in the Middle Ages as protection against the cold.

WYVERN

WREATH—the six-fold band placed on top of a helm in an achievement upon which the crest stands or out of which it issues (*see* 'crest').

WYVERN—a kind of dragon with only two legs and a knowed tail on which he sits in place of his hind legs.

Architectural Periods

It is difficult to give precise details to architectural styles in Wales compared to England since some well-established changes in architecture in England took fifty years or more to appear in the remote rural areas of Wales which were isolated by poor communications from the rest of the country. Since there was a great deal of overlapping of the characteristics of style from one period to another many of the dates given below must be regarded as tentative.

600–1066	Anglo-Saxon	} Romanesque
1066–1189	Norman	
1150–1200	Transitional	} Gothic
1200–1300	Early English	
1300–1377	Decorated	
1377–1485	Perpendicular	
1485–1558	Tudor	} Renaissance
1558–1603	Elizabethan	
1603–1625	Jacobean	
1625–1714	Stuart	
1695–1725	Baroque	} Georgian
1714–1837	Georgian	
1837–1901	Victorian	Gothic Revival
1901–1910	Edwardian	
1910 onwards	Modern	

APPENDIX 2

Valuations of ecclesiastical benefices, 1254-1535

In the accounts of individual churches in the main text, valuation figures are given, where they are available, from the three main assessments of ecclesiastical property made between 1254 and 1535. The Valuation of Norwich, 1254 (so-called because it was undertaken under the supervision of Walter Suffield, Bishop of Norwich) was prompted by Pope Innocent IV's grant in 1250 of a clerical tenth to King Henry III towards a projected crusade, never in fact undertaken. The *Taxatio Ecclesiastica P. Nicholai IV, 1291* arose from Pope Nicholas IV's grant to Edward I in 1291 of six years' tenths from the clergy for a crusade which again was never undertaken. This survey of clerical property remained in force until superseded by the *Valor Ecclesiasticus*. The latter valuation compiled in 1535 became necessary when the Statute of Annates (1534) transferred all first fruits and tenths of benefices to the Crown.

It needs to be stressed that the figures given from the first two valuations do not represent net or gross income but rather the lowest figures at which benefices could be farmed out. The *Valor* figures by contrast approximate more closely to net annual income figures. Taken by themselves the figures for individual churches are not of great significance but they do provide a useful yardstick for comparing the wealth of various benefices within a diocese. They are also by inference a useful comparative index to the wealth of parishes.

Bibliography

MANUSCRIPTS

A. ABERYSTWYTH: NATIONAL LIBRARY OF WALES
 1. Schedules of the Church in Wales records. Diocese of Llandaff. Vol. III. Faculties.
 2. Bishop Shute Barrington's *Llandaff Diocesan Book* NLW/LL/PBEN/1.
 3. Glamorgan visitation returns for 1771. NLW/LL/QA/4.
 4. Description of St. Andrew's Major church made by G. T. Clark circa 1860. NLW 5215E.
 5. Notes on Michaelston-super-Ely church made by G. T. Clark during a visit to the church circa 1859/60. NLW 5212E FOLIOS 89-91.
 6. Traherne-Mansel Franklen Manuscript Collection NLW 6511-6605.
 7. Iolo Morganwg. Notes on St. Andrews & Dynas Powis (1789), (Llanover Manuscript Collection: NLW MSS 13061-185).

B. BIRMINGHAM: CITY OF BIRMINGHAM PUBLIC LIBRARIES DEPARTMENT: REFERENCE LIBRARY
Archives of the firm of John Hardman Studios, artists and craftsmen in stained glass (Correspondence, letter books, ledgers, day books, order books, etc. late 18th century to c. 1920.)

C. BIRMINGHAM: CITY OF BIRMINGHAM: CITY MUSEUMS AND ART GALLERY
Archives of the firm of John Hardman Studios, artists and craftsmen in stained glass.

D. BRIDGEND: MID GLAMORGAN COUNTY COUNCIL: REFERENCE LIBRARY
 1. Aeron Price papers.
 2. Roderick G. Williams' manuscript notes on the Vale of Glamorgan and its churches.

E. CARDIFF: CARDIFF CENTRAL LIBRARY
 1. Evans, T. C. (Cadrawd)—A history of the parish of Llandough. 1902. MS 4.304.
 2. Jones, David (of Wallington). Notes on some Glamorgan churches, 1881-1882. MS 1.187.
 3. Jones, David (of Wallington)—Outline of the history of the parishes of Llysworney, Llanmihangel, Llanmaes with extra-parochial places of Nash and Stembridge. MS 2.355.
 4. Thompson, Herbert M.—Manuscript notes on the old churches of Glamorgan. 1935. 2 vols.
 5. Williams, Roderick G.—Church fonts in the Vale of Glamorgan (circa 1928). MS 2.1329.

F. CARDIFF: GLAMORGAN ARCHIVE SERVICE
    1. Ewenny estate collection. Scrap book of the Turbervill family, 19th century. D/DE 695.
    2. Pedigrees of prominent Glamorgan families with illustrated coats of arms in colour. D/DE 439/440.
    3. Aubrey family of Llantrithyd records. Llantrithyd parish church D/D AU 303/ 1–9.
    4. Schedules of ecclesiastical parish records in Glamorgan. 2 vols.
    5. Records of the Carne family of Nash Manor. E/38 iii–v. Faculty for new pews in Llysworney church 1774 and plan of new seating.

G. CARDIFF: NATIONAL MUSEUM OF WALES: DEPARTMENT OF ARCHAEOLOGY AND NUMISMATICS
    Manuscript notes on the church bells of Glamorgan; by Arthur Wright. NMW A&N 4/Wright.

H. GLOUCESTER: COUNTY RECORD OFFICE
    Repairs to Llancarfan church, Glamorgan 1765–1785. (D936/E210).

I. LONDON: GENERAL SYNOD OF THE CHURCH OF ENGLAND: COUNCIL FOR THE CARE OF CHURCHES
    Manuscripts of the late Canon B. F. L. Clarke on the churches in Glamorgan

J. LONDON: LAMBETH PALACE LIBRARY
    1. *Notitia Episcopatum* 1664–65. MS 932.
    2. Incorporated Church Building Society Files 4170 (Cowbridge); 4404 (St. Bride's Major); 5390 (St. Nicholas); 5660 (Bonvilston); 5836 (St. Mary Church); 5907 (Llandough); 6911 (Wick).

K. LONDON: SOCIETY OF ANTIQUARIES
    Aymer Vallance manuscript notes on Glamorgan churches. 1911.

PRINTED BOOKS

THE HOLY BIBLE

ALDEN, JEFF *Holy Cross Church, Cowbridge.* (Cowbridge, 1985.)

ALEXANDER, D. A. *Glamorgan reminiscences.* (Carmarthen, 1915.)

ANDERSON, M. D. *History and imagery in British churches.* (London, 1971.)

ANGUS, M. *Modern stained glass in British churches.* (Oxford, 1984.)

ANSON, PETER F. *Fashions in church furnishing, 1840–1940.* 2nd ed. (London, 1965.)

ATKINSON, T. D. *A glossary of terms used in English architecture.* 7th ed. (London, 1948.)

ATKINSON, T. D. *Local style in English architecture.* (London, 1947.)

AWBERY, STAN *I searched for Llantwit Major.* (Barry, 1965.)

AWBERY, STAN *Let us talk of Barry.* (Barry, 1954.)

AWBERY, STAN *Llancarfan: the village of a thousand saints.* (Barry, 1957.)

AWBERY, STAN *St. Donat's and the Stradlings.* (Barry, 1966.)

AWBERY, STAN *The story of St. Athan and Aberthaw.* (Barry, 1959.)

BARING-GOULD, SABINE & FISHER, JOHN *The lives of the British saints.* (London, 1907–1913.) 4 vols.

BARTRUM, PETER C. *Welsh genealogies, A.D. 1400–1500.* (Aberystwyth, 1983.) 18 vols.

BEAZLEY, E. A. *Burrow's glossary of church architecture, furnishings and fittings: a concise and reliable handbook for lovers of old churches.* (London, 1937.)

BETJEMAN, JOHN (ed.) *Collins guide to parish churches of England & Wales*; edited by John Betjeman. (London, 1980.)

BEVAN, STANLEY W. *St. Bride's Major, Southerndown and Ogmore-by-sea: a chronicle of a parish in the Vale of Glamorgan.* (Cowbridge, 1980.)

BOND, FRANCIS *The chancel of English churches.* (London, 1916.)

BOND, FRANCIS *Fonts and font covers.* (London, 1908.)

BOTTOMLEY, FRANK *The church explorer's guide to symbols and their meaning.* (London, 1978.)

BOUTELL, CHARLES *Christian monuments in England and Wales: a historical and descriptive sketch.* (London, 1854.)

BOUTELL, CHARLES *Monumental brasses and slabs: a historical and descriptive notice of the incised monumental memorials of the Middle Ages.* (London, 1847.)

BRADLEY, A. G. *Glamorgan and Gower.* (London, 1908.)

BRADNEY, SIR J. A. *Llandaff records.* (Cardiff, 1905-1914.) 5 vols.

BRIGGS, MARTIN S. *Everyman's concise encyclopaedia of architecture.* (London, 1959.)

BRITTON, JOHN *A dictionary of the architecture and archaeology of the Middle Ages.* (London, 1838.)

BROWN, ROGER L. *The records of the Diocese of Llandaff and the local historian.* (Cardiff, 1981.)

BROWN, ROGER L. *The Welsh Evangelicals.* (Tongwynlais, 1985.)

BURGESS, FREDERICK *English churchyard memorials.* (London, 1979.)

BURKE, SIR BERNARD *Burke's genealogical and heraldic history of the landed gentry (including American families with British ancestry).* (London, 1939.)

BURKE, SIR BERNARD *The General Armory of England, Scotland, Ireland and Wales comprising a registry of armorial bearings from the earliest to the present time.* (London, 1884.)

BUTLER, L. A. S. 'Medieval ecclesiastical architecture in Glamorgan and Gower'. (In: *Glamorgan County History*, Vol. III. The Middle Ages, Chapter VIII. pp. 379-415. Cardiff, 1971.)

CAIGER-SMITH, A. *English medieval mural paintings.* (Oxford, 1963.)

CAMP, JOHN *Discovering bells and bellringing.* 2nd ed. (Aylesbury, 1975.)

CARLISLE, N. *A topographical dictionary of the Dominion of Wales.* (London, 1811.)

CAUTLEY, H. MUNRO *Royal Arms and commandments in our churches.* (Ipswich, 1934.)

CHILD, MARK *Discovering church architecture: a glossary of terms.* (Aylesbury, 1976.)

CHILD, MARK *Discovering churchyards.* (Aylesbury, 1982.)

CHILD, MARK *English church architecture: a visual guide.* (London, 1981.)

CLARK, GEORGE T. *Cartae et alia munimenta quae ad Dominium de Glamorgan pertinent.* 2nd ed. (Cardiff, 1910.)

CLARK, GEORGE T. *Limbus patrum Morganiae et Glamorganiae being the genealogies of the older families of the Lordships of Morgan and Glamorgan.* (London, 1886.)

CLARKE, B. F. L. *Church builders of the nineteenth century.* (London, 1938.)

CLIFTON-TAYLOR, ALEC *English parish churches as works of art.* (London, 1974.)

CLOWNEY, PAUL & CLOWNEY, TESSA *Exploring churches: a guide to churches, cathedrals and abbeys.* (Tring, Herts, 1982.)

CLUTTON, CECIL & NILAND, AUSTIN *The British organ.* 2nd ed. (London, 1981.)

COCKE, THOMAS *Recording a church: an illustrated glossary.* (London, 1982.)

COLE, DAVID *The work of Sir Gilbert Scott.* (London, 1980.)

COLVIN, HOWARD *A biographical dictionary of British architects, 1600-1840.* (London, 1978.)

CORBETT, J. A. (ed.) *A book of Glamorganshire antiquities.* (London, 1887.)

CORBETT, J. S. *Glamorgan: papers and notes on the Lordship and its members.* (Cardiff, 1925.)

COWEN, PAINTON *A guide to stained glass in Britain.* (London, 1985.)

COWLEY, F. G. 'The church in Glamorgan from the Norman Conquest to the beginning of the fourteenth century.' (In: *Glamorgan County History,* Vol. III (1971), pp. 87-135.)

COWLEY, F. G. *The monastic order in South Wales, 1066-1349.* (Cardiff, 1977.)

COX, J. C. *Pulpits, lecterns and organs in English churches.* (London, 1915.)

CRIPPS, WILFRED J. *Old English plate: ecclesiastical, decorative, and domestic, its makers and marks.* 11th ed. (London, 1926).

CROSS, F. L. & LIVINGSTONE, E. A. *The Oxford dictionary of the Christian church.* (London, 1974.)

CURL, JAMES STEVENS *English architecture: an illustrated glossary.* (Newton Abbot, 1977.)

CUTTS, EDWARD *A manual for the study of the sepulchral slabs and crosses of the Middle Ages.* (London, 1849.)

CYMMRODORION SOCIETY *Dictionary of Welsh biography down to 1940.* (London, 1959.)

DARBY, MICHAEL *John Pollard Seddon.* (London, 1983.)

DAVID, R. *Notes on St. Illtyd's church.* (Llantwit Major, 1952.)

DAVIES, E. T. (ed.) *The story of the church in Glamorgan, 560-1960.* (London, 1962.)

DAVIES, E. T. 'The Church of England and Schools, 1662-1774.' (In: *Glamorgan County History,* Vol. IV (1974), pp. 432-468.)

DAVIES, E. T. *Religion and society in the nineteenth century.* (Llandybie, 1981.)

DAVIES, IOLO *A certaine school: a history of the Grammar School at Cowbridge.* (Cowbridge, 1967.)

DAVIES, J. CONWAY *Episcopal Acts and cognate documents relating to the Welsh Dioceses, 1066-1272.* (Cardiff, 1946-49.) 2 vols.

DAVIES, WENDY *An early Welsh microcosm: studies in the Llandaff Charters.* (London, 1978.)

DAVIES, WENDY *The Llandaff Charters.* (Aberystwyth, 1979.)

DAVIES, WENDY *Wales in the early Middle Ages.* (Leicester, 1982.)

DINELEY, THOMAS *The account of the official progress of his Grace, Henry the first Duke of Beaufort through Wales in 1684.* (London, 1888.)

DIRSZTAY, PATRICIA *Church furnishings: a NADFAS guide.* (London, 1978.)

DIXON, ROGER & MUTHESIUS, STEFAN *Victorian architecture.* (London, 1978.)

DONOVAN, EDWARD *Descriptive excursions through South Wales and Monmouthshire in the year 1804 and the four preceding Summers,* (London, 1805.) 2 vols.

DOVE, RONALD H. *A bellringer's guide to the church bells of Britain and ringing peals of the World.* 6th ed. (Guildford, 1982.)

ELVIN, CHARLES N. *Elvin's handbook of mottoes.* Rev. ed. (London, 1971.)

ESDAILE, KATHARINE A. *English church monuments, 1510 to 1840.* (London, 1946.)

EVANS, C. J. O. *Glamorgan: its history and topography.* 2nd ed. (Cardiff, 1943.)

EVANS, LESLIE *Margam Abbey.* (Port Talbot, 1958.)

FEARN, JACQUELINE *Discovering heraldry.* (Aylesbury, 1980.)

FLEMING, JOHN *Penguin dictionary of architecture:* by John Fleming (*et al.*). 2nd ed. (Harmondsworth, 1972.)

FLETCHER, H. L. V. *South Wales.* (London, 1956.)

FOLIOT, GILBERT *The letters of Gilbert Foliot, Abbot of Gloucester (1139-48), Bishop of Hereford (1148-63) and London (1163-87)*; edited by C. N. Brooke (*et al.*). (Cambridge, 1967.)

FOSTER, JOSEPH *Alumni Oxoniensis 1715-1886.* (Oxford, 1891.)

FOSTER, JOSEPH *Some feudal coats of arms and others.* (Oxford, 1902.)

FOSTER, RICHARD *Discovering English churches: a beginner's guide to the story of the parish church from before the Conquest to the Gothic Revival.* (London, 1981.)

FOWLER, CHARLES B. *Rambling sketches from the old churches in the Diocese of Llandaff.* (Cardiff, 1896.)

FRANCIS, DAVID *The Border Vale of Glamorgan.* (Barry, 1976.)

GIBBON, S. R. *Guide to the parish church of St. Athan being notes collected by the Reverend S. R. Gibbon, Rector of St. Athan.* (Cowbridge, 1947.)

GLAMORGAN ARCHIVE SERVICE *King Richard III and Holy Cross Church, Cowbridge.* (Cowbridge, 1984.)

GLAMORGAN COUNTY RECORD OFFICE *Guide to the exhibition of the records of the Turbervill family of Ewenny held at County Hall Cardiff 28th March-26th May, 1966.* (Cardiff, 1966.)

GLYNNE, SIR STEPHEN R. *Notes on the older Welsh churches (1824-74).* (London, 1903.)

GOVETT, SHEILA A. S. *The history of St. John the Baptist Church, Sully.* (Barry, 1967.)

GRANT, SIR FRANCIS J. (ed.) *The manual of heraldry:* edited by Francis J. Grant. (Edinburgh, 1962.)

GRAY, A. STUART *Edwardian architecture: a biographical dictionary.* (London, 1985.)

GREEN, C. A. H. *Notes on churches in the Diocese of Llandaff.* (Aberdare, 1906-1907.)

GREENHILL, F. A. *Incised effigial slabs: a study of engraved stone memorials in Latin Christendom c. 1100-c. 1700.* (London, 1976.) 2 vols.

GUNNIS, R. *A dictionary of British sculptors, 1660-1851.* 2nd ed. (London, 1975.)

HALL, JAMES *Dictionary of subjects and symbols in art.* Rev. ed. (London, 1979.)

HALLIDAY, GEORGE E. *Llandaff church plate.* (London, 1901.)

HARRIES, JOHN *Discovering stained glass.* 2nd ed. (Aylesbury, 1980.)

HARRIS, JOHN & LEVER, JILL *Illustrated glossary of architecture, 850-1830.* (London, 1966.)

HARRISON, MARTIN *Victorian stained glass.* (London, 1980.)

HARVEY, JOHN *The Perpendicular style, 1330-1485.* (London, 1978.)

HAWKINS, CHRISTOPHER *Discovering church furniture.* (Tring, Herts, 1969.)

HILLING, JOHN B. *The historic architecture of Wales: an introduction.* (Cardiff, 1976.)

HILLING, JOHN B. *Plans and prospects—architecture in Wales 1780-1914: catalogue of Welsh Arts Council Exhibition 1975.* (Cardiff, 1975.)

HOPKIN-JAMES, LEMUEL JOHN *Old Cowbridge.* (Cardiff, 1922.)

HOWELL, PETER & BEAZLEY, ELISABETH *The companion guide to South Wales.* (London, 1977.)

HURLOW, WINSTON G. *The story of St. Donat's: a history of the Castle and of the Stradling family.* (St. Donat's, 1952.)

JAMES, BRIAN LL. 'Cowbridge' (In: *South Glamorgan: a county history;* edited by Stewart Williams. (Barry, 1975), pp. 225-241.)

JAMES, BRIAN LL. 'Llantwit Major' (In: *South Glamorgan: a county history;* edited by Stewart Williams. (Barry, 1975), pp. 205-224.)

JAMES, BRIAN LL. 'The Vale of Glamorgan' (In: *South Glamorgan: a county history;* edited by Stewart Williams. (Barry, 1975), pp. 163-204.)

JAMES, BRIAN LL. & FRANCIS, DAVID *Cowbridge and Llanblethian: past and present.* (Cowbridge, 1979.)

JAMES, J. W. *A church history of Wales.* (Ilfracombe, 1945.)

JENKINS, J. AUSTEN *Glamorgan at the opening of the 20th century.* (Cardiff, 1907.)

JENKINS, JABEZ E. *Southerndown.* (Carmarthen, 1900.)

JENKINS, PHILIP *The making of a ruling class: the Glamorgan gentry, 1640-1790.* (Cambridge, 1983.)

JOHNSON, A. M. 'Politics and religion in Glamorgan during the Interregnum, 1649-1660.' (In: *Glamorgan County History,* Vol. IV, (1974), pp. 279-309.)

JONES, GLYN M. & SCOURFIELD, ELFYN *Sully: a village and parish in the Vale of Glamorgan.* (Caerphilly, 1986.)

JONES, IEUAN G. 'Ecclesiastical economy: aspects of church building in Victorian Wales.' (In: *Welsh Society and Nationhood: historical essays presented to Glanmor Williams;* edited by R. R. Davies (*et al.*). (Cardiff, 1984), pp. 216-231.)

JONES, IEUAN G. & WILLIAMS, D. (eds.) *The Religious Census of 1851: a Calendar of the Returns relating to Wales. Vol. 1. South Wales;* edited by I. G. Jones and D. Williams. (Cardiff, 1976.)

JONES, L. E. *The Observer's book of Old English churches.* (London, 1965.)

KELLY, L. V. (ed.) *Llantwit Major: a history and guide.* (Llantwit Major, 1971.)

KELLY, L. V. *Llantwit Major in Camera.* (Cowbridge, 1979.)

KEMP, BRIAN *English church monuments.* (London, 1980.)

KNIGHT, J. K. 'Glamorgan A.D. 400-1100: archaeology and history.' (In: *Glamorgan County History,* Vol. II (1984), pp. 315-364.)

KNIGHT, J. K. 'Sources for the early history of Glamorgan.' (In: *Glamorgan County History,* Vol. II (1984), pp. 365-409.)

LELAND, JOHN *The itinerary of John Leland the antiquary relating to Glamorganshire,* Vol. IV. (Oxford, 1769.)

LEWIS, A. JOHN *The parish church of Pendoylan.* (Pendoylan, 1968.)

LEWIS, J. M. *Welsh monumental brasses: a guide.* (Cardiff, 1974.)

LEWIS, SAMUEL *Topographical dictionary of Wales.* (London, 1833.) 2 vols.

LUXTON, BRIAN C. *A history of the old village church Cadoxton-juxta-Barry.* (Barry, 1980.)

MACKINNON, CHARLES *The Observer's book of heraldry.* (London, 1966.)

MALKIN, B. H. *The scenery, antiquities and biography of South Wales.* 2nd ed. (London, 1804.)

MATTHEWS, J. H. (ed.) *Cardiff records, materials for a history of the County Borough.* (Cardiff, 1898-1911.) 6 vols.

MAUNSELL, CHARLES A. & STATHAM, EDWARD P. *Family of Maunsell, (Mansell, Mansel).* (London, 1917-20.) 3 vols.

MAYO, JANET *A history of ecclesiastical dress.* (London, 1984.)

MERRICK, RICE *Morganiae archaiographia: a book of the antiquities of Glamorganshire;* edited by Brian Ll. James. (Barry, 1983) (South Wales Record Society, Vol. 1.)

METFORD, J. C. J. *Dictionary of Christian lore and legend.* (London, 1983.)

MOORE, PATRICIA *Fonmon Castle, South Glamorgan: a residence occupied since the thirteenth century.* (Cardiff, 1976.)

MORGAN, G. H. *Rambles in the Vale.* (London, 1948.)

NASH-WILLIAMS, V. F. *The early Christian monuments of Wales.* (Cardiff, 1950.)

NEWELL, E. J. *Llandaff.* (London, 1902.)

NICHOLAS, THOMAS *The history and antiquities of Glamorganshire and its families.* (London, 1874.)

NORMAN, JOHN *The organs of Britain: an appreciation and gazetteer.* (Newton Abbot, 1984.)

ORRIN, GEOFFREY R. *The Gower Churches.* (Penmaen, 1979.)

PAPWORTH, J. W. *Papworth's ordinary of British armorials.* (Bath, 1977.) (Facsimile reprint of 1874 ed.)

PARKER, JOHN H. *A glossary of terms used in Grecian, Roman, Italian and Gothic architecture.* 5th ed. (Oxford, 1850.) 2 vols. in 3.

PENNY, NICHOLAS *Church monuments in Romantic England.* (New Haven & London, 1977.)

PICTON-TURBERVILL, EDITH *In the land of my fathers.* (Cardiff, 1946.)

PIERCE, GWYNEDD O. *The place-names of Dinas Powis Hundred.* (Cardiff, 1968.)

PINE, L. G. *A dictionary of mottoes.* (London, 1983.)

POST, W. ELLWOOD *Saints, signs and symbols: a concise dictionary.* 2nd ed. (London, 1974.)

PURVIS, J. S. *Dictionary of ecclesiastical terms.* (London, 1962.)

PUTTOCK, A. G. *A dictionary of heraldry and related subjects.* (Exeter, 1985.)

QUIN, W. T. W. *Dunraven Castle, Glamorgan: some notes on its history and associations.* (London, 1926.)

RADFORD, C. A. RALEGH *Ewenny Priory, Glamorgan.* (London, 1952.)

RADFORD, C. A. RALEGH 'The native ecclesiastical architecture of Wales (c. 1100-1285): the study of a regional style.' (In: *Culture and Environment: essays in honour of Sir Cyril Fox*; edited by I. Ll. Foster and L. Alcock. (London, 1963.), pp. 355-372.

RANDALL, GERALD *Church furnishing and decoration in England and Wales.* (London, 1980.)

RANDALL, H. J. *The Vale of Glamorgan.* (Newport, 1961.)

RHOOSE LOCAL HISTORY EXHIBITION *A brief history of Rhoose and District.* (Rhoose, 1970.)

RICHARDS, JOHN *The Cowbridge story: history and anecdotes of the ancient Borough.* (Bridgend, 1956.)

RICHARDS, JOHN *The Ogmore story: notes on the Lordship of Ogmore.* (Bridgend, 1958.)

RICKMAN, THOMAS *An attempt to discriminate the styles of architecture in England from the Conquest to the Reformation.* 6th ed. (Oxford, 1862.)

ROBINSON, DAVID M. *Cowbridge: the archaeology and topography of a small market town in the Vale of Glamorgan.* (Swansea, 1980.)

ROBINSON, DAVID M. *South Glamorgan's heritage: the archaeology of a county.* (Bridgend, 1985.)

ROBERTS, G. M. 'Calvinistic Methodism in Glamorgan, 1737-1773.' (In: *Glamorgan County History*, Vol. IV, (1974), pp. 499-533.)

ROUSE, E. CLIVE *Discovering wall paintings.* 3rd ed. (Aylesbury, 1980.)

ROYAL COMMISSION ON ANCIENT AND HISTORICAL MONUMENTS IN WALES AND MONMOUTHSHIRE *An inventory of the ancient monuments in Glamorgan. Vol. 1. Pre-Norman. Part III. The early Christian period.* (Cardiff, 1976.)

ROYAL COMMISSION ON ANCIENT AND HISTORICAL MONUMENTS IN WALES AND MONMOUTHSHIRE *An inventory of the ancient monuments in Glamorgan. Vol. IV. Domestic architecture from the Reformation to the Industrial Revolution. Part. 1. The Greater houses.* (Cardiff, 1981.)

SCOTT-GILES, C. W. *Boutell's heraldry.* Rev. ed. (London, 1966.)

SHARPE, FREDERICK *The church bells of Cardiganshire: their inscriptions and founders.* (Brackley, 1965.)

SHARPE, FREDERICK *The church bells of Herefordshire: their inscriptions and founders and details of bellframes and gear.* (Brackley, 1976.)

SHEPHERD, CHARLES F. *Annals of St. Fagans with Llanilterne: an ancient Glamorgan parish.* (Cardiff, 1938.)

SHEPHERD, CHARLES F. *Local history: sidelights on some Glamorgan parishes.* (Cardiff, 1946.)

SHEPHERD, CHARLES F. *A short history of St. George-super-Ely.* (Cardiff, 1933.)

SHEPHERD, CHARLES F. *St. Nicholas: a historical survey of a Glamorganshire parish.* (Cardiff, 1934.)

SODEN, R. W. *A guide to Welsh parish churches.* (Llandysul, 1984.)

SPENCER, MARIANNE R. *Annals of South Glamorgan: historical, legendary and descriptive chapters on some leading places of interest.* (Carmarthen, 1913.)

STEPHENS, MEIC (ed.). *Oxford Companion to Welsh literature*; compiled and edited by Meic Stephens. (Oxford, 1986.)

STOTHARD, C. A. *The monumental effigies of Great Britain.* 2nd ed. with additions by John Hewitt. (London, 1876.)

SUMMERS, PETER G. *How to read a coat of arms.* (London, 1967.)

SYMONDS, R. *Diary of the marches of the Royal Army during the great Civil War*; edited by C. E. Long. (London, 1859.)

TAXATIO ECCLESIASTICA *Taxatio ecclesiastica Angliae et Walliae auctoritate P. Nicholai IV circa A.D. 1291.* (London, 1802.)

THOMAS, HILARY M. *The parish church of Llandough (near Cowbridge).* (Cowbridge, 1985.)

THOMAS, HOWARD J. 'Castle, church and village: medieval Barry, 1100-1500.' (In: *Barry: the Centenary Book*; edited by Donald Moore. (Barry, 1985), pp. 57-99.)

THOMAS, LAWRENCE *The Reformation in the Old Diocese of Llandaff.* (Cardiff, 1930.)

TILNEY, CHRYSTAL *A history of the parishes of St. Andrew Major and Michaelston-le-Pit.* (Penarth, 1960.)

TILNEY, CHRYSTAL *St. Andrew's-in-the-Vale, Dinas Powys.* (Caerphilly, 1980.)

TREVELYAN, MARIE *Llantwit Major: its history and antiquities.* (Newport, 1910.)

TUMMERS, H. A. *Early secular effigies in England: the thirteenth century.* (Leiden, 1980.)

TURBERVILL, JOHN P. *Ewenny Priory: monastery and fortress.* (London, 1901.)

VALOR ECCLESIASTICUS *Valor Ecclesiasticus tempore Henr. VIII auctoritate regia institutus.* (London, 1810-34.) 6 vols.

VAUGHAN, HERBERT M. *The South Wales squires.* (London, 1926.)

VENN, JOHN *Alumni Cantabrigiensis—a biographical list of all known students, graduates and holders of office at the University of Cambridge from the earliest times to 1900.* (Cambridge, 1920-54.)

VILE, WALTER B. *A brief description of St. Mary's the parish church of St. Fagans.* (Cardiff, 1978.)

VILE, WALTER B. *A history and description of the parish church of St. Michael, Michaelston-super-Ely.* (Cardiff, 1981.)

WADE, JOSEPH H. *Glamorganshire.* (Cambridge, 1914.)

WALKER, DAVID (ed.) *A history of the Church in Wales.* (Penarth, 1976.)

WALKER, JOHN *An attempt towards recovering an account of the numbers and sufferings of the clergy of the Church of England . . . who were sequestered, harrassed etc. in the late times of the Grand Rebellion . . .* (London, 1714.)

WALL, J. C. *Porches and fonts.* (London, 1912.)

WARNER, MARINA *Alone of all her sex: the myth and cult of the Virgin Mary.* (New York, 1976.)

WEBB, GEOFFREY *Architecture in Britain: the Middle Ages.* (London, 1956.)

WESTWOOD, J. O. *Lapidarium Walliae: the early inscribed and sculptured stones of Wales.* (Oxford, 1876-1879.)

WHITE, JAMES F. *The Cambridge movement: the ecclesiologists and the Gothic Revival.* (Cambridge, 1962.)

WHO'S WHO IN WALES *Who's who in Wales.* First edition: edited by Arthur Mee. (Cardiff, 1921.)

WILLIAMS, A. H. *John Wesley in Wales, 1739-1790.* (Cardiff, 1971.)

WILLIAMS, C. J. & WATTS-WILLIAMS, JOHN *Parish registers of Wales*; compiled by C. J. Williams & J. Watts-Williams. (Aberystwyth, 1986.)

WILLIAMS, FREDERICK R. *Llanfrynach church, Glamorganshire: an ancient parish church without an altar, font, reading desk or lectern.* (Cardiff, 1924.)

WILLIAMS, GLANMOR 'The Dissenters in Glamorgan, 1660-c. 1760.' (In: *Glamorgan County History*, Vol. IV, (1974), pp. 468-498.)

WILLIAMS, GLANMOR 'The Church in Glamorgan from the fourteenth century to the Reformation.' (In: *Glamorgan County History*, Vol. III, (1971), pp. 135-166.)

WILLIAMS, GLANMOR 'The ecclesiastical history of Glamorgan, 1527-1642.' (In: *Glamorgan County History*, Vol. IV, (1974), pp. 203-256.)

WILLIAMS, GLANMOR The Stradling family. (In: *The story of St. Donat's Castle and Atlantic College*; edited by Roy Denning, (Barry, 1983, pp. 17-53.)

WILLIAMS, RODERICK G. *Guide to the Vale of Glamorgan.* (Cardiff, 1932.)

WILLIAMS, RODERICK G. *Llanblethian church.* (Cowbridge, 1937.)

WILLIAMS, STEWART (ed.) *History on my doorstep*; edited by Stewart Williams. (Cowbridge, 1959.) (Vale Series, vol. 1.)

WILLIAMS, STEWART (ed.) *Vale of history*; edited by Stewart Williams. (Cowbridge, 1960.) (Vale Series, vol. 2.)

WILLIAMS, STEWART (ed.) *The Garden of Wales*; edited by Stewart Williams. (Cowbridge, 1961.) (Vale Series, vol. 3.)

WILLIAMS, STEWART (ed.) *Saints and sailing ships*; edited by Stewart Williams. (Cowbridge, 1962.) (Vale Series, vol. 4.)

WILLIAMS, W. P. *A monograph of the Windsor family.* (Cardiff, 1879.)

WRIGHT, ARTHUR *The church bells of Monmouthshire: their inscriptions and founders with a chapter upon the Chepstow foundry.* (Cardiff, 1942.)

YATES, NIGEL *The Oxford Movement and Anglican Ritualism.* (London, 1983.)

PERIODICAL ARTICLES

ADAMS, D. J. 'The Restoration of Margam Abbey Church in the 19th century.' (*Transactions of the Port Talbot Historical Society* Vol. III, no. 3 (1984), pp. 60-67.)

ALLEN, JOHN ROMILLY 'The cylindrical pillar at Llantwit Major, Glamorganshire.' (*Archaeologia Cambrensis*, 1889, pp. 317-326.)

ALLEN, JOHN ROMILLY 'The inscribed and sculptured stones at Llantwit Major, Glamorganshire.' (*Archaeologia Cambrensis*, 1889, pp. 118-126.)

ALLEN, JOHN ROMILLY 'Iolo Morganwg's readings of the inscriptions on the crosses at Llantwit Major.' (*Archaeologia Cambrensis*, 1893, pp. 326-331.)

ALLEN, JOHN ROMILLY 'Notes on Porthkerry church, Glamorganshire with special reference to the churchyard cross.' (*Archaeologia Cambrensis*, 1876, pp. 45-48.)

BADDELEY, W. ST. CLAIR 'Ewenny Priory or St. Michael of Ogmore.' (*Archaeologia Cambrensis*, 1913, pp. 1-50.)

BRAKSPEAR, SIR HAROLD 'Ewenny Priory church.' (*Archaeological Journal*, Vol. LXVIII, pp. 391-396.)

CARTER, JOHN 'The pursuits of architectural innovation: no. LXX. Cardiff, Llantwitt and Ewenny.' (*Gentleman's Magazine*, Vol. 74, Pt. 1. 1804, pp. 324-326.)

CLARK, GEORGE T. 'Contribution towards a history of the parish of Llantrithyd in Glamorgan.' (*Archaeologia Cambrensis*, 1866, pp. 389-397, 1867, pp. 205-233.)

CLARK, GEORGE T. 'The parish of St. Hilary in Glamorganshire and its Lords.' (*Archaeologia Cambrensis*, 1889, pp. 214-223.)

CLARK, GEORGE T. 'Some account of the parish of Llancarvan.' (*Archaeologia Cambrensis*, 1865, pp. 261-276, 343-360, 1866, pp. 1-29.)

CLARK, GEORGE T. & JONES, ROBERT OLIVER 'Some account of the parish of Penmark.' (*Archaeologia Cambrensis*, 1861, pp. 1-22.)

CLARK, GEORGE T. 'Some account of the parishes of St. Nicholas and St. Lythan's, Co. Glamorgan.' (*Archaeologia Cambrensis*, 1862, pp. 92-116, 176-201.)

[THE] CROSS OF ST. DONAT'S. (*Archaeologia Cambrensis*, 1865, pp. 33-48.)

CROSSLEY, F. H. & RIDGEWAY, M. M. 'Screens, lofts and stalls in Wales and Monmouthshire. Section XII. Glamorgan.' (*Archaeologia Cambrensis*, 1958, pp. 72-108.)

CROUCH, DAVID 'An unknown medieval church survey of Llandaff Diocese (1433 A.D.).' (*Morgannwg*, Vol. XXVI, 1982, pp. 8-14.)

DAVID, W. 'The antiquities of St. Fagans: St. Fagan and his church.' (*Transactions of the Cardiff Naturalists' Society*, Vol. IX, 1877, pp. 49-52.)

DAVIES, E. T. 'The Education of the clergy in the Diocese of Llandaff, 1750-1866.' (*Journal of the Historical Society of the Church in Wales*, XXVI (1979), pp. 54-64.)

DAVIES, IOLO 'Holy Cross, Cowbridge, Glam.' (*The Ringing World*, Vol. LXIX, no. 3237, 11th May, 1973, pp. 1-2.)

DAVIES, JAMES CONWAY 'Ewenny Priory: some recently-found records.' (*National Library of Wales Journal*, Vol. III, 1943-44, pp. 107-37.)

DENNING, ROY 'The Rev. John Montgomery Traherne: a nineteenth-century antiquary.' (*Glamorgan Historian*, Vol. 4. 1967, pp. 46-55.)

DENNING, ROY 'William Thomas of Michaelston-super-Ely: the diary and the man.' (*Glamorgan Historian*, Vol. 9, 1973, pp. 143-156.)

EDWIN-COLE, JAMES Memoir of the family of Edwin. (*Herald and Genealogist*, Vol. 6. 1871, pp. 54-62.)

FENN, R. W. D. 'The pre-Norman church in Glamorgan. (*Glamorgan Historian*, Vol. 2. 1965, pp. 145-158.)

FOWLER, CHARLES BUSTEED 'Discoveries at Llanblethian church, Glamorganshire.' (*Archaeologia Cambrensis*, 1898, pp. 121-131.)

FRANCIS, DAVID J. 'Llansannor and the Gwyns.' (*Glamorgan Historian*, Vol. 10, 1974, pp. 9-26.)

FRANCIS, GEORGE GRANT 'Llantwit Major, Glamorganshire. No. III. The carving and heraldry in the church roof.' (*Archaeologia Cambrensis*, 1858, pp. 284-288.)

FREEMAN, EDWARD AUGUSTUS 'Architectural antiquities in Glamorganshire. No. II. Coyty, Coychurch and Ewenny.' (*Archaeologia Cambrensis*, 1857, pp. 100-128.)

FREEMAN, EDWARD AUGUSTUS 'Architectural antiquities in Glamorganshire. No. III. Llantwit Major.' (*Archaeologia Cambrensis*,1858, pp. 31-41.)

GLYNNE, SIR STEPHEN R. 'Notes on the older churches in the four Welsh Dioceses: Llandaff.' (*Archaeologia Cambrensis*, 1901, pp. 245-278.)

GUY, JOHN R. 'Bishop Barrington's Book.' (*Morgannwg*, Vol. XXV, 1981, pp. 112-129.)

GUY, JOHN R. The Churches of the Vale of Glamorgan: 27 articles. (*South Wales Echo*, 22nd March-11th October, 1963.)

GUY, JOHN R. 'The Gamage family: a study in clerical patronage in the seventeenth and eighteenth centuries.' (*Morgannwg*, Vol. XIV, 1970, pp. 35-61.)

GUY, JOHN R. Some ecclesiastical peculiarities of South Glamorgan: human and otherwise. (*Province*, Vol. XVII, no. 3. 1966, pp. 83-87.)

HALLIDAY, GEORGE ELEY 'Gileston church, Glamorgan.' (*Archaeologia Cambrensis*, 1903, pp. 339-344.)

HALLIDAY, GEORGE ELEY 'Llantwit Major church, Glamorganshire.' (*Archaeologia Cambrensis*, 1900, pp. 129-156.)

HALLIDAY, GEORGE ELEY 'Llantwit Major church, Glamorgan.' (*Archaeologia Cambrensis*, 1905, pp. 242-250.)

HALLIDAY, GEORGE ELEY 'The removal of the Cross of Iltyd at Llantwit Major Glamorganshire.' (*Archaeologia Cambrensis*, 1903 pp. 56-64.)

HASLAM, RICHARD 'Ewenny Priory, Mid Glamorgan: the home of Mr. and Mrs. Turbervill.' (*Country Life*, October 23rd, 1986, Vol. 180, (No. 4653), pp. 1270-1275.)

HILLING, J. B. 'The buildings of Llandaff, Penarth and outer Cardiff: an historical survey.' (*Glamorgan Historian*, Vol. 7, 1971, pp. 102-147.)

HOPKINS, T. J. David Jones of Wallington: (1) An introduction to his life and work. (*Glamorgan Historian*, Vol. 4. 1967, pp. 86-95.)

HOPKINS, T. J. 'David Jones of Wallington: (2) His work as a genealogist.' (*Glamorgan Historian*, Vol. 7, 1971, pp. 51-58.)

JAMES, BRIAN LL. 'The Vale of Glamorgan 1840-1860: profile of a rural community.' (*Glamorgan Historian*, Vol. 5, 1968, pp. 13-27.)

JENKINS, PHILIP 'Church patronage and clerical politics in eighteenth-century Glamorgan.' (*Morgannwg*, Vol. XXVIII, 1984, pp. 32-47.)

JONES, DAVID 'On a seventeenth century Welsh inscription at Michaelston-super-Ely, Glamorganshire.' (*Archaeologia Cambrensis*, 1889, pp. 198-213.)

LAW, T. G. The miraculous cross at St. Donat's, 1559-61. (*English Historical Review*, Vol. 1. 1886, pp. 513-517.)

LEWIS, EWART 'The Cowbridge Diocesan Library, 1711-1848.' (*Journal of the Historical Society of the Church in Wales*, IV (1954), pp. 36-43; VII (1957), pp. 80-89.)

McDONALD, R. W. 'The parish registers of Wales.' (*National Library of Wales Journal*, Vol. XIX, 1975-76, pp. 399-429.)

MORGAN, PRYS 'Glamorgan and the Red Book.' (*Morgannwg*, Vol. XXII, 1978, pp. 42-60.)

NORTH, F. J. 'Dean Conybeare Geologist.' (*Transactions of the Cardiff Naturalists' Society*, Vol. LXVI (1933), pp. 15-68.)

PATERSON, D. R. 'The manors of Michaelston-le-Pit and Wrinston and their early owners.' (*Transactions of the Cardiff Naturalists' Society*, Vol. LXV, 1932, pp. 30-40.)

POWELL, KEN 'A local Westminster Abbey? St. Illtyd's church, Llantwit Major, South Glamorgan.' (*Country Life*, October 31st, 1985, Vol. 178 (No. 4602), pp. 1376-1378.)

PRICHARD, T. J. 'The Reformation in the Deanery of Llandaff: a study of changes in its clerical personnel 1534-1609.' (*Morgannwg*, Vol. XIII, 1969, pp. 5-46.)

REES, J. F. 'Politics and religion in the Vale of Glamorgan during the Civil War.' (*Glamorgan Historian*, Vol. 1, (1963), pp. 54-66.)

REES, WILLIAM 'Accounts of the rectory of Cardiff and other possessions of the Abbey of Tewkesbury in Glamorgan for the years 1449-50.' (*South Wales and Monmouth Record Society*: Publications, No. 2 (1950), pp. 129-186.)

RHYS, JOHN 'Some Glamorgan inscriptions.' (*Archaeologia Cambrensis*, 1899, p. 132-168.)

RODGER, JOHN W. 'The stone slabs of South Wales and Monmouthshire.' (*Transactions of the Cardiff Naturalists' Society*, Vol. XLIV (1911), pp. 24-64.)

SAINT, ANDREW 'Charles Buckeridge and his family.' (*Oxoniensia*, Vol. 38, 1973, pp. 357-372.)

RICHARD, ARTHUR J. 'The religious houses of Glamorgan.' (*Glamorgan Historian*, Vol. 2, 1965, pp. 61-75.)

SEWARD, EDWIN 'Penmark, St. Athan's, Llantrithyd.' (*Transactions of the Cardiff Naturalists' Society*. Vol. XIV, 1882, pp. 40-42.)

SEWARD, EDWIN 'Some churches and castles in Glamorgan.' (*Transactions of the Cardiff Naturalists' Society*. Vol. XXXIX, 1906, pp. 78-95.)

SHEPHERD, CHARLES F. 'Admiral Sir Thomas Button.' (*Glamorgan Historian*, Vol. 4, 1967, pp. 121-135.)

SMITH, J. T. 'Medieval roofs: a classification.' (*Archaeological Journal*, Vol. CXV, 1958, pp. 111-148.)

THOMAS, D. R. 'The Norwich Taxation and the Diocese of Llandaff.' (*Archaeologia Cambrensis*, 1889, pp. 106-117.)

THOMAS, PETER H. 'Medical men of Glamorgan: William Salmon of Penllin 1790-1896.' (*Glamorgan Historian*, Vol. 11, 1975, pp. 98-108.)

THOMAS, T. H. 'Calvary crosses, Glamorgan.' (*Transactions of the Cardiff Naturalists' Society*, Vol. 37, 1904, pp. 55-65.)

THOMAS, T. H. 'Inscribed stones: some account of the pre-Norman inscribed and decorated monumental stones of Glamorganshire, being explanatory notes upon the series of photographs made by Mr. T. Mansel Franklen.' (*Transactions of the Cardiff Naturalists' Society*, Vol. XXV, Part 1. 1892-1893, pp. 34-46.)

TILNEY, CHRYSTAL 'An outline history of Dinas Powis.' (*Glamorgan Historian*, Vol. 2, 1965, pp. 197-208.)

TRAHERNE, JOHN MONTGOMERY St. Donat's Cathedral Church, Glamorganshire. *Gentleman's Magazine*, Vol. 91, 1821, part 1, pp. 489-491.

TURBERVILL, THOMAS PICTON 'The history of Ewenny Priory.' (*Transactions of the Cardiff Naturalists' Society*, Vol. VIII, 1876, pp. 41-48.)

TYRRELL-GREEN, EDMUND 'The church architecture of Wales.' (*Transactions of the Honourable Society of Cymmrodorion*, 1916-1917, pp. 52-118.)

TYRRELL-GREEN, EDMUND 'Types of baptismal fonts as illustrated by Welsh examples.' (*Transactions of the Honourable Society of Cymmrodorion*, 1918-1919, pp. 30-127.)

VEYSEY, A. G. 'Ecclesiastical parish records in Wales.' (*Journal of the Society of Archivists*, Vol. 6, 1978-1981, pp. 31-33.)

WALKER, D. G. 'The Welsh Church and Disestablishment.' (*The Modern Churchman*, 14, (1971), pp. 139-54.)

WESTWOOD, J. O. 'On certain peculiarities observable in some of the early monumental effigies in Wales. Part 1.' (*Archaeologia Cambrensis*, 1847, pp. 314-321.)

WILLIAMS, DAVID The miracle at St. Donats. (*Welsh Review* , Vol. VI. no. 1. 1947, pp. 33-38.)

WILLIAMS, RODERICK G. 'Penmark, Glamorgan 'scratch dials'.' (*Archaeologia Cambrensis*, 1936, pp. 316-318.)

WILLIAMS, RODERICK G. Discovery of a 'mass dial' at Ewenny.' (*Transactions of the Aberfan and Margam District Historical Journal*, 1930, pp. 72-74.)

WILLIAMS, STEPHEN W. 'Stone monumental effigies in Wales.' (*Archaeologia Cambrensis*, 1890, pp. 177-195.)

WILLS, W. D. 'The clergy in Society in Mid-Victorian South Wales.' (*Journal of the Historical Society of the Church in Wales*, XXIV, (1974), pp. 27-43.)

WILLS, W. D. 'The Established Church in the Diocese of Llandaff, 1850-70: a study of the Evangelical Movement in the South Wales Coalfield.' (*Welsh History Review*, IV, (1968-69), pp. 235-71.)

WILLS, W. D. 'The Rev. John Griffiths and the Revival of the Established Church in nineteenth-century Glamorgan.' (*Morgannwg*, Vol. XIII, (1969), pp. 75-102.)

WRIGHT, ARTHUR 'The bells of the Diocese of Llandaff: Deanery of Barry.' (*Llandaff Diocesan Magazine*, Vols. 10-11, April 1918-April, 1919.)

UNPUBLISHED DISSERTATIONS

EVANS, CAROLE A. *The Stradling family of St. Donats circa 1498-1609*. (Unpublished University of Wales (Swansea) M.A. Thesis, 1984.)

GUY, JOHN R. *An investigation into the pattern and nature of patronage, plurality and non-residence in the old Diocese of Llandaff between 1660 and the beginning of the 19th century*. (Unpublished University of Wales (Lampeter) Ph.D. Thesis, 1983. 2 vols.)

HIGHAM, ROBERT BRIAN *The life and works of the Reverend David Jones of Llangan 1736-1810*. (Unpublished University of Wales (Aberystwyth) M. Theology Thesis, 1971.)

JAMES, BRIAN LL. *The Vale of Glamorgan 1780-1850: a study in social history with special reference to the ownership and occupation of the land*. (Unpublished University of Wales (Cardiff) M.A. Thesis.)

JENKINS, OLWEN *Illustrative examples of the effect on medieval and later parish church fabric in the post-1844 Archdeaconry of Llandaff of restoration work by John Prichard and John Pollard Seddon*. (Unpublished Thesis for the Diploma in Building Conservation presented to the Architectural Association, London, June, 1985.)

LODWICK, BRIAN MARTIN *The Oxford Movement and the Diocese of Llandaff during the nineteenth century*. (Unpublished University of Leeds M.Phil. Thesis, 1976.)

WILLIS, WILTON D. *Ecclesiastical reorganization and church extension in the Diocese of Llandaff 1830-1870*. (Unpublished University of Wales (Swansea) M.A. Thesis, 1965.)

REPORTS

CAMBRIAN ARCHAEOLOGICAL ASSOCIATION Report of the twenty-third Annual Meeting of the Cambrian Archaeological Association held at Bridgend on Monday, August 9th to Saturday, August 14th, 1869. (*Archaeologia Cambrensis*, 1869, pp. 419-450.)

CAMBRIAN ARCHAEOLOGICAL ASSOCIATION Report of the forty-third Annual Meeting of the Cambrian Archaeological Association held at Cowbridge on Monday, August 13th, 1888 and four following days, (*Archaeologia Cambrensis*, 1888, pp. 372-434.)

CAMBRIAN ARCHAEOLOGICAL ASSOCIATION Report of the sixty-sixth Annual Meeting of the Cambrian Archaeological Association held at Cardiff, July 22nd to July 27th, 1912, (*Archaeologia Cambrensis*, 1913, pp. 65-152.)

CAMBRIAN ARCHAEOLOGICAL ASSOCIATION Report of the eighty-second Annual Meeting of the Cambrian Archaeological Association held at Aberafan, August 13th to August 17th, 1928, (*Archaeologia Cambrensis*, 1928, pp. 363-423.)

CAMBRIAN ARCHAEOLOGICAL ASSOCIATION Report of the eighty-seventh Annual Meeting of the Cambrian Archaeological Association held at Cardiff, August 28th to September 1st, 1933, (*Archaeologia Cambrensis*, 1933, pp. 361-411.)

GLAMORGAN-GWENT ARCHAEOLOGICAL TRUST *Annual report 1981-82. Excavation and survey at Llanfrynach near Cowbridge: a preliminary report (SS 9803 7465): by J. Parkhouse and David M. Robinson, pp. 36-47.*

INCORPORATED CHURCH BUILDING SOCIETY *Annual report 1927. List of grants from 1818-1927. Diocese of Llandaff*, pp. 120-121.

SOCIETY FOR THE PROTECTION OF ANCIENT BUILDINGS (SPAB) *Annual report for 1888. Llantwit Major church, Glamorganshire*, pp. 40-41.

NEWSPAPERS

Bridgend and Neath Chronicle (1888-94)
The Cambrian (1804-1915)
Cardiff and Merthyr Guardian (1845-74)
Cardiff and Suburban News (1929-64)
Cardiff Times (1857-1928)

Central Glamorgan Gazette (1866-94)
Glamorgan Gazette (1894-)
Neath Guardian (1927-)
South Wales Daily News (1872-1918)
Western Mail (1869-)

JOURNALS AND PERIODICALS

Aberafan and Margam District Historical Society: Transactions Vols. 1-6. 1924; 1928; 1929; 1931-32; 1932-33; 1933-34.
The Builder (1842-)
Church Builder (1862-1915)
Ecclesiologist (1841-1868)
Llandaff Diocesan Magazine Vols. 1-11, 1899-1919.
Neath Antiquarian Society Transactions, Second Series Vols. 1-7, 1930-39.

DIRECTORIES

Crockford's Clerical Directory (1858-1986)
Kelly's Directory of Monmouthshire and South Wales 1884, 1895, 1901, 1914, 1920, 1923.
Kelly's Directory of South Wales 1906, 1926.
Worrall's Directory of South Wales 1875.

Index of Architects, Bellfounders, Clockmakers, Organ Builders, Sculptors and Stained Glass Artists

The page numbers after each name refer to reference in the text.

General Index

The page numbers after each name refer to reference in the text.
Those numbers in bold type indicate illustrations.

A

Aaron, St., 3

Aberafan, church, 21

Aberdare, Lord, 177

Aberdare, parish, 30; St. Michael's Theological College, 33, 309

Abergavenny, 231; Grammar School, 21

Aberthaw, St. Peter's church, 302

Aberthin, 25

Ackland-Allen, Lt. Hugh Thomas, 373-4

Act for the Propagation of the Gospel in Wales (1650), 19

Act of Supremacy (1534), 80, 102

Act of Uniformity (1662), 17, 20

Additional Curates Society, 29

Aguod ap Ieuaf, 9

Aissa (Monknash), 287

Alban, St., 3

Alexander, *family*, of Bryneithan, Dinas Powis; 304; David Thomas, 303; John, 304; Margaret, 304; Mary, 304

Algeziras, 395

Allen, *family*, of Gileston; Dr. James, 155, 168, 170; Mary, 53, 168; Winifred, 168

Allen, Rev. Edmund Edward, rector of Porthkerry church, 313

Allen, J. Romilly, 315

Allen, William J. (sailor), 200

Alsop, 19

Amos, Brynley, (soldier), 200

Andrew, St., 319

Andrews, *family*, of Cadoxton Court, 116

Anglo-Catholic (High Church) Movement, 30-1, 72, 416 *See also* Oxford Movement, Tractarian Movement

Anglo-Saxons, 5, 7, 9, 11

Anselm, archbishop of Canterbury (1093-1114), 11

Anthony, St., of Egypt (the Great) (251-356), 7

ap Rhys (Rice), *family*; arms of, 373

Archaeologia Cambrensis, 257, 283, 381

Arles, Council of (314 A.D.), 3

Arminian Methodism, 25

Arminium, Council of, (359 A.D.), 3

Army and Navy Co-operative Society, 315

Artmail, 253

Arts and Crafts Movement, 73, 75

Arundell, Thomas, of Lanherne, Cornwall, 351

Aubrey, *family*, of Llantrithyd, 19, 235, 237; arms of, 233, 236; Charles Aubrey, 233, 312, 391; Frances (*née* Digby), 235; Sir John (d. 1700), 233, 235; Margaret (*née* Lowther), 233 235; Dame Martha (*née* Carter), 235; Mary (*née* Lewis), 235; Mary (*née* Mansel), 234, 236; Richard 235; Sir Thomas (*fl.* 1637), 234-6, 238; Sir Thomas (d. 1786), 235; Sir Thomas Digby, 233, 307, 387

Augustine, St., of Canterbury (d. 605), 5

489

C

I

Iddyn, king of Gwent, 261
Iestyn ap Gwrgant, 122, 282, 300, 308; arms of, 352, 365-6
Illtyd, St., 7, 233, 239, 257; Cross of, 258
Incorporated Church Building Society, 29, 138, 194, 224, 237, 323, 341, 420
Incorporated Society for Promoting the Enlargement of Churches *see* Incorporated Church Building Society
Independents, 27
Insole, *family*, of Ely Court, Llandaff and Tŷ Fry; James Harvey, 72, 294, 296; Mary Ann, 72, 294, 296
Isabella, countess of Gloucester, 297
Ithel ap Athrwys, king, 9, 377
Iuthahelo, king, 253

J

James, St., 417
James I, 20, 82; Royal Arms of, 80, 246
James, Brian Ll., 397
James, Elizabeth (d. 1890), 163
James, John Gibbon (d. 1601), 324
James, Margaret (d. 1631), 324
James, Mary, of The Grange, Wick, 417
James, Rev. S., rector of Flemingston, 163
James, W. A. (builder) of Cardiff, 180, 267
James & Price, (builders) of Cardiff, 376
Jay, Thomas, (churchwarden) of Penmark, 304
Jeaffreson, *family*, of Dullingham, Cambridge; arms of, 300; Colonel John, 305
Jenkin, David, (churchwarden) of St. Athan, 328
Jenkin, Thomas, (churchwarden) of St. Mary Hill, 390
Jenkins, *family*, of Cowbridge; Elizabeth, 175; Evan, 179-80; Jenkin Llewellyn, 175; Sir Leoline, 79, 135, 175, 179-80

Jenkins, *family*, of Flemingston Court; Ann, 161; David James, 161, 164; Jane Elizabeth, 161, 164
Jenkins, *family*, of Llansannor; arms of, 229
Jenkins, Christopher, (churchwarden) of Llancarfan, 188
Jenkins, Cissell, of Cowbridge, 138
Jenkins, Judge David, of Hensol, 133, 295
Jenkins, Rev. David, rector of St. Bride's-super-Ely, 345
Jenkins, Rev. George Morgannwg, rector of Eglwys Brewis and St. Athan, 141, 329
Jenkins, Helen Jane Essyllt, 328
Jenkins, Rev. Isaac Domer, rector of St. Andrew's Major, 321
Jenkins, John (churchwarden) of St. Andrew's Major, 322
Jenkins, Minnie, 345
Jenkins, Rees, of Llanfrynach, 209
Jenkins, William, of Caercady House, Welsh St. Donat's, 408
Jenkins, Rev. William, rector of Cadoxton-juxta-Barry and Merthyr Dyfan, 115, 407
Jenner, *family*, of Wenvoe, 411, 413, 415-6; Rev. Alfred Herbert, rector of Wenvoe, 413; Ann, (of Llanblethian), 178; Birt Wyndham Rous (of Llanblethian), 178; Charles Herbert, 414; Charlotte Anne, 414; Edwin Arthur, 414; Everilda (*née* Thornhill), 413; Fanny, 414; Rev. George Herbert, (Father Jenner), 31, 413, 416, Gilb Birt Price, 413; Henry Augustus, 414; Laura Frances, 115; Robert, 413; Robert Francis, 115, 269, 411; Robert Francis Lascelles, 414-5
Jesus College, Oxford, 30, 79, 130, 135, 173, 175, 199, 386; arms of, 130, 135
Jickells, John, 78, 315
Jickells, Noreen, 78, 315
Johan le Botiler, of Dunraven (*c.* 1285); sepulchral slab of, 50, **51**, 337, 341
John, St., the Baptist, 171, 399
John, king of England, 293
John, abbot of Gloucester, 181

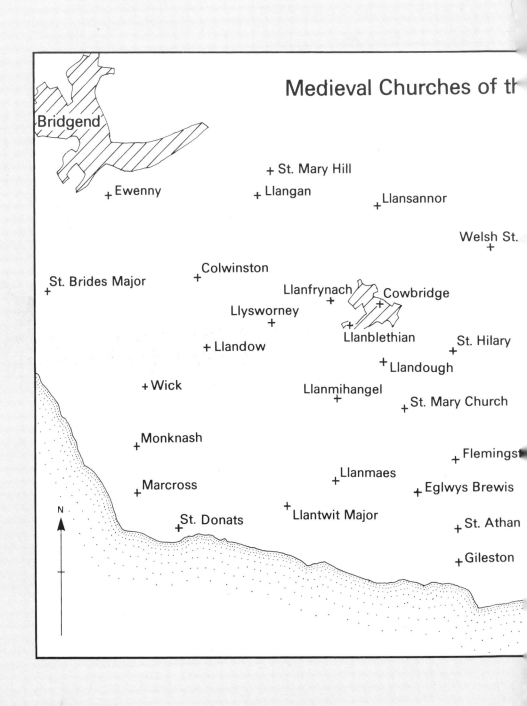

Medieval Churches of th

Bridgend

+ St. Mary Hill
+ Ewenny   + Llangan
+ Llansannor

Welsh St.
+

+ Colwinston
St. Brides Major
+

Llanfrynach   Cowbridge
+   +

Llysworney   Llanblethian
+   +   St. Hilary
+ Llandow   +

+ Llandough

+ Wick   Llanmihangel
+   + St. Mary Church

Monknash
+

+ Flemings

Llanmaes
+   + Eglwys Brewis

Marcross
+   Llantwit Major
+   + St. Athan

St. Donats
+   + Gileston

N